REFLECTING ON NATURE

Readings in Environmental Ethics and Philosophy

Second Edition

EDITED BY

Lori Gruen
Wesleyan University

Dale Jamieson
New York University

Christopher Schlottmann
New York University

New York   Oxford
OXFORD UNIVERSITY PRESS

For our students and other readers,

in the hope that their reflections on nature may help them to protect it.

Oxford University Press is a department of the University of Oxford. It furthers the University's objective of excellence in research, scholarship, and education by publishing worldwide.

Oxford   New York
Auckland   Cape Town   Dar es Salaam   Hong Kong   Karachi
Kuala Lumpur   Madrid   Melbourne   Mexico City   Nairobi
New Delhi   Shanghai   Taipei   Toronto

With offices in
Argentina   Austria   Brazil   Chile   Czech Republic   France   Greece
Guatemala   Hungary   Italy   Japan   Poland   Portugal   Singapore
South Korea   Switzerland   Thailand   Turkey   Ukraine   Vietnam

For titles covered by Section 112 of the US Higher Education Opportunity Act, please visit www.oup.com/us/he for the latest information about pricing and alternate formats.

Published by Oxford University Press.
198 Madison Avenue, New York, New York 10016
www.oup.com

Library of Congress Cataloging-in-Publication Data

Reflecting on nature: readings in environmental ethics and philosophy. —2nd ed. / edited by Lori Gruen, Dale Jamieson, Christopher Schlottmann.
p. cm.
Includes bibliographical references and index.
ISBN 978-0-19-978243-7 (alk. paper)
1. Environmental sciences—Philosophy.   I. Gruen, Lori.   II. Jamieson, Dale.   III. Schlottmann, Christopher, 1980-
GE40.R44 2013
363.7001—dc23   2012017157

Printer number: 9 8 7 6 5 4 3 2 1

Printed in the United States of America
on acid-free paper

The editors wish to express their appreciation to the following for permission to reprint the selections in this volume.

Anil Agarwal and Sunita Narain, "Global Warming in an Unequal World: A Case of Environmental Colonialism," New Delhi: Centre for Science and Environment, 1991. Reprinted by permission of the publisher.

Aristotle, from *Physics* and *Politics*. Translated by Christopher Shields.

Brian Barry, "Sustainability and Intergenerational Justice," *Theoria* 45, no. 89 (June 1997): 43–65. Reprinted by permission of Wiley.

Wendell Berry, "The Ecological Crisis as a Crisis of Agriculture," from *The Unsettling of America: Culture and Agriculture*, 1977. Reprinted by permission of Sierra Club Books.

Daniel Botkin, from *Discordant Harmonies*, 1992. Reprinted by permission of Oxford University Press.

J. Baird Callicott, from *Beyond the Land Ethic*, 1999. Reprinted by permission of State University of New York Press.

Allen Carlson, "Nature and Positive Aesthetics," *Environmental Ethics* (1984). Reprinted by permission of the publisher.

Rachel Carson, from *Silent Spring*, 1962. Reprinted by permission of Houghton Mifflin.

William Cronon, "The Trouble with Wilderness; or, Getting Back to the Wrong Nature," from *Uncommon Ground: Rethinking the Human Place in Nature*, ed. W. Cronon, 1995, pp. 69–90. Reprinted by permission of W. W. Norton.

Cora Diamond, "Eating Meat and Eating People," *Philosophy* 53, no. 206 (Oct. 1978): 465–479. Reprinted by permission of Cambridge University Press.

Robert Elliot, "Normative Ethics," from *Companion to Environmental Philosophy*, ed. D. Jamieson, 2001, 2003. Reprinted by permission of Blackwell Publishers.

John A. Fisher, "Environmental Aesthetics," from *Oxford Handbook of Aesthetics*, ed. J. Levison, 2003, pp. 667–678. Reprinted by permission of Oxford University Press.

Jonathan Safran Foer, from *Eating Animals*, 2009. Reprinted by permission of Little, Brown & Co.

Sheila Foster and Luke Cole, from *From the Ground Up: Environmental Racism and the Rise of the Environmental Justice Movement*, 2001, pp. 54–79. Reprinted by permission of New York University Press.

Lynn White, Jr., "The Historical Roots of Our Ecological Crisis," *Science* 155, no. 3767 (March 10, 1967): 1203–1207. Reprinted by permission of the American Association for the Advancement of Science.

Bernard Williams, "Must a Concern for the Environment be Centred on Human Beings?" Reprinted by permission of the author.

CONTENTS

Preface to
the Second Edition

When the first edition of *Reflecting on Nature* (RON) was published in 1994, it pioneered the idea of an expansive field of environmental philosophy rather than accepting the narrower notion of environmental ethics that was then current. It highlighted the problems of environmental justice and sustainable development, and provided a global perspective on questions of environmental concern. This second edition conserves the most important readings and insights of the first edition, while updating the issues and readings in light of changes in the intellectual climate and in environmental concerns. As environmental problems continue to become increasingly serious, scholarly work that attempts to alter that trajectory has also increased significantly. New generations of students are demanding that their teachers be more responsive to these concerns. Most colleges and universities now offer courses and even majors in environmental studies, and scholars in traditional disciplines are increasingly engaged with environmental topics.

This edition of RON includes a broad range of views and presents a sample of the myriad concerns that make up environmental philosophy. Some of these views may seem anachronistic, others enlightening, and still others may be so much a part of how we view nature that we have trouble seeing them at all. While disagreements will inevitably continue, it is important to recognize that ideas have consequences. They shape the concepts and vocabularies that we use to approach the problems of our time.

For this reason, it is important to examine our intellectual heritage. We may be embarrassed by it or find it ugly or despicable. But through this examination we may also find important threads that can help to illuminate our present problems, as well as suggest future directions. At the very least, from this examination we can learn to better understand ourselves and our place in nature. If we are to do better by nature, then we will have to learn more about ourselves. Examining intellectual histories, scientific practices, and ethical commitments helps us to understand how we got into our present predicament.

CHANGES TO THE SECOND EDITION

While we retained much from the first edition of RON, we also made changes:

- We cut the section on Alternative Perspectives that included ecofeminism and deep ecology since they have now been integrated into many approaches to environmental issues.
- We replaced the section on Sustainable Development with a section on Justice and the Environment that provides a more general framework for the issues and updated readings.

- We revised what was formerly a subsection on Animals and made it a full section.
- We updated the Contemporary Issues and Controversies subsections on Wilderness and Biodiversity and added new subsections on Food, Climate Change, and Aesthetics.

ACKNOWLEDGMENTS

We would like to express our gratitude to the following for helping to make the second edition of RON possible: Robert Miller of Oxford University Press for his early, consistent, and strong support of this project; Christina Mancuso and Kristin Maffei, also of OUP, for leading us through the editorial process; and Amanda Anjum of the New York University Environmental Studies Program for her invaluable administrative support. We also thank those who devoted their precious time to reviewing this volume for OUP: Peggy Hill, University of Tulsa; Adrian Ivakhiv, University of Vermont; Sheldon Krimsky, Tufts University; Paul Nelson, Wittenberg University; Jason Sears, Eckerd College; Kelly Sorenson, Ursinus College; William Stephens, Creighton University; William Storey, Millsaps College; Brian Treanor, Loyola Marymount University and Michael Weber, Bowling Green State University. Our students at Carleton College, Lafayette College, Stanford University, Wesleyan University, and NYU continue to provide us with hope that collectively we can change our destructive ways. LG and CS would like to also thank DJ who really was one of the pioneers of environmental philosophy, continues to work on cutting-edge environmental topics, and has trained many students who not only reflect on nature but work hard to protect what remains.

LG, DJ, and CS
Old Lyme, CT
September 4, 2011

Preface to
the First Edition

Since the 1970s, when courses in environmental ethics were first taught in philosophy departments, the number of courses on the environment has steadily increased and their content expanded. During the 1980s, these courses became increasingly common in departments of politics, sociology, religion, geography, and biology, and even in professional schools such as business, engineering, and law. Nowadays the examination of our place in nature is occurring throughout the university. This book is intended to facilitate this examination.

Philosophical concern for the environment has become more sophisticated in the past decade. In compiling this anthology, we have been able to mine a much richer literature than was available in the early 1980s. As part of this process of maturation, philosophical writing about the environment has spilled beyond the borders of ethics and has involved explorations in the history of philosophy, political philosophy, and the philosophy of science, among other fields. Environmental ethics—the central concern of the 1970s and 1980s—is now just one important dimension of environmental philosophy. This shift is reflected in the structure and title of this book.

For too long environmental philosophy, as influential as it has been in some circles, has been practiced on the margins of its home discipline. Yet some of the questions that environmental philosophers have been struggling with are closely connected to traditional philosophical questions. By bringing the writings of such leading environmental philosophers as Holmes Rolston III and Paul Taylor together with texts by such prominent moral philosophers as Jonathan Glover and Bernard Williams, we have tried to illuminate some of the connections between environmental philosophy and the philosophical tradition.

Another important change from the 1980s is that the environment has become more central in the thought of diverse people all over the globe. The environment is no longer just the province of a few philosophers, historians, and scientists. The environmental issues that are now of major concern are global in scope—ozone depletion, climate change, and biodiversity loss, for example. These problems must be addressed in the context of a world characterized by radical inequality. The problem of international justice cannot be evaded if our environmental crises are to be solved. In this book, we have tried to reflect the changing global discourse by including voices that are not usually heard in philosophical discussions about the environment. A significant number of articles are by women and authors from the developing world.

With the demise of Reaganism and the restoration of mainstream environmentalism in the United States, space has been created for new thinking. Such movements as deep ecology, social ecology, and ecofeminism may move from the margins closer to the center in the 1990s. We have also included these voices in this volume.

In addition to hearing new voices, it is important for us to listen to echoes from the past. Such philosophers as John Stuart Mill and naturalists as John Muir still have important lessons to teach us. Moreover, understanding the diverse images of nature that are part of our cultural heritage is vital for appreciating the environmental crises that we face.

As we approach the end of the twentieth century, our environmental problems continue to worsen. It is difficult to select a few problems as more worthy of attention than others. In this book, we focus on wilderness because the very concept seems endangered, on animals because they continue to suffer in numbers that are almost unimaginable, and on overpopulation and overconsumption because a strong case can be made that they are at the root of our problems. Finally, we have chosen to address biodiversity loss because the issue is so complex and yet so urgent. Never before in the history of the planet has a single species been responsible for such a holocaust.

These problems cannot be solved by a book. A philosophy book is, after all, only a collection of words. Yet words are important to action, in part because in speaking and writing we are doing something. This is part of the reason why language about controversial issues is often itself controversial. In this book, we have adopted various linguistic conventions that we cannot fully defend here. The most that we can do is to make some of these choices explicit.

Like most philosophers, we often use the word "we" to refer to some vaguely defined community of readers. Our use of this term is not meant to be exclusive or patronizing; we use it to refer to our probable readership—college undergraduates in the United States, Canada, Britain, Australia, and New Zealand. Nor do we mean to suggest that this probable readership forms a homogenous group.

In a world of almost 200 countries, each with its own culture, traditions, and institutions, it is difficult to speak in sweeping terms. Yet sometimes it is necessary to do so. We have used the term "developed country" to refer to such countries as the United States, Germany, and Japan, and the term "developing country" to refer to such countries as Kenya, Indonesia, and Brazil because these terms reflect the usage that has become conventional in international forums. However, this vocabulary is controversial and is challenged with good reason by people in all parts of the world.

Occasionally, we use the term "animal" to refer to nonhuman animals. This usage is misleading because it suggests that humans are not animals, thus reinforcing one of the dualisms that may be implicated in our environmental problems. We have been careful to refer to nonhuman animals with gendered pronouns so as not to reinforce the prejudice that they are mere objects, like tables or chairs.

In many cases, we have taken significant liberties with the original texts. Most of the selections are drawn from discussions that are far more extensive and nuanced than the extracts might suggest. For the serious student, there is no substitute for reading the original publications. We have deleted many notes, and in at least one case, we have rearranged some material; however, the linguistic conventions adopted by the authors have not been changed. For example, some use gender-neutral language; some do not.

Producing this anthology was a lot more work than we had anticipated, and many people helped in various ways. Unfortunately, we cannot remember them all here. But we would especially like to thank those whose words we have reproduced, both for their work on the articles presented here and for their larger contributions to environmental theory and practice. Our students—now numbering in the thousands at the University of Colorado, the University of British Columbia, and Cornell University—have been an invaluable source of insight and inspiration. Since 1980, DJ has occasionally co-taught courses on the environment with Micky Glantz, whose influence on this project is deep, if indirect. Alison Jaggar, Linda Nicholson, David Rosenthal, Peter Singer, Bob Solomon, and especially David Tatom were sources of advice and encouragement when we began. Robin Attfield, Andrew Brennan, David Crocker, Robert Elliot, Alastair Gunn, Ned Hettinger, Holmes Rolston, and two anonymous referees made helpful suggestions. Lori Cohen generously provided a comfortable place for LG to work while in Vancouver. John A. Fisher suggested the title, and he, along with Christopher Shields, played supporting roles in this project with their usual flair. Dooley, Grete, Kenny, and Toby were unusually patient, even indulgent. Angela Blackburn and Rob Dilworth shepherded the project through the labyrinth of Oxford University Press, and Angela's enthusiasm for the project from the beginning was contagious and helped to sustain us.

Perhaps most important, this book grows out of a community of thought and action about the environment. Without the efforts, enthusiasm, and interest of many unnamed and unacknowledged people this book would not exist.

LG, DJ
Boulder, Colo.
April 1993

Images of Nature

INTRODUCTION

We live in a world of virtual reality and mass tourism. It is easy to think that reality is what is happening right now and that our lives can be whatever we want them to be. History is the story of distant people who lived in a strange world. What could it possibly have to do with us here and now? In an article published more than forty years ago, the historian Lynn White, Jr. (1907–1987) argued that our current ecological crisis is rooted in the Christian cultural tradition. Some thinkers have argued that White is too hard on the Judeo-Christian tradition, insisting that the God of the Bible did not give the Earth to humans for them to pillage and destroy. Even former Vice President Al Gore has a view on this matter, writing in his book, *Earth in the Balance*, that "the biblical concept of dominion is quite different from the concept of domination," since having dominion over the earth requires believers to " 'care for' the earth even as they 'work' it" (p. 243). Others have thought that White gives too much credit to ideas. On their view, religions and philosophies are created to rationalize what we do for economic or political reasons. The Judeo-Christian tradition could no more be a cause of our ecological crisis than numbers can cause earthquakes.

Virtually all cultures and religious traditions have creation myths. In the Judeo-Christian story, we are told that before creating Adam, God surveyed nonhuman nature and "saw that it was good." In this peaceable kingdom, both humans and animals were vegetarian. But after Adam's sin, violence and corruption swept the Earth and God decided to "make an end to all flesh." Before bringing the flood, however, he commanded Noah to take into his ark two of each animal. After the waters had receded, God gave the animals to Noah for food, but he promised both Noah and the animals that he would never again send a flood to destroy the Earth.

Ancient Greek philosophy was also an important influence on Western culture. Aristotle (384–322 B.C.E.) claimed that everything in nature exists for some purpose. This idea, natural teleology, held that the sky rains in order for corn to grow. According to Aristotle, there is a hierarchy in nature: plants exist for the sake of animals, and animals exist for the sake of humans.

The view that humans are the pinnacle of nature and everything exists for our sake has been an important influence on Western political and legal thought. The British philosopher John Locke (1632–1704) developed a theory of property, according to which God gave all of nature, including the "inferior creatures," to mankind to hold in common. Land that was left idle was without value. By "mixing" his labor with land—tilling, cultivating, planting, and so on, a man improved the land and thereby came to own it.

The idea that humans are at the center of nature, which was created to serve our purposes, received a serious blow from the British scientist Charles Darwin (1809–1882). Darwin showed how purposeless biological processes operating over geological time could have produced the diversity of life that seems so miraculous. Rather than God creating distinct, immutable species arranged in hierarchical order with humans at the top, Darwin argued for the continuity of all life. In his view, humans are not so much fallen angels as risen apes.

John Muir (1838–1914), born in Scotland, was the founder of the Sierra Club and has become the patron saint of the American environmental movement. He spent much of his life on long treks through wilderness areas, writing about what he saw. In a more pointed way than Darwin, Muir ridiculed the idea that it is the purpose of nature to serve human interests. If God created nature solely to serve human interests, then what are we to make of mosquitoes and poisonous plants?

If Muir was the patron saint of the early environmental movement, then Aldo Leopold (1887–1948) was its philosopher. Leopold was trained in wildlife management, but as his career unfolded he produced a remarkable series of essays exploring the values that exist in nature. He argued that our relationship with the land is fundamentally ethical, and he envisioned an expanding circle of morality that might one day lead us to see ourselves as citizens of the "land community" rather than as conquerors of it.

The American Transcendentalist, Henry David Thoreau (1817–1862), was a vegetarian, antiwar activist, and all-around eccentric. In both his life and work, he celebrated the strength, integrity, and life-promoting character of wildness.

The Utilitarian philosopher John Stuart Mill (1806–1873) produced works on moral and political theory, language, logic, and science that are read and admired even today. Less well-known are his views about the importance of reaching a "stationary state" in which population and economic growth stabilize, and we are free to devote ourselves to improving the quality of life. Mill warns of a future in which "solitude is extirpated," and every piece of land is brought into cultivation to feed the growing mass of humanity. Despite his love of nature, he also warns about the fallacy of deriving lessons or prescriptions from the concept of nature.

In recent years, there has been an explosion of writing about nature from many different perspectives. The American ecologist Daniel Botkin argues that instead of viewing nature as a machine and humans as its operators, we should regard nature as a global living system in which humans are active participants. Vandana Shiva is a feminist philosopher and activist who criticizes the traditions of Western science, which she sees as leading to "maldevelopment" and the exploitation of women and nature. Stephen Jay Gould (1941–2002) was a biologist, paleontologist, and historian of science. According to Gould, we have to make a pact with the planet, akin to the Golden Rule, in which we commit ourselves to treating the Earth as we wish to be treated. The Australian philosopher Val Plumwood (1939–2008) often criticized the dualistic thinking that separates humans from animals and the rest of nature. In this selection, she describes a terrifying encounter in which she is hunted by a crocodile.

Arne Naess (1912–2009) was a Norwegian philosopher who was one of the founders of Deep Ecology. He devoted much of his life to spelling out principles of a radically nature-centered theory of value. This section concludes with the words of Rachel Carson (1907–1964), the biologist and nature writer, often credited with catalyzing the modern American environmental movement. In *Silent Spring*, her critique of the uncritical use of synthetic chemicals such as DDT, Carson challenged conventional notions of progress, raising concerns about the consequences of human attempts to change the "nature of the world."

FURTHER READING

Attfield, Robin. *The Ethics of Environmental Concern*. 2nd ed. Athens, GA: University of Georgia Press, 1992. Part 1 is a survey of Judeo-Christian and Enlightenment attitudes toward nature.

Callicott, J. Baird, and Roger Ames, eds. *Nature in Asian Traditions and Thought: Essays in Environmental Philosophy*. Albany, NY: State University of New York Press, 1989. A collection of essays addressing attitudes toward nature in the Chinese, Japanese, and Indian traditions.

Hargrove, Eugene C. *Foundations of Environmental Ethics*. Englewood Cliffs, NJ: Prentice Hall, 1989. Parts 1 and 2 discuss philosophical views of nature, land use, aesthetic and scientific attitudes toward the environment, and wildlife protection.

Jamieson, Dale. ed. *A Companion to Environmental Philosophy*. Malden, MA: Blackwell, 2003. A collection of essays on central topics in environmental philosophy, including cultural traditions, contemporary ethics, and topics such as economics and consumption.

Merchant, Carolyn. *The Death of Nature: Women, Ecology, and the Scientific Revolution*. New York, NY: Harper & Row, 1980. The classic study of how the scientific revolution affected cultural attitudes toward women and nature.

Oelschlaeger, Max. *The Idea of Wilderness Prehistory to the Age of Ecology*. New Haven, CT: Yale University Press, 1991. A historical and philosophical defense of a postmodern conception of wilderness.

Passmore, John. *Man's Responsibility for Nature*. New York, NY: Scribner, 1974. An early book on Western attitudes toward nature and discussions of such topics as pollution, population, conservation, and preservation.

DISCUSSION QUESTIONS

1. How does historical reflection on human relations to the natural world help our understanding of our current situation?
2. To what extent should we be guided by our cultural traditions and to what extent should we challenge them?
3. How do religious beliefs and intellectual traditions inform our attitudes about nature?
4. How might scientific and technological advancement contribute to, or help to curtail, ecological destruction?
5. Are there moral lessons to be learned from the natural world?
6. What is meant by "dualistic thinking" and how may it be implicated in ecological destruction?
7. What is the place of humans in the natural world? How is this affected by modern technologies and development?

Lynn White, Jr.

The Historical Roots of Our Ecological Crisis

A conversation with Aldous Huxley not infrequently put one at the receiving end of an unforgettable monologue. About a year before his lamented death he was discoursing on a favorite topic: man's unnatural treatment of nature and its sad results. To illustrate his point he told how, during the previous summer, he had returned to a little valley in England where he had spent many happy months as a child. Once it had been composed of delightful grassy blades; now it was becoming overgrown with unsightly brush because the rabbits that formerly kept such growth under control had largely succumbed to a disease, myxomatosis, that was deliberately introduced by the local farmers to reduce the rabbits' destruction of crops. Being something of a Philistine, I could be silent no longer, even in the interests of great rhetoric. I interrupted to point out that the rabbit itself had been brought as a domestic animal to England in 1176, presumably to improve the protein diet of the peasantry.

All forms of life modify their contexts. The most spectacular and benign instance is doubtless the coral polyp. By serving its own ends, it has created a vast undersea world favorable to thousands of other kinds of animals and plants. Ever since man became a numerous species he has affected his environment notably. The hypothesis that his fire-drive method of hunting created the world's great grasslands and helped to exterminate the monster mammals of the Pleistocene from much of the globe is plausible, if not proved. For six millennia at least, the banks of the lower Nile have been a human artifact rather than the swampy African jungle which nature, apart from man, would have made it. The Aswan Dam, flooding 5,000 square miles, is only the latest stage in a long process. In many regions terracing or irrigation,

overgrazing, the cutting of forests by Romans to build ships to fight Carthaginians or by Crusaders to solve the logistics problems of their expeditions, have profoundly changed some ecologies. Observation that the French landscape falls into two basic types, the open fields of the north and the *bocage* of the south and west, inspired Marc Bloch to undertake his classic study of medieval agricultural methods. Quite unintentionally, changes in human ways often affect nonhuman nature. It has been noted, for example, that the advent of the automobile eliminated huge flocks of sparrows that once fed on the horse manure littering every street.

The history of ecologic change is still so rudimentary that we know little about what really happened, or what the results were. The extinction of the European aurochs as late as 1627 would seem to have been a simple case of overenthusiastic hunting. On more intricate matters it often is impossible to find solid information. For a thousand years or more the Frisians and Hollanders have been pushing back the North Sea, and the process is culminating in our own time in the reclamation of the Zuider Zee. What, if any, species of animals, birds, fish, shore life, or plants have died out in the process? In their epic combat with Neptune have the Netherlanders overlooked ecological values in such a way that the quality of human life in the Netherlands has suffered? I cannot discover that the questions have ever been asked, much less answered.

People, then, have often been a dynamic element in their own environment, but in the present state of historical scholarship we usually do not know exactly when, where, or with what effects man-induced changes came. As we enter the last third of the twentieth century, however, concern for the problem of ecologic backlash is mounting feverishly. Natural science, conceived as the effort to understand the nature of things, had flourished in several eras and among several peoples. Similarly there had been an age-old accumulation of technological skills, sometimes growing rapidly, sometimes slowly. But it was not until about four generations ago that Western Europe and North America arranged a marriage between science and technology, a union of the theoretical and the empirical approaches to our natural environment. The emergence in widespread practice of the Baconian creed that scientific knowledge means technological power over nature can scarcely be dated before about 1850, save in the chemical industries, where it is anticipated in the eighteenth century. Its acceptance as a normal pattern of action may mark the greatest event in human history since the invention of agriculture, and perhaps in nonhuman terrestrial history as well.

Almost at once the new situation forced the crystallization of the novel concept of ecology; indeed, the word *ecology* first appeared in the English language in 1873. Today, less than a century later, the impact of our race upon the environment has so increased in force that it has changed in essence. When the first cannons were fired, in the early fourteenth century, they affected ecology by sending workers scrambling to the forests and mountains for more potash, sulfur, iron ore, and charcoal, with some resulting erosion and deforestation. Hydrogen bombs are of a different order: a war fought with them might alter the genetics of all life on this planet. By 1285 London had a smog problem arising from the burning of soft coal, but our present combustion of fossil fuels threatens to change the chemistry of the globe's atmosphere as a whole, with consequences which we are only beginning to guess. With the population explosion, the carcinoma of planless urbanism, the new geological deposits of sewage and garbage, surely no creature other than man has ever managed to foul its nest in such short order.

There are many calls to action, but specific proposals, however worthy as individual items, seem too partial, palliative, negative: ban the bomb, tear down the billboards, give the Hindus contraceptives and tell them to eat their sacred cows. The simplest solution to any suspect change is, of course, to stop it, or, better yet, to revert to a romanticized past: make those ugly gasoline stations look like Anne Hathaway's cottage or (in the Far West) like ghost-town saloons. The "wilderness-area" mentality invariably advocates deep-freezing an ecology, whether San Gimignano or the High Sierra, as it was before the first Kleenex was dropped. But neither atavism nor prettification will cope with the ecologic crisis of our time.

What shall we do? No one yet knows. Unless we think about fundamentals, our specific measures may produce new backlashes more serious than those they are designed to remedy.

As a beginning we should try to clarify our thinking by looking, in some historical depth, at the presuppositions that underlie modern technology and science. Science was traditionally aristocratic, speculative, intellectual in intent; technology was lower-class, empirical, action-oriented. The quite sudden fusion of these two, towards the middle of the nineteenth century, is surely related to the slightly prior and contemporary democratic revolutions which, by reducing social barriers, tended to assert a functional unity of brain and hand. Our ecologic crisis is the product of an emerging, entirely novel, democratic culture. The issue is whether a democratized world can survive its own implications. Presumably we cannot unless we rethink our axioms.

THE WESTERN TRADITIONS OF TECHNOLOGY AND SCIENCE

One thing is so certain that it seems stupid to verbalize it: both modern technology and modern science are distinctively *occidental*. Our technology has absorbed elements from all over the world, notably from China, yet everywhere today, whether in Japan or in Nigeria, successful technology is Western. Our science is the heir to all the sciences of the past, especially perhaps to the work of the great Islamic scientists of the Middle Ages, who so often outdid the ancient Greeks in skill and perspicacity: al-Rāzī in medicine, for example; or ibn-al-Haytham in optics; or Omar Khāyyám in mathematics. Indeed, not a few works of such geniuses seem to have vanished in the original Arabic and to survive only in medieval Latin translations that helped to lay the foundations for later Western developments. Today, around the globe, all significant science is Western in style and method, whatever the pigmentation or language of the scientists.

A second pair of facts is less well recognized because they result from quite recent historical scholarship. The leadership of the West, both in technology and in science, is far older than the so-called scientific revolution of the seventeenth century or the so-called industrial revolution of the eighteenth century. These terms are in fact outmoded and obscure the true nature of what they try to describe—significant stages in two long and separate developments. By A.D. 1000 at the latest—and perhaps, feebly, as much as 200 years earlier—the West began to apply water power to industrial processes other than milling grain. This was followed in the late twelfth century by the harnessing of wind power. From simple beginnings, but with remarkable consistency of style, the West rapidly expanded its skills in the development of power machinery, laborsaving devices, and automation. Those who doubt should contemplate that most monumental achievement in the history of automation: the weight-driven mechanical clock, which appeared in two forms in the early fourteenth century. Not in craftsmanship but in basic technological capacity, the Latin West of the later Middle Ages far outstripped its elaborate, sophisticated, and esthetically magnificent sister cultures, Byzantium and Islam. In 1444 a great Greek ecclesiastic, Bessarion, who had gone to Italy, wrote a letter to a prince in Greece. He is amazed by the superiority of Western ships, arms, textiles, glass. But above all he is astonished by the spectacle of waterwheels sawing timbers and pumping the bellows of blast furnaces. Clearly, he had seen nothing of the sort in the Near East.

By the end of the fifteenth century the technological superiority of Europe was such that its small, mutually hostile nations could spill out over all the rest of the world, conquering, looting, and colonizing. The symbol of this technological superiority is the fact that Portugal, one of the weakest states of the Occident, was able to become, and to remain for a century, mistress of the East Indies. And we must remember that the technology of Vasco da Gama and Albuquerque was built by pure empiricism, drawing remarkably little support or inspiration from science.

In the present-day vernacular understanding, modern science is supposed to have begun in 1543, when both Copernicus and Vesalius published their great works. It is no derogation of their accomplishments, however, to point out that such structures as the *Fabrica* and the *De revolutionibus* do not appear overnight. The distinctive Western tradition of science, in fact, began in the late eleventh century with a massive movement of translation of Arabic and Greek scientific works into Latin. A few notable books—Theophrastus', for example—escaped the West's avid new appetite for science, but within less than 200 years effectively the entire corpus of Greek and Muslim science was available in Latin, and was being eagerly read and criticized in the new European universities. Out of criticism arose new observation, speculation, and increasing distrust of ancient authorities. By the late thirteenth century Europe had seized global scientific leadership from the faltering hands of Islam. It would be as absurd to deny the profound originality of Newton, Galileo, or Copernicus as to deny that of the fourteenth-century scholastic scientists like Buridan or Oresme on whose work they built. Before the eleventh century, science scarcely existed in the Latin West, even in Roman times. From the eleventh century onward, the scientific sector of occidental culture has increased in a steady crescendo.

Since both our technological and our scientific movements got their start, acquired their character, and achieved world dominance in the Middle Ages, it would seem that we cannot understand their nature or their present impact upon ecology without examining fundamental medieval assumptions and developments.

MEDIEVAL VIEW OF MAN AND NATURE

Until recently, agriculture has been the chief occupation even in "advanced" societies; hence, any change in methods of tillage has much importance. Early plows, drawn by two oxen, did not normally turn the sod but merely scratched it. Thus, cross-plowing was needed and fields tended to be squarish. In the fairly light soils and semi-arid climates of the Near East and Mediterranean, this worked well. But such a plow was inappropriate to the wet climate and often sticky soils of northern Europe. By the latter part of the seventh century after Christ, however, following obscure beginnings, certain northern peasants were using an entirely new kind of plow, equipped with a vertical knife to cut the line of the furrow, a horizontal share to slice under the sod, and a moldboard to turn it over. The friction of this plow with the soil was so great that it normally required not two but eight oxen. It attacked the land with such violence that cross-plowing was not needed, and fields tended to be shaped in long strips.

In the days of the scratch-plow, fields were distributed generally in units capable of supporting a single family. Subsistence farming was the presupposition. But no peasant owned eight oxen: to use the new and more efficient plow, peasants pooled their oxen to form large plow-teams, originally receiving (it would appear) plowed strips in proportion to their contribution. Thus, distribution of land was based no longer on the needs of a family but, rather, on the capacity of a power machine to till the earth. Man's relation to the soil was profoundly changed. Formerly man had been part of nature; now he was the exploiter of nature. Nowhere else in the world did farmers develop any

analogous agricultural implement. Is it coincidence that modern technology, with its ruthlessness toward nature, has so largely been produced by descendants of these peasants of northern Europe?

This same exploitive attitude appears slightly before A.D. 830 in Western illustrated calendars. In older calendars the months were shown as passive personifications. The new Frankish calendars, which set the style for the Middle Ages, are very different: they show men coercing the world around them—plowing, harvesting, chopping trees, butchering pigs. Man and nature are two things, and man is master.

These novelties seem to be in harmony with larger intellectual patterns. What people do about their ecology depends on what they think about themselves in relation to things around them. Human ecology is deeply conditioned by beliefs about our nature and destiny—that is, by religion. To Western eyes this is very evident in, say, India or Ceylon. It is equally true of ourselves and of our medieval ancestors.

The victory of Christianity over paganism was the greatest psychic revolution in the history of our culture. It has become fashionable today to say that, for better or worse, we live in "the post-Christian age." Certainly the forms of our thinking and language have largely ceased to be Christian, but to my eye the substance often remains amazingly akin to that of the past. Our daily habits of action, for example, are dominated by an implicit faith in perpetual progress which was unknown either to Greco-Roman antiquity or to the Orient. It is rooted in, and is indefensible apart from, Judeo-Christian teleology. The fact that Communists share it merely helps to show what can be demonstrated on many other grounds: that Marxism, like Islam, is a Judeo-Christian heresy. We continue today to live, as we have lived for about 1,700 years, very largely in a context of Christian axioms.

What did Christianity tell people about their relations with the environment?

While many of the world's mythologies provide stories of creation, Greco-Roman mythology was singularly incoherent in this respect. Like Aristotle, the intellectuals of the ancient West denied that the visible world had had a beginning. Indeed, the idea of a beginning was impossible in the framework of their cyclical notion of time. In sharp contrast, Christianity inherited from Judaism not only a concept of time as nonrepetitive and linear but also a striking story of creation. By gradual stages a loving and all-powerful God had created light and darkness, the heavenly bodies, the earth and all its plants, animals, birds, and fishes. Finally, God had created Adam and, as an afterthought, Eve, to keep man from being lonely. Man named all the animals, thus establishing his dominance over them. God planned all of this explicitly for man's benefit and rule: no item in the physical creation had any purpose save to serve man's purposes. And, although man's body is made of clay, he is not simply part of nature: he is made in God's image.

Especially in its Western form, Christianity is the most anthropocentric religion the world has seen. As early as the second century both Tertullian and Saint Irenaeus of Lyons were insisting that when God shaped Adam he was foreshadowing the image of the Incarnate Christ, the Second Adam. Man shares, in great measure, God's transcendence of nature. Christianity, in absolute contrast to ancient paganism and Asia's religions (except, perhaps, Zoroastrianism), not only established a dualism of man and nature but also insisted that it is God's will that man exploit nature for his proper ends.

At the level of the common people this worked out in an interesting way. In antiquity every tree, every spring, every stream, every hill had its own *genius loci*, its guardian spirit. These spirits were accessible to men, but were very unlike men; centaurs, fauns, and mermaids show their ambivalence. Before one cut a tree, mined a mountain, or dammed a brook, it was important to placate the spirit in charge of that particular situation, and to keep it placated. By destroying pagan animism, Christianity made it possible to exploit nature in a mood of indifference to the feelings of natural objects.

It is often said that for animism the Church substituted the cult of saints. True; but the cult of saints is functionally quite different from animism. The saint is not *in* natural objects; he may have special shrines, but his citizenship is in heaven. Moreover, a saint is entirely a man; he can be approached in human terms. In addition to saints, Christianity of course also had angels and demons inherited from Judaism and perhaps, at one remove, from Zoroastrianism. But these were all as mobile as the saints themselves. The spirits *in* natural objects, which formerly had protected nature from man, evaporated. Man's effective monopoly on spirit in this world was confirmed, and the old inhibitions to the exploitation of nature crumbled.

When one speaks in such sweeping terms, a note of caution is in order. Christianity is a complex faith, and its consequences differ in differing contexts. What I have said may well apply to the medieval West, where in fact technology made spectacular advances. But the Greek East, a highly civilized realm of equal Christian devotion, seems to have produced no marked technological innovation after the late seventh century, when Greek fire was invented. The key to the contrast may perhaps be found in a difference in the tonality of piety and thought which students of comparative theology find between the Greek and the Latin churches. The Greeks believed that sin was intellectual blindness, and that salvation was found in illumination, orthodoxy—that is, clear thinking. The Latins, on the other hand, felt that sin was moral evil, and that salvation was to be found in right conduct. Eastern theology has been intellectualist. Western theology has been voluntarist. The Greek saint contemplates; the Western saint acts. The implications of Christianity for the conquest of nature would change more easily in the Western atmosphere.

The Christian dogma of creation, which is found in the first clause of all the Creeds, has another meaning for our comprehension of today's ecologic crisis. By revelation, God had given man the Bible, the Book of Scripture. But since God had made nature, nature also must reveal the divine mentality. The religious study of nature for the better understanding of God was known as natural theology. In the early Church, and always in the Greek East, nature was conceived primarily as a symbolic system through which God speaks to men: the ant is a sermon to sluggards; rising flames are the symbol of the soul's aspiration. This view of nature was essentially artistic rather than scientific. While Byzantium preserved and copied great numbers of ancient Greek scientific texts, science as we conceive it could scarcely flourish in such an ambience.

However, in the Latin West by the early thirteenth century natural theology was following a very different bent. It was ceasing to be the decoding of the physical symbols of God's communication with man and was becoming the effort to understand God's mind by discovering how his creation operates. The rainbow was no longer simply a symbol of hope first sent to Noah after the Deluge: Robert Grosseteste, Friar Roger Bacon, and Theodoric of Freiberg produced startingly sophisticated work on the optics of the rainbow, but they did it as a venture in religious understanding. From the thirteenth century onward, up to and including Leibnitz and Newton, every major scientist, in effect, explained his motivations in religious terms. Indeed, if Galileo had not been so expert an amateur theologian he would have got into far less trouble: the professionals resented his intrusion. And Newton seems to have regarded himself more as a theologian than as a scientist. It was not until the late eighteenth century that the hypothesis of God became unnecessary to many scientists.

It is often hard for the historian to judge, when men explain why they are doing what they want to do, whether they are offering real reasons or merely culturally acceptable reasons. The consistency with which scientists during the long formative centuries of Western science said that the task and the reward of the scientist was "to think God's thoughts after him" leads one to believe that this was their real motivation. If so, then modern Western science was cast in a matrix of Christian theology. The dynamism

of religious devotion, shaped by the Judeo-Christian dogma of creation, gave it impetus.

AN ALTERNATIVE CHRISTIAN VIEW

We would seem to be headed toward conclusions unpalatable to many Christians. Since both *science* and *technology* are blessed words in our contemporary vocabulary, some may be happy at the notions, first, that, viewed historically, modern science is an extrapolation of natural theology and, second, that modern technology is at least partly to be explained as an occidental, voluntarist realization of the Christian dogma of man's transcendence of, and rightful mastery over, nature. But, as we now recognize, somewhat over a century ago science and technology—hitherto quite separate activities—joined to give mankind powers which, to judge by many of the ecologic effects, are out of control. If so, Christianity bears a huge burden of guilt.

I personally doubt that disastrous ecologic backlash can be avoided simply by applying to our problems more science and more technology. Our science and technology have grown out of Christian attitudes toward man's relation to nature which are almost universally held not only by Christians and neo-Christians but also by those who fondly regard themselves as post-Christians. Despite Copernicus, all the cosmos rotates around our little globe. Despite Darwin, we are *not*, in our hearts, part of the natural process. We are superior to nature, contemptuous of it, willing to use it for our slightest whim. The newly elected governor of California, like myself a churchman, but less troubled than I, spoke for the Christian tradition when he said (as is alleged), "When you've seen one redwood tree, you've seen them all." To a Christian a tree can be no more than a physical fact. The whole concept of the sacred grove is alien to Christianity and to the ethos of the West. For nearly two millennia Christian missionaries have been chopping down sacred groves, which are idolatrous because they assume spirit in nature.

What we do about ecology depends on our ideas of the man–nature relationship. More science and more technology are not going to get us out of the present ecologic crisis until we find a new religion, or rethink our old one. The beatniks, who are the basic revolutionaries of our time, show a sound instinct in their affinity for Zen Buddhism, which conceives of the man–nature relationship as very nearly the mirror image of the Christian view. Zen, however, is as deeply conditioned by Asian history as Christianity is by the experience of the West, and I am dubious of its viability among us.

Possibly we should ponder the greatest radical in Christian history since Christ: Saint Francis of Assisi. The prime miracle of Saint Francis is the fact that he did not end at the stake, as many of his left-wing followers did. He was so clearly heretical that a general of the Franciscan Order, Saint Bonaventura, a great and perceptive Christian, tried to suppress the early accounts of Franciscanism. The key to an understanding of Francis is his belief in the virtue of humility—not merely for the individual but for man as a species. Francis tried to depose man from his monarchy over creation and set up a democracy of all God's creatures. With him the ant is no longer simply a homily for the lazy, flames a sign of the thrust of the soul toward union with God; now they are Brother Ant and Sister Fire, praising the Creator in their own ways as Brother Man does in his.

Later commentators have said that Francis preached to the birds as a rebuke to men who would not listen. The records do not read so: he urged the little birds to praise God, and in spiritual ecstasy they flapped their wings and chirped rejoicing. Legends of saints, especially the Irish saints, had long told of their dealings with animals but always, I believe, to show their human dominance over creatures. With Francis it is different. The land around Gubbio in the Apennines was being ravaged by a fierce wolf. Saint Francis, says the legend, talked to the wolf and persuaded him of the error of his ways. The wolf repented, died in the odor of sanctity, and was buried in consecrated ground.

What Sir Steven Ruciman calls "the Franciscan docrine of the animal soul" was quickly stamped out. Quite possibly it was in part inspired, consciously or unconsciously, by the belief in reincarnation held by the Cathar heretics who at that time teemed in Italy and southern France, and who presumably had got it originally from India. It is significant that at just the same moment, about 1200, traces of metempsychosis are found also in western Judaism, in the Provençal *Cabala*. But Francis held neither to transmigration of souls nor to pantheism. His view of nature and of man rested on a unique sort of panpsychism of all things animate and inanimate, designed for the glorification of their transcendent Creator, who, in the ultimate gesture of cosmic humility, assumed flesh, lay helpless in a manger, and hung dying on a scaffold.

I am not suggesting that many contemporary Americans who are concerned about our ecologic crisis will be either able or willing to counsel with wolves or exhort birds. However, the present increasing disruption of the global environment is the product of a dynamic technology and science which were originating in the Western medieval world against which Saint Francis was rebelling in so original a way. Their growth cannot be understood historically apart from distinctive attitudes toward nature which are deeply grounded in Christian dogma. The fact that most people do not think of these attitudes as Christian is irrelevant. No new set of basic values has been accepted in our society to displace those of Christianity. Hence we shall continue to have a worsening ecologic crisis until we reject the Christian axiom that nature has no reason for existence save to serve man.

The greatest spiritual revolutionary in Western history, Saint Francis, proposed what he thought was an alternative Christian view of nature and man's relation to it: he tried to substitute the idea of the equality of all creatures, including man, for the idea of man's limitless rule of creation. He failed. Both our present science and our present technology are so tinctured with orthodox Christian arrogance toward nature that no solution for our ecologic crisis can be expected from them alone. Since the roots of our trouble are so largely religious, the remedy must also be essentially religious, whether we call it that or not. We must rethink and refeel our nature and destiny. The profoundly religious, but hereti-

cal, sense of primitive Franciscans for the spiritual autonomy of all parts of nature may point a direction. I propose Francis as a patron saint for ecologists.

[From] Genesis

CHAPTER 1

In the beginning God created the heavens and the earth.[2] The earth was without form and void, and darkness was upon the face of the deep; and the Spirit of God was moving over the face of the waters.

3 And God said, "Let there be light"; and there was light.[4] And God saw that the light was good; and God separated the light from the darkness.[5] God called the light Day, and the darkness he called Night. And there was evening and there was morning, one day.

6 And God said, "Let there be a firmament in the midst of the waters, and let it separate the waters from the waters." [7] And God made the firmament and separated the waters which were under the firmament from the waters which were above the firmament. And it was so.[8] And God called the firmament Heaven. And there was evening and there was morning, a second day.

9 And God said, "Let the waters under the heavens be gathered together into one place, and let the dry land appear." And it was so. [10] God called the dry land Earth, and the waters that were gathered together he called Seas. And God saw that it was good. [11] And God said, "Let the earth put forth vegetation, plants yielding seed, and fruit trees bearing fruit in which is their

seed, each according to its kind, upon the earth." And it was so. [12] The earth brought forth vegetation, plants yielding seed according to their own kinds, and trees bearing fruit in which is their seed, each according to its kind. And God saw that it was good.[13] And there was evening and there was morning, a third day.

14 And God said, "Let there be lights in the firmament of the heavens to separate the day from the night; and let them be for signs and for seasons and for days and years, [15] and let them be lights in the firmament of the heavens to give light upon the earth." And it was so. [16] And God made the two great lights, the greater light to rule the day, and the lesser light to rule the night; he made the stars also. [17] And God set them in the firmament of the heavens to give light upon the earth, [18] to rule over the day and over the night, and to separate the light from the darkness. And God saw that it was good. [19] And there was evening and there was morning, a fourth day.

20 And God said, "Let the waters bring forth swarms of living creatures, and let birds fly above the earth across the firmament of the heavens." [21] So God created the great sea monsters and every living creature that moves, with which the waters swarm according to their kinds, and every winged bird according to its kind. And God saw that it was good. [22] And God blessed them saying, "Be fruitful

and multiply and fill the waters in the seas, and let the birds multiply on the earth." 23 And there was evening and there was morning, a fifth day.

24 And God said, "Let the earth bring forth living creatures according to their kinds: cattle and creeping things and beasts of the earth according to their kinds." And it was so. 25 And God made the beasts of the earth according to their kinds and the cattle according to their kinds, and everything that creeps upon the ground according to its kind. And God saw that it was good.

26 Then God said, "Let us make man in our image, after our likeness and let them have dominion over the fish of the sea, and over the birds of the air, and over the cattle, and over all the earth, and over every creeping thing that creeps upon the earth." 27 So God created man in his own image, in the image of God he created him; male and female he created them. 28 And God blessed them, and God said to them, "Be fruitful and multiply, and fill the earth and subdue it; and have dominion over the fish of the sea and over the birds of the air and over every living thing that moves upon the earth." 29 And God said, "Behold, I have given you every plant yielding seed which is upon the face of all the earth, and every tree with seed in its fruit; you shall have them for food. 30 And to every beast of the earth, and to every bird of the air, and to everything that creeps on the earth, everything that has the breath of life, I given every green plant for food." And it was so. 31 And God saw everything that he had made, and behold, it was very good. And there was evening and there was morning, a sixth day....

CHAPTER 6

11 Now the earth was corrupt in God's sight, and the earth was filled with violence. 12 And God saw the earth, and behold, it was corrupt; for all flesh had corrupted their way upon the earth. 13 And God said to Noah, "I have determined to make an end of all flesh; for the earth is filled with violence through them; behold, I will destroy them with the earth. 14

Make yourself an ark of gopher wood; make rooms in the ark, and cover it inside and out with pitch. 15 This is how you are to make it: the length of the ark three hundred cubits, its breadth fifty cubits, and its height thirty cubits. 16 Make a roof for the ark, and finish it to a cubit above; and set the door of the ark in its side; make it with lower, second, and third decks. 17 For behold, I will bring a flood of waters upon the earth, to destroy all flesh in which is the breath of life from under heaven; everything that is on the earth shall die. 18 But I will establish my covenant with you; and you shall come into the ark, you, your sons, your wife, and your sons' wives with you. 19 And of every living thing of all flesh, you shall bring two of every sort into the ark, to keep them alive with you; they shall be male and female. 20 Of the birds according to their kinds, and of the animals according to their kinds, of every creeping thing of the ground according to its kind, two of every sort shall come in to you, to keep them alive. 21 Also take with you every sort of food that is eaten, and store it up; and it shall serve as food for you and for them." 22 Noah did this; he did all that God commanded him.

CHAPTER 7

Then the LORD said to Noah, "Go into the ark, you and all your household, for I have seen that you are righteous before me in this generation. 2 Take with you seven pairs of all clean animals, the male and his mate; and a pair of the animals that are not clean, the male and his mate; 3 and seven pairs of the birds of the air also, male and female, to keep their kind alive upon the face of all the earth. 4 For in seven days I will send rain upon the earth forty days and forty nights; and every living thing that I have made I will blot out from the face of the ground." 5 And Noah did all that the LORD had commanded him.

6 Noah was six hundred years old when the flood of waters came upon the earth. 7 And Noah and his sons and his wife and his sons' wives with him went into the ark, to escape the waters of the flood. 8 Of clean animals, and of animals that are not clean, and of birds,

and of everything that creeps on the ground, [9] two and two, male and female, went into the ark with Noah, as God had commanded Noah. [10] And after seven days the waters of the flood came upon the earth.

11 In the six hundredth year of Noah's life, in the second month, on the seventeenth day of the month, on that day all the fountains of the great deep burst forth, and the windows of the heavens were opened. [12] And rain fell upon the earth forty days and forty nights. [13] On the very same day Noah and his sons, Shem and Ham and Japheth, and Noah's wife and the three wives of his sons with them entered the ark, [14] they and every beast according to its kind, and all the cattle according to their kinds, and every creeping thing that creeps on the earth according to its kind, and every bird according to its kind, every bird of every sort. [15] They went into the ark with Noah, two and two of all flesh in which there was the breath of life. [16] And they that entered, male and female of all flesh, went in as God had commanded him; and the LORD shut him in.

17 The flood continued forty days upon the earth; and the waters increased, and bore up the ark, and it rose high above the earth. [18] The waters prevailed and increased greatly upon the earth; and the ark floated on the face of the waters. [19] And the waters prevailed so mightily upon the earth that all the high mountains under the whole heaven were covered; [20] the waters prevailed above the mountains, covering them fifteen cubits deep.[21] And all flesh died that moved upon the earth, birds, cattle, beasts, all swarming creatures that swarm upon the earth, and every man; [22] everything on the dry land in whose nostrils was the breath of life died. [23] He blotted out every living thing that was upon the face of the ground, man and animals and creeping things and birds of the air; they were blotted out from the earth. Only Noah was left, and those that were with him in the ark. [24] And the waters prevailed upon the earth a hundred and fifty days.

CHAPTER 8

But God remembered Noah and all the beasts and all the cattle that were with him in the ark. And God made a wind blow over the earth, and the waters subsided; [2] the fountains of the deep and the windows of the heavens were closed, the rain from the heavens was restrained, [3] and the waters receded from the earth continually. At the end of a hundred and fifty days the waters had abated; [4] and in the seventh month, on the seventeenth day of the month, the ark came to rest upon the mountains of Ar'arat.[5] And the waters continued to abate until the tenth month; in the tenth month, on the first day of the month, the tops of the mountains were seen.

6 At the end of forty days Noah opened the window of the ark which he had made, [7] and sent forth a raven; and it went to and fro until the waters were dried up from the earth. [8] Then he sent forth a dove from him to see if the waters had subsided from the face of the ground; [9] but the dove found no place to set her foot, and she returned to him to the ark, for the waters were still on the face of the whole earth. So he put forth his hand and took her and brought her into the ark with him. [10] He waited another seven days, and again he sent forth the dove out of the ark; [11] and the dove came back to him in the evening, and lo, in her mouth a freshly plucked olive leaf; so Noah knew that the waters had subsided from the earth. [12] Then he waited another seven days, and sent forth the dove; and she did not return to him any more.

13 In the six hundred and first year, in the first month, the first day of the month, the waters were dried from off the earth; and Noah removed the covering of the ark, and looked, and behold, the face of the ground was dry. [14] In the second month, on the twenty-seventh day of the month, the earth was dry. [15] Then God said to Noah, [16] "Go forth from the ark, you and your wife, and your sons and your sons' wives with you. [17] Bring forth with you every living thing that is with you of all flesh—birds and animals and every creeping thing that creeps on the earth— that they may breed abundantly on the earth, and be fruitful and multiply upon the earth." [18] So Noah went forth, and his sons and his wife and his sons' wives with him. [19] And every beast, every creeping thing, and every bird, everything that moves upon the earth, went forth by families out of the ark.

20 Then Noah built an altar to the LORD, and took of every clean animal and of every clean bird, and offered burnt offerings on the altar.²¹ And when the LORD smelled the pleasing odor, the LORD said in his heart, "I will never again curse the ground because of man, for the imagination of man's heart is evil from his youth; neither will I ever again destroy every living creature as I have done.²² While the earth remains, seedtime and harvest, cold and heat, summer and winter, day and night, shall not cease."

CHAPTER 9

And God blessed Noah and his sons, and said to them, "Be fruitful and multiply, and fill the earth. ² The fear of you and the dread of you shall be upon every beast of the earth, and upon every bird of the air, upon everything that creeps on the ground and all the fish of the sea; into your hand they are delivered. ³ Every moving thing that lives shall be food for you; and as I gave you the green plants, I give you everything. ⁴ Only you shall not eat flesh with its life, that is, its blood. ⁵ For your lifeblood I will surely require a reckoning; of every beast I will require it and of man; of every man's brother I will require the life of man. ⁶ Whoever sheds the blood of man, by man shall his blood be shed; for God made man in his own image. ⁷ And you, be fruitful and multiply, bring forth abundantly on the earth and multiply in it."

8 Then God said to Noah and to his sons with him, ⁹ "Behold, I establish my covenant with you and your descendants after you, ¹⁰ and with every living creature that is with you, the birds, the cattle, and every beast of the earth with you, as many as came out of the ark. ¹¹ I establish my covenant with you, that never again shall all flesh be cut off by the waters of a flood, and never again shall there be a flood to destroy the earth." ¹² And God said, "This is the sign of the covenant which I make between me and you and every living creature that is with you, for all future generations."

ARISTOTLE

[From] *Physics*

Why shouldn't nature operate not for the sake of something or because a result is better, but rather from necessity? That is, why shouldn't the sky rain not in order to make the corn grow, but rather of necessity (for, [as one might argue] what is taken up must cool, and what is cooled becomes water and comes down, with the result that the corn grows); similarly, if the corn rots on the threshing-floor, [we do not say that] it rains in order for the corn to rot, but that this [simply] happened. What prevents the parts of nature from being this way, e.g., why [shouldn't we ascribe] our teeth's coming up as they do to necessity?...

It is not possible that things should be this way. For teeth and all other natural things occur in a given way either always or for the most part; but nothing which occurs by chance or spontaneity [occurs always or for the most part]....If then things occur either by coincidence or for the sake of something, it follows that [what occurs by nature] occurs for the sake of something....Therefore, among the things which occur and exist in nature, [some things are] for the sake of something.

ARISTOTLE

[From] *Politics*

Hence it is similarly clear that we must suppose that plants exist on account of animals...and the other animals for the sake of man, the tame ones because of their usefulness and as food, and if not all the wild ones, then most, on account of food and other assistance [they provide, in the form of] clothing and other tools which come from them. If, then, nature does nothing without an end and nothing in vain, it is necessary that nature made all these on account of men. Hence, the craft of war will be by nature a sort of art of acquisition (for hunting is a part of this), which one ought to use against wild beasts and those men who, those naturally ruled, do not submit, since this sort of war is just by nature.

JOHN LOCKE

[From] *The Second Treatise of Government*

27. Though the earth and all inferior creatures be common to all men, yet every man has a property in his own person; this nobody has any right to but himself. The labor of his body and the work of his hands, we may say, are properly his. Whatsoever then he removes out of the state that nature has provided and left it in, he has mixed his labor with, and joined to it something that is his own, and thereby makes it his property.

28. He that is nourished by the acorns he picked up under an oak, or the apples he gathered from the trees in the wood, has certainly appropriated them to himself. Nobody can deny but the nourishment is his. I ask, then, When did they begin to be his? When he digested or when he ate or when he boiled or when he brought them home? Or when he picked them up? And it is plain, if the first gathering made

them not his, nothing else could. That labor put a distinction between them and common; that added something to them more than nature, the common mother of all, had done; and so they became his private right. And will anyone say he had no right to those acorns or apples he thus appropriated because he had not the consent of all mankind to make them his? Was it a robbery thus to assume to himself what belonged to all in common? If such a consent as that was necessary, man had starved, notwithstanding the plenty God had given him. We see in commons, which remain so by compact, that it is the taking any part of what is common and removing it out of the state nature leaves it in which begins the property, without which the common is of no use. And the taking of this or that part does not depend on the express consent of all the commoners. Thus the grass my horse has bit, the turfs my servant has cut, and the ore I have digged in any place where I have a right to them in common with others, become my property without the assignation or consent of anybody. The labor that was mine, removing them out of that common state they were in, has fixed my property in them. . . .

32. But the chief matter of property being now not the fruits of the earth and the beasts that subsist on it, but the earth itself, as that which takes in and carries with it all the rest, I think it is plain that property in that, too, is acquired as the former. As much land as a man tills, plants, improves, cultivates, and can use the product of, so much is his property. He by his labor does, as it were, enclose it from the common. Nor will it invalidate his right to say everybody else has an equal title to it, and therefore he cannot appropriate, he cannot enclose, without the consent of all his fellow commoners—all man-

kind. God, when he gave the world in common to all mankind, commanded man also to labor, and the penury of his condition required it of him. God and his reason commanded him to subdue the earth, i.e., improve it for the benefit of life, and therein lay out something upon it that was his own, his labor. He that in obedience to this command of God subdued, tilled, and sowed any part of it, thereby annexed to it something that was his property, which another had no title to, nor could without injury take from him. . . .

34. God gave the world to men in common; but since he gave it them for their benefit and the greatest conveniences of life they were capable to draw from it, it cannot be supposed he meant it should always remain common and uncultivated. He gave it to the use of the industrious and rational—and labor was to be his title to it—not to the fancy or covetousness of the quarrelsome and contentious. He that had as good left for his improvement as was already taken up needed not complain, ought not to meddle with what was already improved by another's labor; if he did, it is plain he desired the benefit of another's pains which he had no right to, and not the ground which God had given him in common with others to labor on, and whereof there was as good left as that already possessed, and more than he knew what to do with, or his industry could reach to.

35. . . . [H]ence subduing or cultivating the earth and having dominion, we see, are joined together. The one gave title to the other. So that God, by commanding to subdue, gave authority so far to appropriate; and the condition of human life which requires labor and material to work on necessarily introduces private possessions.

CHARLES DARWIN

[From] *On the Origin of Species*

With respect to the belief that organic beings have been created beautiful for the delight of man,—a belief which it has been pronounced is subversive of my whole theory,—I may first remark that the sense of beauty obviously depends on the nature of the mind, irrespective of any real quality in the admired object; and that the idea of what is beautiful, is not innate or unalterable. We see this, for instance, in the men of different races admiring an entirely different standard of beauty in their women. If beautiful objects had been created solely for man's gratification, it ought to be shown that before man appeared, there was less beauty on the face of the earth than since he came on the stage. Were the beautiful volute and cone shells of the Eocene epoch, and the gracefully sculptured ammonites of the Secondary period, created that man might ages afterwards admire them in his cabinet? Few objects are more beautiful than the minute siliceous cases of the diatomaceæ: were these created that they might be examined and admired under the higher powers of the microscope?...

Authors of the highest eminence seem to be fully satisfied with the view that each species has been independently created. To my mind it accords better with what we know of the laws impressed on matter by the Creator, that the production and extinction of the past and present inhabitants of the world should have been due to secondary causes, like those determining the birth and death of the individual. When I view all beings not as special creations, but as the lineal descendants of some few beings which lived long before the first bed of the Cambrian system was deposited, they seem to me to become ennobled. Judging from the past, we may safely infer that not

one living species will transmit its unaltered likeness to a distant futurity. And of the species now living very few will transmit progeny of any kind to a far distant futurity; for the manner in which all organic beings are grouped, shows that the greater number of species in each genus, and all the species in many genera, have left no descendants, but have become utterly extinct. We can so far take a prophetic glance into futurity as to foretell that it will be the common and widely-spread species, belonging to the larger and dominant groups within each class, which will ultimately prevail and procreate new and dominant species. As all the living forms of life are the lineal descendants of those which lived long before the Cambrian epoch, we may feel certain that the ordinary succession by generation has never once been broken, and that no cataclysm has desolated the whole world. Hence we may look with some confidence to a secure future of great length. And as natural selection works solely by and for the good of each being, all corporeal and mental endowments will tend to progress towards perfection.

It is interesting to contemplate a tangled bank, clothed with many plants of many kinds, with birds singing on the bushes, with various insects flitting about, and with worms crawling through the damp earth, and to reflect that these elaborately constructed forms, so different from each other, and dependent upon each other in so complex a manner, have all been produced by laws acting around us. These laws, taken in the largest sense, being Growth with Reproduction; Inheritance which is almost implied by reproduction; Variability from the indirect and direct action of the conditions of life, and from use and disuse: a Ratio of Increase as to lead to a Struggle for Life, and as a consequence to Natural

Selection, entailing Divergence of Character and the Extinction of less-improved forms. Thus, from the war of nature, from famine and death, the most exalted object which we are capable of conceiving, namely, the production of the higher animals, directly follows. There is grandeur in this view of life, with its several powers, having been originally breathed by the Creator into a few forms or into one; and that, whilst this planet has gone cycling on according to the fixed law of gravity, from so simple a beginning endless forms most beautiful and most wonderful have been, and are being evolved.

JOHN MUIR

Anthropocentrism and Predation

The world, we are told, was made especially for man—a presumption not supported by all the facts. A numerous class of men are painfully astonished whenever they find anything, living or dead, in all God's universe, which they cannot eat or render in some way what they call useful to themselves. They have precise dogmatic insight of the intentions of the Creator, and it is hardly possible to be guilty of irreverence in speaking of *their* God any more than of heathen idols. He is regarded as a civilized, law-abiding gentleman in favor either of a republican form of government or of a limited monarchy; believes in the literature and language of England; is a warm supporter of the English constitution and Sunday schools and missionary societies; and is as purely a manufactured article as any puppet of a half-penny theater.

With such views of the Creator it is, of course, not surprising that erroneous views should be entertained of the creation. To such properly trimmed people, the sheep, for example, is an easy problem—food and clothing "for us," eating grass and daisies white by divine appointment for this predestined purpose, on perceiving the demand for wool that would be occasioned by eating of the apple in the Garden of Eden.

In the same distant plan, whales are storehouses of oil for us, to help out the stars in lighting our dark ways until the discovery of the Pennsylvania oil wells. Among plants, hemp, to say nothing of the cereals, is a case of evident destination for ships' rigging, wrapping packages, and hanging the wicked. Cotton is another plain case of clothing. Iron was made for hammers and ploughs, and lead for bullets; all intended for us. And so of other small handfuls of insignificant things.

But if we should ask these profound expositors of God's intentions, How about those man-eating animals—lions, tigers, alligators—which smack their lips over raw man? Or about those myriads of noxious insects that destroy labor and drink his blood? Doubtless man was intended for food and drink for all these? Oh, no! Not at all! These are unresolvable difficulties connected with Eden's apple and the Devil. Why does water drown its lord? Why do so many minerals poison him? Why are so many plants and fishes deadly enemies? Why is the lord of creation subjected to the same laws of life as his subjects? Oh, all these things are satanic, or in some way connected with the first garden.

Now, it never seems to occur to these far-seeking teachers that Nature's object in making animals and plants might possibly be first of all the happiness of each one of them, not the creation of all for the happiness of one. Why should man value himself as more than a small part of the one great unit of creation? And what creature of all that the Lord has taken the pains to make is not essential to the completeness of that unit—the cosmos? The universe would be incomplete without man; but it would also be incomplete without the smallest transmicroscopic creature that dwells beyond our conceitful eyes and knowledge.

From the dust of the earth, from the common elementary fund, the Creator has made *Homo sapiens*. From the same material He has made every other creature, however noxious and insignificant to us. They are earth-born companions and our fellow mortals. The fearfully good, the orthodox, of this laborious patchwork of modern civilization cry "Heresy" on every one whose sympathies reach a single hair's breadth beyond the boundary epidermis of our own species. Not content with taking all of earth, they also claim the celestial country as the only ones who possess the kind of souls for which that imponderable empire was planned.

This star, our own good earth, made many a successful journey around the heavens ere man was made, and whole kingdoms of creatures enjoyed existence and returned to dust ere man appeared to claim them. After human beings have also played their part in Creation's plan, they too may disappear without any general burning or extraordinary commotion whatever.

Plants are credited with but dim and uncertain sensation, and minerals with positively none at all.

But why may not even a mineral arrangement of matter be endowed with sensation of a kind that we in our blind exclusive perfection can have no manner of communication with?

But I have wandered from my object. I stated a page or two back that man claimed the earth was made for him, and I was going to say that venomous beasts, thorny plants, and deadly diseases of certain parts of the earth prove that the whole world was not made for him. When an animal from a tropical climate is taken to high latitudes, it may perish of cold, and we say that such an animal was never intended for so severe a climate. But when man betakes himself to sickly parts of the tropics and perishes, he cannot see that he was never intended for such deadly climates. No, he will rather accuse the first mother of the cause of the difficulty, though she may never have seen a fever district; or will consider it a providential chastisement for some self-invented form of sin.

Furthermore, all uneatable and uncivilizable animals, and all plants which carry prickles, are deplorable evils which, according to closet researches of clergy, require the cleansing chemistry of universal planetary combustion. But more than aught else mankind requires burning, as being in great part wicked, and if that transmundane furnace can be so applied and regulated as to smelt and purify us into conformity with the rest of the terrestrial creation, then the tophetization of the erratic genus *Homo* were a consummation devoutly to be prayed for. But, glad to leave these ecclesiastical fires and blunders, I joyfully return to the immortal truth and immortal beauty of Nature.

ALDO LEOPOLD

[From] The Land Ethic

When god-like Odysseus returned from the wars in Troy, he hanged all on one rope a dozen slave-girls of his household whom he suspected of misbehavior during his absence.

This hanging involved no question of propriety. The girls were property. The disposal of property was then, as now, a matter of expediency, not of right and wrong.

Concepts of right and wrong were not lacking from Odysseus' Greece: witness the fidelity of his wife through the long years before at last his black-prowed galleys clove the wine-dark seas for home. The ethical structure of that day covered wives, but had not yet been extended to human chattels. During the three thousand years which have since elapsed, ethical criteria have been extended to many fields of conduct, with corresponding shrinkages in those judged by expediency only.

THE ETHICAL SEQUENCE

This extension of ethics, so far studied only by philosophers, is actually a process in ecological evolution. Its sequences may be described in ecological as well as in philosophical terms. An ethic, ecologically, is a limitation on freedom of action in the struggle for existence. An ethic, philosophically, is a differentiation of social from anti-social conduct. These are two definitions of one thing. The thing has its origin in the tendency of interdependent individuals or groups to evolve modes of co-operation. The ecologist calls these symbioses. Politics and economics are advanced symbioses in which the original free-for-all competition has been replaced, in part, by co-operative mechanisms with an ethical content.

The complexity of co-operative mechanisms has increased with population density, and with the efficiency of tools. It was simpler, for example, to define the anti-social uses of sticks and stones in the days of the mastodons than of bullets and billboards in the age of motors.

The first ethics dealt with the relation between individuals; the Mosaic Decalogue is an example. Later accretions dealt with the relation between the individual and society. The Golden Rule tries to integrate the individual to society; democracy to integrate social organization to the individual.

There is as yet no ethic dealing with man's relation to land and to the animals and plants which grow upon it. Land, like Odysseus' slave-girls, is still property. The land-relation is still strictly economic, entailing privileges but not obligations.

The extension of ethics to this third element in human environment is, if I read the evidence correctly, an evolutionary possibility and an ecological necessity. It is the third step in a sequence. The first two have already been taken. Individual thinkers since the days of Ezekiel and Isaiah have asserted that the despoliation of land is not only inexpedient but wrong. Society, however, has not yet affirmed their belief. I regard the present conservation movement as the embryo of such an affirmation.

An ethic may be regarded as a mode of guidance for meeting ecological situations so new or intricate, or involving such deferred reactions, that the path of social expediency is not discernible to the average individual. Animal instincts are modes of guidance for the individual in meeting such situations. Ethics are possibly a kind of community instinct in-the-making.

THE COMMUNITY CONCEPT

All ethics so far evolved rest upon a single premise: that the individual is a member of a community of interdependent parts. His instincts prompt him to compete for his place in that community, but his ethics prompt him also to cooperate (perhaps in order that there may be a place to compete for).

The land ethic simply enlarges the boundaries of the community to include soils, waters, plants, and animals, or collectively: the land.

This sounds simple: do we not already sing our love for and obligation to the land of the free and the home of the brave? Yes, but just what and whom do we love? Certainly not the soil, which we are sending helter-skelter downriver. Certainly not the waters, which we assume have no function except to turn turbines, float barges, and carry off sewage. Certainly not the plants, of which we exterminate whole communities without batting an eye. Certainly not

the animals, of which we have already extirpated many of the largest and most beautiful species. A land ethic of course cannot prevent the alteration, management, and use of these "resources," but it does affirm their right to continued existence, and, at least in spots, their continued existence in a natural state.

In short, a land ethic changes the role of *Homo sapiens* from conqueror of the land-community to plain member and citizen of it. It implies respect for his fellow-members, and also respect for the community as such.

In human history, we have learned (I hope) that the conqueror role is eventually self-defeating. Why? Because it is implicit in such a role that the conqueror knows, *ex cathedra*, just what makes the community clock tick, and just what and who is valuable, and what and who is worthless, in community life. It always turns out that he knows neither, and this is why his conquests eventually defeat themselves.

HENRY DAVID THOREAU

[From] Walking

I wish to speak a word for Nature, for absolute freedom and wilderness, as contrasted with a freedom and culture merely civil,—to regard man as an inhtabitant, or a part and parcel of Nature, rather than a member of society. I wish to make an extreme statement, if so I may make an emphatic one, for there are enough champions of civilization: the minister and the school-committee and every one of you will take care of that....

Life consists with wildness. The most alive is the wildest. Not yet subdued to man, its presence refreshes him. One who pressed forward incessantly and never rested from his labors, who grew fast and made infinite demands on life, would always find himself in a new country or wilderness, and surrounded by the raw material of life. He would be climbing over the prostrate stems of primitive forest-trees.

Hope and the future for me are not in lawns and cultivated fields, not in towns and cities, but in the impervious and quaking swamps.

In literature it is only the wild that attracts us. Dullness is but another name for tameness. It is the uncivilized free and wild thinking in "Hamlet" and the "Iliad," in all the Scriptures and Mythologies, not learned in the schools, that delights us. As the wild duck is more swift and beautiful than the tame, so is the wild—the mallard—thought, which 'mid falling dews wings its way above the fens. A truly good book is something as natural, and as unexpectedly and unaccountably fair and perfect, as a wild flower discovered on the prairies of the West or in the jungles of the East. Genius is a light which makes the darkness visible, like the lightning's flash, which perchance shatters the temple of knowledge itself,— and not a taper lighted at the heartstone of the race, which pales before the light of common day.

English literature, from the days of the minstrels to the Lake Poets,—Chaucer and Spenser and Milton, and even Shakespeare, included,—breathes no quite fresh and, in this sense, wild stain. It is an essentially tame and civilized literature, reflecting Greece and Rome. Her wilderness is a greenwood, her wild man a Robin Hood. There is plenty of genial love of Nature, but not so much of Nature herself. Her chronicles inform us when her wild animals, but not when the wild man in her, became extinct.

In short, all good things are wild and free. There is something in a strain of music, whether produced by an instrument or by the human voice,— take the sound of a bugle in a summer night, for instance,—which by its wildness, to speak without satire, reminds me of the cries emitted by wild beasts in their native forests. It is so much of their wildness as I can understand. Give me for my friends and neighbors wild men, not tame ones. The wildness of the savage is but a faint symbol of the awful ferity with which good men and lovers meet.

I love even to see the domestic animals reassert their native rights,—any evidence that they have not wholly lost their original wild habits and vigor; as when my neighbor's cow breaks out of her pasture early in the spring and boldly swims the river, a cold, gray tide, twenty-five or thirty rods wide, swollen by the melted snow. It is the buffalo crossing the Mississippi. This exploit confers some dignity on the herd in my eyes,—already dignified. The seeds of instinct are preserved under the thick hides of cattle and horses, like seeds in the bowels of the earth, an indefinite period. . . .

I rejoice that horses and steers have to be broken before they can be made the slaves of men, and that men themselves have some wild oats still left to sow before they become submissive members of society.

[From] *Principles of Political Economy: With Some of Their Applications to Social Philosophy*

There is room in the world, no doubt, and even in old countries, for a great increase of population, supposing the arts of life to go on improving, and capital to increase. But even if innocuous, I confess I see very little reason for desiring it. The density of population necessary to enable mankind to obtain, in the greatest degree, all the advantages both of co-operation and of social intercourse, has, in all the most populous countries, been attained. A population may be too crowded, though all be amply supplied with food and raiment. It is not good for man to be kept perforce at all times in the presence of his species. A world from which solitude is extirpated, is a very poor ideal. Solitude, in the sense of being often alone, is essential to any depth of meditation or of character; and solitude in the presence of natural beauty and grandeur, is the cradle of thoughts and aspirations which are not only good for the individual, but which society could ill do without. Nor is there much satisfaction in contemplating the world with nothing left to the spontaneous activity of nature; with every rood of land brought into cultivation, which is capable of growing food for human beings; every flowery waste or natural pasture ploughed up, all quadrupeds or birds which are not domesticated for man's use exterminated as his rivals for food, every hedgerow or superfluous tree rooted out, and scarcely a place left where a wild shrub or flower could grow without being eradicated as a weed in the name of improved agriculture. If the earth must lose that great portion of its pleasantness which it owes to things that the unlimited increase of wealth and population would extirpate from it, for the mere purpose of enabling it to support a larger, but not a better or a happier population, I sincerely hope, for the sake of posterity, that they will be content to be stationary, long before necessity compels them to it.

It is scarcely necessary to remark that a stationary condition of capital and population implies no stationary state of human improvement. There would be as much scope as ever for all kinds of mental culture, and moral and social progress; as much room for improving the Art of Living, and much more likelihood of its being improved, when minds ceased to be engrossed by the art of getting on. Even the industrial arts might be as earnestly and as successfully cultivated, with this sole difference, that instead of serving no purpose but the increase of wealth, industrial improvements would produce their legitimate effect, that of abridging labour. Hitherto it is questionable if all the mechanical inventions yet made have lightened the day's toil of any human being. They have enabled a greater population to live the same life of drudgery and imprisonment, and an increased number of manufacturers and others to make fortunes. They have increased the comforts of the middle classes. But they have not yet begun to effect those great changes in human destiny, which it is in their nature and in their futurity to accomplish. Only when, in addition to just institutions, the increase of mankind shall be under the deliberate guidance of judicious foresight, can the conquests made from the powers of nature by the intellect and energy of scientific discoverers, become the common property of the species, and the means of improving and elevating the universal lot.

JOHN STUART MILL

[From] On Nature

"Nature," "natural," and the group of words derived from them, or allied to them in etymology, have at all times filled a great place in the thoughts and taken a strong hold on the feelings of mankind. That they should have done so is not surprising when we consider what the words, in their primitive and most obvious signification, represent; but it is unfortunate that a set of terms which play so great a part in moral and metaphysical speculation should have acquired many meanings different from the primary one, yet sufficiently allied to it to admit of confusion. The words have thus become entangled in so many foreign associations, mostly of a very powerful and tenacious character, that they have come to excite, and to be the symbols of, feelings which their original meaning will by no means justify, and which have made them one of the most copious sources of false taste, false philosophy, false morality, and even bad law. . . .

If there are any marks at all of special design in creation, one of the things most evidently designed is that a large proportion of all animals should pass their existence in tormenting and devouring other animals. They have been lavishly fitted out with the instruments necessary for that purpose; their strongest instincts impel them to it and many of them seem to have been constructed incapable of supporting themselves by any other food. If a tenth part of the pains which have been expended in finding benevolent adaptations in all nature had been employed in collecting evidence to blacken the character of the Creator, what scope for comment would not have been found in the entire existence of the lower animals, divided, with scarcely an exception, into devourers and devoured, and a prey to a thousand ills from which they are denied the faculties

necessary for protecting themselves. If we are not obliged to believe the animal creation to be the work of a demon, it is because we need not suppose it to have been made by a Being of infinite power. But if imitation of the Creator's will as revealed in nature were applied as a rule of action in this case, the most atrocious enormities of the worst men would be more than justified by the apparent intention of Providence that throughout all animated nature the strong should prey upon the weak. . . .

Conformity to nature has no connection whatever with right and wrong. The idea can never be fitly introduced into ethical discussions at all, except, occasionally and partially, into the question of degrees of culpability. To illustrate this point, let us consider the phrase by which the greatest intensity of condemnatory feeling is conveyed in connection with the idea of nature—the word "unnatural." That a thing is unnatural, in any precise meaning which can be attached to the word, is no argument for its being blamable; since the most criminal actions are to a being like man not more unnatural than most of the virtues. The acquisition of virtue has in all ages been accounted a work of labour and difficulty, while the *descensus Averni*, on the contrary, is of proverbial facility; and it assuredly requires in most persons a greater conquest over a greater number of natural inclinations to become eminently virtuous than transcendently vicious. But if an action, or an inclination, has been decided on other grounds to be blamable, it may be a circumstance in aggravation that it is unnatural—that is, repugnant to some strong feeling usually found in human beings; since the bad propensity, whatever it be, has afforded evidence of being both strong and deeply rooted, by having overcome that repugnance. This presumption, of course, fails if the individual never had the repugnance; and the argument, therefore, is not fit to be urged unless the feeling which is violated by the act is not only justifiable and reasonable, but is one which it is blamable to be without.

The corresponding plea in extenuation of a culpable act because it was natural, or because it was prompted by a natural feeling, never, I think, ought to be admitted. There is hardly a bad action ever perpetrated which is not perfectly natural, and the motives to which are not perfectly natural feelings. In the eye of reason, therefore, this is no excuse, but it is quite "natural" that it should be so in the eyes of the multitude; because the meaning of the expression is, that they have a fellow feeling with the offender. When they say that something which they cannot help admitting to be blamable is nevertheless natural, they mean that they can imagine the possibility of their being themselves tempted to commit it. Most people have a considerable amount of indulgence towards all acts of which they feel a possible source within themselves, reserving their rigour for those which, though perhaps really less bad, they cannot in any way understand how it is possible to commit. If an action convinces them (which it often does on very inadequate grounds) that the person who does it must be a being totally unlike themselves, they are seldom particular in examining the precise degree of blame due to it, or even if blame is properly due to it at all. They measure the degree of guilt by the strength of their antipathy; and hence differences of opinion, and even differences of taste, have been objects of as intense moral abhorrence as the most atrocious crimes...

The word "nature" has two principal meanings: it either denotes the entire system of things, with the aggregates of all their properties, or it denotes things as they would be, apart from human intervention.

In the first of these senses, the doctrine that man ought to follow nature is unmeaning; since man has no power to do anything else than follow nature; all his actions are done through, and in obedience to, some one or many of nature's physical or mental laws.

In the other sense of the term, the doctrine that man ought to follow nature, or, in other words, ought to make the spontaneous course of things the model of his voluntary actions, is equally irrational and immoral.

Irrational, because all human action whatever consists in altering, and all useful action in improving, the spontaneous course of nature.

Immoral, because the course of natural phenomena being replete with everything which when committed by human beings is most worthy of abhorrence, any one who endeavoured in his actions to imitate the natural course of things would be universally seen and acknowledged to be the wickedest of men.

The scheme of Nature, regarded in its whole extent, cannot have had, for its sole or even principal object, the good of human or other sentient beings. What good it brings to them is mostly the result of their own exertions. Whatsoever, in nature, gives indication of beneficent design proves this beneficence to be armed only with limited power; and the duty of man is to cooperate with the beneficent powers, not by imitating, but by perpetually striving to amend, the course of nature—and bringing that part of it over which we can exercise control more nearly into conformity with a high standard of justice and goodness.

DANIEL BOTKIN

[From] *Discordant Harmonies: A New Ecology for the Twenty-First Century*

IN THE MIRROR OF NATURE, WE SEE OURSELVES

The answers to old questions—What is the character of nature undisturbed? What is the influence of nature on human beings? What is the influence of human beings on nature?—can no longer be viewed as distinct from one another. Life and the environment are one thing, not two, and people, as all life, are immersed in the one system. When we influence nature, we influence ourselves; when we change nature, we change ourselves. A concern with nature is not merely a scientific curiosity, but a subject that pervades philosophy, theology, aesthetics, and psychology. There are deep reasons that we desire a balance and harmony in the structure of the biological world and that we seek to find that structural balance, just as our ancestors desired and sought that kind of balance in the physical world.

Clearly, to abandon a belief in the constancy of undisturbed nature is psychologically uncomfortable. As long as we could believe that nature undisturbed was constant, we were provided with a simple standard against which to judge our actions, a reflection from a windless pond in which our place was both apparent and fixed, providing us with a sense of continuity and permanence that was comforting. Abandoning these beliefs leaves us in an extreme existential position: we are like small boats without anchors in a sea of time; how we long for safe harbor on a shore.

The change in perception of nature and the new answers to the ancient questions about nature arise from new observations and new ways of thinking that

even now seem radical. The transition that is taking place affects us today and will continue to affect us deeply, in ways that may not be obvious, for decades. These changes strike at the very root of how we see ourselves. We have clouded our perception of nature with false images, and as long as we continue to do that we will cloud our perception of ourselves, cripple our ability to manage natural resources, and choose the wrong approaches to dealing with global environmental concerns. The way to achieve a harmony with nature is first to break free of old metaphors and embrace new ones so that we can lift the veils that prevent us from accepting what we observe, and then to make use of technology to study life and life-supporting systems as they are. A harmony between ourselves and nature depends on—indeed, requires—modern technological tools to teach us about the Earth and to help us manage wisely what we realize we have inadvertently begun to unravel.

Once we realize that we are part of a living system, global in scale, produced and in some ways controlled by life, and once we accept the intrinsic qualities of organic systems—with their ambiguities, variabilities, and complexities—we can feel a part of the world in a way that our nineteenth-century ancestors could not, but our ancestors before them did. We can leave behind the metaphors of the machine, which are so uncomfortable psychologically because they separate us from nature and are so unlifelike and therefore so different from ourselves, and we can arrive, with the best information available for us in our time, at a new organic view of the Earth, a view in which we are a part of a living and changing system whose changes we can accept, use, and control, to make the Earth a comfortable home, for each of us individually and for all of us collectively in our civilizations.

The machine-age view provided simple and immediate answers to the classic questions about the relationship between human beings and nature. Nature knew best; nature undisturbed was constant. Individuals, depending on which of the interpretations of nature they chose, had a certain fixed relationship to their surroundings. From the new perspective, nature does not provide simple answers. People are forced to choose the kind of environment they want, and a "desirable" environment may be one that people have altered, at least in some vicinities some of the time.

An awareness of the power of civilization to change and destroy the biological world has grown since the nineteenth century. We recognize that civilization has had a tremendous impact on nature, and it is tempting to agree with George Perkins Marsh that the absence of structural balance in the biological world is always, or almost always, the result of human activity, that "man is everywhere a disturbing agent. Wherever he plants his foot, the harmonies of nature are tuned to discords."[1] But we understand, in spite of our wishes, that nature moves and changes and involves risks and uncertainties and that our judgments of our own actions must be made against this moving image.

There are ranges within which life can persist, and changes that living systems must undergo in order to persist. We can change structural aspects of life within the acceptable ranges. Those changes that are necessary to the continuation of life we must allow to occur, or substitute for them at huge cost the qualities that otherwise would have been achieved. We can engineer nature at nature's rates and in nature's ways; we must be wary when we engineer nature at an unnatural rate in novel ways. To conserve well is to engineer within the rules of natural changes, patterns, and ambiguities; to engineer well is to conserve, to maintain the dynamics of the living systems. The answer to the question about the human role in nature depends on time, culture, technologies, and peoples. There is no simple, universal (external to all peoples, cultures, times) answer. However, the answer to this question for our time is very much influenced by the fact that we are changing nature at all levels—from the local to the global—that we have the power to mold nature into what we want it to be or to destroy it completely, and that we know we have that power. This leads us to a very different kind of answer from those of the Greek and Roman philosophers, their intellectual descendants in the Middle Ages and Renaissance, or the people of the early and mid-industrial–mechanical age.

Now that we understand that we are changing the environment at a global level, we must accept the responsibility for the actions we have taken and the changes these actions have wrought. It is prudent to minimize these effects and to slow down the rates of change as much as possible. This requires not only information and understanding, but also a political will and social and economic means and policies to accomplish what we need and desire, issues to which little attention has so far been paid. It is uncomfortable to us that the new perspective does not give the same simple answers to all questions, but requires that our management be specific and that answers to questions be dependent on the particular qualities of our goals and the actions open to us. Knowing what to do in each case requires considerable information, surveys, monitoring, knowledge, and understanding, which we as a society have been most reluctant to seek. Perhaps we have been too much like those people Peter Kalm met in eighteenth-century America, who believed that the study of nature was "a mere trifle, and the pastime of fools."[2]

A new awareness of biological nature is coming and is inevitable, and it can easily be misused. If we persist in arguing that what is natural is constant and what is constant is good, then those of us who value wilderness for its intrinsic characteristcs or believe that the biosphere must be maintained within certain bounds will have lost our ability to live in harmony with nature as it really is. If we do not understand the true nature of populations, biological communities, and ecosystems, how can we expect to husband them wisely? When we had less power, we could live with myths. But today, as Joseph Campbell recognized, "Science itself is now the only field through which the dimension of mythology can be again revealed."[3]

The task that I am encouraging the reader to join in continues that begun by George Perkins Marsh, a task that acknowledges the great destructive powers of human civilization but is optimistic that we may begin to choose as a prudent person would in our dealings with nature. The message is consistent with the ethical outlook of Paul Sears, who wrote that "nature is not to be conquered save on her own terms."[4] I have tried simply to give a modern view of "her" terms. It is also consistent with the land ethic of Aldo Leopold: "Conservation is a state of harmony between men and land."[5] We have not abandoned that belief or Leopold's ethic, but have redefined "harmony." To achieve that new harmony, we must understand the character of nature undisturbed, that discordant harmony which has been the topic of this book.

The proper response to the problems we have created for the environment with our technology is not to abandon civilization or modern technology, as some have argued and as seems so comfortable and desirable a course of action to those who have suffered most the destructive effects of human actions against the natural world, or to cling to the belief that everything natural (that is, nonhuman) is desirable and good. Having altered nature with our technology, we must depend on technology to see us through to solutions. The task before us is to understand the biological world to the point that we can learn how to live within the discordant harmonies of our biological surroundings, so that they function not only to promote the continuation of life but also to benefit ourselves: our aesthetics, morality, philosophies, and material needs. We need not only new knowledge, but also new

metaphors, which are arising from an amalgamation of the organic metaphor with a new technological metaphor, evolving from the old machine idea that we have been accustomed to using for the past 200 years.

...Could that most magnificent machine of the twentieth century, the airplane, serve as the proper model for the system of nature visible below? Machines can help us see nature, but they alone are not the proper model, the right metaphor for nature. We have things backward. We use an engineering metaphor and imagine that the Earth is a machine when it is not, but we do not take an engineering approach to nature; we do not borrow the cleverness and the skills of the engineer, which is what we must do. We talk about the spaceship Earth, but who is monitoring the dials and turning the knobs? No one; there are no dials to watch, only occasional alarms made by people peering out the window, who call to us that they see species disappearing, an ozone hole in the upper atmosphere, the climate change, the coasts of all the world polluted. But because we have never created the system of monitoring our environment or devised the understanding of nature's strange ecological systems, we are still like the passengers in the cabin who think they smell smoke or, misunderstanding how a plane flies, mistake light turbulence for trouble. We need to instrument the cockpit of the biosphere and to let up the window shade so that we begin to observe nature as it is, not as we imagine it to be.

NOTES
1. G. P. Marsh, *Man and Nature*, ed. D. Lowenthal (1864; Cambridge, Mass.: Harvard University Press, 1967), 36.

2. P. Kalm, *Travels in North America*, 2 vols., trans. A. B. Benson (New York: Dover, 1966), 308–9.

3. J. Campbell, *The Masks of God: Primitive Mythology* (New York: Viking, 1959), 468.

4. P. Sears, *Deserts on the March* (Norman: University of Oklahoma Press, 1935), 3.

5. A. Leopold, *A Sand County Almanac, and Sketches Here and There* (New York: Oxford University Press, 1949), 207.

Vandana Shiva

[From] *Staying Alive: Women, Ecology and Development*

Contemporary western views of nature are fraught with the dichotomy or duality between man and woman, and person and nature. In Indian cosmology, by contrast, person and nature (Purusha-Prakriti) are a duality in unity. They are inseparable complements of one another in nature, in woman, in man. Every form of creation bears the sign of this dialectical unity, of diversity within a unifying principle, and this dialectical harmony between the male and female principles and between nature and man, becomes the basis of ecological thought and action in India. Since, ontologically, there is no dualism between man and nature and because nature as Prakriti sustains life, nature has been treated as integral and inviolable. Prakriti, far from being an esoteric abstraction, is an everyday concept which organises daily life. There is no separation here between the popular and elite imagery or between the sacred and secular traditions. As an embodiment and manifestation of the feminine principle it is characterized by (1) creativity, activity, productivity; (2) diversity in form and aspect; (3) connectedness and inter-relationship of all beings, including man; (4) continuity between the human and natural; and (5) sanctity of life in nature.

Conceptually, this differs radically from the Cartesian concept of nature as 'environment' or a 'resource'. In it, the environment is seen as separate from man: it is his surrounding, not his substance. The dualism between man and nature has allowed the subjugation of the latter by man and given rise to a new world-view in which nature is (1) inert and passive; (2) uniform and mechanistic; (3) separable and fragmented within itself; (4) separate from man; and (5) inferior, to be dominated and exploited by man.

The rupture within nature and between man and nature, and its associated transformation from a life-force that sustains to an exploitable resource characterises the Cartesian view which has displaced more ecological world-views and created a development paradigm which cripples nature and woman simultaneously.

The ontological shift for an ecologically sustainable future has much to gain from the world-views of ancient civilisations and diverse cultures which survived sustainably over centuries. These were based on an ontology of the feminine as the living principle, and on an ontological continuity between society and nature—the humanisation of nature and the naturalisation of society. Not merely did this result in an ethical context which excluded possibilities of exploitation and domination, it allowed the creation of an earth family.

The dichotomised ontology of man dominating woman and nature generates maldevelopment because it makes the colonising male the agent and model of 'development'. Women, the Third World and nature become underdeveloped, first by definition, and then, through the process of colonisation, in reality....

Ecological ways of knowing nature are necessarily participatory. Nature herself is the experiment and women, as sylviculturalists, agriculturists and water resource managers, the traditional natural scientists. Their knowledge is ecological and plural, reflecting both the diversity of natural ecosystems and the diversity in cultures that nature-based living gives rise to. Throughout the world, the colonisation of diverse peoples was, at its root, a forced subjugation of ecological concepts of nature and of the Earth as the repository of all forms, latencies and powers of creation, the ground and cause of the world. The symbolism of Terra Mater, the earth in the form of the Great Mother, creative and protective, has been a shared but diverse symbol across space and time, and ecology movements in the West today are inspired in large part by the recovery of the concept of Gaia, the earth goddess.

The shift from Prakriti to 'natural resources', from Mater to 'matter' was considered (and in many quarters is still considered) a progressive shift from superstition to rationality. Yet, viewed from the perspective of nature, or women embedded in nature, in the production and preservation of sustenance, the shift is regressive and violent. It entails the disruption of nature's processes and cycles, and her inter-connectedness. For women, whose productivity in the sustaining of life is based on nature's productivity, the death of Prakriti is simultaneously a beginning of their marginalisation, devaluation, displacement and ultimate dispensability. The ecological crisis is, at its root, the death of the feminine principle, symbolically as well as in contexts such as rural India, not merely in form and symbol, but also in the everyday processes of survival and sustenance.

STEPHEN JAY GOULD

[From] The Golden Rule—A Proper Scale for Our Environmental Crisis

...This decade, a prelude to the millennium, is widely and correctly viewed as a turning point that will lead either to environmental perdition or stabilization. We have fouled local nests before and driven regional faunas to extinction, but we have never been able to unleash planetary effects before our current concern with ozone holes and putative global warming. In this context, we are searching for proper themes and language to express our environmental worries.

I don't know that paleontology has a great deal to offer, but I would advance one geological insight to combat a well-meaning, but seriously flawed (and all too common), position and to focus attention on the right issue at the proper scale. Two linked arguments are often promoted as a basis for an environmental ethic:

1. That we live on a fragile planet now subject to permanent derailment and disruption by human intervention;
2. That humans must learn to act as stewards for this threatened world.

Such views, however well intentioned, are rooted in the old sin of pride and exaggerated self-importance. We are one among millions of species, stewards of nothing. By what argument could we, arising just a geological microsecond ago, become responsible for the affairs of a world 4.5 billion years old, teeming with life that has been evolving and diversifying for at least three-quarters of that immense span? Nature does not exist for us, had no idea we were coming, and doesn't give a damn about us. Omar Khayyám was right in all but his crimped view of the earth as battered when he made his brilliant comparison of our world to an eastern hotel:

Think, in this battered Caravanserai
Whose Portals are alternate
Night and Day,
How Sultan after Sultan with his Pomp
Abode his destined Hour, and
    went his way.

This assertion of ultimate impotence could be countered if we, despite our late arrival, now held power over the planet's future (argument number one above). But we don't, despite popular misperception of our might. We are virtually powerless over the earth at our planet's own geological time scale. All the megatonnage in our nuclear arsenals yield but one ten-thousandth the power of the asteroid that might have triggered the Cretaceous mass extinction. Yet the earth survived that larger shock and, in wiping out dinosaurs, paved the road for the evolution of large mammals, including humans. We fear global warming, yet even the most radical model yields an earth far cooler than many happy and prosperous times of a prehuman past. We can surely destroy ourselves, and take many other species with us, but we can barely dent bacterial diversity and will surely not remove many million species of insects and mites. On geological scales, our planet will take good care of itself and let time clear the impact of any human malfeasance. The earth need never seek a henchman to wreak Henry's vengeance upon Thomas à Becket: "Who will free me from this turbulent priest?" Our planet simply waits.

People who do not appreciate the fundamental principle of appropriate scales often misread such an argument as a claim that we may therefore cease to worry about environmental deterioration....But I raise the same counterargument. We cannot threaten at geological scales, but such vastness is entirely inappropriate. We have a legitimately parochial interest in our own lives, the happiness and prosperity of our children, the suffering of our fellows. The planet will recover from nuclear holocaust, but we will be killed

and maimed by the billions, and our cultures will perish. The earth will prosper if polar icecaps melt under a global greenhouse, but most of our major cities, built at sea level as ports and harbors, will founder, and changing agricultural patterns will uproot our populations.

We must squarely face an unpleasant historical fact. The conservation movement was born, in large part, as an elitist attempt by wealthy social leaders to preserve wilderness as a domain for patrician leisure and contemplation (against the image, so to speak, of poor immigrants traipsing in hordes through the woods with their Sunday picnic baskets). We have never entirely shaken this legacy of environmentalism as something opposed to immediate human needs, particularly of the impoverished and unfortunate. But the Third World expands and contains most of the pristine habitat that we yearn to preserve. Environmental movements cannot prevail until they convince people that clean air and water, solar power, recycling, and reforestation are best solutions (as they are) for human needs at human scales—and not for impossibly distant planetary futures.

I have a decidedly unradical suggestion to make about an appropriate environmental ethic—one rooted in the issue of appropriate human scale versus the majesty, but irrelevance, of geological time. I have never been much attracted to the Kantian categorical imperative in searching for an ethic—to moral laws that are absolute and unconditional and do not involve any ulterior motive or end. The world is too complex and sloppy for such uncompromising attitudes (and God help us if we embrace the wrong principle, and then fight wars, kill, and maim in our absolute certainty). I prefer the messier "hypothetical imperatives" that involve desire, negotiation, and reciprocity. Of these "lesser," but altogether wiser and deeper, principles, one has stood out for its independent derivation, with different words but to the same effect, in culture after culture. I imagine that our various societies grope toward this principle because structural stability, and basic decency necessary for any tolerable life, demand such a maxim. Christians call this principle the "golden rule"; Plato, Hillel, and Confucius knew the same maxim by other names. I cannot think of a better principle based on enlightened self-interest. If we all treated others as we wish to be treated ourselves, then decency and stability would have to prevail.

I suggest that we execute such a pact with our planet. She holds all the cards and has immense power over us—so such a compact, which we desperately need but she does not at her own time scale, would be a blessing for us, and an indulgence for her.

We had better sign the papers while she is still willing to make a deal. If we treat her nicely, she will keep us going for a while. If we scratch her, she will bleed, kick us out, bandage up, and go about her business at her planetary scale. Poor Richard told us that "necessity never made a good bargain," but the earth is kinder than human agents in the "art of the deal." She will uphold her end; we must now go and do likewise.

VAL PLUMWOOD

[From] Being Prey

In the early wet season, Kakadu's paperbark wetlands are especially stunning, as the water lilies weave white, pink, and blue patterns of dreamlike beauty over the shining thunderclouds reflected in their still waters. Yesterday, the water lilies and the wonderful bird life had enticed me into a joyous afternoon's idyll as I ventured onto the East Alligator Lagoon for the first time in a canoe lent by the park service. "You can play about on the backwaters," the ranger had said, "but don't go onto the main river channel. The current's too swift, and if you get into trouble, there are the crocodiles. Lots of them along the river!"...

As I pulled the canoe out into the main current, the rain and wind started up again. I had not gone more than five or ten minutes down the channel when, rounding a bend, I saw in midstream what looked like a floating stick—one I did not recall passing on my way up. As the current moved me toward it, the stick developed eyes. A crocodile! It did not look like a large one. I was close to it now but was not especially afraid; an encounter would add interest to the day.

Although I was paddling to miss the crocodile, our paths were strangely convergent. I knew it would be close, but I was totally unprepared for the great blow when it struck the canoe. Again it struck, again and again, now from behind, shuddering the flimsy craft. As I paddled furiously, the blows continued. The unheard of was happening; the canoe was under attack! For the first time, it came to me fully that I was prey....

Few of those who have experienced the crocodile's death roll have lived to describe it. It is, essentially, an experience beyond words of total terror. The crocodile's breathing and heart metabolism are not suited to prolonged struggle, so the roll is an intense burst of power designed to overcome the victim's resistance quickly. The crocodile then holds the feebly struggling prey underwater until it drowns....

Escaping the crocodile was not the end of my struggle to survive. I was alone, severely injured, and many miles from help. During the attack, the pain from the injuries had not fully registered. As

I took my first urgent steps, I knew something was wrong with my leg. . . .

In the end I was found in time and survived against many odds. A similar combination of good fortune and human care enabled me to overcome a leg infection that threatened amputation or worse. . . . I am very lucky that I can still walk well and have lost few of my previous capacities. The wonder of being alive after being held quite literally in the jaws of death has never entirely left me. . . .

It seems to me that in the human supremacist culture of the West there is a strong effort to deny that we humans are also animals positioned in the food chain. This denial that we ourselves are food for others is reflected in many aspects of our death and burial practices; the strong coffin, conventionally buried well below the level of soil fauna activity, and the slab over the grave to prevent any other thing from digging us up, keeps the Western human body from becoming food for other species. Horror movies and stories also reflect this deep-seated dread of becoming food for other forms of life: Horror is the wormy corpse, vampires sucking blood, and alien monsters eating humans. Horror and outrage usually greet stories of other species eating humans. Even being nibbled by leeches, sandflies, and mosquitoes can stir various levels of hysteria.

This concept of human identity positions humans outside and above the food chain, not as part of the feast in a chain of reciprocity but as external manipulators and masters of it: Animals can be our food, but we can never be their food. The outrage we experience at the idea of a human being eaten is certainly not what we experience at the idea of animals as food. The idea of human prey threatens the dualistic vision of human mastery in which we humans manipulate nature from outside, as predators but never prey. We may daily consume other animals by the billions, but we ourselves cannot be food for worms and certainly not meat for crocodiles. This is one reason why we now treat so inhumanely the animals we make our food, for we cannot imagine ourselves similarly positioned as food. We act as if we live in a separate realm of culture in which we are never food, while other animals inhabit a different world of nature in which they are no more than food, and their lives can be utterly distorted in the service of this end.

Before the encounter, it was as if I saw the whole universe as framed by my own narrative, as though the two were joined perfectly and seamlessly together. As my own narrative and the larger story were ripped apart, I glimpsed a shockingly indifferent world in which I had no more significance than any other edible being. The thought, This can't be happening to me, I'm a human being. I am more than just food! was one component of my terminal incredulity. It was a shocking reduction, from a complex human being to a mere piece of meat. Reflection has persuaded me that not just humans but any creature can make the same claim to be more than just food. We are edible, but we are also much more than edible. Respectful, ecological eating must recognize both of these things. I was a vegetarian at the time of my encounter with the crocodile, and remain one today. This is not because I think predation itself is demonic and impure, but because I object to the reduction of animal lives in factory farming systems that treat them as living meat.

Large predators like lions and crocodiles present an important test for us. An ecosystem's ability to support large predators is a mark of its ecological integrity. Crocodiles and other creatures that can take human life also present a test of our acceptance of our ecological identity. When they're allowed to live freely, these creatures indicate our preparedness to coexist with the otherness of the earth, and to recognize ourselves in mutual, ecological terms, as part of the food chain, eaten as well as eater. . . .

ARNE NAESS

[From] The Basics of Deep Ecology

... In the deep ecology movement we are biocentric or ecocentric. For us it is the ecosphere, the whole planet, Gaia, that is the basic unit, and every living being has an intrinsic value.

The supporters of the deep ecology movement agree upon this, but in their very basic views about the universe and themselves, they may well disagree. They may have, for example, a Buddhist-inspired philosophy, or a Christian-inspired philosophy, or a nonreligious approach. At this most basic level we cannot understand each other. We cannot understand five or ten different religions. We shouldn't pretend to. It is culturally disastrous to pretend that we can understand all religions or all philosophies. That is a terrible error on the part of the universities—there are courses in all philosophies and all religions of the world, and the students are supposed to understand philosophers who are miles apart. I feel it is important in the deep ecology movement to have plurality, especially at this deepest level. However, from all religions and philosophical approaches we agree on the following points (comments are in parentheses).

1. The well-being and flourishing of human and nonhuman life on earth have intrinsic value, inherent worth. This value is independent of the usefulness of the nonhuman world for narrow human purposes.
2. Richness and diversity of life-forms contribute to a realization of these values and are also values in themselves. (Richness means we have to have an abundance of life of all kinds. We have to replenish the earth. In this sense, landscapes are living beings and so are rivers. I can't and I don't have to justify that diversity and richness; plurality of life is

good in itself. People who claim to be realistic say, Well, I keep to facts. What, though, is the status of this sentence: *So-and-so is a fact*? In logic you need rules, and the goodness of those rules cannot be shown—they cannot be argued, they cannot come as a conclusion. If you say, "This rule of logic is valid," then I say, "Well, show me that, prove it." You have to use premises to arrive at a conclusion, and to do that, you have to have rules of inference by which you come from the premise to the conclusion. You cannot start by saying "I am for facts," because the term *fact* itself is a tremendously complex affair. Aristotle said that to try to prove everything is a sign of bad education. Diversity of life for us is such a premise; we don't need to waste time proving it.)

3. Human beings have no right to reduce this richness and diversity except to satisfy vital needs. (People say to me, "Oh, but what do you mean by *right*?" I say, "I mean exactly the same as when children say, You have no right to hit my little sister"—and this is established practice among children, so there must be something in it.)
4. The flourishing of human life and culture is compatible with a substantial decrease of the human population. Flourishing of nonhuman life requires such a decrease. (Some people would call this "antihuman," but I believe that it is not good even for human beings that we number five thousand million and are soon going to be eight thousand million. It's not good even for the deep cultural differences on earth; it's very difficult to

have cultural differences with no space in between. This significant decrease in human population will not happen overnight. It may take a thousand years. This is our long-range vision. People say, A thousand years has nothing to do with the problem of today. Yes, it does have to do with today. For example, we have to change our architecture. Old people need small children around because small children are, after all, important. So the architecture will have to be such that there is a common ground, without streets, where small children and old people can get together. If we have two children per couple on an average, then there will be a transition period of hundreds of years but eventually we will have a smaller population.)

5. Present-day human interference with the non-human world is excessive, and the situation is rapidly worsening.

6. Policies must therefore be changed. These policies will affect our basic economic, technological, and ideological structures. (I have not had the courage to go into detail and define what these different structures will be because we are going to have a lot of different green societies. We shouldn't have one set of structures imposed.)

7. The change in our attitudes will bring an appreciation of the quality of life rather than adherence to an increasingly higher standard of living. There will be a profound awareness of the difference between big and great. (We will have a great society with no bigness. I am very much in love with the term *quality of life*. People say, "Well, that's just a slogan. Standard of living is quantitative—that we can discuss and understand—but *quality of life*, what's that?" I am very much for the richness and luxury that I have in my cottage in the high mountains of Norway. For more than ten years of living there, the feeling of richness has been tremendous. This is quality of life, however, not standard of living. If there is snow in winter, I dig down into a lake for water. To heat that water from $-1°$ to $+1°$ takes as many calories as to heat it from $+1°$ to $100°$. So I use cold water for washing, but after one or two months of living there I feel very comfortable.)

   In Great Britain and in Norway we have to accept a drop in our standard of living in order to have a standard that is universalizable. What I am saying is take it easy, take it easy; life quality may still be there, but you will have to shed some of your bad habits that destroy the planet. Much of the high standard of living is sheer bad habits that we cannot sustain because they are ruining the balance of Gaia.

8. Those who subscribe to the foregoing points have an obligation directly or indirectly to try to implement necessary changes.

Rachel Carson

[From] *Silent Spring*

A FABLE FOR TOMORROW

There was once a town in the heart of America where all life seemed to live in harmony with its surroundings. The town lay in the midst of a checkerboard of prosperous farms, with fields of grain and hillsides of orchards where, in spring, white clouds of bloom drifted above the green fields. In autumn, oak and maple and birch set up a blaze of color that flamed and flickered across a backdrop of pines. Then foxes barked in the hills and deer silently crossed the fields, half hidden in the mists of the fall mornings.

Along the roads, laurel, viburnum and alder, great ferns and wildflowers delighted the traveler's eye through much of the year. Even in winter the roadsides were places of beauty, where countless birds came to feed on the berries and on the seed heads of the dried weeds rising above the snow. The countryside was, in fact, famous for the abundance and variety of its bird life, and when the flood of migrants was pouring through in spring and fall people traveled from great distances to observe them. Others came to fish the streams, which flowed clear and cold out of the hills and contained shady pools where trout lay. So it had been from the days many years ago when the first settlers raised their houses, sank their wells, and built their barns.

Then a strange blight crept over the area and everything began to change. Some evil spell had settled on the community: mysterious maladies swept the flocks of chickens; the cattle and sheep sickened and died. Everywhere was a shadow of death. The farmers spoke of much illness among their families. In the town the doctors had become more and more puzzled by new kinds of sickness appearing among their patients. There had been several sudden and unexplained deaths, not only among adults but even among children, who would be stricken suddenly while at play and die within a few hours.

There was a strange stillness. The birds, for example—where had they gone? Many people spoke of them, puzzled and disturbed. The feeding stations in the backyards were deserted. The few birds seen anywhere were moribund; they trembled violently and could not fly. It was a spring without voices. On the mornings that had once throbbed with the dawn chorus of robins, catbirds, doves, jays, wrens, and scores of other bird voices there was now no sound; only silence lay over the fields and woods and marsh.

On the farms the hens brooded, but no chicks hatched. The farmers complained that they were unable to raise any pigs—the litters were small and the young survived only a few days. The apple trees were coming into bloom but no bees droned among the blossoms, so there was no pollination and there would be no fruit.

The roadsides, once so attractive, were now lined with browned and withered vegetation as though swept by fire. These, too, were silent, deserted by all living things. Even the streams were now lifeless. Anglers no longer visited them, for all the fish had died.

In the gutters under the eaves and between the shingles of the roofs, a white granular powder still showed a few patches; some weeks before it had fallen like snow upon the roofs and the lawns, the fields and streams.

No witchcraft, no enemy action had silenced the rebirth of new life in this stricken world. The people had done it themselves.

This town does not actually exist, but it might easily have a thousand counterparts in America or elsewhere in the world. I know of no community that has experienced all the misfortunes I describe. Yet every one of these disasters has actually happened somewhere, and many real communities have already suffered a substantial number of them. A grim specter has crept upon us almost unnoticed, and this imagined tragedy may easily become a stark reality we all shall know.

What has already silenced the voices of spring in countless towns in America?

THE OBLIGATION TO ENDURE

The history of life on earth has been a history of interaction between living things and their surroundings. To a large extent, the physical form and the habits of the earth's vegetation and its animal life have been molded by the environment. Considering the whole span of earthly time, the opposite effect, in which life actually modifies its surroundings, has been relatively slight. Only within the moment of time represented by the present century has one species—man—acquired significant power to alter the nature of his world.

During the past quarter century this power has not only increased to one of disturbing magnitude but it has changed in character. The most alarming of all man's assaults upon the environment is the contamination of air, earth, rivers, and sea with dangerous and even lethal materials. This pollution is for the most part irrecoverable; the chain of evil it initiates not only in the world that must support life but in living tissues is for the most part

irreversible. In this now universal contamination of the environment, chemicals are the sinister and little recognized partners of radiation in changing the very nature of the world—the very nature of its life. Strontium 90, released through nuclear explosions into the air, comes to earth in rain or drifts down as fallout, lodges in soil, enters into the grass or corn or wheat grown there, and in time takes up its abode in the bones of a human being, there to remain until his death Similarly, chemicals sprayed on croplands or forests or gardens lie long in soil, entering into living organisms, passing from one to another in a chain of poisoning and death. Or they pass mysteriously by underground streams until they emerge and through the alchemy of air and sunlight, combine into new forms that kill vegetation, sicken cattle, and work unknown harm on those who drink from once pure wells. As Albert Schweitzer has said, "Man can hardly even recognize the devil of his own creation."

It took hundreds of millions of years to produce the life that now inhabits the earth—eons of time in which that developing and evolving and diversifying life reached a state of adjustment and balance with its surroundings. The environment, rigorously shaping and directing the life it supported, contained elements that were hostile as well as supporting. Certain rocks gave out dangerous radiation; even within the light of the sun, from which all life draws its energy, there were short-wave radiations with power to injure. Given time—time not in years but in millennia—life adjusts, and a balance has been reached. For time is the essential ingredient; but in the modern world there is no time.

Ethics and the Environment

INTRODUCTION

Should we allow loggers to cut ancient forests and jeopardize the survival of the remaining orangutans, elephants, and other endangered species whose lives depend on those forests? Is it wrong to export toxic waste to the developing world? Must consumers refuse to purchase and use products that emit greenhouse gases, cause animal suffering, or generally contribute to environmental degradation? These are a few of the questions that an environmental ethic helps answer. Environmental ethics is the area of philosophy that explores our moral relations to the natural world, the values that underlie those relations, and the principles that shape our attitudes and actions.

Fundamental to all areas of ethics are questions about values. It is important to identify and distinguish three central questions about moral values. First is the question about the source of moral values: Where do values come from? Would there be values if there were no valuers? The second question is about the content of values: What sorts of things are valuable? Are only humans, their capacities, productions, activities, and futures valuable, or is nonhuman nature valuable as well? Finally, there is the question about the role of particular values in our moral outlook: Do we value nonhuman nature for its own sake, much as we value our friends, or do we value it because of its contribution to something else, like the promotion of human interests?

Questions about the roles values play in our thinking and action arise both in abstract thinking about environmental ethics (e.g., what are the values on which our obligations to the natural world rest?), as well as in everyday conversations about how we should relate to nature (e.g., should I buy organic food and use green energy?). Because philosophers who work in environmental ethics are interested in the practical applications of abstract principles, they often find themselves addressing many of the traditional questions of ethics, even while they wonder, as Aldo Leopold did, about the adequacy of traditional theories for guiding our actions in relation to nonhuman nature.

In one of the founding papers of environmental ethics, Richard Routley (later Sylvan) (1935–1996) raised a provocative challenge to traditional ethical theories. He asks us to imagine a world in which there is a lone person who sets about destroying the natural world. According to Routley, traditional ethical theories are unable to articulate what might be wrong with the last person's actions because these theories are "human chauvinist." They place humans first "and everything else a bad last." Accounting for the value of ecosystems, vanishing species, and awe-inspiring natural beauty is a challenge to such theories, and this raises the question of Routley's title: is there a need for a new, an environmental ethic?

Some philosophers who answered Routley's question in the affirmative, such as Holmes Rolston, thought that in order to adequately explain the value of nature, value must exist independently of any valuers. Some have called this mind independent value of nature "intrinsic" or "inherent" value and have set out to develop an environmental ethic based on it. Others, such as Bernard Williams (1929–2003), argued that while humans are the source of value, the content of our values need not be chauvinistic or "anthropocentric" (human-centered). We can value wild rhinoceroses in remote parts of the world and appreciate the value of remarkable living beings in the very deepest parts of the ocean, even if we will never see them or directly benefit from them in any way.

If we put aside questions about the source of values, there is a further question about why we should value deep-sea creatures and wild rhinoceroses. Though we might extend our understanding of who or what is valuable beyond the human species, what is it, precisely, that is to be valued and why? Kenneth Goodpaster argues that valuing humans and nonhumans because they have interests or are sentient is as arbitrary as valuing humans because they are human. He claims that the only nonarbitrary position is to value all living things, including nonsentient living things such as trees and plants, because they are "self-sustaining," have "independent needs," and "capacities for benefit and harm."

If we expand the domain of value beyond humans and those who are similar to them, further ethical questions arise. How should we respond to those things that are valuable? What principles should guide us in our valuing, and in our actions that affect the natural world?

Robert Elliot provides an overview of the ways in which traditional theories can be configured to provide guidance in understanding our responsibilities to the natural world. This includes consequentialist theories (in which the value of consequences is foundational) and deontological theories (in which the rightness of an act is foundational). Ronald Sandler introduces a third model, an environmental virtue ethic, that provides "an account of character dispositions that one ought to have regarding the natural environment." Paul Taylor develops an ethic that has three parts: (1) an ultimate moral attitude of "respect for nature"; (2) a belief system, which he calls "the biocentric outlook"; and (3) a set of rules of duty that express the attitude of respect. All three authors attempt to show how traditional moral philosophies can respond to Routley's challenge.

The environmental ethics discussed by Elliot, Sandler, and Taylor focuses on individuals. Aldo Leopold's "Land Ethic" is a holistic ethic, in which the value of biotic community can take precedence over the value of its individual members. J. Baird Callicott defends Leopold's holistic environmental ethic, which he believes is most responsive to Routley's challenge.

FURTHER READING

Agar, Nicholas. *Life's Intrinsic Value.* New York, NY: Columbia University Press, 2001. An argument for the intrinsic value of all living things.

Cafaro, Phil, and Ronald Sandler, eds. *Environmental Virtue Ethics.* Lanham, MD: Rowman & Littlefield, 2005. A collection of readings on environmental ethics grounded in virtues.

Elliot, Robert. *Faking Nature: The Ethics of Environmental Restoration.* London and New York: Routledge, 1997. An analysis of natural values and a critique of common justifications for restoration.

Jamieson, Dale. *Ethics and the Environment.* New York, NY: Cambridge University Press, 2008. An introduction to philosophical issues related to the environment, and an argument for why environmental issues require ethics to best understand them.

O'Neill, John, Alan Holland, and Andrew Light. *Environmental Values.* New York, NY: Routledge, 2008. An account of the ethical underpinnings of environmental decision-making.

Rolston, Holmes, III. *Environmental Ethics: Duties to and Values in the Natural World.* Philadelphia, PA: Temple University Press, 1988. An early defense of environmental holism.

Varner, Gary. *In Nature's Interest? Interests, Animal Rights and Environmental Ethics.* New York, NY: Oxford University Press, 1998. A defense of biocentric individualism with an emphasis on the place of animals.

DISCUSSION QUESTIONS

1. What are the strengths and weaknesses of various approaches to environmental ethics (e.g., sentientism, biocentrism, holism)?
2. Do we need different ethical concepts to respond to environmental problems that exist at different scales (e.g., global climate change versus local water pollution)?
3. When conflicting values arise (e.g., between habitat preservation and development rights), how might we determine which are relevant to decision-making, and how do we resolve the conflicts?
4. Does environmental ethics require a commitment to mind independent value?
5. What are the best arguments for and against holism in environmental ethics?
6. Do we need a new, environmental ethic?
7. What does respect for nature consist in?

RICHARD ROUTLEY

Is There a Need for a New, an Environmental Ethic?

1

It is increasingly said that civilization, Western civilization at least, stands in need of a new ethic (and derivatively of a new economics) setting out people's relations to the natural environment, in Leopold's words "an ethic dealing with man's relation to land and to the animals and plants which grow upon it."[1] It is not of course that old and prevailing ethics do not deal with man's relation to nature; they do, and on the prevailing view man is free to deal with nature as he pleases, i.e., his relations with nature, insofar at least as they do not affect others, are not subject to moral censure. Thus assertions such as "Crusoe ought not to be mutilating those trees" are significant and morally determinate but, inasmuch at least as Crusoe's actions do not interfere with others, they are false or do not hold—and trees are not, in a good sense, moral objects.[2] It is to this, to the values and evaluations of the prevailing ethics, that Leopold and others in fact take exception. Leopold regards as subject to moral criticism, as wrong, behaviour that on prevailing views is morally permissible. But it is not, as Leopold seems to think, that such behaviour is beyond the scope of the prevailing ethics and that an extension of traditional morality is required to cover such cases, to fill a moral void. If Leopold is right in his criticism of prevailing conduct what is required is a change in the ethics, in attitudes, values and evaluations. For as matters stand, as he himself explains, men do not feel morally ashamed if they interfere with a wilderness, if they maltreat the land, extract from it whatever it will yield, and then move on; and such conduct is not taken to interfere with and does not rouse the moral indignation of others. "A farmer who clears the woods off a 75% slope, turns his cows into the clearing, and dumps its rainfall, rocks, and soil into the community creek, is still (if otherwise decent) a respected member of society."[3] Under what we shall call an *environmental ethic* such traditionally permissible conduct would be accounted morally wrong, and the farmer subject to proper moral criticism.

Let us grant such evaluations for the purpose of the argument. What is not so clear is that a new ethic is required even for such radical judgments. For one thing it is none too clear what is going to count as a new ethic, much as it is often unclear whether a new development in physics counts as a new physics or just as a modification or extension of the old. For, notoriously, ethics are not clearly articulated or at all well worked out, so that the application of identity criteria for ethics may remain obscure...[4] There are two possibilities, apart from a new environmental ethic, which might cater for the evaluations, namely that of an extension or modification of the prevailing ethics or that of the development of principles that are already encompassed or latent within the prevailing ethic. The second possibility, that environmental evaluations can be incorporated within (and ecological problems solved within) the framework of prevailing Western ethics, is open because there isn't a single ethical system uniquely assumed in Western civilization: on many issues, and especially on controversial issues such as infanticide, women's rights, and drugs, there are competing sets of principles. Talk of a new ethic and prevailing ethics tends to suggest a sort of monolithic structure, a uniformity, that prevailing ethics, and even a single ethic, need not have.

Indeed Passmore has mapped out three important traditions in Western ethical views concerning man's relation to nature; a dominant tradition, the despotic position, with man as despot (or tyrant), and two lesser traditions, the stewardship position, with man as custodian, and the co-operative position with man as perfecter.[5] Nor are these the only traditions; primitivism is another, and both romanticism and mysticism have influenced Western views.

The dominant Western view is simply inconsistent with an environmental ethic; for according to it nature is the dominion of man and he is free to deal with it as he pleases (since—at least on the mainstream Stoic-Augustine view—it exists only for his sake), whereas on an environmental ethic man is not so free to do as he pleases. But it is not quite so obvious that an environmental ethic cannot be coupled with one of the lesser traditions. Part of the problem is that the lesser traditions are by no means adequately characterized anywhere, especially when the religious backdrop is removed, e.g. *who* is man steward for and responsible to? However both traditions are inconsistent with an environmental ethic because they imply policies of complete interference, whereas on an environmental ethic some worthwhile parts of the earth's surface should be preserved from substantial human interference, whether of the "improving" sort or not. Both traditions would in fact prefer to see the earth's land surfaces reshaped along the lines of the tame and comfortable north-European small farm and village landscape. According to the co-operative position man's proper role is to develop, cultivate and perfect nature—all nature eventually—by bringing out its potentialities, the test of perfection being primarily usefulness for human purposes; while on the stewardship view man's role, like that of a farm manager, is to make nature productive by his efforts though not by means that will deliberately degrade its resources. Although these positions both depart from the dominant position in a way which enables the incorporation of some

evaluations of an environmental ethic, e.g. some of those concerning the irresponsible farmer, they do not go far enough: for in the present situation of expanding populations confined to finite natural areas, they will lead to, and enjoin, the perfecting, farming and utilizing of all natural areas. Indeed these lesser traditions lead to, what a thoroughgoing environmental ethic would reject, a principle of total use, implying that every natural area should be cultivated or otherwise used for human ends, "humanized."[6]

As the important Western traditions exclude an environmental ethic, it would appear that such an ethic, not primitive, mystical or romantic, would be new all right. The matter is not so straightforward; for the dominant ethic has been substantially qualified by the rider that one is not always entitled to do as one pleases where this physically interferes with others. Maybe some such proviso was implicit all along (despite evidence to the contrary), and it was simply assumed that doing what one pleased with natural items would not affect others (the noninterference assumption). Be this as it may, the *modified* dominant position appears, at least for many thinkers, to have supplanted the dominant position; and the modified position can undoubtedly go much further towards an environmental ethic. For example, the farmer's polluting of a community stream may be ruled immoral on the grounds that it physically interferes with others who use or would use the streams. Likewise business enterprises which destroy the natural environment for no satisfactory returns or which cause pollution deleterious to the health of future humans, can be criticized on the sort of welfare basis that blends with the modified position; and so on.[7] The position may even serve to restrict the sort of family size one is entitled to have since in a finite situation excessive population levels will interfere with future people. Nonetheless neither the modified dominant position nor its Western variants, obtained by combining it with the lesser traditions, is adequate as an environmental ethic, as I shall try to show. A new ethic *is* wanted.

2
_____

As we noticed (an) *ethic* is ambiguous, as between a specific ethical system, a *specific* ethic, and a more generic notion, a super ethic, under which specific ethics cluster.[8] An ethical system S is, near enough, a propositional system (i.e. a structured set of propositions) or theory which includes (like individuals of a theory) a set of values and (like postulates of a theory) a set of general evaluative judgments concerning conduct, typically of what is obligatory, permissible and wrong, of what are rights, what is valued, and so forth. A general or law-like proposition of a system is a principle; and certainly if systems S1 and S2 contain different principles, then they are different systems. It follows that any environmental ethic differs from the important traditional ethics outlined. Moreover if environmental ethics differ from Western ethical systems on some *core* principle embedded in Western systems, then these systems differ from the Western super ethic (assuming, what seems to be so, that it can be uniquely characterized)—in which case if an environmental ethic is needed then a new ethic is wanted. It suffices then to locate a core principle and to provide environmental counter examples to it.

It is commonly assumed that there are, what amount to, core principles of Western ethical systems, principles that will accordingly belong to the super ethic. The fairness principle inscribed in the Golden Rule provides one example. Directly relevant here, as a good stab at a core principle, is the commonly formulated liberal principle of the modified dominance position. A recent formulation runs as follows:

> The liberal philosophy of the Western world holds that one should be able to do what he wishes, providing (1) that he does not harm others and (2) that he is not likely to harm himself irreparably.[9]

Let us call this principle *basic (human) chauvinism*—because under it humans, or people, come first and everything else a bad last—though sometimes the principle is hailed as a *freedom* principle because it gives permission to perform a wide range of actions (including actions which mess up the environment and natural things) providing they do not harm others. In fact it tends to cunningly shift the onus of proof to others. It is worth remarking that *harming others* in the restriction is narrower than a restriction to the (usual) interests of others; it is not enough that it is in my interests, because I detest you, that you stop breathing; you are free to breathe, for the time being anyway, because it does not harm me. There remains a problem however as to exactly what counts as harm or interference. Moreover the width of the principle is so far obscure because "other" may be filled out in significantly different ways: it makes a difference to the extent, and privilege, of the chauvinism whether "other" expands to "other human"—which is too restrictive—or to "other person" or to "other sentient being"; and it makes a difference to the adequacy of the principle, and inversely to its economic applicability, to which class of others it is intended to apply, whether to future as well as to present others, whether to remote future others or only to non-discountable future others and whether to possible others. The latter would make the principle completely unworkable, and it is generally assumed that it applies at most to present and future others.

It is taken for granted in designing counter examples to basic chauvinist principles, that a semantic analysis of permissibility and obligation statements stretches out over ideal situations (which may be incomplete or even inconsistent), so that what is permissible holds in some ideal situation, what is obligatory in every ideal situation, and what is wrong is excluded in every ideal situation. But the main point to grasp for the counter examples that follow, is that ethical principles if correct are universal and are assessed over the class of ideal situations.

(i) The *last man* example. The last man (or person) surviving the collapse of the world system lays about him, eliminating, as far as he can, every living thing, animal or plant (but painlessly if you like, as at the best abattoirs). What he does is quite permissible according to basic chauvinism, but on environmental grounds what he does is wrong. Moreover one does not have to be committed to esoteric values to regard Mr. Last Man as behaving badly (the reason being perhaps that radical thinking and values have shifted in an environmental direction in advance of corresponding shifts in the formulation of fundamental evaluative principles).

(ii) The *last people* example. The last man example can be broadened to the last people example. We can assume that they know they are the last people, e.g. because they are aware that radiation effects have blocked any chance of reproduction. One considers the last people in order to rule out the possibility that what these people do harms or somehow physically interferes with later people. Otherwise one could as well consider science fiction cases where people arrive at a new planet and destroy its ecosystems, whether with good intentions such as perfecting the planet for their ends and making it more fruitful or, forgetting the lesser traditions, just for the hell of it.

Let us assume that the last people are very numerous. They humanely exterminate every wild animal and they eliminate the fish of the seas, they put all arable land under intensive cultivation, and all remaining forests disappear in favour of quarries or plantations, and so on. They may give various familiar reasons for this, e.g. they believe it is the way to salvation or to perfection, or they are simply satisfying reasonable needs, or even that it is needed to keep the last people employed or occupied so that they do not worry too much about their impending extinction. On an environmental ethic the last people have behaved badly; they have simplified and largely destroyed all the natural ecosystems, and with their demise the world will soon be an ugly and largely wrecked place. But this conduct may conform with the basic chauvinist principle, and as well with the principles enjoined by the lesser traditions. Indeed the main point of elaborating this example is because, as the last man example reveals, basic chauvinism may conflict with stewardship or co-operation principles...

The class of permissible actions that rebound on the environment is more narrowly circumscribed on an environmental ethic than it is in the Western super ethic. But aren't environmentalists going too far in claiming that people are behaving, when engaging in environmentally degrading activities of the sort described, in a morally impermissible way? No, what these people do is to a greater or lesser extent evil, and hence in serious cases morally impermissible. For example, insofar as the killing or forced displacement of primitive peoples who stand in the way of an industrial development is morally indefensible and impermissible, so also is the slaughter of the last remaining blue whales for private profit. But how to reformulate basic chauvinism as a satisfactory freedom principle is a more difficult matter. A tentative, but none too adequate beginning might be made by extending (2) to include harm to or interference with others who would be so affected by the action in question were they placed in the environment and (3) to exclude speciecide. It may be preferable, in view of the way the freedom principle sets the onus of proof, simply to scrap it altogether, and instead to specify classes of rights and permissible conduct, as in a bill of rights....

3
_____

An environmental ethic does not commit one to the view that natural objects such as trees have rights (though such a view is occasionally held, e.g. by pantheists. But pantheism is false since artefacts are not alive). For moral prohibitions forbidding certain actions with respect to an object do not award that object a correlative right. That it would be wrong to mutilate a given tree or piece of property does not entail that the tree or piece of property has a correlative right not to be mutilated (without seriously stretching the notion of a right). Environmental views can stick with mainstream theses according to which rights are coupled with corresponding responsibilities and so with bearing obligations, and with corresponding interests and concern; i.e. at least, whatever has a right also has responsibilities and therefore obligations, and whatever has a right has interests. Thus although any person may have a right by no means every living thing can (significantly) have rights, and arguably most sentient objects other than persons cannot have rights. But persons can relate morally, through obligations, prohibitions and so forth, to practically anything at all.

The species bias of certain ethical and economic positions which aim to make principles of conduct or reasonable economic behaviour calculable is easily brought out. These positions typically employ a single criterion p, such as preference or happiness, as a *summum bonnum;* characteristically each individual of some base class, almost always humans, but perhaps including future humans, is supposed to have an ordinal p ranking of the states in question (e.g. of affairs, of the economy); then some principle is supplied to determine a collective p ranking of these states in terms of individual p rankings, and what is best or ought to be done is determined either directly, as in act-utilitarianism under the Greatest Happiness principle, or indirectly, as in rule-utilitarianism, in terms of some optimization principle applied to the collective ranking. The species bias is transparent from the selection of the base class. And even if the base class is extended to embrace persons, or even some animals (at the cost, like that of including remotely future humans, of losing testability), the positions are open to familiar criticism, namely that the whole of the base class may be prejudiced in a way which leads to unjust principles. For example if every member of the base class detests dingoes, on the basis of mistaken data as to dingoes' behaviour, then by the Pareto ranking test the collective ranking will rank states where dingoes are exterminated very highly, from which it will generally be concluded that dingoes ought to be exterminated (the evaluation of most Australian farmers anyway). Likewise it would just be a happy accident, it seems, if collective demand (horizontally summed from individual demand) for a state of the economy with blue whales as a mixed good, were to succeed in outweighing private whaling demands; for if no one in the base class happened to know that blue whales exist or cared a jot that they do then "rational" economic decision-making would do nothing to prevent their extinction. Whether the blue whale survives should not have to depend on what humans know or what they see on television. Human interests and preferences are far too parochial to provide a satisfactory basis for deciding on what is environmentally desirable.

These ethical and economic theories are not alone in their species chauvinism; much the same applies to most going meta-ethical theories which, unlike intuitionistic theories, try to offer some rationale for their basic principles. For instance, on social contract positions obligations are a matter of mutual agreements between individuals of the base class; on a social justice picture rights and obligations spring from the application of symmetrical fairness principles to members of the base class, usually a rather special class of persons, while on a Kantian position which has some vague obligations somehow arise from respect for members of the base class persons. In each case if members of the base class happen to be ill-disposed to items outside the base class then that is too bad for them: that is (rough) justice.

NOTES

1. Aldo Leopold, *A Sand County Almanac with Essays on Conservation from Round River* (New York: Ballantine, 1966), p. 238.

2. A view occasionally tempered by the idea that trees house spirits.

3. Leopold, *Sand County*, p. 245.

4. To the consternation no doubt of Quineans. But the fact is that we can talk perfectly well about inchoate and fragmentary systems the identity of which may be indeterminate.

5. John Passmore, *Man's Responsibility for Nature: Ecological Problems and Western Traditions* (New York: Scribner's, 1974).

6. If "use" is extended, somewhat illicitly, to include use for preservation, this total use principle is rendered innocuous at least as regards its actual effects. Note that the total use principle is tied to the resource view of nature.

7. P. W. Barkley and D. W. Seckler, *Economic Growth and Environmental Decay: The Solution Becomes the Problem* (New York: Harcourt Brace Jovanovich, 1972).

8. A *meta-ethic* is, as usual, a theory about ethics, super ethics, their features and fundamental notions.

9. Barkley and Seckler, *Economic Growth and Environmental Decay*, p. 58. A related principle is that (modified) free enterprise can operate within similar limits.

BERNARD WILLIAMS

Must a Concern for the Environment Be Centered on Human Beings?

If we ask about the relations between environmental questions and human values, there is an important distinction to be made straight away between two issues. It is one thing to ask whose questions these are; it is another matter to ask whose interests will be referred to in the answers. In one sense—the sense corresponding to the first of these two issues—conservation and related matters are uncontestably human issues, because, on this planet at least, only human beings can discuss them and adopt policies that will affect them. That is to say, these are inescapably human questions in the sense that they are questions for humans. This implies something further and perhaps weightier, that the answers must be human answers: they must be based on human values, values that human beings can make part of their lives and understand themselves as pursuing and respecting.

The second issue then comes up, of what the content of those values can be. In particular, we have to ask how our answers should be related to our life. Few who are concerned about conservation and the environment will suppose that the answers have to be exclusively human answers in the further sense that the policies they recommend should exclusively favour human beings. But there are serious questions of how human answers can represent to us the value of things that are valued for reasons that go beyond human interests. Our approach to these issues cannot and should not be narrowly anthropocentric. But what is it that we move to when we move from the narrowly anthropocentric, and by what ethical route do we get there?

Many cases that we have to consider of course do directly concern human interests, and we shall perhaps understand our route best if we start with them.

There is, first, the familiar situation in which an activity conducted by one person, A, and which is profitable and beneficial to A and perhaps to others as well, imposes a cost on someone else, B. Here the basic question is to decide whether B should be compensated; how much; by whom; and on what principles. A further range of problems arises when various further conditions hold. Thus there may be no specific B: the people affected are identified just as those who are exposed to the activity and affected by it, whoever they may be. When this is so, we have unallocated effects (all effects on future generations are unallocated). A different range of questions is raised when we ask whether B is affected in a way that essentially involves B's states of perception or knowledge. Thus B may be affected by the disappearance of song birds or the blighting of a landscape. These are experiential effects. It is important that an effect on B's experience may take the form of a deprivation of which, just because of that deprivation, B is never aware; living under constant atmospheric pollution, B may never know what it is to see the stars.

Beyond this, and leaving aside the experiential effects on human beings, there are effects on animals other than human beings. These are non-human effects. Finally, what is affected may be neither human nor a member of any other animal species: it may, for instance, be a tree or a mountain. These are non-animal effects.

It is of course a major question in very many real cases whether an activity that has one of these other effects on the environment may not also harm human beings: the cutting down of rain forests is an obvious example. To the extent that human interests are still involved, the problems belong with the well-known, if difficult, theory of risk or hazard. This aspect of the problems is properly central to political discussion, and those arguing for conservation and environmental causes reasonably try to mobilise human self-interest as far as possible. But the human concern for other, non-human and non-animal, effects is misrepresented if one tries to reduce it simply to a kind of human self-concern. Since, moreover, the concern for those

other effects is itself a human phenomenon, humanity will be itself misrepresented in the process.

Our attitudes to these further kinds of effect are not directed simply to human interests, and in that sense they are not anthropocentric. But they are still our attitudes, expressing our values. How much of a constraint is that? What is involved in the ineliminable human perspective itself? Where might we look for an understanding of this kind of human concern?

There is a point to be made first about the experiences of non-human animals. I have so far mentioned experiential effects only in the context of effects on human beings, but, of course, there are also effects on the experience of other animals to be taken into account. This is also important, but it is not at the heart of the conservation and environmental concerns that I am considering, which focus typically on the survival of species. An experiential concern is likely to be with individual animals rather than with the survival of species, and it is bound to be less interested in the less complex animals; in these respects it is unlike a conservation concern. It also, of course, has no direct interest in the non-living. In all these ways an environmental concern in the sense relevant to conservation is at least broader than a concern with the experiences of other animals. This particularly helps to bring out the point that an environmental concern is not just motivated by benevolence or altruism. (Inasmuch as vegetarianism is motivated by those feelings, it is not the same as a conservation interest.)

There is a well-known kind of theory which represents our attitudes as still radically anthropocentric, even when they are not directed exclusively to human interests. On this account, our attitudes might be understood in terms of the following prescription: treat the non-animal effects, and also the non-human effects which do not involve other animals' experiences, simply as experiential effects on human beings, as types of state that human beings would prefer not to be in, in the case of what we call good effects, would prefer to be in. The badness of environmental effects would then be measured in terms of the effect on human experience—basically, our dislike or distaste for what is happening. It might be hoped that by exploiting existing economic theory, this way of thinking could generate prices for pollution.

This way of looking at things invovles some basic difficulties, which bring out the fairly obvious fact that this interpretation has not moved far enough from the very simply anthropocentric. This approach reduces the whole problem to human consciousness of these effects, but people's preferences against being conscious of some non-human or non-living effect are in the first instance preferences against the effect itself. A guarantee that no-one would further know about a given effect would not cheer anyone up about its occurring; moreover, if people simply ceased to care, this could not be counted an improvement. A preference of this kind involves a value. A preference not to see a blighted landscape is based on the thought that it is blighted, and one cannot assess the preference—in particular, one cannot decide what kind of weight to give to it—unless one understands that thought, and hence that value.

A different approach is to extend the class of things we may be concerned about beyond ourselves and the sufferings of other animals by supposing that non-animal things, though they have no experiences, do have interests. This directly makes the attitudes in question less anthropocentric, but I myself do not think that it is a way in which we are likely to make progress. To say that a thing has interests will help in these connections only if its interests make a claim on us: we may have to allow in some cases that the claim can be outweighed by other claims, but it will have to be agreed that the interests of these things make some claim on us, if the notion of "interests" is to do the required work. But we cannot plausibly suppose that all the interests which, on this approach, would exist do make a claim on us. If a tree has any interests at all, then it must have an interest in getting better if it is sick; but a sick tree, just as such, makes no claim on us. Moreover, even if individual members of a species had interests, and they made some claims on us, it would remain quite unclear

how a species could have interests: but the species is what is standardly the concern of conservation. Yet again, even if it were agreed that a species or kind of thing could have interests, those interests would certainly often make no claim on us: the interests of the HIV virus make no claim on us, and we offend against nothing if our attitude to it is that we take no prisoners.

These objections seem to me enough to discourage this approach, even if we lay aside the difficulties—which are obvious enough—of making sense in the first place of the idea of a thing's having interests if it cannot have experiences. The idea of ascribing interests to species, natural phenomena and so on, as a way of making sense of our concern for these things, is part of a project of trying to extend into nature our concerns for each other, by moralising our relations to nature. I suspect, however, that this is to look in exactly the wrong direction. If we are to understand these things, we need to look to our ideas of nature itself, and to ways in which it precisely lies outside the domestication of our relations to each other.

The idea of "raw" nature, as opposed to culture and to human production and control, comes into these matters, and fundamentally so, but not in any simple way. If the notion of the "natural" is not to distort discussion in a hopelessly fanciful way, as it has distorted many other discussions in the past, we have to keep firmly in mind a number of considerations. First, a self-conscious concern for preserving nature is not itself a piece of nature: it is an expression of culture, and indeed of a very local culture (though that of course does not mean that it is not important). Second, the disappearance of species is itself natural, if anything is. Third, and conversely, many of the things that we want to preserve under an environmental interest are cultural products, and some of them very obviously so, such as cultivated landscapes, and parks.

Last of these general considerations, it is presumably part of the idea of the natural that kinds of creatures have "natures," and we cannot rule out at the beginning the idea that we might have one, and that if we have one, it might be of a predatory kind. It is one of the stranger paradoxes of many people's attitudes to this subject (and the same applies to some other matters, such as animal rights) that while they supposedly reject traditional pictures of human beings as discontinuous from nature in virtue of reason, and they remind us all the time that other species share the same world with us on (so to speak) equal terms, they unhesitatingly carry over into their picture of human beings a moral transcendence over the rest of nature, which makes us uniquely able, and therefore uniquely obliged, to detach ourselves from any natural determination of our behaviour. Such views in fact firmly preserve the traditional doctrine of our transcendence of nature, and with it our proper monarchy of the earth; they merely ask us to exercise it in a more benevolent manner.

Granted these various considerations, the concept of the "natural" is unlikely to serve us very well as anything like a criterion to guide our activities. Nevertheless, our ideas of nature must play an important part in explaining our attitudes towards these matters. Nature may be seen as offering a boundary to our activities, defining certain interventions and certain uncontrolled effects as transgressive.

Many find it appropriate to speak of such a conception as religious: a sense that human beings should not see the world as simply theirs to control is often thought to have a religious origin, and a "secular" or "humanist" attitude is thought to be in this, as in other respects, anthropocentric. In one way, at least, there must be something too simple in this association; while some traditional religious outlooks have embodied feelings of this kind, there are some religions (including many versions of Christianity) that firmly support images of human domination of the world. However this may be, an appeal to religious origins will in any case not be the end of the matter, for the question will remain of why religious outlooks should have this content, to the extent that they do. In particular, the religious sceptic, if he or she is moved by concerns of conservation, might be thought to be embarrassed by the supposed religious origin of these concerns. Other sceptics might hope to talk that sceptic out of his or her concerns by referring these attitudes back to religion. But they should reflect here, as elsewhere, on the force of *Feuerbach's Axiom*, as it may be called: if religion is false, it cannot ultimately explain anything, but itself needs to be explained. If religion is false, it comes entirely from humanity (indeed if it is true, it comes in good part from humanity). If it tends to embody a sense of nature that should limit our exploitation of it, we may hope to find the source of that sense in humanity itself.

I end with a line of thought about that source; it is offered as no more than a speculation to encourage reflection on the question. Human beings have two basic kinds of emotional relations to nature: gratitude and a sense of peace, on the one hand, terror and stimulation on the other. It needs to elaborate sociobiological speculation to suggest why these relations should be very basic. The two kinds of feelings famously find their place in art, in the form of its concern with the beautiful and with the sublime. We should consider the fact that when the conscious formulation of this distinction became central to the theory of the arts, at the end of the eighteenth century, at the same time the sublimity and the awesomeness of nature themselves became a subject for the arts, to a much greater extent than had been the case before. Art which was sublime and terrifying of course existed before, above all in literature, but its theme was typically not nature in itself, but rather, insofar as it dealt with nature, nature's threat to culture: in Sophocles, for instance,[1] or in *King Lear*. It is tempting to think that earlier ages had no need for art to represent nature as terrifying: that was simply what, a lot of the time, it was. An artistic reaffirmation of the separateness and fearfulness of nature became appropriate at the point at which for the first time the prospect of an ever-increasing technical control of it became obvious.

If we think in these terms, our sense of restraint in the face of nature, a sense very basic to conservation concerns, will be grounded in a form of fear: a fear not just of the power of nature itself, but what might be called Promethean fear, a fear of taking too lightly or inconsiderably our relations to nature. On this showing, the grounds of our attitudes will be very different from that suggested by any appeal to the interests of natural things. It will not be an extension of benevolence or altruism; nor, directly, will it be a sense of community, though it may be a sense of intimate involvement. It will be based rather on a sense of an opposition between ourselves and nature, as an old, unbounded and potentially dangerous enemy, which requires respect. "Respect" is the notion that perhaps more than any other needs examination here—and not first in the sense of respect for a sovereign, but that in which we have a healthy respect for mountainous terrain or treacherous seas.

Not all our environmental concerns will be grounded in Promethean fear. Some of them will be grounded in our need for the other powers of nature, those associated with the beautiful. But the thoughts which, if these speculations point in the right direction, are associated with the sublime and with Promethean fear will be very important, for they particularly affirm our distinction, and that of our culture, from nature, and conversely, the thought that nature is independent of us, something not made, and not adequately controlled.

We should not think that, if the basis of our sentiments is of such a kind, then it is simply an archaic remnant which we can ignore. For, first, Promethean fear is a good, general warning device, reminding us still appropriately of what we may properly fear. But apart from that, if it is something that many people deeply feel, then it is something that is likely to be pervasively connected to things that we value, to what gives life the kinds of significance that it has. We should not suppose that we know how that may be, or that we can be sure that we can do without those things.

As I said earlier, it is not these feelings in themselves that matter. Rather, they embody a value which we have good reason, in terms of our sense of what is worthwhile in human life, to preserve, and to follow, to the extent that we can, in our dealings with nature. But there are, undeniably, at least two large difficulties that present themselves when we try to think of how we may do that. First, as I also implied earlier, there is no simple way to put such values into a political sum. Certainly these philosophical or cultural reflections do not help one to do so. It may well be that our ways of honouring such values cannot take an economic form. The patterns must be political; it can only be the mobilisation, encouragement and expression of these attitudes, their manifest connection with things that people care about, that can give them an adequate place on the agenda.

The second difficulty concerns not the ways in which we might come to do anything about them, but what we might do. What many conservation interests want to preserve is a nature that is not controlled, shaped, or willed by us, a nature which, as against culture, can be thought of as just there. But a nature which is preserved by us is no longer a nature that is simply not controlled. A natural park is not nature, but a park; a wilderness that is preserved is a definite, delimited, wilderness. The paradox is that we have to use our power to preserve a sense of what is not in our power. Anything we leave untouched we have already touched. It will no doubt be best for us not to forget this, if we are to avoid self-deception and eventual despair. It is the final expression of the inescapable truth that our refusal of the anthropocentric must itself be a human refusal.

NOTE

1. As has been admirably shown by C. Segal, *Tragedy and Civilization* (Cambridge, Mass.: Harvard University Press, 1981).

KENNETH E. GOODPASTER

[From] On Being Morally Considerable

A thing is right when it tends to preserve the integrity, stability, and beauty of the biotic community. It is wrong when it tends otherwise.

—ALDO LEOPOLD

What follows is a preliminary inquiry into a question which needs more elaborate treatment than an essay can provide. The question can be and has been addressed in different rhetorical formats, but perhaps G. J. Warnock's formulation of it is the best to start with:

> Let us consider the question to whom principles of morality apply from, so to speak, the other end—from the standpoint not of the agent, but of the "patient." What, we may ask here, is the condition of moral *relevance?* What is the condition of having a claim to be *considered,* by rational agents to whom moral principles apply?[1]

In the terminology of R. M. Hare (or even Kant), the same question might be put thus: In universalizing our putative moral maxims, what is the scope of the variable over which universalization is to range? A more legalistic idiom, employed recently by Christopher D. Stone,[2] might ask: What are the requirements for "having standing" in the moral sphere? However the question gets formulated, the thrust is in the direction of necessary and sufficient conditions on X in

(1) For all A, X deserves moral consideration from A.

where A ranges over rational moral agents and moral 'consideration' is construed broadly to include the most basic forms of practical respect (and so is not restricted to "possession of rights" by X)....

I

Let us begin with Warnock's own answer to the question, now that the question has been clarified somewhat. In setting out his answer, Warnock argues (in my view, persuasively) against two more restrictive candidates. The first, what might be called the *Kantian principle,* amounts to little more than a reflection of the requirements of moral *agency* onto those of moral considerability:

(2) For X to deserve moral consideration from A, X must be a rational human person.

Observing that such a criterion of considerability eliminates children and mentally handicapped adults, among others, Warnock dismisses it as intolerably narrow.

The second candidate, actually a more generous variant of the first, sets the limits of moral considerability by disjoining "potentiality":

(3) For all A, X deserves moral consideration from A if and only if X is a rational human person or is a potential rational human person.

Warnock's reply to this suggestion is also persuasive. Infants and imbeciles are no doubt potentially rational, but this does not appear to be the reason why we should not maltreat them. And we would not say that an imbecile reasonably judged to be incurable would thereby reasonably be taken to have no moral claims (151). In short, it seems arbitrary to draw the boundary of moral *considerability* around rational human beings (actual or potential), however plausible it might be to draw the boundary of moral *responsibility* there.

Warnock then settles upon his own solution. The basis of moral claims, he says, may be put as follows:

> ...just as liability to be judged as a moral agent follows from one's general capability of alleviating, by moral action, the ills of the predicament, and is for that reason confined to rational beings, so the condition of being a proper "beneficiary" of moral action is the capability of *suffering* the ills of the predicament—and for that reason is not confined to rational beings, nor even to potential members of that class. (151)

The criterion of moral considerability then, is located in the *capacity to suffer:*

(4) For all *A, X* deserves moral consideration from *A* if and only if *X* is capable of suffering pain (or experiencing enjoyment).

And the defense involves appeal to what Warnock considers to be (analytically) the *object* of the moral enterprise: amelioration of "the predicament."

Now two issues arise immediately in the wake of this sort of appeal. The first has to do with Warnock's own over-all strategy in the context of the quoted passage. Earlier on in his book, he insists that the appropriate analysis of the concept of morality will lead us to an "object" whose pursuit provides the framework for ethics. But the "object" seems to be more restrictive:

> ...the general object of moral evaluation must be to contribute in some respects, by way of the actions of rational beings, to the amelioration of the human predicament—that is, of the conditions in which *these* rational beings, humans, actually find themselves. (16; emphasis in the original)

It appears that, by the time moral considerability comes up later in the book, Warnock has changed his mind about the object of morality by enlarging the "predicament" to include nonhumans.

The second issue turns on the question of analysis itself.... [I]t is difficult to keep conceptual and substantive questions apart in the present context. We can, of course, stipulatively *define* "morality" as both

having an object and having the object of mitigating suffering. But, in the absence of more argument, such definition is itself in need of a warrant. Twentieth-century preoccupation with the naturalistic or definist fallacy should have taught us at least this much.

Neither of these two observations shows that Warnock's suggested criterion is wrong, of course. But they do, I think, put us in a rather more demanding mood. And the mood is aggravated when we look to two other writers on the subject who appear to hold similar views.

W. K. Frankena, in a recent paper, joins forces:

> Like Warnock, I believe that there are right and wrong ways to treat infants, animals, imbeciles, and idiots even if or even though (as the case may be) they are not persons or human beings—just because they are capable of pleasure and suffering, and not just because their lives happen to have some value to or for those who clearly are persons or human beings.[3]

And Peter Singer writes:

> If a being is not capable of suffering, or of experiencing enjoyment or happiness, there is nothing to be taken into account. This is why the limit of sentience (using the term as a convenient, if not strictly accurate, shorthand for the capacity to suffer or experience enjoyment or happiness) is the only defensible boundary of concern for the interests of others.[4]

I say that the mood is aggravated because, although I acknowledge and even applaud the conviction expressed by these philosophers that the capacity to suffer (or perhaps better, *sentience*) is sufficient for moral considerability, I fail to understand their reasons for thinking such a criterion necessary. To be sure, there are hints at reasons in each case. Warnock implies that nonsentient beings could not be proper "beneficiaries" of moral action. Singer seems to think that beyond sentience "there is nothing to take into account." And Frankena suggests that non-sentient beings simply do not provide us with moral reasons for respecting them unless it be potentiality for sentience. Yet it is so clear that there *is* something to take into account, something that is not merely "potential sentience" and which surely does qualify beings as beneficiaries and capable of harm—namely, *life*—that the hints provided seem to me to fall short of good reasons.

Biologically, it appears that sentience is an adaptive characteristic of living organisms that provides them with a better capacity to anticipate, and so avoid, threats to life. This at least suggests, though of course it does not prove, that the capacities to suffer and to enjoy are ancillary to something more important rather than tickets to considerability in their own right. In the words of one perceptive scientific observer:

> If we view pleasure as rooted in our sensory physiology, it is not difficult to see that our neurophysiological equipment must have evolved via variation and selective retention in such a way as to record a positive signal to adaptationally satisfactory conditions and a negative signal to adaptationally unsatisfactory conditions.... The pleasure signal is only an evolutionarily derived indicator, not the goal itself. It is the applause which signals a job well done, but not the actual completion of the job.[5]

Nor is it absurd to imagine that evolution might have resulted (indeed might still result?) in beings whose capacities to maintain, protect, and advance their lives did not depend upon mechanisms of pain and pleasure at all.

So far, then, we can see that the search for a criterion of moral considerability takes one quickly and plausibly beyond humanism. But there is a tendency, exhibited in the remarks of Warnock, Frankena, and Singer, to draw up the wagons around the notion of sentience. I have suggested that there is reason to go further and not very much in the way of argument not to. But perhaps there is a stronger and more explicit case that can be made for sentience. I think there is, in a way, and I propose to discuss it in detail in the section that follows.

II

Joel Feinberg offers what may be the clearest and most explicit case for a restrictive criterion on moral considerability (restrictive with respect to life).[6] I should mention at the outset, however, that the context for his remarks is

1. the concept of "rights," which, we have seen, is sometimes taken to be narrower than the concept of "considerability"; and
2. the *intelligibility* of rights-attributions, which, we have seen, is problematically related to the more substantive issue of what beings deserve moral consideration.

These two features of Feinberg's discussion might be thought sufficient to invalidate my use of that discussion here. But the context of his remarks is clearly such that "rights" is taken very broadly, much closer to what I am calling moral considerability than to what Passmore calls "rights." And the thrust of the arguments, since they are directed against the *intelligibility* of certain rights attributions, is *a fortiori* relevant to the more substantive issue set out in ([section] I). So I propose to treat Feinberg's arguments as if they were addressed to the considerability issue in its more substantive form, whether or not they were or would be intended to have such general application. I do so with due notice to the possible need for scare-quotes around Feinberg's name, but with the conviction that it is really in Feinberg's discussion that we discover the clearest line of argument in favor of something like sentience, an argument which was only hinted at in the remarks of Warnock, Frankena, and Singer.

The central thesis defended by Feinberg is that a being cannot intelligibly be said to possess moral rights (read: deserve moral consideration) unless that being satisfies the "interest principle," and that only the subclass of humans and higher animals among living beings satisfies this principle:

> ...the sorts of beings who can have rights are precisely those who have (or can have) interests. I have come to this tentative conclusion for two reasons: (1) because a right holder must be capable of being represented and it is impossible to represent a being that has no interests, and (2) because a right holder must be capable of being a beneficiary in his own person, and a being without interests is a being that is incapable of being

harmed or benefited, having no good or "sake" of its own. (51)

Implicit in this passage are the following two arguments, interpreted in terms of moral considerability:

(A1) Only beings who can be represented can deserve moral consideration.
Only beings who have (or can have) interests can be represented.
Therefore, only beings who have (or can have) interests can deserve moral consideration.

(A2) Only beings capable of being beneficiaries can deserve moral consideration.
Only beings who have (or can have) interests are capable of being beneficiaries.
Therefore, only beings who have (or can have) interests can deserve moral consideration.

I suspect that these two arguments are at work between the lines in Warnock, Frankena, and Singer, though of course one can never be sure. In any case, I propose to consider them as the best defense of the sentience criterion in recent literature.

I am prepared to grant, with some reservations, the first premises in each of these obviously valid arguments. The second premises, though, are *both* importantly equivocal. To claim that only beings who have (or can have) interests can be represented might mean that "mere things" cannot be represented because they have nothing to represent, no "interests" as opposed to "usefulness" to defend or protect. Similarly, to claim that only beings who have (or can have) interests are capable of being beneficiaries might mean that "mere things" are incapable of being benefited or harmed— they have no "well-being" to be sought or acknowledged by rational moral agents. So construed, Feinberg seems to be right; but he also seems to be committed to allowing any *living* thing the status of moral considerability. For as he himself admits, even plants

...are not "mere things"; they are vital objects with inherited biological propensities determining their natural growth. Moreover we do say that certain

conditions are "good" or "bad" for plants, thereby suggesting that plants, unlike rocks, are capable of having a "good." (51)

But Feinberg pretty clearly wants to draw the nets tighter than this—and he does so by interpreting the notion of "interests" in the two second premises more narrowly. The contrast term he favors is not "mere things" but "mindless creatures." And he makes this move by insisting that "interests" logically presuppose *desires* or *wants* or *aims*, the equipment for which is not possessed by plants (nor, we might add, by many animals or even some humans?).

But why should we accept this shift in strength of the criterion? In doing so, we clearly abandon one sense in which living organisms like plants do have interests that can be represented. There is no absurdity in imagining the representation of the needs of a tree for sun and water in the face of a proposal to cut it down or pave its immediate radius for a parking lot. We might of course, on reflection, decide to go ahead and cut it down or do the paving, but there is hardly an intelligibility problem about representing the tree's interest in our deciding not to. In the face of their obvious tendencies to maintain and heal themselves, it is very difficult to reject the idea of interests on the part of trees (and plants generally) in remaining alive.

Nor will it do to suggest, as Feinberg does, that the needs (interests) of living things like trees are not really their own but implicitly *ours:* "Plants may need things in order to discharge their functions, but their functions are assigned by human interests, not their own" (54). As if it were human interests that assigned to trees the tasks of growth or maintenance! The interests at stake are clearly those of the living things themselves, not simply those of the owners or users or other human persons involved. Indeed, there is a suggestion in this passage that, to be capable of being represented, an organism must *matter* to human beings somehow—a suggestion whose implications for human rights (disenfranchisement), let alone the rights of animals (inconsistently for Feinberg, I think), are grim.

The truth seems to be that the "interests" that nonsentient beings share with sentient beings (over and against "mere things") are far more plausible as criteria of *considerability* than the "interests" that sentient beings share (over and against "mindless creatures"). This is not to say that interests construed in the latter way are morally irrelevant—for they may play a role as criteria of moral *significance*— but it is to say that psychological or hedonic capacities seem unnecessarily sophisticated when it comes to locating the minimal conditions for something's deserving to be valued for its own sake. Surprisingly, Feinberg's own reflections on "mere things" appear to support this very point:

> …mere things have no conative life: no conscious wishes, desires, and hopes; or urges and impulses; or unconscious drives, aims, and goals; or latent tendencies, direction of growth, and natural fulfillments. Interests must be compounded somehow out of conations; hence mere things have no interests. (49)

Together with the acknowledgment, quoted earlier, that plants, for example, are not "mere things," such observations seem to undermine the interest principle in its more restrictive form. I conclude, with appropriate caution, that the interest principle either grows to fit what we might call a "life principle" or requires an arbitrary stipulation of psychological capacities (for desires, wants, etc.) which are neither warranted by (A1) and (A2) nor independently plausible.

III

Thus far, I have examined the views of four philosophers on the necessity of sentience or interests (narrowly conceived) as a condition on moral considerability. I have maintained that these views are not plausibly supported, when they are supported at all, because of a reluctance to acknowledge in nonsentient living beings the presence of independent needs, capacities for benefit and harm, etc.…

Let us now turn to several objections that might be thought to render a "life principle" of moral considerability untenable quite independently of the adequacy or inadequacy of the sentience or interest principle.

(O1) A principle of moral respect or consideration for life in all its forms is mere Schweitzerian romanticism, even if it does not involve, as it probably does, the projection of mental or psychological categories beyond their responsible boundaries into the realms of plants, insects, and microbes.

(R1) This objection misses the central thrust of my discussion, which is *not* that the sentience criterion is necessary, but applicable to all life forms— rather the point is that the possession of sentience is not necessary for moral considerability. Schweitzer himself may have held the former view—and so have been "romantic"—but this is beside the point.

(O2) To suggest seriously that moral considerability is coextensive with life is to suggest that conscious, feeling beings have no more central role in the moral life than vegetables, which is downright absurd—if not perverse.

(R2) This objection misses the central thrust of my discussion as well, for a different reason. It is consistent with acknowledging the moral considerability of all life forms to go on to point out differences of moral significance among these life forms. And as far as perversion is concerned, history will perhaps be a better judge of our civilization's treatment of animals and the living environment on that score.

(O3) Consideration of life can serve as a criterion only to the degree that life itself can be given a precise definition; and it can't.

(R3) I fail to see why a criterion of moral considerability must be strictly decidable in order to be tenable. Surely rationality, potential rationality, sentience, and the capacity for or possession of interests fare no better here. Moreover, there do seem to be empirically respectable accounts of the nature of living beings available which are not intolerably vague or open-textured:

> The typifying mark of a living system…appears to be its persistent state of low entropy, sustained by metabolic processes for accumulating energy, and maintained in equilibrium with its environment by homeostatic feedback processes.[7]

Granting the need for certain further qualifications, a definition such as this strikes me as not only plausible in its own right, but ethically illuminating, since it suggests that the core of moral concern lies in respect for self-sustaining organization and integration in the face of pressures toward high entropy.

(O4) If life, as understood in the previous response, is really taken as the key to moral considerability, then it is possible that larger systems besides our ordinarily understood "linear" extrapolations from human beings (e.g., animals, plants, etc.) might satisfy the conditions, such as the biosystem as a whole. This surely would be a *reductio* of the life principle.

(R4) At best, it would be a *reductio* of the life principle in this form or without qualification. But it seems to me that such (perhaps surprising) implications, if true, should be taken seriously. There is some evidence that the biosystem as a whole exhibits behavior approximating to the definition sketched above, and I see no reason to deny it moral considerability on that account.[8] Why should the universe of moral considerability map neatly onto our medium-sized framework of organisms?

(O5) There are severe epistemological problems about imputing interests, benefits, harms, etc., to nonsentient beings. What is it for a tree to have needs?

(R5) I am not convinced that the epistemological problems are more severe in this context than they would be in numerous others which the objector would probably not find problematic. Christopher Stone has put this point nicely:

> I am sure I can judge with more certainty and meaningfulness whether and when my lawn wants (needs) water than the Attorney General can judge whether and when the United States wants (needs) to take an appeal from an adverse judgment by a lower court. The lawn tells me that it wants water by a certain dryness of the blades and soil—immediately obvious to the touch—the appearance of bald spots, yellowing, and a lack of springiness after being walked on; how does "the United States" communicate to the Attorney General?[9]

We make decisions in the interests of others or on behalf of others every day—"others" whose wants are far less verifiable than those of most living creatures.

(O6) Whatever the force of the previous objections, the clearest and most decisive refutation of the principle of respect for life is that one cannot *live* according to it, nor is there any indication in nature that we were intended to. We must eat, experiment to gain knowledge, protect ourselves from predation (macroscopic and microscopic), and in general deal with the overwhelming complexities of the moral life while remaining psychologically intact. To take seriously the criterion of considerability being defended, all these things must be seen as somehow morally wrong.

(R6) This objection, if it is not met by implication in (R2), can be met, I think, by … the distinction … between regulative and operative moral consideration. It seems to me that there clearly are limits to the operational character of respect for living things. We must eat, and usually this involves killing (though not always). We must have knowledge, and sometimes this involves experimentation with living things and killing (though not always). We must protect ourselves from predation and disease, and sometimes this involves killing (though not always). The regulative character of the moral consideration due to all living things asks, as far as I can see, for sensitivity and awareness, not for suicide (psychic or otherwise). But it is not vacuous, in that it does provide a *ceteris paribus* encouragement in the direction of nutritional, scientific, and medical practices of a genuinely life-respecting sort.

As for the implicit claim, in the objection, that since nature doesn't respect life, we needn't, there are two rejoinders. The first is that the premise is not so clearly true. Gratuitous killing in nature is rare indeed. The second, and more important, response is that the issue at hand has to do with the appropriate moral demands to be made on rational moral agents, not on beings who are not rational moral agents. Besides, this objection would tell equally against *any* criterion of moral considerability so far as I can see, if the suggestion is that nature is amoral.

I have been discussing the necessary and sufficient conditions that should regulate moral consideration. As indicated earlier, however, numerous other questions are waiting in the wings. Central among them are questions dealing with how to balance competing claims to consideration in a world in which such competing claims seem pervasive. Related to these questions would be problems about the relevance of developing or declining status in life (the very young and the very old) and the relevance of the part-whole relation (leaves to a tree; species to an ecosystem). And there are many others.

Perhaps enough has been said, however, to clarify an important project for contemporary ethics, if not to defend a full-blown account of moral considerability and moral significance. Leopold's ethical vision and its implications for modern society in the form of an environmental ethic are important—so we should proceed with care in assessing it.

NOTES

1. G. J. Warnock, *The Object of Morality* (New York: Methuen, 1971), 148. All parenthetical page references to Warnock are to this book.

2. C. D. Stone, *Should Trees Have Standing? Toward Legal Rights for Natural Objects* (Los Altos, Calif.: William Kaufmann, 1974).

3. W. K. Frankena, "Ethics and the Environment," in *Ethics and Problems of the Twenty-first Century*, ed. K. Goodpaster and K. Sayre (Notre Dame, Ind.: University of Notre Dame Press, 1979).

4. P. Singer, "All Animals Are Equal," in *Animal Rights and Human Obligations*, 2nd ed., ed. T. Regan and P. Singer (Englewood Cliffs, N.J.: Prentice-Hall, 1989), 79.

5. M. W. Lipsey, "Value Science and Developing Society" (Paper presented to the Society for Religion in Higher Education, Institute on Society, Technology and Values, July 1973), 11.

6. J. Feinberg, "The Rights of Animals and Unborn Generations," in *Philosophy and Environmental Crisis*, ed. W. Blackstone (Athens: University of Georgia Press, 1974). All parenthetical page references to Feinberg are to this article.

7. K. M. Sayre, *Cybernetics and the Philosophy of Mind* (New York: Humanities Press, 1976), 91.

8. See J. Lovelock and S. Epton, "The Quest for Gaia," *New Scientist* 935 (February 1975): 304–9.

9. Stone, *Should Trees Have Standing?* 24.

ROBERT ELLIOT

Normative Ethics

The human assault on the terrestrial environment shows no signs of abating and some signs of spilling over into non-terrestrial environments. Deforestation continues, soil is eroded, water and air are poisoned, species are extinguished, human population and resource use are burgeoning, climate change caused by human activity threatens island states with inundation and fertile areas with protracted drought, and human activity generally leaves its unhappy mark on every part of the biosphere, prompting some commentators to proclaim the death of nature. Many are appalled by this destruction, much of it insidious and temporarily hidden, because of what it implies for themselves, their children, their friends, other creatures, the biomass, and the planet we inhabit. This response is in many instances an ethical response. People judge that what is occurring is not merely irritating, inconvenient, disappointing, or unfortunate, but immoral, bad, wrong, or evil.

It is easy to connect with this kind of response and it is worth taking some time unpacking it and working out exactly why the destruction and despoliation of natural systems engenders it. This involves the application of ethical categories to domains in which they have historically not been applied. Ethical categories and ethical systems have for too long had primarily a human focus, with limited application outside the human domain. The recent development of normative environmental ethics has necessitated reviewing these categories and their application. Here, various approaches to normative environmental ethics, that is, to the principles and values in terms of which human impacts on the natural environment might be morally evaluated, are discussed. This is done in two stages. The first discusses the varying scope or content of normative environmental ethics and aims to provide an overview of the kinds of concern that have motivated the development of normative environmental ethics, especially those that are not assimilable to human-centered concerns. The second discusses several important approaches to normative ethics, namely consequentialism, deontology (including Kantianism), and virtue theory, and indicates their ability to accommodate the shifting and expanding concerns identified in the first step.

HUMAN-CENTERED ENVIRONMENTAL ETHICS

Much of the ethical response to environmental destruction is undeniably human-centered and so does not compel a reexamination of ethical concerns and structures. In principle at least, this part, and for some theorists it will be the whole, of normative environmental ethics is simply the application of principles and values that are thoroughly human-centered. Of course the development of adequate policy responses will still be complex, difficult, and fraught. Moreover, the fact that so many environmental issues can be compellingly argued in terms of human-centered concerns massively increases the constituency of environmentalism by appealing to the many who will be, unfortunately, unresponsive to broader concerns. In any case, much environmental concern quite rightly focuses on harm to humans, with some commentators warning that human civilization as such is threatened. Others warn of adverse impacts on human health and well-being and lament the destruction of natural resources which have important economic, scientific, medical, recreational, and aesthetic uses.

There are human-centered environmental ethics which do not emphasize harm to humans. For instance, there are perfectionist ethics which concern themselves not so much with the well-being of particular humans but rather with human accomplishments in general, such as the development of knowledge, the refinement of culture, and the creation of new forms of aesthetic expression. No doubt such accomplishments contribute to the well-being of individual humans, and so are instrumentally valued, however they may be valued intrinsically, that is to say for their own sakes or in their own right, as well. The realization of such perfectionist ideals depends on the preservation of nature and the maintenance of biospheric health, for example as a source of inspiration, as an object of contemplation, or simply as a material precondition for civilized life.

Virtue ethics, which are a kind of perfectionist ethic in that they focus on ideals of human character, might also assist us in understanding the ethical response to environmental destruction. The key idea of virtue ethics is that certain kinds of action, insofar as they manifest particular traits of character, may be ethically laudable—that is to say, virtuous—or ethically dubious—that is to say, vicious. The virtuousness or viciousness of actions is not, according to such ethics, straightforwardly reducible to a consideration of their consequences, although it is difficult to believe that there is no connection between the consequences of actions, or types of action, and the evaluation of the underlying motivational and affective structures as virtuous or vicious. Nor do assessments in terms of virtues and vices reduce to the intrinsic wrongness or rightness of the actions themselves, as deontological ethics, which are discussed below, might suggest. Thus, environmental despoliation is sometimes represented as the exemplification of a vicious, or less than virtuous, character and condemned for that reason. Furthermore, the condemnation of the action implies a condemnation of the character of the person whose action it is. And, plausibly, virtue ethics may be deployed beyond the level of particular individuals, commenting as well on the character of institutions, governments, and even economic systems. This extension is important, since many of the policies and practices that assault the environment result not so much from the personal decisions of particular individuals but from the structures and momentum of the social and economic institutions within which individuals act. This is not to say that individuals are not ultimately responsible; it is, rather, an acknowledgment of the institutional impediments to individuals doing the right thing.

It is important to avoid viewing these human-centered ethics as mutually exclusive. It is helpful instead to think of them as possibly overlapping ways in which we might articulate the basis for our environmental concern. There may be instances in which the pertinent normative principles conflict—for instance considerations to do with well-being might sometimes conflict with virtue considerations or other perfectionist considerations. We are no strangers, though, to situations in which there are good reasons for each of several conflicting actions, and we are usually able to achieve a satisfactory ordering of the reasons so that we might, perhaps with some discomfort, choose a course of action. The same point applies when environmental ethics other than human-centered ones are considered. The

principles and values that emerge from them may be added to the plurality of things that ethically matter.

BEYOND HUMAN-CENTERED ENVIRONMENTAL ETHICS

A human-centered environmental ethic may go quite a way toward articulating the moral responses many have to environmental damage and destruction. But not everyone who endorses environmentalist policies is moved merely by human-centered considerations. Indeed, some might regard them as comparatively insignificant and others would regard them as no more significant than considerations that extend beyond the interests of our own species. The first step outside the circle of human interests is to include the interests of other animals in our ethical deliberations....

While extensions of moral consideration to non-human animals do challenge human chauvinism, some normative environmental ethics hold that it constitutes another unjustifiable chauvinism and that further extensions are required. Thus it has been claimed that all living things are morally considerable (Goodpaster 1978). Here, the moral significance of, for instance, uprooting a bush is not exhausted by the relationship of the act to humans and other animals. The suggestion is that the bush itself has a direct claim to moral consideration. Drawing a boundary that omits some living things fails, so it is argued, to take proper account of what it is to harm a thing or to act contrary to a thing's interests. Limiting the extension to, say, sentient creatures assumes that harm and interests presuppose a capacity for experience, whereas all that is required, or so the argument continues, is some loosely specifiable set of biological goals or states in terms of which a thing could be characterized as flourishing or not flourishing to some degree (Feinberg 1974). Thus there could be a normative environmental ethic based on a principle of respect for the biologically goal-directed activity of natural entities (Taylor 1986). Such an ethic would take biological organization, including biologically-based tendencies and dispositions to behave or act in certain ways, as the defining characteristic of living things. It would urge that these tendencies and dispositions, which define what it is for a living thing to flourish according to its kind, be respected, perhaps equally, in every living thing.

The extension of moral consideration to all living things highlights a problem that is, perhaps, somewhat less obvious where the extension is only to sentient animals. The problem is simply that the flourishing of many living things is inevitably at the expense of the flourishing of others, giving rise to multitudinous cases of conflicting interests. The problem threatens to render the relevant ethic vacuous or at least computationally intractable. It may be possible to ameliorate the problem by introducing, and justifying, principles that establish ethical hierarchies, permitting, for instance, trade-offs between the interests of plants and the interests of humans. Or again the problem might be addressed by extending some but not all moral categories across the whole range of living things. Thus it might be argued that while moral value attaches to the flourishing of plants as much as it does to the flourishing of humans, there is nevertheless no extension of the rights that protect human flourishing to the whole domain of living things. It is also possible to appeal to gradations of value, arguing that the flourishing of a human has more value than the flourishing of a non-human sentient creature which has more value than the flourishing of a non-sentient living thing. While these mechanisms might render normative evaluation more tractable, we are still left with a situation that seems overwhelmingly messy and resistant to clear-cut moral judgments.

Matters become more complicated when we note that important foci of normative environmental judgment are yet to be included. Thus there is an extension even beyond living things that some have suggested, according to which all natural entities are morally considerable, irrespective of whether or not they are living things. Here moral considerability is extended to significant natural entities such as rocks, fossils, mountains, rivers, waterfalls, stalactites, cliffs, glaciers, dunes, asteroids, moons, and ecosystems (Rolston 1988). Some of these entities are hosts to living things, and some, such as ecosystems, crucially involve them, but this mooted extension would give them direct moral standing independently of that extended to the living things they contain. Extensionism carried to this extreme will strike many as implausible, but at least some of these critics might think that the putative inclusion of such items in the domain of the morally considerable points to something important. When some of us worry about the despoliation of the natural world, our focus is clearly on the inert natural structures that gave rise to, and support, living things, as much as on those living things themselves. This kind of concern needs somehow to be inserted into the normative framework.

One response is to say that extensionism is hopelessly atomistic and individualistic. The thought is that it tries to develop an acceptable environmental normative ethic through the application of ideas at home in the human domain to the whole gamut of natural items. In so doing, it arguably fails to recognize, and is in tension with, the compelling claims of a holistic environmental ethic (Callicott 1989). What is supposedly required is a more general alteration in the form of ethical theories to reflect the moral significance of wholes, such as specific ecosystems, sets of ecosystems, bioregions, or the biosphere itself. Extensionism, it is argued, distorts our view of nature, inclining us to see it as an aggregation of individuals as opposed to an integrated, organic, dynamic whole. Some who offer this line of criticism take the view that the value of individuals is purely instrumental and that intrinsic value is exemplified only by certain systemic properties such as the integrity of, and diversity within, ecosystems. It is possible, however, to combine the holistic view with individualistic considerations, taking each into account in evaluating policy (Elliot 1997). Further, an important aspect of the development of normative environmental ethics has been the move from human-centered to non-human-centered concerns. Some of the flavor of this has been provided above. But a normative ethic strives to fit our ethical concerns into a systematic structure that generates principles of action. This takes us to our second stage, namely the investigation of how amenable various styles of normative ethics are to the content constituted by our environmental concerns.

CONSEQUENTIALIST ENVIRONMENTAL ETHICS

The dominant ethical framework in philosophical ethics in the recent past is consequentialism, although it is not widely endorsed by environmental ethicists. Consequentialism defines the obligatory as a function over intrinsic value. In other words, considerations to do with intrinsic value, the value that something has in itself or for its own sake, are taken to exhaust the normative content of consequentialist principles of obligation. These considerations define what, in consequentialist terms, is permissible, obligatory, and impermissible. Other moral concepts, such as duty, will, on the consequentialist view, be similarly defined via the concepts of the permissible, the obligatory, and the impermissible. Consequentialism enjoins examination of the consequences of actions in determining whether they ought to be performed, ought not to be performed, are right, wrong, obligatory, permissible, etc. Specifically, it requires examining the intrinsic values and disvalues attaching to those consequences and to the actions themselves. The most common form of consequentialism directs us to maximize intrinsic value. Another form worth discussing directs us to increase intrinsic value and another directs us to maintain intrinsic value. These variants express obligation generally as a non-maximizing function over value: inserting the relevant values specifies particular obligations.

Consider, first, maximizing consequentialism. It tells us that an action is obligatory if, compared to the other actions that it is open to an agent to perform, it maximizes the expected quantity of intrinsic value, and, further, that only those actions that maximize expected intrinsic value are permissible. The obligatory and the permissible coincide. Utilitarianism is perhaps the best known maximizing consequentialism, recognizing only pleasure or happiness as intrinsic values. It obliges us to maximize expected pleasure or happiness, other actions being impermissible (Singer 1979). Utilitarianism is only one possible kind of maximizing consequentialism. Other versions are identified by the different intrinsic values they specify. The practical outcome of applying these principles of obligation is determined by these intrinsic values. And according to some theorists there are distinctively natural intrinsic values that are exemplified by nature in its relatively unspoiled states (Elliot 1997; Rolston 1988; Sylvan and Bennett 1994). According to maximizing consequentialisms, if failure to preserve wild nature delivers a less than maximal increase in intrinsic value, then there is an obligation to preserve it. Similarly, if restoring a natural area that has been degraded maximizes expected intrinsic value, then there is an obligation to restore it. With all serious variants of consequentialism, the support for environmentalist policies is strongest where nature itself is taken to have intrinsic value. The support will be exceptionally strong where natural values are the only intrinsic values recognized, although a normative environmental ethic that counts only natural values as intrinsic values would be immensely controversial. Support will also be very strong where, even though other values are recognized, natural values are taken to be the most important values.

A further aspect of consequentialisms should be particularly stressed; namely that they permit trade-offs between quantities of the same intrinsic value and also between different intrinsic values. For example, if pleasure is the only intrinsic value, then a maximizing consequentialist would say that it is obligatory to reduce one person's pleasure, or even to inflict pain, in order to maximize pleasure overall. A consequentialist who accepts that there is a plurality of intrinsic values, including natural values, is faced with a very difficult task, having to make comparative judgments not only about different quantities of the same value but also about different quantities of different values. For example, the consequentialist who thinks both pleasure and the acquisition of knowledge are distinct values, has the problem of deciding just how much pleasure should be sacrificed in order to advance some particular area of knowledge and vice versa. Because of the possibility of trade-offs, it is useful to say that if some natural item has intrinsic value it is prima facie obligatory not to destroy it, rather than obligatory all things considered. Noting that something is of intrinsic value puts us on a warning not to destroy it or degrade it unless it really is, and can be shown to be, the case that such an action maximizes value. It is, moreover, always necessary to ensure that there are no alternative actions that might be performed that would increase value to a greater extent. Furthermore, consequentialism takes a global and long-term perspective in delivering its normative assessments. Establishing that some action is permissible, all things considered, requires a serious attempt to assess its impact far from its geographical location and also into the further future. This is especially pertinent where natural ecosystems and processes, upon which all life and well-being depend, are involved.

Still, when relevant consequences, values, and alternative courses of action are assessed and compared, we might discover that the loss of intrinsic value through environmental despoliation could, in principle, be compensated for by increases of intrinsic values that are human-centered. For instance, environmentalist policies are often countered with the claim that the development of some natural area will result in substantially increased benefits for humans, such as employment opportunities and increased material wealth. The implication is that environmentalists have their value priorities wrong or that they are illegitimately discounting the substantial benefits for humans that flow from environmental pillage. The possibility of this style of argument is one reason that many environmental ethicists have been cool toward consequentialism, looking elsewhere for a framework for their normative beliefs (Sylvan and Bennett 1994). Consequentialism, provided it recognizes natural values, nevertheless is in a strong position to defeat this style of argument. This is because such arguments typically exaggerate benefits for humans, underestimate deleterious environmental impacts, ignore alternative means of benefiting humans, do not investigate alternative social and economic arrangements, underestimate the costs of environmental despoliation and degradation to present and future humans and non-humans, and fail to interrogate the connections between quality of life and material wealth. And of course if the consequentialism in question recognized only natural value, although that would constitute an extremely controversial value theory, or give natural values special significance or intensity within a plurality of intrinsic values, then the concern that consequentialism is an inadequate normative environmental ethic should be allayed.

A feature of maximizing consequentialism, noted earlier, is that it does not allow any deep distinction between the obligatory and the permissible. This is sometimes thought to be a weakness of maximizing consequentialism in that, allegedly, the theory asks more of people than a normative ethic could reasonably ask. Some variants of consequentialism, however, do allow that actions that are permissible need not be obligatory. Assume, for example, that there are natural values, and consider improving consequentialism, which says that it is obligatory to act so as to increase, although not necessarily maximize, intrinsic value. Such a view is not, if we think about it, all that odd. It reflects the plausible maxim that we should leave the world better than we found it. This variant of consequentialism is, it seems, less onerous than the maximizing variant, requiring less of agents than a total, all-out effort to maximize value. But environmentalists who were concerned by the

trade-offs implicit in maximizing consequentialism will be concerned here too. In particular, there are cases where some environmental despoliation may lead to an increase in value, but in which some alternative action, not involving environmental destruction, would increase value to a greater extent. Improving consequentialism seems to leave open the possibility that the former action is permissible and the latter not obligatory. There are three reasons, though, for thinking that the implications of adopting an improving consequentialism are not, from an environmentalist perspective, quite so worrying.

First, improving consequentialism does not require us to do the best we can, requiring us only to improve matters to some degree. If, however, a person is willing to make a specific degree of effort to improve things, we might reasonably require that she or he use that degree of effort to produce the best result possible. Improving consequentialism might reasonably be taken to have an efficiency requirement built into it. The upshot would be an obligation not merely to ensure that an action improves value, but also to ensure that no alternative action involving the same degree of effort improves value more. An improving consequentialism that recognized intrinsic natural values and took them to be intense would thus strongly favor environmentalist policies. Second, improving consequentialism also takes a global and long-term perspective, requiring agents to take pains to ensure that their actions are improving from that perspective. Relatedly, improving consequentialism must engage in an honest appraisal of the actual consequences of those actions embarked on in order to improve value. Third, in improving consequentialism there is considerable looseness involved because improvements may be very large or very small. Serious advocates of improving consequentialism might think their position is trivialized if acceptable improvements need only minimally increase value. Instead they might insist, still with a degree of looseness, that significant improvements are required.

Another, still less onerous, variant of consequentialism makes it obligatory to act so as to maintain, although not necessarily increase, let alone maximize, intrinsic value. Maintaining consequentialism might be thought to provide little support for environmentalist policies but initial impressions might here be misleading, especially where natural values are taken to be intensely significant. Thus it is not difficult to imagine the maintaining consequentialist trying to maintain intrinsic natural value in the face of extensive and recurring acts of environmental destruction. Actions, including those which impact directly on wild nature, will, all too frequently, depress intrinsic value. Acting to promote environmentalist policies will be a clear and obvious way to fulfill the requirement to maintain intrinsic value. Ironically, an onerousness objection might be pressed even against maintaining consequentialism, since in a world in which the loss of intrinsic natural value proceeds apace, the requirements of even maintaining consequentialism may be exceptionally demanding.

The three variants of consequentialism considered involve differing relationships between value and obligation, although they have in common the view that figuring out our obligations is nothing more than a matter of calculating values and plugging them into some function, such as a maximizing, improving, or a maintaining one. Each provides a framework for a normative environmental ethic and their adequacy in this regard is crucially dependent on the specific values that are recognized and the comparative primacy given to natural values. Nor should we lose sight of the range of possible values, including those that reflect the interests of humans and other sentient creatures. The assault on the natural environment massively threatens these interests and a consequentialism that recognizes them would certainly compel serious environmentalist policies.

DEONTOLOGICAL ENVIRONMENTAL ETHICS

Let us turn now to another major ethical tradition that is constituted by deontological normative

ethics. Deontological ethics are often characterized as ethics of principle rather than ethics focused on promoting intrinsic value. Unlike consequentialist theories, they offer principles of obligation or duty that do not reduce to functions over value, allowing the judgment that actions are obligatory for reasons in addition to the value of their consequences. Deontological theories claim that certain kinds of action are obligatory, permissible, impermissible, and so on, in virtue of specific, non-consequential properties of that action. They do not, however, necessarily exclude such axiological or value assessments, and complete deontological assessments may require some prior axiological assessments.

Thus it might be claimed that, since some natural object has intrinsic value, it is obligatory not to destroy it. The property of being destructive of a thing with intrinsic value would, according to this ethic, be a wrong-making property; the relevant maxim or principle being "do not destroy things which have intrinsic value." While this maxim has about it the flavor of a consequentialist principle, the normative assessment is not carried out by calculating the loss of intrinsic value associated with the destruction of the object and figuring it into some principle of obligation, such as those variants of consequentialism earlier considered—that is, a function over value. Instead, the wrongness of the act can be established without having to look beyond the fact that it involves destroying something of intrinsic value. There is, then, no suggestion that one need look to the consequences of such acts or that one ought to act in accordance with some function of the intrinsic value of the consequences of the act and that of its alternatives. There is, moreover, no suggestion that it is permissible to destroy something of lesser value in order to protect or create something of greater value, which is one reason some environmentalists have felt less unease about deontology than consequentialism. The difference is akin to the difference between a principle that enjoins us to minimize pain, which is consequentialist, and a principle that forbids us to cause pain, which is not consequentialist. Indeed

it may be impermissible to act in ways that maximize, improve, or even maintain intrinsic value—for instance, in situations where the only means of doing one of these things involves the destruction of something of intrinsic value contrary to the prohibition on destroying such. There is, then, a deontological structure that would sustain a distinctively environmental normative ethic, the scope of which extends beyond human interests and concerns. Thus destroying or degrading the natural environment could be wrong because, among other things, it is an act of destroying things which possess natural intrinsic value. But the wrongness does not result from the reduction of value as such: the wrongness results from an independent non-consequentialist principle.

There are other ways of fitting a distinctively environmental ethic into a deontological structure. Theories of rights, for example, are often presented as deontological theories because they imply the proscription and prescription of acts independently of the consequences of those acts. Thus, someone's right to life might be said to result in an absolute proscription on taking that person's life, except perhaps in self-defense or in a judicial context, irrespective of the consequences. The fact that value is increased as a consequence is not, it is often claimed, an acceptable justification for violating the right. Much environmental ethics might be cast in terms of rights. Most obviously it makes sense to invoke the rights of non-human animals in objecting to the destruction of natural habitat. But some have wanted to extend the concept of rights beyond the set of sentient creatures, suggesting that, in addition, plants have rights, that species have rights, or that ecosystems have rights. This proliferation of rights generates problems. In the first place there is the issue of whether the extension of rights in these ways is conceptually sound (Feinberg 1974). Does it, for example, make sense to attribute rights to entities that do not even have desires, that are not even conscious? And do we even want to suggest that non-living natural items, such as rocks or glaciers or rivers, could have rights?

Equally important is the practical problem of how to process and adjudicate the barrage of rights claims that would be generated by such profligate deontological ethics. The problem would be ameliorated if we could be sure that the rights in question would not conflict, but that is not at all clear even where we are focusing only on the rights of humans. In the context of extended rights theories, conflicting rights seem inevitable, with attendant problems of weighing up, balancing, and adjudicating countless apparently competing rights claims. Furthermore, the problem seems more acute for a deontological theory than a consequentialist theory because the former eschews trade-offs based on consequences. How exactly do we respect the rights of every organism? Is there a hierarchy of rights? Is there a hierarchy of rights-bearing individuals, such that, for example, the rights of humans have priority over the rights of sentient non-humans which have priority over the rights of other living things? The answer, even in theory, is not clear and the ethic that suggests the principle might therefore be thought vacuous. The prospect of vacuousness is brought out if we consider the claim, often associated with the Norwegian philosopher Arne Naess's (1986) deep ecology view, that every living thing has an equal right to flourish. Life on earth is such, though, that particular organisms can flourish only if others do not. Taking the right literally seems to leave no room for action.

Some are tempted to say that the problem just sketched is the general one that affects ethical extensionism as the method for generating an environmental ethic, namely that things go awry when we focus on individual entities at too fine-grained a level. Such theorists might suggest that we should be focusing on macro-entities such as whole ecosystems or the biosphere as the pertinent rights bearers. This move might stem the proliferation of rights but it still leaves the problem of how to make sense of the claim that entities that lack consciousness or desires could have rights. Of course there is no parallel problem in the suggestion that they have intrinsic value, and so no problem in a deontological theory that prohibits the destruction of what has intrinsic value. It is odd, however, to suggest that they have rights in the sense that humans and sentient non-humans have rights. For one thing, unless an entity is conscious there seems no content to the suggestion that from its point of view things are going well or badly. And the point of rights theories seems to be to create a set of entitlements on the part of individuals that allow things to go well from an individual's point of view.

In any case, there would still be a residual ranking problem in working out the respective priorities of the rights of sentient creatures, ecosystems, and the biosphere. A simple solution would be to give absolute priority to biospheric rights. This solution would be unpalatable to many because it would demote human rights to little more than an afterthought, making human interests subservient to those of the biosphere. Perhaps, though, this is an idea that we could get used to if we are convinced of the intense ethical significance of the natural environment. While there are limits to the capacity of a deontological theory based on rights to support the moral sentiments expressed by many environmentalists, such a theory can accommodate many. Certainly, acts of environmental destruction and degradation will be wrong for human-centered and animal-centered reasons that a deontologist would likely find compelling. For example, such damage would wrongfully injure and kill non-humans and wrongfully impose costs and burdens on humans, including future humans. The attendant ethical concerns can be powerfully and coherently expressed in the language of rights.

There is a deontological theory, Kantianism, deriving from the views of the eighteenth-century German philosopher Immanuel Kant, that is similar in structure to the rights-based theories and which deserves some comment. The central tenet of Kantianism is that each person is an end in herself or himself, having a capacity for rational autonomy and therefore requiring respect as a person. The idea of respect for persons indeed might be thought

to be the basis of theories of rights that, among other things, articulate and elaborate the idea of respect for persons. At first sight, Kantianism, emphasizing as it does respect for persons, might not seem to provide an amenable structure for anything much more than a human-centered environmental ethic. At least one prominent theorist, the American philosopher Paul Taylor, has, however, elaborated a normative environmental ethic with a Kantian flavor. Taylor (1986) asks us to see all living things as autonomous, in that, at the very least, they have biologically based goals that are definitive of the kinds of organism they are and that define for them what counts as flourishing. He suggests that just as Kantianism enjoins us to respect the rational autonomy of persons, so too a naturalized Kantianism enjoins us to respect the natural autonomy of all living things. The force of Taylor's position derives from whatever success he might have in convincing us that there is a useful analogy between rational autonomy and natural autonomy, and, of course, our views about the significance of rational autonomy. And Taylor, by the way, does not seem to want natural autonomy to swallow up rational autonomy, seeking instead to maintain a moral distinction, with hierarchical implications, between persons and other living things.

The conceptual and proliferation problems that affected rights-based deontological theories are present in Taylor's theory. The analogy between rational autonomy and natural autonomy might well founder on the fact that so much of the latter involves no consciousness of preferences or desires. Although we might well see the point of allowing that non-sentient living things have a kind of autonomy, we might think the conceptual distance between the autonomy of, say, an orchid and that of a primate is too great to sustain the mooted ethical extension. Moreover, the theory runs into problems of ranking claims based on natural autonomy. How, for instance, do we adjudicate situations in which human welfare is promoted, or rational autonomy protected, at the cost of destroying entities, such as plants or microbes, that have natural autonomy? One response to these problems is to try to render Taylor's insights in a non-Kantian form. Thus we might accept that there is something ethically significant about natural autonomy but suggest that its significance is best articulated through the concept of intrinsic value. We can say that natural autonomy is a basis of intrinsic value and either plug that into a consequentialist framework or into a non-Kantian, non-rights-based deontological framework.

There is a final problem that should be sketched. Taken literally, deontological ethics apparently render impermissible actions that do not seem impermissible and that may even be obligatory. For instance, the degradation of some small area of the natural environment in order to create a firebreak may be necessary to ensure the protection of an extensive area. If what we value is wild nature, then surely it is permissible to make the firebreak even though it involves the destruction of items of value. Thus a strict deontology is likely to deliver normative conclusions that are difficult to accept. One response, not unproblematic, is to suggest a mixed ethic, containing both consequentialist and deontological components. If enough of value is at stake, then it may be judged permissible to act in a way that a strict deontology would proscribe. By the same token, the deontological component would act as a brake on consequentialist justifications of environmental degradation (Sylvan and Bennett 1994)....

REFERENCES

Callicott, J. (1989) *In Defense of the Land Ethic* (Albany: State University of New York Press).

Elliot, R. (1997) *Faking Nature: the Ethics of Environmental Restoration* (London: Routledge).

Feinberg, J. (1974) "The rights of animals and unborn generations," in *Philosophy and Environmental Crisis*, ed. W. Blackstone (Athens, Ga.: University of Georgia Press).

Goodpaster, K. (1978) "On being morally considerable," *Journal of Philosophy 75*, p. 308–25.

Hill, Jr., T. (1983) "Ideals of human excellence and preserving the natural environment," *Environmental Ethics* 5, pp. 211–24.

Naess, A. (1986) "The deep ecological movement: some philosophical aspects," *Philosophical Inquiry* 8.

O'Neill, J. (1993) *Ecology, Policy and Politics: Human Wellbeing and the Natural World* (London: Routledge).

Passmore, J. (1975) "Attitudes to nature," in *Nature and Conduct*, ed. R. S. Peters (London, Macmillan), pp. 251–64.

Plumwood, V. (1993) *Feminism and the Mastery of Nature* (London: Routledge).

Rolston III., H. (1988) *Environmental Ethics: Duties to and Values in the Natural World* (Philadelphia: Temple University Press).

Singer, P. (1979) "Not for humans only," in *Ethics and Problems of the 21st Century* (Notre Dame: University of Notre Dame Press), pp. 191–206.

Sylvan. R. and Bennett, D. (1994) *The Greening of Ethics: from Human Chauvinism to Deep-Green Theory* (Cambridge: Whitehorse Press).

Taylor, P. (1986) *Respect for Nature* (Princeton: Princeton University Press).

RONALD SANDLER

Environmental Virtue Ethics

There is at least one certainty regarding the human relationship with nature: there is no getting away from it. One simply cannot opt out of a relationship with the natural world. On some accounts this is because humans are themselves a part of nature. On others it is because we must breathe, eat, drink, and decompose, each of which involves an exchange with the natural world. But whereas a relationship with nature is given, the nature of that relationship is not. Both human history and the contemporary world are replete with diverse and contradictory ways of conceiving of and interacting with the natural environment. Environmental ethics as a field of inquiry is the attempt to understand the human relationship with the environment (including natural ecosystems, agricultural ecosystems, urban ecosystems, and the individuals that populate and constitute those systems) and determine the norms that should govern our interactions with it. These norms can be either norms of action or norms of character. The project of specifying the latter is *environmental virtue ethics*,

and a particular account of the character dispositions that we ought to have regarding the environment is an *environmental virtue ethic*.

WHY IS THERE A NEED FOR AN ENVIRONMENTAL VIRTUE ETHIC?

The central ethical question is, "How should one live?" Answering this question of course requires providing an account of what actions we ought and ought not to perform. But an account of right action—whether a set of rules, a general principle, or a decision-making procedure—does not answer it entirely. A complete answer will inform not only what we ought to do but also what kind of person we ought to be. An adequate ethical theory must provide an ethic of character, and our lived ethical experience belies the claim that one's character is merely the sum of one's actions. Environmental ethics is simply ethics as it pertains to human–environment interactions and relationships. So an adequate environmental ethic likewise requires not only an ethic of action—one that provides guidance regarding what we ought and ought not to do to the environment—but also an ethic of character—one that provides guidance on what attitudes and dispositions we ought and ought not to have regarding the environment.

Consider four widely regarded environmental heroes: Rachel Carson (naturalist and author of *Silent Spring*), John Muir (naturalist and founder of the Sierra Club), Aldo Leopold (wildlife ecologist and author of *A Sand County Almanac*), and Julia Butterfly Hill (activist who lived two years atop a threatened redwood). Why do we admire these individuals? Is it their accomplishments in defense of the environment? Yes. The sacrifices they made for those accomplishments? Of course. Their capacity to motivate others to take action? To be sure. But it is not only what they have done and the legacy they have left that we admire. It is also them—the individuals who managed those accomplishments, made those sacrifices, and have left those legacies. That is, we admire them also for their character—their fortitude, compassion, wonder, sensitivity, respectfulness, courage, love, appreciation, tenacity, and gratitude.

It is not always easy to keep this dimension of environmentalism in mind. Public discourse regarding the environment tends to be framed almost exclusively in legislative and legal terms, so it is tempting to become fixated on what activities and behaviors regarding the environment are or ought to be legal. After all, we might restrict the use of off-road vehicles in an ecologically sensitive area and take legal action against those who fail to adhere to that boundary; but we will not legislate against ecological insensitivity or indifference itself, and no one will be called to court merely for possessing those attitudes. We legislate regarding behavior, not character; policy concerns actions, not attitudes; and the courts apply the standards accordingly.

But as our environmental heroes remind us—both by example and by word—we must not take so narrow a perspective of our relationship with the environment. It is always *people*—with character traits, attitudes, and dispositions—who perform actions, promote policies, and lobby for laws. So while we decry removing mountaintops, filling wetlands, and poisoning wolves and we make our case against these practices before lawmakers, the courts, and the public, we must also consider the character of persons responsible for them. Indeed, how one interacts with the environment is largely determined by one's disposition toward it, and it seems to many that the enabling cause of reckless environmental exploitation is the attitude that nature is merely a boundless resource for satisfying human wants and needs. In Muir's words, "No dogma taught by the present civilization seems to form so insuperable an obstacle in the way of a right understanding of the relations which culture sustains to wildness as that which regards the world as made especially for the uses of man." So it would seem that any significant change in our environmental practices and policies is going to require a substantial shift in our dispositions toward the environment. In this way proper character is indispensable for facilitating right action and behavior.

But as our environmental heroes also remind us—again, by example and by word—environmental virtue is not merely instrumentally valuable as the disposition to identify and then perform proper actions; it is also valuable in itself. It is life-affirming and life-enhancing. Those who possess it are better off than those who do not, for they are able to find reward, satisfaction, and comfort from their relationship with nature; and it is their character—their capacity to appreciate, respect, and love nature—that opens them to these benefits. "Those who dwell, as scientists or laymen, among the beauties and mysteries of the earth are never alone or weary of life," writes Carson; and according to Muir, "Everybody needs beauty as well as bread, places to play in and pray in, where nature may heal and give strength to body and soul alike." To those who are receptive to it, nature is a source of joy, peace, renewal, and self-knowledge.

Once the need for an environmental virtue ethic is recognized two questions immediately present themselves. First, what are the attitudes and dispositions that constitute environmental virtue? Second, what is the proper role of an ethic of character in an environmental ethic? These two issues—specifying environmental virtue and identifying the appropriate role of virtue in an environmental ethic—are central to environmental virtue ethics and largely orient the philosophical work that appears in this collection. The remainder of this essay is intended to serve as a primer on these issues.

SPECIFYING ENVIRONMENTAL VIRTUE

The environmental virtues are the proper dispositions or character traits for human beings to have regarding their interactions and relationships with the environment. The environmentally virtuous person is disposed to respond—both emotionally and through action—to the environment and the nonhuman individuals (whether inanimate, living, or conscious) that populate it in an excellent or fine way. But although this formal account may be accurate, it does not provide any substantive description of what the environmentally virtuous person will actually be like. So how does one establish which dispositions regarding the environment are constitutive of virtue and which are constitutive of vice (and which are neither)? That is, how does one go about providing a substantive account of the environmental virtues and vices?

Perhaps the most common strategy for specifying environmental virtue is to argue by extension from standard interpersonal virtues, that is, from virtues that are typically applied to relationships among humans. Each interpersonal virtue is normative for a particular range of items, activities, or interactions, and that range is its sphere or field of applicability. For example, the field of honesty is the revealing or withholding of truth; the field of temperance is

bodily pleasures and pains; and the field of generosity is the giving and withholding of material goods. Extensionists attempt to expand the range of certain interpersonal virtues to include nonhuman entities by arguing that the features that characterize their fields in interpersonal interaction or relationships also obtain in (at least some) environmental contexts. The virtues, they conclude, should therefore be normative in those environmental contexts as well. For example, if compassion is the appropriate disposition to have toward the suffering of other human beings and there is no relevant moral difference between human suffering and the suffering of nonhuman animals, then one should be compassionate toward the suffering of nonhuman animals. Or if gratitude is the appropriate disposition toward other human beings from whom one has benefited and one has similarly benefited from the natural environment, then gratitude is also an appropriate disposition to have toward the natural environment. Extension from the substance of the interpersonal virtues is thus one strategy for specifying the environmentally virtuous person.

A second strategy is to appeal to agent benefit. On this approach, what establishes a particular character trait as constitutive of environmental virtue is that it typically benefits its possessor. This is a wide-ranging approach bounded only by the limit to the ways in which the environment benefits moral agents. The environment provides not only material goods—such as clean water and air—but also aesthetic goods, recreational goods, and a location to exercise and develop physically, intellectually, morally, and aesthetically. That the environment can benefit individuals in such ways straightforwardly justifies a disposition to preserve these opportunities and goods. But it does not only justify a disposition toward conservation and preservation. It justifies cultivating the kind of character traits that allow one to enjoy those goods. The natural environment provides the opportunity for aesthetic experience, but that benefit accrues only to those who possess the disposition to appreciate the natural environment in that way. It provides the opportunity for intellectual challenge and reward, but those benefits come only to those who are disposed first to wonder and then to try to understand nature. The natural environment provides plentiful opportunities for meaningful relationships with its denizens, but those relationships are only possible for those who are open to having them. Many religious and environmental thinkers have argued that the natural world provides unique opportunities to commune with the spiritual or divine. But, again, the benefits are only available to those who are disposed to be open to them. So considerations of which environmental dispositions benefit their possessor (and allow their possessor to be benefited by the natural environment) are relevant to the substantive specification of environmental virtue. In this way environmental virtue ethics emphasizes the role that enlightened self-interest can play in promoting or motivating environmental consciousness and its corresponding behavior in a way that reinforces rather than undermines the other-regarding aspects of environmental ethics. It allows for environmental ethics to be self-interested without being egoistic.

A third strategy for the specification of environmental virtue is to argue from considerations of human excellence. On this approach what establishes a particular character trait as constitutive of environmental virtue is that it makes its possessor a good human being. What it means to be a good human being—to flourish as a human being—is typically understood naturalistically. That is, it is understood in terms of the characteristic features of the life of members of the human species. Human beings are, for example, social beings. Excellence as a human being therefore involves character dispositions that promote the good functioning of social groups and encourage one to maintain healthy relationships with members in the group. A human being who is disposed to undermine social cohesion, disrupt the conditions that make cooperation among individuals possible, and sour relationships with others is properly described as a deviant human being. Such

a person fails to be a good human being precisely in virtue of his or her antisocial disposition. Many environmental philosophers have argued that a proper naturalistic understanding of human beings will locate them not only socially (as members of the human community) but also ecologically (as members of the broader biotic community). If this is correct, then excellence as a human being would include dispositions to maintain and promote the well-being of the larger ecological community. Given that the well-being of the ecological community is threatened by further habitation fragmentation and biodiversity loss, a disposition to oppose these would thereby be constitutive of environmental virtue. A human being who lacked these dispositions would, from the perspective of human beings as members of the biotic community, be properly described as deviant. Considerations of human excellence need not, however, be confined to secular or naturalistic accounts of environmental virtue. Human excellence is often understood by religious traditions in a way that transcends the natural by connecting it with divine or cosmic purposes. For example, if it is the divinely prescribed role of human beings that they be stewards of the land, then the environmental virtues will be those character traits or dispositions that make human beings reliable and effective stewards.

A fourth strategy for specifying environmental virtue is to study the character traits of individuals who are recognized as environmental role models. By examining the life, work, and character of exemplars of environmental excellence we may be able to identify particular traits that are conducive to, or constitutive of, that excellence. The lives of John Muir, Rachel Carson, and Aldo Leopold, for example, are not just compelling narratives; they also instruct us on how to improve ourselves and our approach to the natural world. Environmental role models of course need not be such public or renowned figures as Carson, Muir, and Leopold. Exemplars of environmental excellence can be found in local communities and in many organizations working for environmental protection and improvement. No doubt many of us have been benefited by such people, not only by their accomplishments but also by the guidance, inspiration, and example they provide.

These four approaches to the specification of environmental virtue—extensionism, considerations of benefit to agent, considerations of human excellence, and the study of role models—are not mutually exclusive. A particular disposition might draw support from all four approaches. Indeed, one often finds them working in concert. Collectively they provide a rich variety of resources for thinking about the substance of environmental virtue.

THE ROLE OF ENVIRONMENTAL VIRTUE IN ENVIRONMENTAL ETHICS

A complete environmental ethic will include both an account of how one ought to interact with the natural environment and an account of the character dispositions that one ought to have regarding the natural environment. But what is the proper relationship between these two? This is an instance of the more general (and very much live) question in moral philosophy: What is the appropriate role of virtue in ethical theory?

Some moral philosophers believe that the virtues are simply dispositions to do the right thing. In the context of environmental ethics this would imply that environmental virtue is merely the disposition to act according to the rules, principles, or norms of action of the correct environmental ethic. On this account the environmental virtues are strictly instrumental and subordinate to right action. First one determines what the right ways to act or behave regarding the environment are, and then one determines which character dispositions tend to produce that behavior. Those dispositions are the environmental virtues.

I argued earlier that environmental virtue is instrumental to promoting proper action. The environmentally virtuous person—precisely because of his or her virtue—will be disposed both to recognize

the right thing and to do it for the right reasons. However, there is more to how one ought to be in the world than the rules, principles, or guidelines of moral action. For example, it might not be morally required that one appreciate the beauty or complexity of the natural environment, but those who are disposed to do so are benefited and so better off than those who are not. So although it is undoubtedly true that the environmental virtues are dispositions to act well regarding the environment, they are not only that. As we have seen, they can be excellences or beneficial to their possessor in their own right, not merely insofar as they tend to produce right action.

Moreover, environmental virtue might provide the sensitivity or wisdom necessary for the application of action-guiding rules and principles to concrete situations. At a minimum, this sensitivity is required to determine which rules or principles are applicable to which situations, as well as for determining what course of action they recommend in those situations where they are operative. But it may also be indispensable in adjudicating between conflicting demands of morality or resolving moral dilemmas that arise from a plurality of sources of value and justification. Indeed, many moral philosophers have argued that it is implausible and unreasonable to believe that there is some finite set of rules or principles that can be applied by any human moral agent in any situation to determine what the proper course of action is in that situation. If they are correct— if action guidance cannot always be accomplished by moral rules and principles alone—then the wisdom and sensitivity that are part of virtue (including environmental virtue) are in some situations indispensable for determining or identifying right action (including environmentally right action).

Some moral philosophers believe that virtue should play an even more prominent or fundamental role within ethical theory than it is afforded in the previous account. These virtue ethicists consider an ethic of character to be theoretically prior to an ethic of action. On this approach to moral philosophy an action is right if and only if it is the virtuous thing to do, it hits the target of virtue, or it is what the virtuous person would do under the circumstances. So a substantive account of the virtues and the virtuous person informs what actions one ought or ought not to perform. In the context of environmental ethics this would imply that reflections on the content of the virtues and studying the character traits and behavior of environmentally virtuous people are what ultimately inform how we ought to behave regarding the environment.

There is thus a range of roles—from instrumental to foundational—that environmental virtue might play within a complete environmental ethic. This is not, however, to claim that each position is equally defensible. I have, for example, argued that a merely instrumental role for environmental virtue is too narrow. But those arguments notwithstanding, it is very much an unsettled issue what the proper role (or roles) of virtue is in an adequate environmental ethic....

PAUL W. TAYLOR

[From] *Respect for Nature: A Theory of Environmental Ethics*

HAVING AND EXPRESSING THE ATTITUDE OF RESPECT FOR NATURE

The central tenet of the theory of environmental ethics that I am defending is that actions are right and character traits are morally good in virtue of their expressing or embodying a certain ultimate moral attitude, which I call respect for nature. When moral agents adopt the attitude, they thereby subscribe to a set of standards of character and rules of conduct as their own ethical principles. Having the attitude entails being morally committed to fulfilling the standards and complying with the rules. When moral agents then act in accordance with the rules and when they develop character traits that meet the standards, their conduct and character express (give concrete embodiment to) the attitude. Thus ethical action and goodness of character naturally flow from the attitude, and the attitude is made manifest in how one acts and in what sort of person one is.

THE BIOCENTRIC OUTLOOK AND THE ATTITUDE OF RESPECT FOR NATURE

The attitude we think it appropriate to take toward living things depends on how we conceive of them and of our relationship to them. What moral significance the natural world has for us depends on the way we look at the whole system of nature and our role in it. With regard to the attitude of respect for nature, the belief-system that renders it intelligible and on which it depends for its justifiability is the biocentric outlook. This outlook underlies and supports the attitude of respect for nature in the following sense. Unless we grasp what it means to accept that belief-system and so view the natural order from its perspective, we cannot see the point of taking the attitude of respect. But once we do grasp it and shape our world outlook in accordance with it, we immediately understand how and why a person would adopt that attitude as the only appropriate one to have toward nature. Thus the biocentric outlook provides the explanatory and justificatory background that makes sense of and gives point to a person's taking the attitude.

The beliefs that form the core of the biocentric outlook are four in number:

1. The belief that humans are members of the Earth's Community of Life in the same sense and on the same terms in which other living things are members of that Community.
2. The belief that the human species, along with all other species, are integral elements in a system of interdependence such that the survival of each living thing, as well as its chances of faring well or poorly, is determined not only by the physical conditions of its environment but also by its relations to other living things.
3. The belief that all organisms are teleological centers of life in the sense that each is a unique individual pursuing its own good in its own way.
4. The belief that humans are not inherently superior to other living things.

To accept all four of these beliefs is to have a coherent outlook on the natural world and the place of humans in it. It is to take a certain perspective on human life and to conceive of the relation between human and other forms of life in a certain way. Given this world view, the attitude of respect is then seen to be the only suitable, fitting, or appropriate moral attitude to take toward the natural world and its living inhabitants.

THE BASIC RULES OF CONDUCT

... I shall now set out and examine four rules of duty in the domain of environmental ethics. This is not supposed to provide an exhaustive account of every valid duty of the ethics of respect for nature. It is doubtful whether a complete specification of duties is possible in this realm. But however that may be, the duties to be listed here are intended to cover only the more important ones that typically arise in everyday life.... [I]n all situations not explicitly or clearly covered by these rules we should rely on the attitude of respect for nature and the biocentric outlook that together underlie the system as a whole and give it point. Right actions are always actions that express the attitude of respect, whether they are covered by the four rules or not. They must also be actions which we can approve of in the light of the various components of the biocentric outlook.

The four rules will be named (1) the Rule of Nonmaleficence, (2) the Rule of Noninterference, (3) the Rule of Fidelity, and (4) the Rule of Restitutive Justice.

1. *The Rule of Nonmaleficence.* This is the duty not to do harm to any entity in the natural environment that has a good of its own. It includes the duty not to kill an organism and not to destroy a species-population or biotic community, as well as the duty to refrain from any action that would be seriously detrimental to the good of an organism, species-population, or life community. Perhaps the most fundamental wrong in the ethics of respect for nature is to harm something that does not harm us.

The concept of nonmaleficence is here understood to cover only nonperformances or intentional abstentions. The rule defines a negative duty, requiring that moral agents refrain from certain kinds of actions. It does not require the doing of any actions, such as those that *prevent* harm from coming to an entity or those that help to *alleviate* its suffering. Actions of these sorts more properly fall under the heading of benefiting an entity by protecting or promoting its good. (They will be discussed in connection with the Rule of Restitutive Justice.)

The Rule of Nonmaleficence prohibits harmful and destructive acts done by moral agents. It does not apply to the behavior of a nonhuman animal or the activity of a plant that might bring harm to another living thing or cause its death. Suppose, for example, that a Rough-legged Hawk pounces on a field mouse, killing it. Nothing morally wrong has occurred. Although the hawk's behavior can be thought of as something it does intentionally, it is not the action of a moral agent. Thus it does not fall within the range of the Rule of Nonmaleficence. The hawk does not violate any duty because it *has* no duties. Consider, next, a vine which over the years gradually covers a tree and finally kills it. The activity of the vine, which involves goal-oriented movements but not, of course, intentional actions, is not a moral wrongdoing. The vine's killing the tree has no moral properties at all, since it is not the conduct of a moral agent.

Let us now, by way of contrast, consider the following case. A Peregrine Falcon has been taken from the wild by a falconer, who then trains it to hunt, seize, and kill wild birds under his direction. Here there occurs human conduct aimed at controlling and manipulating an organism for the enjoyment of a sport that involves harm to other wild organisms. A wrong is being done but not by the falcon, even though it is the falcon which does the actual killing and even though the birds it kills are its natural prey. The wrong that is done to those birds is a wrong done by the falconer. It is not the action of the Peregrine that breaks the rule of duty but the actions of the one who originally captured it, trained it, and who now uses it for his own amusement. These actions, it might be added, are also violations of the Rule of Noninterference, since the falcon was removed from its wild state. Let us now turn our attention to this second rule of duty.

2. *The Rule of Noninterference.* Under this rule fall two sorts of negative duties, one requiring us to refrain from placing restrictions on the freedom of individual organisms, the other requiring a general "hands off" policy with regard to whole ecosystems and biotic communities, as well as to individual organisms.

Concerning the first sort of duty, the idea of the freedom of individual organisms[,] . . . freedom is

absence of constraint, [and] a constraint is any condition that prevents or hinders the normal activity and healthy development of an animal or plant. A being is free in this sense when any of four types of constraints that could weaken, impair, or destroy its ability to adapt successfully to its environment are absent from its existence and circumstances. To be free is to be free *from* these constraints and to be free *to* pursue the realization of one's good according to the laws of one's nature. The four types of constraints, with some examples of each, are:

1. Positive external constraints (cages; traps).
2. Negative external constraints (no water or food available).
3. Positive internal constraints (diseases; ingested poison or absorbed toxic chemicals).
4. Negative internal constraints (weaknesses and incapacities due to injured organs or tissues).

We humans can restrict the freedom of animals and plants by either directly imposing some of these constraints upon them or by producing changes in their environments which then act as constraints upon them. Either way, if we do these things knowingly we are guilty of violating the Rule of Noninterference.

The second kind of duty that comes under this rule is the duty to let wild creatures live out their lives in freedom. Here freedom means not the absence of constraints but simply being allowed to carry on one's existence in a wild state. With regard to individual organisms, this duty requires us to refrain from capturing them and removing them from their natural habitats, *no matter how well we might then treat them.* We have violated the duty of noninterference even if we "save" them by taking them out of a natural danger or by restoring their health after they have become ill in the wild. (The duty is not violated, however, if we do such things with the intention of returning the creature to the wild as soon as possible, and we fully carry out this intention.) When we take young trees or wildflowers from a natural ecosystem, for example, and transplant them in landscaped grounds, we break the Rule of Noninterference *whether or not we then take good care of them and so enable them to live longer, healthier lives than they would have enjoyed in the wild.* We have done a wrong by not letting them live out their lives in freedom. In all situations like these we intrude into the domain of the natural world and terminate an organism's existence as a wild creature. It does not matter that our treatment of them may improve their strength, promote their growth, and increase their chances for a long, healthy life. By destroying their status as wild animals or plants, our interference in their lives amounts to an absolute negation of their natural freedom. Thus, however "benign" our actions may seem, we are doing what the Rule of Noninterference forbids us to do.

Of still deeper significance, perhaps, is the duty of noninterference as it applies to the freedom of whole species-populations and communities of life. The prohibition against interfering with these entities means that we must not try to manipulate, control, modify, or "manage" natural ecosystems or otherwise intervene in their normal functioning. For any given species-population, freedom is the absence of human intervention of any kind in the natural lawlike processes by which the population preserves itself from generation to generation. Freedom for a whole biotic community is the absence of human intervention in the natural lawlike processes by which all its constituent species-populations undergo changing ecological relationships with one another over time. The duty not to interfere is the duty to respect the freedom of biologically and ecologically organized groups of wild organisms by refraining from those sorts of intervention. Again, this duty holds even if such intervention is motivated by a desire to "help" a species-population survive or a desire to "correct natural imbalances" in a biotic community. (Attempts to save endangered species which have almost been exterminated by past *human* intrusions into nature, and attempts to restore ecological stability and balance to an ecosystem that has

been damaged by past *human* activity are cases that fall under the Rule of Restitutive Justice and may be ethically right. These cases will be considered in connection with that rule.)

The duty of noninterference, like that of nonmaleficence, is a purely negative duty. It does not require us to perform any actions regarding either individual organisms or groups of organisms. We are only required to respect their wild freedom by letting them alone. In this way we allow them, as it were, to fulfill their own destinies. Of course some of them will lose out in their struggle with natural competitors and others will suffer harm from natural causes. But as far as our proper role as moral agents is concerned, we must keep "hands off." By strictly adhering to the Rule of Noninterference, our conduct manifests a profound regard for the integrity of the system of nature. Even when a whole ecosystem has been seriously disturbed by a natural disaster (earthquake, lightning-caused fire, volcanic eruption, flood, prolonged drought, or the like) we are duty-bound not to intervene to try to repair the damage. After all, throughout the long history of life on our planet natural disasters ("disasters," that is, from the standpoint of some particular organism or group of organisms) have always taken their toll in the death of many creatures. Indeed, the very process of natural selection continually leads to the extinction of whole species. After such disasters a gradual readjustment always takes place so that a new set of relations among species-populations emerges. To abstain from intervening in this order of things is a way of expressing our attitude of respect for nature, for we thereby give due recognition to the process of evolutionary change that has been the "story" of life on Earth since its very beginnings.

This general policy of nonintervention is a matter of disinterested principle. We may want to help certain species-populations because we like them or because they are beneficial to us. But the Rule of Noninterference requires that we put aside our personal likes and our human interests with reference to how we treat them. Our respect for nature means that we acknowledge the sufficiency of the natural world to sustain its own proper order throughout the whole domain of life. This is diametrically opposed to the human-centered view of nature as a vast piece of property which we can use as we see fit.

In one sense to have the attitude of respect toward natural ecosystems, toward wild living things, and toward the whole process of evolution is to believe that nothing goes wrong in nature. Even the destruction of an entire biotic community or the extinction of a species is not evidence that something is amiss. If the causes for such events arose within the system of nature itself, nothing improper has happened. In particular, the fact that organisms suffer and die does not itself call for corrective action on the part of humans *when humans have had nothing to do with the cause of that suffering and death*. Suffering and death are integral aspects of the order of nature. So if it is ever the case in our contemporary world that the imminent extinction of a whole species is due to entirely natural causes, we should not try to stop the natural sequence of events from taking place in order to save the species. That sequence of events is governed by the operation of laws that have made the biotic Community of our planet what it is. To respect that Community is to respect the laws that gave rise to it.

In addition to this respect for the sufficiency and integrity of the natural order, a second ethical principle is implicit in the Rule of Noninterference. This is the principle of species-impartiality, which serves as a counterweight to the dispositions of people to favor certain species over others and to want to intervene in behalf of their favorites. These dispositions show themselves in a number of ways. First, consider the reactions of many people to predator–prey relations among wildlife. Watching the wild dogs of the African plains bring down the Wildebeest and begin devouring its underparts while it is still alive, they feel sympathy for the prey and antipathy for the predator. There is a tendency to make moral judgments, to think of the dogs as vicious and cruel, and to consider the Wildebeest an innocent victim. Or

take the situation in which a snake is about to kill a baby bird in its nest. The snake is perceived as wicked and the nestling is seen as not deserving such a fate. Even plant life is looked at in this biased way. People get disturbed by a great tree being "strangled" by a vine. And when it comes to instances of bacteria-caused diseases, almost everyone has a tendency to be on the side of the organism which has the disease rather than viewing the situation from the standpoint of the living bacteria inside the organism. If we accept the biocentric outlook and have genuine respect for nature, however, we remain strictly neutral between predator and prey, parasite and host, the disease-causing and the diseased. To take sides in such struggles, to think of them in moral terms as cases of the maltreatment of innocent victims by evil animals and nasty plants, is to abandon the attitude of respect for all wild living things. It is to count the good of some as having greater value than that of others. This is inconsistent with the fundamental presupposition of the attitude of respect: that all living things in the natural world have the same inherent worth....

3. *The Rule of Fidelity*. This rule applies only to human conduct in relation to individual animals that are in a wild state and are capable of being deceived or betrayed by moral agents. The duties imposed by the Rule of Fidelity, though of restricted range, are so frequently violated by so many people that this rule needs separate study as one of the basic principles of the ethics of respect for nature.

Under this rule fall the duties not to break a trust that a wild animal places in us (as shown by its behavior), not to deceive or mislead any animal capable of being deceived or misled, to uphold an animal's expectations, which it has formed on the basis of one's past actions with it, and to be true to one's intentions as made known to an animal when it has come to rely on one. Although we cannot make mutual agreements with wild animals, we can act in such a manner as to call forth their trust in us. The basic moral requirement imposed by the Rule of Fidelity is that we remain faithful to that trust.

The clearest and commonest examples of transgressions of the rule occur in hunting, trapping, and fishing. Indeed, the breaking of a trust is a key to good (that is, successful) hunting, trapping, and fishing. Deception with intent to harm is of the essence. Therefore, unless there is a weighty moral reason for engaging in these activities, they must be condemned by the ethics of respect for nature. The weighty moral reason in question must itself be grounded on disinterested principle, since the action remains wrong in itself in virtue of its constituting a violation of a valid moral rule. Like all such violations, it can be justified only by appeal to a higher, more stringent duty whose priority over the duty of fidelity is established by a morally valid priority principle.

When a man goes hunting for bear or deer he will walk through a woodland as quietly and unobtrusively as possible. If he is a duck hunter he will hide in a blind, set out decoys, use imitative calls. In either case the purpose, of course, is to get within shooting range of the mammal or bird. Much of the hunter's conduct is designed to deceive the wild creature. As an animal is approaching, the hunter remains quiet, then raises his rifle to take careful aim. Here is a clear situation in which, first, a wild animal acts as if there were no danger; second, the hunter by stealth is deliberately misleading the animal to expect no danger; and third, the hunter is doing this for the immediate purpose of killing the animal. The total performance is one of entrapment and betrayal. The animal is manipulated to be trusting and unsuspicious. It is deliberately kept unaware of something in its environment which is, from the standpoint of its good, of great importance to it. The entire pattern of the hunter's behavior is aimed at taking advantage of an animal's trust. Sometimes an animal is taken advantage of in situations where it may be aware of some danger but instinctively goes to the aid of an injured companion. The hunter uses his knowledge of this to betray the animal. Thus when the hunting of shorebirds used to be legally permitted, a hunter would injure a single bird and leave it out to attract hundreds of its fellows, which would fly in and gather around it. This way the hunter could easily "harvest" vast numbers of shorebirds. Even to this day a similar kind of trickery is used to deceive birds. Crow hunters play recordings of a crow's distress calls out in the field. The recording attracts crows, who are then easy targets to shoot. This aspect of hunting, it should be repeated, is not some peripheral aberration. Much of the excitement and enjoyment of hunting as a sport is the challenge to one's skills in getting animals to be trusting and unsuspecting. The cleverer the deception, the better the skill of the hunter....

It is not a question here of whether the animal being hunted, trapped, or fished has a *right* to expect not to be deceived. The animal is being deceived in order to bring advantage to the deceiver and this itself is the sign that the deceiver considers the animal as either having no inherent worth or as having a lower degree of inherent worth than the deceiver himself. Either way of looking at it is incompatible with the attitude of respect for nature....

Besides breaking the Rule of Fidelity, hunting, trapping, and fishing also, of course, involve gross violations of the Rules of Nonmaleficence and Noninterference. It may be the case that in circumstances where the only means for obtaining food or clothing essential to human survival is by hunting, trapping, or fishing, these actions are morally permissible. The ethical principles that justify them could stem from a system of human ethics based on respect for persons plus a priority principle that makes the duty to provide for human survival outweigh those duties of nonmaleficence, noninterference, and fidelity that are owed to nonhumans. But when hunting and fishing are done for sport or recreation, they cannot be justified on the same grounds.

There are cases of deceiving and breaking faith with an animal, however, which can be justified *within* the system of environmental ethics. These cases occur when deception and betrayal must (reluctantly) be done as a necessary step in a wider action of furthering an animal's good, this wider action being the fulfillment of a duty of restitutive justice.

If breaking faith is a temporary measure absolutely needed to alleviate great suffering or to prevent serious harm coming to an animal, such an act may be required as an instance of restitutive justice. Putting aside for the moment a consideration of the idea of restitutive justice as it applies to environmental ethics, it may be helpful to look at some examples.

Suppose a grizzly bear has wandered into an area close to human habitation. In order to prevent harm coming not only to people but also to the bear (when people demand that it be killed), the bear may be deceived so that it can be shot with harmless tranquilizer darts and then, while it is unconscious, removed to a remote wilderness area. Another example would be the live-trapping of a sick or injured animal so that it can be brought to an animal hospital, treated, and then returned to the wild when it is fully recovered. Still another kind of case occurs when a few birds of an endangered species are captured in order to have them raise young in captivity. The young would then be released in natural habitat areas in an effort to prevent the species from becoming extinct.

These human encroachments upon the wild state of mammals and birds violate both the rule of Noninterference and the Rule of Fidelity. But the whole treatment of these creatures is consistent with the attitude of respect for them. They are not being taken advantage of but rather are being given the opportunity to maintain their existence as wild living things....

Hunters and fishermen often argue that they show true respect for nature because they advocate (and pay for) the preservation of natural areas which benefit wild species-populations and life communities. And it is quite true that the setting aside of many "wildlife refuges," both public and private, has resulted from their efforts. Wild animals and plants have benefited from this. What is being overlooked in this argument is the difference between doing something to benefit oneself which happens also to benefit others, and doing something with the purpose of benefiting others as one's ultimate end of action. Hunters and fishermen want only those areas

of the natural environment protected that will provide for them a constant supply of fish, birds, and mammals as game. Indeed, sportsmen will often urge the killing of nongame animals that prey on "their" (the sportsmen's) animals. In Alaska, for example, hunters have persuaded state officials to "manage" wolves—the method used is to shoot them from helicopters—so as to ensure that a large population of moose is available for hunting. The argument that hunters and fishermen are true conservationists of wildlife will stand up only when we sharply distinguish conservation (saving in the present for future consumption) from preservation (protecting from both present and future consumption). And if the ultimate purpose of conservation programs is future exploitation of wildlife for the enjoyment of outdoor sports and recreation, such conservation activities are not consistent with respect for nature, whatever may be the benefits incidentally brought to some wild creatures. Actions that bring about good consequences for wildlife do not express the attitude of respect unless those actions are motivated in a certain way. It must be the case that the actions are done with the intention of promoting or protecting the good of wild creatures as an end in itself and for the sake of those creatures themselves. Such motivation is precisely what is absent from the conservation activities of sportsmen.

4. *The Rule of Restitutive Justice.* In its most general terms this rule imposes the duty to restore the balance of justice between a moral agent and a moral subject when the subject has been wronged by the agent. Common to all instances in which a duty of restitutive justice arises, an agent has broken a valid moral rule and by doing so has upset the balance of justice between himself or herself and a moral subject. To hold oneself accountable for having done such an act is to acknowledge a special duty one has taken upon oneself by that wrongdoing. This special duty is the duty of restitutive justice. It requires that one make amends to the moral subject by some form of compensation or reparation. This is the way one restores the balance of justice that had held between

oneself and the subject before a rule of duty was transgressed.

The set of rules that makes up a valid system of ethics defines the true moral relations that hold between agents and subjects. When every agent carries out the duties owed to each subject and each subject accordingly receives its proper treatment, no one is wronged or unjustly dealt with. As soon as a rule is willfully violated, the balance of justice is tilted against the agent and in favor of the subject; that is, the agent now has a special burden to bear and the victim is entitled to a special benefit, since the doing of the wrong act gave an undeserved benefit to the agent and placed an unfair burden on the subject. In order to bring the tilted scale of justice back into balance, the agent must make reparation or pay some form of compensation to the subject.

The three rules of duty so far discussed in this section can be understood as defining a moral relationship of justice between humans and wild living things in the Earth's natural ecosystems. This relationship is maintained as long as humans do not harm wild creatures, destroy their habitats, or degrade their environments; as long as humans do not interfere with an animal's or plant's freedom or with the overall workings of ecological interdependence; and as long as humans do not betray a wild animal's trust to take advantage of it. Since these are all ways in which humans can express in their conduct the attitude of respect for nature, they are at the same time ways in which each living thing is given due recognition as an entity possessing inherent worth. The principles of species-impartiality and of equal consideration are adhered to, so that every moral subject is treated as an end in itself, never as a means only.

Now, if moral agents violate any of the three rules, they do an injustice to something in the natural world. The act destroys the balance of justice between humanity and nature, and a special duty is incurred by the agents involved. This is the duty laid down by the fourth rule of environmental ethics, the Rule of Restitutive Justice.

What specific requirements make up the duty in particular cases? Although the detailed facts of each situation of an agent's wrongdoing would have to be known to make a final judgment about what sorts of restitutive acts are called for, we can nevertheless formulate some middle-range principles of justice that generally apply. These principles are to be understood as specifying requirements of restitution for transgressions of *any* of the three rules. In all cases the restitutive measures will take the form of promoting or protecting in one way or another the good of living things in natural ecosystems.

In working out these middle-range principles it will be convenient to distinguish cases according to what type of moral subject has been wronged. We have three possibilities. An action that broke the Rule of Nonmaleficence, of Noninterference, or of Fidelity might have wronged an individual organism, a species-population as a whole, or an entire community. Violations of the Rules in all cases are ultimately wrongs done to individuals, since we can do harm to a population or community only by harming the individual organisms in it (thereby lowering the median level of well-being for the population or community as a whole). The first possibility, however, focuses on the harmed individuals taken separately.

If the organisms have been harmed but have not been killed, then the principle of restitutive justice requires that the agent make reparation by returning those organisms to a condition in which they can pursue their good as well as they did before the injustice was done to them. If this cannot wholly be accomplished, then the agent must further the good of the organisms in some other way, perhaps by making their physical environment more favorable to their continued well-being. Suppose, on the other hand, that an organism has been killed. Then the principle of restitutive justice states that the agent owes some form of compensation to the species-population and/or the life community of which the organism was a member. This would be a natural extension of respect from the individual to its genetic relatives and ecological associates. The compensation would consist in promoting or protecting the good of the species-population or life community in question.

Consider as a second possibility that a whole species-population has been wrongly treated by a violation of either nonmaleficence or noninterference. A typical situation would be one where most of the animals of a "target" species have been killed by excessive hunting, fishing, or trapping in a limited area. As a way of making some effort to right the wrongs that have been committed, it would seem appropriate that the agents at fault be required to ensure that permanent protection be given to all the remaining numbers of the population. Perhaps the agents could contribute to a special fund for the acquisition of land and themselves take on the responsibility of patrolling the area to prevent further human intrusion.

Finally, let us consider those circumstances where an entire biotic community has been destroyed by humans. We have two sorts of cases here, both requiring some form of restitution. The first sort of case occurs when the destructive actions are not only wrong in themselves because they violate duties of nonmaleficence and noninterference but are wrong, all things considered. They are not justified by a rule of *either* environmental ethics *or* of human ethics. The second sort of case is one in which the actions are required by a valid rule of human ethics though they are contrary to valid rules of environmental ethics. Even when greater moral weight is given to the rule of human ethics, so that the actions are justified, all things considered, they still call for some form of restitution on grounds of justice to all beings having inherent worth. This idea holds also within the domain of human ethics.

A duty of restitutive justice (as a corollary of the Rule of Reciprocity) arises whenever one of the other valid rules of human ethics is broken. Even if the action was required by a more stringent duty, a human person has been unjustly treated and therefore some compensation is due her or him. That the action was morally justified, all things consid-

ered, does not license our overlooking the fact that someone has been wronged. Hence the propriety of demanding restitution. So in our present concerns, even if the destruction of a biotic community is entailed by a duty of human ethics that overrides the rules of environmental ethics, an act of restitutive justice is called for in recognition of the inherent worth of what has been destroyed.

There are many instances in which human practices bring about the total obliteration of biotic communities in natural ecosystems. Whether or not these practices are justified by valid rules of human ethics, they all come under the Rule of Restitutive Justice. A northern conifer woodland is cut down to build a vacation resort on the shore of a lake. A housing development is constructed in what had been a pristine wilderness area of cactus desert. A marina and yacht club replace a tidal wetland which had served as a feeding and breeding ground for multitudes of mollusks, crustacea, insects, birds, fish, reptiles, and mammals. A meadow full of wildflowers, both common and rare, is bull-dozed over for a shopping mall. Strip mining takes away one side of a mountain. A prairie is replaced by a wheat farm. In every one of these situations and in countless others of the same kind, wholesale destruction of entire natural ecosystems takes place. Unrestrained violence is done to whole communities of plants and animals. Communities that may have been in existence for tens of thousands of years are completely wiped out in a few weeks or a few days, in some cases in a few hours. What form of restitution can then be made that will restore the balance of justice between humanity and nature? No reparation for damages can possibly be given to the community itself, which exists no more. As is true of a single organism that has been killed, the impossibility of repairing the damage does not get rid of the requirement to make some kind of compensation for having destroyed something of inherent worth.

If restitutive justice is to be done in instances of the foregoing kind, what actions are called for and to whom are they due? Two possibilities suggest

themselves here. One is that compensation should be made to another biotic community which occupies *an ecosystem of the same type* as the one destroyed. If it is a northern conifer woodland, then the organizations or individuals who were responsible for its destruction owe it to the life community of another conifer woodland to help it in some way to further or maintain its well-being. Perhaps a partially damaged area of woodland could be restored to ecological health (removing trash that had been put there, cleaning up a polluted stream flowing through the area, stopping any further contamination by acid rain or other atmospheric pollution, and so on).

The other possible recipient of compensation would be any wild region of nature that is being threatened by human exploitation or consumption. Compensatory action would be taken in behalf of a biotic community somewhere on Earth that might be damaged or destroyed unless special efforts are made to protect it. Acquiring the land and giving it legal status as a nature preserve would be suitable measures.

These suggested middle-range principles are all derived from the one broad Rule of Restitutive Justice: that any agent which has caused an evil to some natural entity that is a proper moral subject owes a duty to bring about a countervailing good, either to the moral subject in question or to some other moral subject. The perpetrating of a harm calls for the producing of a benefit. The greater the harm, the larger the benefit needed to fulfill the moral obligation.

It is worth adding here that all of us who live in modern industrialized societies owe a duty of restitutive justice to the natural world and its wild inhabitants. We have all benefited in countless ways from large-scale technology and advanced modes of economic production. As consumers we not only accept the benefits of industrialization willingly, but spend much of our lives trying to increase those benefits for ourselves and those we love. We are part of a civilization that can only exist by controlling nature and using its resources. Even those who go out to a natural area to enjoy "the wilderness experience" are recipients of the benefits of advanced technology. (What marvels of modern chemistry went into the creation of plastics and synthetic fabrics in their backpacks, tents, sleeping bags, and food containers!) None of us can evade the responsibility that comes with our high standard of living; we all take advantage of the amenities of civilized life in pursuing our individual values and interests. Since it is modern commerce, industry, and technology that make these amenities possible, each of us is a consumer and user of what the natural world can yield for us. Our well-being is constantly being furthered at the expense of the good of the Earth's nonhuman inhabitants. Thus we all should share in the cost of preserving and restoring some areas of wild nature for the sake of the plant and animal communities that live there. Only then can we claim to have genuine respect for nature.

J. BAIRD CALLICOTT

[From] *Beyond the Land Ethic*

THE DARWINIAN ROOTS OF THE LAND ETHIC

Of all the environmental ethics so far devised, the land ethic, first sketched by Aldo Leopold, is most popular among professional conservationists and least popular among professional philosophers. Conservationists are preoccupied with such things as the anthropogenic pollution of air and water by industrial and municipal wastes, the anthropogenic reduction in numbers of species populations, the outright anthropogenic extinction of species, and the invasive anthropogenic introduction of other species into places not their places of evolutionary origin. Conservationists as such are not concerned about the injury, pain, or death of nonhuman specimens—that is, of individual animals and plants—except in those rare cases in which a species' populations are so reduced in number that the conservation of every specimen is vital to the conservation of the species. On the other hand, professional philosophers, most of them schooled in and intellectually committed to the Modern classical theories of ethics, are ill-prepared to comprehend morally such "holistic" concerns. Professional philosophers are inclined to dismiss holistic concerns as nonmoral or to reduce them to concerns about either human welfare or the welfare of nonhuman organisms severally. And they are mystified by the land ethic, unable to grasp its philosophical foundations and pedigree.

Without a grasp of its philosophical foundations and pedigree, however, it is difficult to know how the land ethic might be related to the more familiar moral concerns that loom large in the Modern era (roughly the seventeenth through the twentieth centuries)—such as human happiness, human dignity, and human rights—and how it might be applied to and illuminate cases other than those Leopold himself considers in his brief sketch of it in *A Sand County Almanac*. In this essay, I outline the philosophical foundations and pedigree of the land ethic and indicate how it might be related to more familiar Modern moral concerns and how it might be applied to those contemporary environmental concerns that Leopold himself could not have considered. In particular, I address the most serious and disturbing theoretical and practical challenge to the land ethic raised by professional philosophers—the problem of ecofascism.

To discover its philosophical foundations and pedigree, we may begin by looking for clues in the text of "The Land Ethic." Leopold provides the most important clue in the second section of the essay, entitled The Ethical Sequence. Having observed that ethics have grown considerably in scope and complexity during the three thousand years of recorded history in Western civilization, Leopold (1949, 202) writes,

> This extension of ethics, so far studied only by philosophers [and, Leopold's insinuation is clear, therefore not very revealingly studied] is actually a process in ecological evolution. An ethic, ecologically, is a limitation on freedom of action in the struggle for existence. An ethic, philosophically, is a differentiation of social from anti-social conduct. These are two definitions of one thing. The thing has its origin in the tendency of interdependent individuals or groups to evolve modes of cooperation.

Leopold, I should hasten to point out, was no better a student of philosophy, than most professional philosophers are of conservation and its concerns. Hence his characterization of an ethic, "philosophically," is, put most charitably, incomplete. In any case, what he hints at, rather insistently and

unmistakably, is some sort of evolutionary interpretation of ethics. Leopold's use here of such words and phrases as "evolution," "struggle for existence," "origin," "evolve," "social and anti-social conduct" evokes not only a general evolutionary context in which to locate an understanding ethics, it alludes, more particularly, to the classical evolutionary account of ethics in Charles Darwin's *The Descent of Man*, the third chapter of which is devoted to "the moral sense." Doubtless, therefore, Darwin's account of the origin and development of "the thing" is what mainly informed Leopold's thinking about ethics....

THE HOLISM OF THE LAND ETHIC AND ITS ANTECEDENTS

According to Leopold (1949, 204, emphasis added), "a land ethic implies respect for... fellow-members *and also for the community as such*." The land ethic, in other words, has a holistic dimension to it that is completely foreign to the mainstream Modern moral theories going back to Hobbes. The holistic dimension of the land ethic—respect for the community as such, in addition to respect for its members severally—is, however, not in the least foreign to the Darwinian and Humean theories of ethics upon which it is built. Darwin (1871, 96–97) could hardly be more specific or emphatic on this point: "Actions are regarded by savages and were probably so regarded by primeval man, as good or bad, solely as they obviously affect the welfare of the tribe,—not that of the species, nor that of an individual member of the tribe. This conclusion agrees well with the belief that the so-called moral sense is aboriginally derived from the social instincts, for both relate at first exclusively to the community." Gary Varner (1991, 179) states flatly that "concern for communities as such has no historical antecedent in David Hume." But it does. Demonstrably. Hume ([1751] 1957, 47) insists, evidently against Hobbes and other social contract theorists, that "we must renounce the theory which

accounts for every moral sentiment by the principle of self-love. We must adopt a more publick affection, and allow that the interests of society are not, even on their own account, entirely indifferent to us." Nor is this an isolated remark. Over and over we read in Hume's ethical works such statements as this: "It appears that a tendency to publick good, and to the promoting of peace, harmony, and order in society, does always by affecting the benevolent principles of our frame engage us on the side of the social virtues" (Hume [1751] 1957, 56). And this: "Everything that promotes the interests of society must communicate pleasure, and what is pernicious, give uneasiness" (Hume [1751] 1957, 58).

That is not to say that in Hume, certainly, and even in Darwin there is no theoretical provision for a lively concern for the individual members of society, as well as for society per se. The sentiment of sympathy being so central to it, I should expressly acknowledge that in the moral philosophy of Adam Smith, one finds little ethical holism. *Sympathy* means "with-feeling." And that "all-important emotion of sympathy," as Darwin (1871, 81) styles it, can hardly extend to a transorganismic entity, such as society per se, which has no feelings per se. Hume and Darwin, however, recognized other moral sentiments than sympathy, some of which—patriotism, for example—relate as exclusively and specifically to society as sympathy does to sentient individuals.

In the Leopold land ethic, at any rate, the holistic aspect eventually eclipses the individualistic aspect. Toward the beginning of "The Land Ethic," Leopold, as noted, declares that a land ethic "implies respect for fellow-members" of the biotic community, as well as "for the community as such." Toward the middle of "The Land Ethic," Leopold (1949, 210) speaks of a "biotic right" to "continue" but such a right accrues, as the context indicates, to species, not to specimens. Toward the end of the essay, Leopold (1949, 224–25) writes a summary moral maxim, a golden rule, for the land ethic: "A thing is right when it tends to preserve the integrity, stability, and

beauty of the biotic community. It is wrong when it tends otherwise." In it there is no reference at all to "fellow members." They have gradually dropped out of account as the "The Land Ethic" proceeds to its climax.

Why? One reason has already been noted. Conservationists, among whom Leopold counted himself, are professionally concerned about biological and ecological wholes—populations, species, communities, ecosystems—not their individual constituents. And the land ethic is tailored to suit conservation concerns, which are often confounded by concerns for individual specimens. For example, the conservation of endangered plant species is often most directly and efficiently effected by the deliberate eradication of the feral animals that threaten them. Preserving the integrity of a biotic community often requires reducing the populations of some component species, be they native or nonnative, wild or feral. Certainly animal liberation and animal rights—advocated by Peter Singer and Tom Regan, respectively—would prohibit such convenient but draconian solutions to conservation problems. So would a more inclusive individualistic environmental ethic, such as that proffered by Paul Taylor (1986). Another reason is that ecology is about metaorganismic entities—biotic communities and ecosystems—not individuals, and the land ethic is expressly informed by ecology and reflects an ecological worldview. Its holism is precisely what makes the land ethic the environmental ethic of choice among conservationists and ecologists. In short, its holism is the land ethic's principal asset.

Whether by the end of the essay he forgets it or not, Leopold does say in "The Land Ethic" that "fellow-members" of the "land community" deserve "respect." How can we pretend to respect them if, in the interest of the integrity, stability, and beauty of the biotic community, we chop some down, gun others down, set fire to still others, and so on. Such brutalities are often involved in what conservationists call "wildlife management." Here

again, to resolve this conundrum, we may consult Darwin, who indicates that ethics originated among Homo sapiens in the first place to serve the welfare of the community. Certainly, among the things that threaten to dissolve a human community are "murder, robbery, treachery, &c." However, as ethics evolve correlatively to social evolution, not only do they widen their scope, they change in content, such that what is wrong correlative to one stage of social development, may not be wrong correlative to the next. In a tribal society, as Darwin observes, exogamy is a cardinal precept. It is not in a republic. Nevertheless, in all human communities—from the savage clan to the family of man—the "infamy" of murder, robbery, treachery, etc., remains "everlasting." But the multispecies *biotic* community is so different from all our human communities that we cannot assume that what is wrong for one human being to do to another, even at every level of *social* organization, is wrong for one fellow member of the *biotic* community to do to another.

The currency of the economy of nature, we must remember, is energy. And it passes from one member to another, not from hand to hand like money in the human economy, but from stomach to stomach. As Leopold (1949, 107) observes of the biotic community, "The only truth is that its members must suck hard, live fast, and die often." In the biotic community there are producers and consumers; predators and prey. One might say that the integrity and stability of the biotic community depends upon death as well as life; indeed, one might say further, that the life of one member is premised squarely on the death of another. So one could hardly argue that our killing of fellow members of the biotic community is, prima facie, land ethically wrong. It depends on who is killed, for what reasons, under what circumstances, and how. The filling in of these blanks would provide, in each case, an answer to the question about respect. Models of respectful, but often violent and lethal, use of fellow members of the biotic community are provided by traditional

American Indian peoples (Callicott and Overholt 1993).

THE PROBLEM OF ECOFASCISM

Its holism is the land ethic's principal strength, but also its principal liability. Remember that according to Leopold, evolutionary and ecological biology reveal that "land [is] a community to which we belong" not "a commodity belonging to us" and that from the point of view of a land ethic, we are but "plain members and citizens of the biotic community." Then it would seem that the summary moral maxim of the land ethic applies to Homo sapiens no less than to the other members and citizens of the biotic community, plain or otherwise. A human population of more than six billion individuals is a dire threat to the integrity, stability, and beauty of the biotic community. Thus the existence of such a large human population is land ethically wrong. To right that wrong should we not do what we do when a population of white-tailed deer or some other species irrupts and threatens the integrity, stability, and beauty of the biotic community? We immediately and summarily reduce it, by whatever means necessary, usually by randomly and indiscriminately shooting the members of such a population to death—respectfully, of course—until its numbers are optimized. It did not take the land ethic's critics long to draw out the vitiating—but, as I shall go on to argue directly, only apparent—implication of the land ethic. According to William Aiken (1984, 269), from the point of view of the land ethic, "massive human die-backs would be good. It is our duty to cause them. It is our species' duty, relative to the whole, to eliminate 90 per cent of our numbers." Its requirement that individual organisms, apparently also including individual *human* organisms, be sacrificed for the good of the whole, makes the land ethic, according to Tom Regan (1983, 262), a kind of "environmental fascism." Frederick Ferré (1996a, 18) echoes and amplifies Aiken's and Regan's indictment of the land ethic: "Anything we could do to exterminate excess people…would

be morally 'right'! To refrain from such extermination would be 'wrong'!…Taken as a guide for human culture, the land ethic—despite the best intentions of its supporters—would lead toward classical fascism, the submergence of the individual person in the glorification of the collectivity, race, tribe, or nation." Finally, Kristin Shrader-Frechette adds her voice to those expressing moral outrage at the land "ethic": "In subordinating the welfare of all creatures to the integrity, stability, and beauty of the biotic community, then one subordinates individual human welfare, in all cases, to the welfare of the biotic community" (Shrader-Frechette 1996, 63).

Michael Zimmerman (1995) has defended the land ethic against the charge of ecofascism, pointing out that in addition to subordinating the welfare of the individual to that of the community, fascism involves other characterizing features, salient among them nationalism and militarism. And there is no hint of nationalism and militarism in the land ethic. But however one labels it, if the land ethic implies what Aiken, Regan, Ferré, and Shrader-Frechette allege that it does, it must be rejected as monstrous. Happily, it does not. To think that it does, one must assume that Leopold proffered the land ethic as a substitute for, not an addition to, our venerable and familiar human ethics. But he did not. Leopold refers to the various stages of ethical development—from tribal mores to universal human rights and, finally, to the land ethic—as "accretions." Accretion means an "increase by external addition or accumulation." The land ethic is an accretion—that is, an addition—to our several accumulated social ethics, not something that is supposed to replace them. If, as I here explain, Leopold is building the land ethic on theoretical foundations that he finds in Darwin, then it is obvious that with the advent of each new stage in the accreting development of ethics, the old stages are not erased or replaced, but added to. I, for example, am a citizen of a republic, but I also remain a member of an extended family, and a resident of a municipality. And it is quite evident to us all, from our own moral experience, that the duties attendant on citizenship in a republic (to pay taxes, to

serve in the armed forces or in the Peace Corps, for example) do not cancel or replace the duties attendant on membership in a family (to honor parents, to love and educate children, for example) or residence in a municipality (to support public schools, to attend town meetings). Similarly, it is equally evident—at least to Leopold and his exponents, if not to his critics—that the duties attendant upon citizenship in the biotic community (to preserve its integrity, stability, and beauty) do not cancel or replace the duties attendant on membership in the human global village (to respect human rights).

PRIORITIZING THE DUTIES GENERATED BY MEMBERSHIP IN MULTIPLE COMMUNITIES

This consideration has led Varner (1991) to argue that any proponent of the land ethic, Leopold presumably included, must be a moral pluralist. True enough, if by moral pluralist one means only that one tries simultaneously to adhere to multiple moral maxims (Honor thy Father and thy Mother; Love thy Country; Respect the Rights of All Human Beings Irrespective of Race, Creed, Color, or National Origin; Preserve the Integrity, Stability, and Beauty of the Biotic Community, for example). But if being a moral pluralist means espousing multiple moral philosophies and associated ethical theories, as it does in Christopher Stone's celebrated and influential *The Case for Moral Pluralism* (1987), then proponents of the land ethic are not necessarily committed to pluralism. On the contrary, the univocal theoretical foundations of the land ethic naturally generate multiple sets of moral duties—and correlative maxims, principles, and precepts—each related to a particular social scale (family, republic, global village, biotic community, for parallel example) all within a single moral philosophy. That moral philosophy is the one sketched here, beginning with the Humean social instincts and affections that evolve into ethics proper and grow more expansive and

complicated apace with the Darwinian scenario of social evolution.

The land ethic involves a limited pluralism (multiple moral maxims, multiple sets of duties, or multiple principles and precepts) not a thoroughgoing pluralism of moral philosophies *sensu* Stone (1987)—Aristotelian ethics for this quandary, Kantian ethics for that, utilitarianism here, social-contract theory there. Thus, as Shrader-Frechette (1996, 63) points out, the land ethic must provide "second-order ethical principles and a priority ranking system that specifies the respective conditions under which [first-order] holistic and individualistic ethical principles ought to be recognized." Leopold provides no such second-order principles for prioritizing among first-order principles, but they can be easily derived from the communitarian foundations of the land ethic. By combining two second-order principles we can achieve a priority ranking among first-order principles, when, in a given quandary, they conflict. The first second-order principle (SOP-1) is that obligations generated by membership in more venerable and intimate communities take precedence over those generated in more recently emerged and impersonal communities. I think that most of us, for example, feel that our family duties (to care for aged parents, say, to educate minor children) take precedence over our civic duties (to contribute to United Way charities, say, to vote for higher municipal taxes to better support more indigent persons on the dole), when, because of limited means, we are unable to perform both family and civic duties. The second second-order principle (SOP-2) is that stronger interests (for lack of a better word) generate duties that take precedence over duties generated by weaker interests. For example, while duties to one's own children, all things being equal, properly take precedence over duties toward unrelated children in one's municipality, one would be ethically remiss to shower one's own children with luxuries while unrelated children in one's municipality lacked the bare necessities (food, shelter, clothing, education) for a decent life. Having the bare necessities for a decent

life is a stronger interest than is the enjoyment of luxuries, and our duties to help supply proximate unrelated children with the former take precedence over our duties to supply our own children with the latter.

These second-order principles apply as well in quandaries in which duties to individuals conflict with duties to communities per se. In a case made famous by Jean-Paul Sartre in *L'existentialisme est un Humanisme*, a young man is caught in the dilemma of going off to join the French Free Forces in England during the Nazi occupation of France in World War II or staying home with his mother. Sartre, of course, is interested in the existential choice that this forces on the young man and in pursuing the thesis that his decision in some way makes a moral principle, not that it should be algorithmically determined by the application of various moral principles. But the second-order principles here set out apply to the young man's dilemma quite directly and, one might argue, decisively—existential freedom notwithstanding. SOP-1 requires the young man to give priority to the first-order principle, Honor Thy Father and Thy Mother, over the other first-order principle at play, Serve Thy Country. But SOP-2 reverses the priority dictated by SOP-1. The very existence of France as a transorganismic entity is threatened. The young man's mother has a weaker interest at stake, for, as Sartre reports, his going off—and maybe getting killed—would plunge her into "despair." His mother being plunged into despair would be terrible, but not nearly as terrible as the destruction of France would be if not enough young men fought on her behalf. So the resolution of this young man's dilemma is clear; he should give priority to the first-order principle, Serve Thy Country. Had the young man been an American and had the time been the early 1970s and had the dilemma been stay home with his mother or join the Peace Corps and go to Africa, then he should give priority to the first-order principle Honor Thy Father and Thy Mother and stay home. Had the young man been the same

person as Sartre constructs, but had his mother been a Jew whom the Nazis would have sent to a horrible death in a concentration camp if her son did not stay home and help her hide, then again, he should give priority to the first-order principle, Honor Thy Father and Thy Mother, and stay home.

THE PRIORITY PRINCIPLES APPLIED TO THE OLD-GROWTH FOREST QUANDARY

Let me consider now those kinds of quandaries in which our duties to human beings conflict with our duties to *biotic* communities as such. Varner (1996, 176) supplies a case in point:

> Suppose that an environmentalist enamored with the Leopold land ethic is considering how to vote on a national referendum to preserve the spotted owl by restricting logging in Northwest forests.... He or she would be required to vote, not according to the land ethic, but according to whatever ethic governs closer ties to a human family and/or larger human community. Therefore, if a relative is one of 10,000 loggers who will lose jobs if the referendum passes, the environmentalist is obligated to vote against it. Even if none of the loggers is a family member, the voter is still obligated to vote against the referendum.

The flaw in Varner's reasoning is that he applies only SOP-1—that obligations generated by membership in more venerable and intimate communities take precedence over those generated in more recently emerged and impersonal communities. If that were the only second-order communitarian principle then he would be right. But SOP-2—that stronger interests generate duties that take precedence over duties generated by weaker interests—reverses the priority determined by applying SOP-1 in this case. The spotted owl is threatened with preventable anthropogenic extinction—threatened with biocide, in a word—and the old-growth forest biotic communities of the Pacific Northwest

are threatened with destruction. These threats are the environmental-ethical equivalent of genocide and holocaust. The loggers, on the other hand, are threatened with economic losses, for which they can be compensated dollar for dollar. More important to the loggers, I am told, their lifestyle is threatened. But livelihood and lifestyle, for both of which adequate substitutes can be found, is a lesser interest than life itself. If we faced the choice of cutting down millions of four-hundred-year-old trees or cutting down thousands of forty-year-old loggers, our duties to the loggers would take precedence by SOP-1, nor would SOP-1 be countermanded by SOP-2. But that is not the choice we face. The choice is between cutting down four-hundred-year-old trees, rendering the spotted owl extinct, and destroying the old-growth forest biotic community, on the one hand, and displacing forest workers in an economy that is already displacing them through automation and raw-log exports to Japan and other foreign markets. And the old-growth logging lifestyle is doomed, in any case, to self-destruct, for it will come to an end with the "final solution" to the old-growth forest question, if the jack-booted timber barons (who disingenuously blame the spotted owl for the economic insecurity of loggers and other workers in the timber industry) continue to have their way. With SOP-2 supplementing SOP-1, the indication of the land ethic is crystal clear in the exemplary quandary posed by Varner, and it is opposite to the one Varner, applying only SOP-1, claims it indicates.

CONCLUSION

The holistic Leopold land ethic is not a case of ecofascism. The land ethic is intended to supplement, not replace, the more venerable community-based social ethics, in relation to which it is an accretion or addition. Neither is the land ethic a "paper tiger," an environmental ethic with no teeth (Nelson 1996). Choice among which community-related principle should govern a moral agent's conduct in a given

moral quandary may be determined by the application of two second-order principles. The first, SOP-1, requires an agent to give priority to the first-order principles generated by the more venerable and more intimate community memberships. Thus, when holistic environment-oriented duties are in direct conflict with individualistic human-oriented duties, the human-oriented duties take priority. The land ethic is, therefore, not a case of ecofascism. However, the second second-order principle, SOP-2, requires an agent to give priority to the stronger interests at issue. When the indication determined by the application of SOP-1 is reinforced by the application of SOP-2, an agent's choice is clear. When the indication determined by the application of SOP-1 is contradicted by the application of SOP-2, an agent's choice is equally clear: SOP-2 countermands SOP-1. Thus, when holistic environment-oriented duties are in conflict with individualistic human-oriented duties, and the holistic environmental interests at issue are significantly stronger than the individualistic human interests at issue, the former take priority.

REFERENCES

Aiken, W. 1984. "Ethical Issues in Agriculture." In *Earthbound: New Introductory Essays in Environmental Ethics*, edited by T. Regan, 74–288. New York: Random House.

Callicott, J. B., and T. W. Overholt. 1993. "American Indian Attitudes toward Nature." In *Philosophy from Africa to Zen: An Invitation to World Philosophy*, edited by R. C. Solomon and K. M. Higgins, 55–80. Lanham, Md.: Rowman and Littlefield.

Darwin, C. R. 1871. *The Descent of Man and Selection in Relation to Sex*. London: J. Murray.

Ferré, F. 1996a. "Persons in Nature: Toward an Applicable and Unified Environmental Ethics." *Ethics and the Environment* 1:15–25.

Hume, D. [1751] 1957. *An Enquiry Concerning the Principles of Morals*. Reprint, New York: Library of Liberal Arts.

Leopold, A. 1949. *"A Sand County Almanac" and "Sketches Here and There."* New York: Oxford University Press.

Nelson, M. 1996. "Holists and Fascists and Paper Tigers...Oh My!" *Ethics and the Environment* 2:103–17.

Regan, T. 1983. *The Case for Animal Rights*. Berkeley: University of California Press.

Shrader-Frechette, K. 1996. "Individualism, Holism, and Environmental Ethics." *Ethics and the Environment* 1:55–69.

Stone, C. P. 1987. *Earth and Other Ethics: The Case for Moral Pluralism.* New York: Harper and Row.

Taylor, P. W. 1986. *Respect for Nature: A Theory of Environmental Ethics*. Princeton: Princeton University Press.

Varner, G. E. 1991. "No Holism without Pluralism." *Environmental Ethics* 19:175–79.

Zimmerman, M. E. 1995. "The Threat of Ecofascism." *Social Theory and Practice* 21:207–38.

SECTION III

Justice and the Environment

INTRODUCTION

While many people who are drawn to environmental ethics are interested in articulating and promoting the value of the natural world and its nonhuman inhabitants, there are pressing ethical issues that environmental problems raise about what humans owe to each other. In this section we present readings that focus on issues of justice that help us to understand what obligations we have to humans near and far in space and time.

The idea of environmental justice entered public consciousness a generation ago with some startling events. In 1980, white working-class homeowners in Love Canal, New York, detained officials from the United States Environmental Protection Agency who had come to allay their fears about the fact that their community was built on top of a toxic waste dump. Two years later more than 500 people were arrested in the largely African-American community of Afton, North Carolina, during a campaign of nonviolent civil disobedience directed toward preventing the disposal of PCB-laced soil in the Warren County landfill. In 1984 thousands of people were killed when poisonous gas leaked from a carelessly managed Union Carbide plant in Bhopal, India. The World Commission on Environment and Development, popularly known as the "Brundtland Commission," brought the relationship between justice and the environment to global attention in their 1987 report, *Our Common Future*, which popularized the concept of sustainable development. By the end of the 1980s, the idea that we owe duties of environmental justice both to our contemporaries and to those who will come after us was firmly planted.

Some philosophers, such as Peter Singer, understand justice as a part of our broader impartial ethical obligations. In "One Community," he develops the view that these obligations are reserved not only for those who we know and love, but must extend to strangers and those far away as well. His argument builds on a famous example first presented in the 1970s. He asks us to imagine walking past a shallow pond in which a child is drowning. He tells us that to wade in and save the child will pose no risk to us; we will simply be inconvenienced. When we consider whether we have an obligation to save that drowning child, he believes

the answer is obvious: of course we do! To do nothing and simply walk past a dying child who could easily be saved would be monstrous. But why is it less monstrous to allow those children we happen not to walk past to suffer and die, when it would only involve a small inconvenience to save their lives? Singer argues that distance and nationality are morally irrelevant and that justice demands impartial consideration of the claims of others. Singer's primary focus is on global poverty, but it is not difficult to see how his impartial framework applies to problems of environmental justice as well.

When we think about environmental problems, many of us think about the world that we bequeath to future generations. We live in a world given to us by our predecessors, and our actions impact the world that our successors inherit. We are drawn to protect nature because we believe that we owe it to our children's children to leave them a world at least as livable as the one that we have been given. In other words, we believe that we have obligations to future generations. Brian Barry argues that the considerations of justice that guide our relations with our contemporaries should also apply to our thinking about intergenerational justice. Just as distance should not affect our thinking about what we owe to each other, neither should time. Barry thinks that our duties even go beyond justice, and that to treat the natural world as something that can be exploited simply for the benefit of humanity is wrong. He emphasizes the importance of controlling human population in order to protect the interests of wild, nonhuman animals.

This section ends with a discussion of environmental racism. Both Singer and Barry, indeed virtually all ethical theorists who write about justice, use discrimination based on race and gender as paradigm instances of injustice. Discounting the concerns of someone who is of a different race is at least as suspect as discounting the concerns of those who are remote in space or time. Yet evidence suggests that such discounting may occur in decisions to site toxic waste facilities and other environmentally hazardous industries. A disproportionate number of such facilities are located in communities of color that already suffer the consequences of racial discrimination and are, generally, the least prepared to address these additional environmental burdens. Sheila Foster and Luke Cole present evidence of racial disparities in the locations of environmentally destructive industries, differential exposure to environmental hazards, and unequal enforcement of environmental laws. They also show how these disparities are bound up with deeply entrenched social and institutional structures.

FURTHER READING

Bullard, Robert, ed. *Unequal Protection: Environmental Justice and Communities of Color*. San Francisco, CA: Sierra Club, 1994. This anthology by a sociologist active in developing the field of environmental justice examines the history of environmental racism in the United States.

Dobson, Andrew. *Justice and the Environment: Conceptions of Environmental Sustainability and Theories of Distributive Justice*. New York, NY: Oxford University Press, 1998. An analysis of conceptual issues in environmental justice, including natural value, irreversibility, and distributive justice.

Dobson, Andrew, ed. *Fairness and Futurity: Essays on Environmental Sustainability and Social Justice*. New York, NY: Oxford University Press, 1999. This volume analyzes

contested concepts, including sustainable development, sustainability, and intergenerational justice.

Sandler, Ronald, and Phaedra C. Pezzullo, eds. *Environmental Justice and Environmentalism: The Social Justice Challenge to the Environmental Movement*. Cambridge, MA: MIT Press, 2007. A review and analysis of the tensions between environmentalists.

Schlosberg, David. *Defining Environmental Justice: Theories, Movements, and Nature*. New York, NY: Oxford University Press, 2007. An overview of theories of environmental justice from the perspective of a political theorist.

Shrader-Frachette, Kristin. *Environmental Justice: Creating Equality, Reclaiming Democracy*. New York, NY: Oxford University Press, 2002. A discussion of philosophical questions like distributive, procedural and participatory justice, equality, and duties to future generations, with case studies on nuclear waste, native land rights, and developing nations.

Sikora, R. I., and Brian Barry, eds. *Obligations to Future Generations*. Philadelphia, PA: Temple University Press, 1978. An early collection of essays that includes some of the most influential papers on obligations to future generations.

Taylor, Dorcetta, ed. *Environment and Social Justice: An International Perspective*. Cambridge, MA: Emerald Publishing, 2010. A discussion of environmental justice from an international perspective, focusing on urban environmental issues, water resources, food security, energy, and diversity.

DISCUSSION QUESTIONS

1. How might we extend impartial considerations of justice to poorer countries and their people? Consider some of the economic and environmental implications.

2. What should we pay attention to in order to achieve justice? Want-satisfaction? Equal opportunity? Equal access to clean environments? Equal participation?

3. Is there a just decision-making process for disposing of toxic wastes? What would its most important elements be?

4. If we aim to value future generations, how might this impact our current use of nonrenewable resources or investments?

5. Is it permissible to discount the interests of people who are remote in space or time? Why or why not?

6. What does sustainability consist in? What would it mean for us to live sustainable lives?

PETER SINGER

One Community

...There are more than a billion people in the world living in dire poverty. In the year 2000, Americans made private donations for foreign aid of all kinds totaling about $4 per person in need, or roughly $20 per family. New Yorkers, wealthy or not, living in lower Manhattan on September 11, 2001, were able to receive an average of $5,300 a family.[1] The distance between these amounts symbolizes the way in which, for many people, the circle of concern for others stops at the boundaries of their own nation—if it even extends that far. "Charity begins at home," people say, and more explicitly, "we should take care of poverty in our own country before we tackle poverty abroad." They take it for granted that national boundaries carry moral weight, and that it is worse to leave one of our fellow citizens in need than to leave someone from another country in that state. We put the interests of our fellow citizens far above those of citizens of other nations, whether the reason for doing so is to avoid damaging the economic interests of Americans at the cost of bringing floods to the people of Bangladesh, to avoid risking the lives of NATO troops at the cost of more innocent lives in Kosovo, or to help those in need at home rather than those in need abroad. While we do all these things, most of us unquestioningly support declarations proclaiming that all humans have certain rights, and that all human life is of equal worth. We condemn those who say the life of a person of a different race or nationality is of less account than the life of a person of our own race or nation. Can we reconcile these attitudes? If those "at home" to whom we might give charity are already able to provide for their basic needs, and seem poor only relative to our own high standard of living, is the fact that they

are our compatriots sufficient to give them priority over others with greater needs?...

A PREFERENCE FOR OUR OWN

The popular view that we may, or even should, favor those "of our own kind" conceals a deep disagreement about who "our own kind" are. A century ago Henry Sidgwick, professor of moral philosophy at Cambridge University, described the moral outlook of his Victorian England as follows:

> We should all agree that each of us is bound to show kindness to his parents and spouse and children, and to other kinsmen in a less degree: and to those who have rendered services to him, and any others whom he may have admitted to his intimacy and called friends: and to neighbors and to fellow-countrymen more than others: and perhaps we may say to those of our own race more than to black or yellow men, and generally to human beings in proportion to their affinity to ourselves.[2]

When I read this list to students, they nod their heads in agreement at the various circles of moral concern Sidgwick mentions, until I get to the suggestion that we should give preference to our own race more than to "black or yellow men." At that point they sit up in shock.

Coming a little closer to our own time, we can find defenders of a much more extreme form of partiality:

> we must be honest, decent, loyal and friendly to members of our blood and to no one else. What happens to the Russians, what happens to the Czechs, is a matter of utter indifference to me. Such good blood of our own kind as there may be among the nations we shall acquire for ourselves, if necessary by taking away the children and bringing them up among us. Whether the other races live in comfort or perish of hunger interests

me only in so far as we need them as slaves for our culture; apart from that it does not interest me. Whether or not 10,000 Russian women collapse from exhaustion while digging a tank ditch interests me only in so far as the tank ditch is completed for Germany.[3]

That quotation is from a speech by Heinrich Himmler to SS leaders in Poland in 1943. Why do I quote such dreadful sentiments? Because there are many who think it self-evident that we have special obligations to those nearer to us, including our children, our spouses, lovers and friends, and our compatriots. Reflecting on what Sidgwick and Himmler have said about preference for one's own kind should subvert the belief that this kind of "self-evidence" is a sufficient ground for accepting a view as right. What is self-evident to some is not at all self-evident to others. Instead, we need another test of whether we have special obligations to those closer to us, such as our compatriots.

ETHICS AND IMPARTIALITY

How can we decide whether we have special obligations to "our own kind," and if so, who is "our own kind" in the relevant sense? Let us return for a moment to the countervailing ideal that there is some fundamental sense in which neither race nor nation determines the value of a human being's life and experiences. I would argue that this ideal rests on the element of impartiality that underlies the nature of the moral enterprise, as its most significant thinkers have come to understand it. The twentieth-century Oxford philosopher R. M. Hare argued that for judgments to count as moral judgments they must be universalizable, that is, the speaker must be prepared to prescribe that they be carried out in all real and hypothetical situations, not only those in which she benefits from them but also those in which she is among those who lose.[4] Consistently with Hare's approach, one way of deciding whether there are special duties to "our own kind" is to ask whether accepting the idea of

having these special duties can itself be justified from an impartial perspective.

In proposing that special duties need justification from an impartial perspective, I am reviving a debate that goes back two hundred years to William Godwin, whose *Political Justice* shocked British society at the time of the French Revolution. In the book's most famous passage, Godwin imagined a situation in which a palace is on fire, and two people are trapped inside. One of them is a great benefactor of humanity—Godwin chose as his example Archbishop Fénelon, "at the moment when he was conceiving the project of his immortal *Telemachus*." The other person trapped is the Archbishop's chambermaid. The choice of Fénelon seems odd today, since his "immortal" work is now unread except by scholars, but let's suppose we share Godwin's high opinion of Fénelon. Whom should we save? Godwin answers that we should save Fénelon, because by doing so, we would be helping thousands, those who have been cured of "error, vice and consequent unhappiness" by reading *Telemachus*. Then he goes on to make his most controversial claim:

> Supposing I had been myself the chambermaid, I ought to have chosen to die rather than that Fénelon should have died. The life of Fénelon was really preferable to that of the chambermaid. But understanding is the faculty that perceives the truth of this and similar propositions; and justice is the principle that regulates my conduct accordingly. It would have been just in the chambermaid to have preferred the archbishop to herself. To have done otherwise would have been a breach of justice.
>
> Supposing the chambermaid had been my wife, my mother or my benefactor. That would not alter the truth of the proposition. The life of Fénelon would still be more valuable than that of the chambermaid; and justice—pure, unadulterated justice—would still have preferred that which was most valuable. Justice would have taught me to save the life of Fénelon at the expense of the other. What magic is there in the pronoun "my" to overturn the decisions of everlasting truth? My wife or my mother may be a fool or a prostitute, malicious, lying or dishonest. If they be, of what consequence is it that they are mine?[5]

In 1971, at a time when several million Bengalis were on the edge of starvation, living in refugee camps in India so that they could escape from the massacres that the Pakistani army was carrying out in what was then East Pakistan, I used a different example to argue that we have an obligation to help strangers in distant lands. I asked the reader to imagine that on my way to give a lecture, I pass a shallow pond. As I do so, I see a small child fall into it and realize that she is in danger of drowning. I could easily wade in and pull her out, but that would get my shoes and trousers wet and muddy. I would need to go home and change, I'd have to cancel the lecture, and my shoes might never recover. Nevertheless, it would be grotesque to allow such minor considerations to outweigh the good of saving a child's life. Saving the child is what I ought to do, and if I walk on to the lecture, then no matter how clean, dry, and punctual I may be, I have done something seriously wrong.

Generalizing from this situation, I then argued that we are all, with respect to the Bengali refugees, in the same situation as the person who, at small cost, can save a child's life. For the vast majority of us living in the developed nations of the world have disposable income that we spend on frivolities and luxuries, things of no more importance to us than avoiding getting our shoes and trousers muddy. If we do this when people are in danger of dying of starvation and when there are agencies that can, with reasonable efficiency, turn our modest donations of money into life-saving food and basic medicines, how can we consider ourselves any better than the person who sees the child fall in the pond and walks on? Yet this was the situation at the time: the amount that had been given by the rich nations was less than a sixth of what was needed to sustain the refugees. Britain had given rather more than most countries, but it had still given only one-thirtieth as much as it was prepared to spend on the non-recoverable costs of building the Concorde supersonic jetliner.

I examined various possible differences that people might find between the two situations and argued that they were not sufficiently significant, in moral terms, to deflect the judgment that in failing to give to the Bengali refugees, we were doing something that was seriously wrong. In particular, I wrote:

> it makes no moral difference whether the person I help is a neighbor's child ten yards from me or a Bengali whose name I shall never know, ten thousand miles away.[6]

As far as I am aware, no one has disputed this claim in respect of distance per se—that is, the difference between ten yards and ten thousand miles. Of course, the degree of certainty that we can have that our assistance will get to the right person, and will really help that person, may be affected by distance, and that can make a difference to what we ought to do, but that is a different matter, and it will depend on the particular circumstances in which we find ourselves. What people *have* disputed, however, is that our obligation to help a stranger in another country is as great as the obligation to help one of our own neighbors or compatriots. Surely, they say, we have special obligations to our neighbors and fellow citizens—and to our family and friends—that we do not have to strangers in another country.[7]

Godwin faced similar objections. Samuel Parr, a well-known liberal clergyman of the time, preached and subsequently published a sermon that was a sustained critique of Godwin's "universal philanthropy."[8] As the text for his sermon, Parr takes an injunction from Paul's epistle to the Galatians, in which Paul offers yet another variant on who is "of our own kind": "As we have, therefore, opportunity, let us do good unto all men, especially unto them who are of the household of faith."[9] In Paul's words, Parr finds a Christian text that rejects equal concern for all, instead urging greater concern for those to whom we have a special connection. Parr defends Paul by arguing that to urge us to show impartial concern for all is to demand something that human beings cannot, in general and most of the time, give. "The moral obligations of men," he writes, "cannot be stretched beyond their physical powers."[10] Our real desires, our lasting and strongest passions, are not for the good of our species as a whole, but, at best, for the good of those who are close to us.

Modern critics of impartialism argue that an advocate of an impartial ethic would make a poor parent, lover, spouse, or friend, because the very idea of such personal relationships involves being partial toward the other person with whom one is in the relationship. This means giving more consideration to the interests of your child, lover, spouse, or friend than you give to a stranger, and from the standpoint of an impartial ethic this seems wrong. Feminist philosophers, in particular, tend to stress the importance of personal relationships, which they accuse male moral philosophers of neglecting. Nel Noddings, author of a book called *Caring*, limits our obligation to care to those with whom we can be in some kind of relationship. Hence, she states, we are "not obliged to care for starving children in Africa."[11]

Those who favor an impartial ethic have responded to these objections by denying that they are required to hold that we should be impartial in every aspect of our lives. Godwin himself wrote (in writing a memoir of Mary Wollstonecroft after her death following the birth of their first child):

> A sound morality requires that *nothing human should be regarded by us as indifferent;* but it is impossible we should not feel the strongest interest for those persons whom we know most intimately, and whose welfare and sympathies are united to our own. True wisdom will recommend to us individual attachments; for with them our minds are more thoroughly maintained in activity and life than they can be under the privation of them, and it is better that man should be a living being, than a stock or a stone. True virtue will sanction this recommendation; since it is the object of virtue to produce happiness; and since the man who lives in the midst of domestic relations will have many opportunities of conferring pleasure, minute in the detail, yet not trivial in the amount, without interfering with the purposes of general benevolence. Nay, by kindling his sensibility, and harmonising his soul, they may be expected, if he is endowed with a liberal and manly spirit, to render him more prompt in the service of strangers and the public.[12]

In the wake of his own grieving feelings for his beloved wife from whom he had been so tragically parted, Godwin found an impartial justification for partial affections. In our own times, Hare's two-level version of utilitarianism leads to the same conclusion. Hare argues that in everyday life it will often be too difficult to work out the consequences of every decision we make, and if we were to try to do so, we would risk getting it wrong because of our personal involvement and the pressures of the situation. To guide our everyday conduct we need a set of principles of which we are aware without a lot of reflection. These principles form the intuitive, or everyday, level of morality. In a calmer or more philosophical moment, on the other hand, we can reflect on the nature of our moral intuitions, and ask whether we have developed the right ones, that is, the ones that will lead to the greatest good, impartially considered. When we engage in this reflection, we are moving to the critical level of morality, that which informs our thinking about what principles we should follow at the everyday level. Thus the critical level serves as a testing ground for moral intuitions.[13] We can use it to test the list of special obligations suggested by the common moral sense of Victorian England as described by Henry Sidgwick: to parents, spouse, children, other kin, those who have rendered services to you, friends, neighbors, fellow-countrymen, to "those of our own race . . . and generally to human beings in proportion to their affinity to ourselves." Do any of these survive the demand for impartial justification, and if so, which ones?

ASSESSING PARTIAL PREFERENCES

The first set of preferences mentioned by Sidgwick—family, friends, and those who have rendered services to us—stands up quite well. The love of parents for their children and the desire of parents to give preference to their children over the children of strangers go very deep. It may be rooted in our nature as social mammals with offspring who need our help during a long period of dependence when they are not capable of fending for themselves. We can speculate that the children of parents who did not care for them would have been less likely to survive, and thus uncaring parents did not pass their genes on to future generations as frequently as caring parents did. Bonds between parents and children (and especially between mothers and children, for in earlier periods a baby not breast-fed by its mother was very unlikely to survive) are therefore found in all human cultures.

To say that a certain kind of behavior is universal and has its roots in our evolutionary history does not necessarily mean that it cannot be changed, nor does it mean that it should not be changed. Nevertheless in this particular case the experience of utopian social experiments has shown that the desire of parents to care for their children is highly resistant to change. In the early days of the Israeli kibbutzim the more radical of these socialist agricultural collectives sought to equalize the upbringing of children by having all children born to members of the kibbutz brought up communally, in a special children's house. For parents to show particular love and affection for their own child was frowned upon. Nevertheless, mothers used to sneak into the communal nursery at night to kiss and hold their sleeping children. Presumably, if they shared the ideals of the kibbutz, they felt guilty for doing so.[14]

So even if, like the founders of these collective settlements, we were to decide that it is undesirable for parents to favor their own children, we would find such favoritism very difficult to eradicate. Any attempt to do so would have high costs and would require constant supervision or coercion. Unless we are so intent on suppressing parental bias that we are willing to engage in an all-out campaign of intense moral pressure backed up with coercive measures and draconian sanctions, we are bound to find that most parents constantly favor their children in ways that cannot be directly justified on the basis of equal consideration of interests. If we were to engage in such a campaign, we may well bring about guilt and anxiety in parents who want to do things for their children

that society now regards as wrong. Such guilt will itself be a source of much unhappiness. Will the gains arising from diminished partiality for one's own children outweigh this? That seems unlikely, because for the children themselves, the care of loving and partial parents is likely to be better than the care of impartial parents or impartial community-employed carers. There is evidence, too, that children are more likely to be abused when brought up by people who are not their biological parents.[15] Given the unavoidable constraints of human nature and the importance of bringing children up in loving homes, there is an impartial justification for approving of social practices that presuppose that parents will show some degree of partiality towards their own children.

It is even easier to find an impartial reason for accepting love and friendship. If loving relationships, and relationships of friendship, are necessarily partial, they are also, for most people, at the core of anything that can approximate to a good life. Very few human beings can live happy and fulfilled lives without being attached to particular other human beings. To suppress these partial affections would destroy something of great value, and therefore cannot be justified from an impartial perspective.

Bernard Williams has claimed that this defense of love and friendship demands "one thought too many."[16] We should, he says, visit our sick friend in hospital because he is our friend and is in hospital, not because we have calculated that visiting sick friends is a more efficient way of maximizing utility than anything else we could do with our time. This objection may have some force if pressed against those who claim that we should be thinking about the impartial justification of love or friendship at the time when we are deciding whether to visit our sick friend; but it is precisely the point of two-level utilitarianism to explain why we *should* have an extra thought when we are thinking at the critical level, but not at the level of everyday moral decision-making.

Consider the idea, supported to various degrees in the passages I have quoted from Sidgwick and Himmler, to the effect that whites should care more for, and give priority to, the interests of other whites, or that "Aryans" should give priority to the interests of others "of their blood." These ideas have had, in their time, an intuitive appeal very similar to the intuitive appeal of the idea that we have obligations to favor family and friends. But racist views have contributed to many of the worst crimes of our century, and it is not easy to see that they have done much good, certainly not good that can compensate for the misery to which they have led. Moreover, although the suppression of racism is difficult, it is not impossible, as the existence of genuinely multiracial societies, and even the history of desegregation in the American South, shows. White people in the South no longer think twice about sharing a bus seat with an African American, and even those who fought to defend segregation have, by and large, come to accept that they were wrong. Taking an impartial perspective shows that partialism along racial lines is something that we can and should oppose, because our opposition can be effective in preventing great harm to innocent people.

Thus we can turn Williams' aphorism against him: philosophers who take his view have one thought too few. To be sure, to think *always* as a philosopher would mean that, in our roles as parent, spouse, lover and friend, we would indeed have one thought too many. But if we *are* philosophers, there should be times when we reflect critically on our intuitions—indeed not only philosophers, but all thoughtful people, should do this. If we were all simply to accept our feelings without the kind of extra reflection we have just been engaged in, we would not be able to decide which of our intuitive inclinations to endorse and support and which to oppose. As the quotations from Sidgwick and Himmler indicate, the fact that intuitive responses are widely held is not evidence that they are justified. They are not rational insights into a realm of moral truth. Some of them—roughly, those that we share with others of our species, irrespective of their cultural background—are responses that, for most of our evolutionary history, have been well suited to the survival and reproduction of beings like us. Other intuitive responses—roughly, those that we do not share with humans from different cultures—we have because of our particular cultural history. Neither the biological nor the cultural basis of our intuitive responses provides us with a sound reason for taking them as the basis of morality.

Let us return to the issue of partiality for family, lovers and friends. We have seen that there are impartial reasons for accepting some degree of partiality here. But how much? In broad terms, as much as is necessary to promote the goods mentioned above, but no more. Thus the partiality of parents for their children must extend to providing them with the necessities of life, and also their more important wants, and must allow them to feel loved and protected; but there is no requirement to satisfy every desire a child expresses, and many reasons why we should not do so. In a society like America, we should bring up our children to know that others are in much greater need, and to be aware of the possibility of helping them, if unnecessary spending is reduced. Our children should also learn to think critically about the forces that lead to high levels of consumption, and to be aware of the environmental costs of this way of living. With lovers and friends, something similar applies: the relationships require partiality, but they are stronger where there are shared values, or at least respect for the values that each holds. Where the values shared include concern for the welfare of others, irrespective of whether they are friends or strangers, then the partiality demanded by friendship or love will not be so great as to interfere in a serious way with the capacity for helping those in great need....

Geographical proximity is not in itself of any moral significance, but it may give us more opportunities to enter into relationships of friendship and mutually beneficial reciprocity. Of course, increasing mobility and communication have, over the course of the past century, eroded the extent to which neighbors are important to us. When we run out of sugar, we don't go next door to borrow some, because the supermarket down the street has plenty. We walk past our neighbors, barely nodding at them, as we talk on our cell phones to friends in other cities. In these circumstances it becomes doubtful if we have special duties of kindness to our neighbors at all, apart from, perhaps, a duty to do the things that only neighbors can do, such as feeding the cat when your neighbor goes on vacation.

"Kin" is an expression that ranges from the sibling with whom you played as a child and with whom you may later share the task of caring for your parents, to the distant cousin you have not heard from for decades. The extent to which we have a special obligation to our kin should vary accordingly. Kin networks can be important sources of love, friendship, and mutual support, and then they will generate impartially justifiable reasons for promoting these goods. But if that distant cousin you have not heard from for decades suddenly asks for a loan because she wants to buy a new house, is there an impartially defensible ground for believing that you are under a greater obligation to help her than you would be to help an unrelated equally distant acquaintance? At first glance, no, but perhaps a better answer is that it depends on whether there is a recognized system of cooperation among relatives. In rural areas of India, for example, such relationships between relatives can play an important role in providing assistance when needed, and thus in reducing harm when something goes awry.[17] Under these circumstances there is an impartial reason for recognizing and supporting this practice. In the absence of any such system, there is not. (In different cultures, the more impersonal insurance policy plays the same harm-reduction role, and thus reduces the need for a system of special obligations to kin, no doubt with both good and bad effects.)

THE ETHICAL SIGNIFICANCE OF THE NATION-STATE

Compatriots as Extended Kin

Finally, then, what impartial reasons can there be for favoring one's compatriots over foreigners? On some views of nationality, to be a member of the same nation is like an extended version of being kin. Michael Walzer expresses this view when, in discussing immigration policy, he writes:

> Clearly, citizens often believe themselves morally bound to open the doors of their country—not to anyone who wants to come in, perhaps, but to a particular group of outsiders, recognized as national or ethnic "relatives." In this sense, states are like families rather than clubs, for it is a feature of families that their members are morally connected to people they have not chosen, who live outside the household.[18]

Germany's former citizenship law embodied the sense of nationality that Walzer has in mind. Descendants of German farmers and craft workers who settled in Eastern Europe in the eighteenth century are recognized in the German Constitution as having the right to "return" to Germany and become citizens, although most of them do not speak German and come from families none of whom have set foot in the country for generations. On the other hand, before new citizenship laws came into effect in 2000, foreign guest workers could live in Germany for decades without becoming eligible for citizenship, and the same was true of their children, even though they were born in Germany, educated in German schools, and had never lived anywhere else. Although Germany's pre-2000 laws were an extreme case of racial or ethnic preference, most other nations have, for much of their history, used racist criteria to select immigrants, and thus citizens. As late as 1970, when immigrants of European descent were being actively encouraged to become Australian citizens, the "White Australia" policy prevented non-European immigrants from settling in Australia.

If we reject the idea that we should give preference to members of one's own race, or those "of our blood," it is difficult to defend the intuition that we should favor our fellow citizens, in the sense in which citizenship is seen as a kind of extended kinship, because all citizens are of the same ethnicity or race. The two are simply too close.

A Community of Reciprocity

What if we empty all racist elements from the idea of who our fellow citizens are? We might hold that we have a special obligation to our fellow citizens because we are all taking part in a collective enterprise of some sort. Eammon Callan has suggested that to be a citizen in a state is to be engaged in a community of reciprocity:

> So far as citizens come to think of justice as integral to a particular political community they care about, in which their own fulfillment and that of their fellow citizens are entwined in a common fate, the sacrifices and compromises that justice requires cannot be sheer loss in the pursuit of one's own good.[19]

Walter Feinberg takes a similar view:

> The source of national identity is…connected to a web of mutual aid that extends back in time and creates future obligations and expectations.[20]

The outpouring of help from Americans for the families of the victims of September 11 was a striking instance of this web of mutual aid, based on the sense that Americans will help each other in times of crisis. In more normal times, Americans can still feel that by their taxes they are contributing to the provision of services that benefit their fellow-Americans by providing social security and medical care when they retire or become disabled, fight crime, defend the nation from attack, protect the environment, maintain national parks, educate their children, and come to the rescue in case of floods, earthquakes or other natural disasters. If they are male, and old enough, they may have served in the armed forces in wartime, and if they are younger, they might have to do so in the future.

It is therefore possible to see the obligation to assist one's fellow-citizens ahead of citizens of other countries as an obligation of reciprocity, though one that is attenuated by the size of the community and the lack of direct contact between, or even bare knowledge of, other members of the community. But is this sufficient reason for favoring one's fellow citizens ahead of citizens of other countries whose needs are far more pressing? Most citizens are born into the nation, and many of them care little for the nation's values and traditions. Some may reject them. Beyond the borders of the rich nations are millions of refugees desperate for the opportunity to become part of those national communities. There is no reason to think that, if we admitted them, they would be any less ready than native-born citizens to reciprocate whatever benefits they receive from the community. If we deny admission to these refugees, it hardly seems fair to then turn around and discriminate against them when we make decisions about whom we will aid, on the grounds that they are not members of our community and have no reciprocal relationships with us....

Justice Within States and Between States

Christopher Wellman has suggested three further impartial reasons for thinking that it may be particularly important to prevent economic inequality from becoming too great *within* a society, rather than *between* societies. The first is that political equality within a society may be adversely affected by economic inequality within a society, but is not adversely affected by economic inequality between societies. The second is that inequality is not something that is bad in itself, but rather something that is bad in so far as it leads to oppressive relationships, and hence we are right to be more concerned about inequality among people living in the same nation than we are about inequality between people living in different countries who are not in a meaningful relationship with each other. And the third is a point about the comparative nature of wealth and poverty.[21]

Wellman's first two points are at least partly answered by [recognizing that] we are facing issues that affect the entire planet. Whatever it is we value about political equality, including the opportunity to participate in the decisions that affect us, globalization means that we should value equality between societies, and at the global level, at least as much as we value political equality within one society. Globalization also means that there can be oppressive relationships at the global scale, as well as within a society.

Marx provided the classic formulation of Wellman's third point:

> A house may be large or small; as long as the surrounding houses are equally small it satisfies all social demands for a dwelling. But let a palace arise beside the little house, and it shrinks from a little house to a hut...however high it may shoot up in the course of civilization, if the neighboring palace grows to an equal or even greater extent, the occupant of the relatively small house will feel more and more uncomfortable, dissatisfied and cramped with its four walls.[22]

But today it is a mistake to think that people compare themselves only with their fellow citizens (or with all their fellow citizens). Inhabitants of rural Mississippi, for example, probably do not often compare themselves with New Yorkers, or at least not in regard to income. Their lifestyle is so different that income is merely one element in a whole package. On the other hand, many Mexicans obviously do look longingly north of the border, and think how much better off they would be financially if they could live in the United States. They reveal their thoughts by trying to get across the border. And the same can be true of people who are not in close geographical proximity, as we can see from the desperate attempts of Chinese to travel illegally to the United States, Europe, and Australia, not because they are being politically persecuted, but because they already have enough of an idea about life in those far-away countries to want to live there.

Despite the different picture that globalization gives, let us grant that there are some reasons for thinking that we should place a higher priority on avoiding marked economic inequality within a given society than across the entire range of the planet's inhabitants. Wellman's three points can be given some weight when they are brought against the strong claim that it is *no* less desirable to eliminate marked economic inequality between any of the world's inhabitants than it is to eliminate it within a single society. But the weight we should give them is limited, and subject to particular circumstances. In particular, the question of whether to seek greater equality within societies, or between societies only arises if we cannot do both. Sometimes we can. We can increase taxes on people in rich nations who have higher incomes or leave large sums to their heirs, and use the revenue to increase aid to those people in the world's poorest nations who have incomes well below average even for the nation in which they are living. That would reduce inequality both in the poor nations and between nations.

Granted, if we live in a rich nation, we could reduce equality within our own society even further if we used the revenue generated by taxes on the wealthiest people within our own society to help the worst-off within our own society. But even if we accept Wellman's arguments, that would be the wrong choice. For then we would be choosing to reduce inequality within our own nation rather than reducing both inequality within poor nations, and inequality between nations. Wellman has offered reasons why it may be more important to focus on inequality within a nation than on inequality between nations, but that is not the same as finding reasons for giving greater priority to overcoming inequality within one's *own* society than in any other society. If I, living in America, can do more to reduce inequality in, say, Bangladesh than I can do to reduce inequality [in] my own country, then Wellman has not given me any grounds for preferring to reduce equality in America—and if giving money to those near the bottom of the economic ladder in Bangladesh will both reduce inequality there and reduce inequality between nations, that seems the best thing to do. Wellman has failed to find any magic in the pronoun "my."

In any case, in the present situation we have duties to foreigners that override duties to our fellow citizens. For even if inequality is often relative, the state of absolute poverty that has already been described is a state of poverty that is not relative to someone else's wealth. Reducing the number of human beings living in absolute poverty is surely a more urgent priority than reducing the relative poverty caused by some people living in palaces while others live in houses that are merely adequate. Here Sidgwick's account of the common moral consciousness of his time is in agreement. After giving the list of special obligations I quoted above, he continues:

> And to all men with whom we may be brought into relation we are held to owe slight services, and such as may be rendered without inconvenience: but those who are in distress or urgent need have a claim on us for special kindness.

THE REALITY

When subjected to the test of impartial assessment, there are few strong grounds for giving preference to the interests of one's fellow citizens, and none that can override the obligation that arises whenever we can, at little cost to ourselves, make an absolutely crucial difference to the well-being of another person in real need. Hence the issue of foreign aid is a matter with which citizens of any country of the developed world ought to be concerned. Citizens of the United States should feel particularly troubled about their country's contribution. Among the developed nations of the world, ranked according to the proportion of their Gross National Product that they give as development aid, the United States comes absolutely, indisputably, last.

Many years ago, the United Nations set a target for development aid of 0.7 percent of Gross National Product. A handful of developed nations—Denmark, The Netherlands, Norway and Sweden—meet or surpass this very modest target of giving 70 cents in every $100 that their economy produces to the developing nations. Most of them fail to reach it. Japan, for example, gives 0.27 percent. Overall, among the affluent nations, official development assistance fell from 0.33 percent of their combined GNP in

1985 to 0.22 percent in 2000. But of all the affluent nations, none fails so miserably to meet the United Nations target as the United States, which in 2000, the last year for which figures are available, gave 0.10 percent of GNP, or just 10 cents in every $100 its economy produces, one-seventh of the United Nations target. That is less *in actual U.S. dollars* than Japan gives—about $10 billion for the United States, as compared with $13.5 billion for Japan—although the U.S. economy is roughly twice the size of Japan's. And even that miserly sum exaggerates the U.S. aid to the most needy, for much of it is strategically targeted for political purposes. The largest single recipient of U.S. official development assistance is Egypt. (Russia and Israel get even more aid from the United States than Egypt, but it is not classified as development assistance.) Tiny Bosnia and Herzegovina gets a larger allocation from the United States than India. Japan, on the other hand, gives to Indonesia, China, Thailand, India, the Philippines, and Vietnam, in that order. India, for instance, gets more than five times as much assistance from Japan as it gets from the United States. Only a quarter of U.S. aid, as compared to more than half of Japan's aid, goes to low-income countries.[23] . . .

Despite the lip-service most people pay to human equality, their circle of concern barely extends beyond the boundary of their country. Yet not all the facts point to this bleak verdict. In 1995 the University of Maryland's Program on International Policy Attitudes, or PIPA, asked Americans what they thought about the amount that the United States was spending on foreign aid. A strong majority of those answering thought that the United States was spending too much on foreign aid and that aid should be cut. That response will make the cynics feel justified in their low opinion of human altruism, but when asked to estimate how much of the federal budget (not of GNP) was devoted to foreign aid, the median estimate—that is, the one in the middle of all the responses—was 15 percent. The correct answer is less than 1 percent. And when asked what an appropriate percentage would be, the median response was 5 percent—an increase on the amount actually spent that is beyond the wildest hopes of any foreign aid advocates on Capitol Hill. A few months later the *Washington Post* decided to run its own survey to see if the results held up. It got an even higher median estimate, that 20 percent of the federal budget was spent on foreign aid, and a median "right amount" of 10 percent. Some skeptics thought that the figure might be explained by the fact that people were including military expenditure in defense of other countries, but further research showed that this was not the case.

In 2000, PIPA asked a different sample the same questions. The most striking difference was that the strong majority (64 percent) that had in 1995 wanted U.S. foreign aid cut had shrunk to 40 percent. But when asked how much of the federal budget goes to foreign aid, the public was no better educated than before. The median estimate was 20 percent, the same as in the 1995 *Washington Post* survey. Only one respondent in 20 gave an estimate of 1 percent or less. Even among those with post-graduate education, the median estimate was 8 percent. Asked what would be an appropriate percentage, the median answer was again the same as that found by the earlier *Washington Post* survey, 10 percent.....

Survey results should always be treated with caution, especially when asking about attitudes on topics where people may like to present themselves as more generous than they really are, but it is hard to dismiss the consistent findings that Americans are woefully ignorant about their country's dismal foreign aid record. What people would really want to do, once they knew the truth, is less clear.....

AN ETHICAL CHALLENGE

If America's leaders continue to give only the most trifling attention to the needs of everyone except Americans (and the leaders of other rich nations continue to do only a little better) what should the citizens of those rich countries do? We are not powerless to act on our own. We can take practical steps to expand our concern across national boundaries by supporting organizations working to aid those in need, wherever they may be. But how much should we give?

More than 700 years ago Thomas Aquinas, later canonized by the Catholic Church, faced up to this question without flinching. Material goods are, he wrote, provided for the satisfaction of human needs and should not be divided in a way that hinders that goal. From this he drew the logical conclusion: "whatever a man has in superabundance is owed, of natural right, to the poor for their sustenance." Although Thomas Aquinas has had a major influence on the thinking of the Roman Catholic Church—to such an extent that "Thomism" has been described as the official philosophy of the Church—this particular aspect of his teachings is not one that the Church has chosen to emphasize. But how exactly we are to justify keeping what we have in "superabundance" when others are starving is not so easy to say.

In his book *Living High and Letting Die* New York philosopher Peter Unger presents an ingenious series of imaginary examples designed to probe our intuitions about whether it is wrong to live well without giving substantial amounts of money to help people who are hungry, malnourished, or dying from easily treatable illnesses like diarrhea. Here is my paraphrase of one of these examples.

> Bob is close to retirement. He has invested most of his savings in a very rare and valuable old car, a Bugatti, which he has not been able to insure. The Bugatti is his pride and joy. In addition to the pleasure he gets from driving and caring for his car, Bob knows that its rising market value means that he will always be able to sell it and live comfortably after retirement. One day when Bob is out for a drive, he parks the Bugatti near the end of a disused railway siding and goes for a walk up the track. As he does so, he sees that a runaway train, with no one aboard, is running down the railway track. Looking further down the track he sees the small figure of a child playing in a tunnel and very likely to be killed by the runaway train. He can't stop the train and the child is too far away to warn of the danger, but

12. William Godwin, *Memoirs of the Author of a Vindication of the Rights of Woman*, ch. vi., p. 90, second edition, quoted in William Godwin, *Thoughts Occasioned by the Perusal of Dr Parr's Spital Sermon*, Taylor and Wilks, London, 1801; reprinted in J. Marken and B. Pollin, eds., *Uncollected Writings (1785–1822) by William Godwin*, Gainesville, Fla.: Scholars' Facsimiles & Reprints, 1968, pp. 314–315. As K. Codell Carter notes the passage italicized in the original is from Terence (*Heautontimorumenos*, I. 77), and is usually translated as "nothing human is alien to me." Godwin's argument for the importance of "individual attachments" is reminiscent of Aristotle's discussion of the need for friendship in his *Nicomachean Ethics*, Book IX, sec. 9.

13. R. M. Hare, *Moral Thinking: Its Levels, Method and Point*, Clarendon Press, Oxford, 1981, Part I.

14. See Yonina Talmon, *Family and Community in the Kibbutz*, Harvard University Press, Cambridge, Mass., 1972, pp. 3–34.

15. See Martin Daly and Margo Wilson, *The Truth About Cinderella: A Darwinian View of Parental Love*, Yale University Press, New Haven, 1999.

16. Bernard Williams, "Persons, Character and Morality," in Bernard Williams, *Moral Luck*, Cambridge, Cambridge University Press, 1981, p. 18.

17. M. Rosenzweig, "Risk, Implicit Contracts and the Family in Rural Areas of Low-Income Countries," *Economic Journal*, 98, 1988, pp. 1148–1170; M. Rosenzweig and O. Stark, "Consumption Smoothing, Migration and Marriage: Evidence from Rural India," *Journal of Political Economy*, 97:4, 1989, pp. 905–926. I am grateful to Thomas Pogge for this information.

18. Michael Walzer, *Spheres of Justice*, Basic Books, New York, 1983, p. 12.

19. Eamonn Callan, *Creating Citizens: Political Education and Liberal Democracy*, Clarendon Press, Oxford, 1997, p. 96. This and the following quotation are cited from Melissa Williams, "Citizenship as Identity, Citizenship as Shared Fate, and the Functions of Multicultural Education," in Walter Feinberg and Kevin McDonough, eds., *Collective Identities and Cosmopolitan Values*, Oxford University Press, Oxford, 2002.

20. Walter Feinberg, *Common Schools/Uncommon Identities: National Unity and Cultural Difference*, Yale University Press, New Haven, 1998, p. 119.

21. Christopher Wellman, "Relational Facts in Liberal Political Theory: Is There Magic in the Pronoun 'My,'" *Ethics*, 110:3, 2000, pp. 537–562; the third point is also made by David Miller, *Principles of Social Justice*, Harvard University Press, Cambridge, Mass., 1999, p. 18.

22. Karl Marx, *Wage Labour and Capital*, in David McLellan, ed., *Karl Marx: Selected Writings*, Oxford University Press, Oxford, 1977, p. 259.

23. All figures are from the Organization for Economic Cooperation and Development. Figures on the overall fall in aid from developed countries are from the 2001 Development Co-operation Report, Statistical Annex, table 14; figures for individual nations come from charts under the heading "Aid at a Glance by Donor." These tables and charts are available at www.oecd.org.

24. Peter Unger, *Living High and Letting Die*, Oxford University Press, New York, 1996, p. 136–139.

25. The question is raised by Leif Wenar, "What We Owe to Distant Others," presented at the Global Justice Conference, Center for Law and Philosophy, Columbia Law School, New York, 31 March–1 April 2001. See also David Crocker, "Hunger, Capability and Development," in William Aiken and Hugh LaFollette, eds., *World Hunger and Morality*, second edition, Upper Saddle River, N.J., Prentice Hall, 1996, pp. 211–230.

26. World Bank, *Assessing Aid: What Works, What Doesn't, and Why*, Oxford University Press, Oxford, 1998, p. 1; available at www.worldbank.org/research/aid/aidpub.htm.

27. World Bank, *Assessing Aid: What Works, What Doesn't, and Why*, p. 14.

28. World Bank, News Release 2002/228/S, 11 March 2002, "Now More Than Ever, Aid Is a Catalyst for Change: New Study Shows Effects of Development Assistance over Last 50 Years," http://lnweb18.worldbank.org/news/pressrelease.nsf/673fa6c5a2d50a67852565e200692a79/865e6e90a8a6f97f85256b790050c57c?OpenDocument# paper. An executive summary of the research paper, "The Role and Effectiveness of Development Assistance" is available at the same web address.

29. World Bank, *Assessing Aid: What Works, What Doesn't, and Why*, p. x.

30. Alberto Alesina and David Dollar, "Who Gives Foreign Aid to Whom and Why?" NBER Working Paper 6612, pp. 22–23. Available at www.nber.org/papers/w6612.

31. See, for example, Arthur van Diesen, *The Quality of Aid: Towards an Agenda for More Effective International Development Co-operation*, Christian Aid, London, 2000; available at www.christian-aid.org.uk/indepth/0004qual/quality1.htm.

32. Sidgwick, *The Methods of Ethics*, pp. 489–490.

rich countries have income to spare, after meeting their basic needs; but on the other hand, there are hundreds of millions of rich people who live in poor countries, and they could and should give too. We could, therefore, advocate that everyone with income to spare, after meeting their family's basic needs, should contribute a minimum of 0.4 percent of their income to organizations working to help the world's poorest people. But to do so would be to set our sights too low, for it would take fifteen years even to halve poverty and hunger. During those fifteen years, tens of thousands of children will continue to die every day from poverty-related causes. We should feel a greater sense of urgency to eliminate poverty. Moreover there is nothing especially memorable about 0.4 percent of one's income. A more useful symbolic figure would be 1 percent, and this might indeed be closer to what it would take to eliminate, rather than halve, global poverty.

We could therefore propose, as a public policy likely to produce good consequences, that anyone who has enough money to spend on the luxuries and frivolities so common in affluent societies should give at least 1 cent in every dollar of their income to those who have trouble getting enough to eat, clean water to drink, shelter from the elements, and basic health care. Those who do not meet this standard should be seen as failing to meet their fair share of a global responsibility, and therefore as doing something that is seriously morally wrong. This is the minimum, not the optimal, donation. Those who think carefully about their ethical obligations will realize that—since not everyone will be giving even 1 percent—they should do far more. But if, for the purposes of changing our society's standards in a manner that has a realistic chance of success, we focus on the idea of a bare minimum that we can expect everyone to do, there is something to be said for seeing a 1 percent donation of annual income to overcome world poverty as the minimum that one must do to lead a morally decent life. To give that amount requires no moral heroics. To fail to give it shows indifference to the indefinite continuation of dire poverty and avoidable, poverty-related deaths....

NOTES

1. Joyce Purnick, "Take the Cash. You're Making Us Look Bad," *New York Times*, February 11, 2002, p. B1.

2. Henry Sidgwick, *The Methods of Ethics*, seventh edition, Macmillan, London, 1907, p. 246.

3. Heinrich Himmler, speech to SS leaders in Poznan, Poland, 4 October 1943; cited from www.historyplace.com/worldwar2/timeline/Poznan.htm.

4. R. M. Hare, *Freedom and Reason*, Clarendon Press, Oxford, 1963; *Moral Thinking*, Clarendon Press, Oxford, 1981.

5. William Godwin, *An Enquiry Concerning Political Justice and Its Influence on General Virtue and Happiness*, first edition, first published 1793, edited and abridged by Raymond Preston, Knopf, New York, 1926, pp. 41–42.

6. "Famine, Affluence and Morality," *Philosophy and Public Affairs*, 1:2, 1972, pp. 231–232.

7. See, for example, Raymond D. Gastil, "Beyond a Theory of Justice," *Ethics*, 85:3, 1975, p. 185; Samuel Scheffler, "Relationships and Responsibilities," *Philosophy and Public Affairs*, 26:3, 1997, pp. 189–209, reprinted in Samuel Scheffler, *Boundaries and Allegiances*, Oxford University Press, Oxford, 2001, pp. 97–110; Samuel Scheffler, "Conceptions of Cosmopolitanism," *Utilitas*, 11:3, 1999, pp. 255–276, reprinted in *Boundaries and Allegiances*, pp. 111–130. Note, however, that while Scheffler argues against what he calls "extreme cosmopolitanism" and insists that we have "underived special responsibilities" to those close to us in various ways, he does not take a position on whether we have special responsibilities to our compatriots, as compared to those in other countries. (See *Boundaries and Allegiances*, p. 124.) For an excellent discussion of the extensive literature on this topic, see Darrel Moellendorf, *Cosmopolitan Justice*, Westview, Boulder, Colo., 2002, chapters 3–4.

8. Samuel Parr, *A Spital Sermon*, preached at Christ Church upon Easter Tuesday, 15 April 1800, to which are added notes. J. Mawman, London, 1801.

9. Galatians vi:10.

10. Parr, *A Spital Sermon*, p. 4.

11. Nel Noddings, *Caring: A Feminine Approach to Ethics and Moral Education*, University of California Press, Berkeley, 1986, p. 86; for a related passage see also p. 112.

reasonably good governments that will not misuse the resources given.[30] Only when the biggest donors follow the example of the Nordic countries will we be able to tell how effective government foreign aid can be. Experienced non-government organizations, such as the various national members of the Oxfam International group, provide another model. They have had 50 years of experience in the field and have the ability to learn from their mistakes. There is always more to learn, but there is little doubt that well-intentioned, well-resourced, intelligent people, experienced in the cultural context in which they are working, can do a significant amount of good for those living in extreme poverty.[31]

A different objection to the argument that Unger and I have been putting forward is that it is poor policy to advocate a morality that most people will not follow. If we come to believe that, unless we make real sacrifices for strangers, we are doing wrong, then our response may be, not to give more, but to be less observant of other moral rules that we had previously followed. Making morality so demanding threatens to bring the whole of morality into disrepute. This objection effectively concedes that we ought to do a great deal more than we are now doing but denies that advocating this will really lead to the poor getting more assistance. The question then becomes: What policy will produce the best consequences? If it is true that advocating a highly demanding morality will lead to worse consequences than advocating a less demanding morality, then indeed we ought to advocate a less demanding morality. We could do this, while still knowing that, at the level of critical thinking, impartialism is sound. Here Sidgwick's point holds good: there is a distinction between "what it may be right to do, and privately recommend," and "what it would not be right to advocate openly."[32] We might, among ourselves, feel that we should forgo all "superabundance" in order to help those who are unable to provide for their bare subsistence, whereas in public we might decide to advocate whatever level of giving we believe will yield the greatest amount of assistance, while not making

people feel that morality is so demanding that they will disregard it. If, by advocating that people give $50 a year—just $1 a week—to help the world's poorest people, it really were possible to get donations from the 75 percent of Americans that the 2000 PIPA survey suggested might be willing to give this sum, then that would be a target worth campaigning for. If it were possible to get $100 a year from, say, 60 percent of Americans, that would be better still, especially if the 15 percent willing to give $50 but not $100 would still give their $50. The point is to nominate as a target the figure that will lead to the greatest amount of money being raised. For that it needs to be a target that makes sense to people.

One way of looking at how much we might suggest that people should give is to suppose that the task of eliminating poverty in the world were fairly distributed among all of the 900 million people in high-income countries. How much would each of them have to give? As we have seen, the World Bank estimates that it would cost $40 to $60 billion per year in additional aid to achieve the development goals set at the United Nations Millennium Summit. These goals, calling for poverty and hunger to be halved by 2015, are more modest than the elimination of poverty. They could leave untouched the situation of the poorest of all, in countries where the costs of reaching poor people are higher than they are in countries with better infrastructures. But they are at least a stepping stone on the way to a more complete victory over poverty, so let us ask how much it would require, per person, to raise this sum. There are about 900 million people in the developed world, roughly 600 million of them adults. Hence a donation of about $100 per adult per year for the next fifteen years could achieve the Millennium Summit goals, even at the high end of the World Bank estimates. For someone earning $27,500 per annum, the average salary in the developed world, this is less than 0.4 percent of their annual income, or less than 1 cent in every $2 they earn.

There are many complexities that such figures ignore, but they go both ways. Not all residents of

Consider Bob. How far past losing the Bugatti should he go? Imagine that Bob had got his foot stuck in the track of the siding, and if he diverted the train, then it would amputate his big toe before going on to ram his car. Should he still throw the switch? What if it would amputate his foot? His entire leg? Only when the sacrifices become very significant indeed would most people be prepared to say that Bob does nothing wrong when he decides not to throw the switch. Of course, most people could be wrong; we can't decide moral issues by taking opinion polls. But consider for yourself the level of sacrifice that you would demand of Bob, and then think about how much money you would have to give away in order to make a sacrifice that is roughly equal to that. It's almost certainly much, much more than $200. For most middle-class Americans, it could easily be more like $200,000. When Bob first grasped the dilemma that faced him as he stood by that railway switch, he must have thought how extraordinarily unlucky he was, to be placed in a situation in which he must choose between the life of an innocent child and the sacrifice of most of his savings. But he was not unlucky at all. We are all in that situation.

Some critics have questioned the factual assumptions behind such arguments. There is, they insist, an empirical question to be answered: "How much will each additional dollar of aid, given by me or by my government, contribute to the long-term well-being of people in areas receiving that aid?" It is not enough to find out the cost of delivering a packet of oral rehydration salts to a child who, without it, will die from diarrhea. We must look beyond saving life, to how the lives that are saved will be lived, to see if we have some reason to believe that saving the child will do more than perpetuate the cycle of poverty, misery, and high infant mortality.[25]

A World Bank study, *Assessing Aid*, points out that foreign aid has been both a "spectacular success" and an "unmitigated failure." On the success side:

> Internationally funded and coordinated programs have dramatically reduced such diseases as river blindness and vastly expanded immunization against key childhood diseases. Hundreds of millions of people have had their lives touched, if not transformed, by access to schools, clean water, sanitation, electric power, health clinics, roads, and irrigation—all financed by foreign aid.[26]

Among the failures is the aid that went to Zaire, now the Democratic Republic of the Congo, under the dictatorship of Mobutu. Corruption, incompetence, and misguided policies ensured that it had no impact. Extensive road building in Tanzania failed to improve the road network, because the roads were not maintained. But the World Bank study indicates that we now know more about what will work and what will not. It finds that when a poor country with good management is given aid equivalent to 1 percent of its GDP, poverty and infant mortality falls by 1 percent.[27] A more recent World Bank study has confirmed that the efficacy of aid is improving. Whereas in 1990 $1 billion in aid was sufficient to lift an estimated 105,000 people out of poverty, by 1997 to 1998 the same amount was lifting approximately 284,000 people out of poverty.[28] The tragedy is, as Joseph Stiglitz (then Chief Economist of the World Bank) points out in his foreword to the study, that "just as aid is poised to be its most effective, the volume of aid is declining and is at its lowest level ever."[29]

It is true that in the past government foreign aid has not been as effective in reducing poverty as one might hope. That is, to a significant extent, because it has not been aimed at reducing poverty. In a study titled "Who Gives Foreign Aid to Whom and Why?" Alberto Alesina and David Dollar found that three of the biggest donors—the United States, France, and Japan—direct their aid, not to those countries where it will be most effective in fostering growth and reducing poverty, but to countries where aid will further their own strategic or cultural interests. The United States gives much of its aid to its friends in the Middle East, Israel and Egypt. Japan favors those countries that vote the way it votes in international forums like the United Nations. France gives overwhelmingly to its former colonies. The Nordic countries are the most notable exception to this pattern—they give to countries that are poor but have he can throw a switch that will divert the train down the siding where his Bugatti is parked. Then nobody will be killed—but since the barrier at the end of the siding is in disrepair, the train will destroy his Bugatti. Thinking of his joy in owning the car, and the financial security it represents, Bob decides not to throw the switch. The child is killed. But for many years to come Bob enjoys owning his Bugatti and the financial security it represents.[24]

Bob's conduct, most of us will immediately respond, was gravely wrong. Unger agrees. But then he reminds us that we too have opportunities to save the lives of children. We can give to organizations like UNICEF or Oxfam America. How much would we have to give one of these organizations to have a high probability of saving the life of a child threatened by easily preventable diseases?

In its fund-raising material, the U.S. Committee for UNICEF says that a donation of $17 will provide immunization "to protect a child for life against the six leading child-killing and maiming diseases: measles, polio, diphtheria, whooping cough, tetanus, and tuberculosis," while a donation of $25 will provide "over 400 packets of oral rehydration salts to help save the lives of children suffering from diarrheal dehydration." But these figures do not tell us how many lives are saved by the immunization or rehydration salts, and they do not include the cost of raising the money, administrative expenses, and delivering aid where it is most needed. Unger called some experts to get a rough estimate of these costs and the number of lives likely to be saved and came up with a figure of around $200 per child's life saved. Assuming that this estimate is not too far astray, if you still think that it was very wrong of Bob not to throw the switch that would have diverted the train and saved the child's life, then it is hard to see how you could deny that it is also very wrong not to send at least $200 to one of the organizations listed above. Unless, that is, there is some morally important difference between the two situations. What might that be? Is it the practical uncertainties about whether aid will really reach the people who need it? Nobody who knows the world of overseas aid can doubt that such uncertainties exist. But Unger's figure of $200 to save a child's life was reached after he had made conservative assumptions about the proportion of the money donated that will actually reach its target. One genuine difference between Bob and those who can donate to overseas aid organizations but don't is that only Bob can save the child in the tunnel, whereas there are hundreds of millions of people who can give $200 to overseas aid organizations. The problem is that most of them aren't doing it. Does this mean that it is all right not to do it?

Suppose that there were more owners of priceless vintage cars—Carol, Dave, Emma, Fred, and so on, down to Ziggy—all in exactly the same situation as Bob, with their own siding and their own switch, all sacrificing the child in order to preserve their own cherished car. Would that make it all right for Bob to do the same? To answer this question affirmatively is to endorse follow-the-crowd ethics—the kind of ethics that led many Germans to look away when the Nazi atrocities were being committed. We do not excuse them because others were behaving no better.

We seem to lack a sound basis for drawing a clear moral line between Bob's situation and that of anyone with $200 to spare who does not donate it to an overseas aid agency. These people seem to be acting at least as badly as Bob was acting when he chose to let the runaway train hurtle toward the unsuspecting child. Indeed, they seem to be behaving far worse, because for most Americans, to part with $200 is far less of a sacrifice than Bob would have to make to save the child. So it seems that we must be doing something seriously wrong if we are not prepared to give $200 to UNICEF or Oxfam America to reduce the poverty that causes so many early deaths. Since there are a lot of very needy children in the world, however, this is not the end of the moral claims on us. There will always be another child whose life you could save for another $200. Are we therefore obliged to keep giving until we have nothing left? At what point can we stop?

was 5 percent—an increase on the amount actually spent that is beyond the wildest hopes of any foreign aid advocates on Capitol Hill. A few months later the *Washington Post* decided to run its own survey to see if the results held up. It got an even higher median estimate, that 20 percent of the federal budget was spent on foreign aid, and a median "right amount" of 10 percent. Some skeptics thought that the figure might be explained by the fact that people were including military expenditure in defense of other countries, but further research showed that this was not the case.

In 2000, PIPA asked a different sample the same questions. The most striking difference was that the strong majority (64 percent) that had in 1995 wanted U.S. foreign aid cut had shrunk to 40 percent. But when asked how much of the federal budget goes to foreign aid, the public was no better educated than before. The median estimate was 20 percent, the same as in the 1995 *Washington Post* survey. Only one respondent in 20 gave an estimate of 1 percent or less. Even among those with post-graduate education, the median estimate was 8 percent. Asked what would be an appropriate percentage, the median answer was again the same as that found by the earlier *Washington Post* survey, 10 percent....

Survey results should always be treated with caution, especially when asking about attitudes on topics where people may like to present themselves as more generous than they really are, but it is hard to dismiss the consistent findings that Americans are woefully ignorant about their country's dismal foreign aid record. What people would really want to do, once they knew the truth, is less clear....

AN ETHICAL CHALLENGE

If America's leaders continue to give only the most trifling attention to the needs of everyone except Americans (and the leaders of other rich nations continue to do only a little better) what should the citizens of those rich countries do? We are not

powerless to act on our own. We can take practical steps to expand our concern across national boundaries by supporting organizations working to aid those in need, wherever they may be. But how much should we give?

More than 700 years ago Thomas Aquinas, later canonized by the Catholic Church, faced up to this question without flinching. Material goods are, he wrote, provided for the satisfaction of human needs and should not be divided in a way that hinders that goal. From this he drew the logical conclusion: "whatever a man has in superabundance is owed, of natural right, to the poor for their sustenance." Although Thomas Aquinas has had a major influence on the thinking of the Roman Catholic Church—to such an extent that "Thomism" has been described as the official philosophy of the Church—this particular aspect of his teachings is not one that the Church has chosen to emphasize. But how exactly we are to justify keeping what we have in "superabundance" when others are starving is not so easy to say.

In his book *Living High and Letting Die* New York philosopher Peter Unger presents an ingenious series of imaginary examples designed to probe our intuitions about whether it is wrong to live well without giving substantial amounts of money to help people who are hungry, malnourished, or dying from easily treatable illnesses like diarrhea. Here is my paraphrase of one of these examples.

Bob is close to retirement. He has invested most of his savings in a very rare and valuable old car, a Bugatti, which he has not been able to insure. The Bugatti is his pride and joy. In addition to the pleasure he gets from driving and caring for his car, Bob knows that its rising market value means that he will always be able to sell it and live comfortably after retirement. One day when Bob is out for a drive, he parks the Bugatti near the end of a disused railway siding and goes for a walk up the track. As he does so, he sees that a runaway train, with no one aboard, is running down the railway track. Looking further down the track he sees the small figure of a child playing in a tunnel and very likely to be killed by the runaway train. He can't stop the train and the child is too far away to warn of the danger, but

BRIAN BARRY

[From] Sustainability and Intergenerational Justice

1. THE QUESTION

As temporary custodians of the planet, those who are alive at any given time can do a better or worse job of handing it on to their successors. I take that simple thought to animate concerns about what we ought to be doing to preserve conditions that will make life worth living (or indeed liveable at all) in the future, and especially in the time after those currently alive will have died ("future generations"). There are widespread suspicions that we are not doing enough for future generations, but how do we determine what is enough? Putting the question in that way leads us, I suggest, towards a formulation of it in terms of intergenerational justice.

A methodological principle to which I shall appeal more systematically in section 2 is that we shall make most headway in asking ethical questions about the future if we start by asking them about the present and then see how the results can be extended to apply to the future. The rationale for this procedure is that we are accustomed to thinking about relations among contemporaries and have developed a quite sophisticated apparatus to help us in doing so. We have no similar apparatus to aid our thoughts about relations between people living at different times. Rather than starting from scratch, then, my proposal is that we should move from the familiar to the unfamiliar, making whatever adaptations seem necessary along the way.

If we follow this precept, and start from relations among contemporaries, we shall immediately run into a contrast that virtually all moral systems draw, though they derive it differently and use different vocabularies, between what it would be desirable (virtuous, benevolent, supererogatory) to do for

others and what it would be wrong not to do for them. We may be said to have a duty or an obligation to do things that it is wrong to do, though this entails taking the words outside their natural homes in, respectively, institutionally generated roles and constraints imposed within rule-governed activities (e.g. legal obligations or promissory obligations).

Another family of terms that fits in somewhere here is the one made up of "just," "unjust," "justice," and "injustice." A broad conception would make "unjust" roughly equivalent to "wrong" or "morally impermissible.". . . However, we would not in normal usage describe murder or assault as unjust, even though they are paradigmatically wrong. Rather, we reserve terms from the "justice" family for cases in which some distributive consideration comes into play. For the present purpose, it will make little difference whether we choose the broader or the narrower conception of justice. This is because the questions about intergenerational justice that are liable to create distinctive moral problems are very likely to be issues of justice in the narrow sense: cases where there is (or is believed to be) an intergenerational conflict of interest. Thus, suppose we could provide a benefit or avoid a loss to people in the future at some cost to ourselves, are we morally required to do it? This inter-temporal distributive question falls within the scope of justice in the narrow sense. It is quite true that we can also damage people in the future without benefiting ourselves. But such actions will normally be wrong in relation to contemporaries or at the very least recklessly imprudent. Thus, if the people living at a certain time devastate a large part of the world by fighting a nuclear war, that will obviously be bad for later generations (assuming that human life is not entirely wiped out). But its inflicting immense evils on subsequent people is of a piece, as it were, with its devastating effect on those alive at the time.

I qualified my equation of injustice and wrongness in the broad sense by saying only that they are roughly equivalent. I had in mind two ways in which we can behave wrongly but not unjustly First, I take it to be uncontroversial that we can act wrongly in relation to non-human animals. It is, of course, controversial whether or not certain practices such as using them in medical experiments or raising them for food are wrong. But scarcely anybody would deny that some acts (e.g. torturing them for fun) are wrong. We can, I think, stretch "duty" and "obligation" further beyond their core applications to enable us to talk about duties or obligations to non-human animals. (Even here, though, the core applications exert a pull: we are especially liable to use the vocabulary of duty where a role-related responsibility is at issue.) In contrast, it does not seem to me that the concept of justice can be deployed intelligibly outside the context of relations between human beings. The reason for this is, I suggest, that justice and injustice can be predicated only of relations among creatures who are regarded as moral equals in the sense that they weigh equally in the moral scales.

The second way in which wrongness and injustice come apart is that it is possible to behave wrongly even where the interests of sentient beings are not involved. Here, it is controversial that there are really any cases in which we can treat "nature" wrongly unless the interests of sentient beings are somehow affected. I shall defend the claim below (section 5) though I shall there argue that the common move of appealing to the "independent value of nature" is a mistaken one. For the present purpose, however, I can bracket the validity of the claim. Let me simply say that *if* it is in some circumstances wrong to behave in a certain way in relation to "nature," there is no entity that can properly be described as a victim of injustice.[1] I also believe, incidentally, that talking about duties or obligations to "nature" is misguided. My reason for holding this will, I hope, become apparent when I explain the sense in which I think we can behave wrongly in relation to "nature."

To sum up the discussion this far, behaving unjustly to future generations is wrong but (even in the broad conception of justice) it is not the only thing that those currently alive can do in relation to the distant future that is wrong. Injustice is, however, such a manifestly important aspect of wrongness that it is well worth the amount of attention it gets from political philosophers. Further, if we define "distributive justice" to correspond to the narrow conception of justice, which focuses on conflicts of interest, we may say that questions about intergenerational justice are characteristically questions about intergenerational distributive justice.

With that by way of preamble, I can now set out very quickly what I see as the question to be asked about the ethical status of sustainability. This is as follows: Is sustainability (however we understand the term) either a necessary or a sufficient condition of intergenerational distributive justice?

2. DISTRIBUTIVE JUSTICE

In accordance with the methodological maxim that I laid down at the beginning, I shall approach the question of the demands of intergenerational justice via the question of the demands of distributive justice among contemporaries. The premiss from which I start is one of the fundamental equality of human beings. (It is precisely because this premiss does not make moral standing depend on the time at which people live that principles of justice valid for contemporaries are prima facie valid for intergenerational justice too.)...

I do not know of any way of providing a justification for the premiss of fundamental equality: its status is that of an axiom. I will point out, however, that it is very widely accepted, at least in theory, and attempts to provide a rationale for unequal treatment at least pay lip service to the obligation to square it with the premiss of fundamental equality. Moreover,

it seems to me that there is a good reason for this in that it is very hard to imagine any remotely plausible basis for rejecting the premiss. In any case, it is pre-supposed in what follows.

In brief compass, then, I shall propose four principles which are, I claim, theorems of the premiss of fundamental equality. These are as follows:

1. Equal rights. Prima facie, civil and political rights must be equal. Exceptions can be justified only if they would receive the well-informed assent of those who would be allocated diminished rights compared with others.

2. Responsibility. A legitimate origin of different outcomes for different people is that they have made different voluntary choices. (However, this principle comes into operation fully only against a background of a just system of rights, resources and opportunities.) The obverse of the principle is that bad outcomes for which somebody is not responsible provide a prima-facie case for compensation.

3. Vital interests. There are certain objective requirements for human beings to be able to live healthy lives, raise families, work at full capacity, and take a part in social and political life. Justice requires that a higher priority should be given to ensuring that all human beings have the means to satisfy these vital interests than to satisfying other desires.

4. Mutual advantage. A secondary principle of justice is that, if everyone stands ex ante to gain from a departure from a state of affairs produced by the implementation of the above three principles, it is compatible with justice to make the change. (However, it is not unjust not to.)

What implications do these principles of justice have for justice between generations? Let me take them in turn.

1. Equal rights. I cannot see that this principle has any direct intergenerational application. For it would seem to me absurd to say, e.g.

that it is unfair for a woman to have more rights in Britain now than a century ago, or unfair that a woman had fewer rights then. Surely, the principle of equal rights applies to contemporaries and only to contemporaries. However, the present generation may be able to affect the likelihood that there will be equal rights in the future. Thus, it seems to be a robust generalization that rights suffer at times when large challenges to a system demand rapid and co-ordinated responses. (To offer a relatively modest example, I would guess that all individual university teachers and departments have lost autonomy in the last twenty years.) The more environmental stress we leave our successors to cope with, therefore, the poorer prospects for equal rights.

2. Responsibility. This principle will clearly apply among people who are contemporaries in the future, as it does among people who are contemporaries today, to justify inequalities of outcome that arise from choice. But what place, if any, does it have in relations between different generations? People in the future can scarcely be held responsible for the physical conditions they inherit, so it would seem that it is unjust if people in [the] future are worse off in this respect than we are. (This, of course, leaves open the question of what is the relevant criterion of being well off, and I shall take that up in the next section.) What future people may be held responsible for, however, is how many of them there are at any given time.

Clearly, if we take the view that the principle of responsibility applies to population size, it will have highly significant implications for the requirements of intergenerational justice. I shall pursue this further in section 4.

3. Vital interests. The fundamental idea that location in space and time do not in themselves affect legitimate claims has the immediate implication that the vital interests of

people in the future have the same priority as the vital interests of people in the present. I shall take up the implications of this in section 4.

4. Mutual advantage. In theory, it would be possible for the principle of mutual advantage to have cross-generational implications. That is to say, it could be that there are intertemporally Paretian improvements to be made in comparison with a baseline constituted by the outcomes of the other principles working together. However, I think it quite implausible that there are. The scope of the principle in relation to the distant future is particularly limited because it is explicitly stated in terms of preferences, and the further into the future we look the less confidence we can have about the preferences that people will have.

An objection commonly made against a universalist theory of justice such as this one is that it does not provide an adequate account of motivation to conform to its demands. It is certainly true that it leaves a gap in a way that "communitarian" accounts do not. Consider, for example, Avner de-Shalit's book *Why Posterity Matters*.[2] It seems to me that his account closes the gap only too successfully. For in essence what he is saying is that concern for people in the future is something we naturally have, to the extent that we see them as carrying on with projects that are dear to us, because that gives depth and meaning to our own lives. This is doubtless true to some degree, though it would seem more for some than for others, but (except to the extent that it can generate intragenerational obligations arising from the "principle of fair play") it does not tell people that they have to do what they are not inclined to do anyway. Moreover, because it is a cross-generational form of communitarianism, it cannot offer any reason for people in rich countries to cut back so as to improve the prospects of future people in other communities. Yet that is, as it seems to me, the most important thing for a conception of intergenerational justice to deliver.

In almost all the world, there is discrimination against women: they have fewer legal rights than men, are poorly protected by the law, and even more by its administration, against domestic violence, they have restricted educational and occupational opportunities, and so on. In most countries there are (de facto or de jure) different grades of membership based on race, ethnicity, language, religion, or some other characteristic. Such practices have powerful beneficiaries and it might be said (and is by so-called communitarian political philosophers) that it is "no use" applying universalistic criteria of justice and pointing out that according to these criteria practices such as these are unjust. The only "useful" criticism is "connected" criticism, which deploys already accepted ideas. But this means that criticism cannot get a foothold so long as those who discriminate on the basis of gender or ethnicity have an internally coherent rationale. Meanwhile, it remains none the less true that such practices are unjust. And even if that thought does not have any motivating effect on those within a country who are in a position to change things, it may motivate people outside to organize boycotts and lead international organizations to exclude such countries from the benefits of international trade and aid.

I believe that the core idea of universalism—that place and time do not provide a morally relevant basis on which to differentiate the weight to be given to the interests of different people—has an immense rational appeal. Its corollaries—the illegitimacy of slavery and the impermissibility of assigning women an inferior legal status, for example—have been acted on for the past two centuries in a significant part of the world, despite strongly entrenched interests and beliefs in opposition to them. In the past fifty years, concern for people who are distant in place and time has grown in a quite unprecedented way. The great question for the future is whether or not that concern will grow sufficiently to induce action of the kind called for by the demands of justice. But I can see no reason for supposing that those demands should be scaled back to match pessimistic predictions about the way in which that question

will be answered, even if we believe pessimism to be a reasonable response to the evidence so far.

3. SUSTAINABILITY

Many people who have thought seriously about the matter have reached the conclusion that the concept of sustainability is inherently incapable of carrying the burden it would have to bear if it were to constitute a basic building block in a theory of intergenerational justice. With due diffidence, as a non-expert, I should like to make two observations on the literature that I have read. I first note a tendency to elide an important distinction. I have in mind here on the one hand the problem of producing a definition of sustainability that is coherent and comprehensible, and on the other hand the problem of drawing out concrete policy implications from any such definition. It seems to me that the problem of application is undeniably enormous, but that this should not be allowed too readily to impugn the possibility of achieving a definition of the concept.

The other point that occurs to me about the pessimists is their propensity to cite disagreement about the concept of sustainability as a basis for dismissing it. But we need not despair so long as the disagreements reflect substantive differences of viewpoint. Thus, let us suppose that concern about sustainability takes its origins from the suspicion that I articulated at the beginning: the suspicion that we are shortchanging our successors. If we then take this to mean that we should not act in such a way as to leave them with less of what matters than we enjoy, and call that sustainability, it is clear that the content of sustainability will depend crucially on what we think matters. For example, one writer may assume that what matters is utility, understood as want-satisfaction. (Such a writer is unlikely to be anything other than an economist, but economists loom quite large in the literature of sustainability.) Others will disagree and propose some alternative. There is nothing either mysterious or discreditable

about this. It is, in fact, exactly what we should expect.

The core concept of sustainability is, I suggest, that there is some X whose value should be maintained, in as far as it lies within our power to do so, into the indefinite future. This leaves it open for dispute what the content of X should be. I have already mentioned one candidate: utility, understood (as is orthodox in economics) as the satisfaction of wants or, as they are usually called, preferences. The obvious objection to this criterion is that wants are (quite reasonably) dependent on what is, or is expected to be, available. Perhaps people in the future might learn to find satisfaction in totally artificial landscapes, walking on the astroturf amid the plastic trees while the electronic birds sing overhead. But we cannot but believe that something horrible would have happened to human beings if they did not miss real grass, trees, and birds.

The want-satisfaction criterion does not enable us to explain what would be wrong with such a world. This sheds light on the oft-noted tendency of economists to be disproportionately located at the "brown" end of the spectrum on environmental issues. For economists are also, as I have already noted, the most significant adherents of the want-satisfaction criterion. Combine that criterion with a faith in the adaptability of human preferences and you have a formula that can easily generate optimism about the future. For it will seem plausible that almost any environmental degradation that does not actually undermine productive capacity will be compensable by advances in technology that we can safely assume will continue to occur.

If I am right that substantive disputes about the concept of sustainability reflect disagreements about what matters, we can begin to see why what appear superficially to be technical questions of definition are so intractable. Consider especially the arguments in the literature about the status of "natural capital." For someone who adopts want-satisfaction as a criterion, all resources are in principle fungible: if plastic trees are as satisfying as real ones, there

is no reason for worrying about the destruction of the world's trees so long as the resources exist to enable plastic replacements to be manufactured in sufficient numbers. Those who insist that "natural capital" must be preserved are in effect denying the complete fungibility of all capital. But what is this disagreement actually about? On the interpretation I wish to offer, this is not a disagreement that turns on some matter of fact. It would be quite possible to agree with everything that might be said in favour of fungibility and still deny that it amounts to a case against the special status of "natural capital." For the case in favour of giving the preservation of nature an independent value is that it is important in its own right. If future people are to have access to what matters, and unspoilt nature is an essential part of what matters, then it follows that loss of "natural capital" cannot be traded off against any amount of additional productive capacity. (I leave until section 5 the idea that nature might have value independently of its contribution to human interests, broadly conceived.)

What helps to obscure the point at issue is the terminology of "capital" itself. For this naturally suggests that what is going on is a technical dispute about the conditions of production. On this understanding of the matter, the proponents of "natural capital" are insisting that production has a natural base that cannot be run down beyond a certain point without putting future production in jeopardy, But the "fungibility" school are not committed to denying this. They insist on fungibility in principle; whether or not everything can be substituted for *in* practice is a matter of fact on which they do not have to be dogmatic. But if I am right the real dispute is at the level of principle, and is not perspicuously represented in terms of the properties of different kinds of capital.

"Capital" is a term that is inherently located within economic discourse. A mountain is, in the first instance, just a mountain. To bring it under the category of "capital"—of any kind—is to look at it in a certain light, as an economic asset of some description. But if I want to insist that we should leave future generations mountains that have not been strip-mined, quarried,

despoiled by skislopes, or otherwise tampered with to make somebody a profit, my point will be better made by eschewing talk about "capital" altogether.

Let us dismiss the hypothesis that X is want-satisfaction. What, then, is it? On the strength of the objection urged against want-satisfaction, it might appear that what should be maintained for future generations is their chance to live a good life as we conceive it. But even if "we" agreed on what that is (which is manifestly not the case), this would surely be an objectionable criterion for "what matters." For one of the defining characteristics of human beings is their ability to form their own conceptions of the good life. It would be presumptuous—and unfair—of us to pre-empt their choices in the future. (This is what is wrong with all utopias). We must respect the creativity of people in the future. What this suggests is that the requirement is to provide future generations with the opportunity to live good lives according to their conception of what constitutes a good life. This should surely include their being able to live good lives according to our conception but should leave other options open to them.

This thought leads me to the suggestion (for which I claim no originality) that X needs to be read as some notion of equal opportunity across generations. Unfortunately, however, the concept of equal opportunity is notoriously treacherous. Although, therefore, I do believe this to be the right answer, I have to confess that saying this is not doing a lot more than [to] set out an agenda for further study.

To summarize an extensive and in places technical literature with desperate brevity, there are two natural approaches to the measurement of opportunity, both of which rapidly turn out to be dead ends. One is [to] count opportunities. This has the obvious drawback that three options that are very similar (three apples of the same variety) will have to be said to give more opportunity than two more dissimilar options (an apple and an orange). But why is a greater range more valuable? A natural response might be that a choice between a number of apples is fine if you are an apple-lover but leaves you out of

luck otherwise, whereas a choice between an apple and an orange gives you two shots at getting something you like. We might be tempted to move from this to the conclusion that what makes a range of options valuable is the want-satisfying property of the most preferred item in it. From there it is a short step to identifying the value of a set of opportunities with the utility of the most preferred option in it.

Notice, however, that if we follow this path we shall have insensibly changed the subject. We began by asking for a measure of the amount of opportunity provided by a set of options. What we have now done is come up with a measure of the value of the opportunities provided by a set of options. Even if we concede that the value of the most preferred element is for certain purposes an appropriate measure of the value of a set of options, it is strikingly counterintuitive as a measure of the amount of opportunity offered by a set of options. Thus, for example, it entails that opportunity is not increased by adding any number of desirable options to a singleton choice set, so long as none of those added comes as far up the agent's preference scale as the one option with which we began.

Another way of seeing the inadequacy of this measure of opportunity is to note that it takes preferences as given. But the whole reason for our taking opportunities to be constitutive of X was that we could not accept utility based on given preferences as the criterion of X. If preferences in the future are such that plastic trees (the only kind, let us suppose, that are available) give as much satisfaction to people then as real trees do now to us, the amount of opportunity in the future is not diminished. Thus, if we embrace the measure of opportunity that equates it with the utility of the most preferred item in the choice set, we shall simply be back at utility as the criterion of X. All that will have happened is that it will have been relabelled "opportunity."

The notion of a range of opportunity cannot be reduced either to the sheer number of opportunities or to the utility of the most preferred option. We must define it in a way that tracks our reasons for wishing to make it our criterion of X in the first place. That means taking seriously the idea that conditions must be such as to sustain a range of possible conceptions of the good life. In the nature of the case, we cannot imagine in any detail what may be thought of [as] a good life in the future. But we can be quite confident that it will not include the violation of what I have called vital interests: adequate nutrition, clean drinking-water, clothing and housing, health care and education, for example. We can, in addition, at the very least leave open to people in the future the possibility of living in a world in which nature is not utterly subordinated to the pursuit of consumer satisfaction.

More work, as they say, needs to be done, but I cannot hope to undertake it within the bounds of this chapter. The most important contention that I have tried to establish in this section is that the concept of sustainability is irreducibly normative, so that disputes about its definition will inevitably reflect differing values. If, as I maintain, the root idea of sustainability is the conservation of what matters for future generations, its definition is inescapably bound up with one's conception of what matters.

4. SUSTAINABILITY AND INTERGENERATIONAL JUSTICE

Having said something about intergenerational justice and something about sustainability, it is time to bring them together. We can be encouraged about the prospect of a connection if I am correct in my contention that sustainability is as much a normative concept as is justice. And I believe that there is indeed a close connection. It may be recalled that the question that I formulated at the end of section I asked if sustainability was either a necessary or a sufficient condition of intergenerational justice. It appears that sustainability is at least a necessary condition of justice. For the principle of responsibility says that, unless people in the future can be held responsible for the situation that they find

themselves in, they should not be worse off than we are. And no generation can be held responsible for the state of the planet it inherits.

This suggests that we should at any rate leave people in the future with the possibility of not falling below our level. We cannot, of course, guarantee that our doing this will actually provide people in the further future with what we make possible. The next generation may, for all we can know, go on a gigantic spree and leave their successors relatively impoverished. The potential for sustaining the same level of X as we enjoy depends on each successive generation playing its part. All we can do is leave open the possibility, and that is what we are obliged by justice to do.

An objection sometimes raised to the notion that it would be unjust to let future generations fall below our standard (of whatever is to count as X) is that there is something arbitrary about taking the current position as the baseline. We are, it is argued, better off materially than our ancestors. Suppose we were to pursue policies that ran down resources to such an extent that people in [the] future would be no better off than our ancestors were a hundred years (or two hundred years) ago. Why would that be unjust? What is so special about the present as the point of comparison? In reply, it must be conceded that the expression "intergenerational justice" is potentially misleading—though perhaps it actually misleads only those who are determined to be misled. It is a sort of shorthand for "justice between the present generation and future generations." Because of time's arrow, we cannot do anything to make people in the past better off than they actually were, so it is absurd to say that our relations to them could be either just or unjust. "Ought" implies "can," and the only people whose fate we can affect are those living now and in the future. Taking the present as our reference point is arbitrary only in some cosmic sense in which it might be said to be arbitrary that now is now and not some other time. It is important, however, to understand that "now" means "now" in the timeless sense, not "1998."...Just as "here" does

not mean my flat (though that is where I am as I write this) so in the sentence "We start from now" the meaning of "now" is not rigidly designated.

We now have to face a question of interpretation so far left aside. This is: How are we to deal with population size? On one quite natural interpretation of the concept of sustainability, the X whose value is to be maintained is to be defined over individuals. The demands of justice will then be more stringent the larger we predict the future population to be. Suppose we were simply to extrapolate into the indefinite future growth rates of the order of those seen in past decades. On the hypothesis that numbers double every forty years or so, we shall have a world population after two centuries of around a hundred and fifty billion and in a further two centuries a population of five thousand billion. If the increase were spread evenly round the world, this would imply a population for the UK more than ten times the size of the whole current world population.

It is surely obvious that no degree of self-immiseration that those currently alive could engage in would be capable of providing the possibility of an equal level of X per head even that far inside the future. This would be so on any remotely plausible definition of X. (Indeed, we can be certain that some cataclysm would have occurred long before these numbers were reached.) But even far more modest increases in population would make it impossible to maintain X, if X is taken to include the preservation of so-called "natural capital."

This is worth emphasizing because the "cornucopian" school of optimists about population, such as Julian Simon, cite in support of their ideas the alleged failures of early neo-Malthusians (from the mid-nineteenth century onward) to predict correctly the course of events. But I believe that the pessimists have already been proved right on a central point: the deleterious impact on the quality of life of sheer numbers. Thus, John Stuart Mill's forebodings a century and a half ago (in 1848 to be precise) have, it seems to me, proved quite uncannily prescient. All that he feared has already in large measure come to

pass, and every bit of future population increase will make things that much worse.

Mill was quite prepared to grant the "cornucopian" premiss that material conditions might be able to keep up with a greatly expanded population (or even more than keep up with it). But he still insisted that the population increase should be regretted. "A population may be crowded, though all be amply supplied with food and raiment...A world from which solitude is extirpated, is a very poor ideal...Nor is there much satisfaction in contemplating the world with nothing left to the spontaneous activity of nature; with every rood of land brought into cultivation, which is capable of growing food for human beings; every flowery waste or natural pasture ploughed up, all quadrupeds or birds which are not domesticated for man's use exterminated as his rivals for food, every hedgerow or superfluous tree rooted out, and scarcely a place left where a wild shrub or flower could grow without being eradicated as a weed in the name of improved agriculture."[3]

Treating future population as parametric is in effect assuming it to be beyond human control. But any such assumption is obviously false. I suggest, therefore, that the size of future population should be brought within the scope of the principle of responsibility. We must define intergenerational justice on the assumption that "the increase of mankind shall be under the guidance of judicious foresight," as Mill put it.[4] If future people choose to let population increase, or by default permit it to increase, that is to be at their own cost. There is no reason in justice for our having any obligation to accommodate their profligacy. Concretely, then, the conception of sustainability that makes it appropriate as a necessary condition of intergenerational justice may be formulated as follows: Sustainability requires at any point in time that the value of some X per head of population should be capable of being maintained into the indefinite future, on the assumption that the size of the future population is no greater than the size of the present population.

It is worth emphasizing again that we always start from now, and ask what sustainability requires. The question is: What amount of X could be maintained into the indefinite future, given things as they are now, on the assumption that future population will be the same then as now? The way in which "now" is always moving would not matter if (a) the demands of sustainability were correctly assessed in 1998; (b) sustainability were achieved in 1998 and maintained thereafter; and (c) the assumption of stable population control were in fact accurate. If all these conditions were met, we could substitute "1998" for "now," but not otherwise.

We know that stabilization of population is perfectly possible as a result of voluntary choices made by individuals because a number of Western countries have already arrived at the position at which the (non-immigrant) population is only barely replacing itself, if that. Although they stumbled into it without any particular foresight, the formula is now known and can be applied elsewhere. Women have to be educated and to have a possibility of pursuing rewarding occupations outside the home while at the same time compulsory full-time education and stringent child-labour laws make children an economic burden rather than a benefit.

Unfortunately, however, many countries have such a large proportion of their population below the age of fifteen that their numbers would double before stabilizing even if every female now alive had only two children. Stabilizing population at its current level in these countries can be achieved only if women have only one child. So long as a policy restricting women to one child is operated consistently across the board, it does not contravene any principle of intragenerational justice, and is a requirement of intragenerational justice. Combined, as it has been in China, with a focus on medical care and education for children, there can be no question that it offers the next generation the best chance of living satisfactory lives, and removes a huge burden on future generations.

At this point, however, we must expect the response, already anticipated in general terms, that whether or not this is just it simply conflicts too strongly with religious objections to contraception

and abortion and to powerful pronatalist norms, especially in many parts of the world where great importance is attached to having a male heir. If we are impressed by this, we shall have to say that justice demands more of people than they can reasonably be expected to perform. But what follows from that? At this point, it seems to me unavoidable to enter into the question that I have so far left on one side: the concrete implications of any criterion of sustainability. Suppose we believed that it would be fairly easy to provide the conditions in which X (e.g. some conception of equal opportunity) could be maintained into the indefinite future for a population twice the existing one. We might then treat as parametric the predicted doubling of world population and redefine sustainability accordingly. But my own conjecture is that the criterion of sustainability already proposed is extremely stringent, and that there is little chance of its demands being met. If I am right about this, all we can do is get as close to that as we can, which means doing everything possible to reduce population growth as well as everything possible to conserve resources and reduce depletion.

What then about the future? Suppose that the demographers' (relatively optimistic) projection for world population is correct, so that it stabilizes some time in the next century at double its current size. If we stick to the proposition that intragenerational justice is always a problem for the current generation (because they are the only people in a position to do anything about it), the implication is that sustainability should be redefined by each generation as the indefinite continuation of the level of X over the existing population, whatever it is. Whether people in the past have behaved justly or not is irrelevant. But if I am right in thinking that we are going to fall short of maintaining sustainability even on the basis of the continuation of current population size, it seems highly unlikely that people in the future will achieve it on the basis of a population twice as large. The only ray of light is that getting from a stable population to a gently declining one would not be difficult (nothing like as difficult as stabilizing a rapidly expanding

population), and that the power of compound interest means that even a gradual decline in numbers would suffice to bring world population back well below current levels over a matter of a few centuries.

My conclusion, after this vertiginous speculation, is that we would be doing very well to meet the criterion of sustainability that I originally proposed. The more we fail, and the more that world population is not checked in coming decades, the worse things will be in the future and the smaller the population at which it will be possible to maintain tolerable living conditions. Perhaps the right way to look at the matter is to think of population and resources (in the largest sense) as the two variables that enter into sustainability: we might then say that sustainability is a function of both. Realistically, any given generation can make only a limited impact on either. But what can at least then be said is that if some generation is failing to meet the condition of sustainability (defined in the standard way over a fixed population), it can at least be more just than otherwise towards its successors by ensuring that the dwindling resources will have to spread around over fewer people.

Interpreted on some such lines as these, sustainability is, I suggest, adequate as a necessary condition of intergenerational justice. Is it also a sufficient condition? I feel strongly inclined to say that it is: if we were to satisfy it, we would be doing very well, and it is hard to see that we could reasonably be expected to do more. My only hesitation arises from the application of the vital interests. (I noted in section 2 that this needed later discussion.) Obviously, if we give the principle of vital interests priority over the principle of responsibility, we are liable to be back at a version of the absurd idea that we are obliged to immiserate ourselves to a level capable of sustaining a hugely larger population if we predict there will be one. For if we predict an enormously greater number of people in the future, meeting their vital interests trumps any objective we might have. I have not specified priority relations among the principles, and I do not think this can be done across the board. The principles are guides to thinking, not a piece of machinery that can

be cranked to grind out conclusions. However, in this case it seems to me that giving the principle of vital interests priority produces such absurd results that this cannot possibly be the right thing to do.

Even if we make the principle of vital interests subordinate to the principle of responsibility, there is still a feature of the principle of vital interests that is worth attention. So far "generations" have been treated as collective entities: the question has been posed as one of justice between the present generation as a whole and future generations as wholes. But the principle of vital interests forces us to focus on the fates of individuals. Suppose we leave future generations as collectivities with "enough" between them to satisfy the criterion of sustainability, but it is distributed in such a way that the vital interests of many will predictably fail to be met? Does this possibility suggest that the criterion of sustainability has to be supplemented in order to count as a sufficient condition of intergenerational justice?

What I think it shows is that the distinction between intergenerational and intragenerational justice cannot be made absolute. I pointed out in section 1 that some things that would be wrong in relation to people in the future (e.g. fighting a nuclear war) would in the first instance be wrong among those alive at the time. Similarly, the primary reason for our being able to predict that the vital interests of many people in the world will not be met in the future is that they are not being met in the present. Formally, I suggest we have to say that maldistribution in the future is intragenerational injustice in the future. But we must recognize that intragenerational injustice in the future is the almost inevitable consequence of intragenerational injustice in the present.

5. BEYOND JUSTICE

If the current generation meets the demands of justice, is that enough? In the broad sense of justice, we would not be doing wrong in relation to human beings if we met the demands of justice. But we can (as I

said in section 1) behave wrongly in relation to non-human animals even though this does not fall within the scope of justice. If we factor this in, what difference does it make? As far as I can see, its main effect is to reinforce the importance of keeping the lid on population, since the pressure on the habitats of the remaining wild non-human animals are already being encroached on at an alarming rate as a consequence of the growth of population that has already occurred.

The remaining question is the one that divides environmentalists into those for whom the significance of the environment lies solely in its contribution to human (or if you like animal) welfare from those for whom the environment has some significance beyond that. (Perhaps talking about "the environment" is itself prejudicial since it suggests something in the background to another thing that is more important. But I take it that the distinction is familiar enough in a variety of descriptions.) I have to confess that I cannot quite decide what I think about this question because I find it hard to focus on the question when it is put, as it often is, as one about the "independent value of nature." Let me explain.

In *Principia Ethica*, G. E. Moore sought to discredit Sidgwick's claim that nothing can be said to be good "out of relation to human existence, or at least to some consciousness or feeling." To this end, he asked his reader to consider the following case. Let us imagine one world exceedingly beautiful. Imagine it as beautiful as you can; put into it whatever on this earth you most admire—mountains, rivers, the sea, trees, and sunsets, stars and moon. Imagine these all combined in the most exquisite proportions so that no one thing jars against another but each contributes to increase the beauty of the whole. And then imagine the ugliest world you can possibly conceive. Imagine it simply one heap of filth, containing everything that is most disgusting to us, for whatever reason, and the whole, as far as may be, without one redeeming feature. Such a pair of worlds we are entitled to compare: they fall within Prof. Sidgwick's meaning, and the comparison is highly relevant to it. The only thing we are not entitled to imagine is that any human being ever has or ever, by any possibility, can, live in either, can ever see and enjoy the beauty of the one or hate the foulness of the other. Well, even so, supposing them quite apart from any possible contemplation by human beings; still, is it irrational to hold that it is better that the beautiful world should exist, than the one that is ugly?[5]

It is surely obvious that the question is loaded, because the two worlds are already unavoidably being visited by us, at least in imagination. It requires a self-conscious effort to avoid being affected by that. But if I make that effort conscientiously, I have to say that the whole question strikes me as ridiculous. In what possible sense could the universe be a better or a worse place on one supposition rather than the other? It seems to me an abuse of our language to assume that the word "good" still has application when applied to such a context.

If adherence to the "deep ecological" or "dark green" position entails giving Moore the answer he wanted about the two worlds, I have to be counted out. But I wonder if all (or even many) of those who wish to endorse such a position feel thereby committed to attaching an intrinsic value to nature in the sense suggested by Moore. And, quite apart from that biographical question, there is the philosophical question: is there any way of being "dark green" that does not entail being committed to Moore's preferred answer about the two worlds?

I am inclined to think that there is an attitude (which I share) that is distinguishable from the first position but is perhaps misleadingly expressed in terms of the intrinsic value of nature. This is that it is inappropriate—cosmically unfitting, in some sense—[to] regard nature as nothing more than something to be exploited for the benefit of human beings—or other sentient creatures, if it comes to that. There is an obvious sense in which this is still somehow human-centred, because it is about the right way for human beings to think about nature. But the content of that thought could be expressed by talking about the intrinsic value of nature.

It is important to observe that what I am saying here is not to be equated with the kind of environmental utilitarianism put forward by Robert Goodin in his *Green Political Theory*. According to this, we do as a matter of fact care about unspoilt nature—for example, even the most carefully restored site of open-cast mining is "not the same" as the original, any more than a perfect copy of a statue is "the same" as the original. A sophisticated utilitarianism will therefore take our concerns about nature into account and set more stringent limits on the exploitation of the environment than would be set by our merely regarding the environment as a factor of production. This enables us to press "green" concerns but still within a framework that makes human interests the measure of all things.

What I am saying is quite different from this. For it is a purely contingent matter whether or not people have the attitude to nature attributed to them by Goodin or, if they do, how far it weighs in their utility function compared with, say, cheap hamburgers from the cattle raised on pasture created from the ravaged Brazilian rain forest. The view that I am proposing says bluntly that people behave wrongly if they act out of a wrong attitude to nature. Although this is in a sense a human-centred proposition, it cannot be captured in any utilitarian calculus, however extensive its conception of human well-being.

6. CONCLUSION

I want to conclude by saying that I can understand and indeed sympathize with the impatience that will undoubtedly be felt by any environmental activist into whose hands this might fall. (Jonathon Porritt eloquently expressed such sentiments—and not only in relation to my contribution—during the final session of the Keele seminars on social justice and sustainability.) What the activist wants is ammunition that can be used in the fight for greater ecological awareness and responsibility. Fine-drawn analyses of sustainability such as those offered here are hardly the stuff to give the troops. But is it reasonable to expect them to be?

Let me make what may at first sight seem an eccentric suggestion. This is that it is not terribly difficult to know what needs to be done, though it is of course immensely difficult to get the relevant actors (governmental and other) to do it. I do not deny that there are large areas of scientific uncertainty, and probably always will be (e.g. about global warming), since the interacting processes involved are so complex. But what I am claiming is that virtually everybody who has made a serious study of the situation and whose objectivity is not compromised by either religious beliefs or being in the pay of some multinational corporation has reached the conclusion that the most elementary concern for people in the future demands big changes in the way we do things. These could start with the implementation by all signatories of what was agreed on at the Rio Conference.

Moreover, whatever is actually going to get done in, say, the next decade, to move towards a sustainable balance of population and resources is going to be so pathetically inadequate that it really does not matter how far it falls short. We know the direction in which change is required, and we know that there is absolutely no risk that we shall find ourselves doing more than required. It really does not make any practical difference whether we think a certain given effort represents 10 per cent of what needs to be done, or whether we think it is as much as 20 per cent. Either way, we have good reason to push for more. If I am right about this, it explains the feeling among practitioners that philosophical analyses have little relevance to their concerns. For whether we make the demands of justice more or less stringent, it is going to demand more than is likely to get done in the foreseeable future. What then is the use of pursuing these questions?

One obvious answer is that as political philosophers we are concerned to discover the truth, and

that is an adequate justification for our work. The agenda of a scholarly discipline has its own integrity, which is worthy of respect. Distributive justice among contemporaries and within the boundaries of a state has been at the centre of the dramatic revival of political philosophy in the last quarter century. Extending the inquiry into the nature of distributive justice beyond these limits is a natural and inevitable development. But I think that there is also something to offer to those who are not interested in pursuing these questions for their own sake. It is surely at least something to be able to assure those who spend their days trying to gain support for measures intended to improve the prospects of future generations that such measures do not represent optional benevolence on our part but are demanded by elementary considerations of justice. What I have aimed to do here is show that the application of ideas about justice that are quite familiar in other contexts have radical implications when applied to intergenerational justice, and that there is no reason why they should not be.

NOTES

1. In a paper presented to a seminar, Andrew Dobson wrote of 'the privileging of human welfare over justice to nature'. But perhaps this was not intended to carry a lot of theoretical freight ('Sustainabilities: An Analysis and a Typology', paper presented to the Social Justice and Sustainability Seminars, Keele University, UK, (1996*b*), fo. 11). See also A. Dobson, *Justice and the Environment Conceptions of Environmental Sustainability and Dimensions of Social Justice* (Oxford: Oxford University Press, 1998).

2. A. de-Shalit, *Why Posterity Matters: Environmental Politics and Future Generations* (London: Routledge, 1995).

3. J. S. Mill, *Principles of Political Economy*, ed. Donald Winch (Harmondsworth, Penguin Books, 1970 [1848]), Book IV, ch. 5, 115–16.

4. Ibid. 117.

5. Ibid. 83–4.

SHEILA FOSTER AND LUKE COLE

Environmental Racism

Beyond the Distributive Paradigm

The pattern of siting a disproportionate number of waste facilities in places like Chester, established empirically by national and regional studies, has provided substance to claims of environmental racism. But, as the Chester case study illustrates, the empirical studies and their important conclusions are part of a much larger picture. Chester is not unique as [a] magnet for toxic waste facilities; it shares a social, political, and economic history with other communities that are experiencing a proliferation of unwanted toxic waste sites. Like them, it is a former industrial town now populated by low-income people of color after the flight of businesses and its white, middle-class population. Distributional outcomes are thus produced by, and within, an institutional context and a particular social structure. To understand fully the phenomenon of environmental racism, one must understand the structural processes that underlie the well-documented distributive outcomes. In this sense, unequal distribution is not the sine qua non of environmental racism. Instead, it is a crucial entry point for exploring the social and institutional processes underlying distributional patterns.

THE UNEQUAL DISTRIBUTION OF ENVIRONMENTAL HAZARDS

Since the 1960s, researchers have analyzed the distribution of numerous environmental hazards: garbage dumps, air pollution, lead poisoning, toxic waste production and disposal, pesticide poisoning, noise pollution, occupational hazards, and rat bites. Their overwhelming conclusion is that these environmental hazards are inequitably distributed by income or race. In studies that looked at distribution of these hazards by income *and* race, race was most often found to be the better predictor of exposure to environmental dangers. Later studies have in large part confirmed these conclusions.

Because waste facility siting is the focus of this book, our starting point is the seminal study that documents disproportionate distribution of toxic waste sites on a national level. The 1987 study *Toxic Waste and Race in the United States*, performed by the United Church of Christ's Commission for Racial Justice (CRJ), measured the demographic patterns associated with commercial hazardous waste facilities and uncontrolled toxic sites.[1] The CRJ study found that race was the most significant variable in determining the location of commercial hazardous waste facilities; communities with the greatest number of commercial hazardous waste facilities had the highest percentage of nonwhite residents. The CRJ's study of uncontrolled waste sites produced similar findings: three out of every five African American and Latino residents lived in communities with uncontrolled toxic waste sites. Furthermore, African Americans were heavily overrepresented in the populations of metropolitan areas with the largest number of such sites.[2]

More recent national studies, with a handful of exceptions, continue to document the persistence of racial disparities in the location of waste facilities; some studies report that results vary by ethnic group.[3] Most notably, in 1994, the CRJ updated its 1987 study. Based on its assessment of 530 commercial hazardous waste sites, the CRJ found even greater racial disparities in the demographics of people who live around such facilities. In particular, it found that from 1980 to 1993 the concentration of people of color (defined as the total population less non-Hispanic whites) in all zip codes with toxic waste sites increased from 25 percent to 31 percent. Similarly, in 1993, as in 1980, the percentage of people of color in a community increased as commercial hazardous waste management activity increased. The 1994 CRJ study found the increase statistically significant and concluded that there was little probability that the increase could be attributed to merely random fluctuation.[4] The CRJ was careful to note that the study had measured only the outcomes of environmental hazard distribution and did not determine "the root causes of this pattern."[5] Regardless of the causes, the report advocates toxic use reduction as a solution to disproportionate environmental impacts.

Researchers at the Social and Demographic Research Institute (SADRI) of the University of Massachusetts challenged the findings of the 1987 CRJ study. The SADRI study found that there was *not* a statistically significant pattern of racial or ethnic disparity in the distribution of commercial hazardous waste sites.[6] Though the SADRI study analyzed data similar to those used in the recent CRJ study, its methodology was significantly different. For example, the SADRI study used census tracts from 1980 and 1990, instead of zip codes, as the geographic unit of analysis. The SADRI researchers also used data from only metropolitan or rural counties, not from the entire United States, as their comparison group (nonhost tracts), possibly understating the relationship among race, ethnicity, and siting choices.[7] Moreover, the study looked only at African American and Latino populations and did not measure the proximity of other racial groups, such as Asians and Native Americans, to existing toxic waste sites. Hence, the researchers' conclusions leave out a not-insignificant percentage of the people of color population in the United States and possibly understate racial and ethnic disparities.

The most recent study, by Professor Vicki Been, supports the conclusions of both the 1987 and the 1994 CRJ studies, though it uses census tract data as in the SADRI study.[8] Like the previous studies, Been measured the location of commercial hazardous waste facilities and the demographics of people who live near those facilities. In particular, Been set out to analyze how the demographics of neighborhoods that host toxic waste facilities have changed over time. To do this, she used census data from the past three decades (1970, 1980, and 1990). Unlike the researchers in the SADRI study, who used a limited pool of nonhost tracts, Been compared the demographics of host tracts to those of *all* nonhost tracts. However, similar to that in the SADRI study, her analysis seems to have included only disparities that involved African Americans and Latinos, not those that involved members of other racial groups as defined by the census, such as Native Americans and Asians.

Been's study found that toxic waste sites were disproportionately located near African American and Latino populations. In particular, Been's analysis demonstrated that the percentage of African Americans or Latinos in a census tract in 1990 is a significant predictor of whether or not that tract hosted a toxic waste facility. Been attributed the current inequitable distribution of toxic waste sites in African American neighborhoods to the existence of facilities sited before 1970. On the other hand, she attributed the current inequitable distribution of toxic waste sites in Latino neighborhoods to facilities that were sited after 1970. As to class disparities, Been's study indicated that high poverty rates were "negatively correlated" with the location of toxic waste facilities. Instead, the study concluded, it was working-class and lower-middle-income neighborhoods that contained a disproportionate share of facilities. The study did not measure the effect of the intersection of race and class (e.g., poor African American neighborhoods) on the probability that the tract hosts a facility.

Studies also document the government's unequal enforcement of environmental laws in the waste siting context. A 1992 study by the *National Law Journal* confirmed what environmental justice activists have known for years, that people of color are not protected as vigorously by enforcement of environmental laws as whites. The *National Law*

Journal study found that "[t]here is a racial divide in the way the U.S. government cleans up toxic waste sites and punishes polluters. White communities see faster action, better results and stiffer penalties than communities where blacks, Hispanics and other minorities live. This unequal protection often occurs whether the community is wealthy or poor."[9] The *Journal*'s study found that penalties applied under hazardous waste laws at sites in white communities were about 500 percent higher than were penalties applied at similar sites in communities of color; that for all violations of pollution laws, penalties in white communities were about 46 percent higher than in communities of color; and that under Superfund, the law designed to clean up toxic sites, it took communities of color 20 percent longer to be listed as priority clean-up sites than white communities. The disproportionately greater exposure in communities of color to environmental hazards is undoubtedly exacerbated by unequal enforcement of environmental laws in such communities.

Taken together, the national studies conducted to date provide evidence that people of color bear a disproportionate burden of environmental hazards, particularly toxic waste sites. Numerous local studies, with some exceptions, have, on the basis of their assessment of particular cities, counties or regions, similarly concluded that racial disparities exist in the location of toxic waste facilities. Though researchers will continue to study the distribution of environmental hazards, including toxic waste sites, there is already ample evidence to warrant a closer look at the factors that might lead to the outcomes thus far documented.

THE PROBLEM OF CAUSATION: NAMING THE OUTCOMES AS RACISM

As with most statistical research, studies that chart the disproportionate distribution of waste facilities simply establish *correlations*, not *causation*.

Some commentators therefore question whether the maldistribution of environmental hazards is appropriately attributed to racism or other injustice or to a more benign explanation. Among the alternative explanations offered to explain the racial disparities are (1) that the social status or lifestyle choices of certain racial and ethnic groups result in maldistribution and (2) that maldistribution is a result of the operation of the "free market." What both explanations have in common is their description of existing social practices and social structure as a cause of current distributions. By accepting the existing social structure and practices as the "baseline" for causal analysis, these explanations tend to obscure the injustice of current distributions and dangerously suggest that the inequitable outcomes are a natural and inevitable feature of social and economic life.[10]

"Lifestyle" as Causation

The first explanation, what we call the "lifestyle" explanation, invokes a description of a social situation or status as the causal element explaining the distribution of hazardous wastes and other toxics. The United States Environmental Protection Agency's Environmental Equity Workgroup, for example, after reviewing much of the evidence then available on the disproportionate impact of environmental hazards on people of color, concluded in 1992 that a "person's activity" is the main determinant of how much environmental exposure she bears.[11] The Workgroup further concluded that racially disparate environmental hazard exposure results from the fact that "a large proportion of racial minorities reside in metropolitan areas" and "are more likely to live near a commercial or uncontrolled waste site," that higher levels of certain pesticides in Latinos results from the fact that "racial and ethnic minorities comprise the majority of the documented and undocumented farm work force," and that racial disparities in exposure to contaminated fish result from the fact that some racial groups "consume more fish than the average population."

There is no doubt that certain groups of people, such as recent immigrants with poor English language skills, are concentrated in the most dangerous sectors of our workforce, agriculture and heavy industry. These same people are, not surprisingly, more likely than others to have multiple exposures to environmental dangers; they face more severe hazards on the job, in the home, in the air they breathe, in the water they drink, in the food they eat. Nor is there any dispute that many poor people and people of color are relegated to urban areas; as we explain later, their residential choices are limited by their poverty and by various forms of discrimination. Moreover, while they live with the greatest dangers, poor people and people of color have the least access to health care and often can not get it at all.[12]

That the current social location of certain people overexposes them to contaminated environments raises, rather than answers, important questions about the injustice that underlies environmental distributions. *Why* are African Americans disproportionately segregated in cities and thus overexposed to a variety of pollutants? *Why* are farm-workers disproportionately poor and Latino? *Why* do current environmental laws leave farm-workers unprotected? Why are certain racial groups forced to rely on subsistence fishing or on poisoned fish stocks? Without a further causal analysis of the social processes that constitute the current situatedness of various groups, the tautological "lifestyle" explanation amounts to little more than "blaming the victim."[13] The "lifestyle" approach plays an important social role in naturalizing the unequal distribution of environmental hazards, however, by describing disproportionate exposure as a choice those exposed have made, a decision that could, presumably, be changed. It allows the observer to acknowledge the unequal environmental protection of certain groups and, at the same time, to keep a safe distance from the social context and structural dynamics that produce those outcomes. It also relieves the observer of any culpability for, or responsibility for changing, the unjust situation.

"Market Dynamics" as Causation

The second explanation—"market dynamics"—is by far the most common, and important, causation objection to the empirical evidence of disproportionate impact. Market dynamics adherents ask the question "Which came first, the environmental hazard or the racial/class makeup of the neighborhood?" The suspicion underlying this question is that researchers have failed to compare the demographics of the neighborhoods at the time the facilities were sited and at the time measured by the study. This failure "leaves open the possibility that [the facilities] were not disparately sited in poor and minority neighborhoods" but that the "dynamics of the housing and job markets" led people of color and the poor to "come to the nuisance"—for example, to move to areas that surround waste facilities because those neighborhoods offered the cheapest available housing.[14] A waste facility, for instance, may "cause those who can afford to move to become dissatisfied and leave the neighborhood," or it may "decrease the value of the neighborhood's property, making the housing more available to lower income households and less attractive to higher income households."[15]

Again, the explanation is volitional: people, as rational economic actors, are *choosing* to live in neighborhoods that host dangerous facilities.[16] There is inconclusive empirical support to date for the "market dynamics" explanation for racial or economic disparities in the distribution of hazardous waste facilities.[17] Nevertheless, the market dynamics explanation is continually invoked to account for the racial disparities in environmental hazard distribution, as an alternative to the assumption that racially biased practices account for the disparities. As one commentator sums up, "by failing to address how [facilities] have affected the demographics of their host communities, the current research has ignored the possibility that the correlation between the location of [facilities] and the socio-economic characteristics of neighborhoods may be a function of aspects of our *free market* system."[18] The implications of this alternative causal account is that where market dynamics produce current distributions, this fact renders the outcomes somehow more benign. This implication stands on its own terms, however, only if the market is unaffected by racial discrimination and other unjust processes.

"Free market" explanations, however, are notoriously incomplete. As others have persuasively argued, markets are social institutions shaped by various levels of state and private control. Choices and preferences made in the "market" domain are, as Cass Sunstein explains, "endogenous rather than exogenous"—a function of current information, consumption patterns, existing legal rules, social norms, and culture.[19] For instance, the historical and present reality of race discrimination in the housing market inevitably affects individual preferences and mobility in the housing arena. Given this history and present reality, the "free" nature of market choices must be called into question.

Proponents of the "market dynamics" theory of hazardous waste distribution do acknowledge the influence of well-documented housing discrimination on individual preferences and mobility in the market. Such racial discrimination in the sale and rental of housing, one proponent notes, "relegates people of color (especially African Americans) to the least desirable neighborhoods, regardless of their income level."[20] Moreover, even after a neighborhood becomes predominantly composed of people of color, market dynamics proponents recognize that "racial discrimination in the promulgation and enforcement of zoning and environmental protection laws, the provision of municipal services, and the lending practices of banks, may cause neighborhood quality to decline further" and that the "additional decline . . . will induce those who can leave the neighborhood—the least poor and those least subject to discrimination—to do so."[21] Nevertheless, by continuing to describe the forces that underlie

racially disparate environmental distributions as "free market" dynamics, the explanation tends to subsume social practices of racial discrimination into rational economic processes and choices. The collapse of social practices of racial discrimination into economic processes subtly expands the domain of the "free market" to include, and hence to obscure, racially biased social practices.

The "market dynamics" explanation, like the "lifestyle" explanation, thus rests on a descriptive, rather than a normative, causal account of the racial disparities in environmental justice research. It is important not to confuse the two accounts. Undoubtedly the dynamics of the housing market, broadly construed to include discriminatory practices, can theoretically explain some of the racially disparate outcomes in environmental hazard distribution. As Regina Austin and Michael Schill have pointed out, given the combination of poverty and racially discriminatory practices, there might be a number of developmental patterns that would result in poor people of color either moving to, or being trapped in, neighborhoods with a disproportionate number of hazardous waste sites.[22] For instance, in one pattern, communities where poor people of color now live may have originally been homes to whites who "worked in the facilities that generate toxic emissions." In those communities, Austin and Schill explain, the housing and industry may have "sprang up roughly simultaneously," and whites may have "vacated the housing (but not necessarily the jobs) for better shelter as their socioeconomic status improved." In turn, poorer Latinos and African Americans "who enjoy much less residential mobility" may have taken their place. In another pattern, housing for African Americans and Latinos may have been built in the vicinity of existing industrial operations because "the land was cheap and the people were poor." In still another pattern, sources of toxic pollution may have been placed in existing minority communities. Determining the various factors that contribute to the distributive outcomes is indeed an important epistemological inquiry.

The "chicken-or-egg" question posed by commentators does not, however, answer the more fundamental inquiry posed by environmental justice research. The question underlying environmental justice research is normative; it asks, "What do we mean when we call an outcome racist or evidence of injustice?" The chicken-or-egg inquiry posed by these commentators is empirical; it asks, "Which came first, the waste facilities or the poor people of color?" Answering the second question does not necessarily answer the first. That is, the normative claim embedded in environmental justice research is not answered simply by a descriptive analysis of the forces that underlie a particular distributional pattern. Uncovering the patterns and processes underlying the distributive outcomes is an important first step; a normative evaluation of these patterns and processes is the next crucial step.

The post-siting market dynamics analysis employed is certainly useful in determining whether it is more descriptively correct to attribute environmental disparities to one set of social and/or economic processes than to another. However, even if one could establish that "market dynamics," and not the siting process itself, produce racially disparate outcomes, this would not tell us whether such market forces are just or illicit. Similarly, even if "lifestyle" factors accurately describe the forces that underlie exposure to a particular environmental hazard, further analysis is needed to evaluate whether those forces themselves are attributable to unjust social practices or norms or to some other benign explanation.

STRUCTURAL RACISM VERSUS JUDICIALLY CONSTRUCTED "RACISM"

As Gerald Torres reminds us, in order to make sense of the term "environmental racism," one "must have a clear idea of what it means to call a particular activity racist."[23] Similarly, in order to determine whether

the processes underlying particular distributions are racist, we must be clear on what that term means. On the one hand, as Torres explains, "the term racism draws its contemporary moral strength by being clearly identified with the history of the structural oppression of African Americans and other people of color in this society." On the other hand, judicial constructions of racism have severely narrowed the concept in recent years. The disparate impact of governmental or private action on a historically oppressed group, such as African Americans, is no longer sufficient to establish an actionable claim of race discrimination under the U.S. Constitution and most civil rights laws. Since 1976, the U.S. Supreme Court has construed "race discrimination" to mean intentional or purposeful conduct on the basis of race, or at least some consciousness of race as a factor motivating conduct.[24] This construction requires that the intent be attached to an individual actor. Hence, labeling the outcomes that correlate race and exposure to environmental hazards as "racist" invites the demand for evidence of an overt race-conscious impetus and a "single bad actor."[25]

Not surprisingly, claims of environmental racism have not fit into the existing judicial construction of racism. The invariable judicial response has been to reject environmental racism claims for failure to prove the requisite discriminatory intent attached to an identifiable perpetrator, notwithstanding demonstrations of disparate impact and discriminatory outcomes. For example, in *R.I.S.E., Inc. v. Kay*, a federal district court found no discrimination in the siting of a landfill in a predominantly African American area of a county despite evidence that, during the past twenty years, the County Board of Supervisors had approved three other landfills that were placed within one mile of neighborhoods that were respectively 100 percent, 95 percent, and 100 percent African American.[26] The proposed landfill in *R.I.S.E.* would have been placed within half a mile of a population that was 64 percent African American and 36 percent white. The population of the County was 50 percent African American and

50 percent white. Moreover, in the one instance where the County Board of Supervisors had opposed a landfill in the County, the surrounding community was predominantly white.

The *R.I.S.E.* court reasoned that, although the placement of the proposed facility would have a disproportionate impact on African American residents, "the Equal Protection Clause does not impose an affirmative duty to equalize the impact of official decisions on different racial groups." Instead, the clause "merely prohibits government officials from intentionally discriminating on the basis of race." The plaintiffs, in spite of the facts of the case, failed to meet their burden of proving intentional discrimination. The Court accepted, instead, the County's facially neutral explanation that it was motivated not by racial bias but by other factors. Despite the fact that residents opposed the facility, the Court found that the County Board had been motivated by the economic, environmental, and cultural needs of the African American community.[27]

This prevailing understanding of "racism," molded by judicial constructions, is myopic in its failure to accommodate for the fact that the nature of racism has become appreciably more subtle and structural. Historically, disparate racial treatment and impacts were easily traceable to overt, racially motivated actions. However, partly as a result of laws that punish and forbid such overt behavior, decision makers rarely openly and intentionally seek a discriminatory outcome. As Charles Lawrence argues, requiring conscious intent before characterizing an outcome as racist ignores "the fact that decisions about racial matters are influenced in large part by factors that can be characterized as neither intentional—in the sense that certain outcomes are self-consciously sought—nor unintentional—in the sense that outcomes are random, fortuitous, and uninfluenced by the decision maker's beliefs, desires and wishes."[28] Understanding racism thus requires a broader analysis, beyond legal understandings of this complex social phenomenon.

Judicial notions of "racism" may be necessary for various jurisprudential reasons—for instance, an intent requirement arguably reinforces the separation of powers between courts and political branches by making it difficult for courts to intervene in more democratic processes.[29] However, our definitions of racism and injustice need not be confined to juridical notions. As we have written elsewhere, and as illustrated by the Chester case study, the struggle for environmental justice is primarily a political and economic struggle, with law one facet of that struggle.[30] Understanding environmental racism thus requires a conceptual framework that (1) retains a structural view of economic and social forces as they influence discriminatory outcomes, (2) isolates the dynamics within environmental decision-making processes that further contribute to such outcomes, and (3) normatively evaluates social forces and environmental decision-making processes which contribute to disparities in environmental hazard distribution.[31]

THE SOCIAL STRUCTURE OF ENVIRONMENTAL RACISM: THE ROLE OF RACE AND SPACE

Let us assume that the current physical distribution of hazardous waste facilities could be attributed to the location of older facilities in neighborhoods that subsequently became populated by poor people of color—that "market dynamics" produced the racially disparate outcomes found in some communities. Even accepting that the siting process is not responsible for all racially disparate outcomes in environmental hazard distribution and that instead the demographics of a given community with a waste facility have changed over time, it is not easy to dismiss the notion that racism or injustice produced the results. If existing racially discriminatory processes in the housing market, for example, contribute to the distribution of environmental hazards, or of people of color, then it is entirely appropriate to call such outcomes unjust, and even racist.[32] In this sense, "environmental racism" is not a separate phenomenon at all. Environmental outcomes are instead

a manifestation of racially discriminatory practices that continue to exist in our society.

The inequitable distribution of environmental hazards, particularly commercial waste facilities, can be traced historically to the patterns of residential segregation and its resulting structural inequalities. Spatial segregation and isolation are key features of racial inequality in our society. Racial segregation, in turn, shapes how groups are viewed and what type of resources they get. This spatial inequality creates a vicious, self-perpetuating circle of causation, resulting in uniquely disadvantaged communities. A brief look at the history of spatial segregation confirms that the construction of racial space, and its mechanisms, have had profound consequences in the distribution of social goods. Given this history, it is not difficult to conclude that the physical distribution of hazardous waste facilities is linked to the historical organization of racially identified space and its precipitating social processes and mechanisms—namely, discriminatory zoning, housing, and real estate practices.

In their book *American Apartheid: Segregation and the Making of the Underclass*, Douglas Massey and Nancy Denton chart the course of racially segregated space, beginning in the nineteenth century.[33] As they persuasively argue, residential segregation did not always exist, nor did it come about naturally. Segregation did not result from the "desires" of African Americans and other people of color (the "lifestyle" explanation), "impersonal market forces" (the "market dynamics" explanation), or as "a chance by-product of other socioeconomic processes," explain Massey and Denton. Before 1900, for instance, "blacks and whites lived side by side in American cities" in the north—in places like Chicago, Detroit, and Philadelphia—as well as in the south in cities like Charleston, New Orleans, and Savannah. However, at critical points between the end of the Civil War in 1865 and the passage of the Fair Housing Act in 1968, "white America chose to strengthen the walls of the ghetto." During this time period, residential segregation was constructed

and imposed through various public and private processes—discriminatory real estate practices, exclusionary and expulsive zoning, redlining, and white flight, among others—that both contained growing urban black populations and limited the mobility of blacks and other people of color. Some of these actions and decisions were individual, some were collective, and others reflected "the powers and prerogatives of government"; together, these practices effectively constructed and maintained the residential color line well into the twentieth century and up to the present.

Even if society were to purge itself of racism and become color-blind, and people were to behave purely as rational economic actors in their choices of mobility and residential location, racially segregated space would still persist today absent affirmative efforts to dismantle the vestiges of historical racism. As Richard Ford explains, "race-neutral policy could be expected to entrench segregation and socio-economic stratification in a society with a history of racism."[34] His conclusion rests on the fact that leaving historical residential segregation intact would affect virtually every aspect of social status, including employment opportunities and residential mobility. For instance, because the education system is financed through local taxes, segregated localities would inevitably offer vastly different levels of educational opportunity: "the poor, black cities would have poorer education facilities than the wealthy, white cities." In turn, "whites would be better equipped to obtain high-income employment than would blacks." Whites' increased economic status would likewise translate into an increased ability to buy into economically superior neighborhoods and would mean that the market value of white homes on average would be significantly higher than that of black homes. Thus, "blacks attempting to move into white neighborhoods would, on average, have less collateral with which to obtain new mortgages, or less equity to convert into cash."

Residential segregation would also result in closed social networks, which "form the basis of the

ties and the communities of trust that open the doors of opportunity in the business world," and thus would decrease the likelihood that crucial social connections would be formed between members of different races. Without some intervention to dismantle historical racial segregation, racial stratification on all levels of society would likely perpetuate itself, explains Ford, even in the absence of current racism. Although "there is no racist actor or racist policy in this model," racially defined communities "perform the 'work' of segregation silently." Racially stratified space thus, as Ford concludes, becomes "the inert context in which individuals make rational choices" and "a controlling structure in which seemingly innocuous actions lead to racially detrimental consequences."

Unfortunately, we don't live in a color-blind world, nor one in which legal rules and social action have eliminated either the vestiges of historical racism or even all of the current manifestations of racism. Adding racist actors and current racism to historical patterns, Ford explains, further exacerbates the dynamic of racial stratification and makes possible a number of public activities and private practices that continue to entrench racial inequality. As Massey and Denton document, the systematic segregation and isolation of racial groups continues to this day as a result of exclusionary real estate practices, racial and cultural bias, and pervasive discrimination. Surveys indicate that whites continue to be very apprehensive about racial mixing, fearing declines in property values and other deleterious effect on neighborhood qualities. To a large extent, these fears are based on racial stereotypes about African Americans and other groups.[35] Nevertheless, for whatever reason, white demand decreases for neighborhoods that African Americans and Latinos, in particular, begin to integrate.[36]

Moreover, the cultural differences and socialization resulting from the history of racism and from racial segregation have produced a fear and distrust of whites, particularly by African Americans, who fear white hostility, rejection and/or violence, studies show. As a result, many of them are reluctant to live in white neighborhoods in the absence of a significant number of other African Americans. Thus, even when African Americans *are* able to move into white neighborhoods, "contemporary society imposes significant costs" on integration.[37] "The additional amenities and lower taxes of the white neighborhood [are] often outweighed by the intangible but real costs of living as an isolated minority in an alien and sometimes hostile environment."[38] These costs make it even more difficult for African Americans, and members of other racial groups, to move to predominantly white neighborhoods, regardless of class.

The attitudes and fears of both whites and people of color would not in and of themselves perpetuate racial segregation without discriminatory mechanisms to enforce them. As Massey and Denton have shown, the "segmentation of black and white housing demand" is encouraged and supported by pervasive discrimination in the housing and lending markets. Empirical evidence demonstrates that real estate agents often limit the likelihood of black entry into white neighborhoods "through a series of exclusionary tactics" and "channel black demand for housing into areas that are within or near existing ghettos." This discrimination by realtors is further enforced by the "allocation of mortgages and home improvement loans, which systematically channel money away from integrated areas." In essence, race remains the "dominant organizing principle" for housing and residential patterns in spite of the Fair Housing Act and other civil rights reforms.[39]

In addition to discriminatory real estate and lending practices and "white flight," a variety of facially neutral rules and decisions add to the creation and maintenance of racially identified, and subordinate, neighborhoods. For instance, the MIT economist Yale Rabin has demonstrated that, in communities across the country, many residential neighborhoods composed of people of color have been re-zoned as industrial by white planning boards, a process Rabin calls "expulsive zoning." While these zoning decisions are not made with reference to race, their impact, given racial segregation, has profound racial implications. As Rabin explains, "[b]ecause it appears that [the re-zoned] areas were mainly

black, and because whites who may have been similarly displaced were not subject to racially determined limitations in seeking alternative housing, the adverse impacts of expulsive zoning on blacks were far more severe and included, in addition to accelerated blight, increases in over-crowding and racial segregation." These types of zoning decisions allowed heavy industry to locate in African American residential neighborhoods and also led banks to stop loaning money for home improvement and maintenance because of improper zoning.[40] As we saw in Chester, one of the common attributes of communities that are experiencing a disproportionate influx of waste facilities is their status as former industrial towns, now abandoned by industry and desperate for new economic development. Indeed, as we shall see, waste facility developers affirmatively select sites in heavy industrial areas that have little or no commercial activity.

Physical segregation and isolation thus have intense political and economic consequences, particularly for poor African Americans and Latinos living in inner cities. Segregation not only concentrates poverty but also economically dislocates people.[41] This racialization of space "reaches to the societal processes in which people participate and to the structures and institutions that people produce."[42] Residential location, for instance, is seen as an indication of the attitudes, values, and behavioral inclinations of the types of people who are assumed to live there.[43] Segregated communities are isolated not only geographically and economically, but also socially and culturally; this isolation, in turn, leads to political marginalization.[44] Accordingly, the concerns of such communities are rarely taken seriously in the political process, and are often ignored altogether by decision makers.[45]

SOCIAL STRUCTURE AND THE SITING PROCESS

The preceding assessment of post-siting market dynamics is still an incomplete causal account of environmental injustice in communities such as Chester. Post-siting market dynamics may explain how communities like Chester became predominantly poor and/or of color *after* the influx of older industrial and waste facilities. Post-siting market dynamics does not, however, explain the *current* siting pattern in Chester, nor the wave of environmental disputes arising in many communities across the country. Empirical studies continue to document that new waste facilities are disproportionately sited in low-income communities of color. Moreover, anecdotal accounts of current siting disputes paint a troublesome picture of disproportionate siting patterns in poor communities of color. The Chester experience illustrates one such account. The *R.I.S.E.* case, discussed earlier, illustrates another. There are countless other examples across the country.

Examining the structured inequalities embedded in post-siting "market dynamics" does help one understand and evaluate current siting processes within their social context. Although the siting process does not produce the structured inequalities created in part by racially discriminatory processes, as we have detailed, it is heavily dependent upon them. Conventional industry wisdom counsels private companies to target sites that are in neighborhoods "least likely to express opposition"—those with poorly educated residents of low socioeconomic status. Not surprisingly, many communities that host toxic waste sites possess these characteristics. State permitting laws remain neutral, or blind, toward these inequalities; they therefore perpetuate, and indeed exacerbate, distributional inequalities.[46]

In most states, the hazardous waste siting process begins when the private sector chooses a site for the location of a proposed facility. Because the proposed location of a hazardous waste facility near, particularly, a neighborhood of white people of high socioeconomic status often faces strong public opposition, there is a limited supply of land on which to site such facilities.[47] Inevitably, the siting process focuses on industrial, or rural, communities, many of which are populated predominantly by people of color. Because land values are lower in heavily industrial

and rural communities than in white suburbs, these areas are attractive to industries that are seeking to reduce the cost of doing business.[48] Furthermore, these communities are presumed to pose little threat of political resistance because of their subordinate socioeconomic, and often racial, status.[49]

Rarely does a "smoking gun"—explicit racial criteria or motivation—exist behind the decision to locate a toxic waste facility in a community of color. The reasons frequently given by companies for siting facilities are that such communities have low-cost land, sparse populations, and desirable geological attributes.[50] Notably, however, there is evidence that portions of the waste industry target neighborhoods that possess the attributes of many poor communities of color, using "race-neutral criteria." In 1984, the California Waste Management Board commissioned a study on how to site waste incinerators. The report, written by the political consulting firm Cerrell Associates of Los Angeles and entitled *Political Difficulties Facing Waste-to-Energy Conversion Plant Siting* (popularly known as the Cerrell Report), set out "to assist in selecting a site that offers the least potential of generating public opposition."[51] The report acknowledged that "since the 1970s, political criteria have become every bit as important in determining the outcome of a project as engineering factors." The Cerrell Report suggests that companies target small, rural communities whose residents are low income, older people, or people with a high school education or less; communities with a high proportion of Catholic residents; and communities whose residents are engaged in resource extractive industries such as agriculture, mining, and forestry. Ideally, the report states, "officials and companies should look for lower socioeconomic neighborhoods that are also in a heavy industrial area with little, if any, commercial activity."

While corporations were quick to disavow the use of the study, this community profile just happens to fit all three of the California communities that host the state's commercial toxic waste dumps—Buttonwillow, Kettleman City and Westmorland. Each of

these small, rural communities has a high percentage of residents who live below the poverty line. Each community is predominantly Latino and Catholic, with many farm-workers, and most residents have few years of formal education. Additionally, the Cerrell profile fits another community: Chester, Pennsylvania, is a heavy-industrial inner city with little commercial activity, populated predominantly by working-class and poor people of color.

Likewise, even the "race-neutral" criteria used by government and industry for siting waste facilities—such as the presence of cheap land values, appropriate zoning, low population densities, proximity to transportation routes, and the absence of proximity to institutions such as hospitals and schools—turn out not to be "race neutral" after all, when seen in their social and historical context. Race potentially plays a factor in almost every "neutral" siting criterion used. "Cheap land values" is, understandably, a key siting criteria for the waste industry and other developers. However, because of historical segregation and racism, land values in the United States are integrally tied to race. In urban areas across the United States, this is starkly clear: an acre of land in the San Fernando Valley of Los Angeles has roughly the same physical characteristics as an acre of land in South Central Los Angeles, but people are willing to pay a premium to live in all-white neighborhoods. In rural areas, the pattern is similar: low land values tend to be found in poor areas, and people of color are overrepresented among the rural poverty population.

The land value cycle is vicious, too: once a neighborhood becomes host to industry, land values typically fall or do not increase as quickly as those in purely residential neighborhoods. Thus, a community that initially has low land values because it is home to people of color becomes a community that has low land values because it has a preponderance of industry, which in turn attracts more industry, creating a cumulative effect on land values. As we noted earlier, calling these changes "market driven" naturalizes the underlying racism in the valuation of the land. Thus, when a company makes a siting

decision on the basis of land values in urban areas, far from being "race neutral," it is focusing on land more likely to be in proximity to people of color.

Zoning is inextricably linked with race, as well. As we noted earlier, Yale Rabin's studies of historical zoning decisions have documented numerous instances where stable African American residential communities were "down-zoned" to industrial status by biased decision makers, allowing inappropriate land uses near residents and ruining the social fabric of the neighborhoods. Rabin found that local zoning bodies in the early part of the century routinely zoned as "industrial" many residential African American communities, even as they zoned as "residential" similar white areas. These zoning practices permitted the intrusion of disruptive, incompatible uses and generally undermined the character, quality, and stability of the black residential areas. Such "expulsive zoning," as Rabin calls it, permanently alters the character of a neighborhood, often depressing property values and causing community blight.[52] The lower property values and the zoning status are then easily invoked as "neutral" criteria upon which siting decisions are made.

"Low population density" translates to the siting of facilities in rural areas. In a major region of the country—the U.S. South—rural areas have populations that are disproportionately African American because of the historical influence of slavery on population settlement and distribution patterns.[53] In fact, a study of Mississippi discovered that population density was inversely correlated with race; that is, the less dense the population was, the more African American it became.[54] In other areas such as Texas and California, where historical settlement patterns and the current agricultural economy result in a rural population that is increasingly Latino, low population densities lead to the siting of facilities near farm-worker communities.

Proximity to major transportation routes may also skew the siting process toward communities of color, as freeways appear to be disproportionately sited in such communities.[55] Similarly, locational criteria—prohibitions against the siting of waste facilities near neighborhood amenities like hospitals and schools—skew the process toward underdeveloped communities of color, since such communities are less likely to have hospitals and schools. Hence, siting criteria that prohibit the siting of waste facilities close to such facilities perpetuate the historical lack of such amenities in these communities.

The sociologist Robert Bullard documented this underlying racial discrimination in an otherwise "neutral" siting process. Bullard's documentation was recognized in a 1997 decision by the Nuclear Regulatory Commission's Atomic Safety and Licensing Board, which overturned a facility's permit. In an administrative appeal to block the siting of a uranium enrichment facility in a poor and African American area of Louisiana, Professor Bullard successfully argued that racism more than likely played a significant part in the selection process. Bullard demonstrated (through a statistical analysis) that at each progressively narrower stage of the company's site selection process, the level of poverty and African Americans in the local population rose dramatically until it culminated in the selection of a site whose local population is extremely poor and 97 percent African American. The race-neutral siting criteria—including the criteria of low population and the need to site the facility five miles from institutions such as schools, hospitals, and nursing homes—operated in conjunction with the current racial segregation and the resulting inferior infrastructure (e.g., lack of adequate schools, road paving, water supply) to ensure that the location selected would be a poor community of color. The NRC's licensing board, on the basis of Bullard's evidence, overturned the facility's permit and directed the NRC staff to conduct a "thorough and in-depth investigation" of the site selection process and to determine whether "the selection process was tainted by racial bias." In doing so, it ordered the staff to "lift some rocks and look under them" because racial discrimination is "rarely, if ever, admitted" and is "often rationalized under some other seemingly racially neutral guise,

making it difficult to ferret out," and "direct evidence of racial discrimination is rarely found."[56]...

BEYOND THE DISTRIBUTIVE PARADIGM

The studies that chart the disproportionate distribution of environmental hazards have been a wake up call for those in this country who care about social justice. However, in a sense, the studies are just a beginning in fully understanding the phenomenon of environmental injustice or racism. As we have demonstrated, focusing on distributional results alone obscures the social structure and institutional context in which environmental decisions are made. Absent a deeper focus on the processes that lead to racially disparate outcomes, the studies provide only an incomplete understanding of environmental racism.

This is not to say that distributive patterns are not crucial to the environmental justice inquiry, even when it focuses on environmental decision making. Distributional patterns and decision-making processes are intricately intertwined in important ways. As we have said, distributive patterns are a crucial entry point for exploring the justice of the social processes that underlie those patterns, including environmental decision-making processes. Evaluating decision-making processes, in turn, also requires an evaluation of distributions. For instance, a legitimate decision-making process often depends upon an adequate distribution of various social goods, or rights, that are crucial to participation in that process.[57] In the environmental justice context, for instance, some social groups approach environmental decision-making processes with fewer social goods (e.g., time, money, education, information, specialized knowledge, access, and influence) than more privileged groups. Not surprisingly, these same groups remain disadvantaged in the distribution of goods by those processes.

Environmental decision-making processes are a location of contestation by, and reform through, grassroots struggles. However, formal decision-making processes are not the only area where ordinary citizens are taking control of the decisions that affect their lives. Through direct protests, litigation, and other strategies, environmental justice advocates are questioning the justice of existing decision-making processes and at the same time creating their own organizations and networks to affect the way in which environmental decisions get made.

NOTES

1. Commission for Racial Justice (United Church of Christ), *Toxic Wastes and Race in the United States* xii (1987). The UCC study defines "hazardous wastes" as the term is used by the EPA: as "by-products of industrial production which present particularly troublesome health and environmental problems." Id. The study goes on to explain that

[n]ewly generated hazardous wastes must be managed in an approved "facility," which is defined by the EPA as any land structures thereon which are used for treating, storing or disposing of hazardous wastes (TSD facility). Such facilities may include landfills, surface impoundments or incinerators. A "commercial" facility is defined as any facility (public or private) which accepts hazardous wastes from a third party for a fee or other remuneration.

Id. The term "uncontrolled toxic waste sites" refers to closed and abandoned sites on the EPA's list of sites that pose a present and potential threat to human health and the environment. As of 1985, the EPA inventoried approximately 200 uncontrolled toxic wastes sites across the nation. See id.

2. These areas included Memphis, Tenn. (173 sites), St. Louis, Mo. (160 sites), Houston, Tex. (152 sites), Cleveland, Ohio (106 sites), Chicago, Ill. (103 sites), and Atlanta, Ga. (91 sites). Id.

3. See, e.g., Vicki Been, *Coming to the Nuisance or Going to the Barrios? A Longitudinal Analysis of Environmental Justice Claims*, 24 ECOLOGY LAW QUARTERLY 1 (1997) (finding in a nationwide study that commercial hazardous waste treatment facilities sited between 1970 and 1990 were sited in areas disproportionately populated by lower-income Hispanics, but finding no evidence that these facilities were sited in disproportionately African American areas or in areas with high concentrations

of the poor). Some regional studies also report results that vary by ethnic group. See, e.g., Brett Baden and Don Coursey, *The Locality of Waste Sites within the City of Chicago: A Demographic, Social and Economic Analysis* (Irving B. Harris Graduate School of Public Policy Studies Working Paper Series 97–2, 1997) (finding that, in 1990, waste sites tended to be located in low population density areas near commercial waterways and commercial highways, that more African Americans do appear to live in proximity to historical solid waste disposal sites, that there is no evidence that African Americans live in areas with higher concentrations of hazardous waste than whites or Hispanics, and that the percentage of Hispanics in an area is significant in describing the location of waste sites); Douglas L. Anderton et al., *Hazardous Waste Facilities: "Environmental Equity" Issues in Metropolitan Areas*, 18 EVALUATION REVIEW, 123–40 (April 1994) (finding no racial disparity in the location of commercial hazardous waste facilities, using the 1990 census). The Anderton study was funded by the world's largest waste management firm, WMX Technologies, Inc.

4. See, e.g., Benjamin A. Goldman and Laura Fitton, *Toxic Waste and Race Revisited: An Update of the 1987 Report on the Racial and Socioeconomic Characteristics of Communities with Hazardous Waste Sites I* (Center for Policy Alternatives, NAACP, United Church of Christ Commission for Racial Justice, 1994). Id. at 2 (finding statistical significance at the 0.001 level, which means that the probability that the observed change is merely a random fluctuation is less than one in a thousand). No similar pronounced disparities by socioeconomic status were discovered, though the researchers indicated that the data were not examined with the same detail as in the original 1987 study. Id. at 5 (also noting that sixty-three out of sixty-four of most recent studies continue to document racial disparities in the location of noxious facilities, toxic releases and exposures, ambient levels of air pollution, and environmental health effects). "People of color" includes the total population less non-Hispanic whites. The demographics of the zip code areas, including socioeconomic status, are taken from the 1990 census. Id.

5. Id. at 17 (but also noting that "no matter what the causes, the distribution of these facilities shows how some of the most hazardous inefficiencies of our economy can also pose significant social inequities").

6. Anderton et al., *Hazardous Waste Facilities*, supra; Douglas L. Anderton et al., *Environmental Equity: The Demographics of Dumping*, 31 DEMOGRAPHY 229 (1994) (results using 1980 census data); Andy B. Anderson et al.,

Environmental Equity: Evaluating TSDF Siting over the Past Two Decades, WASTE AGE 83–100 (July 1994).

7. SADRI researchers reasoned that only tracts in the same metropolitan or rural county as a facility could serve as possible alternative sites for the same market. See Andy B. Anderson et al., *Evaluating TSDF Siting*, supra, at 92, 96, 100. For an effective rebuttal of this argument, see Vicki Been, *Analyzing Evidence of Environmental Justice*, 11 JOURNAL OF LAND USE & ENVIRONMENTAL LAW 1, 12–13 (1995) (demonstrating that limiting analysis of census data to metropolitan areas or rural counties that have at least one facility reduces the differences in the ethnic and racial composition of host and nonhost tracts) and Been, *Coming to the Nuisance or Going to the Barrios?* supra, at 15–17 (arguing that the effect of SADRI's limitation reduced the differences between the racial and ethnic composition of host and nonhost tracts).

8. Been, *Coming to the Nuisance or Going to the Barrios?* supra. Been attributes her results, which differ compared to those of the SADRI study, to the fact that the SADRI study "did not control for density." Id. at 34.

9. See, e.g., Marianne Lavelle and Marcia Coyle, *Unequal Protection: The Racial Divide in Environmental Law*, NATIONAL LAW JOURNAL (September 21, 1992), at S1, S2 (concluding that there is a racial disparity in the way the U.S. government cleans up toxic waste sites and punishes polluters). The *National Law Journal* study is not without its critics. See Mary Bryant, *Unequal Justice? Lies, Damn Lies, and Statistics Revisited*, SONREEL (American Bar Association Section of Natural Resources, Energy, and Environmental Law) NEWS (September–October 1993), at 3 (critiquing the NLJ study for not defining key terms, not disclosing sample sizes, not disclosing the size of studied communities, and not adjusting the data for time).

10. The concept of "baselines" belongs to Cass Sunstein. See Cass Sunstein, *The Partial Constitution* 3–4 (1993) (when the state chooses "status quo neutrality," in taking existing social practices and distributions as its baseline for being neutral toward public and private actors, it produces injustice).

11. See Environmental Equity Workgroup, U.S. Environmental Protection Agency, EPA 230-R-92–008, *Environmental Equity: Reducing Risk For All Communities, Workgroup Report to the Administrator* 1 (1992).

12. When it is available to them, people of color have a more difficult time getting adequate medical care than do whites. U.S. General Accounting Office, GAO/PEMD-92–6, Hispanic Access to Health Care: Significant Gaps Exist 10 (1992) (reporting that 33 percent of

Latinos had neither private nor public medical insurance in 1989, compared with 19 percent of blacks and 12 percent of whites); Cassandra Q. Butts, *The Color of Money: Barriers to Access to Private Health Care Facilities for African-Americans*, 26 CLEARINGHOUSE REVIEW 159, 160 n. 5, 161–62 (1992); Marilyn Yaquinto, *Latinos Cited as Having Least Medical Coverage*, LOS ANGELES TIMES (February 19, 1992), at A5; Stephanie Pollack and JoAnn Grozuczak, *Reagan, Toxics & Minorities* 2 (1984) (Policy Report for the Urban Environment Conference, Inc.) (noting that one in six and one-half black families had trouble getting medical care in 1982, as compared to one in eleven white families). As Cassandra Butts notes, African Americans in both urban and rural areas are more likely than whites to face geographic barriers to health care and health care providers, and a disproportionate share of hospital closings affect African Americans, with "the likelihood of closures...directly related to the percentage of African-Americans in the population of a city." Butts, *The Color of Money*, supra. The problem is particularly acute for undocumented Latino farm-workers, who are concentrated in low-paying, high-risk jobs and who are prohibited by law from receiving most government health benefits. See Peter L. Reich, *Jurisprudential Tradition and Undocumented Alien Entitlements*, 6 GEORGETOWN IMMIGRATION LAW JOURNAL 1 (1992); Peter L. Reich, *Public Benefits for Undocumented Aliens: State Law into the Breach Once More*, 21 NEW MEXICO LAW REVIEW 219, 220–23 (1991); Susan B. Drake, *Immigrants' Right to Health Care*, 20 CLEARINGHOUSE REVIEW 498, 503–4 (1986); U.S. General Accounting Office, GAO/HRD-92–46, *Hired Farmworkers: Health and Well-Being at Risk* 3, 24–25 (1992). Additionally, doctors who treat poor people, people of color, and rural residents also often have fewer resources at their disposal and therefore less to offer those patients. Diana B. Dutton, *Children's Health Care: The Myth of Equal Access*, in IV BETTER HEALTH FOR OUR CHILDREN: A NATIONAL STRATEGY 375 (U.S. Department of Health & Human Services, ed., 1981).

13. See Beverly H. Wright, *Effects of Occupational Injury, Illness, and Disease on the Health Status of Black Americans: A Review*, in RACE AND THE INCIDENCE OF ENVIRONMENTAL HAZARDS: A TIME FOR DISCOURSE (Bunyan Bryant and Paul Mohai, eds., 1992), at 118 (explaining "victim blaming").

14. Vicki Been, *What's Fairness Got to Do with It? Environmental Justice and the Siting of Locally Undesirable Land Uses*, 78 CORNELL LAW REVIEW 1001, 1016 (1993); see also Vicki Been, *Locally Undesirable Land Uses in Minority Neighborhoods: Disproportionate Siting or Market Dynamics*, 103 YALE LAW JOURNAL 1383, 1389 (1994). See also Thomas Lambert and Christopher Boerner, *Environmental Inequity: Economic Causes, Economic Solutions*, 14 YALE JOURNAL ON REGULATION 195, 202 (1997); Lynn Blais, *Environmental Racism Reconsidered*, 74 NORTH CAROLINA LAW REVIEW 75, 93 (1996).

15. Been, *Locally Undesirable Land Uses*, supra, at 1388–89.

16. See also Lambert and Boerner, *Environmental Inequity*, supra, at 206, 212 (finding that their analysis supports the theory that "minority and poor [individuals] voluntarily move into areas surrounding industrial and waste sites" in St. Louis).

17. In fact, a chief proponent of such theories has proved the opposite proposition through her empirical research: that market dynamics do *not* lead people of color to "come to the nuisance." See, e.g., Been, *Coming to the Nuisance or Going to the Barrios?* supra (finding that the areas surrounding commercial hazardous waste treatment facilities currently are disproportionately populated by lower-income Hispanics, and finding no evidence that these communities became poorer or increased in minority population after the waste facilities were sited); Been, *Locally Undesirable Land Uses in Minority Neighborhoods*, supra, at 1398–1400 (finding that the southeastern waste sites studied by the U.S. General Accounting Office in 1983 were all in communities that originally had both high levels of poverty and predominantly African American populations; finding that these communities did not become poorer or increase in African American percentage of population after the waste facilities were sited). But see Been, *Locally Undesirable Land Uses in Minority Neighborhoods*, supra, at 1400–1406 (finding that Houston waste sites studied in 1983 by Professor Robert Bullard were originally sited in disproportionately African American communities, but that the communities did not originally have disproportionately low incomes; however, the percentage of African Americans rose and incomes fell after the solid waste facilities were sited); Lambert and Boerner, *Environmental Inequity*, supra, at 206–7 (finding a disproportionate increase of poor and minority individuals around waste sites in St. Louis between 1970 and 1990); Anderton, et al., *Hazardous Waste Facilities*, supra, at 135 (finding evidence of economic decline in communities with commercial hazardous waste facilities but no evidence of "white flight").

18. Been, *Locally Undesirable Land Uses*, supra, at 1389 (emphasis added); see also Lambert and Boerner, *Environmental Inequity*, supra, at 200–202.

19. See, e.g., Cass Sunstein, *Free Markets and Social Justice* 13–31 (1997).

20. Been, *Locally Undesirable Land Uses*, supra, at 1389; Lambert and Boerner, *Environmental Inequity*, supra, at 212 (finding that their analysis supports the theory that "minority and poor [individuals] voluntarily move into areas surrounding industrial and waste sites" in the St. Louis area but cautioning that "the conclusions drawn from this study may provide an incomplete picture of environmental justice" and that "other forms of racial discrimination may have been a factor influencing the subsequent migration of these residents to communities hosting polluting facilities"); Blais, *Environmental Racism*, supra, at 141. See also Douglas S. Massey and Nancy A. Denton, *American Apartheid: Segregation and the Making of the Underclass* 114 (1993) (finding that "race is the dominant organizing principle" for "housing and residential patterns").

21. Been, *Locally Undesirable Land Uses*, supra, at 1389. See also Massey and Denton, AMERICAN APARTHEID, supra, at 114 (describing the various types of "exclusionary tactics" used by realtors to limit the likelihood of black entry into white neighborhoods and to channel black demand for housing into areas that are within or near existing ghettos; detailing the "white prejudice" that accompanies the movement of blacks into certain neighborhoods, making the area unattractive to further white settlement, and leading to "white flight"; and the pervasive discrimination in the allocation of mortgages and home improvement loans).

22. Regina Austin and Michael Schill, *Black, Brown, Poor and Poisoned: Minority Grassroots Environmentalism and the Quest for Eco-Justice*, 1 KANSAS JOURNAL OF LAW AND PUBLIC POLICY 69, 69–70 (1991).

23. Gerald Torres, *Understanding Environmental Racism*, 63 UNIVERSITY OF COLORADO LAW REVIEW 839 (1992).

24. *Washington v. Davis*, 426 U.S. 229 (1976) (adopting intent/purpose requirement as a prerequisite to proving race discrimination in equal protection jurisprudence).

25. See Alan D. Freeman, *Legitimizing Racial Discrimination through Antidiscrimination Law: A Critical Review of Supreme Court Doctrine*, 63 MINNESOTA LAW REVIEW 1049, 1052–57 (1978); Charles R. Lawrence III, *The Id, the Ego, and Equal Protection: Reckoning with Unconscious Racism*, 39 STANFORD LAW REVIEW 317, 318–19 (1987); Luke W. Cole, *Empowerment as the Key to Environmental Protection: The Need for Environmental Poverty Law*, 19 ECOLOGY LAW REVIEW 619, 642 (1992).

26. 768 F.Supp. 1144, 1149 (E.D. Va. 1991), *aff'd*, 977 F.2d 573 (4th Cir. 1992).

27. Id. at 1150. See also *Bean v. Southwestern Waste Management Corp.*, 482 F.Supp. 673 (S.D. Tex. 1979), *aff'd without op.*, 782 F.2d 1038 (5th Cir. 1986); (denying environmental racism claim for lack of discriminatory intent); *East Bibb Twiggs Neighborhood Assn. v. Macon-Bibb County Planning and Zoning Comm'n* 706 F.Supp. 880 (M.D. Ga.), *aff'd* 896 F.2d 1264 (11th Cir.), *opinion replaced by* 846 F.2d 1264 (11th Cir. 1989) (same).

28. Lawrence, *The Id, the Ego, and Equal Protection*, supra at 322.

29. See Sheila Foster, *Intent and Incoherence*, 72 TULANE LAW REVIEW 1065 (1998).

30. Cole, *Empowerment as the Key to Environmental Protection*, supra at 648; Luke W. Cole, *Environmental Justice Litigation: Another Stone in David's Sling*, 21 FORDHAM URBAN LAW JOURNAL 523, 524 (1994); Luke W. Cole, *Remedies for Environmental Racism: A View from the Field*, 90 MICHIGAN LAW REVIEW 1991, 1997 (1992).

31. See, e.g., Michael Gelobter, *Toward a Model of "Environmental Discrimination,"* in RACE AND THE INCIDENCE OF ENVIRONMENTAL HAZARDS: A TIME FOR DISCOURSE (Bunyan Bryant and Paul Mohai, eds., 1992), at 76–80.

32. Presumably, market dynamics adherents would agree with this normative analysis. See Been, *Locally Undesirable Land Uses in Minority Neighborhoods*, supra, at 1391 n. 30 (noting that "[i]f market forces at issue are based on discrimination, i.e., if host neighborhoods became predominantly minority after the [facility] was sited because racial discrimination in the housing market relegated people of color to those neighborhoods, siting practices might have to change to account for persistent discrimination in the housing market").

33. Massey and Denton, *American Apartheid*, supra, at 1–16, 17–60.

34. Richard Ford, *The Boundaries of Race: Political Geography in Legal Analysis*, 107 HARVARD LAW REVIEW 1841, 1847–54 (1994).

35. Massey and Denton, *American Apartheid*, supra, at 83–114.

36. According to one study, among neighborhoods located within five miles of an established black neighborhood, white population loss is extremely likely, and this loss becomes virtually certain as the percentage of blacks increase. This pattern holds true for suburbs as well as for central cities. The probability that a central city tract located within five miles of a black neighborhood would

lose white residents was .85 when its black percentage was 0%–5%; it rose to .92 when the black percentage reached 30%–40%. Massey and Denton, AMERICAN APARTHEID, supra, at 80. See also id. at 74, 113–14 (comparing the segregation of Caribbean Latinos with that of blacks and concluding that the average level of segregation increases steadily as one moves from being identified as white Hispanics, to mixed-race Hispanic to black Hispanic, the last having an "index" of segregation comparable to that for African Americans).

37. Ford, *Boundaries of Race*, supra, at 1857.

38. Id. at 1854.

39. Massey and Denton, *American Apartheid*, supra, at 114, 96–109.

40. Yale Rabin, *Expulsive Zoning: The Inequitable Legacy of* Euclid, in *Zoning and the American Dream 101* (Charles M. Haar and Jerold S. Kayden, eds., 1990).

41. Massey and Denton, *American Apartheid*, supra, 118–30, Ford; *Boundaries of Race*, supra, at 1851–52.

42. John Calmore, *Racialized Space and the Culture of Segregation: "Hewing a Stone of Hope from a Mountain of Despair,"* 143 UNIVERSITY OF PENNSYLVANIA LAW REVIEW 1233, 1235 (1995).

43. Susan J. Smith, *Residential Segregation and the Politics of Racialization*, in *Racism, the City, and the State* 128, 133 (Malcolm Cross and Michael Keith, eds., 1993).

44. William Julius Wilson, *When Work Disappears: The World of the New Urban Poor* 51–86 (1996). Wilson writes that social isolation deprives inner-city residents not only of conventional role models but also of the social resources provided by mainstream social networks that facilitate social and economic advancement in a modern industrial society; social isolation also contributes to the formation and crystallization of ghetto-related cultural traits and behaviors.

45. Margaret Weir, *From Equal Opportunity to the New Social Contract*, in *Racism, the City, and the State* (Malcolm Cross and Michael Keith, eds., 1993), 104; see also Wilson, *When Work Disappears*, supra, at 184–85 ("[t]he growing suburbanization of the population influences the extent to which national politicians will support increased federal aid to large cities and the poor...we can associate the sharp drop in federal support for basic urban programs since 1980 with the declining political influence of cities and the rising influence of electoral coalitions in the suburbs").

46. Sunstein, *The Partial Constitution*, supra, at 3–4 (when the state chooses "status quo neutrality," in taking existing social practices and distributions as its baseline for being neutral toward public and private actors, it produces injustice); see also Ford, *Boundaries of Race*, supra, at 1852 (making similar point in the context of housing segregation).

47. Public opposition, and often direct protest, is considered by industry to be the "greatest single obstacle to the successful siting of" hazardous facilities, with middle and upper socioeconomic groups possessing greater resources to effectuate their opposition. Cerrell Associates, *Political Difficulties Facing Waste-to-Energy Conversion Plant Siting* 43 (1984) (prepared for the California Waste Management Board) (counseling that "middle and higher socioeconomic strata neighborhoods should not fall within the one-mile and five-mile radius of the proposed site"); Richard Lazarus, *Pursuing "Environmental Justice": The Distributional Effects of Environmental Protection*, 87 NORTHWESTERN UNIVERSITY LAW REVIEW 787, 806 (1993) (noting that few proposals survive the public review that often accompanies the announcement of the recommended siting of a hazardous waste facility).

48. Joan Bernstein, *The Siting of Commercial Waste Facilities: An Evolution of Community Land Use Decisions*, 1 KANSAS JOURNAL OF LAW & PUBLIC POLICY 83 (1991) (waste companies look for cheap land); Michael B. Gerrard, *Whose Backyard, Whose Risk: Fear and Fairness* in *Toxic Nuclear Waste Siting* 47 (1994); Paul Mohai and Bunyan Bryant, *Race, Poverty, and the Distribution of Environmental Hazards: Reviewing the Evidence*, in RACE, POVERTY, AND THE ENVIRONMENT (Fall 1991–Winter 1992), at 24.

49. Cerrell Associates, POLITICAL DIFFICULTIES, supra, at 65 (noting that "older, conservative, and lower socioeconomic neighborhoods" are least likely to resist sitings).

50. Bernstein, *The Siting of Commercial Waste Facilities*, supra.

51. Cerrell Associates, *Political Difficulties*, supra, at 29.

52. See Rabin, *Expulsive Zoning*, supra, at 101–2. "Such patterns, once established, are difficult to alter. Locally Unwanted Land Uses (LULUs) result in depressed residential property values which, in turn, reduce the municipal tax base and discourage other upscale development which would help boost property values." Jason Wilson, *Environmental Inequity: Which Came First, Poverty or Pollution*, NEW JERSEY REPORTER 40 (March/April 1997).

53. Conner Bailey and Charles E. Faupel, *Environmentalism and Civil Rights in Sumter County, Alabama*, in *Race and the Incidence of Environmental Hazards: A Time*

for Discourse 140 (Bunyan Bryant and Paul Mohai, eds., 1992) (noting that "among Alabama's 67 counties, the ten with the lowest population densities also have average per capita incomes well below the state average" and noting that blacks are a majority in six of ten Alabama counties with the lowest population densities and lower than average per capita income); Gerrard, *Whose Backyard, Whose Risk*, supra (noting that "most of the anecdotes and much of the data concerning discriminatory siting come from the southeastern United States…[and that] is a region where, for obvious historical reasons, rural areas have large black populations; in the northeast, where the rural areas are mostly white, most proposed sites have been in white areas").

54. *African Americans for Environmental Justice v. Mississippi Department of Environmental Quality*, No. 1R-93-R4 (filed Sept. 24, 1993) (study of Mississippi's siting process revealed that population density in Mississippi was directly inversely correlated with race so that the less dense, the more African American an area was, leading to siting in only black areas). See also Luke W. Cole, *Civil Rights, Environmental Justice, and the EPA: The Brief History of Administrative Complaints under Title VI of the Civil Rights Act of 1964*, 9 JOURNAL OF ENVIRONMENTAL LAW AND LITIGATION 309, 345 (1994).

55. See, e.g., *North Carolina Department of Transportation v. Crest Street Community Council, Inc.*, 479 U.S. 6 (1986) (freeway through African American neighborhood fought on civil rights grounds); *Coalition of Concerned Citizens against I-670 v. Damian*, 608 F.Supp. 110 (S.D. Ohio 1984) (same); *Clean Air Alternatives Coalition v. United States Department of Transportation*, No. C-93-0721-VRW (N.D. Cal. filed March 2, 1993) (same).

56. *In the Matter of Louisiana Energy Services, L.P.*, Decision of the Nuclear Regulatory Commission Atomic Safety and Licensing Board, LBP-97-8, 45 NRC 367, 390–92 (May 1, 1997). On appeal, NRC Commissioners reversed the Board's requirement of an inquiry into racial discrimination in the siting process. It based its reversal on the Board's failure to find that intentional racism had tainted the decisional process and the Board's failure to make clear the legal basis for its decision to order an investigation of possible racism in the section of the site. *In the Matter of Louisiana Energy Services*, Decision of the Nuclear Regulatory Commission, CLI-98-3 (April 3, 1998).

57. See Robert A. Dahl, *Democracy and Its Critics* 163–75 (1989) (arguing that certain rights, goods, and interests are integral to a legitimate democratic process).

Section IV

Animals and the Environment

INTRODUCTION

Not long ago, it seemed unquestionable that cows belonged on plates, rats in laboratories, elephants in zoos, and minks on the backs of the fashionably dressed. Vegetarianism seemed a strange practice and vegan skin care products didn't exist. In a relatively short period of time, much has changed, in large part due to the 1975 publication of Peter Singer's *Animal Liberation*, from which "All Animals Are Equal" is excerpted here. Much as he argued for extending impartial consideration of the interests of all people in the previous section, Singer argues for extending the basic principle of equality beyond the species boundary. Speciesism—the view that denies the equal consideration of interests to other animals, simply because they are members of another species—is, in Singer's view, an unjustified prejudice, like racism and sexism. Rather than excluding other animals because they are not human, Singer focuses on whether a being can be harmed. He argues that all animals, human and nonhuman, who can feel pain have an interest in avoiding harm. The principle of equality requires us to consider all of their interests equally, regardless of species.

Lori Gruen introduces us to the wide range of views about the moral status of animals that has opened up in the wake of Singer's groundbreaking work. Kantians, virtue ethicists, rights theorists, feminists, and utilitarians such as Singer, have all argued for reexamining our ethical practices regarding animals. While these views have very different philosophical foundations, they converge on the conclusion that our everyday practices regarding animals cannot be defended. Kantianism, utilitarianism, and rights theory all stem from eighteenth-century Enlightenment views that emphasized progress through reason. Yet there are important differences between them. Utilitarians such as Singer object primarily to animal suffering. Whether an animal can be killed in a particular case depends enormously on the circumstances. Rights theorists, such as Tom Regan, tend to be absolutist. They object to killing innocent animals, even if this is done painlessly and results in good consequences. Some feminists object to the individualism of both rights theory and utilitarianism. Virtue theorists object to the rationalism of these Enlightenment views and look to Aristotle for guidance.

Mark Sagoff details the differences between animal liberation and environmental ethics. He thinks that any attempt to bring them together would be a bad marriage that should end in a quick divorce. He juxtaposes the individualism of Singer, which treats suffering as the primary evil, with the holism of Leopold, which views pain as simply a product of natural selection. Animal liberation takes the suffering of domesticated animals seriously, while it is a matter of indifference to environmental ethics. According to Sagoff, animal liberation is a humanitarian ethic centered on an appreciation of animal welfare rather than an environmental ethic devoted to the appreciation of nature. For environmentalists, the preservation of endangered species is of paramount importance, while an animal liberationist has a difficult time explaining why the last few polar bears are any more important than members of an overpopulated species such as mule deer. Environmentalists would sacrifice the lives of individual animals in order to preserve the authenticity, integrity, and complexity of ecological systems while animal liberationists would sacrifice ecosystems in order to protect individual animals. Sagoff's conclusion is that environmentalists cannot be animal liberationists and animal liberationists cannot be environmentalists.

Dale Jamieson argues that the differences between animal liberationists and environmentalists are no greater than the differences that exist within each group. Environmentalists do not always see eye to eye, as we have seen throughout this volume, and Gruen has shown us how much diversity exists within the animal liberation community. In this light it is important to recognize what animal liberationists and environmentalists share. The fact that they both object to industrial animal agriculture, even though perhaps on different grounds, illuminates an important common commitment. They both also reject the prevailing view that humans are separate from, and superior to, other animals and the rest of nature. Since we ourselves are animals and other animals are an inseparable part of the environment, any plausible environmental ethic will have to give a consistent and coherent account of humanity's moral relations with other animals and the rest of nature. Environmentalists cannot ignore nonhuman animals, and animal liberationists cannot ignore the environments in which animals live. Rather than seeing animal liberation and environmental ethics as unsuitable suitors, Jamieson sees them as part of the same unruly family.

In recent years both environmentalists and animal liberationists have been accused of terrorism. Both movements have radical wings (e.g., the Earth Liberation Front and the Animal Liberation Front) that commit acts of civil disobedience, crimes against property, and sometimes even threaten or commit acts of violence against people. These tactics have been the source of much debate among both activists and scholars. Tom Regan explores the strategic divides within the animal rights movement, developing an analogy with the antislavery movement. He argues that animal rights violence is often the result of an absolute commitment to principle and an "unwillingness to accept doing evil so that good will come," suggesting that incremental abolition may help to reduce the violence.

FURTHER READING

Beauchamp, Tom L., and R.G. Frey, eds. *The Oxford Handbook of Animal Ethics*. New York, NY: Oxford University Press, 2011. A comprehensive treatment of a wide range of issues in animal ethics.

DeGrazia, David. *Taking Animals Seriously*. Cambridge: Cambridge University Press, 1996. A discussion of animal well-being, attempting to overcome the rights-welfare debates.

Donovan, Josephine, and Carol Adams, eds. *The Feminist Care Tradition in Animal Ethics*. New York: Columbia University Press, 2007. The case for animal rights from an ethics of care perspective.

Gruen, Lori. *Ethics and Animals: An Introduction*. New York, NY: Cambridge University Press, 2011. An introduction to animal ethics, covering such topics as animals in the wild, the ethics of captivity, and animal activism.

Palmer, Clare. *Animal Ethics in Context*. New York, NY: Columbia University Press, 2010. An analysis of animal ethics focusing on capacities and proposing a relational approach.

Regan, Tom. *The Case for Animal Rights*. Berkeley, CA: University of California Press, 1985. The essential defense of animal rights.

Sunstein, Cass, and Martha Nussbaum, eds. *Animal Rights: Current Debates and New Directions*. New York, NY: Oxford University Press, 2004. An edited volume addressing such topics as regulating animal use, animal law, and animal capabilities.

DISCUSSION QUESTIONS

1. In the previous section, Brian Barry said that the concept of justice does not apply to animals. Do you agree?
2. Is suffering the most important thing to avoid in our treatment of animals? Why or why not? What other considerations might be important?
3. Are there any conditions under which violence may be justified in order to protect animals?
4. Can the interests of individual animals be sacrificed in order to protect ecosystems or preserve species? If so, are there limits on the extent of the sacrifice? What are these limits?
5. Is it wrong to painlessly kill animals? Why or why not?
6. Must feminists support animal liberation? Why or why not?
7. How would a virtuous person relate to animals? Would she eat them or use them in research that would benefit only humans?

PETER SINGER

All Animals Are Equal...

or why the ethical principle on which human equality rests requires us to extend equal consideration to animals too

"Animal Liberation" may sound more like a parody of other liberation movements than a serious objective. The idea of "The Rights of Animals" actually was once used to parody the case for women's rights. When Mary Wollstonecraft, a forerunner of today's feminists, published her *Vindication of the Rights of Woman* in 1792, her views were widely regarded as absurd, and before long an anonymous publication appeared entitled *A Vindication of the Rights of Brutes*. The author of this satirical work (now known to have been Thomas Taylor, a distinguished Cambridge philosopher) tried to refute Mary Wollstonecraft's arguments by showing that they could be carried one stage further. If the argument for equality was sound when applied to women, why should it not be applied to dogs, cats, and horses? The reasoning seemed to hold for these "brutes" too; yet to hold that brutes had rights was manifestly absurd. Therefore the reasoning by which this conclusion had been reached must be unsound, and if unsound when applied to brutes, it must also be unsound when applied to women, since the very same arguments had been used in each case.

In order to explain the basis of the case for the equality of animals, it will be helpful to start with an examination of the case for the equality of women. Let us assume that we wish to defend the case for women's rights against the attack by Thomas Taylor. How should we reply?

One way in which we might reply is by saying that the case for equality between men and women cannot validly be extended to nonhuman animals. Women have a right to vote, for instance, because they are just as capable of making rational decisions about the future as men are; dogs, on the other hand, are incapable of understanding the significance of voting, so they cannot have the right to vote. There are many other obvious ways in which men and women resemble each other closely, while humans and animals differ greatly. So, it might be said, men and women are similar beings and should have similar rights, while humans and nonhumans are different and should not have equal rights.

The reasoning behind this reply to Taylor's analogy is correct up to a point, but it does not go far enough. There are obviously important differences between humans and other animals, and these differences must give rise to some differences in the rights that each have. Recognizing this evident fact, however, is no barrier to the case for extending the basic principle of equality to nonhuman animals. The differences that exist between men and women are equally undeniable, and the supporters of Women's Liberation are aware that these differences may give rise to different rights. Many feminists hold that women have the right to an abortion on request. It does not follow that since these same feminists are campaigning for equality between men and women they must support the right of men to have abortions too. Since a man cannot have an abortion, it is meaningless to talk of his right to have one. Since dogs can't vote, it is meaningless to talk of their right to vote. There is no reason why either Women's Liberation or Animal Liberation should get involved in such nonsense. The extension of the basic principle of equality from one group to another does not imply that we must treat both groups in exactly the same way, or grant exactly the same rights to both groups. Whether we should do so will depend on the nature of the members of the two groups. The basic principle of equality does not require equal or identical *treatment*; it requires equal consideration. Equal consideration for different beings may lead to different treatment and different rights.

So there is a different way of replying to Taylor's attempt to parody the case for women's rights, a way that does not deny the obvious differences between human beings and nonhumans but goes more deeply into the question of equality and concludes by finding nothing absurd in the idea that the basic principle of equality applies to so-called brutes. At this point such a conclusion may appear odd; but if we examine more deeply the basis on which our opposition to discrimination on grounds of race or sex ultimately rests, we will see that we would be on shaky ground if we were to demand equality for blacks, women, and other groups of oppressed humans while denying equal consideration to nonhumans. To make this clear we need to see, first, exactly why racism and sexism are wrong. When we say that all human beings, whatever their race, creed, or sex, are equal, what is it that we are asserting? Those who wish to defend hierarchical, inegalitarian societies have often pointed out that by whatever test we choose it simply is not true that all humans are equal. Like it or not we must face the fact that humans come in different shapes and sizes; they come with different moral capacities, different intellectual abilities, different amounts of benevolent feeling and sensitivity to the needs of others, different abilities to communicate effectively, and different capacities to experience pleasure and pain. In short, if the demand for equality were based on the actual equality of all human beings, we would have to stop demanding equality.

Still, one might cling to the view that the demand for equality among human beings is based on the actual equality of the different races and sexes. Although, it may be said, humans differ as individu-

als, there are no differences between the races and sexes as such. From the mere fact that a person is black or a woman we cannot infer anything about that person's intellectual or moral capacities. This, it may be said, is why racism and sexism are wrong. The white racist claims that whites are superior to blacks, but this is false; although there are differences among individuals, some blacks are superior to some whites in all of the capacities and abilities that could conceivably be relevant. The opponent of sexism would say the same: a person's sex is no guide to his or her abilities, and this is why it is unjustifiable to discriminate on the basis of sex.

The existence of individual variations that cut across the lines of race or sex, however, provides us with no defense at all against a more sophisticated opponent of equality, one who proposes that, say, the interests of all those with IQ scores below 100 be given less consideration than the interests of those with ratings over 100. Perhaps those scoring below the mark would, in this society, be made the slaves of those scoring higher. Would a hierarchical society of this sort really be so much better than one based on race or sex? I think not. But if we tie the moral principle of equality to the factual equality of the different races or sexes, taken as a whole, our opposition to racism and sexism does not provide us with any basis for objecting to this kind of inegalitarianism.

There is a second important reason why we ought not to base our opposition to racism and sexism on any kind of factual equality, even the limited kind that asserts that variations in capacities and abilities are spread evenly among the different races and between the sexes: we can have no absolute guarantee that these capacities and abilities really are distributed evenly, without regard to race or sex, among human beings. So far as actual abilities are concerned there do seem to be certain measurable differences both among races and between sexes. These differences do not, of course, appear in every case, but only when averages are taken. More important still, we do not yet know how many of these differences are really due to the different genetic endowments of the different races and sexes, and how many are due to poor schools, poor housing, and other factors that are the result of past and continuing discrimination. Perhaps all of the important differences will eventually prove to be environmental rather than genetic. Anyone opposed to racism and sexism will certainly hope that this will be so, for it will make the task of ending discrimination a lot easier; nevertheless, it would be dangerous to rest the case against racism and sexism on the belief that all significant differences are environmental in origin. The opponent of, say, racism who takes this line will be unable to avoid conceding that if differences in ability did after all prove to have some genetic connection with race, racism would in some way be defensible.

Fortunately there is no need to pin the case for equality to one particular outcome of a scientific investigation. The appropriate response to those who claim to have found evidence of genetically based differences in ability among the races or between the sexes is not to stick to the belief that the genetic explanation must be wrong, whatever evidence to the contrary may turn up; instead we should make it quite clear that the claim to equality does not depend on intelligence, moral capacity, physical strength, or similar matters of fact. Equality is a moral idea, not an assertion of fact. There is no logically compelling reason for assuming that a factual difference in ability between two people justifies any difference in the amount of consideration we give to their needs and interests. *The principle of the equality of human beings is not a description of an alleged actual equality among humans: it is a prescription of how we should treat human beings.*

Jeremy Bentham, the founder of the reforming utilitarian school of moral philosophy, incorporated the essential basis of moral equality into his system of ethics by means of the formula: "Each to count for one and none for more than one." In other words, the interests of every being affected by an action are to be taken into account and given the same weight as the like interests of any other being. A later utili-

tarian, Henry Sidgwick, put the point in this way: "The good of any one individual is of no more importance, from the point of view (if I may say so) of the Universe, than the good of any other." More recently the leading figures in contemporary moral philosophy have shown a great deal of agreement in specifying as a fundamental presupposition of their moral theories some similar requirement that works to give everyone's interests equal consideration—although these writers generally cannot agree on how this requirement is best formulated.[1]

It is an implication of this principle of equality that our concern for others and our readiness to consider their interests ought not to depend on what they are like or on what abilities they may possess. Precisely what our concern or consideration requires us to do may vary according to the characteristics of those affected by what we do: concern for the well-being of children growing up in America would require that we teach them to read; concern for the well-being of pigs may require no more than that we leave them with other pigs in a place where there is adequate food and room to run freely. But the basic element—the taking into account of the interests of the being, whatever those interests may be—must, according to the principle of equality, be extended to all beings, black or white, masculine or feminine, human or nonhuman.

Thomas Jefferson, who was responsible for writing the principle of the equality of men into the American Declaration of Independence, saw this point. It led him to oppose slavery even though he was unable to free himself fully from his slaveholding background. He wrote in a letter to the author of a book that emphasized the notable intellectual achievements of Negroes in order to refute the then common view that they had limited intellectual capacities:

> Be assured that no person living wishes more sincerely than I do, to see a complete refutation of the doubts I myself have entertained and expressed on the grade of understanding allotted to them by nature, and to find that they are on a par with ourselves...but whatever

be their degree of talent it is no measure of their rights. Because Sir Isaac Newton was superior to others in understanding, he was not therefore lord of the property or persons of others.[2]

Similarly, when in the 1850s the call for women's rights was raised in the United States, a remarkable black feminist named Sojourner Truth made the same point in more robust terms at a feminist convention:

> They talk about this thing in the head; what do they call it? ["Intellect," whispered someone nearby.] That's it. What's that got to do with women's rights or Negroes' rights? If my cup won't hold but a pint and yours holds a quart, wouldn't you be mean not to let me have my little half-measure full?[3]

It is on this basis that the case against racism and the case against sexism must both ultimately rest; and it is in accordance with this principle that the attitude that we may call "speciesism," by analogy with racism, must also be condemned. Speciesism— the word is not an attractive one, but I can think of no better term—is a prejudice or attitude of bias in favor of the interests of members of one's own species and against those of members of other species. It should be obvious that the fundamental objections to racism and sexism made by Thomas Jefferson and Sojourner Truth apply equally to speciesism. If possessing a higher degree of intelligence does not entitle one human to use another for his or her own ends, how can it entitle humans to exploit nonhumans for the same purpose?[4]

Many philosophers and other writers have proposed the principle of equal consideration of interests, in some form or other, as a basic moral principle; but not many of them have recognized that this principle applies to members of other species as well as to our own. Jeremy Bentham was one of the few who did realize this. In a forward-looking passage written at a time when black slaves had been freed by the French but in the British dominions were still being treated in the way we now treat animals, Bentham wrote:

> The day *may* come when the rest of the animal creation may acquire those rights which never could have been withholden from them but by the hand of

tyranny. The French have already discovered that the blackness of the skin is no reason why a human being should be abandoned without redress to the caprice of a tormentor. It may one day come to be recognized that the number of the legs, the villosity of the skin, or the termination of the *os sacrum* are reasons equally insufficient for abandoning a sensitive being to the same fate. What else is it that should trace the insuperable line? Is it the faculty of reason, or perhaps the faculty of discourse? But a full-grown horse or dog is beyond comparison a more rational, as well as a more conversable animal, than an infant of a day or a week or even a month, old. But suppose they were otherwise, what would it avail? The question is not, Can they *reason*? nor Can they *talk*? but, Can they *suffer*?[5]

In this passage Bentham points to the capacity for suffering as the vital characteristic that gives a being the right to equal consideration. The capacity for suffering—or more strictly, for suffering and/or enjoyment or happiness—is not just another characteristic like the capacity for language or higher mathematics. Bentham is not saying that those who try to mark "the insuperable line" that determines whether the interests of a being should be considered happen to have chosen the wrong characteristic. By saying that we must consider the interests of all beings with the capacity for suffering or enjoyment Bentham does not arbitrarily exclude from consideration any interests at all—as those who draw the line with reference to the possession of reason or language do. The capacity for suffering and enjoyment is *a prerequisite for having interests at all*, a condition that must be satisfied before we can speak of interests in a meaningful way. It would be nonsense to say that it was not in the interests of a stone to be kicked along the road by a schoolboy. A stone does not have interests because it cannot suffer. Nothing that we can do to it could possibly make any difference to its welfare. The capacity for suffering and enjoyment is, however, not only necessary, but also sufficient for us to say that a being has interests—at an absolute minimum, an interest in not suffering. A mouse, for example, does have an interest in not being kicked along the road, because it will suffer if it is....

If a being suffers there can be no moral justification for refusing to take that suffering into consideration. No matter what the nature of the being, the principle of equality requires that its suffering be counted equally with the like suffering—insofar as rough comparisons can be made—of any other being. If a being is not capable of suffering, or of experiencing enjoyment or happiness, there is nothing to be taken into account. So the limit of sentience (using the term as a convenient if not strictly accurate shorthand for the capacity to suffer and/or experience enjoyment) is the only defensible boundary of concern for the interests of others. To mark this boundary by some other characteristic like intelligence or rationality would be to mark it in an arbitrary manner. Why not choose some other characteristic, like skin color?

Racists violate the principle of equality by giving greater weight to the interests of members of their own race when there is a clash between their interests and the interests of those of another race. Sexists violate the principle of equality by favoring the interests of their own sex. Similarly, speciesists allow the interests of their own species to override the greater interests of members of other species. . . .

Do animals other than humans feel pain? How do we know? Well, how do we know if anyone, human or nonhuman, feels pain? We know that we ourselves can feel pain. We know this from the direct experience of pain that we have when, for instance, somebody presses a lighted cigarette against the back of our hand. But how do we know that anyone else feels pain? We cannot directly experience anyone else's pain, whether that "anyone" is our best friend or a stray dog. Pain is a state of consciousness, a "mental event," and as such it can never be observed. Behavior like writhing, screaming, or drawing one's hand away from the lighted cigarette is not pain itself; nor are the recordings a neurologist might make of activity within the brain observations of pain itself. Pain is something that we feel, and we can only infer that others are feeling it from various external indications.

In theory, we *could* always be mistaken when we assume that other human beings feel pain. It is conceivable that one of our close friends is really a cleverly constructed robot, controlled by a brilliant scientist so as to give all the signs of feeling pain, but really no more sensitive than any other machine. We can never know, with absolute certainty, that this is not the case. But while this might present a puzzle for philosophers, none of us has the slightest real doubt that our close friends feel pain just as we do. This is an inference, but a perfectly reasonable one, based on observations of their behavior in situations in which we would feel pain, and on the fact that we have every reason to assume that our friends are beings like us, with nervous systems like ours that can be assumed to function as ours do and to produce similar feelings in similar circumstances.

If it is justifiable to assume that other human beings feel pain as we do, is there any reason why a similar inference should be unjustifiable in the case of other animals?

Nearly all the external signs that lead us to infer pain in other humans can be seen in other species, especially the species most closely related to us—the species of mammals and birds. The behavioral signs include writhing, facial contortions, moaning, yelping or other forms of calling, attempts to avoid the source of pain, appearance of fear at the prospect of its repetition, and so on. In addition, we know that these animals have nervous systems very like ours, which respond physiologically as ours do when the animal is in circumstances in which we would feel pain: an initial rise of blood pressure, dilated pupils, perspiration, an increased pulse rate, and, if the stimulus continues, a fall in blood pressure. Although human beings have a more developed cerebral cortex than other animals, this part of the brain is concerned with thinking functions rather than with basic impulses, emotions, and feelings. These impulses, emotions, and feelings are located in the diencephalon, which is well developed in many other species of animals, especially mammals and birds.[6]

We also know that the nervous systems of other animals were not artificially constructed—as a robot might be artificially constructed—to mimic the pain behavior of humans. The nervous systems of animals evolved as our own did, and in fact the evolutionary history of human beings and other animals, especially mammals, did not diverge until the central features of our nervous systems were already in existence. A capacity to feel pain obviously enhances a species' prospects of survival, since it causes members of the species to avoid sources of injury. It is surely unreasonable to suppose that nervous systems that are virtually identical physiologically, have a common origin and a common evolutionary function, and result in similar forms of behavior in similar circumstances should actually operate in an entirely different manner on the level of subjective feelings.

It has long been accepted as sound policy in science to search for the simplest possible explanation of whatever it is we are trying to explain. Occasionally it has been claimed that it is for this reason "unscientific" to explain the behavior of animals by theories that refer to the animal's conscious feelings, desires, and so on—the idea being that if the behavior in question can be explained without invoking consciousness or feelings, that will be the simpler theory. Yet we can now see that such explanations, when assessed with respect to the actual behavior of both human and nonhuman animals, are actually far more complex than rival explanations. For we know from our own experience that explanations of our own behavior that did not refer to consciousness and the feeling of pain would be incomplete; and it is simpler to assume that the similar behavior of animals with similar nervous systems is to be explained in the same way than to try to invent some other explanation for the behavior of nonhuman animals as well as an explanation for the divergence between humans and nonhumans in this respect.

The overwhelming majority of scientists who have addressed themselves to this question agree. Lord Brain, one of the most eminent neurologists of our time, has said:

> I personally can see no reason for conceding mind to my fellow men and denying it to animals....I at least cannot doubt that the interests and activities of animals are correlated with awareness and feeling in the same way as my own, and which may be, for aught I know, just as vivid.[7]

The author of a book on pain writes:

> Every particle of factual evidence supports the contention that the higher mammalian vertebrates experience pain sensations at least as acute as our own. To say that they feel less because they are lower animals is an absurdity; it can easily be shown that many of their senses are far more acute than ours—visual acuity in certain birds, hearing in most wild animals, and touch in others; these animals depend more than we do today on the sharpest possible awareness of a hostile environment. Apart from the complexity of the cerebral cortex (which does not directly perceive pain) their nervous systems are almost identical to ours and their reactions to pain remarkably similar, though lacking (so far as we know) the philosophical and moral overtones. The emotional element is all too evident, mainly in the form of fear and anger.[8]

In Britain, three separate expert government committees on matters relating to animals have accepted the conclusion that animals feel pain. After noting the obvious behavioral evidence for this view, the members of the Committee on Cruelty to Wild Animals, set up in 1951, said:

> ...we believe that the physiological, and more particularly the anatomical, evidence fully justifies and reinforces the commonsense belief that animals feel pain.

And after discussing the evolutionary value of pain the committee's report concluded that pain is "of clear-cut biological usefulness" and this is "a third type of evidence that animals feel pain." The committee members then went on to consider forms of suffering other than mere physical pain and added that they were "satisfied that animals do suffer from acute fear and terror." Subsequent reports by British government committees on experiments on animals and on the welfare of animals under intensive farming methods agreed with this view, concluding that animals are capable of suffering both from straightforward physical injuries and from fear, anxiety, stress, and so on.[9] Finally, within the last decade, the publication of scientific studies with titles such as *Animal Thought, Animal Thinking*, and *Animal Suffering: The Science of Animal Welfare* have made it plain that conscious awareness in nonhuman animals is now generally accepted as a serious subject for investigation.[10]

That might well be thought enough to settle the matter; but one more objection needs to be considered. Human beings in pain, after all, have one behavioral sign that nonhuman animals do not have: a developed language. Other animals may communicate with each other, but not, it seems, in the complicated way we do. Some philosophers, including Descartes, have thought it important that while humans can tell each other about their experience of pain in great detail, other animals cannot. (Interestingly, this once neat dividing line between humans and other species has now been threatened by the discovery that chimpanzees can be taught a language.[11] But as Bentham pointed out long ago, the ability to use language is not relevant to the question of how a being ought to be treated—unless that ability can be linked to the capacity to suffer, so that the absence of a language casts doubt on the existence of this capacity.

This link may be attempted in two ways. First, there is a hazy line of philosophical thought, deriving perhaps from some doctrines associated with the influential philosopher Ludwig Wittgenstein, which maintains that we cannot meaningfully attribute states of consciousness to beings without language. This position seems to me very implausible. Language may be necessary for abstract thought, at some level anyway; but states like pain are more primitive, and have nothing to do with language.

The second and more easily understood way of linking language and the existence of pain is to say that the best evidence we can have that other creatures are in pain is that they tell us that they are. This is a distinct line of argument, for it is denying not that non-language-users conceivably *could* suffer,

but only that we could ever have sufficient reason to *believe* that they are suffering. Still, this line of argument fails too. As Jane Goodall has pointed out in her study of chimpanzees, *In the Shadow of Man*, when it comes to the expression of feelings and emotions language is less important than nonlinguistic modes of communication such as a cheering pat on the back, an exuberant embrace, a clasp of the hands, and so on. The basic signals we use to convey pain, fear, anger, love, joy, surprise, sexual arousal, and many other emotional states are not specific to our own species.[12] The statement "I am in pain" may be one piece of evidence for the conclusion that the speaker is in pain, but it is not the only possible evidence, and since people sometimes tell lies, not even the best possible evidence.

Even if there were stronger grounds for refusing to attribute pain to those who do not have a language, the consequences of this refusal might lead us to reject the conclusion. Human infants and young children are unable to use language. Are we to deny that a year-old child can suffer? If not, language cannot be crucial. Of course, most parents understand the responses of their children better than they understand the responses of other animals; but this is just a fact about the relatively greater knowledge that we have of our own species and the greater contact we have with infants as compared to animals. Those who have studied the behavior of other animals and those who have animals as companions soon learn to understand their responses as well as we understand those of an infant, and sometimes better.

So to conclude: there are no good reasons, scientific or philosophical, for denying that animals feel pain. If we do not doubt that other humans feel pain we should not doubt that other animals do so too.

Animals can feel pain. As we saw earlier, there can be no moral justification for regarding the pain (or pleasure) that animals feel as less important than the same amount of pain (or pleasure) felt by humans. But what practical consequences follow from this conclusion? To prevent misunderstanding I shall spell out what I mean a little more fully.

If I give a horse a hard slap across its rump with my open hand, the horse may start, but it presumably feels little pain. Its skin is thick enough to protect it against a mere slap. If I slap a baby in the same way, however, the baby will cry and presumably feel pain, for its skin is more sensitive. So it is worse to slap a baby than a horse, if both slaps are administered with equal force. But there must be some kind of blow—I don't know exactly what it would be, but perhaps a blow with a heavy stick—that would cause the horse as much pain as we cause a baby by slapping it with our hand. That is what I mean by "the same amount of pain," and if we consider it wrong to inflict that much pain on a baby for no good reason then we must, unless we are speciesists, consider it equally wrong to inflict the same amount of pain on a horse for no good reason....

NOTES

1. For Bentham's moral philosophy, see his *Introduction to the Principles of Morals and Legislation*, and for Sidgwick's see *The Methods of Ethics*, 1907 (the passage is quoted from the seventh edition; reprint, London: Macmillan, 1963), p. 382. As examples of leading contemporary moral philosophers who incorporate a requirement of equal consideration of interests, see R. M. Hare, *Freedom and Reason* (New York: Oxford University Press, 1963), and John Rawls, *A Theory of Justice* (Cambridge: Harvard University Press, Belknap Press, 1972). For a brief account of the essential agreement on this issue between these and other positions, see R. M. Hare, "Rules of War and Moral Reasoning," *Philosophy and Public Affairs* 1 (2) (1972).

2. Letter to Henry Gregoire, February 25, 1809.

3. Reminiscences by Francis D. Gage, from Susan B. Anthony, *The History of Woman Suffrage*, vol. 1; the passage is to be found in the extract in Leslie Tanner, ed., *Voices From Women's Liberation* (New York: Signet, 1970).

4. I owe the term "speciesism" to Richard Ryder. It has become accepted in general use since the first edition of this book, and now appears in *The Oxford English Dictionary*, second edition (Oxford: Clarendon Press, 1989).

5. *Introduction to the Principles of Morals and Legislation*, chapter 17.

6. Lord Brain, "Presidential Address," in C.A. Keele and R. Smith, eds., *The Assessment of Pain in Men and Animals* (London: Universities Federation for Animal Welfare, 1962).

7. Lord Brain, "Presidential Address," p. 11.

8. Richard Serjeant, *The Spectrum of Pain* (London: Hart Davis 1969), p. 72.

9. See the reports of the Committee on Cruelty to Wild Animals (Command Paper 8266, 1951), paragraphs 36–42; the Departmental Committee on Experiments on Animals (Command Paper 2641, 1965), paragraphs 179–182; and the Technical Committee to Enquire into the Welfare of Animals Kept under Intensive Livestock Husbandry Systems (Command Paper 2836, 1965), paragraphs 26–28 (London: Her Majesty's Stationery Office).

10. See Stephen Walker, *Animal Thoughts* (London: Routledge and Kegan Paul, 1983); Donald Griffin, *Animal Thinking* (Cambridge: Harvard University Press, 1984); and Marian Stamp Dawkins, *Animal Suffering: The Science of Animal Welfare* (London: Chapman and Hall, 1980).

11. See Eugene Linden, *Apes, Men and Language* (New York: Penguin, 1976); for popular accounts of some more recent work, see Erik Eckholm, "Pygmy Chimp Readily Learns Language Skill," *The New York Times*, June 24, 1985; and "The Wisdom of Animals," *Newsweek*, sMay 23, 1988.

12. *In the Shadow of Man* (Boston: Houghton Mifflin, 1971), p. 22. Michael Peters makes a similar point in "Nature and Culture," Stanley and Roslind Godlovitch and John Harris, eds., *Animals, Men and Morals* (New York: Taplinger, 1972). For examples of some of the inconsistencies in denials that creatures without language can feel pain, see Bernard Rollin, *The Unheeded Cry: Animal Consciousness, Animal Pain, and Science* (Oxford: Oxford University Press, 1989).

LORI GRUEN

The Moral Status of Animals

To say that a being deserves moral consideration is to say that there is a moral claim that this being has on those who can recognize such claims. A morally considerable being is a being who can be wronged in a morally relevant sense. It is generally thought that all and only human beings make such claims, because it is only humans who can respond to these claims. However, when we ask why it is thought that all and only humans are the types of beings that can be wronged, answers are not particularly easy to come by. Humans are members of the species *Homo sapiens*. But species membership does not explain why there is a moral claim made by those that belong to this species and not other species. That humans are members of the species *Homo sapiens* is certainly a distinguishing feature of humans—humans share a genetic make-up and a distinctive physiology, but this is unimportant from the moral point of view. Species membership is a morally irrelevant characteristic, a bit of luck that is no more morally interesting than being born male or female, Malaysian or French. Species membership itself cannot support the view that members of one species, namely ours, deserve moral consideration that is not owed to members of other species. Of course, one might respond that it is not membership in a biological category that matters morally, it is our humanity that grounds the moral claims we make. Humans are morally considerable because of the distinctively human capacities we possess, capacities that only we humans have.

But which capacities mark out all and only humans as the kinds of beings that can be wronged? A number of candidate capacities have been proposed—developing family ties, solving social problems, expressing emotions, starting wars, having sex for pleasure, using language, or thinking abstractly, are just a few. As it turns out, none of these activities is uncontroversially unique to humans. Both scholarly and popular work on animal behavior suggests that many of the activities that are thought to be distinct to humans occurs in non-humans. For example, many species of non-humans develop long lasting kinship ties—orangutan mothers stay with their young for eight to ten years and while they eventually part company, they continue to maintain their relationships. Less solitary animals, such as chimpanzees, baboons, wolves, and elephants maintain extended family units built upon complex individual relationships, for long periods of time. Meerkats in the Kalahari desert are known to sacrifice their own safety by staying with sick or injured family members so that the fatally ill will not die alone. All animals living in socially complex groups must solve various problems that inevitably arise in such groups. Canids and primates are particularly adept at it, yet even chickens and horses are known to recognize large numbers of individuals in their social hierarchies and to maneuver within them. One of the ways that non-human animals negotiate their social environments is by being particularly attentive to the emotional states of others around them. When a conspecific is angry, it is a good idea to get out of his way. Animals that develop life-long bonds are known to suffer terribly from the death of their partners. Some are even said to die of sorrow. Darwin reported this in *The Descent of Man*: "So intense is the grief of female monkeys for the loss of their young, that it invariably caused the death of certain kinds." Jane Goodall's report of the death of the healthy 8-year-old chimpanzee Flint just three weeks after the death of his mother Flo also suggests

that sorrow can have a devastating effect on non-human animals. (see Goodall 2000, p. 140–141 in Bekoff 2000). Coyotes, elephants and killer whales are also among the species for which profound effects of grief have been reported (Bekoff 2000) and many dog owners can provide similar accounts. While the lives of many, perhaps most, non-humans in the wild are consumed with struggle for survival, aggression and battle, there are some non-humans whose lives are characterized by expressions of joy, playfulness, and a great deal of sex (Woods, 2010). Recent studies in cognitive ethology have suggested that some non-humans engage in manipulative and deceptive activity, can construct "cognitive maps" for navigation, and some non-humans appear to understand symbolic representation and are able to use language.[1] It appears then that most of the capacities that are thought to distinguish humans as morally considerable beings, have been observed, often in less elaborate form, in the non-human world. Because human behavior and cognition share deep roots with the behavior and cognition of other animals, approaches that try to find sharp behavioral or cognitive boundaries between humans and other animals remain controversial. For this reason, attempts to establish human uniqueness by identifying certain capacities, like those discussed in this paragraph and perhaps others, are not the most promising when it comes to thinking hard about the moral status of animals.

Nonetheless, there is something important that is thought to distinguish humans from non-humans that is not reducible to the observation of behavior best explained by possessing a certain capacity, namely our "personhood." The notion of personhood identifies a category of morally considerable beings that is thought to be coextensive with humanity. Historically, Kant is the most noted defender of personhood as the quality that makes a being valuable and thus morally considerable. In the *Groundwork*, Kant writes:

> ... every rational being, exists as an end in himself and not merely as a means to be arbitrarily used by this or

that will ... Beings whose existence depends not on our will but on nature have, nevertheless, if they are not rational beings, only a relative value as means and are therefore called things. On the other hand, rational beings are called persons inasmuch as their nature already marks them out as ends in themselves. (Kant, 1785, 428)

And in the *Lectures on Anthropology*:

> The fact that the human being can have the representation "I" raises him infinitely above all the other beings on earth. By this he is a person ... that is, a being altogether different in rank and dignity from things, such as irrational animals, with which one may deal and dispose at one's discretion. (Kant, LA, 7, 127)

More recent work in a Kantian vein develops this idea. Christine Korsgaard, for example, argues that humans "uniquely" face a problem, the problem of normativity. This problem emerges because of the reflective structure of human consciousness. We can, and often do, think about our desires and ask ourselves "Are these desires reasons for action? Do these impulses represent the kind of things I want to act according to?" Our reflective capacities allow us *and* require us to step back from our mere impulses in order to determine when and whether to act on them. In stepping back we gain a certain distance from which we can answer these questions and solve the problem of normativity. We decide whether to treat our desires as reasons for action based on our conceptions of ourselves, on our "practical identities." When we determine whether we should take a particular desire as a reason to act we are engaging in a further level of reflection, a level that requires an endorseable description of ourselves. This endorseable description of ourselves, this practical identity, is a necessary moral identity because without it we cannot view our lives as worth living or our actions as worth doing. Korsgaard suggests that humans face the problem of normativity in a way that non-humans apparently do not:

> A lower animal's attention is fixed on the world. Its perceptions are its beliefs and its desires are its will. It is engaged in conscious activities, but it is not conscious *of* them. That is, they are not the objects of its

attention. But we human animals turn our attention on to our perceptions and desires themselves, on to our own mental activities, and we are conscious *of* them. That is why we can think *about* them…

And this sets us a problem that no other animal has. It is the problem of the normative … The reflective mind cannot settle for perception and desire, not just as such. It needs a reason. (Korsgaard, 1996, 93)

Here, Korsgaard understands "reason" as "a kind of reflective success" and given that non-humans are thought to be unable to reflect in a way that would allow them this sort of success, it appears that they do not act on reasons, at least reasons of this kind. Since non-humans do not act on reasons they do not have a practical identity from which they reflect and for which they act. So humans can be distinguished from non-humans because humans, we might say, are sources of normativity and non-humans are not.

Yet Kant's view of personhood cannot distinguish all and only humans as morally considerable. Personhood is not, in fact, coextensive with humanity when understood as a general description of the group to which human beings belong. And the serious part of this problem is not that there may be some extra-terrestrials or deities who have rational capacities. (It seems likely that Kant recognized this when he wrote "man, and in general every rational being.") The serious problem is that many humans are not persons. Some members of humanity—i.e. infants, children, people with advanced forms of autism or Alzheimer's disease or other cognitive disorders—do not have the rational, self-reflective capacities associated with personhood. This problem, unfortunately known in the literature as the problem of "marginal cases," poses serious difficulties for "personhood" as the criterion of moral considerability. Many beings who's positive moral value we have deeply held intuitions about, and who we treat as morally considerable, will be excluded from consideration by this account.

There are four ways to respond to this counter-intuitive conclusion. One, which can be derived from one interpretation of Kant, is to suggest that non-persons are morally considerable indirectly.

Though Kant believed that animals were mere things it appears he did not genuinely believe we could dispose of them any way we wanted. In the *Lectures on Ethics* he makes it clear that we have indirect duties to animals, duties that are not toward them, but in regard to them insofar as our treatment of them can affect our duties to persons.

> If a man shoots his dog because the animal is no longer capable of service, he does not fail in his duty to the dog, for the dog cannot judge, but his act is inhuman and damages in himself that humanity which it is his duty to show towards mankind. If he is not to stifle his human feelings, he must practice kindness towards animals, for he who is cruel to animals becomes hard also in his dealings with men. (Kant, LE, 240)

And one could argue the same would be true of those human beings who are not persons. We disrespect our humanity when we act in inhumane ways towards nonpersons, whatever their species.

But this indirect view is unsatisfying—it fails to capture the independent wrong that is being done to the non-person. When someone rapes a woman in a coma, or whips a severely brain damaged child, or sets a cat on fire, they are not simply disrespecting humanity or themselves as representatives of it, they are wronging these non-persons. So, a second way to avoid the counter-intuitive conclusion is to argue that such non-persons stand in the proper relations to "rational nature" such that they should be thought of as morally considerable. Allen Wood (1998) argues in this way and suggests that all beings that potentially have a rational nature, or who virtually have it, or who have had it, or who have part of it, or who have the necessary conditions of it, what he calls "the infrastructure of rational nature," should be directly morally considerable. Insofar as a being stands in this relation to rational nature, they are the kinds of beings that can be wronged.

This response is not unlike that of noted animal rights proponent, Tom Regan, who argues that what is important for moral consideration are not the differences between humans and non-humans but the similarities. Regan argues that because persons share with certain non-persons (which includes

those humans and non-humans who have a certain level of organized cognitive function) the ability to be experiencing subject of a life and to have an individual welfare that matters to them regardless of what others might think, both deserve moral consideration. Regan argues that subjects of a life

> want and prefer things, believe and feel things, recall and expect things. And all these dimensions of our life, including our pleasure and pain, our enjoyment and suffering, our satisfaction and frustration, our continued existence or our untimely death—all make a difference to the quality of our life as lived, as experienced, by us as individuals. As the same is true of ... animals ... they too must be viewed as the experiencing subjects of a life, with inherent value of their own. (Regan, 1985)

A third way of addressing this problem has been taken up by Korsgaard who maintains that there is a big difference between those with normative, rational capacities and those without, but unlike Kant, believes both humans and non-humans are the proper objects of our moral concern. She argues that those without normative, rational capacities share certain "natural" capacities with persons, and these natural capacities are often the content of the moral demands that persons make on each other. She writes, "what we demand, when we demand ... recognition, is that our natural concerns—the objects of our natural desires and interests and affections—be accorded the status of values, values that must be respected as far as possible by others. And many of those natural concerns—the desire to avoid pain is an obvious example—spring from our animal nature, not from our rational nature" (Korsgaard 2007). What moral agents construct as valuable and normatively binding is not only our rational or autonomous capacities, but the needs and desires we have as living, embodied beings. Insofar as these needs and desires are valuable for agents, the ability to experience similar needs and desires in patients should also be valued.

A final response is simply to reject rational nature as the touchstone of moral considerability. This is the kind of direct argument that utilitarians have traditionally made. They argue that the truly mor-

ally important feature of beings is unappreciated when we focus on personhood or the rational, self-reflective nature of humans, or the relation a being stands in to such nature, or being the subject of a life. What is really important, utilitarians maintain, is the promotion of happiness, or pleasure, or the satisfaction of interests, and the avoidance of pain, or suffering, or frustration of interests...

Contemporary utilitarians, such as Peter Singer (1990, 1993), suggest that there is no morally justifiable way to exclude from moral consideration non-humans or non-persons who can clearly suffer. Any being that has an interest in not suffering deserves to have that interest taken into account. And a non-human who acts to avoid pain can be thought to have just such an interest. Even contemporary Kantians have acknowledged the moral force of the experience of pain. Korsgaard, for example, writes "it is a pain to be in pain. And that is not a trivial fact" (1996, 154).

> When you pity a suffering animal, it is because you are perceiving a reason. An animal's cries express pain, and they mean that there is a reason, a reason to change its conditions. And you can no more hear the cries of an animal as mere noise than you can the words of a person. Another animal can obligate you in exactly the same way another person can ... So of course we have obligations to animals. (Korsgaard, 1996, 153)

When we encounter an animal in pain we recognize their claim on us, and thus beings who can suffer are morally considerable.

That non-human animals can make moral claims on us does not in itself indicate how such claims are to be assessed and conflicting claims adjudicated. Being morally considerable is like showing up on a moral radar screen—how strong the signal is or where it is located on the screen are separate questions. Of course, how one argues for the moral considerability of non-human animals will inform how we are to understand the force of an animal's claims.

According to the view that an animal's moral claim is equivalent to a moral right, any action that fails to treat the animal as a being with inherent worth would violate that animal's right and is thus morally

objectionable. According to the animal rights position, to treat an animal as a means to some human end, as many humans do when they eat animals or experiment on them, is to violate that animal's right. As Tom Regan has written,

> …animals are treated routinely, systematically as if their value were reducible to their usefulness to others, they are routinely, systematically treated with a lack of respect, and thus are their rights routinely, systematically violated. (Regan, 1985)

The animal rights position is an absolutist position. Any being that is a subject of a life has inherent worth and the rights that protect such worth, and all subjects of a life have these rights equally. Thus any practice that fails to respect the rights of those animals who have them, e.g. eating animals, hunting animals, experimenting on animals, using animals for entertainment, is wrong, irrespective of human need, context, or culture.

The utilitarian position on animals, most commonly associated with Singer and popularly, though erroneously, referred to as an animal rights position, is actually quite distinct. Here the moral significance of the claims of animals depends on what other morally significant competing claims might be in play in any given situation. While the equal interests of all morally considerable beings are considered equally, the practices in question may end up violating or frustrating some interests but would not be considered morally wrong if, when all equal interests are considered, more of these interests are satisfied than frustrated. For utilitarians like Singer, what matters are the strength and nature of interests, not whose interests these are. So, if the only options available in order to save the life of one morally considerable being is to cause harm, but not death, to another morally considerable being, then according to a utilitarian position, causing this harm may be morally justifiable. Similarly, if there are two courses of action, one which causes extreme amounts of suffering and ultimate death, and one which causes much less suffering and painless death, then the latter would be morally preferable to the former.

Consider factory farming, the most common method used to convert animal bodies into relatively inexpensive food in industrialized societies today. An estimated 8 billion animals in the United States are born, confined, biologically manipulated, transported and ultimately slaughtered each year so that humans can consume them. The conditions in which these animals are raised and the method of slaughter causes vast amounts of suffering. (See, for example, Mason and Singer 1990.) Given that animals suffer under such conditions and assuming that suffering is not in their interests, then the practice of factory farming would only be morally justifiable if its abolition were to cause greater suffering or a greater amount of interest frustration. Certainly humans who take pleasure in eating animals will find it harder to satisfy these interests in the absence of factory farms; it may cost more and require more effort to obtain animal products. The factory farmers, and the industries that support factory farming, will also have certain interests frustrated if factory farming were to be abolished. How much interest frustration and interest satisfaction would be associated with the end to factory farming is largely an empirical question. But utilitarians are not making unreasonable predictions when they argue that on balance the suffering and interest frustration that animals experience in modern day meat production is greater than the suffering that humans would endure if they had to alter their current practices.

Importantly, the utilitarian argument for the moral significance of animal suffering in meat production is not an argument for vegetarianism. If an animal lived a happy life and was painlessly killed and then eaten by people who would otherwise suffer hunger or malnutrition by not eating the animal, then painlessly killing and eating the animal would be the morally justified thing to do. In many parts of the world where economic, cultural, or climate conditions make it virtually impossible for people to sustain themselves on plant based diets, killing and eating animals that previously led relatively unconstrained lives and are painlessly killed, would not be morally objectionable. The utilitarian position can thus avoid certain charges of cultural chauvinism and moralism, charges that the animal rights position apparently cannot avoid.

It might be objected that to suggest that it is morally acceptable to hunt and eat animals for those people living in arctic regions, or for nomadic cultures, or for poor rural peoples, for example, is to potentially condone painlessly killing other morally considerable beings, like humans, for food consumption in similar situations. If violating the rights of an animal can be morally tolerated, especially a right to life, then similar rights violations can be morally tolerated. In failing to recognize the inviolability of the moral claims of all morally considerable beings, utilitarianism cannot accommodate one of our most basic prima facie principles, namely that killing a morally considerable being is wrong.

There are at least two replies to this sort of objection. The first appeals to the negative side effects that killing may promote. If, to draw on an overused and sadly sophomoric counter-example, one person can be kidnapped and painlessly killed in order to provide body parts for four individuals who will die without them, there will inevitably be negative side-effects that all things considered would make the kidnapping wrong. Healthy people, knowing they could be used for spare parts, might make themselves unhealthy to avoid such a fate or they may have so much stress and fear that the overall state of affairs would be worse than that in which four people died. Appealing to side-effects when it comes to the wrong of killing is certainly plausible, but it fails to capture what is directly wrong with killing.

A more satisfying reply would have us adopt what might be called a multi-factor perspective, one that takes into account the kinds of interest that are possible for certain kinds of morally considerable beings, the content of interests of the beings in question, their relative weight, and the context of those who have them. Consider a seal who has spent his life freely roaming the oceans and ice flats and who is suddenly and painlessly killed to provide food for

a human family struggling to survive a bitter winter in far northern climes. While it is probably true that the seal had an immediate interest in avoiding suffering, it is less clear that the seal has a future directed interest in continued existence. If the seal lacks this future directed interest, then painlessly killing him does not violate this interest. The same cannot be said for the human explorer who finds himself face to face with a hungry Inuit family. Persons generally have interests in continued existence, interests that, arguably, non-persons do not have. So one factor that can be appealed to is that non-persons may not have the range of interests that persons do.

An additional factor is the type of interest in question. We can think of interests as scalar; crucial interests are weightier than important interests, important interests are weightier than replaceable interests, and all are weightier than trivial interests or mere whims. When there is a conflict of interests, crucial interests will always override important interests, important interests will always override replaceable interests, etc. So if an animal has an interest in not suffering, which is arguably a crucial interest, or at least an important one, and a person has an interest in eating that animal when there are other things to eat, meaning that interest is replaceable, then the animal has the stronger interest and it would be wrong to violate that interest by killing the animal for food if there is another source of food available.

Often, however, conflicts of interests are within the same category. The Inuit's interest in food is crucial and the explorer's interest in life is crucial. If we assume that the explorer cannot otherwise provide food for the hunter, then it looks as if there is a conflict within the same category. If you take the interests of an indigenous hunter's whole family into account, then their combined interest in their own survival appears to outweigh the hapless explorer's interest in continued existence. Indeed, if painlessly killing and eating the explorer were the only way for the family to survive, then perhaps this action would be morally condoned. But this is a rather extreme sort of example, one in which even our deepest held convictions are strained. So it is quite hard to know what to make of the clash between what a utilitarian would condone and what our intuitions tell us we should believe here. Our most basic prima facie principles arise and are accepted under ordinary circumstances. Extraordinary circumstances are precisely those in which such principles or precepts give way.[2]

The multi-factor utilitarian perspective is particularly helpful when considering the use of animals in medical research. According to the animal rights position, the use of animals in experimental procedures is a clear violation of their rights—they are being used as a mere means to some possible end—and thus animal rights proponents are in favor of the abolition of all laboratory research. The utilitarian position, particularly one that incorporates some kind of multi-factor perspective, might allow some research on animals under very specific conditions. Before exploring what a utilitarian might condone in the way of animal experimentation, let us first quickly consider what would be morally prohibited. All research that involves invasive procedures, constant confinement, and ultimate death can be said to violate the animal's crucial interests. Thus any experiments that are designed to enhance the important, replaceable, or trivial interests of humans or other animals would be prohibited. That would mean that experiments for cosmetics or household products are prohibited, as there are non-animal tested alternatives and many options already available for consumers. Experiments to determine the effects of recreational drugs, cigarettes, and alcohol would also be prohibited. Certain psychological experiments, such as those in which infant primates are separated from their mothers and exposed to frightening stimuli in an effort to understand problems teenagers have when they enter high school, would also come into question. There are many examples of experiments that violate an animal's crucial interests in the hopes of satisfying the lesser interests of some other morally considerable being, all of which would be objectionable from this perspective.

There are some laboratory experiments, however, that from a multi-factor utilitarian perspective may be permitted. These are experiments in which the probability of satisfying crucial or important interests for many who suffer from some debilitating or fatal disease is high, and the numbers of non-human animals who's crucial interests are violated is low. The psychological complexity of the non-humans may also be significant in determining whether the experiment is morally justified. In the case of experimenting in these limited number of cases, presumably a parallel argument could be made about experimenting on humans. If the chances are very high that experimenting on one human, who is a far superior experimental animal when it comes to human disease, can prevent great suffering or death in many humans, then the utilitarian may, if side effects are minimal, condone such an experiment. Of course, it is easier to imagine this sort of extreme case in the abstract, what a utilitarian would think actually morally justified, again depends on the specific empirical data.

In sum, the animal rights position takes the significance of morally considerable claims to be absolute. Thus, any use of animals that involves a disregard for their moral claims is problematic. The significance of an animal's morally considerable interests according to a utilitarian is variable. Whether an action is morally justified or permissible will depend on a number of factors. The utilitarian position on animals would condemn a large number of practices that involve the suffering and death of billions of animals, but there are cases in which some use of non-human animals, and perhaps even human animals, may be morally justified.

Given the long-standing view that non-humans are mere things, there are still many who reject the arguments presented here for the moral considerability of non-humans and the significance of their interests. Nonetheless, most now realize that the task of arguing that humans have a unique and exclusive moral status is rather difficult. Yet even amongst those who do view animals as within the sphere of moral concern, there is disagreement about the nature and usefulness of the arguments presented on behalf of the moral status of animals.

Some, in the neo-Aristotelian or "virtue ethics" tradition, have argued that while our behavior towards animals is indeed subject to moral scrutiny, the kinds of arguments that have been presented frame the issues in the wrong way. According to many in this tradition, rational argumentation fails to capture those features of moral experience that allow us to really see why treating animals badly is wrong. The point, according to commentators such as Stephen R. L. Clark and Cora Diamond, for example, is that members of our communities, however we conceive of them, pull on us and it is in virtue of this indescribable pull that we recognize what is wrong with cruelty. Animals are individuals with whom we share a common life and this recognition allows us to see them as they are. A person striving for virtue comes to see that eating animals is wrong not because it is a violation of the animal's rights or because on balance such an act creates more suffering than other acts, but rather because in eating animals or using them in other harmful ways, we do not display the traits of character that kind, sensitive, compassionate, mature, and thoughtful members of a moral community should display. And carefully worked out arguments in which the moral considerability and moral significance of animals are laid out will have little if any grip on our thoughts and actions. Rather, by perceiving the attitudes that underlie the use and abuse of non-human animals as shallow or cruel, one interested in living a virtuous life will change their attitudes and come to reject treating animals as food or tools for research. As Rosalind Hursthouse recognized after having been exposed to alternative ways of seeing animals:[3]

> I began to see [my attitudes] that related to my conception of flesh-foods as unnecessary, greedy, self-indulgent, childish, my attitude to shopping and cooking in order to produce lavish dinner parties as parochial, gross, even dissolute. I saw my interest and delight in nature programmes about the lives of animals on tel-

evision and my enjoyment of meat as side by side at odds with one another ... Without thinking animals had rights, I began to see both the wild ones and the ones we usually eat as having lives of their own, which they should be left to enjoy. And so I changed. My perception of the moral landscape and where I and the other animals were situated in it shifted. (Hursthouse, 2000, 165–166)

Feminists too have taken issue with the methods of argumentation used to establish the moral status of animals. For many feminists the traditional methods of rational argumentation fail to take into account the feelings of sympathy or empathy that humans have towards non-humans, feelings they believe are central to a full account of what we owe non-humans and why. While many feminists believe, following Hume, that our moral emotions are what ultimately move us to act compassionately towards animals, they do not reject the conclusions that the rights-based theorists or the utilitarian theorists draw. Rather, their criticisms are directed at the idea that these conclusions, drawn through reason alone, can change our behaviors. (See Adams and Donovan 1995.)

Feminist philosophers have also challenged the individualism that is central in the arguments for the moral status of animals. Rather than identifying intrinsic or innate properties that non-humans share with humans, properties that are thought to be morally valuable in themselves, some feminists have argued instead that we ought to understand moral status in relational terms given that moral recognition is invariably a social practice. As Elizabeth Anderson has written: "Moral considerability is not an intrinsic property of any creature, nor is it supervenient on only its intrinsic properties, such as its capacities. It depends, deeply, on the kind of relations they can have with us" (Anderson, 2004, 289).

Similarly ecological feminists have also argued that the standard approaches to determining the moral status of animals are flawed. For these critics, the focus on individuals in isolation from their context fails to capture the political structures, particularly

the structures of power, that underlie current practices in which animals are used. According to some eco-feminists there is a conceptual link between the "logic of domination" that operates to reinforce sexism and the logic that supports the oppression of non-human animals, a link that translates into individual and institutional practices that are harmful to both women and animals. Gender hierarchies, in which men are thought to be separate from and superior to women share the same structure, according to this analysis, as hierarchies that separate humans from other animals and justify human dominance over the allegedly inferior others. According to an ecological feminist perspective, differences between groups and individuals can be acknowledged without attributing greater or lesser moral worth to those groups or individuals within them and just social relations require that such valuations be avoided. Like many social justice perspectives, the eco-feminist perspective maintains that no one will be free unless everyone is free, and that includes non-human animals. (See, for example, Gaard 1993.)

NOTES

1. For one of many summaries of tool-use in animals, see Griffin 1992, Ch. 5. See also Attenborough 1998, Ch. 5. For primary research see, for example, S. Chevalier-Skolnikoff 1989; Weir, Chappell, and Kacelnik 2002, and Visalberghi 1997. For elaborate stories of family-ties, see Galdikas 1995 and Goodall 1986 & 2000. For an interesting discussion of Meerkats see "All For One: Meerkats," National Geographic. For examples of non-human "culture" in chimpanzees, see Whiten, Goodall, et al. 1999; in whales and dolphins see Rendell and Whitehead 2001; and for a general discussion Griffin 1992, Ch. 4. Two useful discussions of non-human "social knowledge" can be found in Cheney & Seyfarth 1990, and Tomasello & Call 1997, Part II. See Bekoff 2000 for an account of animal emotion. For a discussion of warlike behavior and alliance building see de Waal 1989. Bonobos have sex not just for reproduction, but to relax, to bond, or just for pleasure. They also don't seem to have taboos about who they have sex with or how. For a discussion see de Waal and Lanting 1997. See Bekoff and Byers 1998 for discussion of play among many different species. Studies of language use among non-humans have a long and interesting history. See, for example, Pepperberg 1999 and Premack 1986. Critics have contended that while some animals can be taught to use words they do not use a language with syntax, defenders have argued that the non-human animals in the language studies, particularly the bonobos, not only have large vocabularies, but are capable of communicating novel information, of combining words in new ways, and of following simple syntactic rules. See Rumbaugh & Savage-Rumbaugh 1999. For a discussion of deception see, for example, Whiten and Byrne 1988 (I) and 1997 (II). For a nice introductory discussion of other forms of cognition see Roberts 1998. See also Hauser and Carey 1997 and Bekoff, Allen, and Burghardt 2002.

2. Unfortunately, in our complex world, it does appear that the extraordinary is becoming more ordinary; that conflicts of crucial interests are occurring more regularly. Some have suggested that in order to cope with such conflicts additional factors be considered in the process of conflict resolution. Donald VanDeVeer has proposed that the level of psychological complexity be a determining factor such that if a being has a higher level of this complexity then his crucial interest would outweigh the crucial interests of a being with lesser complexity. There are clearly refinements needed with this proposal. See VanDeVeer 1979, 55–70.

3. See also Diamond 2001 (esp. Chs. 11 and 13), and Clarke 1977.

REFERENCES

Adams, C., and Donovan, J. (eds.), 1995, *Animals and Women: Feminist Theoretical Explorations*, Durham: Duke University Press.

Anderson, E., 2004, "Animal Rights and the Values of Nonhuman Life," in *Animal Rights: Current Debates and New Directions*, Sunstein, C. R. and Nussbaum, M. (eds.). Oxford: Oxford University Press.

Bekoff, M., 2000, *The Smile of a Dolphin: Remarkable Accounts of Animal Emotion*, Discovery Channel Books.

Bentham, J., 1781, *An Introduction to the Principles of Morals and Legislation*, edited by J. H. Burns and H. L. A. Hart, London: Methuen, 1982.

Darwin, C., 1883, *The Descent of Man*, New York: Appleton & Co.

Donovan, J. and Adams, C. (eds.), 2007, *The Feminist Care Tradition in Animal Ethics*, New York: Columbia University Press.

Gaard, G. (ed.), 1993, *Ecofeminism: Women, Animals, Nature*, Philadelphia: Temple University Press.

Goodall, J., 1986, *The Chimpanzees of Gombe*, Cambridge, MA: Harvard University Press.

———, 2000, *In the Shadow of Man*, revised edition, New York: Houghton Mifflin Co.

Hursthouse, R., 2000, *Ethics, Humans and Other Animals*, London: Routledge.

Kant, I., 1785, *The Groundwork for the Metaphysics of Morals*, Mary J. Gregor (trans.), Cambridge: Cambridge University Press, 1998.

———, [LA], *Lectures on Anthropology*, Akademie-Textausgabe, Berlin.

———, [LE], *Lectures on Ethics*, translated and edited by P. Heath and J. B. Schneewind, Cambridge: Cambridge University Press, 1997.

Korsgaard, C., 1996, *The Sources of Normativity*, Cambridge: Cambridge University Press.

———, 2007, "Facing the Animal You See in the Mirror," *Harvard Review of Philosophy*, 16: 2–7.

Mason, J., and Singer, P., 1990, *Animal Factories*, New York: Harmony Books.

Regan, T., 1985, "The Case for Animal Rights," in P. Singer (ed.), *In Defence of Animals*, Oxford: Basil Blackwell.

Singer, P., 1990, *Animal Liberation*, 2nd edition, New York: New York Review.

———, 1993, *Practical Ethics*, Cambridge: Cambridge University Press.

Wood, A., 1998, "Kant on Duties Regarding Nonrational Nature," *Proceedings of the Aristotelian Society Supplement*, LXXII: 189–210.

Woods, V., 2010, *Bonobo Handshake*, New York: Gotham Books.

MARK SAGOFF

Animal Liberation and Environmental Ethics: Bad Marriage, Quick Divorce

I

"The land ethic," Aldo Leopold wrote in *A Sand County Almanac*, "simply enlarges the boundaries of the community to include soils, waters, plants, and animals, or collectively, the land."[1] What kind of community does Leopold refer to? He might mean a *moral* community, for example, a group of individuals who respect each other's right to treatment as equals or who regard one another's interests with equal respect and concern. He may also mean an *ecological* community, that is, a community tied together by biological relationships in interdependent webs or systems of life.[2]

Let us suppose, for a moment, that Leopold has a *moral* community in mind; he would expand our *moral* boundaries to include not only human beings, but also soils, waters, plants and animals. Leopold's view, then, might not differ in principle from that of Christopher Stone, who has suggested that animals and even trees be given legal standing, so that their interests may be represented in court.[3] Stone sees the expansion of our moral consciousness in this way as part of a historical progress by which societies have recognized the equality of groups of oppressed people, notably blacks, women and children.[4] Laurence Tribe eloquently makes the same point:

> What is crucial to recognize is that the human capacity for empathy and identification is not static; the very process of recognizing rights in those higher vertebrates with whom we can already empathize could well pave the way for still further extensions as we move upward along the spiral of moral evolution. It is not only the human liberation movements—involving first blacks, then women, and now children—that advance in waves of increased consciousness.[5]

Peter Singer, perhaps more than any other writer, has emphasized the analogy between human

liberation movements (for example, abolitionism and sufferagism) and "animal liberation" or the "expansion of our moral horizons" to include members of other species in the "basic principle of equality."[6] Singer differs from Stone and Tribe, however, in two respects. First, he argues that the capacity of animals to suffer pain or to enjoy pleasure or happiness places people under a moral obligation which does not need to be enhanced by a doctrine about rights. Second, while Stone is willing to speak of the interests of his lawn in being watered,[7] Singer argues that "only a being with subjective experiences, such as the experience of pleasure or the experience of pain, can have interests in the full sense of the term."[8] A tree, as Singer explains, may be said to have an "interest" in being watered, but all this means is that it needs water to grow properly as an automobile needs oil to function properly.[9] Thus, Singer would not include rocks, trees, lakes, rivers or mountains in the moral community or the community of morally equal beings.

Singer's thesis, then, is not necessarily that animals have rights which we are to respect. Instead, he argues that they have utilities that ought to be treated on an equal basis with those of human beings. Whether Tribe and Stone argue a weaker or a different thesis depends upon the rights they believe animals and other natural things to have. They may believe that all animals have a right to be treated as equals, in effect, they may agree with Singer that the interests of *all* animals should receive equal respect and concern. On the other hand, Tribe, Stone or both may believe that animals have a right only to life or only to those very minimal and basic rights without which they could not conceivably enjoy any other right.[10] I will, for the moment, assume that Tribe and Stone agree that animals have basic rights, for example, a right to live or a right not to be killed for their meat. I will consider later the possibility that environmental law might protect the rights of animals without necessarily improving their welfare or protecting their lives.

Moral obligations to animals, to their well-being or to their rights, may arise in either of two ways.

First, duties to non-human animals may be based on the principle that cruelty to animals is obnoxious, a principle nobody denies. Muckraking journalists (thank God for them) who depict the horrors which all too often occur in laboratories and on farms, appeal quite properly to the conviction and intuition that people should never inflict needless pain on animals and especially not for the sake of profit. When television documentaries or newspaper articles report the horrid ways in which domestic animals are often treated, the response is, as it should be, moral revulsion. This anger is directed at human responsibility for the callous, wanton and needless cruelty human beings inflict on domestic animals. It is not simply the pain but the way it is caused which justifies moral outrage.

Moral obligations, however, might rest instead on a stronger contention, which is that human beings are obliged to prevent and to relieve animal suffering however it is caused. Now, insofar as the animal equality or animal liberation movement makes a philosophically interesting claim, it insists on the stronger thesis, that there is an obligation to serve the interests, or at least to protect the lives, of *all* animals who suffer or are killed, whether on the farm or in the wild. Singer, for example, does not stop with the stultifying platitude that human beings ought not to be cruel to animals. No; he argues the controversial thesis that society has an obligation to prevent the killing of animals and even to relieve their suffering wherever, however, and as much as it is able, at a reasonable cost to itself.

II

I began by supposing that Aldo Leopold viewed the community of nature as a *moral* community—one in which human beings, as members, have obligations to all other animals, presumably to minimize their pain. I suggested that Leopold, like Singer, may be committed to the idea that the natural environment should be preserved and protected only insofar as,

and because, its protection satisfies the needs or promotes the welfare of individual animals and perhaps other living things. I believe, however, that this is plainly not Leopold's view. The principle of natural selection is not obviously a humanitarian principle; the predator-prey relation does not depend on moral empathy. Nature ruthlessly limits animal populations by doing violence to virtually every individual before it reaches maturity; these conditions respect animal equality only in the darkest sense. Yet these are precisely the ecological relationships which Leopold admires; they are the conditions which he would not interfere with, but protect. Apparently, Leopold does not think that an ecological system has to be an egalitarian moral system in order to deserve love and admiration. An ecological system has a beauty and an authenticity that demands respect—but plainly not on humanitarian grounds.

In a persuasive essay, J. Baird Callicott describes a number of differences between the ideas of Leopold and those of Singer—differences which suggest that Leopold's environmental ethic and Singer's humane utilitarianism lead in opposite directions. First, while Singer and other animal liberationists deplore the suffering of domestic animals, "Leopold manifests an attitude that can only be described as indifference."[11] Second, while Leopold expresses an urgent concern about the disappearance of species, Singer, consistently with his premises, is concerned with the welfare of individual animals, without special regard to their status as endangered species. Third, the preservation of wilderness, according to Leopold, provides "a means of perpetuating, in sport form, the more virile and primitive skills. . . ."[12] He had hunting in mind. Leopold recognized that since top predators are gone, hunters may serve an important ecological function. Leopold was himself an enthusiastic hunter and wrote unabashedly about his exploits pursuing game. The term "game" as applied to animals, Callicott wryly comments, "appears to be morally equivalent to referring to a sexually appealing young woman as a 'piece' or to a strong, young black man as a 'buck'—if animal rights, that is, are

to be considered on par with women's rights and the rights of formerly enslaved races."[13]

Singer expresses disdain and chagrin at what he calls "environmentalist" organizations such as the Sierra Club and the Wildlife Fund, which actively support or refuse to oppose hunting. I can appreciate Singer's aversion to hunting, but why does he place the word "environmentalist" in shudder quotes when he refers to organizations like the Sierra Club? Environmentalist and conservationist organizations traditionally have been concerned with ecological, not humanitarian issues. They make no pretense of acting for the sake of individual animals; rather, they attempt to maintain the diversity, integrity, beauty and authenticity of the natural environment. These goals are ecological, not eleemosynary. Their goals are entirely consistent, then, with licensing hunters to shoot animals whose populations exceed the carrying capacity of their habitats. Perhaps hunting is immoral; if so, environmentalism is consistent with an immoral practice, but it is environmentalism without quotes nonetheless. The policies environmentalists recommend are informed by the concepts of population biology, not the concepts of animal equality. The S.P.C.A. does not set the agenda for the Sierra Club.

I do not in any way mean to support the practice of hunting; nor am I advocating environmentalism at this time. I merely want to point out that groups like the Sierra Club, the Wilderness Society and the World Wildlife Fund do not fail in their mission insofar as they devote themselves to causes other than the happiness or welfare of individual creatures; that never was their mission. These organizations, which promote a love and respect for the functioning of natural ecosystems, differ ideologically from organizations that make the suffering of animals their primary concern—groups like the Fund for Animals, the Animal Protection Institute, Friends of Animals, the American Humane Association, and various single issue groups such as Friends of the Sea Otter, Beaver Defenders, Friends of the Earthworm, and Worldwide Fair Play for Frogs.[14]

D. G. Ritchie, writing in 1916, posed a difficulty for those who argue that animals have rights or that we have obligations to them created simply by their capacity to suffer. If the suffering of animals creates a human obligation to mitigate it, is there not as much an obligation to prevent a cat from killing a mouse as to prevent a hunter from killing a deer? "Are we not to vindicate the rights of the persecuted prey of the stronger?" Ritchie asks. "Or is our declaration of the rights of every creeping thing to remain a mere hypocritical formula to gratify pug-loving sentimentalists?"[15]

If the animal liberation or animal equality movement is not to deteriorate into "a hypocritical formula to gratify pug-loving sentimentalists," it must insist, as Singer does, that moral obligations to animals are justified, in the first place, by their distress, and, in the second place, by human ability to relieve that distress. The liberationist must morally require society to relieve animal suffering wherever it can and at a lesser cost to itself, whether in the chicken coop or in the wild. Otherwise, the animal liberationist thesis becomes interchangeable with the platitude one learns along with how to tie shoestrings: people ought not to be cruel to animals. I do not deny that human beings are cruel to animals, that they ought not to be, that this cruelty should be stopped and that sermons to this effect are entirely appropriate and necessary. I deny only that these sermons have anything to do with environmentalism or provide a basis for an environmental ethic.

III

In discussing the rights of human beings, Henry Shue describes two that are basic in the sense that "the enjoyment of them is essential to the enjoyment of all other rights."[16] These are the right to physical security and the right to minimum subsistence. These are positive, not merely negative rights. In other words, these rights require governments to provide security and subsistence, not merely to refrain from

invading security and denying subsistence. These basic rights require society, where possible, to rescue individuals from starvation; this is more than the merely negative obligation not to cause starvation. No; if people have basic rights—and I have no doubt they do—then society has a positive obligation to satisfy those rights. It is not enough for society simply to refrain from violating them.

This, surely, is true of the basic rights of animals as well, if we are to give the conception of "right" the same meaning for both people and animals. For example, to allow animals to be killed for food or to permit them to die of disease or starvation when it is within human power to prevent it, does not seem to balance fairly the interests of animals with those of human beings. To speak of the rights of animals, of treating them as equals, of liberating them, and at the same time to let nearly all of them perish unnecessarily in the most brutal and horrible ways is not to display humanity but hypocrisy in the extreme.

Where should society concentrate its efforts to provide for the basic welfare—the security and subsistence—of animals? Plainly, where animals most lack this security, when their basic rights, needs, or interests are most thwarted and where their suffering is most intense. Alas, this is in nature. Ever since Darwin, we have been aware that few organisms survive to reach sexual maturity; most are quickly annihilated in the struggle for existence. Consider as a rough but reasonable statement of the facts the following:

> All species reproduce in excess, way past the carrying capacity of their niche. In her lifetime a lioness might have 20 cubs; a pigeon, 150 chicks; a mouse, 1,000 kits; a trout, 20,000 fry, a tuna or cod, a million fry or more; an elm tree, several million seeds; and an oyster, perhaps a hundred million spat. If one assumes that the population of each of these species is, from generation to generation, roughly equal, then on the average only one offspring will survive to replace each parent. All the other thousands and millions will die, one way or another.[17]

The ways in which creatures in nature die are typically violent: predation, starvation, disease,

parasitism, cold. The dying animal in the wild does not understand the vast ocean of misery into which it and billions of other animals are born only to drown. If the wild animal understood the conditions into which it is born, what would it think? It might reasonably prefer to be raised on a farm, where the chances of survival for a year or more would be good, and to escape from the wild, where they are negligible. Either way, the animal will be eaten: few die of old age. The path from birth to slaughter, however, is often longer and less painful in the barnyard than in the woods. Comparisons, sad as they are, must be made to recognize where a great opportunity lies to prevent or mitigate suffering. The misery of animals in nature—which humans can do much to relieve—makes every other form of suffering pale in comparison. Mother Nature is so cruel to her children she makes Frank Perdue look like a saint.

What is the practical course society should take once it climbs the spiral of moral evolution high enough to recognize its obligation to value the basic rights of animals equally with that of human beings? I do not know how animal liberationists, such as Singer, propose to relieve animal suffering in nature (where most of it occurs), but there are many ways to do so at little cost. Singer has suggested, with respect to pest control, that animals might be fed contraceptive chemicals rather than poisons.[18] It may not be beyond the reach of science to attempt a broad program of contraceptive care for animals in nature so that fewer will fall victim to an early and horrible death. The government is spending hundreds of millions of dollars to store millions of tons of grain. Why not lay out this food, laced with contraceptives, for wild creatures to feed upon? Farms which so overproduce for human needs might then satisfy the needs of animals. The day may come when entitlement programs which now extend only to human beings are offered to animals as well.

One may modestly propose the conversion of national wilderness areas, especially national parks, into farms in order to replace violent wild areas with more humane and managed environments. Starving

deer in the woods might be adopted as pets. They might be fed in kennels; animals that once wandered the wilds in misery might get fat in feedlots instead. Birds that now kill earthworms may repair instead to birdhouses stocked with food, including textured soybean protein that looks and smells like worms. And to protect the brutes from cold, their dens could be heated, or shelters provided for the all too many who will otherwise freeze. The list of obligations is long, but for that reason it is more, not less, compelling. The welfare of all animals is in human hands. Society must attend not solely to the needs of domestic animals, for they are in a privileged class, but to the needs of all animals, especially those which without help, would die miserably in the wild.

Now, whether you believe that this harangue is a *reductio* of Singer's position, and thus that it agrees in principle with Ritchie, or whether you think it should be taken seriously as an ideal is of no concern to me. I merely wish to point out that an environmentalist must take what I have said as a *reductio*, whereas an animal liberationist must regard it as stating a serious position, at least if the liberationist shares Singer's commitment to utilitarianism. Environmentalists cannot be animal liberationists. Animal liberationists cannot be environmentalists. The environmentalist would sacrifice the lives of individual creatures to preserve the authenticity, integrity and complexity of ecological systems. The liberationist—if the reduction of animal misery is taken seriously as a goal—must be willing, in principle, to sacrifice the authenticity, integrity and complexity of ecosystems to protect the rights, or guard the lives, of animals.

IV

A defender of the rights of animals may answer that my argument applies only to someone like Singer who is strongly committed to a utilitarian ethic. Those who emphasize the rights of animals, however, need not argue that society should enter the interests of animals equitably into the felicific calculus on

which policy is based. For example, Laurence Tribe appeals to the rights of animals not to broaden the class of wants to be included in a Benthamite calculus but to "move beyond wants" and thus to affirm duties "ultimately independent of a desire-satisfying conception."[19] Tribe writes:

> To speak of "rights" rather than "wants," after all, is to acknowledge the possibility that want-maximizing or utility-maximizing actions will be ruled out in particular cases as inconsistent with a structure of agreed-upon obligations. It is Kant, not Bentham, whose thought suggests the first step toward making us "different persons from the manipulators and subjugators we are in danger of becoming."[20]

It is difficult to see how an appeal to rights helps society to "move beyond wants" or to affirm duties "ultimately independent of a desire-satisfying conception." Most writers in the Kantian tradition analyze rights as claims to something in which the claimant has an interest.[21] Thus, rights-theorists oppose utilitarianism not to go beyond wants but because they believe that some wants or interests are moral "trumps" over other wants and interests.[22] To say innocent people have a right not to be hanged for crimes they have not committed, even when hanging them would serve the general welfare, is to say that the interest of innocent people not to be hanged should outweigh the general interest in deterring crime. To take rights seriously, then, is simply to take some interests, or the general interest, more seriously than other interests for moral reasons. The appeal to rights simply is a variation on utilitarianism, in that it accepts the general framework of interests, but presupposes that there are certain interests that should not be traded off against others.[23]

A second problem with Tribe's reply is more damaging than the first. Only *individuals* may have rights, but environmentalists think in terms of protecting *collections, systems* and *communities.* Consider Aldo Leopold's oft-quoted remark: "A thing is right when it tends to preserve the integrity, stability, and beauty of the biotic community. It is wrong when it tends to do otherwise."[24] The obligation to preserve the "integrity, stability, and beauty of the biotic community," whatever those words mean, implies no duties whatever to individual animals in the community, except in the rare instance in which an individual is important to functioning of that community. For the most part, individual animals are completely expendable. An environmentalist is concerned only with maintaining a population. Accordingly, the moral obligation Leopold describes cannot be grounded in or derived from the rights of individuals. Therefore, it has no basis in rights at all.[25]

Consider another example: the protection of endangered species. An individual whale may be said to have rights, but the species cannot; a whale does not suddenly have rights when its kind becomes endangered.[26] No; the moral obligation to preserve species is not an obligation to individual creatures. It cannot, then, be an obligation that rests on rights. This is not to say that there is no moral obligation with regard to endangered species, animals or the environment. It is only to say that moral obligations to nature cannot be enlightened or explained—one cannot even take the first step—by appealing to the rights of animals and other natural things.

V.

Garrett Hardin, in his "Foreword" to *Should Trees Have Standing?* suggests that Stone's essay answers Leopold's call for a "new ethic to protect land and other natural amenities...."[27] But as one reviewer has pointed out,

> Stone himself never refers to Leopold, and with good reason; he comes from a different place, and his proposal to grant rights to natural objects has emerged not from an ecological sensibility but as an extension of the philosophy of the humane movement.[28]

A humanitarian ethic—an appreciation not of nature, but of the welfare of animals—will not help us to understand or to justify an environmental ethic. It will not provide necessary or valid foundations for environmental law.

NOTES

1. Leopold, *A Sand County Almanac* (Oxford University Press, 1949) at 204.

2. For discussion, see Heffernan, "The Land Ethic: A Critical Appraisal," *Environmental Ethics* 4 (1982): 235. Heffernan notes that "when Leopold talks of preserving the 'integrity, stability and beauty of the biotic community' he is referring to preserving the characteristic structure of an ecosystem and its capacity to withstand change or stress." Leopold, *A Sand County Almanac* at 237.

3. Stone, *Should Trees Have Standing?* (Los Altos: William Kaufmann, 1974).

4. Stone, *Should Trees Have Standing?* at p. 44.

5. Tribe, "Ways Not to Think About Plastic Trees: New Foundations in Environmental Law," *Yale Law Journal* 83 (1973): 1315. See p. 1345.

6. Singer, "All Animals Are Equal" *Philosophic Exchange* 1 (1974): 103.

7. Stone, *Should Trees Have Standing?*, 24.

8. Singer, "Not For Humans Only: The Place of Nonhumans in Environmental Issues," in *Ethics and the Problems of the Twenty-first Century*, ed. Goodpaster and Sayre (1979), p. 194.

9. Singer, "Not For Humans Only," p. 195.

10. For a discussion of basic rights, see Shue, *Basic Rights* (1980).

11. Callicott, *Animal Liberation: A Triangular Affair* (1980), *Environmental Ethics* 2 (1980): 311. See p. 315.

12. Leopold, *A Sand County Almanac*, p. 269.

13. Callicott, "Animal Liberation," p. 314–15.

14. Singer, "Not For Humans Only," p. 201.

15. Ritchie, *Natural Rights* (3rd ed., 1916), p. 107. For an excellent discussion of this passage, see Clark, "The Rights of Wild Things," *Inquiry* 22 (1979): 171.

16. Shue, *Basic Rights*, p. 18–29.

17. Hapgood, *Why Males Exist* (1979). See p. 34.

18. Singer, "Not For Humans Only," p. 198.

19. Tribe, "From Environmental Foundations to Constitutional Structures: Learning From Nature's Future," *Yale Law Journal* 84 (1974): 545. See pp. 551–52.

20. Tribe, "From Environmental Foundations," p. 552.

21. For discussion, see Feinberg, "Duties, Rights, and Claims," *American Philosophical Quarterly* 3 (1966): 137.

22. See Dworkin, "Liberalism," in *Public and Private Morality* (1978), ed. Stuart Hampshire. See pages 113–43. Rights "function as trump cards held by individuals." See p. 136.

23. Barry observes: "On the surface, rights theories stand in opposition to utilitarianism, for rights, whatever their foundation (or lack thereof), are supposed to trump claims that might be made on behalf of the general welfare. The point here is, however, that the whole notion of rights is simply a variation on utilitarianism in that it accepts the definition of the ethical problem as conterminous with the problem of conflicting interests, and replaces the felicific calculus (in which the interests are simply added) with one which does not permit certain interests to be traded off against others." Barry, "Self-government Revisited," *The Nature of Political Theory* (1983), ed. Miller and Siedentop. See p. 125; see generally pp. 121–54.

24. Leopold, *A Sand County Almanac*, p. 262.

25. For discussion of this point, see Katz, "Is There A Place For Animals in the Moral Consideration of Nature," *Ethics and Animals* 4 (1983): 74; Norton, "Environmental Ethics and Nonhuman Rights," (1982), *Environmental Ethics* 4 (1982): 17; Rodman, "The Liberation of Nature?" *Inquiry* 20 (1977): 83; Goodpaster, "On Being Morally Considerable" *Journal of Philosophy* 75 (1978): 308.

Tom Regan discusses this issue in *The Case for Animal Liberation* (1983). See p. 362.

Because paradigmatic rights-holders are individuals, and because the dominant thrust of contemporary environmental efforts (e.g., wilderness preservation) is to focus on the whole rather than on the part (i.e., the individual), there is an understandable reluctance on the part of environmentalists to "take rights seriously" or at least a reluctance to take them as seriously as the rights view contends we should....A rights-based environmental ethic...ought not to be dismissed out of hand by environmentalists as being in principle antagonistic to the goals for which they work. It isn't. Were we to show proper respect for the rights of individuals who make up the biotic community, would not the *community* be preserved?

I believe this is an empirical question, the answer to which is "no." The environmentalist is concerned about preserving evolutionary processes; whether these processes, e.g., natural selection, have deep enough respect for the rights of individuals to be preserved on those grounds, is a question that might best be addressed by an evolutionary biologist.

26. Feinberg, "The Rights of Animals and Unborn Generations," in *Philosophy and the Environmental Crisis*, ed. Blackstone (1974), 43–end. See pp. 55–56.

27. Hardin, "Foreword," in Stone, *Should Trees Have Standing?* See p. xii.

28. Rodman, "The Liberation of Nature?" See p. 110.

DALE JAMIESON

Animal Liberation Is an Environmental Ethic

In an influential essay first published in 1980, J. Baird Callicott argued that animal liberation and environmental ethics are distinct and inconsistent perspectives.[1] Callicott had harsh words both for animals and animal liberationists. He referred to domestic animals as "living artifacts" and claimed that it is "incoherent" to speak of their natural behaviour (1980/1989:30). He wrote that it is a "logical impossibility" to liberate domestic animals and that "the value commitments of the humane movement seem at bottom to betray a world-denying or rather a life-loathing philosophy" (p. 31). All of this is in distinction to Aldo Leopold's "land ethic" which, according to Callicott, is holistic: "[It] locates ultimate value in the biotic community and assigns differential moral value to the constitutive individuals relatively to that standard" (p. 58). "Some bacteria, for example, may be of greater value to the health or economy of nature than dogs, and thus command more respect" (p. 39). From the perspective of the land ethic, "inanimate entities such as oceans and lakes, mountains, forests, and wetlands are assigned a greater value than individual animals" (p. 58). While Callicott grants that a variety of environmental ethics may exist, he suggests that "the extent to which an ethical system resembles Leopold's land ethic might be used...as a criterion to measure the extent to which it is or is not of the environmental sort" (pp. 30–1). Animal liberation fails to satisfy this criterion since, according to Callicott, animal liberation and conventional anthropocentric ethics "have much more in common with one another than either has with environmental or land ethics" (p. 57).[2]

The idea that environmental ethics and animal liberation are conceptually distinct, and that animal

liberation has more in common with conventional morality than with environmental ethics, would come as a surprise to many people concerned about the human domination of nature. For one thing, environmentalists and animal liberationists have many of the same enemies: those who dump poisons into the air and water, drive whales to extinction, or clear rainforests to create pastures for cattle, to name just a few. Moreover, however one traces the history of the environmental movement, it is clear that it comes out of a tradition that expresses strong concern for animal suffering and autonomy. Certainly both the modern environmental and animal liberation movements spring from the same sources in the post–World War II period: a disgust with the sacrifice of everything else to the construction of military machines, the creation of a culture which views humans and other animals as replaceable commodities, and the prevailing faith in the ability of science to solve all of our problems. It is no coincidence that, in the United States at least, both of these movements developed during the same period. Peter Singer's first article on animal liberation (1973) appeared less than three years after the first Earth Day. Even today people who identify themselves as environmentalists are likely to be as concerned about spotted owls as old growth forests and to think that vegetarianism is a good idea. Many people are members of both environmental and animal liberation organizations and feel no tension between these commitments.

This is not to say that there are no differences between environmentalists and animal liberationists.[3] Such differences exist, but so do deep divisions among environmentalists and among animal liberationists. My thesis is that the divisions within each of these groups are just as deep and profound as the differences between them. Leopold's land ethic is one environmental ethic on offer, but so is animal liberation. The superiority of one to the other must be demonstrated by argument, not by appeal to paradigm cases or established by definitional fiat.

I begin by briefly tracing the history of the split between environmental ethics and animal liberation, go on to sketch a theory of value that I think is implicit in animal liberation, and explain how this theory is consistent with strong environmental commitments. I conclude with some observations about problems that remain.

1. ORIGINS

I have already mentioned Callicott's role in setting environmental ethics against animal liberation. However, he does not deserve all the blame. In order to see why we must recover some recent history.

The origins of the contemporary environmental movement were deeply entangled in the counter-culture of the 1960s. Generally in the counter-culture there was a feeling that sex was good, drugs were liberating, opposing the government was a moral obligation, and that new values were needed to vindicate, sustain, and encourage this shift in outlook and behaviour. In 1967 (during the "Summer of Love" in San Francisco's Haight-Ashbury), the UCLA historian Lynn White Jr. published an essay in which he argued that the dominant tendencies in the Judaeo-Christian tradition were the real source of our environmental problems. Only by overthrowing these traditions and embracing the suppressed insights of other traditions could we come to live peaceably with nature.

This view gained philosophical expression in a 1973 paper by Richard Routley. Routley produced a series of cases about which he thought we have moral intuitions that cannot be accounted for by traditional ethics. Routley asked us to consider a "last man" whose final act is to destroy such natu-

ral objects as mountains and salt marshes. Although these natural objects would not be appreciated by conscious beings even if they were not destroyed, Routley thought that it would still be wrong for the "last man" to destroy them. These intuitions were widely shared, and many environmental philosophers thought that they could only be explained by supposing that non-sentient nature has mind-independent value.[4]

Throughout the 1970s there was a great deal of discussion about whether a new environment ethic was needed, possible, or defensible. In a widely discussed 1981 paper Tom Regan clearly distinguished what he called an "environmental ethic" from a "management ethic." In order to be an environmental ethic, according to Regan, a theory must hold that there are non-conscious beings that have "moral standing." Passmore had argued in his 1974 book that such an ethic was not required to explain our duties concerning nature, but in a 1973 paper Naess had already begun the attempt to develop a new ethic that he called Deep Ecology.[5]

At the time Callicott was writing his 1980/1989 essay the very possibility of an environmental ethic was up for grabs. Animal liberationist views, on the other hand, were already well-developed and comparatively well-established. Peter Singer's *Animal Liberation* (1975/2001) and Stephen Clark's *The Moral Status of Animals* were in print, and Bernard Rollin's *Animal Rights and Human Morality* was about to go to press. *Animals, Men and Morals*, the influential anthology edited by Stanley Godlovitch, Rosalind Godlovitch, and John Harris had appeared in 1972, and the first edition of *Animal Rights and Human Obligations*, edited by Regan and Singer, appeared in 1976. By 1980 the philosophical literature already included contributions by such philosophers as Thomas Auxter, Cora Diamond, Joel Feinberg, Colin McGinn, Mary Midgley, Timothy Sprigge, and Donald VanDeVeer, in addition to those mentioned above. Callicott hoped to gain a hearing for a new environmental ethic by rejecting as inadequate and denouncing as conceptually conservative both what he calls "ethical humanism" and "humane moralism." Ethical theory should become a "triangular affair," with the land ethic as the third player.

Callicott is correct in pointing out the close affinities between animal liberationist ethics and traditional ethics. There are utilitarian, Kantian, libertarian, Aristotelian, and communitarian animal liberationists. Animal liberationists typically accept the projects of traditional Western ethics, then go on to argue that in their applications they have arbitrarily and inconsistently excluded non-human animals. Part of the explanation for the comparative conceptual conservatism of animal liberationist philosophers is that, for the most part, they have been educated in the mainstream traditions of Anglo-American philosophy, while environmental ethicists often have been educated outside the mainstream and are influenced by continental philosophers, "process" philosophers, or theologians. The split between environmental ethics and animal liberation is as much cultural and sociological as philosophical.[6]

Despite the weakness of the argument and the caricaturing of animal liberationist views, Callicott's 1980 article was remarkably influential within the environmental ethics community.[7] Some of Callicott's themes were echoed by Mark Sagoff in an influential 1984 paper.[8] Sagoff charged that if animal liberationists had their way they would institute such anti-environmentalist policies as contraceptively eliminating wild animals so that fewer would suffer and die, converting wilderness areas into farms where animals could be well taken care of, and adopting starving deer as pets. Sagoff concludes that "[a] humanitarian ethic—an appreciation not of nature, but of the welfare of animals—will not help us to understand or to justify an environmental ethic."[9]

By the early 1980s it seemed clear that environmental ethics and animal liberation were conceptually distinct. To be an environmental ethicist one had to embrace new values. One had to believe that some non-sentient entities have inherent value; that these entities include such collectives as species, ecosystems, and the community of the land; and that value is mind-independent in the following respect: even if there were no conscious beings, aspects of nature would still be inherently valuable. What remained to be seen was whether any plausible ethic satisfied these conditions.

2. CANONICAL ENVIRONMENTAL ETHICS

Once it became clear what was required for membership in the club of environmental ethicists, most animal liberationists did not want to join. Some began to fling Callicott's rhetoric back in his direction. In 1983 Tom Regan wrote that

> The implications of [Leopold's maxim] include the clear prospect that the individual may be sacrificed for the greater biotic good...It is difficult to see how the notion of rights of the individual could find a home within a view that...might be fairly dubbed "environmental fascism"...Environmental fascism and the rights view are like oil and water: they don't mix.[10]

Almost immediately some environmental philosophers abandoned one or more of the conditions that had been thought to be definitive of an environmental ethic. By 1986 Callicott himself had given up his belief in the mind-independence of value and had adopted a value theory that he attributed to Hume and Darwin.[11] Collectives such as species, ecosystems, and the land have inherent value, according to Callicott, but the existence of valuers is a necessary condition for their having value.

Holmes Rolston III emerged as the most prominent spokesperson for the old-time religion. He vigorously attacked Callicott for having departed from the true path and having abandoned the idea that "nature is of value in itself" (1992). The philosophy that Rolston has developed satisfies all of the conditions for an environmental ethic: value is mind-independent and exists at several different levels including those of "higher" animals, organisms, species, and ecosystems (1988). Although Rolston has an environmental ethic by anyone's standards, it has not commanded widespread assent. As it has become clearer in his work what mind-independent values would have to be like, there have been few who have been willing to follow him. When the normative implications of his views have been made explicit—that, for example, we should sometimes let animals suffer when we could easily intervene, that on many occasions we should prefer the lives of plants to those of animals, that we have a positive duty not to be vegetarian—few have been willing to embrace his philosophy.

During the 1980s the new environmental ethic that Routley wanted was, to some extent, developed. The problem was that not many philosophers found it plausible. In recent years environmental philosophers have begun to return to more conventional views in value theory. But this makes one wonder what happened to the titanic struggle between environmental ethics and animal liberation which some seem to think continues unabated.

3. TOGETHER AGAIN?

Callicott has expressed regret for the rhetoric of his 1980 essay and, by his own lights anyway, attempted a reconciliation between animal liberation and environmental ethics. In an essay published in the late 1980s Callicott wrote that "[a]nimal liberation and environmental ethics may thus be united under a common theoretical umbrella" (1989: 59), but in the same article he wrote that there is nothing wrong with slaughtering "meat animals" for food so long as this is not in violation "of a kind of evolved and unspoken social contract between man and beast" (p. 56) and claimed that animal liberationist philosophers must favour protecting "innocent vegetarian animals from their carnivorous predators" (p. 57). When his 1980 essay was reprinted in his 1989 book, Callicott wrote that

"this is the one [of all the essays reprinted] that I would most like to revise (censor) for this publication" (p. 6). When the same essay was reprinted in a 1995 collection Callicott wrote that "I now think that we do in fact have duties and obligations...to domestic animals," and that "a vegetarian diet is indicated by the land ethic." However he also says, puzzlingly enough, that "the land ethic leaves our traditional human morality quite intact and preemptive."[12]

I suspect that what is going on in part is that Callicott senses that, since he is no longer a canonical environmental ethicist, the differences between his views and those of animal liberationists cannot be as philosophically deep as they once appeared. Yet the revolutionary idea, rooted in the culture of the 1960s, that what we need is a new environmental ethic is one that dies hard. In the next section I will show how an animal liberationist ethic, rooted in traditional views of value and obligation, can take non-sentient nature seriously. A deep green ethic does not require strange views about value.

4. ANIMAL LIBERATION AND THE VALUE OF NATURE

In my view any plausible ethic must address concerns about both animals and the environment. Some issues that directly concern animals are obviously of great environmental import as well. The production and consumption of beef may well be the most important of them.[13] The addiction to beef that is characteristic of people in the industrialized countries is not only a moral atrocity for animals but also causes health problems for consumers, reduces grain supplies for the poor, precipitates social divisions in developing countries, contributes to climate change, leads to the conversion of forests to pasture lands, is a causal factor in overgrazing, and is implicated in the destruction of native plants and animals. If there is one issue on which animal

liberationists and environmentalists should speak with a single voice it is on this issue. To his credit Callicott appears to have recognized this, but many environmental philosophers have not.

In addition to there being clear issues on which animal liberationists and environmentalists should agree, it is also important to remember that non-human animals, like humans, live in environments. One reason to oppose the destruction of wilderness and the poisoning of nature is that these actions harm both human and non-human animals. I believe that one can go quite far towards protecting the environment solely on the basis of concern for animals.

Finally, and most importantly, environmental ethicists have no monopoly on valuing such collectives as species, ecosystems, and the community of the land. It has only seemed that they do because parties to the dispute have not attended to the proper distinctions.

One relevant distinction, noted by Callicott in different language, is between the source and content of values.[14] We can be sentientist with respect to the source of values, yet non-sentientist with respect to their content. Were there no sentient beings there would be no values but it doesn't follow from this that only sentient beings are valuable.[15]

The second important distinction is between primary and derivative value. Creatures who can suffer, take pleasure in their experiences, and whose lives go better or worse from their own point of view are of primary value. Failure to value them involves failures of objectivity or impartiality in our reasoning or sentiments....

Non-sentient entities are not of primary value because they do not have a perspective from which their lives go better or worse. Ultimately the value of non-sentient entities rests on how they fit into the lives of sentient beings. But although non-sentient entities are not of primary value, their value can be very great and urgent. In some cases their value may even trump the value of sentient entities. The distinction between primary and derivative value is not a distinction in degree of value, but rather in the ways different entities can be valuable....

The main point I am making here is that many people have traditional evaluational outlooks yet value works of art intrinsically and intensely. There is no great puzzle about how they can both intrinsically value persons and works of art. Similarly, animal liberationists can value nature intrinsically and intensely, even though they believe that non-sentient nature is of derivative value. Because what is of derivative value can be valued intensely and intrinsically, animal liberationists can join environmental ethicists in fighting for the preservation of wild rivers and wilderness areas. Indeed, rightly understood, they can even agree with environmental ethicists that these natural features are valuable for their own sakes.

But at this point an objection may arise. The most that I have shown is that non-sentient entities can be intrinsically valued. I have not shown that they ought to be intrinsically valued. Canonical environmentalists can give a reason for intrinsically valuing non-sentient nature that animal liberationists cannot: aspects of non-sentient nature are valuable independently of any conscious being.

The objection is correct in that environmental ethicists who believe in mind-independent value can appeal to normative high ground that is not available to those philosophers who do not believe in mind-independent value. However, it should be noted that even if the value of non-sentient nature were mind-independent, it would not immediately follow that non-sentient nature should be valued intrinsically or that its value would be of greater urgency than that of other entities. But putting that point aside, the fundamental problem with this attempt to seize the normative heights is that they are a mirage. There is no mind-independent value, but none is required in order for nature to be valued intrinsically. Still, having said this, some account needs to be given of how my kind of environmental philosopher moves from the claim that wilderness can be intrinsically valued

to the claim that wilderness ought to be intrinsically valued.

First, we should see that this question plunges us into the familiar if difficult problem of how first-order value claims can be defended and justified.[16] In order to give an account of this, very close attention would have to be paid to our everyday moral practices and our strategies of defence, offence, justification, and capitulation. I doubt that very much of general interest can be said about this. But as a first approximation, we might say that in order to see how environmentalist claims are justified, we should look at the practices of persuasion that environmentalists employ. Consider an example.

Many people think of deserts as horrible places that are not worth protecting. I disagree. I value deserts intrinsically and think you should too. How do I proceed? One thing I might do is take you camping with me. We might see the desert's nocturnal inhabitants, the plants that have adapted to these conditions, the shifting colours of the landscape as the day wears on, and the rising of the moon on stark features of the desert. Together we might experience the feel of the desert wind, hear the silence of the desert, and sense its solitude. You may become interested in how it is that this place was formed, what sustains it, how its plants and animals make a living. As you learn more about the desert, you may come to see it differently and to value it more. This may lead you to spend more time in the desert, seeing it in different seasons, watching the spring with its incredible array of flowers turn to the haunting stillness of summer. You might start reading some desert literature, from the monastic fathers of the church to Edward Abbey. Your appreciation would continue to grow.

But there is no guarantee that things will go this way. You may return from your time in the desert hot, dirty, hungry for a burger, thirsty for a beer, and ready to volunteer your services to the US Army Corps of Engineers (whose *raison d'être* seems to be to flood as much of the earth's surface as possible). Similarly, some people see Venice as a dysfunctional collection of dirty old buildings, find Kant boring and wrong, and hear Mahler as both excessively romantic and annoyingly dissonant. More experience only makes matters worse.

If someone fails to appreciate the desert, Venice, or Mahler, they need not have made any logical error. Our evaluative responses are not uniquely determined by our constitution or the world. This fact provokes anxiety in some philosophers. They fear that unless value is mind-independent, anything goes. Experience machines are as good as experience, Disney-desert is the same as the real thing, and the Spice Girls and Mahler are colleagues in the same business (one strikingly more successful than the other). Those who suffer this anxiety confuse a requirement for value with how value is constituted. Value is mind-dependent, but it is things in the world that are valuable or not. The fact that we draw attention to features of objects in our evaluative discourse is the common property of all theories of value.

These anxious philosophers also fail to appreciate how powerful psychological and cultural mechanisms can be in constituting objectivity. Culture, history, tradition, knowledge, and convention mediate our constitutions and the world. Culture, together with our constitutions and the world, determines our evaluative practices. Since the world and our constitutions alone are not sufficient for determining them, common values should be seen in part as cultural achievements rather than simply as true reports about the nature of things or expressions of what we are essentially. Evaluative practices are in the domain of negotiation and collective construction, as well as reflection and recognition. But the fact that these practices are in part constructed does not mean that they cannot be rigid and compelling. We can be brought to appreciate Venice, Mahler, or the desert by collectively and interactively educating our sensibilities, tastes, and judgements, but such change often involves a deep reorientation of how we see the world. When I try to get you to appreciate the desert I direct your attention to objects in your visual field, but I am trying to change your way of seeing and thinking and your whole outlook towards

nature. I am also trying to change our relationship from one of difference to one of solidarity. Similarly, when advocates of the enterprise society point to missed opportunities for profit and competitiveness, they are trying to educate our sensibilities as well as referring us to economic facts. Their descriptions of how economies work are to a great extent stories about the social world they want to construct.

What I have argued in this section is that animal liberationists can hold many of the same normative views as environmental ethicists. This is because many of our most important issues involve serious threats to both humans and animals as well as to the non-sentient environment; because animal liberationists can value nature as a home for sentient beings; and because animal liberationists can embrace environmental values as intensely as environmental ethicists, though they see them as derivative rather than primary values. What animal liberationists cannot do is claim the moral high ground of the mind-independent value of nature which, since the early days of the movement environmental ethicists have attempted to secure. But, as I have argued, this moral high ground is not there to be claimed anyway. Those who are deep green should not despair because some of our environmental values are to a great extent socially constructed. Constructivism is a story about how our practices come to be, not about how real, rigid, or compelling they are.

Still, many will think that this is a flabby ethic that leans too far in the direction of subjectivism, relativism, constructivism, or some other postmodern heresy. One way of making their point is to return to the distinction between primary and derivative value. Imagine two people: Robin, who thinks that trees are of primary value, and Ted, who denies that humans or gorillas are included in this class. What kind of a mistake are Robin and Ted making? If I say they are making a conceptual mistake then I will be dismissing some very influential views as non-starters; if I say they are making a normative mistake then my view of what has primary and derivative value will turn out to be just as subjective as my view that deserts are

valuable, and therefore just as vulnerable to other people's lack of responsiveness to my concerns.

I want to reiterate that first-order value judgements can be both rigid and compelling, even though to some extent they are relative and socially constructed. But having said this, I want to reject the idea that Robin and Ted are making a logical or grammatical error. Robin, Ted, and I have a real normative dispute about how to determine what is of primary value. At the same time this dispute has a different feel to it than first-order normative disputes (e.g. the dispute about whether or not to value the desert). We can bring out this difference by saying as a first approximation that someone who fails to value deserts lacks sensitivity while someone who fails to value people or gorillas lacks objectivity. Although in both cases the dispute involves how we see ourselves in relation to the world, to a great extent different considerations are relevant in each case. Because questions about primary values are at the centre of how we take the world, abstract principles (e.g. those that concern objectivity and impartiality) are most relevant to settling these disputes. Differences about whether or not to value deserts, on the other hand, turn on a panoply of considerations, some of which I have already discussed.[17]

In this section I have argued that there is a great deal of theoretical convergence between animal liberationists and environmental ethicists. There is also a strong case for convergence at the practical and political level. The environmental movement has numbers and wealth while the animal liberation movement has personal commitment. Both environmental and animal issues figure in the choices people make in their daily lives, but they are so glaringly obvious in the case of animals that they cannot be evaded. Anyone who eats or dresses makes ethical choices that affect animals. Refraining from eating meat makes one part of a social movement: rather than being an abstainer, one is characterized positively as "a vegetarian." While other consumer choices also have profound environmental consequences, somehow they are less visible than

the choice of whether to eat meat. This is part of the reason why self-identified environmentalists are often less motivated to save energy, reduce consumption, or refrain from purchasing toxic substances than animal liberationists are to seek out vegetarian alternatives.[18] Not only is animal liberation an environmental ethic, but animal liberation can also help to empower the environmental movement.

5. REMAINING CONUNDRUMS AND COMPLEXITIES

Where Callicott saw a "triangular affair" and Sagoff saw "divorce," I see the potential for Hollywood romance. It might be objected that my rosy view only survives because I have not dealt in detail with specific issues that divide animal liberationists and environmental ethicists. For example, there are many cases in which environmentalists may favour "culling" (a polite term for "killing") some animals for the good of a population. In other cases environmentalists may favour eliminating a population of common animals in order to preserve a rare plant. Hovering in the background is the image of "hunt saboteurs," trying to stop not only fox hunting but also the fox's hunting.

These difficult issues cannot be resolved here.[19] For present purposes, what is important to see is that while animal liberationists and environmentalists may have different tendencies, the turf doesn't divide quite so neatly as some may think. Consider one example.

Gary Varner (1995), who writes as an animal liberationist, has defended what he calls "therapeutic hunting" in some circumstances. He defines "therapeutic hunting" as "hunting motivated by and designed to secure the aggregate welfare of the target species and/or the integrity of its ecosystem" (ibid. 257). Varner goes on to argue that animal liberationists can support this kind of hunting and that this is the only kind of hunting that environmentalists are compelled to support. What might have appeared as a clear difference between the two groups turns out to be more complex.

In addition to such "convergence" arguments, it is important to recognize the diversity of views that exists within both the environmental and animal liberation movements. Differences between animal liberationists are obvious and on the table. At a practical level animal liberation groups are notorious for their sectarianism. At a philosophical level Tom Regan has spent much of the last fifteen years distinguishing his view from that of Peter Singer's, and I have already mentioned other diverse animal liberationist voices. In recent years the same kinds of divisions have broken out among environmental philosophers, with the rhetoric between Callicott and Rolston (and more recently Callicott and Norton) increasingly resembling that between Singer and Regan. Generally within the community of environmental philosophers there are disagreements about the nature and value of wilderness, the importance of biodiversity, and approaches to controlling population. At a practical level there are disagreements about the very goals of the movement. Some would say that preservation of nature's diversity is the ultimate goal; others would counter that it is the preservation of evolutionary processes that matters. Sometimes people assert both without appreciating that they can come into conflict.[20]

There are many practical issues on which neither animal liberationists nor environmentalists are of one mind. For example, South African, American, and German scientists working for the South African National Parks Board, with support from the Humane Society of the United States, are currently testing contraceptives on elephants in Kruger National Park as an alternative to "culling." The Worldwide Fund for Nature is divided about the project, with its local branch opposing it.[21]

Part of the reason for the divisions within both the environmental and animal liberation movements is that contemporary Western cultures have little by way of positive images of how to relate to animals and nature. Most of us know what is bad—wiping out songbird populations, polluting water ways, causing cats to suffer, contributing to smog, and so on. But when asked to provide a positive vision many people turn to the past,

to their conception of what life is like for indigenous peoples, or what it is to be "natural." None of this will do. So long as we have a paucity of positive visions, different views, theories, and philosophies will compete for attention, with no obvious way of resolving some of the most profound disagreements.

These are early days for those who are sensitive to the interests of nature and animals. We are in the midst of a transition from a culture which sees nature as material for exploitation, to one which asserts the importance of living in harmony with nature. It will take a long time to understand exactly what are the terms of the debate. What is important to recognize now is that animal liberationists and environmental ethicists are on the same side in this transition. Animal liberation is not the only environmental ethic, but neither is it some alien ideology. Rather, as I have argued, animal liberation is an environmental ethic and should be welcomed back into the family.

NOTES

This essay began life as a lecture to the Gruppo di Studio "Scienza & Etica" at the Politecnico di Milano in Italy. Subsequent versions were presented in the Faculty of Philosophy at Monash University in Australia, to an environmental ethics seminar in Oxford, and to an environmental ethics conference in London. I have benefited from the probing questions and comments of many people, especially Paola Cavalieri, Roger Crisp, Lori Gruen, Alan Holland, Steve Kramer, and Rae Langton.

1. 1980/1989. Callicott expresses some misgivings about this essay in the introduction to his 1989 and in a new preface to the original paper published in Robert Elliot's (1995) collection.

2. For Leopold's land ethic see Leopold (1949).

3. The Norwegian government has appealed to theoretical differences between environmental ethics and animal liberation in its attempt to reconcile its reputation as an environmental leader with its flouting of the international consensus against whaling.

4. The intuition that it would be wrong for the last man to destroy non-sentient natural features can also be explained by concerns about character or by appeal to transworld evaluations. For the first strategy see Hill (1983); for the second strategy see Elliot (1985). Routley himself adopted a version of the second strategy.

5. Other important early publications directed towards developing a new environmental ethic include Stone (1974) and Rolston III (1975).

6. Obviously in part this is an empirical claim that would require systematic investigation to establish fully. I believe that it is true based on my general knowledge of the development of the field.

7. As Edward Johnson (1981) points out in his neglected but definitive refutation, Callicott seems to think that all animal liberationists are hedonistic utilitarians; he neglects to distinguish pain being evil from its being evil all things considered; and his claims about the ecological consequences of widespread vegetarianism are downright preposterous.

8. Sagoff (1984/1993).

9. ibid. 92. However, it is important to note that Sagoff explicitly states that he is not advocating environmentalism in this article (p. 87).

10. Regan (1983: 361–2).

11. "In my own papers, going back to 1979, I have also affirmed the importance of the value question in environmental ethics and early on endorsed the postulate of nature's objective, intrinsic value…After thinking very hard, during the mid-1980s, about the ontology of value finally I came reluctantly to the conclusion that intrinsic value cannot exist objectively" (Callicott 1992a; 131–2). For further discussion of Callicott's value theory, see Norton (1995a); Callicott (1996); and Lee (1996).

12. These quotations are from Callicott's new preface to "Animal Liberation: A Triangular Affair," in Elliot (1995: 29–30).

13. The case for this has been very convincingly argued by Jeremy Rifkin (1992).

14. John O'Neill (1993, ch. 2) also makes a similar distinction.

15. Here we border on some important issues in philosophy of mind that cannot be discussed here. For present purposes I assume that sentience and consciousness determine the same class, and that there is something that it is like to be a "merely conscious" (as well as self-conscious) entity, although a "merely conscious" entity cannot reflect on what it is like to be itself. I say a little more about these matters in Jamieson (1983). See also various papers collected in Bekoff and Jamieson (1996).

16. I have discussed the relation between moral practice and moral theorizing in Jamieson (1991). See also Weston (1985).

17. There is much more to say about these questions than I can say here. However, it may help to locate my views if I invoke the Quinian image of the web of belief in which what is at the centre of the web is defended in different

ways from what is at the periphery, not because such beliefs enjoy some special epistemological status, but because of the density of their connections to other beliefs.

18. These and related issues are discussed in two reports to the United States Environmental Protection Agency (Jamieson and VanderWerf 1993, 1995).

19. For my approach to some of these conflicts see Jamieson (1995).

20. To some degree differences among environmentalists have been obscured by the rise of "managerialist" forms of environmentalism which are favoured by many scientists and are highly visible in the media. For a critique, see Jamieson (1990). For alternative forms of environmentalism, see Sachs (1993).

21. "Villagers Slam 'Pill for Elephants,' " *New Scientist*, 9 (1996).

REFERENCES

Bekoff, M and D. Jamieson, eds. (1990). *Interpretation and Explanation in the Study of Animal Behavior*, vol. i: *Interpretation, Intentionality, and Communication*, vol ii: *Explanation, Evolution, and Adaptation*. Boulder, Colo.: Westview Press.

—— (1996). Readings in Animal Cognition. Cambridge, Mass.: MIT Press.

Callicott, J. B. (1980/1989). "Animal Liberation: A Triangular Affair". In Callicott (1989): 15–38.

—— (1989). *In Defense of the Land Ethic: Essays in Environmental Philosophy*. Albany, NY: SUNY Press.

—— (1992a). "Rolston on Intrinsic Value: A Deconstruction". *Environmental Ethics*, 14/2: 129–43.

—— (1992b). "Aldo Leopold's Metaphor". In Costanza *et al.* (1992): 42–56.

—— (1995). "A Review of Some Problems with the Concept of Ecosystem Health". *Ecosystem Health*, 2/1: 101–12.

—— (1996). "On Norton and the Failure of Monistic Inherentism". *Environmental Ethics*, 18/2: 219–21.

Elliot, R. (1985). "Metaethics and Environmental Ethics". *Metaphilosopy*, 16: 103–17.

Elliot, R. ed. (1995). *Environmental Ethics*. Oxford: Oxford University Press.

Hill, T., Jr. (1983). "Ideals of Human Excellence and Preserving Natural Environments". *Environmental Ethics*, 5: 211–24.

Jamieson, D. (1983). "Killing Persons and Other Beings". In Miller and Williams (1983): 135–46.

Jamieson, D. (1990). "Managing the Future: Public Policy, Scientific Uncertainty, and Global Warming". In

D. Scherer, *Upstream/Downstream: Essays in Environmental Ethics*. Philadelphia: Temple University Press: 67–89.

—— (1991). "Method and Moral Theory". In Singer (1991): 476–87.

—— (1995). "Wildlife Conservation and Individual Animal Welfare". In Norton *et al.* (1995): 69–73.

Jamieson, D and K. VanderWerf (1993). "Cultural Barriers to Behavior Change: General Recommendations and Resources for State Pollution Prevention Programs, A Report to US EPA". Boulder, Colo.: Center for Values and Social Policy, University of Colorado.

—— (1995). "Preventing Pollution: Perspectives on Cultural Barriers and Facilitators, A Report to US EPA." Boulder, Colo.: Center for Values and Social Policy, University of Colorado.

Johnson, E. (1981). "Animal Liberation versus the Land Ethic". *Environmental Ethics*, 3/3: 265–73.

Lee, K (1996). "The Source and Locus of Intrinsic Value". *Environmental Ethics*, 18/3: 297–309.

Leopold, A. (1949). *A Sand County Almanac*. Oxford: Oxford University Press.

Norton, B. G. (1995a). "Why I am Not a Nonanthropocentrist: Callicott and the Failure of Monistic Inherentism". *Environmental Ethics*, 17/4: 341–58.

O'Neill, J. (1993). *Ecology, Policy and Politics: Human Well-Being and the Natural World*. London: Routledge.

Regan, T. (1983). *The Case for Animal Rights*. Berkeley: University of California Press.

Rifkin, J. (1992). *Beyond Beef*. New York: Penguin Books.

Rolston III, H. (1975). "Is There an Ecological Ethic?" *Ethics*, 85/1: 93–109.

—— (1988). *Environmental Ethics, Duties to and Values in the Natural World*. Philadelphia: Temple University Press.

Sagoff, M. (1984/1993). "Animal Liberation and Environmental Ethics: Bad Marriage, Quick Divorce". In Zimmerman *et al.* (1993): 84–94.

Singer, P. (1973). "Animal Liberation". *New York Review of Books* (5 Apr.).

—— (1975/2001). *Animal Liberation*. New York: Ecco Press Books.

Stone, C. (1974). *Should Trees Have Standing?* Los Altos, Calif.: William Kaufmann.

Varner, G. (1995). "Can Animal Rights Activists be Environmentalists?" In C. Pierce and D. VanDeVeer, *People, Penguins, and Plastic Trees*. Belmont, Calif.: Wadsworth: 254–73.

Weston, A. (1985). "Beyond Intrinsic Value: Pragmatism in Environmental Ethics". *Environmental Ethics*, 7: 321–39.

TOM REGAN

Understanding Animal Rights Violence

Few issues divide animal rights advocates more than the role violence should play in forwarding their objectives. Moreover, few matters unite opponents of animal rights more than the condemnation of the violence some attribute indiscriminately to all animal rights advocates. Whether advocate or opponent, one thing is clear: when it comes to discussions of animal rights and violence, there is a lot more heat than light.

Three important questions need to be distinguished. The first asks what violence is; the second, whether and, if so, when violence can be morally justified; and the third, why people use it. Concerning the first question, many animal rights advocates maintain that violence can be directed only against sentient forms of life, human and otherwise. As long as no one is hurt, no violence is done. Given this way of understanding violence, advocates who destroy only property—say, fire-bombing laboratories on university campuses or sinking pirate whaling ships on the high seas—can describe themselves as being engaged in nonviolent activism.

I do not think the concept of violence is limited in this way. Someone who sets fire to a vacant abortion clinic or torches an empty church causes no physical injury to any sentient being, but to suppose that these acts of arson are nonviolent seems to me badly to distort what *violence* means. We do not need to hurt someone to use violence against something. To the extent that animal rights advocates engage in activities that damage or destroy property, they engage in violence.

Part of the reason some advocates define violence as they do can be traced to the way they answer the second question. Most advocates are pacifists; that

is, most believe that violence is wrong. Because some of those advocates who view themselves as pacifists do not think it is wrong to blow up trucks loaded with furs or meat, the definition of violence is tailored to fit the demands of pacifism. All violence is wrong; since blowing up a truck is not wrong, it must not be violent.

The truth of the matter, I think, is different. If someone blows up a truck, torches a lab, or sinks an illegal whaling vessel, they do serious violence even if no one is hurt. To describe these acts as "nonviolent" is to misdescribe them, the way the military does when it describes civilians who are killed or maimed as "collateral damage." Nonetheless, the fact that the destruction of property counts as violence does not by itself make such destruction wrong. Whether the act is wrong remains an open question, one that cannot be answered merely by appealing to what words mean. No other moral question can be answered in this way. There is no reason to think that asking about the morality of violence should be answered any differently.

Of the three questions distinguished previously, it is the third one (the one that asks why animal advocates use violence) that I explore in the following pages. Near the end, however, I offer some suggestions concerning steps that could be taken to reduce the amount of violence committed in the name of animal rights. What violence is, and when, if ever, violence against property or sentient forms of life is morally justified are questions left for possible exploration on some future occasion.

"Understanding Animal Rights Violence" was originally presented at a 1993 meeting sponsored by the organization Public Responsibility in Medicine and Research Science in the Public Interest.

Those people who view themselves as advocates of animal rights—and I certainly include myself among them—also see themselves as part of a social justice movement: the animal rights movement. In this respect, animal rights advocates believe that common bonds unite them with those who have worked for justice in other quarters: for example, for women, people of color, the poor, and gays and lesbians. The struggle for equal rights for and among these people is hardly complete; the struggle for the rights of animals has only begun, and this latter struggle promises to be, if anything, more difficult and protracted than any of its social justice relatives. For while demands for equal rights for many historically disfranchised people face formidable obstacles, they have one advantage over the struggle for animal rights. None of the other movements I have mentioned challenges the conception of the moral community that has dominated Western thought and traditions, the one that includes *humans only*; rather, all these struggles work with rather than against this conception, demanding only (and I do not mean to minimize the enormous difficulties such a demand inevitably faces) that the boundaries of the moral community expand to include previously excluded human beings—Native Americans, for example, or humans who suffer from various physical or mental disabilities.

The struggle for animal rights is different; it calls for a deeper, more fundamental change in the way we think about membership in the moral community. It demands not an expansion but a dismantling of the for-humans-only conception, to be replaced by one that includes other-than-human animals.

Not surprisingly, therefore, any obstacle that stands in the way of greater justice for people of color or the poor, for example, also stands in the way of greater justice for chimpanzees and chickens, whereas the struggle for justice for chimpanzees and chickens encounters obstacles at once more fundamental and unique, including the resistance or disdain of people who are among the most enlightened when it comes to injustice done to humans. Any doubt about this can be readily dispelled by gauging the indifference and hostility showered on the very idea of animal rights by both many of the leaders and most of the rank and file in any human rights movement, including, for example, those committed to justice and equality for women and racial minorities.

Despite these differences, those of us involved in the struggle for animal rights need to remember that we share many of the challenges other social justice movements face. How these movements respond to these challenges, therefore, is something worthy of our study, something from which we can learn. But this is a subject for another occasion. Here, a related set of questions takes pride of place. These concern not external obstacles to social justice movements but internal divisions within them. By way of illustration, I want to explore a few of the similarities between the nineteenth-century antislavery movement in America and today's animal rights movement.

Before doing this, I want to try to defuse a possible misunderstanding. I am not in any way suggesting that the animal rights movement and the antislavery movement are in every respect the same (clearly, they are not), any more than I would be suggesting that all African Americans must be either gay or lesbian because there are similarities between the movement to liberate slaves, on the one hand, and the gay and lesbian movement, on the other. Similarities are just that: similarities. And one thing similarities are not is sameness.

Nevertheless, attending to the similarities I have in mind is not idle. A clearer understanding of the ideology of the antislavery movement and an appreciation of that movement's internal divisions can help us better understand the animal rights movement. In particular, understanding disagreements about the role of violence in the former can help us better understand debates about its role in the latter—or so I believe and hope to be able to explain.

First, however, some stage setting regarding the idea of animal rights is in order.

ANIMAL RIGHTS VERSUS ANIMAL WELFARE

When it comes to what we humans are morally permitted to do to other animals, it is safe to say that opinion is divided. Some people (abolitionists) believe that we should stop using nonhuman animals, whether as sources of food, as trained performers, or as models of various diseases, for example. Others (welfarists) think such utilization is permissible as long as it is done humanely. Those who accept the former outlook object to such utilization in principle and believe it should end in practice. Those who accept the latter outlook accept such utilization in principle and believe it may continue in practice, provided the welfare of animals is not unduly compromised, in which case these practices will need to be appropriately reformed. Clearly real differences separate these two ways of thinking, one abolitionist at its core, the other not. Anyone who would deny or attempt to minimize these differences would distort rather than describe the truth.

Language users that we are, we have a shared need for intelligible verbal markers, some word or phrase that captures and conveys these differences. It is against this larger background of philosophical disagreement and linguistic need that the expressions "animal rights" and "animal rights movement," on the one hand, and "animal welfare" and "animal welfare movement," on the other, have been introduced, with the former pair of expressions commonly used to refer to the abolitionist and the latter pair, to the reformist.

Language is an imperfect instrument, of course, and for all I know there may be better words to mark the differences at hand. I do not care what words we use. What I do care about is (1) the plain truth that such differences exist and (2) our willingness to acknowledge the existence of these differences honestly and forthrightly rather than to pretend or suggest that "it's all a matter of words," that "it really

doesn't matter what we say, since it all comes to the same thing." That not only is not true; among people who know better, it is not honest.

One area where these differences can make a difference is the particular matter before us. For it is among abolitionists, not reformists—among animal rightists, not animal welfarists—that we find those willing to commit acts of violence in the name of animal liberation. Nevertheless—and this is of great importance—not all animal rightists are prepared to go this far. That is, within the animal rights movement one finds deep, protracted, principled disagreements about the limits of protest in general and the permissibility of using violence in particular.

Analogous ideological and tactical themes are to be found in the antislavery movement. That movement was anything but monolithic. True, all abolitionists shared a common goal: slavery in America had to end. Beyond their agreement concerning this unifying goal, however, partisans of emancipation divided over a rich, complex fabric of well-considered, passionately espoused, and irreconcilable disagreements concerning the appropriate means of ending it. For my purposes, reference to just three areas of disagreement will suffice.

ABOLITION FIRST VERSUS ABOLITION LATER

Following the lead of William Lloyd Garrison (1831), some abolitionists called for the unconditional emancipation of slaves, insisting as well that former slave owners not receive compensation for their financial losses. "Immediatists" (as they were called) wanted to end slavery first and then go forward with various plans to educate and in other ways prepare the newly freed slaves for the responsibilities of full citizenship. Other abolitionists (Channing 1835) favored a "gradualist" approach: complete emancipation was the eventual goal, but only after various alternatives to slave labor and improvements in the life of the slaves were in place. Thus, some gradualists sought freedom for slaves after (not before) those in bondage had received at least a rudimentary education or acquired a marketable skill or after (not before) a plan of financial compensation to former slave owners, or another plan calling for voluntary recolonization, had been implemented.

To any and all such proposals, Garrison spoke for his fellow immediatists, declaring that gradualist steps would have opponents of slavery accept the moral absurdity of tolerating the very thing they opposed as a means to ending it. For immediatists, any proposal that required the continued bondage of some slaves today as the price of emancipating others tomorrow was morally unacceptable because it violated a higher moral law: the law that we are not to do evil that good may come.

This split between slavery's immediatists and gradualists is mirrored in today's animal rights movement. Some people who profess belief in the movement's abolitionist goals also believe that these goals can be achieved by using gradualist means— for example, by supporting protocols that aim to reduce or refine animal use in a scientific setting, with replacement possibly achieved later on, or by decreasing the number of hens raised in cages today as a step along the way to emptying cages tomorrow. In this way, it is believed, we can succeed both in making the lives of some animals better today and in ending all animal exploitation in the future.

Other animal rights abolitionists are cut from more Garrison-like cloth. For these animal rightists, *how* we get to the abolitionist goal, not just *that* we get there, matters morally (Francione and Regan 1992). Following the higher moral law that we are not to do evil that good may come, these activists believe that they should not tacitly support violating the rights of some animals today in the hope of freeing others tomorrow. For these activists, as was true of their counterparts in the antislavery movement, it is not a question of first finding an alternative to the evil being done before deciding whether to stop doing it; instead, one must first decide to end the evil and then look for another way to achieve the goals one seeks.

For these animal rights activists, then, our first obligation is to stop using animals as we do; after we have satisfied this obligation, there will be plenty of time to search for alternative ways of doing what it is we want to do. To end evil now rather than later is what conformity to the higher moral law requires....

VIOLENCE VERSUS NONVIOLENCE

Despite his belief in the necessity of working with the government, [Frederick] Douglass was to his dying day a staunch supporter of "agitation," a commitment poignantly captured by Philip Foner's description of a meeting that took place some weeks before Douglass's death. "In the early days of 1895, a young Negro student living in New England journeyed to Providence, Rhode Island, to seek the advice of the aged Frederick Douglass who was visiting that city. As the interview drew to a close the youth said, 'Mr. Douglass, you have lived in both the old and new dispensations. What have you to say to a young Negro just starting out? What should he do?' The patriarch lifted his head and replied, 'Agitate! Agitate! Agitate!'" (Foner 1950:371).

To our ears, Douglass's prescription might sound like a license to lawlessness, but this is not what he meant. For most of his life, Douglass, like the vast majority of abolitionists, favored only nonviolent forms of agitation: peaceful assemblies, rallies, the distribution of pamphlets and other materials depicting the plight of slaves, and petitions—measures that collectively were referred to as "moral suasion." People were to be persuaded that slavery was wrong and ought to be abolished through appeals to their reason, their sense of justice, and their human compassion, not coerced to agree through violence or intimidation.

On this point Garrison and Douglass, who disagreed about much, spoke with one voice. When Garrison said abolitionists were not to do evil that good may come, he meant that they were not to do evil *even to slaveholders, even in pursuit of emancipation.* As he saw it, respect for the higher moral law requires that all efforts made in the name of emancipation, whether immediatist or gradualist and whether in concert with the Union or apart from it, treat all persons respectfully and thus nonviolently.

Not all abolitionists agreed. David Walker (1830) was one; a free black from Virginia, Walker called for massive slave uprisings. "Kill or be killed," he cried out. His *Appeal,* first published in 1829, is said to have influenced Nat Turner as he planned his bloody insurrection in Southampton, Virginia. John Brown was another who did not agree. His legendary raid on Harpers Ferry divided the nation. Southern slave interests with one voice condemned his band of terrorists even as many abolitionists, including Henry David Thoreau, viewed the same acts as noble and inspiring. Brown, Thoreau observes, had the "peculiar doctrine that a man has a perfect right to interfere by force with the slave holder, in order to rescue the slave." And Thoreau's judgment? "I agree with him" (in Oates 1984:365). Although Captain Brown's raid was a military disaster, his call to arms was a portent of things to come, and his last words, written just before his execution, proved to be prophetic: "I, John Brown, am now convinced that the crimes of this guilty land cannot be purged except by blood" (in ibid.:351). In less than a year, the country was at war with itself.

On this matter, today's animal rightists, if not unanimously then at least solidly, align themselves with Garrison and Douglass. Evil, in the form of violence, should not be done to any human being, even in pursuit of animal liberation, and anyone who would perform such an act, whatever that person might say or believe, would not be acting according to the higher moral law that should guide and inform the animal rights movement.

This prohibition against violence to human and other forms of sentient life, however, does not necessarily carry over to property. Most of slavery's opponents understood this. If the cost of freeing a slave was damaged, destroyed, or in the case of slaves

themselves, stolen property, then Garrison, Douglass, and most (but not all) of their abolitionist peers were prepared to accept such violence.

The same is true of many of today's animal rights advocates. Let me be perfectly honest. Some animal rightists obviously believe that violent acts against property carried out in the name of animal liberation, as well as the liberation of animals themselves (the theft of property, given current law), are perfectly justified. Other animal rightists disagree, believing that a principled commitment to the "higher moral law" of nonviolence must be maintained even in the treatment of property.

How many believe the one, how many believe the other, no one, I think, can say. What we can say, and what we should say, is this: it is just as false, just as misleading, and possibly just as dishonest to say that the animal rights movement is a nonviolent movement as it is to say that it is a terrorist movement. The movement to abolish slavery was neither just the one nor just the other. Of the movement to abolish animal exploitation, the same can and should be said. Those who do not say it, whatever their motivations, distort rather than describe the truth. Or so I believe.

UNDERSTANDING ANIMAL RIGHTS VIOLENCE

But if we cannot know how many activists are prepared to use violence against property in the name of animal liberation, the preceding remarks may at least help us understand why they are prepared to do so. Their reasons, I suggest, are as follows.

To understand their motivation, it is not enough to say, "They are abolitionists," since some abolitionists abjure the use of violence not only against persons but also against property. Rather, those who are prepared to use violence are likely to be abolitionists who, first, cannot morally accept reformist means toward realizing their abolitionist ends (for example, they insist on replacement before, not after, reduction and refinement in the case of animals used in research) and, second, cannot rationally believe that the government, as presently or foreseeably constituted, can or will be of any real help in achieving the kind of revolutionary animal liberation they envision.

These activists, I conjecture, reject reformist measures because, like Garrison, they are not willing to accept "doing evil that good may come." Moreover, they have abandoned faith in the government, again like Garrison, because they see the government as being in collusion with and promoting the interests of those who perpetuate the evil they wish to see abolished: the evil of animal exploitation. Impatient with the pace and manner of change and convinced of the prejudice and injustice of the government, which by its laws makes animal exploitation possible, these activists have recourse to the only meaningful form of protest they believe is available to them: violent protest, in the form of damage to or destruction of property. Many there are who will view such behavior as immoral or imprudent. Whether it is the one or the other, my more modest point is that it is intelligible, predictable even, and that those who wish to understand animal rights violence do well first to understand the convictions that fueled the activism of Garrison, Douglass, John Brown, and their followers.

HOW TO LESSEN ANIMAL RIGHTS VIOLENCE

This violence is something that everyone, both friend and foe of animal rights, must lament, something we all wish could be prevented. The question is how to do so. How might we prevent if not all then at least many of the acts we all wish would not occur?

Here we arrive at a question that should give all people of goodwill pause. It is this question, I think, rather than questions about the moral or legal justification of violence, to which we might more profitably give our time, attention, imagination, and labor.

My own (very) modest proposal is this. Although Garrison-like abolitionists cannot support reformist measures, they can support *incremental abolitionist change*, change that involves stopping the utilization of nonhuman animals for one purpose or another. One goal, for example, might be not fewer animals used in cosmetic or industrial testing but no animals used for this purpose. Other goals might be not fewer dogs "sacrificed" in dog labs, or fewer primates "studied" in maternal deprivation research, or fewer goats shot and killed in weapons testing, but no animals used in each of these (and an indefinite number of other possible) cases.

A shared agenda of this type could set forth objectives that animal rights abolitionists, scientific policy makers, and biomedical researchers, for example, could agree on and work collaboratively to achieve; as such, it would go a long way toward reducing animal rights violence. It would demonstrate that it is possible to achieve incremental abolitionist goals by acting nonviolently within the system. This in turn would help defuse the idea that such goals can be achieved only by acting violently outside the system.

I neither say nor believe that such bold steps would eliminate all animal rights violence. What I do believe is that they would help lessen the amount of violence. I also believe that unless we find imaginative, good-faith ways of trying to prevent animal rights violence instead of simply devising more (and more severe) ways of punishing its perpetrators (which is the way defenders of slavery attempted to deal with those who used violence in the name of slave liberation), unless we practice preventive ethics in this quarter, animal rights violence will increase in the coming months and years. Indeed, as things stand at present, the wonder of it is not that there is animal rights violence but that there is not more of it.

REFERENCES

Channing, William Ellery. 1835. "Essay on Slavery." In *The Works of William E. Channing*, 6 vols., 2:123–33. Boston: Anti-Slavery Office.

Douglass, Frederick. 1845. *Narrative of the Life of Frederick Douglass, an American Slave. Written by Himself*. Boston: Anti-Slavery Office.

Foner, Philip S. 1950. *Frederick Douglass: A Biography*. New York: Citadel.

Francione, Gary, and Tom Regan. 1992. "A Movement's Means Create Its Ends." *The Animals' Agenda*, January/February, pp. 40–43.

Garrison, William Lloyd. 1831. "Immediate Emancipation." *The Liberator*, September 3, pp. 1–2.

Oates, Stephen B. 1984. *To Purge This Land with Blood: A Biography of John Brown*. Amherst: University of Massachusetts Press.

Walker, David, 1830. *Walker's Appeal, in Four Articles; together with a Preamble, to the Colored Citizens of the World, and Very Expressly, to Those of the United States of America*. Boston: David Walker.

SECTION V

Contemporary Issues and Controversies

FOOD

Eating is a daily and intimate activity and no matter where we live or how mindful of it we are, food invariably connects us to the environment. Increasingly, questions about the environmental and social impacts of our food choices are being raised. Should we eat meat, purchase only fair trade coffee, avoid genetically engineered foods, and only eat locally grown foods? What qualifies as sustainable food systems? The readings in this section illustrate the myriad of questions that are raised by the food we consume.

Wendell Berry is a defender of traditional agrarian society with its small farms and diverse landscapes and he is critical of those environmentalists who have not come to terms with our inevitable need to use land, particularly for food. In contrast to abusing land "by proxy," he proposes a "kindly use" of nature and argues for eating more "thoughtfully."

Jonathan Safran Foer baldly states that those who regularly eat factory-farmed animal products are not environmentalists. He brings out the fact that many of our most profound environmental problems, including deforestation, water pollution, air pollution, resource depletion, and biodiversity loss, are deeply intertwined with our treatment of animals used for food.

A contrasting view is offered by farmer Blake Hurst. Hurst asks "agri-intellectuals," those who write about food without participating in its production, to reconsider their opposition to industrial agriculture. He argues that the idea of sustainable agriculture is more complex than it may seem, that it has important limitations, and even a dark side, as it is currently practiced. Interestingly, Peter Singer and Jim Mason also note complexities in the growing trend toward "eating locally." They point out, for example, that an American consumer will lower her energy footprint by choosing rice produced in Bangladesh rather than rice produced in California.

Cora Diamond raises important questions about our food preferences. Why don't we eat dead people rather than raising and killing animals who we know suffer from their treatment?

The answer, she thinks, does not turn directly on arguments about rights or interests. Instead, who or what counts as food rests on the relationships that have been established between those who sit at the table and those who are served on it.

Evelyn Pluhar analyzes the variety of ways in which sentient beings are raised and killed for food, and analyzes these practices from the point of view of various moral theories. She argues that vegetarianism is justified, while both factory and humane animal farming are not, for environmental, animal welfare, and human health reasons. She urges us to take seriously the possibility of in vitro meat production that would deliver familiar pleasures of the palate without harming animals.

FURTHER READINGS

Fairlie, Simon. *Meat: A Benign Extravagance*. White River Junction, VT: Chelsea Green, 2010. A defense of small-scale animal agriculture, focusing on food security and land management.

Lappe, Anna. *Diet for a Hot Planet*. New York, NY: Bloomsbury, 2010. A detailed assessment of food's significant contribution to climate change, with a focus on social engagement, justice, and corporate responsibility.

McWilliams, James. *Just Food*. New York, NY: Little, Brown, 2009. A skeptical analysis of some popular environmentalist views about genetically modified organisms, organic agriculture, and "food miles."

Pollan, Michael. *Omnivore's Dilemma*. New York, NY: Penguin, 2006. A "natural history of four meals," tracing foods through their histories and production cycle.

Ronald, Pamela, and Raoul Adamchak. *Tomorrow's Table*. New York, NY: Oxford University Press, 2008. A plant geneticist and organic farmer defend organic, genetically engineered foods as environmentally beneficial.

DISCUSSION QUESTIONS

1. If Foer and others are correct that animal agriculture is one of the largest contributors to environmental problems, what implications does this have for traditional environmental ethics that do not focus on food?

2. Because determining the environmental impacts of food choices is often complex, are there simple guidelines to help people make decisions? Do terms like 'natural,' 'nonindustrial,' 'local,' or 'small-scale' normally indicate environmentally benign foods? If not, are there viable alternatives?

3. How much do environmental and agricultural problems reflect a crisis of culture, as Berry argues, or are they solvable by improving large-scale, industrial technology, as Hurst argues?

4. Is test-tube meat a solution to the problems of animal agriculture? Would you choose it rather than meat produced from raising and slaughtering animals? Why or why not?

5. Does the perception that something is like us (or not like us) justify our eating it? What role does similarity or difference play in our food choices?

WENDELL BERRY

[From] The Ecological Crisis as a Crisis of Agriculture

...The typical present-day conservationist will fight to preserve what he enjoys; he will fight whatever directly threatens his health; he will oppose any ecological violence large or dramatic enough to attract his attention. But he has not yet worried much about the impact of his own livelihood, habits, pleasures, or appetites. He has not, in short, addressed himself to the problem of use. He does not have a definition of his relationship to the world that is sufficiently elaborate and exact.

The problem is well defined in a letter I received from David Budbill of Wolcott, Vermont:

> What I've noticed around here with the militant ecology people (don't get me wrong, I, like you, consider myself one of them) is a syndrome I call the Terrarium View of the World: nature always at a distance, under glass....

We cannot hope—for reasons practical and humane, we cannot even wish—to preserve more than a small portion of the land in wilderness. Most of it we will have to use. The conservation mentality swings from self-righteous outrage to self-deprecation because it has neglected this issue. Its self-contradictions can only be reconciled—and the conservation impulse made to function as ubiquitously and variously as it needs to—by understanding, imagining, and living out the possibility of "kindly use." Only that can dissolve the boundaries that divide people from the land and its care, which together are the source of human life. There are many kinds of land use, but the one that is most widespread and in need of consideration is that of agriculture.

For us, the possibility of kindly use is weighted with problems. In the first place, this is not ultimately an organizational or institutional solution. Institutional solutions tend to narrow and simplify as they approach action. A large number of people can act together only by defining the point or the line on which their various interests converge. Organizations tend to move toward single objectives—a ruling, a vote, a law—and they find it relatively simple to cohere under acronyms and slogans.

But kindly use is a concept that of necessity broadens, becoming more complex and diverse, as it approaches action. The land is too various in its kinds, climates, conditions, declivities, aspects, and histories to conform to any generalized understanding or to prosper under generalized treatment. The use of land cannot be both general and kindly—just as the forms of good manners, generally applied (applied, that is, without consideration of differences), are experienced as indifference, bad manners. To treat every field, or every part of every field, with the same consideration is not farming but industry. Kindly use depends upon intimate knowledge, the most sensitive responsiveness and responsibility. As knowledge (hence, use) is generalized, essential values are destroyed. As the householder evolves into a consumer, the farm evolves into a factory—with results that are potentially calamitous for both.

The understanding of kindly use in agriculture must encompass both farm and household, for the mutuality of influence between them is profound. Once, of course, the idea of a farm included the idea of a household: an integral and major part of a farm's economy was the economy of its own household; the family that owned and worked the farm lived from it. But the farm also helped to feed other households in towns and cities. These households were dependent on the farms, but not passively so, for their dependence was limited in two ways. For one thing, the town or city household was itself often a producer of

food: at one time town and city lots routinely included garden space and often included pens and buildings to accommodate milk cows, fattening hogs, and flocks of poultry. For another thing, the urban household carefully selected and prepared the food that it bought; the neighborhood shops were suppliers of kitchen raw materials to local households, of whose needs and tastes the shopkeepers had personal knowledge. The shopkeepers were under the direct influence and discipline of their customers' wants, which they had to supply honestly if they hoped to prosper. The household was therefore not merely a unit in the economy of food production; its members practiced essential productive skills. The consumers of food were also producers or processors of food, or both....

Social fashion, delusion, and propaganda have combined to persuade the public that our agriculture is for the best of reasons the envy of the Modern World. American citizens are now ready to believe without question that it is entirely good, a grand accomplishment, that each American farmer now "feeds himself and 56 others." They are willing to hear that "96 percent of America's manpower is freed from food production"—without asking what it may have been "freed" *for*, or how many as a consequence have been "freed" from employment of any kind. The "climate of opinion" is now such that a recent assistant secretary of agriculture could condemn the principle of crop rotation without even an acknowledgment of the probable costs in soil depletion and erosion, and former Secretary of Agriculture Butz could say with approval that in 1974 "only 4 percent of all U.S. farms...produced almost 50 percent of all farm goods," without acknowledging the human—and, indeed, the agricultural—penalties.

What these men were praising—what such men have been praising for so long that the praise can be uttered without thought—is a disaster that is both agricultural and cultural: the generalization of the relationship between people and land. That one American farmer can now feed himself and fifty-six other people may be, within the narrow view of the specialist, a triumph of technology; by no stretch of reason can it be considered a triumph of agriculture or of culture. It has been made possible by the substitution of energy for knowledge, of methodology for care, of technology for morality....

The estrangement of consumer and producer, their evolution from collaborators in food production to competitors in the food market, involves a process of oversimplification on both sides. The consumer withdraws from the problems of food production, hence becomes ignorant of them and often scornful of them; the producer no longer sees himself as intermediary between people and land—the people's representative on the land—and becomes interested only in production. The consumer eats worse, and the producer farms worse. And, in their estrangement, waste is institutionalized. Without regret, with less and less interest in the disciplines of thrift and conservation, with, in fact, the assumption that this is the way of the world, our present agriculture wastes topsoil, water, fossil fuel, and human energy—to name only the most noticeable things. Consumers participate "innocently" or ignorantly in all these farm wastes and add to them wastes that are urban or consumptive in nature: mainly all the materials and energy that go into unnecessary processing and packaging, as well as tons of organic matter (highly valuable—and certainly, in the long run, necessary—as fertilizer) that they flush down their drains or throw out as garbage.

What this means for conservationists is that, as consumers, they may be using—and abusing—more land by proxy than they are conserving by the intervention of their organizations. We now have more people using the land (that is, living from it) and fewer thinking about it than ever before. We are eating thoughtlessly, as no other entire society ever has been able to do. We are eating—drawing our lives out of our land—thoughtlessly. If we study carefully the implications of that, we will see that the agricultural crisis is not merely a matter of supply and demand to be remedied by some change of government policy or some technological "breakthrough." It is a crisis of culture.

JONATHAN SAFRAN FOER

[From] *Eating Animals*

Concern for the preservation and restoration of natural resources and the ecological systems that sustain human life. There are grander definitions I could get more excited about, but this is in fact what is usually meant by the term, at least for the moment. Some environmentalists include animals as resources. What is meant by *animals* here is usually endangered or hunted species, rather than those most populous on earth, which are most in need of preservation and restoration.

A University of Chicago study recently found that our food choices contribute at least as much as our transportation choices to global warming. More recent and authoritative studies by the United Nations and the Pew Commission show conclusively that globally, farmed animals contribute *more* to climate change than transport. According to the UN, the livestock sector is responsible for 18 percent of greenhouse gas emissions, around 40 percent more than the entire transport sector—cars, trucks, planes, trains, and ships—combined. Animal agriculture is responsible for 37 percent of anthropogenic methane, which offers twenty-three times the global warming potential (GWP) of CO_2, as well as 65 percent of anthropogenic nitrous oxide, which provides a staggering 296 times the GWP of CO_2. The most current data even quantifies the role of diet: omnivores contribute seven times the volume of greenhouse gases that vegans do.

The UN summarized the environmental effects of the meat industry this way: raising animals for food (whether on factory or traditional farms) "is one of the top two or three most significant contributors to the most serious environmental problems, at every scale from local to global.... [Animal agriculture] should be a major policy focus when dealing with problems of land degradation, climate change and air pollution, water shortage and water pollution and loss of biodiversity. Livestock's contribution to environmental problems is on a massive scale."[1] In other words, if one cares about the environment, and if one accepts the scientific results of such sources as the UN (or the Intergovernmental Panel on Climate Change, or the Center for Science in the Public Interest, or the Pew Commission, or the Union of Concerned Scientists, or the Worldwatch Institute...), one *must* care about eating animals.[2]

Most simply put, someone who regularly eats factory-farmed animal products cannot call himself an environmentalist without divorcing that word from its meaning....

NOTES

1. *Animal agriculture is responsible*...Food and Agriculture Organization, "Livestock's Long Shadow," xxi.

omnivores contribute seven times...AFP, "Going veggie can slash your carbon footprint: Study," August 26, 2008, http://afp.google.com/ article/ALeqM5gb6B3_ItBZn0mNPPt8J5nxjgtllw.

"is one of the top two or three..." Food and Agriculture Organization, "Livestock's Long Shadow," 391.

2. *In other words, if one cares*...Food and Agriculture Organization, "Livestock's Long Shadow"; FAO Fisheries and Aquaculture Department, "The State of World Fisheries and Aquaculture 2008," Food and Agriculture Organization of the United Nations, Rome, 2009, http:// www.fao.org/fishery/sofia/en (accessed August 11, 2009).

Intergovernmental Panel on Climate Change...P. Smith, D. Martino, Z. Cai, D. Gwary, H. Janzen, P. Kumar, B. McCarl, S. Ogle, F. O'Mara, C. Rice, B. Scholes, and

O. Sirotenko, "Agriculture," in *Climate Change 2007: Mitigation.*

Center for Science in the Public Interest...Michael Jacobsen et al., "Six Arguments for a Greener Diet," Center for Science in the Public Interest, 2006, http://www.cspinet.org/EatingGreen/ (accessed August 12, 2009).

Pew Commission...Pew Charitable Trusts et al., "Putting Meat on the Table."

Union of Concerned Scientists...Doug Gurian-Sherman, "CAFOs Uncovered: The Untold Costs of Confined Animal Feeding Operations," Union of Concerned Scientists, 2008, http://www.ucsusa.org/food_and_agriculture/science_and_impacts/impacts_industrial_agriculture/cafos-uncovered.html; Margaret Mellon, "Hogging It: Estimates of Antimicrobial Abuse in Livestock," Union of Concerned Scientists, January 2001, http://www.ucsusa.org/publications/#Food_and_Environment.

Worldwatch Institute...Sara J. Scherr and Sajal Sthapit, "Mitigating Climate Change Through Food and Land Use," Worldwatch Institute, 2009, https://www.worldwatch.org/node/6128.; Christopher Flavin et al., "State of the World 2008," Worldwatch Institute, 2008, https: www.worldwatch.org/node/5561#toc.

BLAKE HURST

The Omnivore's Delusion: Against the Agri-intellectuals

Critics of "industrial farming" spend most of their time concerned with the processes by which food is raised. This is because the results of organic production are so, well, troublesome. With the subtraction of every "unnatural" additive, molds, fungus, and bugs increase. Since it is difficult to sell a religion with so many readily quantifiable bad results, the trusty family farmer has to be thrown into the breach, saving the whole organic movement by his saintly presence, chewing on his straw, plodding along, at one with his environment, his community, his neighborhood. Except that some of the largest farms in the country are organic—and are giant organizations dependent upon lots of hired stoop labor doing the most backbreaking of tasks in order to save the sensitive conscience of my fellow passenger the merest whiff of pesticide contamination. They do not spend much time talking about that at the Whole Foods store. The most delicious irony is this: the parts of farming that are the most "industrial" are the most likely to be owned by the kind of family farmers that elicit such a positive response from the consumer. Corn farms are almost all owned and managed by small family farmers. But corn farmers salivate at the thought of one more biotech breakthrough, use vast amounts of energy to increase production, and raise large quantities of an indistinguishable commodity to sell to huge corporations that turn that corn into thousands of industrial products....

On the desk in front of me are a dozen books, all hugely critical of present-day farming. Farmers are often given a pass in these books, painted as either naïve tools of corporate greed, or economic nullities forced into their present circumstances by the unrelenting forces of the twin grindstones of corporate greed and unfeeling markets. To the farmer on the ground, though, a farmer blessed with free choice

and hard won experience, the moral choices aren't quite so easy. Biotech crops actually cut the use of chemicals, and increase food safety. Are people who refuse to use them my moral superiors? Herbicides cut the need for tillage, which decreases soil erosion by millions of tons. The biggest environmental harm I have done as a farmer is the topsoil (and nutrients) I used to send down the Missouri River to the Gulf of Mexico before we began to practice no-till farming, made possible only by the use of herbicides. The combination of herbicides and genetically modified seed has made my farm more sustainable, not less, and actually reduces the pollution I send down the river.

…Consumers benefit from cheap food. If you think they don't, just remember the headlines after food prices began increasing in 2007 and 2008, including the study by the Food and Agriculture Organization of the United Nations announcing that 50 million additional people are now hungry because of increasing food prices. Only "industrial farming" can possibly meet the demands of an increasing population and increased demand for food as a result of growing incomes….

Much of farming is more "industrial," more technical, and more complex than it used to be. Farmers farm more acres, and are less close to the ground and their animals than they were in the past. Almost all critics of industrial agriculture bemoan this loss of closeness, this "connectedness," to use author Rod Dreher's term. It is a given in most of the writing about agriculture that the knowledge and experience of the organic farmer is what makes him so unique and so important. The "industrial farmer," on the other hand, is a mere pawn of Cargill, backed into his ignorant way of life by forces too large, too far from the farm, and too powerful to resist. Concern about this alienation, both between farmers and the land, and between consumers and their food supply, is what drives much of the literature about agriculture.

The distance between the farmer and what he grows has certainly increased, but, believe me, if we weren't closely connected, we wouldn't still be farming. It's important to our critics that they emphasize this alienation, because they have to ignore the "industrial" farmer's experience and knowledge to say the things they do about farming.

But farmers have reasons for their actions, and society should listen to them as we embark upon this reappraisal of our agricultural system. I use chemicals and diesel fuel to accomplish the tasks my grandfather used to do with sweat, and I use a computer instead of a lined notebook and a pencil, but I'm still farming the same land he did 80 years ago, and the fund of knowledge that our family has accumulated about our small part of Missouri is valuable. And everything I know and I have learned tells me this: we have to farm "industrially" to feed the world, and by using those "industrial" tools sensibly, we can accomplish that task and leave my grandchildren a prosperous and productive farm, while protecting the land, water, and air around us.

PETER SINGER AND JIM MASON

[From] *The Ethics of What We Eat*

…The increasing amount of food being sent by air is a major problem, because air freight uses almost twice as much energy per ton/mile as road freight. Currently, about half of the freight sent by air travels in the hold of passenger flights when they have spare capacity, which is more efficient than sending it on freight-only aircraft, but the use of air freight is growing more rapidly than passenger travel, and so more freight-only aircraft are flying. It has been predicted that aviation will account for 15 percent of all greenhouse-gas emissions by 2050. Although most of that will still be from personal travel, air freight will account for an increasing proportion of that very significant total, and by 2050 could make up nearly a third of the total commercial aviation fleet. Moreover, some experts believe that aviation makes a contribution to the greenhouse effect that goes beyond its energy use, because planes put particulates and water vapor into the upper atmosphere and create additional cloud cover. All of this has a heat-trapping effect that is difficult to quantify but could double that caused by carbon-dioxide emissions alone.[1]

The environmental problems of air travel can create some ethical dilemmas. Consider the genuinely free-range New Zealand eggs available in the western United States. Eggs are much lighter, on a calorie-to-weight basis, than tomatoes, but even so, it takes the energy equivalent of almost a gallon of diesel fuel to fly three dozen large eggs (weighing about 4 pounds, including the cartons), from Auckland to Los Angeles. Is it justifiable to use that amount of energy to give hens a better life? If no other humanely produced eggs are available, maybe we shouldn't be eating eggs at all.

If air freight is the most energy-extravagant way of moving food, sending it by sea or rail are the most economical ways. Rice is grown in California, under irrigation, but it takes a lot of energy to grow it there—about 15 to 25 times as much energy as it takes to grow rice by low-energy input methods in Bangladesh.[2] The energy used in shipping a ton of rice from Bangladesh to San Francisco is less than the difference between the amount of energy it takes to grow it in California and in Bangladesh, so if you live in San Francisco, you would save energy by buying rice that has traveled thousands of miles by sea, rather than locally-grown rice.

To put the energy involved in sea transport in perspective with other energy uses, taking the average car just five extra miles to visit a local farm or market will put as much carbon dioxide into the atmosphere as shipping 17 pounds of onions halfway around the world, from New Zealand to London.[3] That doesn't include the energy used to truck the onions to and from the docks in New Zealand and Britain, and it assumes that refrigeration was not required to store them, but it does show that proximity to the place of production is not necessarily a reliable guide to energy savings.

Other factors to take into account include the use of energy to sort, deliver, and store produce, especially if it has to be kept frozen, and to load and unload trucks, as well as tallying the efficiency of distribution to each store. A local farm may not incur those costs. But the situation is different for stores in town that sell local produce. Suppose an individual farmer has to take small quantities of produce to five local stores in five different nearby towns. Small vans use more fuel and emit more greenhouse gases, in terms of pounds per mile carried, than large trucks, so distribution to small stores may be less efficient, per pound, than an entire truckload of produce going to a large supermarket....

NOTES

1. Intergovernmental Panel on Climate Change, *Aviation and the Global Atmosphere*, Cambridge University Press, 1999; J. Whitelegg and N. Williams, *The Plane Truth: Aviation and the Environment*, Transport 2000 and Ashden Trust, London, 2001; we owe these references to Tara Garnett, *Wise Moves*, Transport 2000, p. 23.

2. J. Pretty and A. Ball, "Agricultural Influences on Carbon Emissions and Sequestration: A Review of Evidence and the Emerging Trading Options," Centre for Environment and Society Occasional Paper 2001–03, University of Essex, 2001.

3. Andy Jones, *Eating Oil*, Sustain & Elm Farm Research Centre, London, 2001, Case Study 2. www.sustainweb.org/chain_fm_eat.asp.

CORA DIAMOND

Eating Meat and Eating People

I

...Discussions of vegetarianism and animals' rights often start with discussion of human rights. We may then be asked what it is that grounds the claims that people have such rights, and whether similar grounds may not after all be found in the case of animals.

All such discussions are beside the point. For they ask why we do not kill people (very irrational ones, let us say) for food, or why we do not treat people in ways which would cause them distress or anxiety and so on, when for the sake of meat we are willing enough to kill *animals* or treat them in ways which cause them distress. This is a totally wrong way of beginning the discussion, because it ignores certain quite central facts—facts which, if attended to, would make it clear that *rights* are not what is crucial. *We do not eat our dead*, even when they have died in automobile accidents or been struck by lightning, and their flesh might be first class. We do not eat them; or if we do, it is a

matter of extreme need, or of some special ritual—and even in cases of obvious extreme need, there is very great reluctance. We also do not eat our amputated limbs. (Or if we did, it would be in the same kinds of special circumstances in which we eat our dead.) Now the fact that we do not eat our dead is not a consequence—not a direct one in any event—of our unwillingness to kill people for food or other purposes. It is not a direct consequence of our unwillingness to cause distress to people. Of course it *would* cause distress to people to think that they might be eaten when they were dead, but it causes distress because of what it is to eat a dead person. Hence we cannot elucidate what (if anything) is wrong—if that is the word—with eating people by appealing to the distress it would cause, in the way we can point to the distress caused by stamping on someone's toe as a reason why we regard it as a wrong to him. Now if we do not eat people who are already dead and also do not kill people for food, it is at least prima facie plausible that our reasons in the two cases might be related, and hence must be looked into by anyone who wants to claim that we have no good reasons for not eating people which are not also good reasons for not eating animals. Anyone who, in discussing this issue, focuses on our reasons for not killing people or our reasons for not causing them suffering quite evidently runs a risk of leaving altogether out of his discussion those fundamental features of our relationship to other human beings which are involved in our not eating them.

It is in fact part of the way this point is usually missed that arguments are given for not eating animals, for respecting their rights to life and not making them suffer, which imply that there is absolutely nothing queer, nothing at all odd, in the vegetarian eating the cow that has obligingly been struck by lightning. That is to say, there is nothing in the discussion which suggests that a cow is *not* something to eat; it is only that one must not help the process along: one must not, that is, interfere with those rights that we should usually have to interfere with if we are to eat animals at all conveniently. But if the point of the Singer–Regan vegetarian's argument is to show that the eating of meat is, morally, in the same position as the eating of human flesh, he is not consistent unless he says that it is just squeamishness, or something like that, which stops us eating our dead. If he admitted that what underlies our attitude to dining on ourselves is the view that *a person is not something to eat*, he could not focus on the cow's right not to be killed or maltreated, as if that were the heart of it.

I write this as a vegetarian, but one distressed by the obtuseness of the normal arguments, in particular, I should say, the arguments of Singer and Regan. For if vegetarians give arguments which do not begin to get near the considerations which are involved in our not eating people, those to whom their arguments are addressed may not be certain how to reply, but they will not be convinced either, and really are quite right. They themselves may not be able to make explicit what it is they object to in the way the vegetarian presents our attitude to

not eating people, but they will be left feeling that beyond all the natter about "speciesism" and equality and the rest, there is a difference between human beings and animals which is being ignored. This is not just connected with the difference between what it is to eat the one and what it is to eat the other. It is connected with the difference between giving people a funeral and giving a dog one, with the difference between miscegenation and *chacun à son goût* with consenting adult gorillas....And so on. It is a mark of the shallowness of these discussions of vegetarianism that the only tool used in them to explain what differences in treatment are justified is the appeal to the capacities of the beings in question. That is to say, such-and-such a being—a dog, say—might be said to have, like us, a right to have its interests taken into account; but its interests will be different because its capacities are. Such an appeal may then be used by the vegetarian to explain why he need not in consistency demand votes for dogs (though even there it is not really adequate), but as an explanation of the appropriateness of a funeral for a child two days old and not for a puppy it will not do; and the vegetarian is forced to explain that—if he tries at all—in terms of what it is *to us*, a form of explanation which for him is evidently dangerous. Indeed, it is normally the case that vegetarians do not touch the issue of our attitude to the dead. They accuse philosophers of ignoring the problems created by animals in their discussions of *human* rights, but they equally may be accused of ignoring the hard cases for their own view. (The hardness of the case for them, though, is a matter of its hardness for any approach to morality deriving much from utilitarianism—deriving much, that is, from a utilitarian conception of what makes something a possible object of moral concern.)

I do not think it an accident that the arguments of vegetarians have a nagging moralistic tone. They are an attempt to show something to be morally wrong, on the assumption that *we all agree* that it is morally wrong to raise people for meat, and so on. Now the objection to saying that *that* is morally wrong is not, or not merely, that it is too weak. What we should be going against in adopting Swift's "Modest Proposal" is something we should be going against in salvaging the dead more generally: useful organs for transplantation, and the rest for supper or the compost heap. And "morally wrong" is not too weak for that, but in the wrong dimension. One could say that it would be impious to treat the dead so, but the word "impious" does not make for clarity, it only asks for explanation. We can most naturally speak of a kind of action as morally wrong when we have some firm grasp of what *kind* of beings are involved. But there are some actions, like giving people names, that are part of the way we come to understand and indicate our recognition of *what* kind it is with which we are concerned. And "morally wrong" will often not fit our refusals to act in such a way, or our acting in an opposed sort of way, as when Gradgrind calls a child "Girl number twenty." Doing her out of a name is not like doing her out of an inheritance to which she has a right and in which she has an interest. Rather, Gradgrind lives in a world, or would like to, in which it makes no difference whether she has a name, a number being more efficient, and in which a human being is not *something to be named and not numbered*. Again, it is not "morally wrong" to eat our pets; people who ate their pets would not have pets in the same sense of that term. (If we call an animal that we are fattening for the table a pet, we are making a crude joke of a familiar sort.) A pet is not something to eat, it is given a name, is let into our houses and may be spoken to in ways in which we do not normally speak to cows or squirrels. That is to say, it is given some part of the character of a person. (This may be more or less sentimental; it need not be sentimental at all.) Treating pets in these ways is not at all a matter of recognizing some *interest* which pets have in being so treated. There is not a class of beings, pets, whose nature, whose capacities, are such that we owe it to them to treat them in

these ways. Similarly, it is not out of respect for the interests of beings of the class to which we belong that we give names to each other, or that we treat human sexuality or birth or death as we do, marking them—in their various ways—as significant or serious. And again, it is not respect for our interests which is involved in our not eating each other. These are all things that go to determine what sort of concept "human being" is. Similarly with having duties to human beings. This is not a consequence of what human beings are, it is not justified by what human beings are: it is itself one of the things which go to build our notion of human beings. And so too—very much so—the idea of the difference between human beings and animals. We learn what a human being is in—among other ways—sitting at a table where *WE* eat *THEM*. We are around the table and they are on it. The difference between human beings and animals is not to be discovered by studies of Washoe or the activities of dolphins. It is not that sort of study or ethology or evolutionary theory that is going to tell us the difference between us and animals: the difference is, as I have suggested, a central concept for human life and is more an object of contemplation than observation (though that might be misunderstood; I am not suggesting it is a matter of intuition). One source of confusion here is that we fail to distinguish between "the difference between animals and people" and "the differences between animals and people"; the same sort of confusion occurs in discussions of the relationship of men and women. In both cases people appeal to scientific evidence to show that "the difference" is not as deep as we think; but all that such evidence can show, or show directly, is that the differences are less sharp than we think. In the case of the difference between animals and people, it is clear that we form the idea of this difference, create the concept of the difference, knowing perfectly well the overwhelmingly obvious similarities....

Evelyn Pluhar

Meat and Morality: Alternatives to Factory Farming

…Intensive confinement and mechanized production methods create an enormous volume of flesh for consumption. According to the U. S. Department of Agriculture, 10.378 billion U. S. land animals were slaughtered for food in 2007 (World Farm Animals 2008). This accounts for nearly 25% of the total estimated number of non-aquatic animals killed for food in the world (United Poultry Concerns 2008).[1] The American appetite for flesh has grown from 234 lbs. per capita in 1980 to 273 lbs. in 2007 (Lavelle and Garber 2008). Worldwide demand for meat is likewise increasing as developing nations become more able to afford it. China, for example, has been doubling its demand for meat every 10 years (Paper says edible meat 2005). Meanwhile, the human population is nearing 7 billion with no downturn in sight. The United Nations Population Division estimates that there will be 9 billion humans on the planet by 2050 (Lederer 2009). According to the FAO (Food and Agriculture Organization, United Nations), meat production will double worldwide by that same year, 2050, unless demand falters (2006, p. 1). Even at current levels, the only way to sustain meat consumption is to industrialize its production (Bittman 2009, p. 13). Yet, as the Pew Commission recognizes, factory farming is unsustainable and grossly deleterious to humans and nonhumans alike, as well as to the ecosystems that sustain us all.

Let us consider just some of the side effects of a system of meat production that has created unparalleled volume to meet unparalleled demand. The humans most directly and most badly affected are those who must work in such facilities, including slaughterhouses. The emotional effects of such employment, especially at the end stage, are considerable. According to slaughterhouse expert Temple Grandin, it is not unusual for the employees to become sadistic, literally brutalized by what they must do hourly and daily (Pollan 2006, p. 233). In terms of physical health alone, the consequences are serious for factory farm-related employees. Michael Pollan recounts being asked to don a biohazard suit before visiting a brooder house (Pollan 2006, p. 221). Communities surrounding such operations suffer from pollution and increased disease susceptibility as well (Sayre and Laura 2009).

Everyone, however, even vegetarians, are at risk from the pathogens released by stressed, immune-compromised, contaminant-filled nonhuman food animals (Bittman 2009, p. 28). Contributing to the problem are routine nontherapeutic doses of antibiotics in animal feed. Although the European Union banned the practice in 2006 (Union of Concerned Scientists Food and agriculture report 2009), it continues in the United States, accompanied by the emergence of increasingly antibiotic-resistant strains of Campylobacter, MRSA, Salmonella, E. Coli, and Enterococcus (Sayre and Laura 2009). In the United States alone 76 million are stricken annually by fouled food, 5,000 of them fatally (Harris 2009). Even those who avoid factory-farmed meat are at risk from these new strains, which enter water, contaminate produce, and invade hospitals. Ironically, Johns Hopkins researchers have compared concentrated animal feeding operations (CAFOs) themselves to nightmare hospitals "where everyone is given antibiotics, patients lie in unchanged beds, hygiene is nonexistent, infections and re-infections are rife, waste is thrown out the window, and visitors enter and leave at will" (Sayre and Laura 2009, p. 78)….

The effects on wild flora, fauna, and the environment in general are also predictably severe. Apart

from overwhelming pollution, one must consider the impact of energy-intensive factory farming on greenhouse emissions. Astonishingly, the FAO documents that the livestock industry contributes more to these emissions—a full 20% of the total—than all of transportation (Bittman 2009, p. 1)! A typical American meat eater contributes one and one-half tons more CO_2 to the environment than a vegetarian. Mark Bittman brings this figure to life by noting that for a typical family of four to enjoy a steak dinner is equivalent to joy-riding in an SUV for 3 hours after leaving all the lights on at home (Bittman 2009, p. 17)....

VEGETARIANISM

The dangerous consequences of factory farming for the environment, human health, and animal well being could obviously be largely avoided by the shift to vegetarianism. Vegan diets are fully compatible with this aim. Dairy products could be permitted as well, so long as they do not exact suffering and death. Depending on one's vegetarian belief system, some egg consumption might also be permissible, although the way eggs come on the market now (most are factory-farmed, male chicks are killed even in "cage-free" operations) is not ethically acceptable. The environmental advantages of a low-on-the-food chain diet are too numerous to recount....Biocentrists and environmental holists join sentience-centrists in decrying these effects. Intensive practices are hugely wasteful drains on the planet and on the food supply itself.

Even from the anthropocentric point of view, continuing as we are is unjustifiable. The USDA documents that animals fed plant proteins edible by humans yield large net protein losses. For example, 1 lb. of beef requires 7 lbs. of corn, 1 lb. of pork requires 6.5 lbs. of corn, and only 1 lb. of chicken results from 2.8 lbs. of corn (Lavelle and Garber 2008). This is ironic indeed, considering the concomitant growth in the human population and the

increasing appetite for large quantities of meat: if industrialized meat production is the only way to sate that appetite, humans are eating themselves into starvation. Vegetarianism would free vast stores of protein for current and future human generations.

The healthfulness of a well-balanced vegetarian (including vegan) regime is likewise acknowledged by mainstream nutritional research (ADA Reports 2003).[2] Eating pesticide- and herbicide-treated produce, including produce genetically modified to be resistant to such agents, is not risk-free, but at least the toxins are not exponentially concentrated in flesh featured on the dining table. Consumers with access to organic or minimally treated produce are in the best position. These options are becoming more available as demand for them increases. According to nutrition research, compared to the traditionally meat-heavy omnivorous American diet, vegetarianism has health advantages for the prevention and amelioration of various diseases (ADA Reports 2003).

Nonhuman sentient beings by the billions yearly suffer intensive confinement with its attendant stress-caused pathogen shedding; transportation and slaughter impose additional agonies. Vegetarians take the moral high ground when they point out that this pain and death is not necessary for human health. Contemporary utilitarians like Singer (2004) and Gruzalski (2004) make the case against eating animals raised and killed for their flesh in classic Benthamite terms: the ethical goal of maximizing utility (happiness) and minimizing disutility (suffering) requires us to cease current practices. Those who hold that sentient beings have justified claims not to be harmed or killed unnecessarily; i.e., rights theorists, go further. Besides contributing mightily to disutility in the world by raising and slaughtering sentient beings for food, we violate their basic moral rights (Regan 1983, pp. 330–351; Pluhar 2004). Vegetarian feminists such as Adams (1990), Curtin (2004), and Gruen (2004) likewise enjoin humanity to stop what they see as outright barbarism. Eliminating sentient beings from our plates eliminates agony and wrongful death....

The moral case for vegetarianism as an alternative to consuming factory-farmed animals is very strong. Nonetheless, some object that as a matter of simple fact most human omnivores will not be persuaded to stop eating animal flesh. Many humans who have participated in meat eating all or most of their lives have a very difficult time letting go of that practice. The numbers of vegetarians in the U. S., for example, probably do not exceed more than 2–3% of the population (How many vegetarians 2006). Some estimates are as high as 7%, but these figures are suspect. One *Vegetarian Times* poll found that most of the respondents who identified themselves as vegetarian actually ate fish, poultry, or beef (Akers 2008)! Many vegetarians can tell you about friends or wait-staff who assume they eat seafood and sometimes chicken; "vegetarian" seems to be confused with "almost-vegetarian." Even the 2.8% estimate (by a 2003 Harris Poll) is questionable, since the margin of error for a 1,000 adult sample is 3% (Akers 2008).

It may well be the case that more extensive education about the effects of factory farming on animals raised for food, on human health, and upon the environment would push the number of vegetarians significantly upward. At present, however, the vegetarian option is largely soft-pedaled on the assumption that as long as meat-eating options are available, most will prefer to exercise that option. Much effort is given to persuading human omnivores to eat less meat by moving it out of the center of the plate. Few seem to think outright vegetarianism is acceptable to most consumers, even though "In some ways it [cutting back] is harder than quitting" (Bittman 2008). On the other end of the meat-eating spectrum, we find that those who never had much often crave more. As we have seen, consumers in rising developing countries who are accustomed to eating little meat tend to demand more as they become able to afford it.

Nevertheless, if humans are able to make the full empathetic connection to nonhumans formerly regarded as food, it becomes increasingly difficult to consume them. The taboos we usually have against eating other humans expand as the moral circle we draw around significant beings expands. Provided that healthy alternative food sources are available, vegetarianism becomes a justified and strongly appealing choice for many. Mutually beneficial relationships with cows, chickens, and goats, for example, could be part of this picture, so long as they do not suffer and die for us. Humans and nonhumans alike can gain from the respectful refusal to eat meat.

Barring extensive reeducation and the full extension of empathy to "food animals," however, many meat-eating humans will be reluctant to become vegetarians. Learning about the hazards of factory farming may lead them to the second option below.

HUMANE ANIMAL FARMING

Many who are not willing to become vegetarians are willing to consider the option of consuming humanely farmed animals. Smaller, more numerous family farms that practice sustainable agriculture and humanely raise the animals they market for food would impose much less of a burden on the environment. Animals raised in much less stressful conditions would shed fewer pathogens. They would not be pumped with hormones and nontherapeutic doses of antibiotics; their feed would not be contaminated with cattle parts and poultry litter. The animals would also suffer much less. Non-vegetarians as well as vegetarians are often horrified when they learn about the conditions under which factory farmed animals live and die. There was general outrage in the U. S. when clandestinely made recordings of sick downer cows being kicked and even forklifted on their way into the slaughter house were widely televised in 2008 (Martin 2008). The growing success of humanely obtained eggs, milk, beef, and chicken is due to consumer education and subsequent demand for healthier and "happier" food (Pfister 2008). As the trend continues, such farms

could eventually replace factory farms, offering many people the products they crave, albeit in lesser amounts. Bittman (2009) observes, for example, that available pasture on the earth could not sustain the 1.3 billion cattle now raised and slaughtered for food in CAFOs. Trading the currently high available volume of meat for healthier eating patterns, a less-stressed planet, and happier "food animals" is not unattractive, however....

Anthropocentrists would be supportive of this option, but it does face objections from other ethical perspectives. Feminist theorists would look askance at an option which "commodifies" and kills sentient beings unnecessarily, albeit humanely. Biocentrists and environmental ethicists in general would also question the emphasis on domestic food animal production, given its displacement of wild flora and fauna. While the humane farming option would exact a much smaller toll on the environment and its denizens than factory farming, displacement would still be a factor. This objection to some extent would also apply to vegetarianism, since that option also calls for land cultivation. However, eating low on the food chain is more protein-efficient and therefore easier on the land than the alternatives. The best favor we could do for the environment is to choose to keep our numbers from further exploding and use the land as responsibly as possible....

One final alternative to factory farming may avoid some of the objections to humane meat farming while satisfying the taste so many have for flesh: in-vitro meat production.

IN-VITRO MEAT

In April 2008, the In Vitro Meat Consortium held its first international conference in Norway (Revkin 2008). The conference reflects the significant progress that has been made in the production of laboratory-cultured meat. The technique calls for a single stem cell to mature and divide in a nutrient-rich soup, eventually resulting in billions of cells fused into a solid slab of meat. So far, a pig muscle cell has been cultured into a very thin bologna slice (Kruglinski 2008). If progress continues, a single muscle cell extracted from a living cow, for example, could in principle produce enough meat to satisfy the annual world demand for beef (Scientists aim for lab-grown meat 2005). Not all cravings are apt to be satisfied by current technology. Steaks cannot be reproduced because blood vessels would have to be coaxed somehow to grow in beef tissue. However, lab-grown chicken nuggets and minced pork or cow meat are real possibilities (Revkin 2008). In the hope of speeding the process along, People for the Ethical Treatment of Animals (PETA) has offered $1 million to the first scientist who can produce affordable chicken nuggets that can pass a blind taste-test (Scientists offered $1 million 2008). PETA's deadline is summer 2012. The taste is likely less of a challenge than the price. The minimum cost with present techniques is a staggering $1,000 per pound. U. S. and Dutch researchers hope that a price equivalent to $1 per pound is a reachable goal (Sandhana 2006).

Were such cultured meat to become affordable and available, the advantages for humans, nonhuman livestock, and the environment might be considerable, depending on production methods. Most of the protein fed to livestock, 75–95%, is lost to metabolism or inedible structures; there would be no such negative protein conversion in the laboratory (Sandhana 2006). The meat would simply be grown. Of course energy would be needed in the production process, but so is it needed to produce, transport, and slaughter livestock. The Dutch government is actively supporting the in-vitro meat initiative in good part to mitigate the environmental damage caused by the livestock industry (Paper says edible meat 2005). From the human health perspective, one can see that the cultured meat consumer would not be exposed to antibiotics, hormones, downer cow tissues, or chicken-feces-fed livestock. Cultured meat would also have a big health advantage compared to organically grown

livestock: the heart-threatening Omega 6 fatty acids existing in high levels in most consumed livestock could be replaced with beneficial Omega 3 fatty acids (Sandhana 2006). Finally, if many flesh-lovers turned to cultured meat, the cruelty inflicted in factory farming would be reduced, as well as the fear and pain of slaughter for factory-farmed and "humanely" farmed animals alike....

The initial reaction of many meat-eaters to the in-vitro meat initiative is repulsion. An unscientific poll conducted by this author elicited comments such as "That's disgusting!" and "Who knows what they would put in that stuff?" They envision meat cells replicating like mold in a laboratory, injected with dubious additives by white-coated Frankensteins. Currently, production does involve a queasiness factor: cells mature in "fetal bovine serum." Researchers are at work substituting a plant-based nutrient agent, however, well aware that this would be advantageous in marketing the product to erstwhile vegetarians as well as meat-eaters with humane concerns (Kruglinski 2008). The in-vitro meat industry, should it become potentially viable, would have to convince consumers that there are no horrors and objectionable additives in the laboratory. If the industry can truthfully point to safe production and persuade people of this fact, and meat-lovers could see how advantageous cultured meat is to humans, cows, pigs, chickens, and the environment, it is probable that attitudes would adjust. Perhaps it is not an impossible dream to foresee a future in which meat-lovers are horrified by our past farming practices?...

Despite these considerations, many are troubled by the new initiative. The discomfort and outright revulsion that many rights theorists, feminists and, quite simply, vegetarians experience at the prospect of in-vitro meat stems, this author believes, from the association the new practice has with the raising and killing of animals for food. One is obtaining cells from animals once destined for consumption, thus continuing a habit that has resulted in the violent deaths of trillions of sentient beings. Why would one wish to support the continued and unnecessary consumption of flesh, given the history of such consumption? This is a question many vegetarians will answer in the negative. Suppose that, as Jonathan Swift's savage satire suggested, the English had actually established the practice of "farming" succulent Irish babies:

> ...a young, healthy child well nursed is at a year old a most delicious, nourishing and healthy food, whether stewed, roasted, baked or boiled...when the family dines alone, the fore or hind quarter will make a reasonable dish, and seasoned with pepper or salt will be very good boiled on the fourth day, especially in winter (Swift 1729).

Now let us suppose that enlightenment dawns after nearly 300 years, and the horrified English populace abolishes the practice. Still, many fondly remember the unparalleled taste of Irish rump roast. Picture, then, the enterprising researchers who learn to clone cells from happy babies (whose parents, of course, consent) to culture into delicious nonsentient baby meat. Would this new product be an easy sell? For many (not all!) the gut reaction would be very negative indeed, a harkening back to abomination. This is precisely the sentiment of many current vegetarians at the prospect of in-vitro meat.

However, this is not a good argument against the practice of meat culturing. Guilt by association arguments are logically unacceptable, albeit psychologically appealing....

CONCLUSION

From various ethical perspectives, including utilitarianism and moral rights theory, avoiding flesh farming through vegetarianism is morally justified. Potentially, so is the production and consumption of in-vitro meat. The continued raising and killing of sentient beings for our dinner tables is not, although switching from factory farming to humane food animal farming would be an improvement for humans, nonhuman food animals, and the environment.

NOTES

1. No statistics are available for the number of aquatic animals slaughtered; however, it is thought that this number is likely equal to the land animals killed (HSUS 2008).

2. The one case where supplementation or fortification is required for vegans concerns vitamin B-12. Found in dairy products, eggs, and meat, B-12 does not occur naturally in plants. Fortified sources of B-12, such as cereals, are readily available.

REFERENCES

Adams, C. (1990). *The sexual politics of meat*. New York, NY: Continuum.

Akers, K. (2008). How many vegetarians? Vegetarian Society of Colorado. http://www.vsc.org/1103-How-Many-Veggies.htm. Accessed 14 August 2008.

ADA Reports. (2003). Position of the American dietetic association and dieticians of Canada: Vegetarian diets. *Journal of the American Dietetic Association*, 103, 748–765.

Bentham, J. (1789, 1988 reprint). *The principles of morals and legislation*. Amherst, NY: Prometheus Books.

Bittman, Mark. (2008). Putting meat back in its place. *The New York Times*. http://www.nytimes.com/. Accessed 11 June 2008.

Bittman, Mark. (2009). *Food matters: A guide to conscious eating*. New York, NY: Simon & Shuster.

Callicott, J. B. (1980). Animal liberation: A triangular affair. *Environmental Ethics*, 2, 311–328.

Clark, S. R. L. (2006). Respecting sentient beings. *Organization and Environment*, 19, 280–283.

Curtin, D. (2004). Contextual moral vegetarianism. In S. Sapontzis (Ed.), *Food for thought* (pp. 272–283). Amherst, NY: Prometheus Books.

DeVault, G. (2008). Which comes first: The chicken or the profit? *Mother Earth News*, p. 25.

FDA Unveils Proposal to Fight Mad Cow. (2005). REDORBIT NEWS. http://www.redorbit.com/. Accessed 26 July 2007.

FAO. (2006). Livestock a major threat to environment. http://www.fao.org/. Accessed 29 November 2009.

Frey, R. G. (1989). The case against animal rights. In T. Regan & P. Singer (Eds.), *Animal rights and human obligations* (2nd ed., pp. 115–118). Englewood Cliffs, NJ: Prentice-Hall.

Frey, R. G. (2004). Utilitarianism and moral vegetarianism again: Protest or effectiveness? In S. Sapontzis (Ed.), *Food for thought* (pp. 118–123). Amherst, NY: Prometheus Books.

Frey, R. G., & Paton, W. (1989). Vivisection, morals, and medicine: An exchange. In T. Regan & P. Singer (Eds.), *Animal rights and human obligations* (2nd ed., pp. 223–236). Englewood Cliffs, NJ: Prentice-Hall.

Gruen, L. (2004). Empathy and vegetarian commitments. In S. Sapontzis (Ed.), *Food for thought* (pp. 124–137). Amherst, NY: Prometheus Books.

Gruzalski, B. (2004). Why it's wrong to eat animals raised and slaughtered for food. In S. Sapontzis (Ed.), *Food for thought* (pp. 124–137). Amherst, NY: Prometheus Books.

Harris, G. (2009). President promises to bolster food safety. *The New York Times*. http://www.nytimes.com/2009/03/15/us/politics/15address.html. Accessed 15 March 2009.

How many vegetarians are there in the US? (2006). Vegetarian Basic 101—Care2.com. http://www.care2.com/. Accessed 14 August 2008.

Humane Society of the United States (HSUS). (2008). An HSUS report: The welfare of animals in the meat, egg, and dairy industries. http://www.hsus.org/farm/resources/research/welfare/welfare_overview.html. Accessed 4 August 2008.

Hunger Notes. (2008). Pew Commission says industrial scale farm animal production poses "unacceptable" risks to public health, environment. http://www.world-hunger.org/articles/08/us/pew2.htm. Accessed 4 May 2008.

Kruglinski, S. (2008). Building a better burger. *Discover Magazine*, pp. 36–37.

Lavelle, M., & Garber, K. (2008). Fixing the food crisis. *U. S. News and World Report*, pp. 36–42.

Lederer, E. M. (2009). UN says world population to hit 7 billion by 2012. Associated Press. Yahoo News. http://news.yahoo.com/. Accessed 14 March 2009.

Martin, A. (2007). Meat processors look for ways to keep ground beef safe. *The New York Times*. http://www.nytimes.com/. Accessed 8 December 2007.

Martin, A. (2008). Largest recall of ground beef is ordered. *The New York Times*. http://www.nytimes.com/2008. Accessed 13 August 2008.

Paper says edible meat can be grown in a lab on industrial scale. (2005). University of Maryland Newsdesk. http://www.newsdesk.umd.edu/schtech/print.cfm?articleID+1098. Accessed 13 June 2008.

Pfister, B. (2008). Meat CSAs catching on. *Pittsburgh Tribune-Review*. http://pittsburghlive.come/x/pittsburghtrib/news/cityregion/print_571712.html. Accessed 9 June 2008.

Pluhar, E. B. (1995). *Beyond prejudice: The moral significance of human and nonhuman animals*. Durham, NC: Duke U. Press.

Pluhar, E. B. (2004). The right not to be eaten. In S. Sapontzis (Ed.), *Food for thought* (pp. 92–107). Amherst, NY: Prometheus Books.

Pollan, M. (2006). *The omnivore's dilemma*. New York, NY: Penguin Books.

Rawls, J. (1971). *A theory of justice*. Cambridge, MA: Harvard U. Press.

Regan, T. (1983). *The case for animal rights*. Berkeley: U. of California Press.

Regan, T. (2001). *Defending animal rights*. Urbana: U. of Illinois Press.

Revkin, A. (2008). Can people have meat and a planet too? *The New York Times*. dotearth.blogs.nytimes.com/2008/04/11. Accessed 11 April 2008.

Sagoff, M. (1984). Animal liberation and environmental ethics: Bad marriage, quick divorce. *Osgood Hall Law Journal*, 22, 303–304.

Sandhana, L. (2006). Test tube meat nears dinner table. Common Dreams News Center. http://www.commondreams.org/. Accessed 13 June 2008.

Sayre, Laura. (2009). The hidden link between factory farms and human illness. *Mother Earth News*, pp. 76–83.

Scientists aim for lab-grown meat. (2005). BBC News. http://newsvote.bbc.co.uk/. Accessed 13 June 2008.

Scientists offered $1 million to grow laboratory chicken. (2008). CNN Headline News. http://www.cnn.com/. Accessed 13 June.

Seven children wait for their IVF sibling. (2008). Baby Web. http://www.babyweb.com. Accessed 1 September 2008.

Singer, P. (1990). *Animal liberation* (2nd ed.). New York: Random House.

Singer, P. (2004). Animal liberation: Vegetarianism as protest. In S. Sapontzis (Ed.), *Food for thought* (pp. 108–117). Amherst, NY: Prometheus Books.

Swift, Jonathan. (1729, 1976 reprint). A modest proposal for preventing the children of poor people from being a burthen to their parents or country, and for making them beneficial to the publick. In R. Regan and P. Singer (Eds.), *Animal rights and human obligations* (pp. 234–237). Englewood Cliffs, NJ: Prentice-Hall.

Union of Concerned Scientists. (2009). Food and agriculture report: European Union bans antibiotics for growth production. http://www.ucsusa.org/. Accessed 11 March 2009.

United Poultry Concerns. (2008). Animals killed for food in the United States in 2000 (millions). http://www.upc-online.org/slaughter_stats.html. Accessed 1 August 2008.

Walker, Alice. (1988). *Am I blue? Living by the word*. New York, NY: Harcourt Brace Jovanovich.

World Farm Animals Day. (2008). U. S. animal death statistics. http://www.wfad.org/statistics/. Accessed 4 August 2008.

WILDERNESS

What is "wilderness" and what is the connection between it and what we think of as "wild"? Can an ecosystem be wilderness if it is designated and managed by humans? What is its value? What are the relationships between wilderness and human improvement, animal protection, and the preservation of biodiversity?

Jack Turner offers an uncompromising defense of wildness. After noting that most, if not all, designated wilderness areas are not wild, Turner argues that wilderness is "not defined by the absence of people, but by the relationship between people and place." He distinguishes between the "autonomy of natural systems," which is what wildness consists of, and management or control, exemplified by "biological inventories, species recovery, surveillance and monitoring." The heart of autonomy and wildness is to be self-willed. Wilderness exists when nature is running the show, not park rangers, outfitters, or conservation biologists. Turner asks us to imagine an alternative to our current model of wilderness that would allow for "wilderness again [to] become a blank on our maps."

Both Turner and William Cronon challenge us to rethink the concept of wilderness but in very different ways. For Turner, wilderness is as radically independent of human control as anything can be. For Cronon, wilderness is a "product of civilization." Cronon reminds us that wilderness has a history, even though its creation is designed in part to allow us to forget this story. In the United States, uninhabited wilderness was created by relocating the Native Americans who lived there. What is the value of wilderness on such a view? Cronon largely leaves this question unanswered. Our work is to be at home in the world, according to Cronon, and the world includes much more than what we call wilderness.

Ramachandra Guha offers a critique of what he regards as the distinctly American (or at least Western) notion of wilderness: He argues that this idea of wilderness can be damaging, particularly when exported to developing countries. Implementing the wilderness idea in such societies can lead to uprooting people (often poor peasants) from land on which they have survived for generations. These decisions about designating and managing parks and wilderness are typically made by scientists and government elites who are part of the global middle class that is already causing a disproportionate share of environmental damages. Local people who are most directly affected by these policies are often excluded from the decision-making process. This transformation of traditional lands to parks and wilderness can be seen as another violation of environmental justice. It is also self-defeating, since attempts to protect nature will not succeed unless they enlist the efforts of those whose lives most depend upon it.

FURTHER READING

Callicott, J. Baird, and Michael Nelson, eds. *The Great New Wilderness Debate*. Athens, GA: University of Georgia Press, 1998. A comprehensive collection of essays on the idea of wilderness, its history, and value.

Fraser, Caroline. *Rewilding the World: Dispatches from the Conservation Revolution*. Picador, 2010. An argument for rewilding as a response to biodiversity loss.

Lewis, Michael, ed. *American Wilderness: A New History*. New York, NY: Oxford University Press, 2007. Contemporary essays responding to Nash's history of wilderness.

Nash, Roderick. *Wilderness and the American Mind*. 4th ed. New Haven, CT: Yale University Press, 2001. The canonical history of the concept of wilderness in American culture.

Sax, Joseph. *Mountains without Handrails: Reflections on the National Parks*. Ann Arbor, MI: University of Michigan Press, 1980. A classic defense of wilderness as a place for contemplation and reflection.

DISCUSSION QUESTIONS

1. If Cronon is right in thinking that wilderness is culturally constructed, is it therefore less valuable than it would be on Turner's conception?
2. Can the views of Turner and Cronon be reconciled in any way? Why or why not?
3. Is Guha right in thinking that the idea of wilderness is a Western notion? If so, what does that mean for the designation of wilderness areas in non-Western countries?
4. Let us suppose, as many say, that human activity has impacted every aspect of nature. Does this mean that no wilderness exists?
5. What are the best reasons for preserving wilderness?

JACK TURNER

[From] *The Abstract Wild*

I

...To construct a new conservation ethic, we need first to understand why we impose a human order on nonhuman orders. We do so for gain, the gain being in prediction, efficiency, and, hence, control. Faced with the accelerating destruction of ecosystems and the extinction of species, we believe our only option lies in increased prediction, efficiency, and control. So we fight to preserve ecosystems and species, and we accept their diminished wildness. This wins the fight but loses the war, and in the process we simply stop talking about wildness.

There are many ways we do this. For instance, we begin to substitute "wilderness" for "wildness," as in Thoreau's commonly misquoted saying "In *wilderness* is the preservation of the world."[1] But most (all?) of our designated Wilderness Act-wilderness is not wild. Take, for example, the Gila Wilderness, which is a pasture, not self-willed land. Thoreau did not claim that in ranching is the preservation of the world.

We also tend to equate wildness with biodiversity. For example, chapter 2 of Roger DiSilvestro's *Reclaiming the Last Wild Places: A New Agenda for Biodiversity* is entitled "Biodiversity: Saving Wildness," and there are phrases like "wildness in nature, which is what we preserve when we protect biodiversity" and "protection of biodiversity, of wildness" (25). But wildness is not biodiversity. Indeed, wildness may be inversely correlated with biodiversity. In *The Desert Smells Like Rain*, Gary Nabhan describes two oases. The oasis occupied by the Papagos had twice as many bird species as the "wild" one preserved in Organ Pipe National Monument.[2] Neither oasis is wild in any meaningful sense of the term, and more remote and wilder desert oases might

very well contain even fewer species. If so, so what? Is wildness less important than biodiversity? Should we preserve the latter at the cost of the former? What criteria would we use to decide the issue?

For many conservation biologists (though not, of course, for Nabhan) the important distinction is between "in the wild" and "in captivity," with "in the wild" now meaning a managed ecosystem. But if grizzlies are controlled in wilderness with radio collars and relocation policies, then what was for Thoreau the central question—freedom—simply drops out of the discourse on preservation.

We also ignore wildness when we define wilderness in terms of human absence. In "Aldo Leopold's Metaphor," J. Baird Callicott points out that with the exception of Antarctica, there has been no land mass without human presence, and therefore the wilderness of the Wilderness Act is an "incoherent" idea (45). Other people deny the existence of wildness on the grounds that any human influence on a species or an ecosystem destroys wildness, and since human influence has been around a long time...again, no wildness. This is absurd, and one wonders what Lewis and Clark, standing on the banks of the Missouri, would have thought of such talk. "This isn't wilderness. Why, there are millions of humans out there. And it isn't wild, either. Human influence has been mucking up this place for 10,000 years."

Something is wrong here, and I believe it can be traced to the fact that most people writing and thinking about wilderness issues know only Wilderness Act-wilderness. A week in the Amazon, the high Arctic, or the northern side of the western Himalayas would suggest that what counts as wildness and wilderness is determined not by the absence of people, but by the

relationship between people and place. A place is wild when its order is created according to its own principles of organization—when it is self-willed land. Native peoples usually (though definitely not always) "fit" that order, influencing it but not controlling it, though probably not from a superior set of values but because they lack the technical means. Control increases with civilization, and modern civilization, being largely about control—an ideology of control projected onto the entire world—must control or deny wildness. This prospect is most clearly represented by the dystopian novels, beginning with Yevgeny Zamyatin's *We*.

Although autonomy is often confused with radical separation and complete independence, the autonomy of systems (and, I would argue, human freedom) is strengthened by interconnectedness, elaborate iteration, and feedback—that is, influence. Indeed, these processes create that possibility of change without which there is no freedom. Determinism and autonomy are as inseparable as the multiple aspects of a gestalt drawing.

The important point is that whatever kind of autonomy is in question—human freedom, self-willed land, self-ordering systems, self-organizing systems, autopoiesis—all are incompatible with external control. To take wildness seriously is to take the issue of control seriously, and because the disciplines of applied biology do not take the issue of control seriously, they are littered with paradoxes—"wildlife management," "wilderness management," "managing for change," "managing natural systems," "mimicking natural disturbance"—what we might call the paradoxes of autonomy. Collections of paradoxes are usually bad news for scientific paradigms, and I think the biological sciences face a major revolution.[3] …

II

In this situation, one would like to believe that radical environmentalists can offer something different from what mainstream environmental organizations and conservation biology offer. Unfortunately, this is no longer obvious.

During the past five years conservation biology has extended its influence to radical environmentalism, inverting themes that once legitimized its radical content. The transformation of part of Earth First! into Wild Earth was a movement from personal trust and confrontation to trust in abstractions and conciliation with technology. In this transition it gained new followers (and much financial support), and lost others. It certainly lost me. Whereas science, technology, and modernity were once part of the problem, now they are a large part of the solution, and I fear that the Wildlands Project may reduce Wild Earth—certainly one of our best radical environmental organizations—to the political arm of a scientific discipline.

But, again, the key issue is control and autonomy, not science. Recent issues of *Wild Earth* and *Conservation Biology* have run debates about the management of wilderness and wild systems, but they haven't penetrated to the heart of the problem. Writing in *Wild Earth*, Mike Seidman concluded his exchange by saying, "It seems that the depth of my critique of management went unnoticed." Seidman was being a gentleman, since the other side of the "debate" was an extended non sequitur.[4]

The autonomy of natural systems is the skeleton in the closet of our conservation ethic, and although it is recognized, no one is dealing honestly with the issue. The problem appears in many forms. It explains the growing discontent with our control of predators, the elk hunts in Grand Teton National Park, the slaughter of elephants for management, and the trapping and training of the last condors. It explains the increasing discontent surrounding the reintroduction of wolves to Yellowstone National Park. For a decade, environmentalists fought for an experimental population; now, faced with the biological and political control on that experimental population, many people would have preferred natural recovery—no matter how long it takes.

Biological controls are now ubiquitous. Biologists control grizzlies, they trap and radio-collar cranes, they have cute little radio backpacks for frogs, they bolt brightly colored plastic buttons to the beaks of harlequin ducks, they even put radio transmitters on minnows. And always for the same reason: more information for a better, healthier ecosystem. Information and control are indivisible, a point made in great detail by James R. Benninger in *The Control Revolution: Technological and Economic Origins of the Information Society*. It is the main point, perhaps the only point, of surveillance.

The great need, now, is to begin to imagine an alternative: Perhaps we don't need more information; maybe the emphasis on biological inventories, species recovery, surveillance, and monitoring is a further step in the wrong direction. And what could possibly be radical about all this? The Nature Conservancy has been doing it for years, and the Department of the Interior is going to do it too. Trying to be radical about, say, biological inventories is like trying to be radical about laundromats: it just isn't big enough, conceptually, to reach the source of the problem.

The radical environmentalist's obsession with roads and dams betrays a crude, industrial idea of destroying nature and blinds us to less visible modern control technologies that imply even more potent modes of destruction. But instead of a general critique of control we have deep ecologists like George Sessions and Arne Naess supporting, in principle or in practice, genetic engineering.[5]

Somehow the key issue is increasingly veiled by lesser issues. We need big wilderness, big natural habitat, not more technological information about big wilderness. Why not work to set aside vast areas where we limit all forms of human influence: no conservation strategies, no designer wilderness, no roads, no trails, no satellite surveillance, no overflights with helicopters, no radio collars, no measuring devices, no photographs, no GPS data, no databases stuffed with the location of every draba of the summit of Mt. Moran, no guidebooks, no topographical maps. Let whatever habitat we can preserve go back to its own self-order as much as possible. Let wilderness again become a blank on our maps. Why don't the radical environmental organizations push for that? I suspect a large part of

the answer is this: there is no money in it, and like all nonprofits, they need a lot of money just to survive, much less achieve a goal.

III

There are two senses of "preservation," and most preservationist efforts have followed the first: the preservation of things. Strawberry preserves epitomize this kind of preservation. The other sense is the preservation of process: leaving things be. Doug Peacock presents the second sense with great clarity, calling biology "Biofuck" and saying, "Leave the fucking bears alone."[6] This echoes Abbey's "Let being be," a quote from Heidegger, who stole it from Lao Tzu:

Do you want to improve the world?
I don't think it can be done.

The world is sacred.
It can't be improved.
If you tamper with it, you'll ruin it.
If you treat it like an object, you'll lose it.

The Master sees things as they are,
without trying to control them.
She lets them go their own way,
and resides at the center of the circle.[7]

Although most of the public believes this is the preservation ethic, leaving things alone is definitely the new minority tradition among preservationists. But consider carefully the admonition that "If you tamper with it, you'll ruin it. / If you treat it like an object, you'll lose it." This goes to the heart of what I call "the abstract wild"—wildness objectified and filtered through concepts, theories, institutions, and technology.

What if the effect of scientific experts creating environments, treating ecosystems, and managing species is (sometimes, often, always?) as bad, or worse, than the effects of unmanaged nature? In short, leave aside the question of "Should we manage nature?" and ask "How well does (can) managing

nature actually work?" Ecologists tend not to talk about this for fear of giving aid to the enemy, but the subject demands careful examination.

In an essay entitled "Down from the Pedestal: A New Role for Experts," David Ehrenfeld, for many years the editor of *Conservation Biology*, presents several examples of predictive failure in ecology and the unfortunate consequences for natural systems. Consider, for instance, the introduction of opossum shrimp into northwestern lakes with the purpose of increasing the production of kokanee salmon. "The story is complicated, involving nutrient loads, water levels, algae, various invertebrates, and lake trout, all interacting. But the bottom line is that the kokanee salmon population went way down rather than way up, and this in turn affected populations of bald eagles, various species of gulls and ducks, coyotes, minks, river otters, grizzly bears, and human visitors to Glacier National Park." Indeed, Ehrenfeld goes on to say that "biological complexity, with its myriad internal and external variables, with its open-endedness, pushes ecology and wildlife management a little closer to the economics…end of the range of expert reliability" (148–150).

Economics? Really? This from one of the deans of conservation biology? We are to entrust the management of nature to experts whose reliability is akin to economists? This removes a bit of the glitter from the remaking nature agenda, doesn't it? I wouldn't let them manage my front yard.

Ecologists are compared with economists because of their problems with prediction. Prediction (some think) is the essence of science: No prediction, no science; lousy prediction, lousy science. Unless (according to this view) the biological sciences can generate accurate, testable, quantitative predictions, they are well on their way to joining the dismal science of, say, astrology. Well, if your idea of good science requires quantitative prediction, particularly long-term quantitative predictions, then all the sciences are looking a bit dismal, ecology especially so.[8]

The historian of ecology Donald Worster, in his essay "The Ecology of Order and Chaos," notes that "Despite the obvious complexity of their subject matter, ecologists have been among the slowest to join the cross-disciplinary science of chaos" (168). This is not quite fair. Robert May, a mathematical ecologist at Oxford, is one of the pioneers of chaos theory, and his book *Stability and Complexity in Model Ecosystems* remains a classic. But Worster's point is still telling, and one suspects that the ecologists' lack of openness on the subject probably has something to do with the unsettling consequences for the practical application of their discipline—and hence their paychecks. They keep hanging on to the hope of better computer models and more information, but as Brecht said in another context, "If you're still smiling, you don't understand the news."

Most of the rapidly growing literature on chaos and complexity is either journalistic or extremely technical.[9] Of greater importance for radical thinking about the environment are the philosophical implications of chaos and complexity and their impact on those biological disciplines we depend on to guide environmental policy. An excellent examination of the former is in Stephen H. Kellert's *In the Wake of Chaos: Unpredictable Order in Dynamical Systems*, which suggests, as Ehrenfeld's examples suggest, that the problems facing the practical applications of ecology and biology are more formidable than the disciplines are willing to admit.[10] For the impact of chaos theory on ecological theory, required reading is Stuart L. Pimm, "Nonlinear Dynamics, Strange Attractors, and Chaos," in *The Balance of Nature? Ecological Issues in the Conservation of Species and Communities*, a sobering book for anyone who believes the issues are either understood or that we have sufficient empirical data to make intelligent decisions about long-term ecosystem management.

Many biologists and ecologists believe the autonomy of nature is a naive ideal, and that we must now attempt to control the Earth. Ironically, this view is widespread despite recent work in nonlinear dynamics that demonstrates nature's talent for self-organization, indeed its talent for organizing itself to critical states that collapse unpredictably with avalanches

of the very events that so disturb us—earthquakes, wildfires, extinctions, epidemics. Indeed, many natural systems seem attracted to disequilibrium (or, I would say, wildness).[11] Some of the largest, most catastrophic events—like the Yellowstone fires in 1988—are precisely the unpredictable events that are the key to forming the vegetation architecture basic to the order of an ecosystem. And yet these are the events we most wish to manage.

What emerges from the recent work on chaos and complexity is the final dismemberment of the metaphor of the world as machine, and the emergence of a new metaphor—a view of a world that is characterized by vitality and autonomy, one which is close to Thoreau's sense of wildness, a view that, of course, goes well beyond him, but one he would no doubt find glorious. Instead of a vast machine, much of nature turns out to be a collection of dynamic systems, rather like the mean eddy lines in Lava Falls, where the description of the turbulence is a nonlinear differential equation containing complex functions with "free" variables that prevent a (closed form) solution. Such natural systems are unstable; they never settle into equilibrium. (Kayakers know this in their bodies.) They are aperiodic; like the weather, they never repeat themselves but forever generate new changes, one of the most important of which is evolution. Life evolves at the edge of chaos, the area of maximum vitality and change.

Dynamic systems marked by chaos and complexity do have an order, and the order can be described mathematically. They are deterministic, and we can (usually) calculate probabilities and make qualitative predictions—how the system will behave *in general*. But with chaos and complexity, scientific knowledge is again limited in ways similar to the limits of incompleteness, uncertainty, and relativity.

That does not end science; all that drops out, really, is long-term quantitative prediction, and that affects most science primarily in one way: control. But that's the nut of the problem. As John Ralston Saul has said, "The essence of rational leadership is control justified by expertise."[12] Without control, there is no expertise.

The biological sciences lose their leadership of the conservation ethic. The "preservation as management" tradition that began with Leopold is finished because there is little reason to trust the experts to make intelligent long-range decisions about nature.

What happens to the rationality of managing species and ecosystems without accurate prediction and control? If the microsystems of an ecosystem—from vascular flows to genetic drift to turbulence—plus all of the natural disturbances to ecosystems—weather, fire (the front of a wildfire is a fractal), wind, earthquakes, avalanches—if all these exhibit chaotic and/or complex behavior, and some organize themselves at a global level to critical states resulting in catastrophic events, and further, if such behavior does not allow long-term quantitative predictions, then isn't ecosystems management a bit of a sham? The management of grizzlies and wolves at best a travesty? If an ecosystem can't be known or controlled with scientific data, then why don't we simply can all the talk of ecosystem health and integrity and admit, honestly, that it's just public policy, not science?

Much of the best intellectual labor of this century has led to the admission of various limits in science and mathematics—of axiom systems, observation, objectivity, measurement. This should have a humbling effect on all of us, and the limits of our knowledge should define the limits of our practice. The biological sciences should draw the line of their operations at wilderness—core wilderness, Wilderness Act-wilderness, any wilderness—for the same reasons atomic scientists should accept limits on messing with the atom, and geneticists should accept limits on messing with the structure of DNA: *We are not that wise, nor can we be.*

The issue is not the legitimacy of science in general, nor the legitimacy of a particular scientific discipline, but the appropriate limits to be placed on any scientific discipline in light of limited knowledge. To ignore these limits is to refuse humility and undermine the foundations of the preservation movement. Accepting these limits and imagining a new conservation ethic based on wildness and humble,

careful, non-intrusive practice would unite Thoreau's insight that "in Wildness is the preservation of the World" and the traditions of ancient wisdom with the intuitions of our most radical wilderness lovers, ecofeminists, and cutting-edge mathematicians and physicists. This is as consoling as it is charming.

All knowledge has its shadow. The advance of biological knowledge into what we call the natural world simultaneously advances the processes of normalization and control, forces that erode the wildness that arises from nature's own order, the very order that, presumably, is the point of preservation. At the core of the present conjunction of preservation and biological science—the heritage of Leopold—lies a contradiction. We face a choice, a choice that is fundamentally moral. To ignore it is mere cowardice. Shall we remake nature according to biological theory? Shall we accept the wild?

Wildness is out there. The most vital beings and systems hang out at the edge of wildness. The next time you howl in delight like a wolf, howl for unstable aperiodic behavior in deterministic nonlinear dynamical systems. Lao Tzu and Thoreau and Abbey will be pleased.

NOTES

1. Richard B. Primack committed this common error in *Essentials of Conservation Biology*, 13.

2. Nabhan, *The Desert Smells Like Rain*, chapter 7. See also Peter Sauer's introduction to *Finding Home*.

3. See Paul Hoyningen-Huene, *Reconstructing Scientific Revolutions*, on paradox in scientific theories.

4. Mike Seidman's original letter appeared in *Wild Earth* 2 (fall 1992): 9–10. Responses to his letter by Reed F. Noss, W. S. Alverson, and D. M. Waller appeared in *Wild Earth* 2 (winter 1992/93): 8–10. Seidman's reply is in *Wild Earth* 3 (spring 1993): 7–8.

5. Salleh, "Class, Race, and Gender," 233.

6. Quoted in Rick Bass, "Grizzlies: Are They Out There?"

7. Lao Tzu, *Tao Te Ching*, chapter 29, trans. Stephen Mitchell. Mitchell deserves the Nobel Peace Prize for his use of the feminine pronoun.

8. For chaos and predictive failure in classical economics, see Richard H. Day, "The Emergence of Chaos from Classical Economic Growth."

9. The classic, of course, is James Gleick's *Chaos: Making A New Science*. See also M. Mitchell Waldrop, *Complexity: The Emerging Science at the Edge of Order and Chaos*, and Roger Lewin, *Complexity: Life at the Edge of Chaos*. The most accessible introduction to the technical issues is John Biggs and F. David Peat, *Turbulent Mirror*. For discussions of chaos in fields ranging from ecology to quantum physics, see Nina Hall (ed.), *Exploring Chaos: A Guide to the New Science of Disorder*.

10. For a general introduction to the problem of prediction see John L. Casti, *Searching For Certainty*.

11. See Per Bak and Kan Chen, "Self-Organized Criticality," and Per Bak, "Self-Organized Criticality and Gaia."

12. Saul, *Voltaire's Bastards*, 10.

REFERENCES

Bak, Per, and Kan Chen. "Self-Organized Criticality." *Scientific American*, January 1991.

Bass, Rick. "Grizzlies: Are They Out There?" *Audubon* 95 (Sept.–Oct. 1993).

Biggs, John, and F. David Peat. *Turbulent Mirror*. New York: Harper & Row, 1989.

Casti, John L. *Searching For Certainty*. New York: William Morrow and Company, 1990.

Day, Richard H. "The Emergence of Chaos from Classical Economic Growth." *Quarterly Journal of Economics*, May 1983.

Gleick, James. *Chaos: Making a New Science*. New York: Penguin Books, 1987.

Hall, Nina, ed. *Exploring Chaos: A Guide to the New Science of Disorder*. New York: W. W. Norton & Company, 1991.

Lao Tzu. *Tao Te Ching*. Translated by Stephen Mitchell. New York: Harper-Collins, 1988.

Lewin, Roger. *Complexity: Life at the Edge of Chaos*. New York: Macmillan, 1992.

Saul, John Ralston. *Voltaire's Bastards: The Dictatorship of Reason in the West*. New York: Random House, 1992.

Waldrop, M. Mitchell. *Complexity: The Emerging Science at the Edge of Order and Chaos*. New York: Simon and Schuster, 1992.

WILLIAM CRONON

The Trouble with Wilderness; or, Getting Back to the Wrong Nature

The time has come to rethink wilderness.

This will seem a heretical claim to many environmentalists, since the idea of wilderness has for decades been a fundamental tenet—indeed, a passion—of the environmental movement, especially in the United States. For many Americans wilderness stands as the last remaining place where civilization, that all too human disease, has not fully infected the earth. It is an island in the polluted sea of urban-industrial modernity, the one place we can turn for escape from our own too-muchness. Seen in this way, wilderness presents itself as the best antidote to our human selves, a refuge we must somehow recover if we hope to save the planet. As Henry David Thoreau once famously declared, "In Wildness is the preservation of the World."[1]

But is it? The more one knows of its peculiar history, the more one realizes that wilderness is not quite what it seems. Far from being the one place on earth that stands apart from humanity, it is quite profoundly a human creation—indeed, the creation of very particular human cultures at very particular moments in human history. It is not a pristine sanctuary where the last remnant of an untouched, endangered, but still transcendent nature can for at least a little while longer be encountered without the contaminating taint of civilization. Instead, it is a product of that civilization, and could hardly be contaminated by the very stuff of which it is made. Wilderness hides its unnaturalness behind a mask that is all the more beguiling because it seems so natural. As we gaze into the mirror it holds up for us, we too easily imagine that what we behold is Nature when in fact we see the reflection of our own unexamined longings and desires. For this reason, we mistake ourselves when we suppose that wilderness can be the solution to our culture's problematic relationships with the nonhuman world, for wilderness is itself no small part of the problem.

To assert the unnaturalness of so natural a place will no doubt seem absurd or even perverse to many readers, so let me hasten to add that the nonhuman world we encounter in wilderness is far from being merely our own invention. I celebrate with others who love wilderness the beauty and power of the things it contains. Each of us who has spent time there can conjure images and sensations that seem all the more hauntingly real for having engraved themselves so indelibly on our memories. Such memories may be uniquely our own, but they are also familiar enough to be instantly recognizable to others. Remember this? The torrents of mist shoot out from the base of a great waterfall in the depths of a Sierra canyon, the tiny droplets cooling your face as you listen to the roar of the water and gaze up toward the sky through a rainbow that hovers just out of reach. Remember this too: looking out across a desert canyon in the evening air, the only sound a lone raven calling in the distance, the rock walls dropping away into a chasm so deep that its bottom all but vanishes as you squint into the amber light of the setting sun. And this: the moment beside the trail as you sit on a sandstone ledge, your boots damp with the morning dew while you take in the rich smell of the pines, and the small red fox—or maybe for you it was a raccoon or a coyote or a deer—that suddenly ambles across your path, stopping

for a long moment to gaze in your direction with cautious indifference before continuing on its way. Remember the feelings of such moments, and you will know as well as I do that you were in the presence of something irreducibly nonhuman, something profoundly Other than yourself. Wilderness is made of that too.

And yet: what brought each of us to the places where such memories became possible is entirely a cultural invention. Go back 250 years in American and European history, and you do not find nearly so many people wandering around remote corners of the planet looking for what today we would call "the wilderness experience." As late as the eighteenth century, the most common usage of the word "wilderness" in the English language referred to landscapes that generally carried adjectives far different from the ones they attract today. To be a wilderness then was to be "deserted," "savage," "desolate," "barren"—in short, a "waste," the word's nearest synonym. Its connotations were anything but positive, and the emotion one was most likely to feel in its presence was "bewilderment"—or terror.[2]

Many of the word's strongest associations then were biblical, for it is used over and over again in the King James Version to refer to places on the margins of civilization where it is all too easy to lose oneself in moral confusion and despair. The wilderness was where Moses had wandered with his people for forty years, and where they had nearly abandoned their God to worship a golden idol.[3] "For Pharoah will say of the Children of Israel," we read in Exodus, "They are entangled in the land, the wilderness hath shut them in."[4] The wilderness was where Christ had struggled with the devil and endured his temptations: "And immediately the Spirit driveth him into the wilderness. And he was there in the wilderness for forty days tempted of Satan; and was with the wild beasts; and the angels ministered unto him."[5] The "delicious Paradise" of John Milton's Eden was surrounded by "a steep wilderness, whose hairy sides / Access denied" to all who sought entry.[6] When Adam and Eve were driven from that garden, the world they entered was a wilderness that only their labor and pain could redeem. Wilderness, in short, was a place to which one came only against one's will, and always in fear and trembling. Whatever value it might have arose solely from the possibility that it might be "reclaimed" and turned toward human ends—planted as a garden, say, or a city upon a hill.[7] In its raw state, it had little or nothing to offer civilized men and women.

But by the end of the nineteenth century, all this had changed. The wastelands that had once seemed worthless had for some people come to seem almost beyond price. That Thoreau in 1862 could declare wildness to be the preservation of the world suggests the sea change that was going on. Wilderness had once been the antithesis of all that was orderly and good—it had been the darkness, one might say, on the far side of the garden wall—and yet now it was frequently likened to Eden itself. When John Muir arrived in the Sierra Nevada in 1869, he would declare, "No description of Heaven that I have ever heard or read of seems half so fine."[8] He was hardly alone in expressing such emotions. One by one, various corners of the American map came to be designated as sites whose wild beauty was so spectacular that a growing number of citizens had to visit and see them for themselves. Niagara Falls was the first to undergo this transformation, but it was soon followed by the Catskills, the Adirondacks, Yosemite, Yellowstone, and others. Yosemite was deeded by the U.S. government to the state of California in 1864 as the nation's first wildland park, and Yellowstone became the first true national park in 1872.[9]

By the first decade of the twentieth century, in the single most famous episode in American conservation history, a national debate had exploded over whether the city of San Francisco should be permitted to augment its water supply by damming the Tuolumne River in Hetch Hetchy valley, well within the boundaries of Yosemite National Park. The dam was eventually built, but what today seems no less significant is that so many people fought to prevent its completion. Even as the fight was being lost, Hetch Hetchy became the battle cry of an emerging movement to preserve wilderness. Fifty years earlier, such opposition would have been unthinkable. Few would have questioned the merits of "reclaiming" a wasteland like this in order to put it to human use. Now the defenders of Hetch Hetchy attracted widespread national attention by portraying such an act not as improvement or progress but as desecration and vandalism. Lest one doubt that the old biblical metaphors had been turned completely on their heads, listen to John Muir attack the dam's defenders. "Their arguments," he wrote, "are curiously like those of the devil, devised for the destruction of the first garden—so much of the very best Eden fruit going to waste; so much of the best Tuolumne water and Tuolumne scenery going to waste."[10] For Muir and the growing number of Americans who shared his views, Satan's home had become God's own temple.

The sources of this rather astonishing transformation were many, but for the purposes of this essay they can be gathered under two broad headings: the sublime and the frontier. Of the two, the sublime is the older and more pervasive cultural construct, being one of the most important expressions of that broad transatlantic movement we today label as romanticism; the frontier is more peculiarly American, though it too had its European antecedents and parallels. The two converged to remake wilderness in their own image, freighting it with moral values and cultural symbols that it carries to this day. Indeed, it is not too much to say that the modern environmental movement is itself a grandchild of romanticism and post-frontier ideology, which is why it is no accident that so much environmentalist discourse takes its bearings from the wilderness these intellectual movements helped create. Although wilderness may today seem to be just one environmental concern among many, it in fact serves as the foundation for a long list of other such concerns that on their face seem quite remote from it. That is why its influence is so pervasive and, potentially, so insidious....

The removal of Indians to create an "uninhabited wilderness"—uninhabited as never before in the human history of the place—reminds us just how invented, just how constructed, the American wilderness really is. To return to my opening argument: there is nothing natural about the concept of wilderness. It is entirely a creation of the culture that holds it dear, a product of the very history it seeks to deny. Indeed, one of the most striking proofs of the cultural invention of wilderness is its thoroughgoing erasure of the history from which it sprang. In virtually all of its manifestations, wilderness represents a flight from history. Seen as the original garden, it is a place outside of time, from which human beings had to be ejected before the fallen world of history could properly begin. Seen as the frontier, it is a savage world at the dawn of civilization, whose transformation represents the very beginning of the national historical epic. Seen as the bold landscape of frontier heroism, it is the place of youth and childhood, into which men escape by abandoning their pasts and entering a world of freedom where the constraints of civilization fade into memory. Seen as the sacred sublime, it is the home of a God who transcends history by standing as the One who remains untouched and unchanged by time's arrow. No matter what the angle from which we regard it, wilderness offers us the illusion that we can escape the cares and troubles of the world in which our past has ensnared us.[11]

This escape from history is one reason why the language we use to talk about wilderness is often permeated with spiritual and religious values that reflect human ideals far more than the material world of physical nature. Wilderness fulfills the old romantic project of secularizing Judeo-Christian values so as to make a new cathedral not in some petty human building but in God's own creation, Nature itself. Many environmentalists who reject traditional notions of the Godhead and who regard themselves as agnostics or even atheists nonetheless express feelings tantamount to religious awe when in the presence of wilderness—a fact that testifies to the success of the romantic project. Those who have no difficulty seeing God as the expression of our human dreams and desires nonetheless have trouble recognizing that in a secular age Nature can offer precisely the same sort of mirror.

Thus it is that wilderness serves as the unexamined foundation on which so many of the quasi-religious values of modern environmentalism rest. The critique of modernity that is one of environmentalism's most important contributions to the moral and political discourse of our time more often than not appeals, explicitly or implicitly, to wilderness as the standard against which to measure the failings of our human world. Wilderness is the natural, unfallen antithesis of an unnatural civilization that has lost its soul. It is a place of freedom in which we can recover the true selves we have lost to the corrupting influences of our artificial lives. Most of all, it is the ultimate landscape of authenticity. Combining the sacred grandeur of the sublime with the primitive simplicity of the frontier, it is the place where we can see the world as it really is, and so know ourselves as we really are—or ought to be.

But the trouble with wilderness is that it quietly expresses and reproduces the very values its devotees seek to reject. The flight from history that is very nearly the core of wilderness represents the false hope of an escape from responsibility, the illusion that we can somehow wipe clean the slate of our past and return to the tabula rasa that supposedly existed before we began to leave our marks on the world. The dream of an unworked natural landscape is very much the fantasy of people who have never themselves had to work the land to make a living—urban folk for whom food comes from a supermarket or a restaurant instead of a field, and for whom the wooden houses in which they live and work apparently have no meaningful connection to the forests in which trees grow and die. Only people whose relation to the land was already alienated could hold up wilderness as a model for human life in nature, for the romantic ideology of wilderness

leaves precisely nowhere for human beings actually to make their living from the land.

This, then, is the central paradox: wilderness embodies a dualistic vision in which the human is entirely outside the natural. If we allow ourselves to believe that nature, to be true, must also be wild, then our very presence in nature represents its fall. The place where we are is the place where nature is not. If this is so—if by definition wilderness leaves no place for human beings, save perhaps as contemplative sojourners enjoying their leisurely reverie in God's natural cathedral—then also by definition it can offer no solution to the environmental and other problems that confront us. To the extent that we celebrate wilderness as the measure with which we judge civilization, we reproduce the dualism that sets humanity and nature at opposite poles. We thereby leave ourselves little hope of discovering what an ethical, sustainable, *honorable* human place in nature might actually look like.

Worse: to the extent that we live in an urban-industrial civilization but at the same time pretend to ourselves that our *real* home is in the wilderness, to just that extent we give ourselves permission to evade responsibility for the lives we actually lead. We inhabit civilization while holding some part of ourselves—what we imagine to be the most precious part—aloof from its entanglements. We work our nine-to-five jobs in its institutions, we eat its food, we drive its cars (not least to reach the wilderness), we benefit from the intricate and all too invisible networks with which it shelters us, all the while pretending that these things are not an essential part of who we are. By imagining that our true home is in the wilderness, we forgive ourselves the homes we actually inhabit. In its flight from history, in its siren song of escape, in its reproduction of the dangerous dualism that sets human beings outside of nature—in all of these ways, wilderness poses a serious threat to responsible environmentalism at the end of the twentieth century...

Perhaps partly because our own conflicts over such places and organisms have become so messy, the convergence of wilderness values with concerns about biological diversity and endangered species has helped produce a deep fascination for remote ecosystems, where it is easier to imagine that nature might somehow be "left alone" to flourish by its own pristine devices. The classic example is the tropical rain forest, which since the 1970s has become the most powerful modern icon of unfallen, sacred land—a veritable Garden of Eden—for many Americans and Europeans. And yet protecting the rain forest in the eyes of First World environmentalists all too often means protecting it from the people who live there. Those who seek to preserve such "wilderness" from the activities of native peoples run the risk of reproducing the same tragedy—being forceably removed from an ancient home—that befell American Indians. Third World countries face massive environmental problems and deep social conflicts, but these are not likely to be solved by a cultural myth that encourages us to "preserve" peopleless landscapes that have not existed in such places for millennia. At its worst, as environmentalists are beginning to realize, exporting American notions of wilderness in this way can become an unthinking and self-defeating form of cultural imperialism.[12]

Perhaps the most suggestive example of the way that wilderness thinking can underpin other environmental concerns has emerged in the recent debate about "global change." In 1989 the journalist Bill McKibben published a book entitled *The End of Nature*, in which he argued that the prospect of global climate change as a result of unintentional human manipulation of the atmosphere means that nature as we once knew it no longer exists.[13] Whereas earlier generations inhabited a natural world that remained more or less unaffected by their actions, our own generation is uniquely different. We and our children will henceforth live in a biosphere completely altered by our own activity, a planet in which the human and the natural can no longer be distinguished, because the one has overwhelmed the other. In McKibben's view, nature has

died, and we are responsible for killing it. "The planet," he declares, "is utterly different now."[14]

But such a perspective is possible only if we accept the wilderness premise that nature, to be natural, must also be pristine—remote from humanity and untouched by our common past. In fact, everything we know about environmental history suggests that people have been manipulating the natural world on various scales for as long as we have a record of their passing. Moreover, we have unassailable evidence that many of the environmental changes we now face also occurred quite apart from human intervention at one time or another in the earth's past.[15] The point is not that our current problems are trivial, or that our devastating effects on the earth's ecosystems should be accepted as inevitable or "natural." It is rather that we seem unlikely to make much progress in solving these problems if we hold up to ourselves as the mirror of nature a wilderness we ourselves cannot inhabit.

To do so is merely to take to a logical extreme the paradox that was built into wilderness from the beginning: if nature dies because we enter it, then the only way to save nature is to kill ourselves. The absurdity of this proposition flows from the underlying dualism it expresses. Not only does it ascribe greater power to humanity than we in fact possess—physical and biological nature will surely survive in some form or another long after we ourselves have gone the way of all flesh—but in the end it offers us little more than a self-defeating counsel of despair. The tautology gives us no way out: if wild nature is the only thing worth saving, and if our mere presence destroys it, then the sole solution to our own unnaturalness, the only way to protect sacred wilderness from profane humanity, would seem to be suicide. It is not a proposition that seems likely to produce very positive or practical results....

However much one may be attracted to such a vision, it entails problematic consequences. For one, it makes wilderness the locus for an epic struggle between malign civilization and benign nature, compared with which all other social, political, and moral concerns seem trivial. Foreman writes, "The preservation of wildness and native diversity is *the* most important issue. Issues directly affecting only humans pale in comparison."[16] Presumably so do any environmental problems whose victims are mainly people, for such problems usually surface in land-scapes that have already "fallen" and are no longer wild. This would seem to exclude from the radical environmentalist agenda problems of occupational health and safety in industrial settings, problems of toxic waste exposure on "unnatural" urban and agricultural sites, problems of poor children poisoned by lead exposure in the inner city, problems of famine and poverty and human suffering in the "overpopulated" places of the earth—problems, in short, of environmental justice. If we set too high a stock on wilderness, too many other corners of the earth become less than natural and too many other people become less than human, thereby giving us permission not to care much about their suffering or their fate.

It is no accident that these supposedly inconse-quential environmental problems affect mainly poor people, for the long affiliation between wilderness and wealth means that the only poor people who count when wilderness is *the* issue are hunter-gatherers, who presumably do not consider them-selves to be poor in the first place. The dualism at the heart of wilderness encourages its advocates to conceive of its protection as a crude conflict between the "human" and the "nonhuman"—or, more often, between those who value the nonhuman and those who do not. This in turn tempts one to ignore crucial differences *among* humans and the complex cultural and historical reasons why different peoples may feel very differently about the meaning of wilderness.

Why, for instance, is the "wilderness experi-ence" so often conceived as a form of recreation best enjoyed by those whose class privileges give them the time and resources to leave their jobs behind and "get away from it all"? Why does the protection of wilderness so often seem to pit urban recreationists against rural people who actually earn their living from the land (excepting those who sell goods and services to the tourists themselves)? Why in the debates about pristine natural areas are "primitive" peoples idealized, even sentimental-ized, until the moment they do something unprimi-tive, modern, and unnatural, and thereby fall from environmental grace? What are the consequences of a wilderness ideology that devalues productive labor and the very concrete knowledge that comes from working the land with one's own hands?[17] All of these questions imply conflicts among different groups of people, conflicts that are obscured behind the deceptive clarity of "human" vs. "nonhuman." If in answering these knotty questions we resort to so simplistic an opposition, we are almost certain to ignore the very subtleties and complexities we need to understand.

But the most troubling cultural baggage that accompanies the celebration of wilderness has less to do with remote rain forests and peoples than with the ways we think about ourselves—we American environmentalists who quite rightly worry about the future of the earth and the threats we pose to the natural world. Idealizing a distant wilderness too often means not idealizing the environment in which we actually live, the landscape that for better or worse we call home. Most of our most serious environmental problems start right here, at home, and if we are to solve those problems, we need an environmental ethic that will tell us as much about *using* nature as about *not* using it. The wilderness dualism tends to cast any use as *ab*-use, and thereby denies us a middle ground in which responsible use and non-use might attain some kind of balanced, sustainable relationship. My own belief is that only by exploring this middle ground will we learn ways of imagining a better world for all of us: humans and nonhumans, rich people and poor, women and men, First Worlders and Third Worlders, white folks and people of color, consumers and producers—a world better for humanity in all of its diversity and for all the rest of nature too. The middle ground is where we actually live. It is where we—all of us, in our different places and ways—make our homes. . . .

Wilderness gets us into trouble only if we imagine that this experience of wonder and otherness is limited to the remote corners of the planet, or that it somehow depends on pristine landscapes we ourselves do not inhabit. Nothing could be more misleading. The tree in the garden is in reality no less other, no less worthy of our wonder and respect, than the tree in an ancient forest that has never known an ax or a saw—even though the tree in the forest reflects a more intricate web of ecological relationships. The tree in the garden could easily have sprung from the same seed as the tree in the forest, and we can claim only its location and perhaps its form as our own. Both trees stand apart from us; both share our common world. The special power of the tree in the wilderness is to remind us of this fact. It can teach us to recognize the wildness we did not see in the tree we planted in our own backyard. By seeing the otherness in that which is most unfamiliar, we can learn to see it too in that which at first seemed merely ordinary. If wilderness can do this—if it can help us perceive and respect a nature we had forgotten to recognize as natural—then it will become part of the solution to our environmental dilemmas rather than part of the problem.

This will only happen, however, if we abandon the dualism that sees the tree in the garden as artificial—completely fallen and unnatural—and the tree in the wilderness as natural—completely pristine and wild. Both trees in some ultimate sense are wild; both in a practical sense now depend on our management and care. We are responsible for both, even though we can claim credit for neither. Our challenge is to stop thinking of such things according to a set of bipolar moral scales in which the human and the nonhuman, the unnatural and the natural, the fallen and the unfallen, serve as our conceptual map for understanding and valuing the world. Instead, we need to embrace the full continuum of a natural landscape that is also cultural, in which the city, the suburb, the pastoral, and the wild each has its proper place, which we permit ourselves to celebrate without needlessly denigrating the others. We need to honor the Other within and the Other next door as much as we do the exotic Other that lives far away—a lesson that applies as much to people as it does to (other) natural things. In particular, we need to discover a common middle ground in which all of these things, from the city to the wilderness, can somehow be encompassed in the word "home." Home, after all, is the place where finally we make our living. It is the place for which we take responsibility, the place we try to sustain so we can pass on what is best in it (and in ourselves) to our children.[18]

The task of making a home in nature is what Wendell Berry has called "the forever unfinished lifework of our species." "The only thing we have to preserve nature with," he writes, "is culture; the only thing we have to preserve wildness with is domesticity."[19] Calling a place home inevitably means that we will *use* the nature we find in it, for there can be no escape from manipulating and working and even killing some parts of nature to make our home. But if we acknowledge the autonomy and otherness of the things and creatures around us—an autonomy our culture has taught us to label with the word "wild"—then we will at least think carefully about the uses to which we put them, and even ask if we should use them at all. Just so can we still join Thoreau in declaring that "in Wildness is the preservation of the World," for *wild*ness (as opposed to wilderness) can be found anywhere: in the seemingly tame fields and woodlots of Massachusetts, in the cracks of a Manhattan sidewalk, even in the cells of our own bodies. As Gary Snyder has wisely said, "A person with a clear heart and open mind can experience the wilderness anywhere on earth. It is a quality of one's own consciousness. The planet is a wild place and always will be."[20] To think ourselves capable of causing "the end of nature" is an act of great hubris, for it means forgetting the wildness that dwells everywhere within and around us.

Learning to honor the wild—learning to remember and acknowledge the autonomy of the other—means striving for critical self-consciousness in all of our actions. It means that deep reflection and respect must accompany each act of use, and means too that we must always consider the possibility of non-use. It means looking at the part of nature we intend to turn toward our own ends and asking whether we can use it again and again and again—sustainably—without its being diminished in the process. It means never imagining that we can flee into a mythical wilderness to escape history and the obligation to take responsibility for our own actions that history inescapably entails. Most of all, it means practicing remembrance and gratitude, for thanksgiving is the simplest and most basic of ways for us to recollect the nature, the culture, and the history that have come together to make the world as we know it. If wildness can stop being (just) out there and start being (also) in here, if it can start being as humane as it is natural, then perhaps we can get on with the unending task of struggling to live rightly in the world—not just in the garden, not just in the wilderness, but in the home that encompasses them both.

NOTES

1. Henry David Thoreau, "Walking," *The Works of Thoreau*, ed. Henry S. Canby (Boston: Houghton Mifflin, 1937), 672.

2. *Oxford English Dictionary*, s.v. "wilderness"; see also Roderick Nash, *Wilderness and the American Mind*, 3rd ed. (New Haven: Yale Univ. Press, 1982), 1–22; and Max Oelschlaeger, *The Idea of Wilderness: From Prehistory to the Age of Ecology* (New Haven: Yale Univ. Press, 1991).

3. Exodus 32:1–35, KJV.

4. Exodus 14:3, KJV.

5. Mark 1:12–13, KJV; see also Matthew 4:1–11; Luke 4:1–13.

6. John Milton, "Paradise Lost," *John Milton: Complete Poems and Major Prose*, ed. Merritt Y. Hughes (New York: Odyssey Press, 1957), 280–81, lines 131–42.

7. I have discussed this theme at length in "Landscapes of Abundance and Scarcity," in Clyde Milner et al., eds., *Oxford History of the American West* (New York: Oxford Univ. Press, 1994), 603–37. The classic work on the Puritan "city on a hill" in colonial New England is Perry Miller, *Errand into the Wilderness* (Cambridge: Harvard Univ. Press, 1956).

8. John Muir, *My First Summer in the Sierra* (1911), reprinted in *John Muir: The Eight Wilderness Discovery Books* (London: Diadem; Seattle: Mountaineers, 1992), 211.

9. Alfred Runte, *National Parks: The American Experience*, 2nd ed. (Lincoln: Univ. of Nebraska Press, 1987).

10. John Muir, *The Yosemite* (1912), reprinted in *John Muir: Eight Wilderness Discovery Books*, 715.

11. Wilderness also lies at the foundation of the Clementsian ecological concept of the climax.

12. This argument has been powerfully made by Ramachandra Guha, "Radical American Environmentalism: A Third World Critique," *Environmental Ethics* 11 (1989): 71–83.

13. Bill McKibben, *The End of Nature* (New York: Random House, 1989).

14. Ibid., 49.

15. Even comparable extinction rates have occurred before, though we surely would not want to emulate the Cretaceous-Tertiary boundary extinctions as a model for responsible manipulation of the biosphere!

16. David Foreman, *Confessions of an Eco-Warrior*, New York: Harmony Books, 1991, 27.

17. It is not much of an exaggeration to say that the wilderness experience is essentially consumerist in its impulses.

18. Analogous arguments can be found in John Brinckerhoff Jackson, "Beyond Wilderness," *A Sense of Place, a Sense of Time* (New Haven: Yale Univ. Press, 1994), 71–91, and in the wonderful collection of essays by Michael Pollan, *Second Nature: A Gardener's Education* (New York: Atlantic Monthly Press, 1991).

19. Wendell Berry, *Home Economics* (San Francisco: North Point, 1987), 138, 143.

20. Gary Snyder, quoted in *New York Times*, "Week in Review," Sept. 18, 1994, 6.

Ramachandra Guha

Radical American Environmentalism and Wilderness Preservation: A Third World Critique

INTRODUCTION

The respected radical journalist Kirkpatrick Sale recently celebrated "the passion of a new and growing movement that has become disenchanted with the environmental establishment and has in recent years mounted a serious and sweeping attack on it—style, substance, systems, sensibilities and all."[1] The vision of those whom Sale calls the "New Ecologists"—and what I refer to in this article as deep ecology—is a compelling one. Decrying the narrowly economic goals of mainstream environmentalism, this new movement aims at nothing less than a philosophical and cultural revolution in human attitudes toward nature. In contrast to the conventional lobbying efforts of environmental professionals based in Washington, it proposes a militant defence of "Mother Earth," an unflinching opposition to human attacks on undisturbed wilderness. With their goals ranging from the spiritual to the political, the adherents of deep ecology span a wide spectrum of the American environmental movement. As Sale correctly notes, this emerging strand has in a matter of a few years made its presence felt in a number of fields: from academic philosophy (as in the journal *Environmental Ethics*) to popular environmentalism (e.g., the group Earth First!).

In this article I develop a critique of deep ecology from the perspective of a sympathetic outsider. I critique deep ecology not as a general (or even a foot soldier) in the continuing struggle between the ghosts of Gifford Pinchot and John Muir over control of the U.S. environmental movement, but as an outsider to these battles. I speak admittedly as a partisan, but of the environmental movement in India, a country with an ecological diversity comparable to [that of] the United States, but with a radically dissimilar cultural and social history.

My treatment of deep ecology is primarily historical and sociological, rather than philosophical, in nature. Specifically, I examine the cultural rootedness of a philosophy that likes to present itself in universalistic terms. I make two main arguments: first, that deep ecology is uniquely American, and despite superficial similarities in rhetorical style, the social and political goals of radical environmentalism in other cultural contexts (e.g., West Germany and India) are quite different; second, that the social consequences of putting deep ecology into practice on a worldwide basis (what its practitioners are aiming for) are very grave indeed.

THE TENETS OF DEEP ECOLOGY

While I am aware that the term *deep ecology* was coined by the Norwegian philosopher Arne Naess, this article refers specifically to the American variant. Adherents of the deep ecological perspective in this country, while arguing intensely among themselves over its political and philosophical implications, share some fundamental premises about human–nature interactions. As I see it, the defining characteristics of deep ecology are fourfold.

First, deep ecology argues that the environmental movement must shift from an "anthropocentric" to a "biocentric" perspective. In many respects, an acceptance of the primacy of this distinction constitutes the litmus test of deep ecology. A considerable effort is expended by deep ecologists in showing that the dominant motif in Western philosophy has been anthropocentric—the belief that man and his works are the center of the universe—and conversely, in identifying those lonely thinkers (Leopold, Thoreau, Muir, Aldous Huxley, Santayana, etc.) who, in assigning man a more humble place in the natural order, anticipated deep ecological thinking. In the political realm, meanwhile, establishment environmentalism (shallow ecology) is chided for casting its arguments in human-centered terms. Preserving nature, the deep ecologists say, has an intrinsic worth quite apart from any benefits preservation may convey to future human generations. The anthropocentric–biocentric distinction is accepted as axiomatic by deep ecologists, it structures their discourse, and much of the present discussion remains mired within it.

The second characteristic of deep ecology is its focus on the preservation of unspoilt wilderness and the restoration of degraded areas to a more pristine condition—to the relative (and sometimes absolute) neglect of other issues on the environmental agenda. I later identify the cultural roots and portentous consequences of this obsession with wilderness. For the moment, let me indicate three distinct sources from which it springs. Historically, it represents a playing out of the preservationist (read *radical*) and utilitarian (read *reformist*) dichotomy that has plagued American environmentalism since the turn of the century. Morally, it is an imperative that follows from the biocentric perspective; other species of plants and animals, and nature itself, have an intrinsic right to exist. And finally, the preservation of wilderness also turns on a scientific argument—viz., the value of biological diversity in stabilizing ecological regimes and in retaining a gene pool for future generations. Truly radical policy proposals have been put forward by deep ecologists on the basis of these arguments. The influential poet Gary Snyder, for example, would like to see a 90 percent reduction in human populations to allow a restoration of pristine environments, while others have argued forcefully that a large portion of the globe must be immediately cordoned off from human beings.[2]

Third, there is a widespread invocation of Eastern spiritual traditions as forerunners of deep ecology. Deep ecology, it is suggested, was practiced both by major religious traditions and at a more popular level by "primal" peoples in non-Western settings. This complements the search for an authentic lineage in Western thought. At one level, the task is to recover those dissenting voices within the Judeo-Christian tradition; at another, to suggest that religious traditions in other cultures are, in contrast, dominantly if not exclusively "biocentric" in their orientation. This coupling of (ancient) Eastern and (modern) ecological wisdom seemingly helps consolidate the claim that deep ecology is a philosophy of universal significance.

Fourth, deep ecologists, whatever their internal differences, share the belief that they are the "leading edge" of the environmental movement. As the polarity of the shallow–deep and anthropocentric–biocentric distinctions makes clear, they see themselves as the spiritual, philosophical, and political vanguard of American and world environmentalism.

TOWARD A CRITIQUE

Although I analyze each of these tenets independently, it is important to recognize, as deep ecologists are fond of remarking in reference to nature, the interconnectedness and unity of these individual themes.

1. Insofar as it has begun to act as a check on man's arrogance and ecological hubris, the transition from an anthropocentric (human-centered) to a biocentric (humans as only one element in the ecosystem) view in both religious and scientific traditions is only to be welcomed. What is unacceptable are the radical conclusions drawn by deep ecology, in particular, that intervention in nature should be guided primarily by the need to preserve biotic integrity rather than by the needs of humans. The latter for deep ecologists is anthropocentric, the former biocentric. This dichotomy is, however, of very little

use in understanding the dynamics of environmental degradation. The two fundamental ecological problems facing the globe are (i) overconsumption by the industrialized world and by urban elites in the Third World and (ii) growing militarization, both in a short-term sense (i.e., ongoing regional wars) and in a long-term sense (i.e., the arms race and the prospect of nuclear annihilation). Neither of these problems has any tangible connection to the anthropocentric–biocentric distinction. Indeed, the agents of these processes would barely comprehend this philosophical dichotomy. The proximate causes of the ecologically wasteful characteristics of industrial society and of militarization are far more mundane: at an aggregate level, the dialectic of economic and political structures, and at a micro-level, the life style choices of individuals. These causes cannot be reduced, whatever the level of analysis, to a deeper anthropocentric attitude toward nature; on the contrary, by constituting a grave threat to human survival, the ecological degradation they cause does not even serve the best interests of human beings! If my identification of the major dangers to the integrity of the natural world is correct, invoking the bogy of anthropocentricism is at best irrelevant and at worst a dangerous obfuscation.

2. If the above dichotomy is irrelevant, the emphasis on wilderness is positively harmful when applied to the Third World. If in the United States the preservationist–utilitarian division is seen as mirroring the conflict between "people" and "interests," in countries such as India the situation is very nearly the reverse. Because India is a long settled and densely populated country in which agrarian populations have a finely balanced relationship with nature, the setting aside of wilderness areas has resulted in a direct transfer of resources from the poor to the rich. Thus, Project Tiger, a network of parks hailed by the international conservation community as an outstanding success, sharply posits the interests of the tiger against those of poor peasants living in and around the reserve. The designation of tiger reserves was made possible only by the physical displacement of existing villages and their inhabitants; their management requires the continuing exclusion of peasants and livestock. The initial impetus for setting up parks for the tiger and other large mammals such as the rhinoceros and elephant came from two social groups, first, a class of ex-hunters turned conservationists belonging mostly to the declining Indian feudal elite and second, representatives of international agencies, such as the World Wildlife Fund (WWF) and the International Union for the Conservation of Nature and Natural Resources (IUCN), seeking to transplant the American system of national parks onto Indian soil. In no case have the needs of the local population been taken into account, and as in many parts of Africa, the designated wildlands are managed primarily for the benefit of rich tourists. Until very recently, wildlands preservation has been identified with environmentalism by the state and the conservation elite; in consequence, environmental problems that impinge far more directly on the lives of the poor—e.g., fuel, fodder, water shortages, soil erosion, and air and water pollution—have not been adequately addressed.[3]

Deep ecology provides, perhaps unwittingly, a justification for the continuation of such narrow and inequitable conservation practices under a newly acquired radical guise. Increasingly, the international conservation elite is using the philosophical, moral, and scientific arguments used by deep ecologists in advancing their wilderness crusade. A striking but by no means atypical example is the recent plea by a prominent American biologist for the takeover of large portions of the globe by the author and his scientific colleagues. Writing in a prestigious scientific forum, the *Annual Review of Ecology and Systematics*, Daniel Janzen argues that only biologists have the competence to decide how the tropical landscape should be used. As "the representatives of the natural world," biologists are "in charge of the future of tropical ecology," and only they have the expertise and mandate to "determine whether the tropical agroscape is to be populated only by humans, their mutualists, commensals, and parasites, or whether it will also contain some islands of the greater nature—the nature that spawned humans, yet has been vanquished by them." Janzen exhorts his colleagues to advance their territorial claims on the tropical world more forcefully, warning that the very existence of these areas is at stake: "if biologists want a tropics in which to biologize, they are going to have to buy it with care, energy, effort, strategy, tactics, time, and cash."[4]

This frankly imperialist manifesto highlights the multiple dangers of the preoccupation with wilderness preservation that is characteristic of deep ecology. As I have suggested, it seriously compounds the neglect by the American movement of far more pressing environmental problems within the Third World. But perhaps more importantly, and in a more insidious fashion, it also provides an impetus to the imperialist yearning of Western biologists and their financial sponsors, organizations such as the WWF and IUCN. The wholesale transfer of a movement culturally rooted in American conservation history can only result in the social uprooting of human populations in other parts of the globe.

3. I come now to the persistent invocation of Eastern philosophies as antecedent in point of time but convergent in their structure with deep ecology. Complex and internally differentiated religious traditions—Hinduism, Buddhism, and Taoism—are lumped together as holding a view of nature believed to be quintessentially biocentric. Individual philosophers such as the Taoist Lao Tzu are identified as being forerunners of deep ecology. Even an intensely political, pragmatic, and Christian-influenced thinker such as Gandhi has been accorded a wholly undeserved place in the deep ecological pantheon. Thus the Zen teacher Robert Aitken Roshi makes the strange claim that Gandhi's thought was not human-centered and that he practiced an embryonic form of deep ecology which is "traditionally Eastern and is found with differing emphasis in Hinduism, Taoism and in Theravada and Mahayana Buddhism."[5] Moving away from the realm of high philosophy and scriptural religion, deep ecologists make the further

claim that at the level of material and spiritual practice "primal" peoples subordinated themselves to the integrity of the biotic universe they inhabited.

I have indicated that this appropriation of Eastern traditions is in part dictated by the need to construct an authentic lineage and in part a desire to present deep ecology as a universalistic philosophy. Indeed, in his substantial and quixotic biography of John Muir, Michael Cohen goes so far as to suggest that Muir was the "Taoist of the [American] West."[6] This reading of Eastern traditions is selective and does not bother to differentiate between alternate (and changing) religious and cultural traditions; as it stands, it does considerable violence to the historical record. Throughout most recorded history the characteristic form of human activity in the "East" has been a finely tuned but nonetheless conscious and dynamic manipulation of nature. Although mystics such as Lao Tzu did reflect on the spiritual essence of human relations with nature, it must be recognized that such ascetics and their reflections were supported by a society of cultivators whose relationship with nature was a far more *active* one. Many agricultural communities do have a sophisticated knowledge of the natural environment that may equal (and sometimes surpass) codified "scientific" knowledge; yet, the elaboration of such traditional ecological knowledge (in both material and spiritual contexts) can hardly be said to rest on a mystical affinity with nature of a deep ecological kind. Nor is such knowledge infallible; as the archaeological record powerfully suggests, modern Western man has no monopoly on ecological disasters.

In a brilliant article, the Chicago historian Ronald Inden points out that this romantic and essentially positive view of the East is a mirror image of the scientific and essentially pejorative view normally upheld by Western scholars of the Orient. In either case, the East constitutes the Other, a body wholly separate and alien from the West; it is defined by a uniquely spiritual and nonrational "essence," even if this essence is valorized quite differently by the two schools. Eastern man exhibits a spiritual dependence with respect to nature—on the one hand, this is symptomatic of his prescientific and backward self, on the other, of his ecological wisdom and deep ecological consciousness. Both views are monolithic, simplistic, and have the characteristic effect—intended in one case, perhaps unintended in the other—of denying agency and reason to the East and making it the privileged orbit of Western thinkers.

The two apparently opposed perspectives have then a common underlying structure of discourse in which the East merely serves as a vehicle for Western projections. Varying images of the East are raw material for political and cultural battles being played out in the West; they tell us far more about the Western commentator and his desires than about the "East." Inden's remarks apply not merely to Western scholarship on India, but to Orientalist constructions of China and Japan as well:

> Although these two views appear to be strongly opposed, they often combine together. Both have a similar interest in sustaining the Otherness of India. The holders of the dominant view, best exemplified in the past in imperial administrative discourse (and today probably by that of "development economics"), would place a traditional, superstition-ridden India in a position of perpetual tutelage to a modern, rational West. The adherents of the romantic view, best exemplified academically in the discourses of Christian liberalism and analytic psychology, concede the realm of the public and impersonal to the positivist. Taking their succour not from governments and big business, but from a plethora of religious foundations and self-help institutes, and from allies in the "consciousness industry," not to mention the important industry of tourism, the romantics insist that India embodies a private realm of the imagination and the religious which modern, western man lacks but needs. They, therefore, like the positivists, but for just the opposite reason, have a vested interest in seeing that the Orientalist view of India as "spiritual," "mysterious," and "exotic" is perpetuated.[7]

4. How radical, finally, are the deep ecologists? Notwithstanding their self-image and strident rhetoric (in which the label "shallow ecology" has an opprobrium similar to that reserved for "social democratic" by Marxist-Leninists), even within the American context their radicalism is limited and it manifests itself quite differently elsewhere.

To my mind, deep ecology is best viewed as a radical trend within the wilderness preservation movement. Although advancing philosophical rather than aesthetic arguments and encouraging political militancy rather than negotiation, its practical emphasis—viz., preservation of unspoilt nature—is virtually identical. For the mainstream movement, the function of wilderness is to provide a temporary antidote to modern civilization. As a special institution within an industrialized society, the national park "provides an opportunity for respite, contrast, contemplation, and affirmation of values for those who live most of their lives in the workaday world."[8] Indeed, the rapid increase in visitations to the national parks in postwar America is a direct consequence of economic expansion. The emergence of a popular interest in wilderness sites, the historian Samuel Hays points out, was "not a throwback to the primitive, but an integral part of the modern standard of living as people sought to add new 'amenity' and 'aesthetic' goals and desires to their earlier preoccupation with necessities and conveniences."[9]

Here, the enjoyment of nature is an integral part of the consumer society. The private automobile (and the life style it has spawned) is in many respects the ultimate ecological villain, and an untouched wilderness the prototype of ecological harmony; yet, for most Americans it is perfectly consistent to drive a thousand miles to spend a holiday in a national park. They possess a vast, beautiful, and sparsely populated continent and are also able to draw upon the natural resources of large portions of the globe by virtue of their economic and political dominance. In consequence, America can simultaneously enjoy the material benefits of an expanding economy and the aesthetic benefits of unspoilt nature. The two poles of "wilderness" and "civilization" mutually coexist in an internally coherent whole, and philosophers of both poles are assigned a prominent place in this culture. Paradoxically as it may seem, it is no accident that Star Wars technology and deep ecology both find their fullest expression in that leading sector of Western civilization, California.

Deep ecology runs parallel to the consumer society without seriously questioning its ecological and socio-political basis. In its celebration of American wilderness, it also displays an uncomfortable convergence with the prevailing climate of nationalism in the American wilderness movement. For spokesmen such as the historian Roderick Nash, the national park system is America's distinctive cultural contribution to the world, reflective not merely of its economic but of its philosophical and ecological maturity as well. In what Walter Lippmann called the American century, the "American invention of national parks" must be exported worldwide. Betraying an economic determinism that would make even a Marxist shudder, Nash believes that environmental preservation is a "full stomach" phenomenon that is confined to the rich, urban, and sophisticated. Nonetheless, he hopes that "the less developed nations may eventually evolve economically and intellectually to the point where nature preservation is more than a business."[10]

The error which Nash makes (and which deep ecology in some respects encourages) is to equate environmental protection with the protection of wilderness. This is a distinctively American notion, borne out of a unique social and environmental history. The archetypal concerns of radical environmentalists in other cultural contexts are in fact quite different. The German Greens, for example, have elaborated a devastating critique of industrial society which turns on the acceptance of environmental limits to growth. Pointing to the intimate links between industrialization, militarization, and conquest, the Greens argue that economic growth in the West has historically rested on the economic and ecological exploitation of the Third World. Rudolf Bahro is characteristically blunt:

> The working class here [in the West] is the richest lower class in the world. And if I look at the problem from the point of view of the whole of humanity, not just from that of Europe, then I must say that the metropolitan working class is the worst exploiting class in history.... What made poverty bearable in eighteenth- or nineteenth-century Europe was the prospect of escaping it through exploitation of the periphery. But this is no longer a possibility, and continued industrialism in the Third World will mean poverty for whole generation s and hunger for millions.[11]

Here the roots of global ecological problems lie in the disproportionate share of resources consumed by the industrialized countries as a whole *and* the urban elite within the Third World. Since it is impossible to reproduce an industrial monoculture worldwide, the ecological movement in the West must begin by cleaning up its own act. The Greens advocate the creation of a "no growth" economy, to be achieved by scaling down current (and clearly unsustainable) consumption levels. This radical shift in consumption and production patterns requires the creation of alternate economic and political structures—smaller in scale and more amenable to social participation—but it rests equally on a shift in cultural values. The expansionist character of modern Western man will have to give way to an ethic of renunciation and self-limitation, in which spiritual and communal values play an increasing role in sustaining social life. This revolution in cultural values, however, has as its point of departure an understanding of environmental processes quite different from deep ecology.

Many elements of the Green program find a strong resonance in countries such as India, where a history of Western colonialism and industrial development has benefited only a tiny elite while exacting tremendous social and environmental costs. The ecological battles presently being fought in India have as their epicenter the conflict over nature between the subsistence and largely rural sector and the vastly more powerful commercial-industrial sector. Perhaps the most celebrated of these battles concerns the Chipko (Hug the Tree) movement, a peasant movement against deforestation in the Himalayan foothills. Chipko is only one of several movements that have sharply questioned the nonsustainable demand being placed on the land and vegetative base by urban centers and industry. These include opposition to large dams by displaced peasants, the conflict between small artisan fishing and large-scale trawler fishing for export, the countrywide movements against commercial forest operations, and opposition to industrial pollution among downstream agricultural and fishing communities.[12]

Two features distinguish these environmental movements from their Western counterparts. First, for the sections of society most critically affected by environmental degradation—poor and landless peasants, women, and tribals—it is a question of sheer survival, not of enhancing the quality of life. Second, and as a consequence, the environmental solutions they articulate deeply involve questions of equity as well as economic and political redistribution. Highlighting these differences, a leading Indian environmentalist stresses that "environmental protection per se is of least concern to most of these groups. Their main concern is about the use of the environment and who should benefit from it."[13] They seek to wrest control of nature away from the state and the industrial sector and place it in the hands of rural communities who live within that environment but are increasingly denied access to it. These communities have far more basic needs, their demands on the environment are far less intense, and they can draw upon a reservoir of cooperative social institutions and local ecological knowledge in managing the "commons"—forests, grasslands, and the waters—on a sustainable basis. If colonial and capitalist expansion has both accentuated social inequalities and signaled a precipitous fall in ecological wisdom, an alternate ecology must rest on an alternate society and polity as well.

This brief overview of German and Indian environmentalism has some major implications for deep ecology. Both German and Indian environmental traditions allow for a greater integration of ecological concerns with livelihood and work. They also place a greater emphasis on equity and social justice (both within individual countries and on a global scale) on the grounds that in the absence of social regeneration environmental regeneration has very little chance of succeeding. Finally, and perhaps most significantly, they have escaped the preoccupation with wilderness perservation so characteristic of American cultural and environmental history.

A HOMILY

In 1958, the economist J. K. Galbraith referred to overconsumption as the unasked question of the American conservation movement. There is a marked selectivity, he wrote, "in the conservationists approach to materials consumption. If we are concerned about our great appetite for materials, it is plausible to seek to increase the supply, to decrease waste, to make better use of the stocks available, and to develop substitutes. But what of the appetite itself? Surely this is the ultimate source of the problem. If it continues its geometric course, will it not one day have to be restrained? Yet in the literature of the resource problem this is the forbidden question. Over it hangs a nearly total silence."[14]

The consumer economy and society have expanded tremendously in the three decades since Galbraith penned these words; yet his criticisms are nearly as valid today. I have said "nearly," for there are some hopeful signs. Within the environmental movement several dispersed groups are working to develop ecologically benign technologies and to encourage less wasteful life styles. Moreover, outside the self-defined boundaries of American environmentalism, opposition to the permanent war economy is being carried on by a peace movement that has a distinguished history and impeccable moral and political credentials.

It is precisely these (to my mind, most hopeful) components of the American social scene that are missing from deep ecology. In their widely noticed book, Bill Devall and George Sessions make no mention of militarization or the movements for peace, while activists whose practical focus is on developing ecologically responsible life styles (e.g., Wendell Berry) are derided as "falling short of deep ecological awareness."[15] A truly radical ecology in the American context ought to work toward a synthesis of the appropriate technology, alternate life style, and peace movements. By making the (largely spurious) anthropocentric–biocentric distinction central to the debate, deep ecologists may have appropriated the moral high ground, but they are at the same time doing a serious disservice to American and global environmentalism.[16]

NOTES

I am grateful to Mike Bell, Tom Birch, Bill Burch, Bill Cronon, Diane Mayerfeld, David Rothenberg, Kirkpatrick Sale, Joel Seton, Tim Weiskel, and Don Worster for helpful comments.

1. K. Sale, "The Forest for the Trees: Can Today's Environmentalists Tell the Difference," *Mother Jones* 11 (November 1986): 26.

2. Quoted in ibid., 32.

3. See Centre for Science and Environment, *India: The State of the Environment 1982: A Citizens Report* (New Delhi: Centre for Science and Environment, 1982), and R. Sukumar, "Elephant–Man Conflict in Karnataka," in *The State of Karnataka's Environment*, ed. C. Saldanha (Bangalore: Centre for Taxonomic Studies, 1985). For Africa, see the brilliant analysis by H. Kjekshus, *Ecology Control and Economic Development in East African History* (Berkeley: University of California Press, 1977).

4. D. Janzen, "The Future of Tropical Ecology," *Annual Review of Ecology and Systematics* 17 (1986): 305–6.

5. R. A. Roshi, "Gandhi, Dogen, and Deep Ecology," reprinted as appendix C in B. Devall and G. Sessions, *Deep Ecology: Living as if Nature Mattered* (Salt Lake City: Peregrine Smith, 1985). For Gandhi's own views on social reconstruction, see the excellent three-volume collection edited by R. Iyer, *The Moral and Political Writings of Mahatma Gandhi* (Oxford: Clarendon Press, 1986–1987).

6. M. Cohen, *The Pathless Way* (Madison: University of Wisconsin Press, 1984), 120.

7. R. Inden, "Orientalist Constructions of India," *Modern Asian Studies* 20 (1986): 442. Inden draws inspiration from E. Said's forceful polemic, *Orientalism* (New York: Basic Books, 1980). It must be noted, however, that there is a salient difference between Western perceptions of Middle Eastern and Far Eastern cultures, respectively. Due perhaps to the long history of Christian conflict with Islam, Middle Eastern cultures (as Said documents) are consistently presented in pejorative terms. The juxtaposition of hostile and worshipping attitudes that Inden talks of applies only to Western attitudes toward Buddhist and Hindu societies.

8. J. Sax, *Mountains Without Handrails: Reflections on the National Parks* (Ann Arbor: University of Michigan Press, 1980), 42.

9. S. P. Hays, "From Conservation to Environment: Environmental Politics in the United States since World War Two," *Environmental Review* 6 (1982): 21. See also S. P. Hays, *Beauty, Health, and Permanence: Environmental Politics in the United States, 1955–1985* (Cambridge: Cambridge University Press, 1987).

10. R. Nash, *Wilderness and the American Mind*, 3rd ed. (New Haven, Conn.: Yale University Press, 1982).

11. R. Bahro, *From Red to Green* (London: Verso Books, 1984).

12. For an excellent review, see A. Agarwal and S. Narain, eds., *India: The State of the Environment, 1984–1985: A Citizens Report* (New Delhi: Centre for Science and Environment, 1985). See also R. Guha, *The Unquiet Woods: Ecological Change and Peasant Resistance in the Indian Himalaya* (Berkeley: University of California Press, 1990).

13. A. Agarwal, "Human–Nature Interactions in a Third World Country," *Environmentalist* 6 (1986): 167.

14. J. K. Galbraith, "How Much Should a Country Consume?" in *Perspectives on Conservation*, ed. Henry Jarrett (Baltimore: Johns Hopkins University Press, 1958), 91–92.

15. Devall and Sessions, *Deep Ecology*, 122. For Wendell Berry's own assessment of deep ecology, see his "Amplications: Preserving Wildness," *Wilderness* 50 (1987): 39–40, 50–54.

16. In this sense, my critique of deep ecology, although that of an outsider, may facilitate the reassertion of those elements in the American environmental tradition for which there is a profound sympathy in other parts of the globe. A global perspective may also lead to a critical reassessment of figures such as Aldo Leopold and John Muir, the two patron saints of deep ecology. As Donald Worster has pointed out, the message of Muir (and, I would argue, of Leopold as well) makes sense only in an American context; he has very little to say to other cultures. See Worster's review of Stephen Fox's *John Muir and His Legacy*, in *Environmental Ethics* 5 (1983): 277–81.

BIODIVERSITY

The word "biodiversity" was coined by scientists in the 1980s. While the term is not easy to define precisely, biodiversity generally refers to the variety of life on the planet, including plants, animals, genetic material, ecosystems, and the relations between them. Biodiversity is often associated with other important environmental values such as wilderness, ecological health, and species conservation. The academic field most concerned with the maintenance and study of biodiversity is conservation biology. The Endangered Species Act is the US federal law that is most relevant to protecting biodiversity, though it does not use this term. Biodiversity may be an unfamiliar or even confusing concept, but preserving biodiversity is one of the central goals of the modern environmental movement and is extremely motivating for many activists. Yet there are deep philosophical questions about what biodiversity is, why we should protect it, and what exactly such a commitment would require us to do.

Elliott Sober asks about the value of biodiversity when he writes that "[t]he problem for environmentalism stems from the idea that species and ecosystems ought to be preserved for reasons additional to their known value as resources for human use." He notes that there is a "stark contrast between an ethic in which it is the life situation of individuals that matters and an ethic in which stability and diversity of populations of individuals are what matter." Sober concludes by suggesting that much of the interest that environmentalists have in preserving biodiversity may actually be based on aesthetic considerations.

Sahotra Sarkar discusses biodiversity not just as a value to protect for its own sake but also as a dynamic resource that can transform our lives. An evocative experience in a threatened forest can transform a tourist into an activist or even a scientist, in much the same way that attending a concert at an early age may turn an aspiring scientist into a musician. According to Sarkar, supposing that biodiversity has transformative value is consistent with supposing that it has intrinsic value as well. However, in both cases, the value of biodiversity is "intellectual," not just narrowly pragmatic, and that may be part of the explanation of why it is so difficult to make a convincing public case for its value.

Focusing on biodiversity shifts our attention from individuals to systems, if for no other reason than that individual plants or animals require an ecosystem in which to survive. Holmes Rolston goes further in defending the moral importance of holistic entities such as species and argues that attempts to assign them economic value fails to uncover their most fundamental and profound value. For Rolston, what matters even more than biodiversity is the natural processes that create it. If a species goes extinct through natural processes we have no obligation to preserve it ("Nature doesn't care, so why should we?"). Our fundamental duty is not to protect everything that exists at any given moment but to respect "species, speciation, and the cumulative biodiversity."

FURTHER READING

Faith, Daniel P. "Biodiversity," *Stanford Encyclopedia of Philosophy*. http://plato.stanford.edu/ archives/fall2008/entries/biodiversity/, 2008. A good introduction to central philosophical questions regarding biodiversity.

McLaurin, James, and Kim Sterelny. *What is Biodiversity?* Chicago, IL: University of Chicago, 2008. The best recent discussion of the concept of biodiversity and reasons for preserving it.

Norton, Bryan. G. *Why Preserve Natural Variety?* Princeton, NJ: Princeton University Press, 1987. The book that introduced the idea of "transformative" value.

Oksanen, Markku, and Juhani Pietarinen, eds. *Philosophy and Biodiversity*. Cambridge: Cambridge University Press, 2004. A collection of philosophical papers on understanding, valuing, and protecting biodiversity.

Wilson, E. O., ed. *Biodiversity*, Washington, DC: National Academy of Sciences/Smithsonian Institution, 1988. An important collection of scientific writings that popularized the term "biodiversity."

DISCUSSION QUESTIONS

1. What is biodiversity?
2. What, if anything, makes biodiversity valuable?
3. Is protecting biodiversity an important enough value to justify exterminating unwanted species or setting aside land for conservation?
4. How does a concern with biodiversity complement or conflict with other environmental values?
5. What are the relations between the value of biodiversity and the value of individual plants or animals?

ELLIOTT SOBER

Philosophical Problems for Environmentalism

INTRODUCTION

Preserving an endangered species or ecosystem poses no special conceptual problem when the instrumental value of that species or ecosystem is known. When we have reason to think that some natural object represents a resource to us, we obviously ought to take that fact into account in deciding what to do. A variety of potential uses may be under discussion, including food supply, medical applications, recreational use, and so on. As with any complex decision, it may be difficult even to agree on how to compare the competing values that may be involved. Willingness to pay in dollars is a familiar least common denominator, although it poses a number of problems. But here we have nothing that is specifically a problem for environmentalism.

The problem for environmentalism stems from the idea that species and ecosystems ought to be preserved for reasons additional to their known value as resources for human use. The feeling is that even when we cannot say what nutritional, medicinal, or recreational benefit the preservation provides, there still is a value in preservation. It is the search for a rationale for this feeling that constitutes the main conceptual problem for environmentalism.

The problem is especially difficult in view of the holistic (as opposed to individualistic) character of the things being assigned value. Put simply, what is special about environmentalism is that it values the preservation of species, communities, or ecosystems, rather than the individual organisms of which they are composed. "Animal liberationists" have urged that we should take the suffering of sentient animals into account in ethical deliberation. Such beasts are not mere things to be used as cruelly as we like no

matter how trivial the benefit we derive. But in "widening the ethical circle," we are simply including in the community more individual organisms whose costs and benefits we compare. Animal liberationists are extending an old and familiar ethical doctrine—namely, utilitarianism—to take account of the welfare of other individuals. Although the practical consequences of this point of view may be revolutionary, the theoretical perspective is not at all novel. If suffering is bad, then it is bad for any individual who suffers. Animal liberationists merely remind us of the consequences of familiar principles.

But trees, mountains, and salt marshes do not suffer. They do not experience pleasure and pain, because, evidently, they do not have experiences at all. The same is true of species. Granted, individual organisms may have mental states; but the species—taken to be a population of organisms connected by certain sorts of interactions (preeminently, that of exchanging genetic material in reproduction)—does not. Or put more carefully, we might say that the only sense in which species have experiences is that their member organisms do: the attribution at the population level, if true, is true simply in virtue of its being true at the individual level. Here is a case where reductionism is correct.

So perhaps it is true in this reductive sense that some species experience pain. But the values that environmentalists attach to preserving species do not reduce to any value of preserving organisms. It is in this sense that environmentalists espouse a holistic value system. Environmentalists care about entities that by no stretch of the imagination have experiences (e.g., mountains). What is more, their position does not force them to care if individual organisms suffer pain, so long as the species is

preserved. Steel traps may outrage an animal liberationist because of the suffering they inflict, but an environmentalist aiming just at the preservation of a balanced ecosystem might see here no cause for complaint. Similarly, environmentalists think that the distinction between wild and domesticated organisms is important, in that it is the preservation of "natural" (i.e., not created by the "artificial interference" of human beings) objects that matters, whereas animal liberationists see the main problem in terms of the suffering of any organism—domesticated or not. And finally, environmentalists and animal liberationists diverge on what might be called the $n + m$ question. If two species—say blue and sperm whales—have roughly comparable capacities for experiencing pain, an animal liberationist might tend to think of the preservation of a sperm whale as wholly on an ethical par with the preservation of a blue whale. The fact that one organism is part of an endangered species while the other is not does not make the rare individual more intrinsically important. But for an environmentalist, this holistic property—membership in an endangered species—makes all the difference in the world: a world with n sperm and m blue whales is far better than a world with $n + m$ sperm and 0 blue whales. Here we have a stark contrast between an ethic in which it is the life situation of individuals that matters, and an ethic in which the stability and diversity of populations of individuals are what matter.

Both animal liberationists and environmentalists wish to broaden our ethical horizons—to make us realize that it is not just human welfare that counts. But they do this in very different, often conflicting, ways. It is no accident that at the level of practical politics the two points of view increasingly find themselves at loggerheads. This practical conflict is the expression of a deep theoretical divide.[1]

THE IGNORANCE ARGUMENT

"Although we might not now know what use a particular endangered species might be to us, allowing it to go extinct forever closes off the possibility of discovering and exploiting a future use." According to this point of view, our ignorance of value is turned into a reason for action. The scenario envisaged in this environmentalist argument is not without precedent; who could have guessed that penicillin would be good for something other than turning out cheese? But there is a fatal defect in such arguments, which we might summarize with the phrase *out of nothing, nothing comes*: rational decisions require assumptions about what is true and what is valuable (in decision-theoretic jargon, the inputs must be probabilities and utilities). If you are completely ignorant of values, then you are incapable of making a rational decision, either for or against preserving some species. The fact that you do not know the value of a species, by itself, cannot count as a reason for wanting one thing rather than another to happen to it.

And there are so many species. How many geese that lay golden eggs are there apt to be in that number? It is hard to assign probabilities and utilities precisely here, but an analogy will perhaps reveal the problem confronting this environmentalist argument. Most of us willingly fly on airplanes, when safer (but less convenient) alternative forms of transportation are available. Is this rational? Suppose it were argued that there is a small probability that the next flight you take will crash. This would be very bad for you. Is it not crazy for you to risk this, given that the only gain to you is that you can reduce your travel time by a few hours (by not going by train, say)? Those of us who not only fly, but congratulate ourselves for being rational in doing so, reject this argument. We are prepared to accept a small chance of a great disaster in return for the high probability of a rather modest benefit. If this is rational, no wonder that we might consistently be willing to allow a species to go extinct in order to build a hydroelectric plant.

That the argument from ignorance is no argument at all can be seen from another angle. If we literally do not know what consequences the extinction of this or that species may bring, then we should take seriously

the possibility that the extinction may be beneficial as well as the possibility that it may be deleterious. It may sound deep to insist that we preserve endangered species precisely because we do not know why they are valuable. But ignorance on a scale like this cannot provide the basis for any rational action.

Rather than invoke some unspecified future benefit, an environmentalist may argue that the species in question plays a crucial role in stabilizing the ecosystem of which it is a part. This will undoubtedly be true for carefully chosen species and ecosystems, but one should not generalize this argument into a global claim to the effect that *every* species is crucial to a balanced ecosystem. Although ecologists used to agree that the complexity of an ecosystem stabilizes it, this hypothesis has been subject to a number of criticisms and qualifications, both from a theoretical and an empirical perspective.[2] And for certain kinds of species (those which occupy a rather small area and whose normal population is small) we can argue that extinction would probably not disrupt the community. However fragile the biosphere may be, the extreme view that everything is crucial is almost certainly not true.

But, of course, environmentalists are often concerned by the fact that extinctions are occurring now at a rate much higher than in earlier times. It is mass extinction that threatens the biosphere, they say, and this claim avoids the spurious assertion that communities are so fragile that even one extinction will cause a crash. However, if the point is to avoid a mass extinction of species, how does this provide a rationale for preserving a species of the kind just described, of which we rationally believe that its passing will not destabilize the ecosystem? And, more generally, if mass extinction is known to be a danger to us, how does this translate into a value for preserving any particular species? Notice that we have now passed beyond the confines of the argument from ignorance; we are taking as a premise the idea that mass extinction would be a catastrophe (since it would destroy the ecosystem on which we depend). But how should that premise affect our

valuing the California condor, the blue whale, or the snail darter?

THE SLIPPERY SLOPE ARGUMENT

Environmentalists sometimes find themselves asked to explain why each species matters so much to them, when there are, after all, so many. We may know of special reasons for valuing particular species, but how can we justify thinking that each and every species is important? "Each extinction impoverishes the biosphere" is often the answer given, but it really fails to resolve the issue. Granted, each extinction impoverishes, but it only impoverishes a little bit. So if it is the *wholesale* impoverishment of the biosphere that matters, one would apparently have to concede that each extinction matters a little, but only a little. But environmentalists may be loathe to concede this, for if they concede that each species matters only a little, they seem to be inviting the wholesale impoverishment that would be an unambiguous disaster. So they dig in their heels and insist that each species matters a lot. But to take this line, one must find some other rationale than the idea that mass extinction would be a great harm. Some of these alternative rationales we will examine later. For now, let us take a closer look at the train of thought involved here.

Slippery slopes are curious things: if you take even one step onto them, you inevitably slide all the way to the bottom. So if you want to avoid finding yourself at the bottom, you must avoid stepping onto them at all. To mix metaphors, stepping onto a slippery slope is to invite being nickeled and dimed to death.

Slippery slope arguments have played a powerful role in a number of recent ethical debates. One often hears people defend the legitimacy of abortions by arguing that since it is permissible to abort a single-celled fertilized egg, it must be permissible to abort a foetus of any age, since there is no place to draw the line from 0 to 9 months. Antiabortionists, on the other hand, sometimes argue in the other direction:

since infanticide of newborns is not permissible, abortion at any earlier time is also not allowed, since there is no place to draw the line. Although these two arguments reach opposite conclusions about the permissibility of abortions, they agree on the following idea: since there is no principled place to draw the line on the continuum from newly fertilized egg to foetus gone to term, one must treat all these cases in the same way. Either abortion is always permitted or it never is, since there is no place to draw the line. Both sides run their favorite slippery slope arguments, but try to precipitate slides in opposite directions.

Starting with 10 million extant species, and valuing overall diversity, the environmentalist does not want to grant that each species matters only a little. For having granted this, commercial expansion and other causes will reduce the tally to 9,999,999. And then the argument is repeated, with each species valued only a little, and diversity declines another notch. And so we are well on our way to a considerably impoverished biosphere, a little at a time. Better to reject the starting premise—namely, that each species matters only a little—so that the slippery slope can be avoided.

Slippery slopes should hold no terror for environmentalists, because it is often a mistake to demand that a line be drawn. Let me illustrate by an example. What is the difference between being bald and not? Presumably, the difference concerns the number of hairs you have on your head. But what is the precise number of hairs marking the boundary between baldness and not being bald? There is no such number. Yet, it would be a fallacy to conclude that there is no difference between baldness and hairiness. The fact that you cannot draw a line does not force you to say that the two alleged categories collapse into one. In the abortion case, this means that even if there is no precise point in foetal development that involves some discontinuous, qualitative change, one is still not obliged to think of newly fertilized eggs and foetuses gone to term as morally on a par. Since the biological differences are ones of degree, not kind,

one may want to adopt the position that the moral differences are likewise matters of degree. This may lead to the view that a woman should have a better reason for having an abortion, the more developed her foetus is. Of course, this position does not logically follow from the idea that there is no place to draw the line; my point is just that differences in degree do not demolish the possibility of there being real moral differences.

In the environmental case, if one places a value on diversity, then each species becomes more valuable as the overall diversity declines. If we begin with 10 million species, each may matter little, but as extinctions continue, the remaining ones matter more and more. According to this outlook, a better and better reason would be demanded for allowing yet another species to go extinct. Perhaps certain sorts of economic development would justify the extinction of a species at one time. But granting this does not oblige one to conclude that the same sort of decision would have to be made further down the road. This means that one can value diversity without being obliged to take the somewhat exaggerated position that each species, no matter how many there are, is terribly precious in virtue of its contribution to that diversity.

Yet, one can understand that environmentalists might be reluctant to concede this point. They may fear that if one now allows that most species contribute only a little to overall diversity, one will set in motion a political process that cannot correct itself later. The worry is that even when the overall diversity has been drastically reduced, our ecological sensitivities will have been so coarsened that we will no longer be in a position to realize (or to implement policies fostering) the preciousness of what is left. This fear may be quite justified, but it is important to realize that it does not conflict with what was argued above. The political utility of making an argument should not be confused with the argument's soundness.

The fact that you are on a slippery slope, by itself, does not tell you whether you are near the beginning,

in the middle, or at the end. If species diversity is a matter of degree, where do we currently find ourselves—on the verge of catastrophe, well on our way in that direction, or at some distance from a global crash? Environmentalists often urge that we are fast approaching a precipice; if we are, then the reduction in diversity that every succeeding extinction engenders should be all we need to justify species preservation.

Sometimes, however, environmentalists advance a kind of argument not predicated on the idea of fast approaching doom. The goal is to show that there is something wrong with allowing a species to go extinct (or with causing it to go extinct), even if overall diversity is not affected much. I now turn to one argument of this kind.

APPEALS TO WHAT IS NATURAL

I noted earlier that environmentalists and animal liberationists disagree over the significance of the distinction between wild and domesticated animals. Since both types of organisms can experience pain, animal liberationists will think of each as meriting ethical consideration. But environmentalists will typically not put wild and domesticated organisms on a par. Environmentalists typically are interested in preserving what is natural, be it a species living in the wild or a wilderness ecosystem. If a kind of domesticated chicken were threatened with extinction, I doubt that environmental groups would be up in arms. And if certain unique types of human environments—say urban slums in the United States—were "endangered," it is similarly unlikely that environmentalists would view this process as a deplorable impoverishment of the biosphere.

The environmentalist's lack of concern for humanly created organisms and environments may be practical rather than principled. It may be that at the level of values, no such bifurcation is legitimate, but that from the point of view of practical political action, it makes sense to put one's energies

into saving items that exist in the wild. This subject has not been discussed much in the literature, so it is hard to tell. But I sense that the distinction between wild and domesticated has a certain theoretical importance to many environmentalists. They perhaps think that the difference is that we created domesticated organisms which would otherwise not exist, and so are entitled to use them solely for our own interests. But we did not create wild organisms and environments, so it is the height of presumption to expropriate them for our benefit. A more fitting posture would be one of "stewardship": we have come on the scene and found a treasure not of our making. Given this, we ought to preserve this treasure in its natural state.

I do not wish to contest the appropriateness of "stewardship." It is the dichotomy between artificial (domesticated) and natural (wild) that strikes me as wrong-headed. I want to suggest that to the degree that "natural" means anything biologically, it means very little ethically. And, conversely, to the degree that "natural" is understood as a normative concept, it has very little to do with biology.

Environmentalists often express regret that we human beings find it so hard to remember that we are part of nature—one species among many others—rather than something standing outside of nature. I will not consider here whether this attitude is cause for complaint; the important point is that seeing us as part of nature rules out the environmentalist's use of the distinction between artificial-domesticated and natural-wild described above. *If we are part of nature, then everything we do is part of nature, and is natural in that primary sense.* When we domesticate organisms and bring them into a state of dependence on us, this is simply an example of one species exerting a selection pressure on another. If one calls this "unnatural," one might just as well say the same of parasitism or symbiosis (compare human domestication of animals and plants and "slave-making" in the social insects).

The concept of naturalness is subject to the same abuses as the concept of normalcy. *Normal* can mean

usual or it can mean *desirable*. Although only the total pessimist will think that the two concepts are mutually exclusive, it is generally recognized that the mere fact that something is common does not by itself count as a reason for thinking that it is desirable. This distinction is quite familiar now in popular discussions of mental health, for example. Yet, when it comes to environmental issues, the concept of naturalness continues to live a double life. The destruction of wilderness areas by increased industrialization is bad because it is unnatural. And it is unnatural because it involves transforming a natural into an artificial habitat. Or one might hear that although extinction is a natural process, the kind of mass extinction currently being precipitated by our species is unprecedented, and so is unnatural. Environmentalists should look elsewhere for a defense of their policies, lest conservation simply become a variant of uncritical conservatism in which the axiom "Whatever is, is right" is modified to read "Whatever is (before human beings come on the scene), is right."

This conflation of the biological with the normative sense of "natural" sometimes comes to the fore when environmentalists attack animal liberationists for naive do-goodism. Callicott writes:

> ...the value commitments of the humane movement seem at bottom to betray a world-denying or rather a life-loathing philosophy. The natural world as actually constituted is one in which one being lives at the expense of others. Each organism, in Darwin's metaphor, struggles to maintain its own organic integrity....To live *is* to be anxious about life, to feel pain and pleasure in a fitting mixture, and sooner or later to die. That is the way the system works. *If nature as a whole is good, then pain and death are also good.* Environmental ethics in general require people to play fair in the natural system. The neo-Benthamites have in a sense taken the uncourageous approach. People have attempted to exempt themselves from the life/death reciprocities of natural processes and from ecological limitations in the name of a prophylactic ethic of maximizing rewards (pleasure) and minimizing unwelcome information (pain). To be fair, the humane moralists seem to suggest that we should attempt to project the same values into the nonhuman animal world and to widen the charmed

circle—no matter that it would be biologically unrealistic to do so or biologically ruinous if, per impossible, such an environmental ethic were implemented.

There is another approach. Rather than imposing our alienation from nature and natural processes and cycles of life on other animals, we human beings could reaffirm our participation in nature by accepting life as it is given without a sugar coating....[3]

On the same page, Callicott quotes with approval Shepard's remark that "the humanitarian's projection onto nature of illegal murder and the rights of civilized people to safety not only misses the point but is exactly contrary to fundamental ecological reality: the structure of nature is a sequence of killings."[4]

Thinking that what is found in nature is beyond ethical defect has not always been popular. Darwin wrote:

> ...That there is much suffering in the world no one disputes.
>
> Some have attempted to explain this in reference to man by imagining that it serves for his moral improvement. But the number of men in the world is as nothing compared with that of all other sentient beings, and these often suffer greatly without any moral improvement. A being so powerful and so full of knowledge as a God who could create the universe, is to our finite minds omnipotent and omniscient, and it revolts our understanding to suppose that his benevolence is not unbounded, for what advantage can there be in the sufferings of millions of the lower animals throughout almost endless time? This very old argument from the existence of suffering against the existence of an intelligent first cause seems to me a strong one; whereas, as just remarked, the presence of much suffering agrees well with the view that all organic beings have been developed through variation and natural selection.[5]

Darwin apparently viewed the quantity of pain found in nature as a melancholy and sobering consequence of the struggle for existence. But once we adopt the Panglossian attitude that this is the best of all possible worlds ("there is just the right amount of pain," etc.), a failure to identify what is natural with what is good can only seem "world-denying," "life-loathing," "in a sense uncourageous," and "contrary to fundamental ecological reality."[6]

Earlier in his essay, Callicott expresses distress that animal liberationists fail to draw a sharp distinction "between the very different plights (and rights) of wild and domestic animals."[7] Domestic animals are creations of man, he says. "They are living artifacts, but artifacts nevertheless....There is thus something profoundly incoherent (and insensitive as well) in the complaint of some animal liberationists that the 'natural behavior' of chickens and bobby calves is cruelly frustrated on factory farms. It would make almost as much sense to speak of the natural behavior of tables and chairs."[8] Here again we see teleology playing a decisive role: wild organisms do not have the natural function of serving human ends, but domesticated animals do. Cheetahs in zoos are crimes against what is natural; veal calves in boxes are not.

The idea of "natural tendency" played a decisive role in pre-Darwinian biological thinking. Aristotle's entire science—both his physics and his biology—is articulated in terms of specifying the natural tendencies of kinds of objects and the interfering forces that can prevent an object from achieving its intended state. Heavy objects in the sublunar sphere have location at the center of the earth as their natural state; each tends to go there, but is prevented from doing so. Organisms likewise are conceptualized in terms of this natural state model:

> ...[for] any living thing that has reached its normal development and which is unmutilated, and whose mode of generation is not spontaneous, the most natural act is the production of another like itself, an animal producing an animal, a plant a plant....[9]

But many interfering forces are possible, and in fact the occurrence of "monsters" is anything but uncommon. According to Aristotle, mules (sterile hybrids) count as deviations from the natural state. In fact, females are monsters as well, since the natural tendency of sexual reproduction is for the offspring to perfectly resemble the father, who, according to Aristotle, provides the "genetic instructions" (to put the idea anachronistically) while the female provides only the matter.

What has happened to the natural state model in modern science? In physics, the idea of describing what a class of objects will do in the absence of "interference" lives on: Newton specified this "zero-force state" as rest or uniform motion, and in general relativity, this state is understood in terms of motion along geodesics. But one of the most profound achievements of Darwinian biology has been the jettisoning of this kind of model. It isn't just that Aristotle was wrong in his detailed claims about mules and women; the whole structure of the natural state model has been discarded. Population biology is not conceptualized in terms of positing some characteristic that all members of a species would have in common, were interfering forces absent. Variation is not thought of as a deflection from the natural state of uniformity. Rather, variation is taken to be a fundamental property in its own right. Nor, at the level of individual biology, does the natural state model find an application. Developmental theory is not articulated by specifying a natural tendency and a set of interfering forces....The idea that a corn plant might have some "natural height," which can be augmented or diminished by "interfering forces" is entirely alien to post-Darwinian biology.

The fact that the concepts of natural state and interfering force have lapsed from biological thought does not prevent environmentalists from inventing them anew. Perhaps these concepts can be provided with some sort of normative content; after all, the normative idea of "human rights" may make sense even if it is not a theoretical underpinning of any empirical science. But environmentalists should not assume that they can rely on some previously articulated scientific conception of "natural."

APPEALS TO NEEDS AND INTERESTS

The version of utilitarianism considered earlier (according to which something merits ethical consideration if it can experience pleasure and/or pain) leaves the environmentalist in the lurch. But there is

an alternative to Bentham's hedonistic utilitarianism that has been thought by some to be a foundation for environmentalism. Preference utilitarianism says that an object's having interests, needs, or preferences gives it ethical status. This doctrine is at the core of Stone's affirmative answer to the title question of his book *Should Trees Have Standing?*[10] "Natural objects *can* communicate their wants (needs) to us, and in ways that are not terribly ambiguous....The lawn tells me that it wants water by a certain dryness of the blades and soil—immediately obvious to the touch—the appearance of bald spots, yellowing, and a lack of springiness after being walked on." And if plants can do this, presumably so can mountain ranges, and endangered species. Preference utilitarianism may thereby seem to grant intrinsic ethical importance to precisely the sorts of objects about which environmentalists have expressed concern.

The problems with this perspective have been detailed by Sagoff.[11] If one does not require of an object that it have a mind for it to have wants or needs, what *is* required for the possession of these ethically relevant properties? Suppose one says that an object needs something if it will cease to exist if it does not get it. Then species, plants, and mountain ranges have needs, but only in the sense that automobiles, garbage dumps, and buildings do too. If everything has needs, the advice to take needs into account in ethical deliberation is empty, unless it is supplemented by some technique for weighting and comparing the needs of different objects. A corporation will go bankrupt unless a highway is built. But the swamp will cease to exist if the highway is built. Perhaps one should take into account all relevant needs, but the question is how to do this in the event that needs conflict.

Although the concept of needs can be provided with a permissive, all-inclusive definition, it is less easy to see how to do this with the concept of want. Why think that a mountain range "wants" to retain its unspoiled appearance, rather than house a new amusement park? Needs are not at issue here, since in either case, the mountain continues to exist. One

might be tempted to think that natural objects like mountains and species have "natural tendencies," and that the concept of want should be liberalized so as to mean that natural objects "want" to persist in their natural states. This Aristotelian view, as I argued in the previous section, simply makes no sense. Granted, a commercially undeveloped mountain will persist in this state, unless it is commercially developed. But it is equally true that a commercially untouched hill will become commercially developed, unless something causes this not to happen. I see no hope for extending the concept of wants to the full range of objects valued by environmentalists.

The same problems emerge when we try to apply the concepts of needs and wants to species. A species may need various resources, in the sense that these are necessary for its continued existence. But what do species want? Do they want to remain stable in numbers, neither growing nor shrinking? Or since most species have gone extinct, perhaps what species really want is to go extinct, and it is human meddlesomeness that frustrates this natural tendency? Preference utilitarianism is no more likely than hedonistic utilitarianism to secure autonomous ethical status for endangered species.

Ehrenfeld describes a related distortion that has been inflicted on the diversity/stability hypothesis in theoretical ecology. If it were true that increasing the diversity of an ecosystem causes it to be more stable, this might encourage the Aristotelian idea that ecosystems have a natural tendency to increase their diversity. The full realization of this tendency— the natural state that is the goal of ecosystems—is the "climax" or "mature" community. Extinction diminishes diversity, so it frustrates ecosystems from attaining their goal. Since the hypothesis that diversity causes stability is now considered controversial (to say the least), this line of thinking will not be very tempting. But even if the diversity/stability hypothesis were true, it would not permit the environmentalist to conclude that ecosystems have an interest in retaining their diversity.

Darwinism has not banished the idea that parts of the natural world are goal-directed systems, but has furnished this idea with a natural mechanism. We properly conceive of organisms (or genes, sometimes) as being in the business of maximizing their chances of survival and reproduction. We describe characteristics as adaptations—as devices that exist for the furtherance of these ends. Natural selection makes this perspective intelligible. But Darwinism is a profoundly individualistic doctrine.[12] Darwinism rejects the idea that species, communities, and ecosystems have adaptations that exist for their own benefit. These higher-level entities are not conceptualized as goal-directed systems; what properties of organization they possess are viewed as artifacts of processes operating at lower levels of organization. An environmentalism based on the idea that the ecosystem is directed toward stability and diversity must find its foundation elsewhere.

GRANTING WHOLES AUTONOMOUS VALUE

A number of environmentalists have asserted that environmental values cannot be grounded in values based on regard for individual welfare. Aldo Leopold wrote in *A Sand County Almanac* that "a thing is right when it tends to preserve the integrity, stability, and beauty of the biotic community. It is wrong when it tends otherwise."[13] Callicott develops this idea at some length, and ascribes to ethical environmentalism the view that "the preciousness of individual deer, *as of any other specimen*, is inversely proportional to the population of the species."[14] In his *Desert Solitaire*, Edward Abbey notes that he would sooner shoot a man than a snake.[15] And Garrett Hardin asserts that human beings injured in wilderness areas ought not to be rescued: making great and spectacular efforts to save the life of an individual "makes sense only when there is a shortage of people. I have not lately heard that there is a shortage of people."[16] The point of view suggested by these quotations is quite clear. It isn't that preserving the integrity of ecosystems has autonomous value, to be taken into account just as the quite distinct value of individual human welfare is. Rather, the idea is that the only value is the holistic one of maintaining ecological balance and diversity. Here we have a view that is just as monolithic as the most single-minded individualism; the difference is that the unit of value is thought to exist at a higher level of organization.

It is hard to know what to say to someone who would save a mosquito, just because it is rare, rather than a human being, if there were a choice. In ethics, as in any other subject, rationally persuading another person requires the existence of shared assumptions. If this monolithic environmentalist view is based on the notion that ecosystems have needs and interests, and that these take total precedence over the rights and interests of individual human beings, then the discussion of the previous sections is relevant. And even supposing that these higher-level entities have needs and wants, what reason is there to suppose that these matter and that the wants and needs of individuals matter not at all? But if this source of defense is jettisoned, and it is merely asserted that only ecosystems have value, with no substantive defense being offered, one must begin by requesting an argument: *why* is ecosystem stability and diversity the only value?

Some environmentalists have seen the individualist bias of utilitarianism as being harmful in ways additional to its impact on our perception of ecological values. Thus, Callicott writes:

> On the level of social organization, the interests of society may not always coincide with the sum of the interests of its parts. Discipline, sacrifice, and individual restraint are often necessary in the social sphere to maintain social integrity as within the bodily organism. A society, indeed, is particularly vulnerable to disintegration when its members become preoccupied totally with their own particular interest, and ignore those distinct and independent interests of the community as a whole. One example, unfortunately, our own society, is altogether too close at hand to be examined with strict academic detachment. The United States

seems to pursue uncritically a social policy of reductive utilitarianism, aimed at promoting the happiness of all its members severally. Each special interest accordingly clamors more loudly to be satisfied while the community as a whole becomes noticeably more and more infirm economically, environmentally, and politically.[17]

Callicott apparently sees the emergence of individualism and alienation from nature as two aspects of the same process. He values "the symbiotic relationship of Stone Age man to the natural environment" and regrets that "civilization has insulated and alienated us from the rigors and challenges of the natural environment. The hidden agenda of the humane ethic," he says, "is the imposition of the anti-natural prophylactic ethos of comfort and soft pleasure on an even wider scale. The land ethic, on the other hand, requires a shrinkage, if at all possible, of the domestic sphere; it rejoices in a recrudescence of the wilderness and a renaissance of tribal cultural experience."[18]

Callicott is right that "strict academic detachment" is difficult here. The reader will have to decide whether the United States currently suffers from too much or too little regard "for the happiness of all its members severally" and whether we should feel nostalgia or pity in contemplating what the Stone Age experience of nature was like.

THE DEMARCATION PROBLEM

Perhaps the most fundamental theoretical problem confronting an environmentalist who wishes to claim that species and ecosystems have autonomous value is what I will call the *problem of demarcation*. Every ethical theory must provide principles that describe which objects matter for their own sakes and which do not. Besides marking the boundary between these two classes by enumerating a set of ethically relevant properties, an ethical theory must say why the properties named, rather than others, are the ones that count. Thus, for example, hedonistic utilitarianism cites the capacity to experience pleasure and/

or pain as the decisive criterion; preference utilitarianism cites the having of preferences (or wants, or interests) as the decisive property. And a Kantian ethical theory will include an individual in the ethical community only if it is capable of rational reflection and autonomy. Not that justifying these various proposed solutions to the demarcation problem is easy; indeed, since this issue is so fundamental, it will be very difficult to justify one proposal as opposed to another. Still, a substantive ethical theory is obliged to try.

Environmentalists, wishing to avoid the allegedly distorting perspective of individualism, frequently want to claim autonomous value for wholes. This may take the form of a monolithic doctrine according to which the only thing that matters is the stability of the ecosystem. Or it may embody a pluralistic outlook according to which ecosystem stability and species preservation have an importance additional to the welfare of individual organisms. But an environmentalist theory shares with all ethical theories an interest in not saying that everything has autonomous value. The reason this position is proscribed is that it makes the adjudication of ethical conflict very difficult indeed. (In addition, it is radically implausible, but we can set that objection to one side.)

Environmentalists, as we have seen, may think of natural objects, like mountains, species, and ecosystems, as mattering for their own sake, but of artificial objects, like highway systems and domesticated animals, as having only instrumental value. If a mountain and a highway are both made of rock, it seems unlikely that the difference between them arises from the fact that mountains have wants, interests, and preferences, but highway systems do not. But perhaps the place to look for the relevant difference is not in their present physical composition, but in the historical fact of how each came into existence. Mountains were created by natural processes, whereas highways are humanly constructed. But once we realize that organisms construct their environments in nature, this contrast begins to cloud. Organisms do not passively reside in an environment

whose properties are independently determined. Organisms transform their environments by physically interacting with them. An anthill is an artifact just as a highway is. Granted, a difference obtains at the level of whether conscious deliberation played a role, but can one take seriously the view that artifacts produced by conscious planning are thereby *less* valuable than ones that arise without the intervention of mentality? As we have noted before, although environmentalists often accuse their critics of failing to think in a biologically realistic way, their use of the distinction between "natural" and "artificial" is just the sort of idea that stands in need of a more realistic biological perspective.

My suspicion is that the distinction between natural and artificial is not the crucial one. On the contrary, certain features of environmental concerns imply that natural objects are exactly on a par with certain artificial ones. Here the intended comparison is not between mountains and highways, but between mountains and works of art. My goal in what follows is not to sketch a substantive conception of what determines the value of objects in these two domains, but to motivate an analogy.

For both natural objects and works of art, our values extend beyond the concerns we have for experiencing pleasure. Most of us value seeing an original painting more than we value seeing a copy, even when we could not tell the difference. When we experience works of art, often what we value is not just the kinds of experiences we have, but, in addition, the connections we usually have with certain real objects. Routley and Routley have made an analogous point about valuing the wilderness experience: a "wilderness experience machine" that caused certain sorts of hallucinations would be no substitute for actually going into the wild.[19] Nor is this fact about our valuation limited to such aesthetic and environmentalist contexts. We love various people in our lives. If a molecule-for-molecule replica of a beloved person were created, you would not love that individual, but would continue to love the individual to whom you actually were historically related. Here again, our attachments are to objects and people as they really are, and not just to the experiences that they facilitate.

Another parallel between environmentalist concerns and aesthetic values concerns the issue of context. Although environmentalists often stress the importance of preserving endangered species, they would not be completely satisfied if an endangered species were preserved by putting a number of specimens in a zoo or in a humanly constructed preserve. What is taken to be important is preserving the species in its natural habitat. This leads to the more holistic position that preserving ecosystems, and not simply preserving certain member species, is of primary importance. Aesthetic concerns often lead in the same direction. It was not merely saving a fresco or an altar piece that motivated art historians after the most recent flood in Florence. Rather, they wanted to save these works of art in their original ("natural") settings. Not just the painting, but the church that housed it; not just the church, but the city itself. The idea of objects residing in a "fitting" environment plays a powerful role in both domains.

Environmentalism and aesthetics both see value in rarity. Of two whales, why should one be more worthy of aid than another, just because one belongs to an endangered species? Here we have the $n + m$ question mentioned [earlier]. As an ethical concern, rarity is difficult to understand. Perhaps this is because our ethical ideas concerning justice and equity (note the word) are saturated with individualism. But in the context of aesthetics, the concept of rarity is far from alien. A work of art may have enhanced value simply because there are very few other works by the same artist, or from the same historical period, or in the same style. It isn't that the price of the item may go up with rarity; I am talking about aesthetic value, not monetary worth. Viewed as valuable aesthetic objects, rare organisms may be valuable because they are rare.

A disanalogy may suggest itself. It may be objected that works of art are of instrumental value only, but that species and ecosystems have intrinsic value. Perhaps it is true, as claimed before, that

our attachment to works of art, to nature, and to our loved ones extends beyond the experiences they allow us to have. But it may be argued that what is valuable in the aesthetic case is always the relation of a valuer to a valued object. When we experience a work of art, the value is not simply in the experience, but in the composite fact that we and the work of art are related in certain ways. This immediately suggests that if there were no valuers in the world, nothing would have value, since such relational facts could no longer obtain. So, to adapt Routley and Routley's "last man argument," it would seem that if an ecological crisis precipitated a collapse of the world system, the last human being (whom we may assume for the purposes of this example to be the last valuer) could set about destroying all works of art, and there would be nothing wrong in this.[20] That is, if aesthetic objects are valuable only in so far as valuers can stand in certain relations to them, then when valuers disappear, so does the possibility of aesthetic value. This would deny, in one sense, that aesthetic objects are intrinsically valuable: it isn't they, in themselves, but rather the relational facts that they are part of, that are valuable.

In contrast, it has been claimed that the "last man" would be wrong to destroy natural objects such as mountains, salt marshes, and species. (So as to avoid confusing the issue by bringing in the welfare of individual organisms, Routley and Routley imagine that destruction and mass extinctions can be caused painlessly, so that there would be nothing wrong about this undertaking from the point of view of the nonhuman organisms involved.) If the last man ought to preserve these natural objects, then these objects appear to have a kind of autonomous value; their value would extend beyond their possible relations to valuers. If all this were true, we would have here a contrast between aesthetic and natural objects, one that implies that natural objects are more valuable than works of art.

Routley and Routley advance the last man argument as if it were decisive in showing that environmental objects such as mountains and salt marshes have autonomous value. I find the example more

puzzling than decisive. But, in the present context, we do not have to decide whether Routley and Routley are right. We only have to decide whether this imagined situation brings out any relevant difference between aesthetic and environmental values. Were the last man to look up on a certain hillside, he would see a striking rock formation next to the ruins of a Greek temple. Long ago the temple was built from some of the very rocks that still stud the slope. Both promontory and temple have a history, and both have been transformed by the biotic and the abiotic environments. I myself find it impossible to advise the last man that the peak matters more than the temple. I do not see a relevant difference. Environmentalists, if they hold that the solution to the problem of demarcation is to be found in the distinction between natural and artificial, will have to find such a distinction. But if environmental values are aesthetic, no difference need be discovered.

Environmentalists may be reluctant to classify their concern as aesthetic. Perhaps they will feel that aesthetic concerns are frivolous. Perhaps they will feel that the aesthetic regard for artifacts that has been made possible by culture is antithetical to a proper regard for wilderness. But such contrasts are illusory. Concern for environmental values does not require a stripping away of the perspective afforded by civilization; to value the wild, one does not have to "become wild" oneself (whatever that may mean). Rather, it is the material comforts of civilization that make possible a serious concern for both aesthetic and environmental values. These are concerns that can become pressing in developed nations in part because the populations of those countries now enjoy a certain substantial level of prosperity. It would be the height of condescension to expect a nation experiencing hunger and chronic disease to be inordinately concerned with the autonomous value of ecosystems or with creating and preserving works of art. Such values are not frivolous, but they can become important to us only after certain fundamental human needs are satisfied. Instead of radically jettisoning individualist ethics, environmentalists may find a more hospitable home for their values in a category of value that has existed all along.

NOTES

I am grateful to Donald Crawford, Jon Moline, Bryan Norton, Robert Stauffer, and Daniel Wikler for useful discussion. I also wish to thank the National Science Foundation and the Graduate School of the University of Wisconsin–Madison for financial support.

1. See, for example, J. B. Callicott, "Animal Liberation: A Triangular Affair," *Environmental Ethics* 2 (1980): 311–38.

2. D. Ehrenfeld, "The Conservation of Non-Resources," *American Scientist* 64 (1976): 648–56; R. M. May, *Stability and Complexity in Model Ecosystems* (Princeton, N.J.: Princeton University Press, 1973).

3. Callicott, "Animal Liberation," 333–34 (my emphasis).

4. P. Shepard, "Animal Rights and Human Rites," *North American Review* (1974): 35–41.

5. C. Darwin, *The Autobiography of Charles Darwin* (1876; London: Collins, 1958), 90.

6. The idea that the natural world is perfect, besides being suspect as an ethical principle, is also controversial as biology. In spite of Callicott's confidence that the amount of pain found in nature is biologically optimal, this adaptationist outlook is now much debated. See, for example, R. Lewontin and S. J. Gould, "The Spandrels of San Marco and the Panglossian Paradigm: A Critique of the Adaptionist Programme," *Proceedings of the Royal Society of London* 205 (1979): 581–98.

7. Callicott, "Animal Liberation," 330.

8. Ibid., 330.

9. Aristotle, *De Anima*, 415a26.

10. C. D. Stone, *Should Trees Have Standing? Toward Legal Rights for Natural Objects* (Los Altos, Calif.: William Kaufmann, 1974), 24.

11. M. Sagoff, "On Preserving the Natural Environment," *Yale Law Review* 84 (1974): 220–24.

12. See G. C. Williams, *Adaptation and Natural Selection* (Princeton, N.J.: Princeton University Press, 1966); and E. Sober, *The Nature of Selection* (Cambridge, Mass.: MIT Press, 1984).

13. A. Leopold, *A Sand County Almanac, and Sketches Here and There* (New York: Oxford University Press, 1949), 224–25.

14. Callicott, "Animal Liberation," 326.

15. E. Abbey, *Desert Solitaire* (New York: Ballantine, 1968), 20.

16. G. Hardin, "The Economics of Wilderness," *Natural History* 78 (1969): 176.

17. Callicott, "Animal Liberation," 323.

18. Ibid., 335.

19. R. Routley and V. Routley, "Human Chauvinism and Environmental Ethics," in *Environmental Philosophy*, Monograph Series 2, ed. D. S. Mannison, M. A. McRobbie, and R. Routley (Canberra: Philosophy Department, Australian National University, 1980), 154.

20. Ibid., 121–22.

SAHOTRA SARKAR

[From] *Biodiversity and Environmental Philosophy*

TRANSFORMATIVE VALUES

Suppose that you are given a ticket to a classical concert.[1] Also suppose that you believe that you do not like classical music but you have never been exposed to it (or, at least, not in a concert setting). You know that you like blues, jazz, rock, and so on, but not classical music. Then the ticket you were given has no demand value for you: you would not have been willing to pay

for it. But suppose that, on a whim, you decide to go to the concert and that you enjoy it immensely. Your horizons have widened. Now you also like classical music.[2] From now, on you will be willing to pay some amount for tickets to classical concerts. Your demand values have thus been transformed by your experience at the concert. Moreover, suppose that you decide on the basis of this experience that you had been narrow-minded about presuming that you did not like certain

genres of music even before being properly exposed to them. From now on, you are willing to pay some amount, though perhaps only a very small amount, for tickets to concerts of every genre of music to which you have not had prior exposure. If this is true, your demand values have been transformed quite significantly. Further, suppose that your experience has been significant enough that you begin to exhibit the same attitude toward many other forms of art, not just toward music. Your demand values have undergone an even more radical transformation.

Experiences such as the one you had in your first classical concert transformed you; because of that, the ticket you were given has "transformative" value, that is, the ability to transform demand values. It has this value in spite of having no demand value. The position advocated here is that biodiversity has value for us because of its ability to transform our demand values. There are at least two related ways, which are not mutually exclusive, in which biodiversity has such a value:

(i) *directly*, when the experience of biodiversity brings about a transformation of our demand values—immediately of features related to biodiversity but sometimes, less immediately, also of other entities. Suppose that you experience a neotropical rainforest—say, in Costa Rica—for the first time. You are overwhelmed by the majesty of the forest, the enclosed canopy above you, the green light filtering through the leaves, and the color and variety of the insects, amphibians, and reptiles around you. From this point onward, you are willing to contribute something for the protection of tropical rainforests. This is an experience that many of those who live in the North have had during the last two decades. For some, such a transformation has occurred through merely vicarious experiences of rainforests, through television, films, or photographs. All such experiences of biodiversity, vicarious or not, have immediate (direct) transformative value in the

sense just indicated. Turning to what were called "less immediate" transformations, suppose that, after your experience of the rainforest, you are outraged that the rainforests of central America have been destroyed only for the sake of creating unsustainable pastures for the production of beef. This cheap beef has decreased the price of hamburgers in the United States by about five cents.[3] You are now more than willing to pay the additional five cents for every hamburger that you consume.[4] Thus some of your demand values, but now for features not immediately associated with biodiversity, have again been directly transformed by your experience of biodiversity.

(ii) *indirectly*, when the experience of biodiversity directly leads to other developments that, in turn, lead to a transformation of the demand values of many features that may or may not themselves be associated with biodiversity. Both Wallace and Darwin came upon the theory of evolution by natural selection through their observations of the biogeographical distributions of related species. For Wallace, the crucial observations were of the distribution of plants and insects in the Amazon basin and, especially, in the Malay archipelago. These observations first led to the formulation of the "Sarawak Law," that every species comes into being in temporal and spatial contiguity with some other species closely resembling it.[5] The Sarawak Law then set the stage for the formulation of the principle of divergence of species from common ancestors, which, in turn, paved the way for the full theory of evolution by natural selection.[6] For Darwin, the crucial observations were those of the geographical variation in the beaks and other morphological features of the finches of the Galápagos. The theory of evolution is perhaps the most spectacular contribution that biodiversity has made to human knowledge. But there are many others, from Wallace's discovery of the biogeographical line named after him (which separates Indian-type and Australian-type fauna in the Malay archipelago, for instance, the placental and marsupial mammals) to the latitudinal gradient of species richness (the steady increase in the number of native species from the poles to the equator). The promise of new insights from biodiversity seems endless.

The important point is that such scientific developments critically alter demand values. The theory of evolution has transformed human values to an unprecedented extent. But there are many less striking examples of scientific developments dependent on biodiversity that have also transformed our demand values. For those developments that even indirectly affect human technological capacities, this is an easily demonstrable point. At first glance, biodiversity studies do not appear to lead to developments of this sort, or at least not as directly as discoveries in molecular biology or in many areas of physics. However, this appearance is misleading. At the very least, knowledge of the bewildering variety of organic life has led to an understanding of the many different ways in which organisms accomplish basic functions such as locomotion, signal detection, and foraging for food. Humans can co-opt many of these for human use, thus again transforming human values. Velcro was designed in a conscious attempt to mimic the grappling hooks of some seeds.[7] Orville and Wilbur Wright are supposed to have carefully observed the flight of vultures to learn the intricacies of drag and lift.[8] Learning the exquisite details of photosynthesis and mimicking it may well be the best solution for our energy needs of the future. If achievements such as these become commonplace, we will probably reconstruct the history of science and technology very differently than we do today: James Watt's achievement in inventing the steam engine will be dwarfed by those of the biomimics of the future. Technology may soon become associated more

with discoveries in biology rather than with invention and construction using inorganic materials. The demand values of many materials will change: if photosynthesis becomes the staple of energy production, fossil fuels will disappear from the marketplace, removing one of our most serious environmental problems. The invention of Velcro presumably changed the demand value of many binding techniques. The advent of airplanes forever changed the demand value of oceanic travel.

Returning to Darwin, Wallace, and the theory of evolution, to a rather remarkable extent evolutionary theory has led us to recalibrate our concept of what it is to be human. Consequently, this is a case where it can plausibly be argued that a scientific development has had a transformative capacity beyond the power of money and thus beyond what can be captured by any demand value. Because of its contribution to evolutionary biology, observing and understanding biodiversity has at least indirectly transformed all human values, including demand values, more radically than any other development in human history. We no longer treat primates in the same way that we treat more distant animals. Most of us are less inclined to contribute lavishly to religious institutions because of a fear of the "Almighty." Wallace and Darwin have probably contributed more to the decline of the demand value of religion than any other individuals in history. Lesser developments than the theory of evolution are equally important. Wallace's biogeography helped to establish the theory of continental drift.[9] Even the destruction of biodiversity may lead to an understanding of the many services that natural ecosystems perform, as we see such services disappear and begin to model that process. (In this case, even the destruction of biodiversity has in a sense some positive transformative value, but only because it had so far been conserved. Since the knowledge obtained could almost certainly have been obtained in other ways, the positive transformative value of continued conservation of biodiversity far outweighs that of its destruction.)

Biodiversity is thus signally valuable because of its intellectual interest. A proactive role in its conservation is required because it is irreplaceable—extinctions are forever. Arguments from intellectual interest may seem unconvincing to those who demand immediate pragmatic virtues in the narrowest sense of immediate utility. This attitude is typical in the United States, where, for instance, the accepted legal defense of a controversial sexually explicit work of art is to claim that it has redeeming social value, not that it is, after all, a work of art. Nevertheless, the best argument for the conservation of biodiversity remains its intellectual promise. Narrow pragmatism would lead to a devaluation not just of biodiversity but of the entire scientific enterprise, if not of every intellectual and aesthetic aspect of human culture.[10] We should not be embarrassed to defend the importance of our intellectual interests and pursuits. All the comforts of life that are traded in the marketplace are ultimately the products of human intellectual life, of our culture, and very often—but obviously not always—of that part of our intellectual culture that we identify as science. Thus even narrow pragmatism dictates the attribution of a high value to intellectual life and science; without them, pragmatism would be useless. Janzen was correct to note that biologists have a *professional* imperative to conserve biodiversity. Nonbiologists share that imperative to the extent that they value biology as a field of endeavor that should be pursued in any society that can afford it. Moreover, there is nothing that says that nonbiologists cannot share the pleasure of the knowledge that the professional pursuit of biology generates.[11] The world is interesting. We enjoy knowing about it, though some of us may cherish this knowledge more than others. Finally, for many individuals, not limited to professional scientists, scientific knowledge of the world, the sense that we are beginning to understand our surroundings, deeply affects our most basic attitudes toward all aspects of life.[12] Science has a cultural value beyond the technology that it provides.[13]

Finally, it should be emphasized again that both these ways of attributing transformative value do not necessarily deny that the value of biodiversity may be intrinsic$_1$. Both of them rely as much on the relations that hold between internal features of the components of biodiversity as they do on the particular relations that hold between these entities and external human observers. This should not really come as a surprise—there is no contradiction between some entity's simultaneously having anthropocentric value and intrinsic$_1$ value.

REFERENCES

Benyus, J. M. 1997. *Biomimicry*. New York: William Morrow.

Caufield, C. 1984. *In the Rainforest: Report from a Strange, Beautiful, Imperiled World*. Chicago: University of Chicago Press.

Elliot, R. 2001. "Normative Ethics." In Jamieson, D., ed., *A Companion to Environmental Philosophy*. Malden, UK: Blackwell, pp. 175–191.

George, W. 1981. "Wallace and His Line." In Whitmore, T. C., ed., *Wallace's Line and Plate Tectonics*. Oxford: Clarendon Press, pp. 3–8.

Norton, B. G. 1987. *Why Preserve Natural Variety?* Princeton, NJ: Princeton University Press.

O'Neill, J. 1993. *Ecology, Policy and Politics: Human Well-Being and the Natural World*. London: Routledge.

O'Neill, J. 2001. "Meta-ethics." In Jamieson, D., ed., *A Companion to Environmental Philosophy*. Malden, MA: Blackwell, pp. 163–176.

Voss, J., and Sarkar, S. 2003. "Depictions as Surrogates for Places: From Wallace's Biogeography to Koch's Dioramas." *Philosophy & Geography* **6**: 60–81.

Wallace, A. R. 1855. "On the Law Which Has Regulated the Introduction of New Species." *Annals and Magazine of Natural History* **16**: 184–196.

Wallace, A. R. 1858. "On the Tendency of Varieties to Depart Indefinitely from the Original Type." *Journal of the Proceedings of the Linnaean Society. Zoology* **3**: 53–62.

NOTES

1. This example is essentially due to Norton (1987), pp. 10–11.

2. For the sake of this argument, it does not matter how much you like it, nor does it matter whether you like it as much as other genres of music.

3. See Caufield (1984), p. 109, for this figure, which is based on United States government estimates.

4. Note that this argument is different from one for, say, the consumption of organically grown food if, in the latter case, the concern is for our own health, not for that of some other entity. If, though, the rejection of nonorganically grown food is based on a concern for the health of future generations—ensuring that soil is not "polluted" with fertilizers—then the situation is closer to the one discussed in the text. Finally, suppose that we decide not to consume a certain good because it is produced by child or slave labor. That situation is similar to the one discussed in the text.

5. Wallace (1855). Contiguity suggests that the newer species arose by transformation of older ones; in this way, this law was an important step toward the theory of evolution.

6. Wallace (1858) is the first full statement of the theory of evolution by natural selection. Though Darwin is believed to have arrived at the same theory earlier, it remained unpublished.

7. See Benyus (1997), p. 4; she provides a systematic and highly readable account of such biomimicry.

8. See Benyus (1997), p. 8, for this example, which may be apocryphal.

9. See George (1981) for a history; see Voss and Sarkar (2003) for a résumé of Wallace's biogeography.

10. This, as Bryan G. Norton (personal communication) has pointed out, is a nonphilosophical use of "pragmatism." Note that Norton's (1987) account of transformative value emphasizes the psychological or spiritual transformative power of biodiversity over its scientific value. However, Norton's discussion is more geared toward the preservation of nature in general (including wilderness in addition to biodiversity) than toward, specifically, biodiversity.

11. Obviously, the same argument can be made for every other aspect of the scientific enterprise.

12. There is an interesting and obvious connection between such an appeal to transformative values and what O'Neill (1993, 2001) calls a traditional Aristotelian account: "The flourishing of many other living things ought to be promoted because they are constitutive of our flourishing" (2001, p. 170).

13. Thus, appreciating the transformative value of biodiversity in individual human beings can be part of a perfectionist (including a virtue-based) ethics of biodiversity conservation. Of course, perfectionism typically puts as much emphasis on nonintellectual features as on intellectual ones. See also Elliot (2001).

HOLMES ROLSTON III

Biodiversity

When animals, birds, and plants vanish from the landscape, this raises public concern. Initially, the focus was on endangered species, which are still central, but in recent years attention has widened to other levels of biodiversity, such as types of ecosystems at a regional level, or genetic diversity at the microbiological level. Species are a more evident, mid-range, natural kind, which can be located in breeding populations. The US Congress, deploring the lack of "adequate concern (for) and conservation (of)" species, passed the Endangered Species Act (US Congress 1973, Sec. 2(a)(1)). The United Nations has negotiated a Biodiversity Convention, signed by more than 100 nations.

Such concern is unfamiliar to traditional philosophical analysis. John Rawls, for example, advocating his most perceptive contemporary theory of justice, admits that in his theory "no account is given of right conduct in regard to animals and the rest of nature." Nevertheless, he claims, "Certainly…the destruction of a whole species can be a great evil" (Rawls 1971, p. 512). But one will search past philosophical literature in vain for much help giving reasons why. This [essay] first asks how far classical humanistic ethics can be applied to conserve biodiversity and then turns to explore novel problems in emerging human responsibilities of caring for endangered species.

The legislation to protect endangered species has often been used to protect as well the ecosystems of which they are part (such as the old growth forests of the Pacific Northwest, containing the spotted owl). An ecosystems approach is increasingly regarded as more efficient than a single-species approach. DNA sequencing and new possibilities in genetic technology have intensified concern for saving genetic diversity. At the same time, saving every genetic variant is evidently impossible even if it were desirable. Some recent studies find more diversity among microbes than among all the higher forms of life. Evaluating this spectrum of diversity, from genes through species to ecosystems to the biosphere, is one of the challenges in environmental ethics.

The implications of the Endangered Species Act have been unfolding over the last quarter century. The Act was passed mostly with the charismatic megafauna in mind (grizzly bears and whooping cranes), though the Act has always permitted listing less glamorous species. On rare inland dunes in California, the Delhi Sands Flower-loving Fly (*Rhaphiomidas terminatus abdominalis*), a huge and unusual fly, on the US endangered species list, is said (in the rhetoric of debate at least) to stand in the way of industrial development that would create 20,000 jobs, although the fly only needs about 300 acres of habitat (Booth 1997).

In later amendments Congress has increasingly extended protection to plants. Court decisions have protected habitat as essential to the survival of species. When the Act is applied to private lands, this has raised the "takings" issue, with landowners claiming that compensation is due, and environmentalists replying the rights to land do not include the right to extinguish species.

Ethics is a matter of duty, in classical categories, or of appropriate caring, as some now prefer to say. Whether humans have duties to endangered species is a significant theoretical and an urgent practical question. Why ought we to care? In the larger picture, the question of duties to ecosystems will arise. It would seem awkward to ask about duties to genes, although proper to ask why we should care about preserving genetic diversity. We will focus on the species question, as this opens up these philosophical issues.

Few persons doubt that humans have some obligations concerning endangered species, because persons are helped or hurt by the condition of their environment, which includes a wealth of wild species. Taking or jeopardizing listed endangered species is illegal and, many think, immoral. But these might be all obligations to persons who are benefited or harmed by species as resources. Is there a human duty directly to species? An answer is vital to the more comprehensive question of the conservation of biodiversity.

SAVING SPECIES FOR PEOPLE

A rationale for saving species that centers on their worth to humans is anthropocentric, where species have instrumental values. A rationale that includes their intrinsic and ecosystemic values, in addition to or independently of persons, is naturalistic, sometimes said to be biocentric. "The preservation of species," by the usual humanistic utilitarian account, reported by Stuart Hampshire, is "to be aimed at and commended only in so far as human beings are, or will be emotionally and sentimentally interested" (Hampshire 1972, pp. 3–4).

This includes duties to future humans. Joel Feinberg says, "We do have duties to protect threatened species, not duties to the species themselves as such, but rather duties to future human beings, duties derived from our housekeeping role as temporary inhabitants of this planet" (Feinberg 1974, p. 56). Persons have a strong duty not to harm others (a duty of non-maleficence) and a weaker, though important, duty to help others (a duty of beneficence).

Many endangered species—which ones we may not now know—are expected to have agricultural, industrial, and medical benefits. Loss of the wild stocks of the cultivars leaves humans genetically vulnerable, so it is prudent to save the native materials. In an interesting example, an obscure Yellowstone thermophilic microbe, *Thermophus aquaticus*, was discovered to supply a heat-stable enzyme, which can be used to drive the polymerase chain reaction (PCR), used in a revolutionary gene-copying technique. The rights to the process sold in 1991 for $300 million, and the process is now earning $100 million a year.

According to this reasoning, the protection of nature is ultimately for the purpose of its enlightened exploitation. Norman Myers urges "conserving our global stock" (Myers 1979). But critics reply that examples of high economic value obtained from rare species are anomalous and that, on statistical average, most endangered species have little probability of significant economic value. Debates have also followed about who owns wild species, if anyone, or who owns rights to them or to products derived from them. These issues are especially problematic in many relatively species-rich and technologically poor developing nations, when wealthier nations come prospecting, or when development is curtailed to save biodiversity.

Where not directly useful, wild species may be indirectly important for the roles they play in ecosystems. They are "rivets" in the airplane, the earthship in which we humans are flying (Ehrlich and Ehrlich 1981). The loss of a few species may have no evident results now, but the loss of many species imperils the resilience and stability of the ecosystems on which humans depend. The danger increases exponentially with subtractions from the ecosystem, a slippery slope into serious troubles. Even species that have no obvious or current direct value to humans are part of the biodiversity that keeps ecosystems healthy. One team of economists estimates the value of the world's ecosystem services, though largely off the market, to be in the range of $16–54 trillion per year, compared to the global gross national product total of $18 trillion per year (Costanza et al. 1997). Even those doubtful of the numbers concede that the aggregate benefits are huge.

Some benefits are less tangible. Species that are too rare to play roles in ecosystems can have recreational and aesthetic value. Biodiversity enriches the landscapes on which humans reside; people enjoy variety in wildlife and wildflowers. Those who see bears or wolves in Yellowstone report that this is the highlight of their experience. The aesthetic experience of nature differs importantly from that of artworks; seeing whooping cranes in flight is unlike visiting an art museum. The wealth of species is aesthetic, an amenity value, as much as it is economic, a commodity value. At least in developed nations, where consumer goods are not in short supply but opportunities to experience nature are diminishing, it seems probable that, in the decades ahead, the quality of life will decline in proportion to the loss of biotic diversity.

Species can be curiosities. The rare species fascinate enthusiastic naturalists and are often key scientific study species. They may serve as indicators of ecosystem health. They can be clues to understanding natural history. Destroying species is like tearing pages out of an unread book, written in a language humans hardly know how to read, about the place where we live. This is the Rosetta Stone argument (named after the obelisk found at Rosetta in Egypt in 1799, which enabled the deciphering of forgotten languages of the ancient past). Humans need insight into the full text of natural history. They need to understand the evolving world in which they are placed.

Following this logic, humans do not have duties to the book, the stone, or the species, but to themselves—duties both of prudence and education. Such anthropogenic reasons are pragmatic and impressive. They are also moral, since persons are benefited or harmed.

AN ETHICS FOR SPECIES?

Can all duties concerning species be analyzed as duties to persons? Many endangered species have no resource value, nor are they particularly important for the other reasons given above. Beggar's ticks, with their stick-tight seeds, are a common nuisance weed through much of the United States. However, one species, the tidal shore beggar's tick (*Bidens bidentoides*), which differs little from the others in appearance, is increasingly endangered. It seems unlikely that it is either a rivet or a potential resource. Its extinction might be good riddance.

Are there completely worthless species? If so, is there any reason or duty to save them? A primary environmental ethics answer is that species are good in their own right, whether or not they are any good for humans. The duties-to-persons-only line of argument leaves deeper reasons untouched. Those calling for a more objective, or biocentric, environmental ethics argue that the deeper problem with the anthropocentric rationale is that its justifications are submoral and fundamentally exploitive and self-serving, even if subtly so. This is not true intraspecifically among humans, when out of a sense of duty an individual defers to the values of fellow humans. But it is true interspecifically, since, under this rationale, *Homo sapiens* treats all other species as rivets, resources, study materials, or entertainments.

Ethics has always been about partners with entwined destinies. But it has never been very convincing when pleaded as enlightened self-interest (I ought always to act in my best self-interest), including class self-interest (we ought always to act in our group self-interest). This is true even though ethics makes a place for self-interest (myself and my group being treated justly, fairly). Ethics brings benefits to those who are ethical; it conveys mutual advantage;

it is good for people. But it also enlarges spheres of care and concern. To value all other species in our human group's self-interest is rather like a nation arguing all its foreign policy in terms of national self-interest. Neither seems fully moral.

Nevertheless, those who try to articulate a deeper environmental ethic often get lost in unfamiliar territory. Natural kinds, if that is what species are, are obscure objects of concern. Species, as such, cannot be directly helped or hurt, though individual tokens of the species type can be. Species, as such, don't care, though individual animals can care. Species require habitats, embedded in ecosystems that evolve and change. Of the species that have inhabited earth, 98 percent are extinct, replaced by other species. Nature doesn't care, so why should we?

All the familiar moral landmarks of classical ethics seem to be gone. One has moved beyond caring about humans, or culture, or moral agents, or individual animals that are close kin, or can suffer, or experience anything, or are sentient. Species are not valuers with preferences that can be satisfied or frustrated. It seems odd to say that species have rights. Tom Regan says, for example, "The rights view is a view about the moral rights of individuals, and the rights view does not recognize the moral rights of species to anything, including survival" (Regan 1983, p. 359).

It seems odd to say that species need our sympathy, or that we should consider their point of view. Nor is it clear that species have interests. Nicholas Rescher says:

> Moral obligation is thus always interest-oriented. But only individuals can be said to have interests; one only has moral obligations to particular individuals or particular groups thereof. Accordingly, the duty to save a species is not a matter of moral duty toward it, because moral duties are only oriented to individuals. A species as such is the wrong sort of target for a moral obligation. (Rescher 1980, p. 83)

So it is hard to figure concern for species within the coordinates of prevailing ethical systems.

In fact, ethics and biology have had uncertain relations. An often-heard argument forbids moving from what *is* the case (a species exists) to what *ought to be* (a species ought to exist); any who do so commit, it is alleged, the naturalistic fallacy. On the other hand, if species are of objective value, and if humans encounter and jeopardize such value, it would seem that humans ought not to destroy values in nature, not at least without overriding justification producing greater value. A species is of *value*—this may be the intermediate premise. We might make a humanistic mistake if we arrogantly take value to lie exclusively in the satisfaction of our human preferences. What is at jeopardy and what are our duties?

THE THREAT OF EXTINCTION

Although projections vary, reliable estimates are that about 20 percent of earth's species may be lost within a few decades, if present trends go unreversed. These losses will be about evenly distributed through major groups of plants and animals in both developed and developing nations, although the most intense concerns are in tropical forests (Wilson 1992; Ehrlich and Ehrlich 1981). At least 500 species, subspecies, and varieties of fauna have been lost in the United States since 1600. The natural rate would have been about ten. Islands have been a special concern. In Hawaii, of 68 species of birds unique to the islands, 41 are extinct or virtually so. Half the 2,200 native plants are endangered or threatened. Covering all states, a candidate list of US plants contains more than 2,000 taxa considered to be endangered, threatened, or of concern. A candidate list of animals contains about 1,800 entries. Humans approach, and, in places, have even exceeded the catastrophic rates of natural extinction spasms of the geological past.

QUESTIONS OF FACT: WHAT ARE SPECIES?

There are problems at two levels: one is about facts (a scientific issue—about species), one is about values (an ethical issue—involving duties). There are several differing concepts of species within biology.

By some accounts any species concept is arbitrary, conventional—a mapping device that is only theoretical. Darwin wrote, "I look at the term species, as one arbitrarily given for the sake of convenience to a set of individuals closely resembling each other" (Darwin 1968 [1872], p. 108). Is there enough factual reality in species to base duty there?

No one doubts that individual organisms exist, but are species discovered? Or made up? Indeed, do species exist at all? Systematists regularly revise species designations and routinely put after a species the name of the "author" who, they say, "erected" the taxon. If a species is only a category or class, boundary lines may be arbitrarily drawn, and the species is nothing more than an artifact of the classifier's thoughts and aims. Some natural properties are used—reproductive structures, bones, teeth, or perhaps ancestry, or genes, or ecological roles. But which properties are selected and where the lines are drawn are decisions that vary with systematists.

Botanists are divided whether *Iliamna remota*, the Kankakee mallow in Illinois, and *Iliamna corei* in Virginia, which are both rare, are distinct species. Perhaps all that exists objectively in the world are the individual mallow plants; whether there are two species or one is a fuss about which label to use. A species is some kind of fiction, like a center of gravity or a statistical average. Almost no one proposes duties to genera, families, orders, phyla; biologists concede that these do not exist in nature, even though we may think that two species in different orders represent more biodiversity, with more genetic distance between them, than two in the same genus. If this approach is pressed, species can become something like the lines of longitude and latitude, or like map contour lines, or time of day, or dates on a calendar. Sometimes endangered species designations have altered when systematists decided to lump or split previous groupings.

A debate has continued over whether the red wolf is a species or a long-established hybrid of the gray wolf and the coyote. The distinction affects the considerable efforts to save this wolf in the southeastern United States. The tuatara is a large, iguana-like

reptile with a third eye in the center of its head, which survives on a few islands off the coast of New Zealand. Because systematists earlier recognized one species rather than the three now claimed, tuataras have received inadequate protection, and one of the three species is now extinct. Depending on the degree to which species are or are not artifacts of those doing the taxonomy, duties to save them can seem more convincing or unconvincing.

There are four main concepts of species: (1) morphological, asking whether organisms have the same anatomy and functions; (2) biological (so-called), asking whether organisms can interbreed; (3) evolutionary, asking whether organisms have the same lineage historically; and (4) genetic, asking whether they have a common genome. But these concepts are not mutually exclusive; organisms that have enough common ancestry will have a similar morphology and function; they will be able to interbreed, and they can do so because they have similar genomes.

All these concepts combine for a more realist account. A species is a living historical form (Latin: *species*), propagated in individual organisms, which flows dynamically over generations. Species are dynamic natural kinds, historically particular lineages. A species is a coherent, ongoing natural kind expressed in organisms that interbreed because that kind is encoded in gene flow, the genes determining the organism's morphology and functions, the kind shaped by its environment. In one sense, the genes are what is reproduced, if one chooses to focus on that level; but in another sense the natural kind (species) is what is reproduced. There is genome producing genome producing genome, with genetic variation. There is also tiger producing tiger producing tiger. The coding is at the genetic level; the coping is at the native range level of organisms with adapted fit in ecosystems. A gene is an information-bit about how the species makes its way through the world.

In this sense, species are objectively there as living processes in the evolutionary ecosystem—found, not made by taxonomists. Species are real

historical entities, interbreeding populations. By contrast, families, orders, and genera are not levels where biological reproduction takes place. So far from being arbitrary, species are the real evolutionary units of biodiversity. This claim—that there are specific forms of life historically maintained in their environments over time—is not fictional, but, rather, seems as certain as anything else we believe about the empirical world, even though at times scientists revise the theories and taxa with which they map these forms.

Species are more like mountains and rivers, phenomena that are objectively there to be mapped. The edges of such natural kinds will sometimes be fuzzy, to some extent discretionary. We can expect that one species will modify into another over evolutionary time, often gradually, sometimes more quickly. But it does not follow from the fact that speciation is sometimes in progress that species are merely made up, instead of found as evolutionary lines articulated into diverse forms, each with its more or less distinct integrity, breeding population, gene pool, and role in its ecosystem. It is quite objective to claim that evolutionary lines are articulated into diverse kinds of life. What taxonomists do, or should do, is "carve nature at the joints" (Plato).

G. G. Simpson concludes, "An evolutionary species is a lineage (an ancestral-descendant sequence of populations) evolving separately from others and with its own unitary evolutionary role and tendencies" (1961, p. 153). Niles Eldredge and Joel Cracraft insist, with emphasis, that species are *"discrete entities in time as well as space"* (1980, p. 92). The various criteria for defining species (recent descent, reproductive isolation, morphology, distinct gene pool) come together at least in providing evidence that species are really there. What survives for a few months, years, or decades is the individual animal or plant, what survives for millennia is the kind as a lineage. Life is something passing through the individual as much as something it possesses on its own. Even a species defends itself; that is one way to interpret reproduction. The individual organism resists death; the species resists extinction through

reproduction with variation. At both levels, biological identity is conserved over time.

QUESTIONS OF DUTY: OUGHT SPECIES BE SAVED?

Why ought species to be protected? One reply is that nature is a kind of wonderland. Humans ought to preserve an environment adequate to match their capacity to wonder. But nature as a wonderland introduces the question whether preserving resources for wonder is not better seen as preserving a remarkable natural history that has objective worth. Valuing speciation directly, however, seems to attach value to the evolutionary process (the wonderland), not merely to subjective experiences that arise when humans reflect over it (the wonder).

One might say that humans of decent character will refrain from needless destruction of all kinds. Vandals destroying art objects do not so much hurt statues as do they cheapen their own character. By this account, the duty to save endangered species is really a matter of cultivating human excellences. It is philistine to destroy species carelessly. It is uncalled for. But such a prohibition seems to depend on some value in the species as such, for there need be no prohibition against destroying a valueless thing. Why are such insensitive actions "uncalled for" unless there is something in the species itself that "calls for" a more appropriate attitude? If the excellence of character really comes from appreciating something wonderful, then why not attach value to this other? It seems unexcellent—cheap and philistine—to say that excellence of human character is what we are after. One ought to want virtue in the human beholder that recognizes value in the endangered species. Excellence of human character does indeed result, but let the human virtue come tributary to value found in nature. An enriched humanity results, with values in the species and values in persons compounded—but only if the loci of value are not confounded.

A naturalistic account values species, speciation, and the cumulative biodiversity intrinsically. Humans ought to respect these dynamic life forms preserved in historical lines. It is not *form* (species) as mere morphology, but the *formative* (speciating) process that humans ought to preserve, although the process cannot be preserved without some of its products, and the products (species) are valuable as results of the creative process. An ethic about species sees that the species is a bigger event than the individual organism. Biological conservation goes on at this level too; and in a sense this level is more appropriate for moral concern, since the species with its populations is a comprehensive evolutionary unit.

A consideration of species is both revealing and challenging because it offers a biologically based counterexample to the focus on individuals—typically sentient animals and usually individual persons—that has been so characteristic in western ethics. As evolution takes place in ecosystems, it is not mere individuality that counts. The individual represents (re-presents) a species in each new generation. It is a token of a type, and the type is more important than the token. A biological identity—a kind of value—is here defended. The achievement resides in the dynamic form; the individual inherits this, exemplifies it, and passes it on. The evolutionary history that the particular individual has is something passing through it during its life, passed to it and passed on during reproduction, as much as something it intrinsically possesses. Having a biological identity reasserted genetically over time is as true of the species as of the individual. That identity includes its evolutionary achievements, the know-how to perpetuate that kind in the midst of its perpetual perishing, its location as an adapted fit in its ecosystem, filling its niche in the biotic community; respecting this identity generates duties to species.

When a rhododendron plant dies, another one replaces it. But when *Rhododendron chapmanii*—an endangered species in the US Southeast—goes extinct, the species terminates forever. Death of a

token is radically different from death of a type; death of an individual different from death of an entire lineage. The deaths of individual rhododendrons in perennial turnover are even necessary if the species is to persist. Seeds are dispersed and replacement rhododendrons grow elsewhere in the pinewood forests, as landscapes change or succession shifts. Latercoming replacements, mutants as well as replacements, are selected for or against in a stable or changing environment. Individuals improve in fitness and the species adapts to an altering climate or competitive pressures. Tracking its environment over time, the species is conserved, modified, and continues on.

With extinction, this stops. Extinction shuts down the generative processes, a kind of superkilling. This kills forms (*species*)—not just individuals. This kills "essences" beyond "existences," collectively, not just distributively. To kill a particular plant is to stop a life of a few years, while other lives of such kind continue unabated, and the possibilities for the future are unaffected; to superkill a particular species is to shut down a story of many millennia, and leave no future possibilities.

A species lacks moral agency, reflective self-awareness, sentience, or organic individuality. Some are tempted to say that specific-level processes cannot count morally. But each ongoing species defends a form of life, and these forms are, on the whole, good kinds. Such speciation has achieved all the planetary richness of life. Virtually all ethicists say that in *Homo sapiens* one species has appeared that not only exists but ought to continue to exist. Everyone concerned for children, grandchildren, and future generations believes that. A naturalistic ethic refuses to say this exclusively of a late-coming, highly developed form and asks whether this duty ought not to extend more broadly to the other species—though not with equal intensity over them all, in view of varied levels of development.

The wrong that humans are doing, or are allowing to happen through carelessness, is stopping the historical gene flow in which the vitality of life is laid, which, viewed at another level, is the same as the flow of natural kinds, which is the drama of biodiversity. A shutdown of the life stream is the most destructive event possible. The duty to species can be overridden, for example with pests or disease organisms. But a prima facie duty stands nevertheless.

The question is not: What is this rare plant or animal good for? But: What good is here? Not: Is this species good for my kind, *Homo sapiens*. But: Is *Rhododendron chapmanii* a good of its kind, a good kind? To care directly about a plant or animal species is to be quite non-anthropocentric and objective about botanical and zoological processes that take place independently of human preferences.

Never before has this level of question been faced, which is why philosophical ethicists have been stuttering about it. Previously, humans did not have much power to cause extinctions, or knowledge about what they were inadvertently doing. But today humans have more understanding than ever of the natural world they inhabit, of the speciating processes, more predictive power to foresee the intended and unintended results of their actions, and more power to reverse the undesirable consequences. The duties that such power and vision generate no longer attach simply to individuals or persons but are emerging duties to specific forms of life.

A consideration of species strains any ethic fixed on individual organisms, much less on sentience or persons. But the resulting ethic can be biologically sounder, though it revises what was formerly thought logically permissible or ethically binding. When ethics is informed by this kind of biology, it is appropriate to attach duty dynamically to the specific form of life. The species line is the more fundamental living system, the whole, of which individual organisms are the essential parts. The appropriate survival unit is the appropriate level of moral concern. Concern for biodiversity will always, by this account, be concern centrally for species. Saving endangered species can even, at times, take priority over the preferences of persons—or even the lives of

persons, as with the shoot-to-kill policies for poachers of elephants and rhinoceros (Rolston 1996).

SPECIES IN ECOSYSTEMS

A species is what it is inseparably from the environmental niche into which it fits. Habitats are essential to species, and an endangered species often means an endangered habitat. The species and the community are complementary goods in synthesis, parallel to, but a level above, the way the species and individual organisms have distinguishable but entwined goods. From this viewpoint, it is not preservation of *species* that we wish, but the preservation of *species in the system*. It is not merely *what* they are, but *where* they are that humans must value correctly. Appropriate concern for species is impossible without concern for the diverse ecosystems that they inhabit.

This limits the otherwise important role that zoos and botanical gardens can play in conservation. They can provide research, a refuge for species, breeding programs, aid in public education, and so forth; but they cannot simulate the ongoing dynamism of gene flow over time under the selection pressures in a wild biome. They only lock up a collection of individuals; they amputate the species from its habitat. The species can only be preserved *in situ*; the species ought to be preserved *in situ*. That does move from scientific facts to ethical duties, but what ought to be has to be based on what can be.

Neither individual nor species stands alone; both are embedded in an ecosystem. Every species came to be what it is where it is, shaped as an adaptive fit. (A problem with exotic species, introduced by humans, is often that they are not good fits in their alien ecosystems.) The product, a species, is the outcome of entwined genetic and ecological processes; the generative impulse springs from the gene pool, defended by information coded there. But the whole population or species survives when selection by natural forces tests the member individuals for their adapted fitness in the environmental niche the species occupies.

In an ethic of endangered species, one ought to admire the evolutionary or creative process as much as the product, since these two are interwined. A species is an ongoing historical event, not just a collection of individuals produced. This involves regular species turnover when a species becomes unfit in its habitat, goes extinct, or tracks a changing environment until transformed into something else. On evolutionary timescales, species too are ephemeral. But the speciating process is not. Persisting through vicissitudes for two and a half billion years, speciation is about as long-continuing as anything on earth can be.

NATURAL AND HUMAN-CAUSED EXTINCTIONS

It might seem that for humans to terminate species now and again is quite natural. Species go extinct all the time in natural history. But there are important theoretical and practical differences between natural and anthropogenic (human-caused) extinctions. In natural extinction, a species dies out when it has become unfit in habitat, and other existing or novel species appear in its place. Such extinction is normal turnover in ongoing speciation. Though harmful to a species, extinction in nature seldom impoverishes the system. It is rather the key to tomorrow. The species is employed in, but abandoned to, the larger historical evolution of life.

By contrast, artificial extinction typically shuts down future evolution because it shuts down speciating processes dependent on those species. One opens doors, the other closes them. Humans generate and regenerate nothing; they only dead-end these lines. Relevant differences make the two as morally distinct as death by natural causes is from murder. Anthropogenic extinction differs from evolutionary extinction in that hundreds of thousands of species will perish because of culturally altered

environments that are radically different from the spontaneous environments in which such species evolved and in which they sometimes go extinct. In natural extinction, nature takes away life when it has become unfit in a habitat, or when the habitat alters, and typically supplies other life in its place. Natural extinction occurs with transformation, either of the extinct line or related or competing lines. Artificial extinction is without issue.

From this perspective, humans have no duty to preserve species from natural extinctions, although they might have a duty to other humans to save such species as resources or museum pieces. Some have claimed that the Uncompahgre fritillary (*Boloria acrocnema*), known from two alpine mountain peaks in Colorado, is going extinct naturally, and that, therefore, no effort should be made to save it. (Others claim that livestock are a decisive factor.) No species has a "right to life" apart from the continued existence of the ecosystem with which it is able to cofit. But humans do have a duty to avoid artificial extinction.

Over evolutionary time, though extinguishing species, nature has provided new species at a higher rate than the extinction rate; hence the accumulated global biodiversity. There have been infrequent catastrophic extinction events, anomalies in the record, each succeeded by a recovery of previous diversity. Typically, however, the biological processes that characterize earth are prolific. Uninterrupted by accident, or even interrupted so, they have rather steadily increased the numbers of species.

An ethicist has to be circumspect. An argument might commit what logicians call the genetic fallacy to suppose that present value depended upon origins. Species judged today to have intrinsic value might have arisen anciently and anomalously from a valueless context, akin to the way in which life arose mysteriously from nonliving materials. But in an ecosystem, what a thing is differentiates poorly from the generating and sustaining matrix. The individual and the species have what value they have to some extent inevitably in the context of the forces that beget them. There is something awesome about an earth that begins with zero and runs up toward five to ten million species in several billion years, setbacks notwithstanding. Were the moral species, *Homo sapiens*, to conserve all Earth's species merely as resources for human preference satisfaction, we would not yet know the truth about what we ought to do in biological conservation.

RESPECT FOR LIFE: BIODIVERSITY AND RARITY

Duties to endangered species will be especially concerned with a respect for rare life. Such respect must ask about the role of rarity in generating respect. Rarity is not, as such, an intrinsically valuable property in fauna and flora, or in human experiences (even though people take an interest in things just because they are rare). Certain diseases are rare, and people are glad of it. Monsters and other sports of nature, such as albinos, are rare, and of no particular intrinsic value for their rarity, curiosities though they sometimes become. Indeed, if a species is naturally rare, that initially suggests its insignificance in an ecosystem. Rarity is no automatic cause for respect. Nevertheless, something about the rarity of endangered species heightens the element of respect, and accompanying duty.

Naturally rare species, as much as common or frequent species, signify exuberance in nature; they add to the biodiversity. A rare species may be barely hanging on, surviving by mere luck. But a rare species may be quite competent in its niche, not at all nearing extinction if left on its own; it is only facing extinction when made artificially more rare by human disruptions. The rare flower is a botanical achievement, a bit of brilliance, an ecological problem resolved, an evolutionary threshold crossed. The locally endemic species, perhaps one specialized for an unusual habitat, represents a rare discovery in nature, before it provides a rare human adventure in finding it.

Naturally rare species—if one insists on a restricted evolutionary theory—are random accidents (as in some sense also are the common ones), resulting from a cumulation of mutations. But this mutational fertility generates creativity, and, equally by the theory, surviving species must be more or less satisfactory fits in their environments. Sometimes they live on the cutting edge of exploratory probing; sometimes they are relics of the past. Either way they offer promise and memory of an inventive natural history. Life is a many-splendored thing; extinction of the rare dims this luster. From this arises the respect that generates a duty to save rare lives.

A six-year study sponsored by the National Science Foundation surveyed environmental attitudes in the general public. The survey tested support for the claim: "Our obligation to preserve nature isn't just a responsibility to other people but to the environment itself"; and, perhaps surprisingly, found agreeing not only 97 percent of Earth First! members but also 82 percent of sawmill workers from the Pacific Northwest. The public average was 87 percent. For the claim: "Justice is not just for human beings. We need to be as fair to plants and animals as we are towards people," the agreements are similar: 97 percent, 63 percent, and an average of 90 percent. The survey authors conclude: "An environmental view of the world is more universal than previous studies have suggested" (Kempton et al. 1995, pp. 113, ix).

The seriousness of respect for biodiversity is further illustrated when the idea approaches a "reverence" for life. Surveys also show that for many this is the most important value at stake, often taking a monotheistic form. Species are the creation itself, the "swarms of living creatures" (biodiversity) that "the earth brought forth" at the divine imperative; "God saw that it was good" and "blessed them" (Genesis 1). Noah's ark was the aboriginal endangered species project; God commanded, "Keep them alive with you" (Genesis 6). Any who decide to destroy species take, fearfully, the prerogative of God. When one is conserving life, ultimacy is always nearby.

Extinction is forever; and, when danger is ultimate, absolutes become relevant. The motivation to save endangered species can and ought to be pragmatic, economic, political, and scientific; deeper down it is moral, philosophical, and religious. Species embody a fertility on earth that is sacred.

On the scale of evolutionary time, humans appear late and suddenly, a few hundred thousand years on a scale of billions of years, analogous to a few seconds in a twenty-four-hour day. Even more lately and suddenly they increase the extinction rate dramatically, as we have done in this one last century among several thousand years of recorded history. What is offensive in such conduct is not merely the loss of resources, but the maelstrom of killing and insensitivity to forms of life. What is required is not prudence but principled responsibility to the biospheric earth. Only the human species contains moral agents, but conscience ought not to be used to exempt every other form of life from consideration, with the resulting paradox that the sole moral species acts only in its collective self-interest toward all the rest.

Several billion years worth of creative toil, several million species of teeming life, have been handed over to the care of the latecoming species in which the mind has flowered and morals have emerged. On the naturalistic account, the host of species has a claim to care in its own right. There is something Newtonian, not yet Einsteinian, besides something morally naive, about living in a reference frame where one species takes itself as absolute and values everything else relative to its utility.

REFERENCES

Booth, William (1997) "Developers wish huge fly would buzz off," *Washington Post*, April 4, p. A1.

Costanza, Robert, et al. (1997) "The value of the world's ecosystem services and natural capital," *Nature* 387, pp. 253–9.

Darwin, Charles (1968 [1872]) *The Origin of Species* (Baltimore: Penguin Books).

Ehrlich, Paul and Ehrlich, Anne (1981) *Extinction* (New York: Random House).

Eldredge, Niles and Cracraft, Joel (1980) *Phylogenetic Patterns and the Evolutionary Process* (New York: Columbia University Press).

Feinberg, Joel (1974) "The rights of animals and unborn generations," in *Philosophy and Environmental Crisis*, ed. W. T. Blackstone (Athens, GA: University of Georgia Press), pp. 43–68.

Hampshire, Stuart (1972) *Morality and Pessimism* (New York: Cambridge University Press).

Kempton, Willett M., Boster, James S., and Hartley, Jennifer A. (1995) *Environmental Values in American Culture* (Cambridge, MA: MIT Press).

Myers, Norman (1979) "Conserving our global stock," *Environment* 21, no. 9 (November): pp. 25–33.

Rawls, John (1971) *A Theory of Justice* (Cambridge, MA: Harvard University Press).

Regan, Tom (1983) *The Case for Animal Rights* (Berkeley CA: University of California Press).

Rescher, Nicholas (1980) "Why save endangered species?" in *Unpopular Essays on Technological Progress* (Pittsburgh, PA: University of Pittsburgh Press), pp. 79–92.

Rolston III, Holmes (1996) "Feeding people versus saving nature," in *World Hunger and Morality*, 2nd edn, ed. William Aiken and Hugh LaFollette (Upper Saddle River, NJ: Prentice-Hall), pp. 248–67.

Simpson, G. G. (1961) *Principles of Animal Taxonomy* (New York: Columbia University Press).

US Congress (1973) *Endangered Species Act of 1973*. 87 Stat. 884. Public Law 93–205.

Wilson, Edward O. (1992) *The Diversity of Life* (Cambridge, MA: Harvard University Press).

CLIMATE CHANGE

Anthropogenic climate change may be the central environmental problem of our age. Some of the impacts of climate change are well established. These include erratic weather patterns, rising sea levels, and changes in disease vectors. Other impacts are difficult to assess since we don't yet know enough about the consequences of changing the earth's climate. The scale and reach of climate change, both in space and time, raise new philosophical concerns about standard accounts of causation and responsibility, as well as pose familiar problems concerning distributive justice, duties to future generations, and the value of nature.

Writing in the early 1990s, the Indian environmentalists Anil Agarwal and Sunita Narain rejected the idea that poor, developing countries are to any extent responsible for climate change. It is an example of environmental colonialism when environmental groups in the rich countries of the North use the rhetoric of "our common future" and "the global environmental crisis" to shift the burden of responsibility to the poor countries of the South. Agarwal and Narain distinguish between greenhouse gas emissions required for subsistence and those produced by the pursuit of luxury, and propose that the rich countries of the North pay the "true ecological cost" of their overconsumption. They go on to identify the role of Western media and the lack of Third World research in perpetuating environmental colonialism.

Philosopher Stephen Gardiner surveys a broad range of central themes in climate ethics including the role of climate economics, risk management, the precautionary principle, responsibility for the past, and how to allocate future emissions. The public and political debate surrounding climate change is often "simplistic, misleading, and awash with conceptual confusion," and Gardiner concludes with a plea for greater attention to the ethics of climate change and greater clarity in discussions about this pressing environmental problem.

Law professors Eric Posner and Cass Sunstein ask what justice requires of the United States, which is historically the most significant emitter of greenhouse gases. They argue that asking the United States to bear disproportionate costs in order to reduce its emissions is an inefficient way to address global inequality. They also claim that viewing the United States as wronging vulnerable people and countries through its emissions is a "highly imperfect" metaphor for what has actually occurred. This essay brings out the difficulty of applying our familiar theories of justice to the problem of climate change.

FURTHER READINGS

Gardiner, Stephen. *A Perfect Moral Storm: The Ethical Tragedy of Climate Change*. New York, NY: Oxford University Press, 2011. An analysis of the theoretical, global, and intergenerational challenges posed by climate change.

Gardiner, Stephen, Simon Caney, Dale Jamieson, and Henry Shue, eds. *Climate Ethics: Essential Readings*. New York, NY: Oxford University Press, 2010. A collection of central texts in the ethics of climate change addressing global justice, future generations, policy responses, and individual responsibility.

McKibben, Bill. *The End of Nature*. New York, NY: Random House, 1989. The book that brought global warming to public attention argues that nature has ended since nothing on the planet is now beyond the reach of human influence.

McKinnon, Catriona. *Climate Change and Future Justice*. New York, NY: Routledge, 2011. This book defends an approach to justice for future generations inspired by the work of John Rawls.

Moore, Kathleen Dean, and Michael Nelson, eds. *Moral Ground: Ethical Action for a Planet in Peril*. San Antonio, TX: Trinity University Press, 2010. Short articles by one hundred theologians and religious leaders, scientists, poets, business leaders, activists, and philosophers addressing the question of how to live in a greenhouse world.

DISCUSSION QUESTIONS

1. If industrialized countries have primarily caused climate change, who is responsible now and in the future? Are we only ethically responsible for the damage we cause?
2. How should we think about decision-making when so much is uncertain, as is the case with climate change?
3. Is climate change different from other environmental issues? If so, how?
4. Is climate change fundamentally a moral issue?
5. How do you think we should respond to climate change? Should we focus on reducing our emissions, adapting to the changes that are occurring, or try to intervene directly to intentionally control climate?

ANIL AGARWAL AND SUNITA NARAIN

[From] Global Warming in an Unequal World

The idea that developing countries like India and China must share the blame for heating up the earth and destabilising its climate, as espoused in a recent study published in the United States by the World Resources Institute in collaboration with the United Nations, is an excellent example of *environmental colonialism.*

The report of the World Resources Institute (WRI), a Washington-based private research group, is based less on science and more on politically motivated and mathematical jugglery.[1] Its main intention seems to be to blame developing countries for global warming and perpetuate the current global inequality in the use of the earth's environment and its resources.

A detailed look at the data presented by WRI itself leads to the conclusion that India and China cannot be held responsible even for a single kg of carbon dioxide or methane that is accumulating in the earth's atmosphere. Carbon dioxide and methane are two of the important gases contributing to global warming. The accumulation in the earth's atmosphere of these gases is mainly the result of the gargantuan consumption of the developed countries, particularly the United States.

The WRI report is entirely designed to blame developing countries for sharing the responsibility for global warming. Global warming is a phenomenon that could lead to major climatic disturbances, drying up of rain over large areas, and melting of the ice caps leading to countries like Maldives disappearing completely and India and Bangladesh losing a large part of their coastline.

The WRI report is already being quoted widely and its figures will definitely be used to influence the deliberations on the proposed, legally-binding, global climate convention. This kind of data will be used by the US government to strengthen its position, which it took during the ozone negotiations, that it will not pay for ecological reparations. The US government agreed to the paltry amounts negotiated at the London 1990 meeting for a global ozone fund only after considerable pressure from European countries, particularly the Scandinavian countries.

Many developing countries fear that the proposed climate convention will put serious brakes on their development by limiting their ability to produce energy, particularly from coal (which is responsible for producing carbon dioxide), and undertake rice agriculture and animal care programmes (activities which produce methane).

Behind the global rules and the global discipline that is being thrust upon the hapless Third World, there is precious little global sharing or even an effort by the West to understand the perspectives of the other two-thirds. How can we visualise any kind of global management, in a world so highly divided between the rich and the poor, the powerful and the powerless, which does not have a basic element of economic justice and equity. One American is equal to, god knows, how many Indians or Africans in terms of global resource consumption.

The entire debate on the prospects of impending doom is, in many ways, an excellent opportunity for the world to truly realise the concept of one world. A world which is interdependent and which cannot withstand the current levels of consumption and exploitation, especially the levels now prevalent in the West. We had hoped that Western environmentalists would seize this opportunity to force their countries to "dedevelop" as they have used up the world's ecological capital and continue to overuse it even today. Sadly, instead, the focus today is on poor developing countries and their miniscule resource use is frowned upon as hysteria is built up about their potential increase in consumption. For instance, in the negotiations to reduce ozone destructive gases, the common refrain has been that the future potential of CFC production in India and China—which together produce only 2 per cent of the responsible chemicals today—constitutes a threat to global survival. As their consumption is bound to increase, the dream of every Chinese to own a refrigerator is being described as a global curse.

The Washington-based Worldwatch Institute points out in a recent paper: "...there remains the extraordinarily difficult question of whether carbon emissions should be limited in developing countries, and if so at what level. It is a simple fact of atmospheric science that the planet will never be able to support a population of 10 billion people emitting carbon at, say, the rate of Western Europe today. This would imply carbon emission's of four times the current level, or as high as 23 billion tonnes per year."[2]

Gus Speth, WRI's president in an article in Environment magazine puts it more bluntly "Deforestation and other land use changes now account for about one-third of the carbon dioxide produced by human activity and some of the methane. If just China and India were to increase their greenhouse gas emissions to the global average per capita rate, today's global total would rise 28 per cent; if these two countries matched France's per capita rate, the total would be 68 per cent higher." Speth, therefore, concludes: "As a practical matter, developing countries expect industrial countries to take the first and strongest actions on global warming. These developing nations want to see the seriousness of the threat validated, and they conclude correctly that industrial nations are largely responsible for the problem and have the most resources to do something about it. *But carrying this argument too far could lead to a tragic stalemate.*"[3]

It is constantly mentioned that the efforts of the West to check pollution and global warming could be torpedoed by a rise in coal burning in the developing world. Why should we do anything if you are also going to want cars, electricity or refrigerators is the underlining statement. Recently, the head of the environmental group of the International Energy Agency (IEA) based in Brussels—an agency which looks after the energy interests of rich countries—told the press that the coal use in developing countries could have very dramatic environmental implications. "The levels of coal use predicted for India and China could have a very dramatic environmental impact indeed. If developing countries keep to the sort of forecasts of coal consumption now being bandied about, they would negate any effort by Western countries to control emissions of greenhouse gases," the IEA official recently told Reuters.[4]

We consider such statements, now commonplace in the West, both irresponsible and highly partisan. They constitute the worst form of preaching the world has ever seen—literally amounting to blaming the victim. If anything, the available figures show that the West must immediately put its own house in order.

And this is when Western nations themselves are talking, at most, about stabilising their current consumption of energy use or reducing them marginally. The US has in fact rejected even discussions about stabilising its consumption as US President George Bush now considers the global warming debate a mere myth. But even stabilising energy consumption means maintaining the manifold inequity in resource consumption between the developed and developing worlds. Does this mean that developing countries will be "allowed" to reach these levels or is our quota of the global atmosphere finished?

India and China today account for more than one-third of the world's population. The question to be asked is whether we are consuming one-third of the world's resources or contributing one-third of the muck and dirt in the atmosphere or the oceans. If not then surely these countries should be lauded for keeping the world in balance because of their parsimonious consumption despite the Western rape and pillage of the world's resources.

The California based International Project for Sustainable Energy Paths (IPSEP) in its report on Energy Policy in the Greenhouse has warned against any trend towards "environmental colonialism in which the climate issues is inadvertently or deliberately used to reinforce traditional agendas that are in conflict with the North-South combine."[5] The report, which the British newsmagazine, *New Scientist*, called the first detailed formula for reducing releases of carbon dioxide by the year 2005, has argued for substantial and urgent reductions of emissions of industrialised countries, who depending on the mathematical calculations, have already either used up their entire quota of emissions to the atmosphere until 2100 or will be doing so by 1997.[6]

The manner in which the global warming debate is being carried out is only sharpening and deepening the North–South divide. Given this new found interest in the so-called Our Common Future and future generations, it is time for the Third World to ask the West, "whose future generations are we seeking to protect, the Western World's or the Third World's?"

WRI report reinforces this divide. By shifting the onus onto the developing world, it whitewashes the role and the responsibility of the West in destroying our "common future." James Gus Speth, WRI's president says diplomatically about his report, "the new information means that industrial and developing countries must work together to begin reducing emissions of greenhouse gases and we need a new era of environmental cooperation." Third World environmentalists must not get taken for a ride by this highly partisan "one worldism."...

TRADEABLE EMISSIONS

The latest literature on management of common property resources shows clearly that an exploitation system based on gifts and a free for all inevitably leads to its degradation—the well-known "tragedy of the commons." In order that all those countries which are overusing or misusing the world's environment pay a price, CSE proposes a two-tier system—one set will consist of charges and another of fines—to bring rationality into the global use of the atmosphere.

In all market economies of the world, pollution control economists are now talking about the concept of tradeable emission quotas, which allow low-level polluters to trade their unused permissible emissions with high-level polluters. Overall, this system leads to better economics as it provides an economic incentive to the low-level polluters to keep their pollution levels low and an economic disincentive to the high-level polluters to reduce their emissions. Expecting everyone to adhere to a standard pollution limit does not provide any incentive to low-level polluters to keep their pollution levels low. In other words, what the world needs is a system which encourages a country like India to keep its emissions as low as possible and pushes a country like USA to reduce its emissions fast.

CSE believes that a system of global tradeable permits should be introduced to control global greenhouse gas emissions. All countries should be given tradeable quotas in proportion to their population share and the total quotas should equal the world's natural sinks. The quantity of unused permissible emissions can be sold by low-level greenhouse gas emitting countries to high-level greenhouse gas producers at a certain fixed rate.

But any excess discharges which lead to an accumulation in the atmosphere and, thus, constitute a global threat for climate destabilisation, should be fined at a higher rate and given over to a "global climate protection fund." The fund can be used to assist those countries which are affected by climate destabilisation and to develop technologies that will reduce greenhouse gas emissions. These technologies can then be used by all humankind. Such a system should provide an incentive to countries like India to keep their share of greenhouse gas emissions low and force countries like USA to reduce their emissions rapidly—and, thus, all will join the race to save the planet.

What charges should low emitters levy on high emitters for a share in their tradeable emissions? The IPSEP study, which was carried out for the Dutch government, suggests that such the charge could be pegged at $15 per 1000 tonnes of carbon emitted into the air (which is equivalent to 3.7 tonnes of carbon dioxide and 0.5 tonne of methane). This amount in 1986, taking into account the global fuel mix in that year, would have been roughly equal to a ten per cent increase in that year's crude oil prices.

Using the same figure, CSE finds that India would be able to charge excess emitters a sum of US $8.3 billion per year for its share in permissible emissions (or about 50 per cent of the country's annual investment in the power sector during the Seventh Plan) whereas USA would have to pay US $6.3 billion to purchase unused permissible emission quotas. Twenty developing countries together would receive about US $30 billion—China $11.31 billion, India $8.3 billion, Pakistan $2.08 billion, Nigeria $1.45 billion and Bangladesh $1.06 billion every year.

But if the nonpermissible emissions that finally accumulate in the atmosphere are fined at a higher rate of US $25 per tonne of carbon equivalent emissions, then a Global Climate Protection Fund of about US $90 billion annually could be created from the contributions of developed countries and oil-rich countries like Saudi Arabia. USA alone would have to pay a sum of US $38.3 billion to the global fund....

IMPACT OF WESTERN MEDIA

The manner in which the WRI report has been flashed across the world raises serious questions about the role of the Western mass media. It is strange that the IPSEP report received no publicity as compared to the WRI report even though the IPSEP study was undertaken by well-known energy analysts. IPSEP's main authors were Floretin Krause, an energy analyst

at the Lawrence Berkeley Laboratory in the US, and Wilfrid Bach, a climatologist who is a member of the West German parliament's special commission on preventing global warming.

The media blitz of the WRI report has been so powerful that even several Indian commentators and environmentalists have accepted the report unquestioningly and have called upon the Indian people to accept their share of the blame. India's Doordarshan even showed, on its prime time news programme, the press conference in Washington DC at which the WRI data was released. It did not care to ask Indian scientists about the veracity of the data, as one of them complained at a recent CSE meeting.

LACK OF THIRD WORLD RESEARCH

The entire episode also emphasises the fact that Third World nations must undertake their own research in this crucial area. They cannot depend on Western institutions to present a true picture of the global situation and safeguard their interests. The manner in which the methane and carbon dioxide emissions of several developing countries have been calculated is itself open to questions. The data base on contributions from deforestation, irrigated rice farming and livestock management is still poor. It is vital that a reliable system of measuring deforestation annually on a global and national basis is developed urgently.

POLITICAL SAGACITY AND FARSIGHTEDNESS

But most of all, the Third World today needs farsighted political leadership. For the first time, the Western world and its environmental movements are arguing that we have to manage the world as one entity. But the same Western politicians—from

Margaret Thatcher to George Bush—who talk so glibly about an interdependent world show no interest in the travails of the Third World. Through quotas, embargoes and subsidies to their own farmers, and through emerging biotechnology, they consistently depress Third World commodity prices. The West has never been prepared to pay the true ecological costs of the goodies it consumes—from bananas, tea, coffee and cocoa to prawns.

All over the world, there is growing consciousness about "Green Economics" and the need to incorporate ecological costs of production into national income and wealth accounts. But what is the point of doing this in a developing country if the rich and powerful consumers of the world are not prepared to pay the true cost of their consumption? *That is not an economic issue but an intensely political issue....*

NOTES

1. World Resources Institute 1990, *World Resources 1990–91: A Guide to the Global Environment*, Oxford University Press, New York.

2. Christopher Flavin 1989, *Slowing Global Warming: A Worldwide Strategy*, Worldwatch paper 91, Worldwatch Institute, Washington, DC.

3. James Gustave Speth 1990, Coming to Terms: Toward a North South compact for the Environment, in *Environment*, Vol. 32, No 5, June 1990, Heldref Publications, Washington, DC.

4. Michael Stott 1989, Third World Fossil Fuel Pollution Prompts Worries, in *Los Angeles Times*, November 19, Los Angeles.

5. Floretin Krause, Wilfrid Bach and Jon Koomey 1989, *Energy Policy in the Greenhouse*, Vol. 1, International Project for Sustainable Energy Paths, El Cerrito.

6. Roger Milne 1989, "Industrialised countries must make deepest carbon cuts," in *New Scientist,* December 2, London.

STEPHEN M. GARDINER

Ethics and Climate Change

Climate ethics is an emerging field. This paper serves as a critical introductory overview. It focuses on five areas of discussion that are particularly relevant to substantive climate policy: the treatment of scientific uncertainty, responsibility for past emissions, the setting of mitigation targets, and the places of adaptation and geoengineering in the policy portfolio. © 2010 John Wiley & Sons, Ltd. *WIREs Clim Change* 2010 1 54–66.

Significant values are incorporated into the foundations of international climate policy, and necessarily so. As the leading scientific authority on climate change, the United Nations' Intergovernmental Panel on Climate Change (IPCC), recognized at the outset of one of its recent reports, while "natural, technical, and social sciences can provide essential information and evidence needed for decisions . . . at the same time, *such decisions are value judgments . . .*" [1, p. 2, emphasis added]. With this in mind, it is no surprise that ethical concepts play a leading role in the way the issue is set out in the foundational legal document, the United Nations framework convention on climate change of 1992.[2] This treaty states as its motivation the "protection of current and future generations of mankind," declares as its major objective the prevention of "dangerous anthropogenic interference" with the climate system, and announces that this objective must be achieved while also protecting ecological, subsistence, and economic values. In addition, the text goes on to list a number of principles to guide the fulfillment of these objectives, and these make heavy use of value-laden concepts. For example, appeals are made to "equity," "common but differentiated responsibilities" (Article 3.1), the "special needs" of developing countries (Article 3.2), the "right" to development (Article 3.4), and the aim of promoting a supportive, open, sustainable, and nondiscriminatory international economic system (Article 3.5). There is no doubt then that ethical concerns are central to climate policy. Still, important questions arise concerning how to interpret, reconcile, and implement the relevant values, and whether the legal account of them should be challenged or extended. This brings us squarely into the realm of moral and political philosophy, broadly construed.

In this brief introduction to the subject, I will not attempt the large project of assessing the values of the framework convention. Instead, my aim is to indicate how ethical analysis can make a contribution to five central concerns of climate policy: the treatment of scientific uncertainty, responsibility for past emissions, the setting of mitigation targets, and the places of adaptation and geoengineering in the policy portfolio. Inevitably, the account I offer here will be too simplistic and selective. Still, I hope that it provides a useful gateway into the emerging literature (see also[3]).

SKEPTICISMS

On the face of it, the claim that climate change poses a real threat that justifies serious action is supported by a broad scientific consensus.[4,5] Still, in the public realm this claim has been subject to three prominent challenges.

The first asserts that the science remains uncertain, so that current action is unjustified. This claim raises important epistemic and normative questions about what constitutes relevant uncertainty, and what amounts to appropriate action under it. We can make some progress on the first question if we begin with a distinction. In economics, situations involving uncertainty are distinguished from those involving risk. Suppose one can identify a possible negative outcome of some action. That outcome is a risk if one can also identify, or reliably estimate, the probability of its occurrence; it is uncertain if one cannot.[6] On this account, it is unclear whether the science is uncertain in the technical sense. On the one hand, the IPCC does assign probabilities to many of its projections, making the situation one of risk. Moreover, many of these assignments are both high, and associated with substantial negative damages; hence, they do seem sufficient to justify significant action.

On the other hand, most of the IPCC's probability assignments are based on expert judgment, rather than direct appeals to causal mechanisms. Hence, these are "subjective," rather than objective probabilities. Appeal to subjective probabilities is common in many approaches to risk. Indeed, some claim that all probabilities are ultimately subjective (e.g.,[7]). But if one is suspicious of subjective probabilities in general, or has particular reasons to be skeptical in this case, one might reject the IPCC assignments and continue to regard climate change as genuinely uncertain in the technical sense.

Still, granting this concession is not enough by itself to make the skeptic's case. Suppose that we do lack robust probability information about climate change. Still, there is something troubling about the claim that one should refuse to act just because of this. We do not get to pick and choose the problems we face, and ignoring those whose shapes we do not like seems both a bizarre strategy, and also out of step with how we behave elsewhere. Many important life decisions come without good probability information attached (e.g., who to marry, what career path to follow, where to live). But this does not paralyze us there.

This brings us to the issue of precaution. The framework convention makes the claim that "where there are threats of serious or irreversible damage, lack of full scientific certainty should not be used as a reason for postponing (precautionary) measures (to anticipate, prevent, or minimize the causes of climate change and mitigate its adverse effects)" (Article 3.3). Hence, the treaty explicitly rules out some kinds of appeal to uncertainty as justifications for inaction.

Stated as it is in the convention, this appeal to precaution is extremely minimal and underdeveloped. However, some have tried to generate a more general precautionary principle. According to one standard statement, this asserts "when an activity raises threats of harm to human health or the environment, precautionary measures should be taken even if some cause and effect relationship[s] are not fully established scientifically."[8] However, such claims have frequently been dismissed as extreme, myopic, and ultimately vacuous. Could not a precautionary principle be invoked to stop *any* activity, however beneficial, on the basis of any kind of worry, however fanciful? If so, the critics charge, surely it is irrational, and ought to be neglected. This is the second challenge to action on climate change.

Understood in a completely open-ended way, the precautionary principle may be vulnerable to such objections. However, it is plausible to try to restrict its application by introducing criteria to guide when the principle ought to be applied.[9] In previous work, I have tried to illustrate this using John Rawls' criteria for the application of a maximin principle: that the situation is uncertain, in the sense that the parties lack reliable probability information; that they care little for potential gains above the minimum they can secure by acting in a precautionary manner; and that they face outcomes that are unacceptable [10,

p. 134]. This approach not only diffuses the original objections, but suggests that many disputes about precaution ultimately do not rest on a rejection of the principle, but rather on disagreement about whether the relevant criteria are met. This significantly reframes the theoretical debate.

At a more practical level, a reasonable case can be made that the Rawlsian precautionary principle applies to climate change. First, presumably some of the projected impacts, being severe or catastrophic, are morally unacceptable. Second, we have already seen that there may be uncertainty in the technical sense. However, third, the claim that we care little for the gains that can be made beyond those secured by precautionary action is more contentious. On the one hand, Cass Sunstein has argued that this condition threatens to confine the Rawlsian version of the principle to trivial cases, and moreover undermines the application to global warming because the costs of mitigation amount to hundreds of millions of dollars [11, p. 112]. (Because of this, he tries to "build on" the Rawlsian version to develop an alternative catastrophic harm precautionary principle [12, p. 168].) On the other hand, though Sunstein is surely right that more work needs to be done in fleshing out the precautionary principle, it is not clear that the problem is that the Rawlsian version is "trivial." Remember that Rawls is speaking of gains that can be made *above some minimum we can guarantee* through eliminating the worst case scenario. Hence, much depends on how one understands the alternative options. Suppose, e.g., that we could avoid the possibility of catastrophic climate change and guarantee a decent quality of life for everyone, all at the cost of slowing down our rate of accumulation of purely *luxury* goods by two years (*cf.*[13]). This might satisfy the "care little for gains" condition even if the cost of those luxury goods in dollar terms were very large. For example, the importance of averting catastrophic climate change might simply make such a loss relatively unimportant. Given this point, the real issue seems to revolve around the interpretation and elaboration of the "care little for gains" condition,

rather than whether it is "too stringent" (pace.[12], p. 156). In my view, resolving this issue is likely to involve a substantive project in normative ethics.

The issue of how to understand the costs of climate change brings us to the third challenge. Many economists maintain that only modest steps should be taken, since (they say) the costs of substantial action outweigh the benefits.[14–16] This result, however, is hardly robust, and other prominent economists argue for the contrary conclusion, that substantial action is strongly justified.[17,18] There are many reasons for this disagreement. One concerns the integrity of the relevant calculations. Some distinguished economists argue that economic costs and benefits simply cannot be projected with any precision over the relevant timeframes (of a century or more), so that fine-grained calculations amount to "self-deception."[19,20] But it is also true that long-range economic models must implicitly make many important ethical judgments, about which there is substantial disagreement. These include issues such as the distribution of benefits and burdens across individuals, countries, and time, and the correct way to deal with noneconomic (e.g., interpersonal, aesthetic, and natural) values.

Most prominently, conventional economics adopts the practice of discounting future costs and benefits at a uniform rate of 2–10% per year. This has the effect of sharply reducing the impact of high values in the future, especially when the rates are high.[21] Some argue that this practice is unethical, since it discriminates against future generations. Moreover, its theoretical foundations appear to be weak. Several distinct rationales are offered for discounting, and these often seem to pull in different directions.[22,23] More importantly, many of the rationales are essentially ethical: they claim that future people will be better off and so should pay more, or that the current generation ought to be able to protect itself from excessive demands by the future, or that political institutions ought to respect the pure time preference of the present generation (if it has one). Given this, what might initially appear to be merely a "technical issue" within economics turns on substantive (and controversial) claims in ethical theory.

PAST EMISSIONS

If action is warranted, who should take it, and what should be done? One proposal is that responsibility should be assigned in light of past emissions. Two kinds of argument are prominent. The first invokes historical principles of responsibility, along the lines of the commonsense ideals of "you broke it, you fix it" and "clean up your own mess."[24,25] Such principles are already familiar in environmental law and regulation, appearing, e.g., in various versions of the "polluter pays" principle (PPP). They imply that those who cause a problem have an obligation to rectify it, and also assume additional liabilities, such as for compensation, if the problem imposes costs or harms on others. The second kind of argument appeals to fair access. The thought is that the atmosphere's capacity to absorb greenhouse gases without adverse effects is a limited resource that is, or ought to be, held in common. If some have used up the resource, and in doing so denied others access to it, then compensation may be owed. The latecomers have been deprived of their fair share.

Such rationales for considering past emissions seem straightforward and readily applicable to climate change. However, this application has been subject to four prominent objections.

The first objection asserts that past polluters were ignorant of the adverse effects of their emissions, and so ought not to be blamed. They neither intended nor foresaw the effects of their behavior, and so should not be held responsible. This objection initially seems compelling, but turns out to be more complicated when pressed. First, it is worth distinguishing blame as such from responsibility. Though it is true that we do not usually blame those ignorant of what they do, still we often hold them responsible. Hence, showing that blame is inappropriate is insufficient to dismiss past emissions.[24] Second, there are reasons

for holding the ignorant responsible in this case. On the one hand, consider the "you broke it, you fix it" rationale. If I accidentally break something of yours, we usually think that I have some obligation to fix it, even if I was ignorant that my behavior was dangerous, and perhaps even if I could not have known. It remains true that I broke it, and in many contexts that is sufficient. After all, if I am not to fix it, who will? Even if it is not completely fair that I bear the burden, is it not at least less unfair than leaving you to bear it alone?[24,26] On the other hand, consider the fair access rationale. Suppose that I unwittingly deprive you of your share of something and benefit from doing so. Is it not natural to think that I should step in to help when the problem is discovered? For example, suppose that everyone in the office chips in to order pizza for lunch. You have to dash out for a meeting, and so leave your slices in the refrigerator. I (having already eaten my slices) discover and eat yours because I assume that they must be going spare. You return to find that you now do not have any lunch. Is this simply your problem? We do not usually think so. Even though I did not realize at the time that I was taking your pizza, this does not mean that I have no special obligations. The fact that I ate your lunch remains morally relevant.

The second objection emerges from the claim that there is a disanalogy between the pizza case and that of past emissions. In the pizza case, you have a clear right to the eaten slices, because you have already paid for them. But in the case of emissions, where the shares of the latecomers are used up by those who come earlier, it might be maintained that the latecomers have no such claim. Perhaps it is simply "first-come, first-served," and hard luck to the tardy.

In my view, this response is too quick. We must ask what justifies a policy like "first-come, first-served" in the first place. To see why, consider one natural explanation. If a resource initially appears to be unlimited, then those who want to consume it might simply assume at the outset that no issues of allocation arise. Everyone can take whatever they

want, with no adverse consequences for others. In this case, the principle is not really "first-come, first-served" (which implies that the resource is limited, so that some may lose out), but rather "free for all" (which does not). Since it is assumed that there is more than enough for everyone, no principle of allocation is needed.

But what if the assumption that the resource is unlimited turns out to be mistaken, so that "free for all" is untenable? Do those who have already consumed large shares have no special responsibility to those who have not, and now cannot? Does the original argument for "free for all" justify ignoring the past? Arguably not. After all, if the parties had considered at the outset the possibility that the resource might turn out to be limited, which allocation principle would have seemed more reasonable and fair: "free for all, with no special responsibility for the early users if the resource turns out to be unlimited," or "free for all, but with early users liable to extra responsibilities if the assumption of unlimitedness turns out to be mistaken?" Offhand, it is difficult to see why ignoring the past would be favored. Indeed, there seem to be clear reasons to reject it: it makes later users vulnerable in an unnecessary way, and provides a potentially costly incentive to consume early if possible. Given this, "first-come, first-served" looks unmotivated. Why adopt an allocation rule that so thoroughly exempts early users from responsibility? Clearly, more needs to be said.

The third objection to considering past emissions emphasizes that, since significant anthropogenic emissions have been occurring since 1750, many past polluters are now dead. Given this, it is said that "polluter pays" principles no longer really apply to a substantial proportion of past emissions; instead, what is really being proposed under the banner "polluter pays" is that the descendents of the original polluters should pay for those emissions, because they have benefited from the past pollution (because of industrialization in their countries). However, the argument continues, this "beneficiary

pays principle" (BPP) is unjust because it holds current individuals responsible for emissions that they did not cause (and could not have prevented), and in ways which diminish their own opportunities.[27,28]

Much could be said about this objection (see also[29] and[30]), but here let me make just two comments. First, the claim that polluter pays does not apply is more complex than it first seems. For example, it does apply if it refers not to individuals as such but to some entity to which they are connected, such as a country, people or corporation. Moreover, this is the case in climate change, where polluter pays is usually invoked to suggest that countries should be held responsible for their past emissions, and these typically have persisted over the time period envisioned.

Many proponents of the objection recognize this complication. To meet it, they typically reject the moral relevance of states, and instead invoke a strong individualism that claims that only individuals should matter ultimately from the moral point of view. Still (second) it should be noted that this move makes the argument more controversial than it initially appears. On the one hand, even many individualists would argue that states often play the role of representing individuals and discharging many of their moral responsibilities. Given this, more needs to be said about why the fact of membership is irrelevant for assigning responsibility. On the other hand, the argument ignores the issue that a very strong individualism would also call into question many other practices surrounding inherited rights and responsibility. Put most baldly, if we are not responsible for at least some of the debts incurred by our ancestors, why are we entitled to inherit all of the benefits of their activities? Hence, if we disavow their emissions, must we also relinquish the territory and infrastructure they left to us? The worry here is that, if successful, the attempt to undermine the PPP and BPP is liable to prove too much, or at least to presuppose a radical rethinking of global politics.

The fourth objection to taking past emissions seriously claims that doing so would be impractical. Instead, it is said, if agreement is to be politically feasible, we should be forward-looking in our approach. The most prominent response to this objection is that it makes a rash claim about political reality. On the contrary, it might be said, since a genuinely global agreement is needed to tackle climate change, and since many nations of the world would not accept an agreement that did not explicitly or implicitly recognize past disparities, any attempt to exclude the past from consideration is itself seriously unrealistic.

FUTURE EMISSIONS

Whatever we say about the past, most people accept that something should be done to limit future emissions. Such a limit would transform an open access resource into one that must be distributed. This raises profound ethical questions, and especially ones of procedural and distributive justice.

Procedurally, the main issue is how to get an agreement that pays due respect to all of the parties involved. In practice, international discussion has treated emissions reductions as a matter for political horse-trading. Individual nations offer cuts in terms of their own emissions in exchange for cuts from the others, and other non-climate-related benefits. However, in an international system characterized by historical injustice and large imbalances of power, the prospect that such bargaining will be fair to all parties seems dim. Moreover, as Henry Shue argues, there is a threat of compound injustice.[31] Those treated unfairly in the past are likely to be more vulnerable to current injustices because of their past treatment. Finally, there are worries that the interests of those most affected by future climate change—future generations, the very poor, animals and nature—are not adequately represented. Why expect an agreement driven by representatives of the current generation of the world's most affluent people to produce justice in this context?

The question of how to arrange a climate regime that is procedurally fair is an important one. But

some of the concerns might be met if we had a good idea of what a fair distributive outcome might look like. At the theoretical level, this issue is complex. But one natural way to frame it is in terms of two questions.

The first question is what the appropriate trajectory of global carbon emissions should be over the long term. To answer this question, we need technical information about what kinds of emissions scenarios produce what kinds of impacts over time, and what kinds of technological and social changes—especially away from a carbon economy—we can expect, or bring about, and on what time scale. Still, as the IPCC recognizes above, we also need to make value judgments. For example, importantly, we need to know how to reconcile the concerns of present and future generations. Presumably, other things being equal, it would be better for the future if we reduced our emissions faster, and so diminished the risks of severe climate change; but, on the other hand, it would be better for the present if we minimized the impacts on our own social infrastructure, and so proceeded more slowly. So what balance should we strike between these concerns? Similarly, presumably there would remain something wrong if we succeeded in protecting future and current people, but allowed the natural world to be devastated. So deciding what trajectory to aim for raises issues about our responsibilities with respect to animals and nature.

Interestingly, there has been very little explicit discussion of the ethical dimension of the trajectory question. Instead, policy has been framed in terms of quantitative targets (such as avoiding a temperature rise of 2 °C, or limiting atmospheric concentration of carbon dioxide to 450 or 550 ppm) without much attention to what justifies such targets, or how we might cho[o]se between them. This approach tends to hide the relevant value judgments. For example, if limiting climate change to 2.3 rather than 2 °C makes a significant difference to specific populations or industries, how is the lower benchmark to be justified? As time goes on, such issues will no doubt become increasingly important.

The second theoretical question about distribution is how emissions allowed under the overall trajectory at a particular time should be allocated. This question has received much more attention than the first, in politics and academia. Here I shall review just three basic proposals, to get a sense of the terrain. [Of course, more complex proposals exist (cf.[32] and[33]). But my remarks here should provide an entry point into thinking about those too.]

The first proposal is that of equal per capita entitlements (e.g.,[25,34–37]). The intuitive idea is that, other things being equal, permissible carbon emissions should be distributed equally across the world population, because no individual has a presumptive right to more than an equal share. Such a position has significant initial appeal. However, it also faces a number of prominent obstacles.

First, people in different parts of the world have different energy needs. For example, those in northern Canada require fuel for heating whereas those in more temperate zones do not. Hence, there is a question about whether equal entitlements really do treat people as equals. This resonates with a deep issue in political philosophy about what the appropriate aim of equality should be: equality of resources, welfare, capabilities, or something else.[38–40]

Second, a shift to per capita entitlements is likely to have radically different implications for different nations. Recent figures show that in 2005, global per capita emissions were at 1.23 metric tons of carbon. But national averages show wide discrepancies. In the United States, e.g., the average in 2005 was 5.32; in the United Kingtom it was 2.47; in China 1.16; in India 0.35; and in Bangladesh 0.08.[41] This raises serious issues. Suppose, e.g., that we were to call for roughly a 20% cut in global emissions in the next decade, and distribute the remaining emissions on a per capita basis, at roughly 1 metric ton each. This would imply that citizens of the United States would have to cut their emissions by more than 80%, those of the UK by nearly 60%, and those of China by around 14%, while the Indians could increase their emissions by around 285% and

the Bangladeshis by 1250%. In short, on the face of it, the burden of the shift to equal per capita entitlements seems very different in different countries. In particular, it is often said that it would be more dislocating for those who emit the most to make such drastic cuts, since much of their infrastructure depends on much higher rates of emission.

In practice, most proponents of the equal per capita approach suggest that this problem can be dealt with by making the right to pollute tradable once allocated. Hence, on this version of the proposal, those for whom the costs of reduction are high can buy unused allocations from others whose costs are low. Moreover, for administrative simplicity, it is usually thought that allocations will actually be made to states on the basis of their populations, rather than directly to individuals. In practice, then, the thought is that the effect of the per capita proposal is that developed nations will end up buying large amounts of currently unused capacity from the developing world in order to make their own cuts more manageable.

This more complex proposal raises many new issues. On the one hand, there are concerns about feasibility. For one thing, on the face of it, trading seems to involve a massive transfer of wealth from the rich to the poor nations. For another, the proposal of giving the allowances to states may lead far away from the initial intuition toward equality. In many countries, the thought goes, such allowances are likely to become just another resource for the elite to plunder, perhaps in collusion with, and on behalf of, outside forces. What then of individuals in poor countries to whom the right is nominally given? Does the appeal to individualism turn out merely to be a convenient illusion? On the other hand, concerns about fairness remain. Do tradable allowances simply allow the rich countries to continue their polluting habits by "buying off" the poor? Perhaps they are morally akin to environmental indulgences, simply a fancy way for the rich to spend their way out of the implications of their bad behavior[42]; and perhaps they also undermine a sense of collective moral endeavor.[43,44]

More generally, it may be that in practice the main appeal of the "equal per capita plus trading" proposal lies not in equal division, but elsewhere, in the way it appears to reconcile concern for the future with recognition of the past, and with global justice more generally. After all, the trading mechanism provides a mechanism for the rich nations to provide some compensation to the developing world (and without clearly appearing to do so). If the numbers had worked out differently (if, i.e., the poor countries turned out to be the big current polluters per capita), then it may be that the modified per capita approach would have little support.

The second proposal for allocating emissions initially appears to overcome some of the worries about the modified per capita approach by putting concern for the poor and for individuals right at the heart of its approach. Henry Shue maintains that individuals have an inalienable right to the emissions necessary for their survival or some minimum level of quality of life. He proposes that such emissions should be open neither to trading, nor appropriation by governments, and that they ought to be sharply distinguished from other emissions, especially those associated with luxury goods.[13] At first glance, this proposal has a sharply different logic than that of tradable per capita rights. On the one hand, subsistence emissions rights are inalienable, suggesting not only that they cannot be exchanged but also that they should be guaranteed even if this would predictably lead to serious harm to others, such as future generations. On the other hand, subsistence emissions are subject to a strict threshold, suggesting that emissions above that threshold might be distributed according to principles other than equality.

Of course, the subsistence emissions proposal also raises new difficulties. Most obviously, what counts as a "subsistence emission?" After all, former US President George H. Bush infamously stated at the Rio Earth Summit in 1992 that "the American way of life is not up for negotiation." Does that mean that we should regard an emissions rate of 5.32 metric tons per capita as the subsistence level for Americans?

Surely not. Yet even subsistence at a minimal level of quality of life presumably does include some social and cultural factors,[45] and these may involve different levels of absolute emissions. So how do we decide what is necessary and what is not? Again, some moral and political philosophy seems needed.

Less obviously, in practice it is not clear that the proposal has real advantages over the equal per capita approach. On the one hand, the two may not be easily separable. Given the fungibility of the notion of "subsistence," it seems likely that the task of determining an adequate minimum may turn out to be very close to that of deciding on an appropriate trajectory and then assigning equal per capita rights. On the other hand, if the two approaches do diverge, it is not clear that the subsistence approach does a better job of protecting vulnerable individuals. For example, if culturally sensitive subsistence emissions overshoot the equal per capita allocation, then they justify an increase in the burdens on future generations. Alternatively, if they undershoot that allocation, then the "excess" emissions need to be distributed in some other way. If this is equal per capita, then (again) the two approaches may amount to much the same thing. But if it is not—in particular if they are to be distributed by market forces—then the subsistence approach may end up being less favorable to the poor than equal per capita.

The third allocation proposal is that nations should share the costs of mitigation fairly among themselves by trying to equalize their marginal costs in reducing emissions. This is presumably part of the appeal of nations declaring percentage reduction targets. The thought is that if each reduces their own emissions by, say, 20% in a given period, then all take on equal burdens. Martino Traxler suggests that this approach has major political advantages. No nation has any stronger reason to defect than any other, and each experiences the maximum moral pressure to participate.[45]

I am not so sure. First, the proposal is entirely future-oriented. Not only does it ignore past emissions but also has it the effect of embedding recent emissions levels. For example, a cut of 20% reduces per capital levels in the United States to 4.26 and in India to 0.28. Is this fair, given that the United States is so much richer? Even more starkly, if ultimately the global cut needs to be 80%, is it fair that the equal percentage cut approach reduces the United States to 1.64 per capita, when this is still significantly higher than current Chinese and Indian levels, and when Bangladesh is pushed down to a miniscule 0.1 per capita?

Second, as the first point already suggests, the correct measure of "equal burdens" is morally contentious. Consider just three proposals. The first aims to equalize the marginal economic cost of reduction in each country. Say that this turns out to be $50 per metric ton. Does it matter that this amounts to the cost of [a] nice evening out for the average American, but more than a month's income for the average Bangladeshi? Presumably, it does. Given this, a second proposal might aim at equalizing marginal welfare instead. But what if the worst-off are in so wretched a condition that taking more from them will make little difference to their misery, but the very well-off are so accustomed to luxury that even small losses hit their subjective states very hard? Does this justify taking more from the poor? Again, presumably not. Finally, as a third proposal, suppose that we adopt a more substantive account of goods, distinguishing (for example) between luxuries and subsistence goods, and differentiating their importance to welfare. Then we could protect the poor from additional deprivation by insisting that the rich should give up all their luxuries before the poor give up anything.[31,45] However, even if this is morally correct, it seems highly politically controversial, and so undermines many of the (alleged) practical advantages of the "equal burdens" approach.

IMPACTS

Efforts to reach agreement on mitigation are complicated by the further issue of adaptation. Clearly, at this point, adaptation measures must be part of any sensible climate policy, because we are already committed to some warming due to past emissions, and because almost all of the proposed abatement strategies envisage that overall global emissions will continue at a high level for at least the next few decades, committing us to even more. However, it is also sometimes maintained that adaptation should be our predominant or even sole strategy. Some maintain that the key problems are human vulnerability to weather and the social conditions that lead to environmental degradation, and that these are strongly influenced by poverty and global population. Given this, the argument continues, these issues should be our focus rather than emissions reductions.[46]

In this vein, Bjorn Lomborg has argued that the climate change problem ultimately reduces to the question of whether to help poor inhabitants of the poor countries now or their richer descendents later, and that the right answer is to help the current poor now, because they are poorer than their descendents will be, because they are more easily (i.e., cheaply) helped, and since in helping them, one also helps their descendents. For example, Lomborg claims that a mitigation project like Kyoto "will likely cost at least $150 billion a year, and possibly much more," whereas "just $70–80 billion a year could give all third world inhabitants access to the basics like health, education, water, and sanitation."[15,16]

Lomborg's approach incorporates two main ideas. The first is a straightforward appeal to opportunity costs: the resources used for climate change mitigation could produce greater net benefits if employed elsewhere.[15] Mitigation efforts like Kyoto are, Lomborg says, a "bad deal."[16]

In some contexts, opportunity cost arguments are compelling. But we should be careful about their import for climate change. The first worry concerns Lomborg's framing of the issue. The claim that the choice is between current and future generations of the world's poor assumes that climate change poses no serious threats to (say) current or future inhabitants of richer countries, to animals, or to the rest of nature. This seems either false, or highly optimistic. In addition, the choice seems to represent a false dichotomy. Helping the poor does not foreclose the option of mitigating climate change. Perhaps we can do both. Moreover, plausibly, the two are inextricably linked. Perhaps digging new wells in Africa would not make much difference if climate change induces severe drought (perhaps it will even be simply a waste of resources), and perhaps some mitigation projects also help the poor (e.g., by reducing air pollution).

A second worry concerns the compensation rationale. It turns out that "even hard-nosed benefit–cost analysts" agree that the claim that future people could be compensated by an alternative policy loses relevance if we know that the compensation would not actually be paid, or would not suffice [[47], p. 6–7]. This may be so if catastrophic climate change undercuts our efforts to grow the global economy,[17] or if an otherwise richer future beset by severe climate change is not better off than a poorer one without such problems, perhaps because throwing money at the problem does not help that much.

The third worry about the opportunity cost argument is that, because it assumes that we can compensate the future for failure to act on climate change with a larger economy, the argument overlooks the possibility that future people may be entitled to both. If we owe it to our successors both that we refrain from climate disruption and that we try to improve their material conditions, then we cannot simply substitute one for the other and say that we are even. This would be a morally mischievous slight of hand. It would be like arguing that we should not save for our own retirements but invest in our kids' education instead, because then they will be able to look after us (better) in our old age. On a standard view of things, we owe our children freedom from the burdens of supporting us when we are older, and also some help in securing a good education. The one obligation cannot simply be silenced by the other.

This brings us to Lomborg's second main idea, that future people will be better off and so should pay more. This position is also open to challenge in the case of climate change. First, the approach ignores all issues of responsibility. If our generation causes the climate problem, it is far from clear that the future victims should pay to fix it (or pay disproportionately). This is so even if they happen to have more resources. We do not *always* think that those who have a greater ability to pay should pay (or pay more). Sometimes we think that those who caused the problem should pay instead. Second, future people may not be richer. For one thing, many of the world's poorer people in 2050 or 2100 may be better off than the poor are today, but still much worse off than the current global rich. So there is no reason to make them pay more. For another, if climate change has severe effects on matters such as food, water, disease, and the regional economies, then many people in the future may be worse off than people now.

Even if adaptation ought not to be our sole concern, it is clearly a crucial component of any defensible climate policy. Unfortunately, very little philosophical work has been done on this topic to date (exceptions include[48] and[49]), although some of the discussion about past emissions and mitigation remains relevant, as does development ethics more generally (e.g.,[50,51]). Still, it may be worth noting two initial points.

First, much resistance to mitigation seems implicitly bound up with the idea that it will be difficult for existing economic systems to "adapt" to emissions restrictions, but not to climate impacts. This is a surprising assumption. Other things being equal, one might think that it would be easier for economic institutions to cope with sensibly managed regulation than with specific climate impacts, since the former could be designed to be gradual, predictable, and incremental, whereas the latter are likely to be sudden, unpredictable, and potentially large-scale. But whatever we say about this, it seems clear that at least some of the existing climate debate turns on background assumptions about the relative resilience of different kinds of social and natural systems. This complicated the ethics of adaptation.

Second, the natural world interacts in complex ways with the social so that it will often be very difficult to separate climate impacts from other factors.

Hence, the harms and costs of failures to adapt will often be hidden—as Dale Jamieson puts it, no one's death certificate will ever read "climate change."[49] Given this, it is difficult to address adaptation without engaging with issues of global poverty and injustice more generally.

DIRECT INTERVENTION

A different approach to climate policy would have us try to make the planet "adapt" to us. Perhaps, the thought goes, we should try a "techno-fix." Why not directly intervene in the climate system in order to prevent emissions from having negative effects? Such "geoengineering" solutions to climate change have been proposed for decades, but have recently gained some prominence. Proposals include deploying space mirrors to reflect incoming sunlight, "fertilizing" the ocean with iron in order to suck carbon dioxide from the atmosphere, and pumping emissions from coal-burning power plants deep underground into sedimentary rock.

Philosophically, it is not clear that all such interventions are best grouped together, in part, because they seem to raise different ethical issues. However, here I shall not try to develop a general definition of geoengineering. Instead, I shall merely gesture at the idea that geoengineering involves something "global, intentional, and unnatural."[52] Wherever it makes a difference, the reader should assume that I am taking, as my model, the proposal that is currently the most popular—that of trying to manage the earth's albedo through injecting sulfur into the stratosphere.[53] I take this to be a paradigm case of geoengineering.[54]

Different arguments can be (and often are) offered in favor of various interventions. For example, some advocate a given approach because they think it much more cost-effective than mitigation (*cf.*[52] and[55]), others say that it will "buy time" while mitigation measures are implemented,[56] and still others claim that geoengineering should only be implemented as a last resort, to stave off a catastrophe.[53,57] Differences

in rationale are important because they often have divergent implications for research, governance, and policy, affecting what kinds of geoengineering should be pursued, to what extent, and with what safeguards. Given this, it is good to be clear about *why* an intervention is proposed.

Consider a few prominent arguments.[54] The first claims that geoengineering is relatively cheap and administratively simple.[53] Thus far, this argument has not proven very persuasive. The claim that geoengineering is cheap focuses on the costs of implementation, but appears to ignore the risk of dangerous side effects, and the fact that many geoengineering options leave some aspects of the carbon dioxide problem (such as ocean acidification) unaffected. The claim that it is administratively simple relies on the idea that it would be technically feasible for one country or corporation to undertake a serious geoengineering project. This ignores the moral and political implications of unilateral geoengineering, and the real possibility of geopolitical conflict.[58] More widely, some worry that this argument fails to take seriously the wider context of global environmental problems and the problematic human relationship to nature that they reflect.

A second argument for geoengineering suggests that we can adopt a "research-only" approach. For example, Ralph Cicerone, the President of the National Academy of Sciences, maintains that we should do further research in order to eliminate bad geoengineering options and discover if there are good ones, because there is a presumption in favor of freedom of enquiry since it promotes the acquisition of knowledge. While this is happening, he adds, there should be a moratorium on deployment and field testing. If promising proposals emerge, scientists can then bring these to the wider community so that political and ethical considerations may be brought to bear.[59]

There is something attractive about this proposal, and about the model it implies of science and its role in society. However, there are concerns about how good that model really is, and in particular how it holds up in the real social and political world in which

we live. One concern is that it is not obvious that any particular research project should be supported just because it enhances knowledge. After all, there are limited resources for research. If we prioritize geoengineering, other knowledge-enhancing projects will be displaced. Some rationale is needed for this displacement. In addition, some kinds of knowledge enhancement seem trivial. This is relevant because some experts claim that geoengineering research is highly unlikely to yield the kind of results needed to justify action on the timescale envisioned,[60] and that the rate of technological progress is so fast that it may make little sense even to try.[52]

A second concern about the research-only approach is that there is a crucial ambiguity in the notion of "supporting research." There are major differences between, e.g., individual scientists and journals being willing to review and publish papers, major funding agencies encouraging geoengineering proposals, and governments providing massive resources for a geoengineering "Manhattan Project." Importantly, giving preeminence to the cause of geoengineering research cannot be justified merely by appealing to the value of knowledge for its own sake. Instead, a much more robust argument is needed.

The final concern is that it is not clear that geoengineering activities can really be limited to research. First, there is such a thing as institutional momentum. In our culture, big projects that are started tend to get done.[61] Second, there are real worries about the idea of a moratorium. After all, if the results of research are to be published in mainstream journals that are freely available online or in libraries across the world, what is to stop a rogue scientist, engineer, or government deciding to use that research? Third, there are issues about who gets to make such decisions and why, and about how they are enforced. If the future of the planet is at stake, why is it that the rest of humanity should cede the floor to a "gentleman's agreement" among a specific set of scientists? Fourth, there are issues about conducting geoengineering research in isolation from public input, and in particular divorced from discussions about the ethics of deployment. The background assumption that is being made seems to

be that such input and discussion has *nothing to tell us* about the goals of geoengineering research or how it should be conducted. But it is not clear why we should accept this assumption (*cf.*[61]).

A third argument for pursuing geoengineering argues that "arming the future" with geoengineering is the lesser of two evils. The argument begins with the thought that if the current failure to act aggressively on mitigation continues, then at some point (probably 40 years or more into the future) we may end up facing a choice between allowing catastrophic impacts to occur, or engaging in geoengineering. Both, it is conceded, are bad options. But engaging in geoengineering is less bad than allowing catastrophic climate change. Therefore, if it comes to it, we should choose geoengineering. However, if we do not start doing serious research now, then we will not be in a position to choose geoengineering should the nightmare scenario arise. Therefore, we should start doing the research.[53]

This argument initially seems both straightforward and irresistible. However, it is subject to a number of important challenges.[54] First, it is not clear that the nightmare choice scenario it describes is the one we should prepare for. Perhaps other nightmares are more likely, such as having to cope with catastrophic change that is already upon us, or with a geopolitical catastrophe caused by unilateral or predatory geoengineering. Second, there may be other ways to prepare. Perhaps a Manhattan Project for alternative energy, or a massive climate assistance and refugee program, or a Strategic Solar Panel Reserve, would be better than geoengineering. Such alternatives should at least be considered. Third, if the nightmare scenario comes about because of our inaction on mitigation, then this seems to be a moral failure on our part, for which we may owe the future compensation beyond that of geoengineering research. The "arm the future" argument is thus too limited in describing our obligations. Fourth, similarly, the argument is silent on the issue of how to make geoengineering intervention politically legitimate and broadly in keeping with norms of global justice and community (e.g., not seriously unfair or parochial in its concerns). For example, a basic principle of modern political thought is that political institutions are legitimate only if they are justifiable to those governed by them. How then are geoengineering institutions to be justified, and what does this imply for global ethics and political philosophy? The final challenge concerns how we are to understand such issues in a context where the need to geoengineer is to be brought on by our failure to mitigate and adapt. Are just and effective geoengineering policies any more likely than just and effective mitigation policies? And if not, what can we say about the ethics of any likely decision to geoengineering?

In addition to the major arguments for pursuing geoengineering, there are also significant arguments against it. One prominent argument concerns how risky it is likely to be, and whether we are morally entitled to take this risk, especially in a context where ethical norms are not in place to protect the victims of side effects (for a first step toward such norms, see[61]). A second argument concerns what kind of people we aim to be. Many people, including a number of climate scientists, appear to believe that the attempt to geoengineer is not only risky, but also both an attempt to divert attention from the obligation to reduce emissions, and ultimately a sign of hubris. This argument sees the decision to pursue geoengineering in a wider context, raising questions that go beyond consideration of what the narrow consequences of this or that intervention are likely to be. If the decision to pursue geoengineering is made in the context of serious inertia on mitigation and adaptation for climate change, and a more general indifference to global environmental problems, the claim is that this reflects badly on the particular societies and generations who make that decision and perhaps on humanity as such. On one way of looking at things, having created a problem, we are obstinately refusing to face it in a serious way, but instead doing whatever we can to defer action, impose the burden on others, and obfuscate matters by arguing that we must hold out for a less demanding solution (however unrealistic that may be). What kind of people would do such a thing?[54,62–64]

CONCLUSION

In this introduction to ethics and climate change, I have tried to illustrate how ethical analysis contributes to our understanding of five central areas of climate policy: the treatment of scientific uncertainty, responsibility for past emissions, the setting of mitigation targets, and the places of adaptation and geoengineering in the policy portfolio. Much more can (and should) be said about these topics, and many other important ethical issues that I have not discussed. Of special interest is the place of climate policy within wider approaches to global justice, environmental ethics, and the ethics of human well-being. In particular, much of the current discussion (including those aspects I have emphasized above) tends to assume that we must work more-or-less within the constraints of the current geopolitical system. But, of course, climate change might be thought to pose a practical and philosophical challenge to that system.[65] If so, then much current writing is at best work on what one might call the "ethics of the transition," helping us to bridge the gap between what is and what should be. Vitally important though that project is, presumably we also need help in working out what we should ultimately be aiming for, in terms of better institutions and ways of life. Ethics should be a central part of this "ideal" project too.

NOTES

Earlier versions of this paper were presented at the University of Oslo and at a National Academies of Science workshop on America's Climate Choices. I thank those audiences, two anonymous referees, and Dale Jamieson for their comments. Some sections of the paper rely on and update material from Ref. 66; the section Direct Intervention draws on Ref. 54.

1. Intergovernmental Panel on Climate Change (IPCC). *Climate Change 2001: The Synthesis Report*. Cambridge, UK: Cambridge University Press.

2. United Nations Framework Convention on Climate Change. *Framework Convention on Climate Change*. 1992. Available at: http://unfccc.int/essential_background/convention/background/items/1349.php.

3. Gardiner S, Caney S, Jamieson D, Shue H eds. *Climate Ethics: Essential Readings*. Oxford: Oxford University Press; 2010. In press.

4. Intergovernmental Panel on Climate Change (IPCC). *Climate Change 2007: The Physical Science Basis*. Cambridge: Cambridge University Press; 2007.

5. Oreskes N. The scientific consensus on climate change. *Science* 2004, 306:1686.

6. Knight F. *Risk, Uncertainty, and Profit*. Boston, MA: Houghton Mifflin Company; 1921.

7. Friedman M. *Price Theory*. Chicago, IL: Aldine; 1976.

8. *Wingspread Statement*. 1998. Available at http://www. gdrc.org/u-gov/precaution-3.html.

9. Gardiner S. A core precautionary principle. *J Polit Philos* 2006, 14:33–60.

10. Rawls J. *A Theory of Justice*. Revised ed. Cambridge, MA: Harvard University Press; 1999.

11. Sunstein C. *The Laws of Fear*. Cambridge: Cambridge University Press; 2005.

12. Sunstein C. Irreversible and catastrophic. *Cornell Law Rev* 2006, 91:841.

13. Shue H. Subsistence emissions and luxury emissions. *Law and Policy* 1993, 15:39–59.

14. Nordhaus WD, Boyer JG. *Warming the World: Economic Models of Global Warming*. Cambridge, MA: MIT Press; 2000.

15. Lomborg B. *The Sceptical Environmentalist*. Cambridge: Cambridge University Press; 2001.

16. Lomborg B. *Cool It: The Skeptical Environmentalist's Guide to Global Warming*. London: Marshall Cavendish; 2007.

17. Stern N. *The Economics of Climate Change: The Stern Review*. Cambridge: Cambridge University Press; 2007.

18. Stern N. The economics of climate change. *Am Econ Rev* 2008, 98:1–37.

19. Broome J. *Counting the Cost of Global Warming*. Isle of Harris, UK: White Horse Press; 1992.

20. Spash C. The economics of climate change impacts a la Stern: novel and nuanced or rhetorically restricted? *Ecol Econ* 2007, 63:706–713.

21. Broome J. The ethics of climate change. *Sci Am* 2008, 298(6):97–102.

22. Cowen T, Derek P. Against the social discount rate. In: Laslett P, Fishkin J, eds. *Justice Between Age Groups and Generations*. New Haven, CT: Yale University Press; 2001, 144–161.

23. Caney S. Human rights, climate change and discounting. *Env Polit* 2008, 17:536–555.

24. Shue H. Global environment and international inequality. *Int Aff* 1999, 75:531–545.

25. Singer P. *One World: The Ethics of Globalization.* New Haven, CT: Yale University Press; 2002.

26. Shue H. *Historical Responsibility. Technical Briefing for Ad Hoc Working Group on Long-term Cooperative Action under the Convention [AWG-LCA], SBSTA, UNFCC, Bonn, 4 June 2009.* 2009. Available at: http://unfccc.int/files/meetings/ad_hoc_working_groups/lca/application/pdf/1_shue_rev.pdf.

27. Caney S. Cosmopolitan justice, responsibility and global climate change. *Leiden J Int Law* 2005, 18:747–775.

28. Posner E, Sunstein C. Climate change justice. *Georgetown Law J* 2008, 96:1565–1612.

29. Gosseries A. Historical emissions and free riding. In: Meyer L, ed. *Justice in Time: Responding to Historical Injustice.* Baden-Baden, Germany: Nomos; 2003, 355–382.

30. Meyer L, Roser D. Distributive justice and climate change: the allocation of emission rights. *Analyse Kritik* 2006, 28:223–249.

31. Shue H. The unavoidability of justice. In: Hurrell A, Kingsbury B, eds. *The International Politics of the Environment.* Oxford: Oxford University Press; 1992, 373–397.

32. Baer P, Athanasiou T, Kartha S. *The Right to Development in a Climate Constrained World: The Greenhouse Development Rights Framework.* London: Christian Aid; 2007.

33. Chakravarty S, Chikkatur A, de Coninck H, Pacala, S, Socolow R, et al. Sharing global CO_2 emission reductions among one billion high emitters. *Proc Natl Acad Sci USA.* 106(29):11884–11888, DOI:10.1073_pnas.0905232106.

34. Agarwal A, Narain S. *Global Warming in an Unequal World: A Case of Environmental Colonialism.* New Delhi: Centre for Science and Environment; 1991.

35. Meyer A. *Contraction and Convergence.* Dartington, UK: Green Books; 2000.

36. Jamieson D. Climate change and global environmental justice. In: Edwards P, Miller C, eds. *Changing the Atmosphere: Expert Knowledge and Global Environmental Governance.* Cambridge, MA: MIT Press; 2001, 287–307.

37. Athanasiou T, Baer P. *Dead Heat: Global Justice and Global Warming.* New York: Seven Stories Press; 2002.

38. Sen A. Equality of what? In: McMurrin S, ed. *Tanner Lectures on Human Values.* Cambridge: Cambridge University Press; 1980.

39. Dworkin R. *Sovereign Virtue: The Theory and Practice of Equality.* Cambridge, MA: Harvard University Press; 2002.

40. Page E. *Climate Change, Justice and Future Generations.* Cheltenham: Elgar; 2007.

41. Marland G, Boden T, Andreas RJ. *Global CO_2 Emissions from Fossil-Fuel Burning, Cement Manufacture, and Gas Flaring.* Dept of Energy, United States: Carbon Dioxide Information Center. 2008, 1751–2005. Available at: http://cdiac.oml.gov/trends/emiss/em_cont.html.

42. Goodin R. Selling environmental indulgences. *Kyklos* 1994, 47:573–596.

43. Sandel M. Should we buy the right to pollute? In: Sandel M, ed. *Public Philosophy: Essays on Morality in Politics*: Cambridge, MA: Harvard University Press; 2005.

44. Sagoff M. Controlling global climate: the debate over pollution trading. *Rep Inst Philos Publ Pol* 1999, 19:1–6.

45. Traxler M. Fair chore division for climate change. *Soc Theory Pract* 2002, 28:101–134.

46. Sarewitz D, Roger P Jr. *Breaking the global warming gridlock. Atl Mon* 2000, July. Available at: http://www.theatlantic.com/doc/200007/global-warming/5.

47. Portney PR, Weylant JP. Introduction. In: Portney, PR, Weylant JP, eds. *Discounting and Intergenerational Equity.* Washington, DC: Resources for the Future; 1999.

48. Adger N, Huq S, Mace M, Paavola J, eds. *Fairness in Adapting to Climate Change.* Cambridge, MA: MIT Press; 2005.

49. Jamieson D. Adaptation, mitigation, and justice. In: Sinnott-Armstrong W, Howarth R, eds. *Perspectives on Climate Change*: Elsevier; 2005, 221–253.

50. Nussbaum M. *Women and Human Development.* Cambridge: Cambridge University Press; 2001.

51. Crocker D. *Ethics of Global Development: Agency, Capability and Deliberative Democracy* Cambridge: Cambridge University Press; 2008.

52. Schelling T. The economic diplomacy of geoengineering. *Clim Change* 1996, 33:303–307.

53. Crutzen P. Albedo enhancement by stratospheric sulphur injections: a contribution to resolve a policy dilemma? *Clim Change* 2006, 77:211–219.

54. Gardiner S. Is "arming the future" with geoengineering really the lesser evil? Some doubts about the ethics of intentionally manipulating the climate system. In: Gardiner S, Caney S, Jamieson D, Shue H eds. *Climate Ethics: Essential Readings.* Oxford: Oxford University Press; 2010.

55. Barrett S. The incredible economics of geoengineering. *Environ Res Econ* 2008, 39:45–54.

56. Wigley TML. A combined mitigation/geoengineering approach to climate stabilization. *Science* 2006, 314:452–454.

57. Victor D, Morgan MG, Apt J, Steinbruner J, Ricke K. The geoengineering option: a last resort against global warming? *Foreign Aff* 2009, 88(2):64–72.

58. Bodansky D. May we engineer the climate? *Clim Change* 1996, 33:309–321.

59. Cicerone R. Geoengineering: encouraging research and overseeing implementation. *Clim Change* 2006, 77:221–226.

60. Bengtsson L. Geoengineering to confine climate change: is it at all feasible? *Clim Change* 2006, 77:229–234.

61. Jamieson D. Intentional climate change. *Clim Change* 2006, 33:323–336.

62. Kiehl J. Geoengineering climate change: treating the symptom over the cause? *Clim Change* 2006, 77:227–228.

63. Schneider S. Geoengineering: could we or should we make it work? *Philos Trans R Soc A* 2008, 366:3843–3862.

64. Schmidt G. Geoengineering in vogue. *Real Clim* 2006, 28 June. Available at: http://www.realclimate.org.

65. Gardiner S. Climate change as a global test for contemporary political institutions and theories. In: O'Brien K, Clair AL St, Kristoffersen B, eds. *Climate Change, Ethics and Human Security*. Cambridge, UK: Cambridge University Press. In press.

66. Gardiner S. Ethics and global climate change. *Ethics* 2004, 114:555–600.

FURTHER READING

Garvey J. *The Ethics of Climate Change: Right and Wrong in a Warming World*. London: Continuum; 2008. Vanderheiden, S. *Atmospheric Justice: A Political Theory of Climate Change*. Oxford: Oxford University Press; 2008.

Gardiner S, Caney S, Jamieson D, Shue H, eds. *Climate Ethics: Essential Readings*. Oxford: Oxford University Press; 2010. In press.

Page E. *Climate Change, Justice and Future Generations*. Cheltenham: Elgar; 2007.

Eric A. Posner and Cass R. Sunstein

[From] Climate Change Justice

I. CLIMATE CHANGE AND DISTRIBUTIVE JUSTICE

A. The Asteroid

Imagine that India faces a serious new threat of some kind—say, a threat of a collision with a large asteroid. Imagine too that the threat will not materialize for a century. Imagine finally that the threat can be eliminated, today, at a cost. India would be devastated by having to bear that cost now; as a practical matter, it lacks the resources to do so. But if the world acts as a whole, it can begin to build technology that will allow it to divert the asteroid, thus ensuring that it does not collide with India a century hence. The cost is high, but it is lower than the discounted benefit of eliminating the threat. If the world delays, it might also be able to eliminate the threat or reduce the damage if it comes to fruition. But many scientists believe that the best approach, considering relevant costs and benefits, is to start immediately to build technology that will divert the asteroid.

Are wealthy nations, such the United States, obliged to contribute significant sums of money to protect India from the asteroid? On grounds of distributive justice, it is tempting to think so. But if we reach that conclusion, how is the case different from one in which India contends, now, that it would be able to prevent millions of premature deaths from disease and malnutrition if the United States gave it (say) some small fraction of its Gross Domestic Product? If one nation is threatened by malaria or a tsunami, other nations might well agree that it is appropriate to help; it is certainly generous and in that sense commendable to assist those in need. But even generous nations do not conventionally think that a threatened nation has an entitlement to their assistance. For those who believe that there is such an entitlement,[1] the puzzle remains: Why is there an entitlement to help in avoiding future harm from an asteroid, rather than current harms from other sources?...

B. Climate Change: From Whom To Whom?

In terms of distributive justice, the problem of climate change is closely analogous to the asteroid problem. From that problem, three general questions emerge. First, why should redistribution take the form of an in-kind benefit, rather than a general grant of money that poor nations could use as they wish? Second, why should rich nations help poor nations in the future, rather than poor nations now? Third, if redistribution is the goal, why should it take the form of action by rich nations that would hurt many poor people in those nations and benefit many rich people in rich nations? To sharpen these questions, suppose that an international agreement to cut greenhouse gas emissions would cost the United States $325 billion.[2] If distributive justice is the goal, should the United States spend $325 billion on climate change, or instead on other imaginable steps to help people who are in need? If the goal is to assist poor people, perhaps there would be far better means than emissions reductions.

In fact, the argument from distributive justice runs into an additional problem in the context of climate change. No one would gain from an asteroid collision, but millions of people would benefit from climate change.[3] Many people die from cold, and to the extent that warming reduces cold, it will save lives.[4] Warming will also produce monetary benefits in many places, such as Russia, due to increases in agricultural productivity.[5] Indeed, many millions of poor people in such countries may benefit from climate change.[6] Some of them will live when they would otherwise die from extreme cold.[7] In China, many millions of people living in rural areas continue to be extremely poor despite the increasing prosperity of the nation as a whole. These people are among the poorest in the world. For at least some of these people, climate change could well provide benefits by increasing the productivity of their land.[8]

In addition, many millions of poor people would be hurt by the cost of emissions reductions. They would bear that cost in the form of higher energy bills, lost jobs, and increased poverty. Recall too that industrialized and relatively wealthy European nations have been found to be at greater risk than the relatively poorer China.[9]

It follows that purely as an instrument of redistribution, emission reductions on the part of the United States are quite crude. True, a suitably designed emissions control agreement would almost certainly help poor people more than it would hurt them, because disadvantaged people in sub-Saharan Africa and India are at such grave risk.[10] And true, an agreement in which the United States pays more than its self-interest dictates might well be better, from the standpoint of distributive justice, than the status quo, or than an agreement that would simply require all nations to scale back their emissions by a specified amount.[11] But there is a highly imperfect connection between distributive goals on the one hand and requiring wealthy countries to pay for emissions reductions on the other.

To see the problem more concretely, suppose that Americans (and the same could be said about citizens in other wealthy countries) are willing to devote a certain portion, X, of their national income to helping people living in poor countries. The question is,

How is X best spent? If X is committed to emissions controls, then X is being spent to benefit wealthy Europeans as well as impoverished Indians, and X is also being spent to harm some or many impoverished people living in China and Russia by denying them the benefit of increased agricultural productivity that warming will bring. And if all of X is spent on global emissions control, then none of X is being spent to purchase malaria nets or to distribute AIDS drugs—which are highly effective ways of helping poor people who are alive today rather than poor people who will be alive in 100 years.[12]

One response to this argument is that Americans should pay more than X: they should pay 2X or 5X or 100X. But this argument is not responsive. If Americans are willing to pay 2X or 5X or 100X, the question remains how this money should be used, and it is quite possible that 100X is better spent on malaria nets and AIDS drugs than on global emissions control, if the only goal is to help the poor. To be sure, it may be that, in fact, the best way to spend X is to cut greenhouse gas emissions. It is possible, for example, that more lives are saved from cutting greenhouse gas emissions than from distributing malaria nets and AIDS drugs, given a constant amount of money and taking into account that future lives and current lives must be put on a common metric. We cannot exclude this possibility, but we can say that the match between greenhouse gas reductions and distributive justice is quite crude.

C. Two Counterarguments

There are two tempting counterarguments. The first involves the risk of catastrophe. The second involves the fact that cash transfers will go to governments that may be ineffective or corrupt.

1. Catastrophe

On certain assumptions about the science, greenhouse gas cuts are necessary to prevent a catastrophic loss of life.[13] Suppose, by way of imperfect analogy, that a genocide is occurring in some nation.

For multiple reasons, it would not be sensible to say that rich countries should give money to such a nation, rather than acting to prevent the genocide. Or suppose that a nation is threatened by a natural disaster that would wipe out millions of lives; if other nations could eliminate the harms associated with such a disaster, it would be hard to object that they should offer cash payments instead. One reason is that if many lives are at risk, and if they can be saved through identifiable steps, taking those steps would seem to be the most effective response to the problem, and cash transfers would have little or no advantage.

Suppose that climate change threatens to create massive losses of life in various countries. In light of the risk of catastrophe, perhaps emissions reductions are preferable to other redistributive strategies. The catastrophic scenario is a way of saying that the future benefits of cuts could be exceptionally high rather than merely high. If poor people in poor nations face a serious risk of catastrophe, then greenhouse gas abatement *could* turn out to be the best way to redistribute wealth (or, more accurately, welfare) to people who would otherwise die in the future.

Ultimately the strength of the argument turns on the extent of the risk. To the extent that the risk of catastrophe is not low, and to the extent that it is faced mostly by people living in difficult or desperate conditions, the argument from distributive justice does gain a great deal of force. To the extent that the catastrophic scenario remains highly unlikely,[14] the argument is weakened. We cannot exclude the possibility that the argument is correct; it depends on the scientific evidence for the truly catastrophic scenarios.

2. Ineffective or Corrupt Governments

We have emphasized that development aid is likely to be more effective than greenhouse gas restrictions as a method of helping poor people in poor nations. A legitimate response is that cutting greenhouse gas emissions bypasses the governments of poor states more completely than other forms of development aid do. This might be counted as a virtue because the governments of many poor states are either inefficient or corrupt (or both), and partly for that reason, ordinary development aid has not been very effective.[15]

But here too there are counterarguments. As we have stressed, this form of redistribution does not help existing poor people at all; it can, at best, help poor people in future generations. And it is far from clear that donor states can avoid the pathologies of development aid by, in effect, transferring resources to the future rather than to the present, or by transferring resources directly to the people rather than to corrupt governments. Benefits received by individuals can be expropriated, or taxed away, by governments that do not respect the rule of law. This is just as true for the future as for the present. If abatement efforts today result in higher crop yields in Chad in 100 years than would otherwise occur, Chadians might be better off, of course, but it is also possible that a future authoritarian government would expropriate these gains for itself, or that they would be squandered as a result of bad economic policy, or that in the meantime Chad has become a completely different place that does best by importing food from elsewhere.

Even more important, the claim that emissions reductions avoid corruption overlooks the fact that emissions abatement does not occur by itself but must take place through the activity of governments, including those in developing countries. In cap-and-trade systems, for example, the government of a poor country would be given permits that it could then sell to industry, raising enormous sums of money that the government could spend however it chose. Corrupt governments would spend this money badly, perhaps using it to finance political repression, while also possibly accepting bribes from local industry that chooses not to buy permits, in return for non-enforcement of the country's treaty obligations.[16] To be sure, significant emissions reductions by wealthy nations would directly benefit poor nations.

Notwithstanding the complexities here, the basic point remains: in principle, greenhouse gas cuts do not seem to be the most direct or effective means of helping poor people or poor nations. We cannot exclude the possibility that the more direct methods are inferior, for example because it is not feasible to provide that direct aid; but it would remain necessary to explain why a crude form of redistribution is feasible when a less crude form is not. . . .

II. CORRECTIVE JUSTICE

Climate change differs from our asteroid example in another way. In the asteroid example, no one can be blamed for the appearance of the asteroid and the threat that it poses to India (or the world). But many people believe that by virtue of its past actions and policies, the United States, along with other developed nations, is particularly to blame for the problem of climate change.[17] In the international arena, the argument that the United States has an obligation to devote significant resources to reducing greenhouse gas emissions is not solely and perhaps not even mainly an argument about distributive justice. The argument also rests on moral intuitions about corrective justice—about wrongdoers and their victims.[18]

A. The Basic Argument

Corrective justice arguments are backward-looking, focused on wrongful behavior that occurred in the past.[19] Corrective justice therefore requires us to look at stocks rather than flows. Even though China is now the world's leading greenhouse gas emitter, the United States has been the largest emitter historically and thus has the greater responsibility for the stock of greenhouse gases in the atmosphere.[20] Of course, a disproportionate share of the stock of greenhouse gases can be attributed to other long-industrialized countries as well, such as Germany and Japan, and so what we say here about the United States can be applied, *mutatis mutandi*, to those other countries. The emphasis on the United States is warranted by the fact that the United States has contributed more to the existing stock than any other nation (nearly 30%).

In the context of climate change, the corrective justice argument is that the United States wrongfully harmed the rest of the world—especially low-lying states and others that are most vulnerable to global warming—by emitting greenhouse gases in vast quantities. On a widespread view, corrective justice requires that the United States devote significant resources to remedying the problem[21]—perhaps by paying damages, agreeing to extensive emissions reductions, or participating in a climate pact that is not in its self-interest. India, for example, might be thought to have a moral claim against the United States—one derived from the principles of corrective justice—and on this view the United States has an obligation to provide a compensatory remedy to India. (Because India is especially vulnerable to climate change,[22] we use that nation as a placeholder for those at particular risk.)

This argument enjoys a great deal of support in certain circles and seems intuitively correct. The apparent simplicity of the argument, however, masks some serious difficulties. We shall identify a large number of problems here, and the discussion will be lamentably complex. The most general point, summarizing the argument as a whole, is that the climate change problem poorly fits the corrective justice model because the consequence of tort-like thinking would be to force many people who have not acted wrongfully to provide a remedy to many people who have not been victimized. Some of the problems we identify could be reduced if it were possible to trace complex causal chains with great precision; unfortunately, legal systems lack the necessary tools to do so.

B. The Wrongdoer Identity Problem

The current stock of greenhouse gases in the atmosphere is a result of the behavior of people living in the past. Much of it is due to the behavior of people who are dead. The basic problem for corrective justice is that dead wrongdoers cannot be punished or held responsible for their behavior, or forced to compensate those they have harmed. At first glance, holding Americans today responsible for the activities of their ancestors is not fair or reasonable on corrective justice grounds, because current Americans are not the relevant wrongdoers; they are not responsible for the harm.

Indeed, many Americans today do not support the current American energy policy and already make some sacrifices to reduce the greenhouse gas emissions that result from their behavior. They avoid driving, they turn down the heat in their homes, and they support electoral candidates who advocate greener policies. Holding these people responsible for the wrongful activities of people who lived in the past seems perverse. An approach that emphasized corrective justice would attempt to be more finely tuned, focusing on particular actors, rather than Americans as a class, which would appear to violate deeply held moral objections to collective responsibility.[23] The task would be to distinguish between the contributions of those who are living and those who are dead.

The most natural and best response to this point is to insist that all or most Americans today benefit from the greenhouse gas emitting activities of Americans living in the past, and therefore it would not be wrong to require Americans today to pay for abatement measures. This argument is familiar from debates about slave reparations, where it is argued that Americans today have benefited from the toil of slaves 150 years ago.[24] To the extent that members of current generations have gained from past wrongdoing, it may well make sense to ask them to make compensation to those harmed as a result. On one view, compensation can work to restore the status quo ante, that is, to put members of different groups, and citizens of different nations, in the position that they would have occupied if the wrongdoing had not occurred.

In the context of climate however, this argument runs into serious problems. The most obvious difficulty is empirical. It is true that many Americans benefit from past greenhouse-gas-emissions, but how many benefit, and how much do they benefit? Many Americans today are, of course, immigrants or children of immigrants, and so not the descendants of greenhouse-gas-emitting Americans of the past. Such people may nonetheless gain from past emissions, because they enjoy the kind of technological advance and material wealth that those emissions made possible. But have they actually benefited, and to what degree? Further, not all Americans inherit the wealth of their ancestors, and even those who do would not necessarily have inherited less if their ancestors' generations had not engaged in the greenhouse-gas-emitting activities. The idea of corrective justice, building on the tort analogy, does not seem to fit the climate change situation.

Suppose that these various obstacles could be overcome and that we could trace, with sufficient accuracy, the extent to which current Americans have benefited from past emissions. As long as the costs are being toted up, the benefits should be as well, and used to offset the requirements of corrective justice. We have noted that climate change is itself anticipated to produce benefits for many nations, both by increasing agricultural productivity and by reducing extremes of cold.[25] And if past generations of Americans have imposed costs on the rest of the world, they have also conferred substantial benefits. American industrial activity has produced products that were consumed in foreign countries, for example, and has driven technological advances from which citizens in other countries have gained. Many of these benefits are positive externalities, for which Americans have not been fully compensated. To be sure, many citizens in, say, India have not much benefited from those advances, just as many citizens of the United States have not much benefited from them. But what would the world, or India, look like if the United States had engaged in 10% of its level of greenhouse gas emissions, or 20%, or 40%? For

purposes of corrective justice, a proper accounting would seem to be necessary, and it presents formidable empirical and conceptual problems.

In the context of slave reparations, the analogous points have led to interminable debates, again empirical and conceptual, about historical causation and difficult counterfactuals.[26] But for causation arguments, used in standard legal analysis and conventional for purposes of conventional justice, present serious and perhaps insuperable problems when applied historically. We can meaningfully ask whether an accident would have occurred if the driver had operated the vehicle more carefully, but conceptual and empirical questions make it difficult to answer the question whether and to what extent white Americans today would have been worse off if there had been no slavery—and difficult too to ask whether Indians would be better off today if Americans of prior generations had not emitted greenhouse gases. What kind of a question is that? In this hypothetical world of limited industrialization in the United States, India would be an entirely different country, and the rest of the world would be unrecognizably different as well.

Proponents of slave reparations have sometimes appealed to principles of corporate liability. Corporations can be immortal, and many corporations today benefited from the slave economy in the nineteenth century. Corporations are collectivities, not individuals, yet they can be held liable for their actions, which means that shareholders today are "punished" (in the sense of losing share value) as a result of actions taken by managers and employees long before the shareholders obtained their ownership interest. If innocent shareholders can be made to pay for the wrongdoing of employees who are long gone, why can't citizens be made to pay for the wrongful actions of citizens who lived in the past?

The best answer is that corporate liability is most easily justified on grounds other than corrective justice. Shareholder liability can be defended on the basis of consent or (in our view most plausibly) on the welfarist ground that corporate liability deters employees from engaging in wrongdoing on behalf of the corporate entity.[27] A factor that distinguishes corporate liability is that purchasing shares is a voluntary activity and one does so with the knowledge that the share price will decline if a past legal violation comes to light, and this is reflected in the share price at the time of purchase. (One also benefits if an unknown past action enhances the value of the company.) But because the corporate form itself is a fiction, and the shareholders today are different from the wrongdoers yesterday, corporate liability cannot be grounded in corrective justice.[28] Thus, it provides no analogy on behalf of corrective justice for the climate change debate.

C. The Victim/Claimant Identity Problem

As usually understood, corrective justice requires an identity between the victim and the claimant: the person who is injured by the wrongdoer must be the same as the person who has a claim against the wrongdoer.[29] In limited circumstances, a child or other dependent might inherit that claim, but usually one thinks of the dependent as having a separate claim, deriving from the wrongdoer's presumed knowledge that by harming the victim she also harms the victim's dependents.

Who are the victims of climate change? Most of them live in the future. Thus, their claims have not matured. To say that future Indians might have a valid claim against Americans today, or Americans of the past, is not the same as saying that Americans today have a duty to help Indians today. To be sure, some people are now harmed by climate change.[30] In addition, people living in low-lying islands or coastal regions can plausibly contend that a particular flood or storm has some probabilistic relationship with climate change—but from the standpoint of corrective justice, this group presents its own difficulties (a point to which we will return shortly). What remains plausible is the claim that future Indians would have corrective justice claims against current and past Americans.

A successful abatement program would, of course, benefit many people living in the future, albeit by preventing them from becoming victims in the first place or reducing the magnitude of their injury, rather than compensating them for harm. One might justify the abatement approach on welfarist grounds: perhaps the welfare benefits for people living in the future exceed the welfare losses to people living today. One could also make an argument that people living today have a nonwelfarist obligation to refrain from engaging in actions today that harm people in the future. The point for present purposes is that both arguments are forward-looking: the obligation, whether welfarist or nonwelfarist, is not based on past actions, and thus a nation's relative contribution to the current greenhouse gas stock in the atmosphere would not be a relevant consideration in the design of the greenhouse gas abatement program, as we have been arguing. By contrast, the corrective justice argument is that the United States should contribute the most to abatement efforts because it has caused the most damage to the carbon-absorbing capacity of the atmosphere.[31]

The argument that we owe duties to the future, on welfarist or other grounds, seems right, but as a basis for current abatement efforts, it runs into a complication. Suppose that activities in the United States that produce greenhouse gases (a) do harm people in the future by contributing to climate change, but also (b) benefit people in the future by amassing capital on which they can draw to reduce poverty and illness and to protect against a range of social ills. Supposing, as we agree, that present generations are obliged not to render future generations miserable, it is necessary to ask whether current activities create benefits that are equivalent to, or higher than, costs for those generations. As our discussion of distributive justice suggests, it is possible that greenhouse gas abatement programs—as opposed to, say, research and development or promoting economic growth in poor countries—are not the best way to ensure that the appropriate level of intergenerational equity is achieved. This point is simply the intertemporal version of the argument against redistribution by greenhouse gas abatement that we made above. Of course, it remains empirically possible that abatement programs would produce significant benefits for future generations without imposing equally significant burdens—in which case they would be justified on welfarist grounds. And we have agreed that, on those grounds, some kind of greenhouse gas abatement program, including all the leading contributors, would be justified. But this is not a point about corrective or distributive justice.

D. The Causation Problem

Corrective justice requires that the wrongdoing cause the harm. In ordinary person-to-person encounters, this requirement is straightforward. But in the context of climate change, causation poses formidable challenges, especially when we are trying to attribute particular losses to a warmer climate.

To see why, consider a village in India that is wiped out by a monsoon. One might make a plausible argument that the flooding was more likely than it would otherwise have been, as a result of rising sea levels caused by climate change. But it might well be impossible to show that greenhouse gas emissions in the United States "caused" the flooding, in the sense that they were a necessary and sufficient condition, and difficult even to show that they even contributed to it.[32] If the flooding was in a probabilistic sense the result of greenhouse gas activities around the world, its likelihood was also increased by complex natural phenomena that are poorly understood. And to the extent that the United States was involved, much of the contribution was probably due to people who died years ago.

Causation problems are not fatal to corrective justice claims, but they significantly weaken them. In tort law, courts are occasionally willing to assign liability according to market share when multiple firms contribute to a harm—for example, pollution or dangerous products whose provenance cannot be traced.[33] Perhaps scientific and economic

studies could find, with sufficient accuracy, aggregate national losses. And it would be plausible to understand corrective justice, in this domain, in probabilistic terms, with the thought that victims should receive "probabilistic recoveries," understood as the fraction of their injury that is probabilistically connected with climate change. It is unclear, however, that statistical relationships can be established with sufficient clarity to support a claim sounding in corrective justice.[34]...

CONCLUSION

...Our narrow goal has been to investigate considerations of distributive justice and corrective justice. If the United States wants to use its wealth to help to protect India or Africa or impoverished people generally, there can be no reason for complaint. The question remains, however, what is the best way to help disadvantaged people around the world. It is plausible that protecting other countries from genocide or poverty or famine is such a way. It is far from clear that greenhouse gas restrictions on the part of the United States are the best way to help the most disadvantaged citizens of the world.

It is tempting to treat climate change as a kind of tort, committed by the United States against those who are most vulnerable. But we have seen that principles of corrective justice have an awkward relationship to the problem of climate change. Many of the relevant actors are long dead, and a general transfer from the United States to those in places especially threatened by climate change is not an apt way of restoring some imagined status quo. In this context, the idea of corrective justice is a metaphor, and a highly imperfect one....

NOTES

1. Some scholars believe that poor nations have an entitlement to help from wealthy nations. See, e.g., Nussbaum, note 28, at 316–17, 324 (arguing that among the principles required to achieve social justice by meeting

basic human needs is an obligation of richer nations to provide "a substantial portion of their GDP to poorer nations"). And on welfarist grounds, we accept the conclusion that wealthy nations should transfer resources to poor people in poor nations. Posner, note 26, at 499–500. But even if this is so, assistance in the case we are describing is less valuable than direct financial aid—a point we shall be emphasizing.

2. See Nordhaus & Boyer, note 5, at 159, 161 (estimating $325 billion in abatement costs imposed on the United States by the Kyoto Protocol).

3. See Todd Sandler, *Global Public Goods* (2004); Lomborg, note 9.

4. See Lomborg, note 9.

5. See Nordhaus & Boyer, note 5, at 91 tbl.4.10; Cline, note 12, at 67–71.

6. Cf. Nordhaus & Boyer, note 5, at 91 tbl.4.10 (estimating agricultural benefits from warming in China and Russia—both countries with substantial low-income populations); *Cline*, note 12, at 67–71 (showing agricultural benefits without carbon fertilization to New Zealand and agricultural benefits with carbon fertilization to many nations, including China, Russia, and the United States).

7. See Lomborg, note 9.

8. See Nordhaus & Boyer, note 5, at 76 (showing agricultural gain of $3 billion from CO_2 doubling); Cline, note 12, at 68 (showing significant benefits to China, at least with carbon sequestration).

9. We acknowledge that greenhouse gas reductions might be accompanied by efforts to soften the economic hardship faced by poor people, as, for example, by cash subsidies to offset the increase in energy prices.

10. See Nordhaus & Boyer, note 5, at 81 tbl.4.7, 82, 83 tbl.4.8, 91 tbl.4.10; Cline, note 12, at 67–71.

11. On some of the complexities here, see Eric A. Posner & Cass R. Sunstein, *Should Greenhouse Gas Permits Be Allocated on a Per Capita Basis? Cal. L. Rev.* (2009). 97:51, 50–94.

12. For this argument in the more general context of tort and regulatory standards, see Eric A. Posner & Cass R. Sunstein, *Dollars and Death*, 72 *U. Chi. L. Rev.* 537, 583–84 (2005).

13. See Weitzman, note 88, at 7–8 (discussing potential impacts from dramatic increases in global temperatures).

14. See, e.g., Nordhaus & Boyer, note 5, at 81–83 (noting vulnerabilities to climate change in India and sub-Saharan Africa).

15. Cf. William Easterly, *The White Man's Burden* 131–34, 136–37, 147–57 (2006) (discussing corruption in some poor countries receiving development aid and

recommending new aid strategies for donor countries and institutions, including bypassing corrupt governments when direct aid to government does not produce results for the poor).

16. Cf. Nordhaus, note 1, at 130–31 (noting that limitations on emissions creates resource rents that can be exploited or abused under corrupt regimes).

17. See, e.g., Jiahua Pan, *Common but Differentiated Commitments: A Practical Approach to Engaging Large Developing Emitters Under L20* (2004), http://www.l20.org/publications/6_5c_climate_pan1.pdf; *Singer*, note 20, at 44–45.

18. We do not address whether there are *legal* challenges, specifically tort challenges, to greenhouse gas emissions. There is an extensive literature on this topic. See, e.g., David A. Grossman, *Warming Up to a Not-So-Radical Idea: Tort-Based Climate Change Litigation*, 28 *Colum. J. Envtl. L.* 1 (2003); David Hunter & James Salzman, *Negligence in the Air: The Duty of Care in Climate Change Litigation*, 155 *U. Pa. L. Rev.* 1741 (2007); Eduardo M. Penalver, *Acts of God or Toxic Torts? Applying Tort Principles to the Problem of Climate Change*, 38 *Nat. Resources J.* 563 (1998). For a discussion of the possibility of tort claims brought under the Alien Tort Statute, see Eric A. Posner, *Climate Change and International Human Rights Litigation: A Critical Appraisal*, 155 *U. Pa. L. Rev.* 1925 (2007). However, the tort claim and the moral claim are overlapping.

19. For this reason, corrective justice claims will not be appealing to welfarists, who tend to think that corrective justice is relevant, if at all, because it serves as a proxy for what welfarism requires. See Louis Kaplow & Steven Shavell, *Fairness Versus Welfare* 12 (2005). We tend to think that welfarists are generally correct here but bracket that point and the associated complexities for purposes of discussion.

20. We assume this point throughout, but if current trends continue, China will, in a matter of decades, exceed the United States in terms of both stocks and flows. We put this point to one side for now.

21. See, e.g., Daniel A. Farber, *Basic Compensation for Victims of Climate Change*, 155 *U. Pa. L. Rev.* 1605, 1641–42 (2007).

22. See Nordhaus & Boyer, note 5, at 91; Cline, note 12, at 69.

23. See, e.g., H.D. Lewis, *Collective Responsibility*, in *Collective Responsibility: Five Decades of Debate in Theoretical and Applied Ethics* 17, 17–34 (Larry May & Stacey Hoffman eds., 1991).

24. See Stephen Kershnar, *The Inheritance-Based Claim to Reparations*, 8 *Legal Theory* 243, 266–67 (2002) (describing and criticizing these arguments). These argu-

ments are often analogized to unjust enrichment arguments. See Eric A. Posner & Adrian Vermeule, *Reparations for Slavery and Other Historical Injustices*, 103 *Colum. L. Rev.* 689, 698 (2003).

25. See Cline, note 12, at 67–71; *Lomborg*, note 9, at 14, 104; Nordhaus & Boyer, note 5, at 76.

26. See Posner & Vermeule, note 127, at 699–703.

27. See id. at 703–08.

28. In recent years, some philosophers have challenged traditional criticisms of collective responsibility, but these philosophers tend to ground collective responsibility in individual failures to act when action was possible and likely to be effective, and when the person in question knew or should have known that she could have prevented the harm. See, e.g., Larry May, *Sharing Responsibility* 1 (1992); cf. Brent Fisse & John Braithwaite, *Corporations, Crime and Accountability* 50 (1993) (explaining why collective responsibility is appropriate in terms of corporate wrongdoing); Christopher Kutz. *Complicity: Ethics and Law for a Collective Age* 166–253 (2000) (explaining why individuals should be held accountable for certain collective harms); David Copp, *Responsibility for Collective Inaction. J. Soc. Phil.*, Fall 1991, at 71, 71 (explaining that "certain collective entities…have moral responsibility for their actions"). These arguments do not carry over to the greenhouse gas case.

29. See Posner & Vermeule, note 127, at 699.

30. The World Health Organization estimates that climate change produces 150,000 annual deaths and 5 million annual illnesses. See Jonathan Patz et al. *Impact of Regional Climate Change on Human Health*, 438 *Nature* 310, 313 (2005); Juliet Eilpern, *Climate Shift Tied to 150,000 Fatalities, Wash. Post*, Nov. 17, 2005, at A20, *available at* http://www.washingtonpost.com/.

31. We might also think that Americans of, say, the last decade or two can be held responsible for their greenhouse gas emissions; because most of them are alive today, they might be considered obliged to provide a remedy.

32. See R.A. Pielke et al., *Hurricanes and Global Warming*, 86 *Bull. Am. Meteorological Soc.* 1571, 1574 (2005) (discussing the uncertain connection between increased hurricane intensity and climate change).

33. See generally Michael Saks & Peter Blanck, *Justice Improved: The Unrecognized Benefits of Aggregation and Sampling in the Trial of Mass Torts*, 44 *Stan. L. Rev.* 815 (1992).

34. For more on the causation problem, see generally Posner, *supra* note 121.

REFERENCES

William Nordhaus and Joseph Boyer, *Warming the World* 91 (2000).

Todd Sandler, *Global Public Goods* (2004)

Bjorn Lomborg, *Cool It* (2007)

William Cline, *Climate Change, in Global Problems, Global Solutions 13* (Bjorn Lomborg ed. 2004)

Martin Weitzman, Structural Uncertainty and the Value of a Statistical Life in the Economics of Catastrophic Climate Change (2007), available at http://www.aei-brookings.org/publications/abstract.php?pid=1196

Eric A. Posner and Adrian Vermeule, Reparations for Slavery and Other Historical Injustices, 103 *Colum. L. Rev.* 689 (2003).

Eric A. Posner, International Law: A Welfarist Approach, 73 *U. Chi. L. Rev.* 487 (2006)

AESTHETICS

Many people love nature because of its aesthetic power. This aesthetic appreciation often provides a strong motivation for protecting the natural world, yet people are sometimes embarrassed that this reason seems sentimental or inconsequential. They worry that aesthetic considerations are flimsy compared to hard economic calculations or the possibility of finding new medicines or energy supplies in nature preserves. But are aesthetic considerations flimsy? People all over the world spend large sums of money buying, visiting, and preserving works of art and architecture, and much of this is motivated by aesthetic considerations. In 2005, Willem de Kooning's *Woman III*, a painting that measures 68 by 48½ inches, sold for $137.5 million. It is hard to think of much besides a work of art that has sold for more than $41,000 per square inch. If artworks are so valuable, why shouldn't the works of nature be considered valuable for similar reasons?

John Fisher provides an introduction to the field of environmental aesthetics. He discusses such topics as the aesthetic value of nature, environmentalism, and environmental art. He focuses especially on the roles that art plays in bringing us to value nature aesthetically as well as the roles of science and other human practices in the appreciation of nature.

Allen Carlson sets out the view that he calls "positive aesthetics": the claim that the entire natural world is beautiful and that the untouched natural environment has mainly positive aesthetic qualities. He traces the history of this view from nineteenth-century artists and aestheticians, through the work of contemporary writers and philosophers. He argues that science was important in the development of this view, and that it is central to the aesthetic appreciation of nature.

Ned Hettinger is concerned with how appeals to the aesthetics of nature provide reasons for environmental protection. He points out that many people think that beauty is in the eye of the beholder and is "merely" a matter of taste. Hettinger thinks that environmental aesthetics "needs some sort of objectivity if it is to help us adjudicate between developers who like strip malls and environmentalists who do not." However, he argues that Carlson overstates the objectivity of aesthetic judgments. Hettinger goes on to consider the views of those who doubt the objectivity of environmental appreciation and argue for relativity in environmental aesthetics. They too overstate their case: "The negative aesthetic value judgment about swamps as bug-infested wastelands is . . . [an] ignorant aesthetic response . . . that need not be taken seriously." Hettinger defends a middle-ground position, "critical pluralism," which he thinks is objective enough to make the case for protecting nature on aesthetic grounds. Hettinger concludes that "environmental aesthetics is important to environmental protection."

FURTHER READING

Brady, Emily. *Aesthetics of the Natural Environment*. Edinburgh: Edinburgh University Press, 2003. A discussion of aesthetic experience and aesthetic qualities, as well as early theories of aesthetic appreciation of nature, including the beautiful, the sublime, and the picturesque.

Budd, Malcolm. *The Aesthetic Appreciation of Nature*. Oxford: Oxford University Press, 2002. An original theory that critically engages with Kant's views on the aesthetics of nature.

Carlson, Allen. *Nature and Landscape: An Introduction to Environmental Aesthetics*. New York, NY: Columbia University Press, 2008. A good introduction to the field and the most recent statement by the leading advocate of "positive aesthetics."

Carlson, Allen, and Sheila Lintott, eds. *Nature, Aesthetics, and Environmentalism: From Beauty to Duty*. New York, NY: Columbia University Press, 2007. A collection of recent papers by leading scholars in the field.

Moore, Ronald. *Natural Beauty: A Theory of Aesthetics Beyond the Arts*. Buffalo, NY: Broadview Press, 2007. A systematic and original book on the philosophy of beauty.

DISCUSSION QUESTIONS

1. How would you characterize environmental aesthetics?
2. Is beauty the only aesthetic property that matters for making the case for environmental protection on aesthetic grounds?
3. What is the thesis of "positive aesthetics"? What arguments can be given for and against it?
4. What is the case for relativity in environmental aesthetics? Does it succeed in undermining the role of environmental aesthetics in making the case for the preservation of nature?
5. What does Hettinger mean by "critical pluralism" about aesthetic responses to the environment? Is he right that this is a strong enough view to underwrite the case for protecting nature on aesthetic grounds?

JOHN A. FISHER

Environmental Aesthetics

The rapid growth of concern for the natural environment over the last third of the twentieth century has brought the welcome reintroduction of nature as a significant topic in aesthetics. In virtue of transforming previous attitudes towards nature, environmentalist thinking has posed questions about how we conceptualize our aesthetic interactions with nature, the aesthetic value of nature, and the status of art about nature. Although environmental concerns have undoubtedly motivated the new aesthetic interest in nature, the term "environmental aesthetics" connotes two overlapping but distinct themes, one emphasizing the aesthetics of nature as understood by environmentalism, the second focusing on the notion of environments of all sorts as objects of appreciation.

First, the environmental roots. Beginning in the romantic era, poets and painters began to represent nature as more than merely the backdrop of human enterprise and drama. Nature began to be seen as comprising landscapes compelling in their own wild beauty and objects valuable in their smallest natural detail. Writing later in the nineteenth century, Henry David Thoreau and John Muir in different ways emphasized hands-on interactions with wilderness. In doing so, they introduced the radical notions that wild nature is in many respects superior to civilization and its products, and that harmonious, non-exploitative encounters with it are of transformative value.

To this must be added the Darwinian revolution, locating humans as merely an element within nature rather than masters of it, and the development of ecological thinking: the notion that elements of nature are thoroughly interdependent. This interrelation of natural elements led Aldo Leopold in the 1940s to formulate the Land Ethic: "A thing is right when it tends to preserve the integrity, stability, and beauty of the biotic community. It is wrong when it tends otherwise" (Leopold 1966: 240). Leopold's Land Ethic shifts the centre of moral gravity from humans to the larger nature of which they are a part, and it also allots a central place to the aesthetic value of nature.

From this perspective, nature is regarded not as an adversary or resource to be subdued and exploited, but as something with an autonomous and worthy existence in itself. In contrast to prior European attitudes, wilderness is regarded not as ugly or as a blemish on existence, but as something not only admirable, but admirable aesthetically. Indeed, environmental thinkers often indict traditional ways of understanding and regarding nature for being "anthropocentric."

The label "environmental aesthetics" applies naturally to the ensuing wave of investigations of the aesthetics of nature conducted under the influence of environmental concerns. (Berleant 1998 suggests that environmental aesthetics is actually the successor to nature aesthetics.) Also important, however, is a broader use of the label championed by Berleant (1992) and Carlson (1992), who use it to cover aesthetic investigation of our experience of all sorts of environments, man-made as well as natural. This broader category of environmental aesthetics incorporates such diverse fields as city planning, landscape architecture, and environmental design, and it is significant because, whether applied to nature or built environments, it directly challenges the object-at-a-distance model associated with standard theories in aesthetics. That said, the majority of new work that falls notionally under this broader definition of environment grows out of concerns about nature instigated by environmentalism, and it concentrates on natural environments. Accordingly, most of the work to be explored in this chapter will be of this specific sort. As Berleant acknowledges, "An interest in the aesthetics of environment is part of a broader response to environmental problems...and to public awareness and action on environmental issues" (1992: xii).

In environmental thinking and the attendant interest in environments in the broad sense, some thinkers see implications for the general practice of aesthetics, a discipline that in the twentieth century persistently ignored nature in favour of theories based on the arts. Environmental thinking, however, has begun to place strain on the assumption that aesthetic concepts drawn from the arts are also adequate to nature and to everyday life.

1. THE AESTHETIC VALUE OF NATURE

Although beauty has been out of fashion in the high arts throughout much of the twentieth century, most people happily view and describe nature as beautiful. Indeed, whereas disagreement about the aesthetic quality of artworks is commonplace, typically there is less disagreement about ascribing positive aesthetic qualities, such as beauty or grandeur, to individual objects (Siberian tigers) and places (Grand Canyon) in nature. What *is* accepted without question about artworks as a class (setting aside the avant-garde) is that they have *value*. Further, it is natural to think of this value as a *non-instrumental*, i.e. intrinsic, value. For instance, we do not lightly contemplate destroying art even if it would be convenient or profitable—indeed, even if preservation comes at a considerable cost.

Environmentalist thinking impacts aesthetics precisely in the thought that nature should be treated in the same way. Hargrove (1989) and Thompson (1995), for example, have noted that

we value artworks as a class and accept obligations concerning their preservation. They do not regard this valuation as an arbitrary convention; the various aesthetic properties and meanings possessed by artworks give them an aesthetic value deriving from these aesthetic features. Hargrove and Thompson argue that nature is similarly valuable and worthy of preserving because of its aesthetic qualities. Thompson urges that, just as we accept an obligation to preserve beautiful artworks, we have obligations to preserve aesthetically valuable nature areas. (For a critique of such aesthetic preservationism see Godlovitch 1989.) Thompson also claims that the same sort of critical and evaluative discourse that applies to the arts appropriately applies to nature; the same patterns of reasoning that lead us to conclude that artworks have high aesthetic quality can be applied to parts of nature. It is not only that there are beautiful details and magnificent and rich structures in nature, but also that, like art, natural objects and sites can provide challenges to our conventional ways of perception, as well as to cultural significance, connection with the past, and so forth.

Because it plays a key role in preservationist arguments, aesthetic value is a more consequential concept in environmental aesthetics than it is in contemporary art aesthetics. Artworks as a class are regarded in modern society as having little instrumental value; they have no other use than to be appreciated. But nature clearly is another story. Humans, modern or not, need to exploit many aspects of nature, and we have the capacity thoroughly to develop almost all of it, if we choose. Nature, in short, has great instrumental value. If, as aesthetic preservationists argue, the aesthetic value of undeveloped nature ought to restrain our use of it for resource extraction, industry, recreation, etc., then aesthetic value has to bear significant weight.

Preservationist reasoning implies that the aesthetic value of undeveloped or wild nature is superior to that of developed nature. For example, an artificial lake will not possess the aesthetic value of the valleys or canyons that were flooded to make it, even though superficially it may be attractive. This suggests that it is unlikely that mere formal features (shapes, colours, reflecting surfaces, etc.) will fully account for the aesthetic value of nature. But what then needs to be added to formal properties, and where and how do we draw the line between nature (canyon) and artefact (lake)?

Environmentalist thinkers find difficulty with treatments of aesthetic value simply in terms of pleasure (as in Beardsley 1982). Brady (1998) classifies such approaches as "hedonist models" of aesthetic appreciation. She says that the "hedonist model classifies aesthetic value as a type of amenity value, where nature is valued for the aesthetic pleasure that it provides to inhabitants or visitors" (p. 97). She argues that such an emphasis on subjective pleasure will not support the conservation of a natural area as against, for instance, a potentially colourful recreational development. As an alternative, she proposes that an updated version of Kantian disinterestedness—with its eschewal of self-interest and utility—provides a better account of the aesthetic stance appropriately underpinning appreciation of nature. (For critiques of disinterestedness applied to nature appreciation, see Berleant 1992; Miller 1993.)

Clearly, then, environmental thinkers have to account for the difference between authentic or wild nature and an artificial nature that might be perceptually similar. Accordingly, the notion of indiscernible counterparts plays a key role in environmental aesthetics, just as it has in recent art aesthetics, where philosophers (e.g. Walton, Danto, Levinson, Currie) have used examples of indiscernible objects one of which is an artwork and the other of which is a different artwork or no artwork at all to argue against the idea that the status and the aesthetic qualities of artworks are determined solely by their inherent perceptual properties. For nature, the aesthetic difference between perceptually similar states of affairs becomes practically important in the context of restoration ecology, the field that proposes to restore or recreate natural areas that have been degraded by human development (see Elliot 1997). Regardless of

whether this is biologically possible, the aesthetic question is whether nature can be exploited—e.g. by mining—and then restored to its original state with similar aesthetic qualities.

The first question is whether one can appreciate an artefactualized segment of "nature" as if it were natural. Carlson (1981) considers the difference between a natural coastline and a hypothetical one that is perceptually indistinguishable but created by removal of structures, large-scale earth, rock and sand movement, landscaping with similar plants, and so on. He argues that these two coastlines should be perceived differently, one as an artefact, the other as a natural coastline. Although they may have similar curves, lines, colours and shapes, he asserts that we properly ascribe many different second-order properties to these similar perceptual patterns. For example, the curve of one coast is *very ingenious*, whereas the curve of the natural coast is no such thing, but rather is the product of erosion by the sea. On the other hand, perhaps the natural coast *expresses the power of the sea*, whereas the artefact coast does no such thing. Carlson concludes that, because we are led to ascribe different properties to the object, it is aesthetically important to perceive an object under the category to which it belongs, as either an artefact or the product of natural forces, just as it is aesthetically important to perceive an artwork in its true art historical category (cf. Walton 1970).

It is natural to suppose that the aesthetic *value* of an item increases with its aesthetic *quality*. Applying this relation to nature seems to imply that some parts of nature have greater aesthetic value than other parts. Some thinkers (e.g. Thompson 1995) accept this, but many others reject the idea that nature can be aesthetically evaluated and ranked in a way parallel to artworks.

A common view among environmental thinkers is that dubbed "positive aesthetics" by Allen Carlson. The strongest version of this position holds that all virgin nature is beautiful (Carlson 1984: 10). A weaker formulation is that the "natural environment, in so far as it is untouched by man, has mainly positive aesthetic qualities; it is, for example, graceful, delicate, intense, unified, and orderly, rather than bland, dull, insipid, incoherent, and chaotic" (Carlson 1984:5). The weaker version clearly does not entail that all parts of nature are equally beautiful, and so it may leave undefended the claim implied by the stronger version: namely, that we cannot maintain that one part of nature is aesthetically superior to another part. The proponent of positive aesthetics rejects conventional aesthetic hierarchies concerning nature—e.g., majestic mountain *v.* bland prairie *v.* dank swamp. Although the aesthetic evaluation of artworks may vary from great to mediocre to poor, and their qualities from beautiful to boring to ugly, this is exactly what is different about nature, according to positive aesthetics.

Positive aesthetics can be understood as the result of two intuitions. First, that aesthetic assessment of art involves criticism, judgement and ultimately *comparison*. But such comparative judgements are appropriate only for artefacts, which are intended to be a certain way or to accomplish certain goals, not for nature. Second, our tendency to find some parts of nature bland, boring, or even distasteful are all based on projecting *inappropriate* ideas or comparisons on to the objects of our experience, for example looking for a view of nature that is similar to a beautifully framed and balanced art representation, or looking at a dark forest as full of evil spirits. Nature properly understood—that is, against a background of biology, geology, and ecology—is, as a matter of fact beautiful, or at least aesthetically good, in many ways.

As Callicott notes, paraphrasing Leopold, knowledge of the ecological relationships between the organisms, the evolutionary and geological history, and so forth can transform a marsh "from a 'waste,' 'God-forsaken' mosquito swamp, into a thing of precious beauty" (Callicott 1987: 162). We see that the marsh is a thing of beauty when we appreciate it as the habitat of the sandhill crane, when we understand that the cranes originated in distant geological

ages, when we understand the intricate interrelations of all of the organisms in the marsh, and so on. Conversely, superficially attractive but non-native plants and animals may be seen as disharmonious interlopers that undermine the balance of nature. (For a sympathetic critique of positive aesthetics, see Godlovitch 1998.)

2. ENVIRONMENTALISM AND THE APPRECIATION OF NATURE

Of the many questions that environmentalist claims give rise to, perhaps none is more fundamental than the question whether nature can be appropriately appreciated with the same methods and assumptions with which we appreciate art. The model of appreciation at the heart of standard art aesthetics is roughly this: it is an interpretive judgement of a demarcated object based on a conventionally circumscribed perception of it. Environmentally inclined aestheticians have found difficulty with many aspects of this model. The environmental tradition gives rise to a preference for a more active relationship with, and within, a natural world of interconnected elements. These points lead to the notion (Carlson 1979; Berleant 1992) that environmental appreciation (*a*) is typically a physically active interaction, (*b*) involves integrated and self-conscious use of all the senses, including touch and smell (Tuan 1993), and (*c*) does not privilege any one vantage point or small set of vantage points as the correct place from which to experience the natural setting or objects.

Are these conditions sufficient for aesthetic experience of nature (or any environment)? If so, then would any self-conscious interaction with nature, e.g. pleasurably basking in the sun, be an aesthetic experience? If not, then what more needs to be added? Carlson (1979) argues that the further feature required is that one's sensory interaction be guided by commonsense/scientific knowledge about nature. Without this cognition, our experience is a blooming, buzzing confusion; but with such science-based cognition our raw experience acquires determinate centres of aesthetic significance and is made harmonious and meaningful.

Another question stimulated by the environmentalist model is whether an aesthetic response to a natural environment is, as in conventional aesthetics, in essence a perceptual–judgemental one, or whether it can be an *action*, such as rock climbing, hiking, or Thoreauvian digging and planting beans. An example of an action or series of actions that are usually regarded as highly aesthetic occurs in the Japanese tea ceremony, where respect for the utensils, ingredients, and the nature setting of the tea house is an integral part of the ceremony, and one of the basic goals of the ceremony is to exemplify harmony between the host and the setting. Even such examples, however, exhibit highly refined perception as an integral component of the actions. So, one could propose that in general actions can be aesthetic if, first of all, they are responses *to* objects and situations, and second, the response is founded upon an aesthetic perception of the situation.

Carlson's (1979, 1981) science-based model of aesthetic appreciation of nature (extended by Carlson, 1985, to all environments) has received considerable attention. For instance, Saito (1984) questions the necessity, and Rolston (1995) the sufficiency, of a science-based appreciation of nature such as Carlson advocates. Carroll further argues that there are alternatives to Carlson's picture, insisting that an emotional response to nature "can be an appropriate form of nature appreciation" (Carroll 1993: 253) and that such a response need not be based on scientific knowledge: it could simply involve, say, being overwhelmed by the grandeur of "a towering cascade." Carroll thus proposes a pluralist model that allows as one sort of legitimate aesthetic appreciation of nature a kind of response that, although based on perception of salient natural features, is not grounded in scientifically informed perception.

The main argument for a science-based appreciation of nature is that we require an objective basis for appreciating nature as it truly is, not as we wish it or

fear it to be, and that science is our best procedure for understanding nature objectively. Godlovitch (1994) finds that this argument does not go far enough. He emphasizes the environmentalist desideratum that we regard nature "as it is and not merely as it is for us" (p. 16). Accordingly, he claims that a "natural aesthetic must forswear the anthropocentric limits which fittingly define and dominate our aesthetic response to and regard for cultural objects" (p. 16). He argues that even science is too much a reflection of human sensibilities to constitute the basis of a true environmentalist aesthetic, which would be *acentric*, privileging no point of view, least of all a human one: "Centric [e.g. anthropocentric and biocentric] environmentalism fails to reflect Nature as a whole because Nature is apportioned and segmented by it" (p. 17). But is it possible for us to adopt a regard of nature that eschews human perspectives, and if it is, can we still regard this as involving aesthetic appreciation?

3. ENVIRONMENTAL ART?

Nature art has obviously been a key factor in a general increase of appreciation of wild nature and in the growth of environmentalism—witness the importance of nature photography to the efforts of conservation groups. There is a certain irony, then, in the fact that environmentalist arguments concerning how we ought to appreciate nature threaten to undermine the legitimacy of nature art and to raise questions as well about other sorts of art about nature.

Within the generic category of art *about* nature, we can define the familiar genre of "nature art" as representations of nature in any art medium—principally, literature and the visual arts—that have nature, not humans, as their main subject. In addition, nature art is usually thought of as exhibiting the same favourable regard to nature as positive aesthetics; even fierce, barren, or threatening landscapes are presented as being admirable or as having positive aesthetic features.

Although nature art inspires appreciation of nature, does it reflect the aesthetics of nature as environmental aesthetics understands it? One aspect of this broad question can be stated as follows: can works of nature art *exhibit or represent* the aesthetic qualities of the nature represented?

Carlson (1979) gives an influential argument—endorsed by Callicott (1987), Carroll (1993), and Godlovitch (1994)—for rejecting the "object" and "landscape" models of nature appreciation, which appears relevant to the question of aesthetic adequacy. Based on art appreciation, these models involve looking at objects in nature for their formal and expressive qualities, abstracting them from their context as if they were sculpture, or framing and perceiving sites as if in a landscape painting. Carlson argues that neither of these methods respects the actual nature of nature. To appreciate nature as nature, we must regard nature as an *environment* (in the broad sense) and as *natural*, but not as art. This means that we cannot, as in the object model, remove objects from their environments. If we remove them, even notionally, we change their aesthetic qualities, which the objects have only in relation to the whole environment. For example, a rock considered by itself may lack the qualities that it has in nature, where it is related to the forces that shaped it (glaciation, volcanism, erosion). The problem with the landscape model is that it involves perceiving nature "as a grandiose prospect seen from a specific standpoint and distance" (Carlson 1979: 131). Carlson describes appreciating nature this way as dividing nature up into blocks of scenery to be viewed from a certain vantage point, "not unlike a walk through a gallery of landscape paintings" (p. 132). But, as he notes, "the environment is not a scene, not a representation, not static, and not two-dimensional" (p. 133).

Yet, if this is the wrong way to experience nature aesthetically, can we experience nature aesthetically (albeit indirectly) or experience the aesthetic properties of nature through appreciating nature art? Carlson's argument raises the question whether we can experience the beauty of a natural environment by appreciating the beauty of a photograph of that environment. However, might not nature art exhibit how a part of nature actually appeared at a certain moment from a certain point of view? Even though limited and incomplete, why must a representation be seen as necessarily unable authentically to exhibit *some* of the aesthetic qualities of the represented objects or scenes?

Different issues are raised by non-representational art about nature, for instance artworks that incorporate natural objects, sites, or processes as elements. Such features by themselves, of course, do not necessarily determine that an artwork is *about* nature. Some artworks that superficially relate to a natural site, such as sculpture placed in a nature setting (e.g. sculpture parks), as well as works that use natural elements, such as Jeff Koons's 1992 *Puppy* (a 43-foot-high West Highland Terrier form covered with thousands of live flowers), are plainly not *about* nature. Carlson helpfully defines the class of "environmental artworks" as works that "are in or on the land in a way such that part of nature constitutes a part of the relevant object . . . not only is the site of an environmental work an environmental site, but the site itself is an aspect of the work" (1986: 636).

Given the deep divide separating the arts and environmental thought, it is essential to contrast their perspectives concerning this large domain of artefacts. From the perspective of the arts, attention naturally focuses on how to interpret and appreciate environmental works *as art*. What issues about nature and culture does the artist deal with? How does the piece relate to trends in recent art? What attitudes does it express? And so on. For example, Gilbert-Rolfe interprets Smithson's *Spiral Jetty* in relation to film: "In Smithson the idea of the work lies as much in the film of the work as in the work" (Gilbert-Rolfe 1988: 72). And Smithson (1973), as theorist of earthworks art, interprets Central Park as a landscape inspired by the eighteenth-century picturesque. Finally, Ross proposes that environmental artworks as a class are the descendants of the eighteenth-century high art

of gardening, that "environmental art is *gardening's avant-garde*" (Ross 1993: 153).

There is also the issue of whether gardens and parks, the environments seemingly most intermediate between the arts and nature, are full-fledged artworks. Certainly many examples of both types of artefact have a strong claim to the status of art. Smithson (1973) argues, for example, that New York's Central Park is a great artwork, exemplifying many of the dialectical principles of his own earthworks. Miller urges that gardens constitute an artkind, on a par with painting or sculpture. This is so clear that it leads to a puzzle: "Why then, if current theories of art show no grounds for excluding them…and if gardens have a history of being regarded as an artkind and can be shown to have form as beautiful, as original, and as self-conscious as the other arts, are gardens currently excluded from the category of art?" (Miller 1993: 72). She resolves this by noting the ways that gardens—by their essence tied to particular sites, ever-changing because of the natural elements, etc.—present multiple challenges to standard preferences of art theory, such as for complete artistic control of the work and for consistent qualities of the work over time.

From the perspective of environmental thought, however, with its inherent rejection of any activity or stance that regards nature as something to be used or as something whose purpose is to be determined by cultural perspectives, the issues point in a different direction, towards how environmental artworks deal with nature. Thus, because earthworks since their inception have often inspired opposition from environmentalists, it is not surprising that the question whether environmental artworks are an *affront* to nature has been explored (Carlson 1986). Less severe questions can also be raised, such as whether environmental artworks are based on an adequate conception of nature and whether they enfranchise an appropriate aesthetic relationship with nature. Topiary, for example, is intriguing as an artform. But by imposing artificial (geometric, representational) forms on to natural objects (trees and shrubs)

topiary does not illuminate the aesthetic properties of nature as nature: it suggests not only that nature can be improved upon aesthetically, but that nature provides sculptural material to be manipulated and exploited.

Ross (1993) organizes environmental art into seven categories, such as "masculine gestures in the environment" (Heizer, Smithson, De Maria), "ephemeral gestures in the environment" (Singer, Long, Fulton, Goldsworthy), and "proto-gardens" (Sonfist, Irwin). Some of this work is clearly troubling in how it uses and/or regards nature, for example Heizer's *Double Negative* (1969–70)—a 50 ft × 30 ft × 1500 ft bulldozed double cut in Virgin River Mesa, displacing 240,000 tons of rhyolite and sandstone—and Christo's *Surrounded Islands* (1983)—eleven islands in Biscayne Bay surrounded for two weeks by sheets of bright pink plastic floating in the water extended 200 ft from the islands into the Bay.

Carlson (1986) rebuts several common defences of such intrusive artworks, for example that they are temporary (Christo), that they improve nature, or that the artist's actions are no different from the alteration of a site by natural processes (Smithson's argument). In spite of this, there are other works of environmental art, such as Sonfist's *Time Landscape* (1965–78), in which the artist attempts to recreate an urban area's lost native flora on a vacant urban lot, that cannot be regarded as affronts to nature, since they do not alter natural aesthetic qualities. Because they respect nature as nature, such works, as well as the conceptual walks and environmental gestures of Long, Fulton, and Goldsworthy, can also be regarded as adequate aesthetically to nature, that is as reflecting nature's actual aesthetic qualities.

Still, there remains a nagging question: can this art contribute to the appreciation of nature? Carlson (1986) wonders why the aesthetic interest in nature can be recognized only if it is first considered art. There seems, in fact, to be a dilemma. Either a work alters nature (e.g. "masculine gestures"), in which case it may affront and misunderstand nature as nature,

or it does not (e.g. "ephemeral gestures"), in which case what does it add to the appreciation of nature? It might be replied that at least such art leads the viewer to notice aspects of nature that had escaped her attention. But more might be claimed. The arts have always been one way to explore the world and our feelings and ideas about it. Environmental art explores our ideas about nature and our changing relations with it. As such, works may not always express the most environmentally enlightened perspectives, and works in the past—for example formal gardens—probably did not. Still, are inadequate conceptions of nature entirely wrong? Can't there be aspects of nature that are usefully brought out even by such works? In any event, those environmental artworks that do adopt environmentally enlightened perspectives can be viewed as addressing in unique ways questions about how we can interact with nature aesthetically while at the same time respecting nature for what it is.

REFERENCES

Beardsley, M. (1982). "The Aesthetic Point of View," reprinted in M. J. Wreen and D. M. Callen (eds.), *The Aesthetic Point of View: Selected Essays*. Ithaca, NY: Cornell University Press, pp. 15–34.

Berleant, A. (1992). *The Aesthetics of Environment*. Philadelphia: Temple University Press.

—— (1998). "Environmental Aesthetics," in M. Kelly (ed.), *Encyclopedia of Aesthetics*. New York: Oxford University Press, pp. 114–20.

—— and Carlson, A. (1998). "Introduction to Special Issue on Environmental Aesthetics." *Journal of Aesthetics and Art Criticism* 56: 97–100.

Brady, E. (1998). "Imagination and the Aesthetic Appreciation of Nature." *Journal of Aesthetics and Art Criticism* 56: 139–47.

Callicott, J. (1987). "The Land Aesthetic," in J. Callicott (ed.), *Companion to* A Sand County Almanac: *Interpretive and Critical Essays*. Madison: University of Wisconsin Press, pp. 157–71.

Carlson, A. (1979). "Appreciation and the Natural Environment." *Journal of Aesthetics and Art Criticism* 37: 267–75.

—— (1981). "Nature, Aesthetic Judgment, and Objectivity." *Journal of Aesthetics and Art Criticism* 40: 15–27.

—— (1984). "Nature and Positive Aesthetics." *Environmental Ethics* 6: 5–34.

—— (1985). "On Appreciating Agricultural Landscapes." *Journal of Aesthetics and Art Criticism* 43: 301–12.

—— (1986). "Is Environmental Art an Aesthetic Affront to Nature?" *Canadian Journal of Philosophy* 16: 635–50.

—— (1992). "Environmental Aesthetics," in D. Cooper (ed.), *A Companion to Aesthetics*. Oxford: Blackwell, pp. 142–4.

—— (2000). *Aesthetics and the Environment: The Appreciation of Nature, Art and Architecture*. London: Routledge.

Carroll, N. (1993). "On Being Moved by Nature: Between Religion and Natural History," in S. Kemal and I. Gaskell (eds.), *Landscape, Natural Beauty and the Arts*. Cambridge: Cambridge University Press, pp. 244–66.

Elliot, R. (1997). *Faking Nature: The Ethics of Environmental Restoration*. London: Routledge.

Fisher, J. (1998). "What the Hills Are Alive with: In Defense of the Sounds of Nature." *Journal of Aesthetics and Art Criticism* 56: 167–79.

Gilbert-Rolfe, J. (1988). "Sculpture as Everything Else, or Twenty Years or So of the Question of Landscape." *Arts Magazine* January: 71–5.

Godlovitch, S. (1989). "Aesthetic Protectionism." *Journal of Applied Philosophy* 6: 171–80.

—— (1994). "Icebreakers: Environmentalism and Natural Aesthetics." *Journal of Applied Philosophy* 11: 15–30.

—— (1998). "Valuing Nature and the Autonomy of Natural Aesthetics." *British Journal of Aesthetics* 38: 180–97.

Hargrove, E. C. (1989). *Foundations of Environmental Ethics*. Englewood Cliffs, NJ: Prentice-Hall.

Leopold, A. (1966). *Sand County Almanac, with Other Essays on Conservation from Round River*. New York: Oxford University Press. First published 1949.

Miller, M. (1993). *The Garden as an Art*. Albany, NY: State University of New York Press.

Rolston, H. III (1995). "Does Aesthetic Appreciation of Landscapes Need to be Science-based?" *British Journal of Aesthetics* 35: 374–86.

Ross, S. (1993). "Gardens, Earthworks, and Environmental Art," in S. Kemal and I. Gaskell (eds.), *Landscape, Natural Beauty and the Arts*. Cambridge: Cambridge University Press, pp. 158–82.

———— (1998). *What Gardens Mean*. Chicago: University of Chicago Press.

Saito, Y. (1984). "Is There a Correct Aesthetic Appreciation of Nature?" *Journal of Aesthetic Education* 18: 35–46.

———— (1998). "The Aesthetics of Unscenic Nature." *Journal of Aesthetics and Art Criticism* 56: 100–11.

Sepanmaa, Y. (1993). *Beauty of Environment: A General Model for Environmental Aesthetics*. 2nd edn. Denton, Tex.: Environmental Ethics Books.

Smithson, R. (1973). "Frederick Law Olmstead and the Dialectical Landscape." *Artforum* February; reprinted in N. Holt (ed.), *The Writings of Robert Smithson: Essays with Illustrations*. New York: New York University Press, 1979, pp. 117–28.

Thompson, J. (1995). "Aesthetics and the Value of Nature." *Environmental Ethics* 17: 291–305.

Tuan, Y. (1993). *Passing Strange and Wonderful: Aesthetics, Nature, and Culture*. New York: Kodansha International.

Walton, K. (1970). "Categories of Art." *Philosophical Review* 79: 334–67.

ALLEN CARLSON

Nature and Positive Aesthetics

THE DEVELOPMENT OF POSITIVE AESTHETICS

In this chapter I examine the view that all the natural world is beautiful. According to this view, the natural environment, insofar as it is untouched by humans, has mainly positive aesthetic qualities: it is, for example, graceful, delicate, intense, unified, and orderly, rather than bland, dull, insipid, incoherent, and chaotic. All virgin nature, in short, is essentially aesthetically good. The appropriate or correct aesthetic appreciation of the natural world is basically positive and negative aesthetic judgments have little or no place.

Such a view of the appropriate aesthetic appreciation of the natural world is initially implausible. Concerning the aesthetic appreciation of art, for example, a comparable view would not warrant serious consideration, for it is not the case that all art is essentially aesthetically good; in such appreciation, negative aesthetic judgments have a significant place. In spite of this initial implausibility, the view that all virgin nature is essentially aesthetically good has numerous supporters, particularly among those who have given serious thought to the natural environment. Thus, it deserves careful consideration. In what follows I elaborate it by reference to some historical and contemporary sources and examine various justifications that may be offered for it.

The roots of the view may be traced to at least eighteenth-century ideas concerning the primacy of natural beauty and the beauty of nature as a norm for art.[1] In the nineteenth century it becomes explicit in the writings of landscape artists and others concerned with nature. For example, 1821 marks landscape painter John Constable's much quoted comment: "I

never saw an ugly thing in my life."[2] At this time the idea of nature as essentially beautiful is also interwoven with a developing awareness of the negative effects of human intervention. Thus, in 1857 John Ruskin, in giving counsel to landscape artists, can find the certainty of beauty only in that which he takes to be beyond the reach of humanity:

> Passing then to skies, note that there is this great peculiarity about sky subject, as distinguished from earth subject;—that the clouds, not being much liable to man's interference, are always beautifully arranged. You cannot be sure of this in any other features of landscape.[3]

By the second half of the nineteenth century the view can also be found in the work of individuals who are best described as environmental reformers. For example, 1864 dates the publication of George Marsh's *Man and Nature*, which has been described as "the fountainhead of the conservation movement" and "the beginning of land wisdom in this country [the United States]."[4] Here Marsh develops two hypotheses—that "nature left alone is in harmony" and that humanity is "the great disturber of nature's harmonies." Early in the book, he enumerates nature's "manifold blessings" for humanity. All, he points out, "must be earned by toil" and are "gradually ennobled by the art of man," with one exception—natural beauty. This blessing is only disturbed, not ennobled, by humans; for it, Marsh says, "unaided nature make[s] provision." He suggests that these beauties "that now, even in their degraded state, enchant every eye" could be fully and universally appreciated "only in the infancy of lands where all the earth was fair."[5]

The related ideas of humanity as the destroyer of nature's beauty and of "all the earth" as beautiful

except for humanity's influence are not limited to somewhat scholarly works such as *Man and Nature*. By the end of the nineteenth century they are key notions in movements of social reform. In public lectures given in the 1880s, artist, poet, and social critic William Morris preaches:

> For surely there is no square mile of earth's inhabitable surface that is not beautiful in its own way, if we men will only abstain from wilfully destroying that beauty; and it is this reasonable share in the beauty of the earth that I claim as the right of every man who will earn it by due labor.[6]

At about the same time, writing in the *Atlantic Monthly*, John Muir promotes wild land preservation with similar themes: "None of Nature's landscapes are ugly so long as they are wild ... But the continent's outer beauty is fast passing away."[7]

In the twentieth century these themes, although perhaps neither fully developed nor completely entrenched, have gained a foothold in the public mind. David Lowenthal, a geographer, characterizes the received opinion in our time as follows:

> Nature is ... thought preferable to artifice. The favored landscapes are wild; landscapes altered or disturbed or built on by man are considered beneath attention or beyond repair ... Conservationist organizations contrast sordid scenes dominated by man with lovely landscapes devoid of human activity ... The implication is clear: man is dreadful, nature is sublime.[8]

The most recent expressions of the view that the natural world is essentially aesthetically good are found in philosophical writings that address environmental issues. Unlike artists and reformers, however, contemporary philosophers are not given to absolute or universal claims. Nonetheless, there is what Leonard Fels describes as one "basic assumption for aesthetic judgments." It is "that anything natural is probably good. Much that is natural is also thought of as inherently beautiful."[9] This attribution of aesthetic goodness, inherent beauty, or more particular positive aesthetic qualities to all that is natural is illustrated by a number of current discussions. For example, in considering the preservation of species,

Lilly-Marlene Russow, while expressing worries about "species such as the snail darter," claims that:

> ...aesthetic value can cover a surprising range of things: a tiger may be simply beautiful; a blue whale is awe-inspiring; a bird might be decorative; an Appaloosa is of interest because of its historical significance; and even a drab little plant may inspire admiration for the marvelous way it has been adapted to a special environment.[10]

The same idea occurs in attempts to analyze the qualities and values that justify preservation. For example, Kenneth Simonsen holds:

> There is ... something astonishing in this world which has been brought into being by obscure if not blind forces ... it is perhaps this realization which is at the root of our wonder at wild things. Once this attitude comes to pervade our response to nature, we feel more than admiring respect. Rather, for us, all wild things become invested with a sense of awe.[11]

Similarly, Holmes Rolston argues:

> Wild nature has a kind of integrity ... The Matterhorn leaves us in awe, but so does the fall foliage on any New England hillside, or the rhododendron on Roan Mountain. Those who linger with nature find this integrity where it is not at first suspected, in the copperhead and the alligator, in the tarantula and the morel, in the wind-stunted banner spruce and the straggly box elder, in the stormy sea and the wintry tundra ... This value is often artistic or aesthetic, and is invariably so if we examine a natural entity at the proper level of observation or in terms of its ecological setting. An ordinary rock in micro section is an extraordinary crystal mosaic. The humus from a rotting log supports an exquisite hemlock ... Natural value is further resident in the vitality of things, in their struggle and zest, and it is in this sense that we often speak of a reverence for life, lovely or not. Or should we say that we find all life beautiful.[12]

Other contemporary writers defend a related but more moderate point of view, arguing that although not every kind of thing in the natural world is aesthetically good, being natural is nonetheless essentially connected with positive aesthetic qualities and value. For example, Joseph Meeker, while suggesting that a "burned forest is ugly because it represents a truncated system of growth,"[13] in general holds that:

> The human experience of beauty is rooted in natural forms and processes ... and our esthetic values are really no more—nor any less—than abstract formulations of the natural ... What is exclusively human is generally not beautiful to us, and we find beauty in human art only when it is compatible with forms and processes in nature.[14]

The moderate view is developed in more detail by Robert Elliot. Elliot explicitly states that "I do not want to be taken as claiming that what is natural is good and what is non-natural is not. The distinction between natural and non-natural connects with valuation in a much more subtle way than that."[15] He elaborates: "Sickness and disease are natural in a straightforward sense and are certainly not good. Natural phenomena such as fires, hurricanes, volcanic eruptions can totally alter landscapes and alter them for the worse."[16] With this qualification, Elliot's view is that "the naturalness of a landscape is a reason for preserving it, a determinant of its value ... What the environmentalist insists on is that naturalness is one factor in determining the value of pieces of the environment."[17] He argues for this view by reference to analogies between artistic fakes and "faked" nature.[18]

Reflection on these and related themes in the aesthetic appreciation of nature has led Aarne Kinnunen to sharply distinguish the aesthetics of nature from the aesthetics of art. He claims the former is positive and the latter critical. Critical aesthetics, he argues, allows for negative aesthetic criticism and is appropriate for art, and for nature only when it has been affected by humans. Positive aesthetics, on the other hand, does not involve negative aesthetic judgment, but only the acceptance and aesthetic appreciation of something for what it is. According to Kinnunen, the aesthetics of nature is essentially positive in that all virgin nature is beautiful. He writes:

> ... all untouched parts of nature are beautiful. To be able to enjoy nature aesthetically is distinct from judgment. The aesthetics of nature is positive. Negative

criticism comes into play only when man's part in affecting nature is considered.[19]

Kinnunen's remarks summarize the pattern of thought I have elaborated here. Consequently I label the view under consideration in this article the "positive aesthetics" position....

SCIENCE AND AESTHETIC APPRECIATION OF NATURE

In the remaining sections of this chapter I explore the role of natural science in our aesthetic appreciation of nature. Consideration of science suggests a more plausible justification for positive aesthetics than any of those examined in the last three sections.

The importance of science in the development of the aesthetic appreciation of nature is brought out in Marjorie Hope Nicolson's classic *Mountain Gloom and Mountain Glory*. Arguing that appeal to the history of art does not provide the complete account, Nicolson elaborates the growth of the "aesthetics of the infinite."[20] Here science plays the essential role. Seventeenth-century developments in astronomy and physics, followed by those in geology and geography, explain and expand the natural world such that the notion of the sublime can find a place in its appreciation. Wonder and awe, formerly thought appropriate only for a deity, now become aesthetic responses to the seemingly infinite natural world; and especially to landscapes such as Nicolson's prime example, mountainscapes. Moreover, all landscapes become objects of appreciation as a function of the continued advances of the natural sciences. Speaking of landscape painting as a reflection of landscape appreciation, Romanenko claims: "Realistic landscape ... reached a flourishing stage in the nineteenth century and ... its development was definitely related to the rapid advance in all fields of natural science, especially geography, biology, geology."[21]

In the nineteenth century, in addition to geography and geology, biology becomes particularly important.

Scientists of that century, especially Darwin, turned the previous practice of collecting and naming into the science of the day, thereby accomplishing for flora and fauna what sciences such as astronomy and geology had earlier accomplished for landscapes:

> Everything, which before the days of Darwin had borne the stamp of "divine origin," the beauty of nature included, was passed down to the earth from heaven. The idea of man's unity with nature, since the days of Darwin, received particularly wide recognition, and his evolutionary theory, his methodology and the principles of his historical approach began, in the latter part of the nineteenth century, to exercise a revolutionizing influence on a subject so remote from exact natural science as aesthetics.[22]

With the growth of our aesthetic appreciation of nature in general science shares credit with art. However, in the more recent development of positive aesthetics, science is the main if not exclusive factor. The individuals who hold the positive aesthetics position take science to have a special relevance to their views. This is particularly true of Marsh; simply a glance at *Man and Nature* reveals the importance in his thought of both the theoretical and the applied science of his day. Moreover, Constable and Ruskin can be seen as no less under the spell of science. Constable is famous for his claim that "painting is a science, and should be pursued as an inquiry into the laws of nature." He asks: "Why, then, may not landscape painting be considered as a branch of natural philosophy, of which pictures are but the experiments?"[23] Equally significant is the following remark: "I must say that the sister arts have less hold on my mind ... than the sciences, especially the study of geology, which, more than any other, seems to satisfy my mind."[24] And it is well known that Ruskin's descriptions of nature compare favorably with those of his scientific contemporaries in accuracy and detail. Ronald Rees claims that "parts 2, 5 and 7 of 'Modern Painters' in effect offer a course in physical geography for landscape painters."[25]

Contemporary advocates of positive aesthetics have a similar regard for science. The main

difference is that now the relevant sciences are not primarily geography and geology, but rather biology and the all encompassing "science" of ecology. The issues these writers frequently address, such as the survival of species and the value and preservation of wild lands, are themselves issues of biological and ecological importance. Their orientation is even revealed in their titles: "Aesthetic Decision-Making and Human Ecology," "The Biology of Beauty," "Can and Ought We to Follow Nature?" "Is There an Ecological Ethic?" "The Value of Wildness," "Ecological Esthetics."[26] More significant is the way they bring biological and ecological insight to the positions they develop. For example, in discussing "languages" of art and "languages" of nature in aesthetic appreciation, Kinnunen characterizes the latter as "ecological languages."[27] Elliot endorses the view that "the understanding of the complexity, diversity, and integration of the natural world which ecology affords us, opens up a new area of valuation."[28] Rolston in speaking of "wild value" claims that "this value is often artistic or aesthetic," but "also has to do with the intelligibility of each of the natural members; and here natural science, especially ecology, has greatly helped us."[29] He also argues that "environmental science" invites us "to see the ecosystem not merely in awe, but in 'love, respect, and admiration.' "[30] As Meeker suggests: "Esthetic theory may be more successful in defining beauty when it has incorporated some of the conceptions of nature and its processes which have been formulated by contemporary biologists and ecologists."[31] It seems no exaggeration to say that this is what these individuals are attempting to do.

That science has played a role in the development of both the aesthetic appreciation of nature and the positive aesthetics position is, I think, clear. What is less clear is exactly why this should be so, although in general the answer is obvious enough: science provides knowledge about nature. For example, even though Biese's *The Development of the Feeling for Nature in the Middle Ages and Modern Times* is mainly an account of art's role in nature appreciation,

Biese concludes that the "present intensity" (1905) of the feeling for nature "is due to the growth of science, for although feeling has become more realistic and matter-of-fact in these days of electricity and the microscope, love for Nature has increased with knowledge."[32] In a similar vein Val Routley argues that the knowledge that science has gathered within the last three hundred years and that has only recently been generally disseminated "makes natural areas intelligible" and "as usual, information is an important adjunct to appreciation, as much so with the natural area as with the string quartet."[33] Following Routley, Elliot takes note of the knowledge provided by ecology. Of those who value wilderness, he says:

> What they do see, and what they value, is very much a function of the degree to which they understand the ecological mechanisms which maintain the landscape and which determine that it appears the way it does. Similarly, knowledge of art history, of painting techniques, and the like will inform aesthetic evaluations and alter aesthetic perceptions. Knowledge of this kind is capable of transforming a hitherto uninteresting landscape into one that is compelling.[34]

I think there is no doubt that scientific knowledge, as Elliot suggests, can transform the landscape, in fact the natural world, but there is yet the question of how and why this transformation occurs: how and why does scientific knowledge make the natural world seem beautiful? The beginnings of an answer are suggested by Rolston when he says:

> Ecological description finds unity, harmony, interdependence, stability, etc. . . . earlier data are not denied, only redescribed or set in a larger ecological context, and somewhere enroute our notions of harmony, stability, etc., have shifted too and we see beauty now where we could not see it before.[35]

Similarly Routley suggests: "The informed person . . . sees a pattern and harmony where the less informed may see a meaningless jumble."[36] Scientific information and redescription make us see beauty where we could not see it before, pattern and harmony instead of meaningless jumble. If these suggestions are

correct, they begin to explain the relationship between scientific knowledge and the aesthetic appreciation of nature. They begin to account for the way in which the two have developed hand in hand and why, in light of scientific knowledge, the natural world seems aesthetically good. However, as they stand they do not do justice to the complexity of aesthetic appreciation, and by themselves they do not provide a justification for the positive aesthetics position. . . .

SCIENCE AND POSITIVE AESTHETICS

. . . It is now possible to summarize the suggested justification for the positive aesthetics position. The key to the justification lies in the kind of thing nature is as opposed to art and the kinds of categories that are correct for it as opposed to those for art. Art is created, while nature is discovered. The determinations of categories of art and of their correctness are in general prior to and independent of aesthetic considerations, while the determinations of categories of nature and of their correctness are in an important sense dependent upon aesthetic considerations. These two differences are closely related. Since nature is discovered, rather than created, in science, unlike in art, creativity plays its major role in the determinations of categories and of their correctness; and considerations of aesthetic goodness come into play at this creative level. Thus, our science creates categories of nature in part in light of aesthetic goodness and in so doing makes the natural world appear aesthetically good to us. Moreover, the categories created in this way are the correct categories—those that involve appropriate aesthetic appreciation and reveal the aesthetic qualities and value of the objects of that appreciation. Thus, these categories not only make the natural world appear aesthetically good, but in virtue of being correct determine that it is aesthetically good. Or to put the point in a simpler way: the aesthetic situation concerning virgin nature in our world is essentially analogous to that concerning art in our previously imagined world. Our natural objects and landscapes, like its works of art, are discovered and categories are created for them. Our scientists, like its artists, create these categories in virtue of these given objects and, over the long run, with an eye toward aesthetic goodness. And in each world these categories are the correct categories. Thus, our natural objects and landscapes, like its works of art, are essentially aesthetically good. The result is that we have positive aesthetics concerning nature as it would have positive aesthetics concerning its art.

If this line of thought yields a justification for the positive aesthetics position, it does so with an important qualification. The justification is not of the same kind as those rejected earlier. For example, the divine justification, if adequate, would support the claim not simply that virgin nature is aesthetically good, but also that it always has been and always will be—whether anyone ever notices or not. The justification developed here, however, regards the aesthetic appreciation of nature as significantly informed by science and positive aesthetics as intimately related to the development of science. Consequently, although aesthetic appreciation of nature is perhaps informed by whatever world view is available, it seems that, outside the temporal and spatial boundaries of the scientific world view, it is not informed by science. Thus, positive aesthetics may not be a justifiable position outside these boundaries. This justification is, as it were, within the scope of the scientific world view. The nature and extent of positive aesthetics that is justified, therefore, seemingly depends upon interpretations of science. In light of various views about science, positive aesthetics might be, for example, absolute, culturally relative, or paradigm relative.[37]

To some this potential limitation of the positive aesthetic position may seem unfortunate, but it nonetheless adds plausibility to the justification itself. It helps to explain the close correlation between the development of natural science and the development of the aesthetic appreciation of nature noted in the two previous sections of this chapter. Moreover, if we construe the development of science as the attempt to make the natural world seem more and more comprehensible to us, by continual self-revision, whenever it appears less then fully comprehensible, then we also have an explanation of the growth of positive aesthetics. If comprehensibility is in part a function of qualities such as order, regularity, harmony, and balance, which we find aesthetically good, then the development of science and its continual self-revision constitutes a movement toward the aesthetically good. Or perhaps less misleadingly, it constitutes a movement that puts the natural world in an increasingly favorable aesthetic light. Such a movement seems evident in general and also at more specific levels. The positive aesthetic appreciation of previously abhorred landscapes, such as mountains and jungles, seems to have followed developments in geology and geography.[38] Likewise, the positive aesthetic appreciation of previously abhorred life forms, such as insects and reptiles, seems to have followed developments in biology.[39] In retrospect, many of the advances in natural science can be viewed as heralding a corresponding advance in positive aesthetics. This in itself gives support to the justification suggested in this section.

In a similar way, if this justification is correct, another connection noted in preceding sections falls into place—the connection between the development of positive aesthetics as a position concerning the natural world in general and the birth and growth of ecology. This is understandable in light of the fact that ecology not only is in certain respects all encompassing, but also puts considerable emphasis on qualities such as unity, harmony, and balance—ones we find particularly aesthetically good. I indicated that the positive aesthetics position is most evident in the writings of contemporary individuals especially concerned with ecology and ecological issues. Perhaps this position is not simply to be justified as a scientific aesthetic but is indeed what one individual terms the "ecological esthetic."[40] The position has seemingly come into its own with the development of ecology and seemingly continues to grow in light of it. Some of the individuals noted earlier suggest this. For example, Rolston writes:

We do not live in Eden, yet the trend is there, as ecological advance increasingly finds in the natural given stability, beauty, and integrity, and we are henceforth as willing to open our concepts to reformation by the world as to prejudge the natural order.[41]

Perhaps someday, at least concerning the natural world, we may all agree with Constable, saying "I never saw an ugly thing in my life."[42]

NOTES

1. For an enumeration of uses of "nature" in the appeal to nature for norms of art, especially with reference to the eighteenth century, see Arthur Lovejoy, " 'Nature' as Aesthetic Norm," *Modern Language Notes*, 1927, vol. 42, pp. 444–50. For a brief discussion of the eighteenth-century point of view, see Harold Osborne, "The Use of Nature in Art," *British Journal of Aesthetics*, 1962, vol. 2, pp. 318–27.

2. The comment is quoted and dated in Andrew Forge, "Art/Nature," *Philosophy and the Arts: Royal Institute of Philosophy Lectures*, London, Macmillan, 1973, vol. 6, pp. 231. Forge remarks: "The position that he was affirming was to be an ingredient in almost all the most vital painting of the next sixty years."

3. John Ruskin, *The Elements of Drawing* [1857], New York, Dover, 1971, pp. 128–9. The passage continues:

The rock on which the effect of a mountain scene especially depends is always precisely that which the roadmaker blasts or the landlord quarries; and the spot of green which Nature left with a special purpose by her dark forest sides, and finished with her most delicate grasses, is always that which the farmer ploughs or builds upon. But the clouds...cannot be quarried nor built over, and they are always therefore gloriously arranged;...they all move and burn together in a marvellous harmony; not a cloud of them is out of its appointed place, or fails of its part.

4. The two characterizations are from respectively Lewis Mumford, *The Brown Decades: A Study of the Arts in America, 1865–1895*, New York, Harcourt, Brace and Co., 1931, p. 78 and Stewart L. Udall, *The Quiet Crisis*, New York, Holt, Rinehart and Winston, 1963, p. 82. Both are quoted by David Lowenthal in his introduction to George Perkins Marsh, *Man and Nature* [1864], Cambridge, Harvard University Press, 1965, pp. ix and xxii.

5. Ibid., pp. 8–9.

6. William Morris, *Art and the Beauty of the Earth: A Lecture Delivered at Burslem Town Hall on October 13, 1881*, London, Longmans and Company, 1898, p. 24. For Morris's thoughts on landscape reform, see William Morris, *The Beauty of Life: An Address Delivered at the Town Hall, Birmingham, in 1880*, London, Brethan Press, 1974, especially pp. 10–18.

7. John Muir, "The Wild Parks and Forest Reservations of the West," in *Our National Parks*, Boston, Houghton Mifflin, 1916, pp. 6–7.

8. David Lowenthal, "The American Scene," *Geographical Review*, 1968, vol. 58, p. 81.

9. Leonard A. Fels, "Aesthetic Decision-Making and Human Ecology," in *Proceedings of the VIIth International Congress of Aesthetics*, Bucharest, Editura Academiei Republic Socialist Romania, 1977, p. 369.

10. Lilly-Marlene Russow, "Why Do Species Matter?" *Environmental Ethics*, 1981, vol. 3. p. 109.

11. Kenneth H. Simonsen, "The Value of Wildness," *Environmental Ethics*, 1981, vol. 3, p. 263.

12. Holmes Rolston, III, "Can and Ought We to Follow Nature?" *Environmental Ethics*, 1979, vol. 1, pp. 23–4. Later in the article Rolston qualifies this claim somewhat: "My concept of the good is not coextensive with the natural, but it does greatly overlap it; and I find my estimate steadily enlarging that overlap" (p. 28). See also Holmes Rolston, III, "Is There an Ecological Ethic?" *Ethics*, 1975, vol. 85, pp. 102–3.

13. Joseph W. Meeker, *The Comedy of Survival: Studies in Literary Ecology*, New York, Charles Scribner's Sons, 1974, p. 129. Meeker, following Konrad Lorenz, holds that in both animals and man "wild" characteristics are beautiful and "virtually all characters we perceive as specifically ugly are genuine domestication effects" (see pp. 121–4). The source is Konrad Lorenz, *Studies in Animal and Human Behavior*, London, Methuen, 1971. See also Yi-Fu Tuan, "Visual Blight: Exercises in Interpretation," *Visual Blight in America*, Commission on College Geography Resource Paper no. 23, Washington, D.C., Association of American Geographers, 1973, p. 27. Tuan attributes the root idea to Susanne Langer, *Feeling and Form*, New York, Charles Scribner's Sons, 1953.

14. Meeker, op. cit., p. 136.

15. Robert Elliot, "Faking Nature," *Inquiry*, 1982, vol. 25, p. 84. Elliot does not take himself to be discussing aesthetic appreciation and evaluation in this article, but rather what he terms "environmental evaluation," which

he holds is differentiated from aesthetic evaluation by "the judgmental element" in the latter (see p. 90). I believe that the argument for making this differentiation is not adequate and that he is mistaken in thinking that the relevant judgments and evaluations are not genuinely aesthetic. Consequently I consider his view a moderate version of positive aesthetics.

16. Ibid., pp. 86–7.

17. Ibid., p. 87.

18. Elliot's argument is similar to that of Nelson Goodman in Chapter 3 of *Languages of Art*, Indianapolis, Bobbs-Merrill, 1968.

19. Aarne Kinnunen, "Luonnonestetiikka," in Aarne Kinnunen and Yrjo Sepanmaa (eds) *Ymparistoestetiikka*, Helsinki, Gaudeamus, 1981, p. 49. The quote is translated from the original Finnish by Anja Sahuri. Kinnunen's idea of positive aesthetics is also discussed in Yrjo Sepanmaa, "Ymparistoestetiikka," in Yrjo Varpio (ed.) *Taiteentutkimaksen Perusteet*, Helsinki, Werner Soderstrom Osakeyhtio, 1982, pp. 33–46. I am grateful to Yrjo Sepanmaa for his contribution to my thinking about the topic of this chapter. Many of the relevant ideas and sources came to my attention during a series of fruitful discussions with him throughout 1982. I also thank J. Baird Callicott and Mark Sagoff for helpful comments.

20. Marjorie Hope Nicolson, *Mountain Gloom and Mountain Glory*, Ithaca, Cornell University Press, 1959. It is generally accepted that art, especially landscape painting, has played an important role in the development of nature appreciation. See, for example, Alfred Biese, *The Development of the Feeling for Nature in the Middle Ages and Modern Times*, New York, Burt Franklin, 1905, E. W. Manwaring, *Italian Landscape in XVIII Century England*, New York, Oxford University Press, 1925, or Christopher Hussey, *The Picturesque*, London, G. P. Putnam's, 1927. To understand the complexity of the subtle interplay between art, science, and nature appreciation, in particular in relation to North American environmental attitudes, see Eugene Hargrove, "The Historical Foundations of American Environmental Attitudes," *Environmental Ethics*, 1979, vol. 1, pp. 209–40.

21. Romanenko, op. cit., p. 143.

22. Ibid., p. 141.

23. John Constable, from his last public lecture, delivered at the Royal Institution of Great Britain in 1836. Quoted in Ronald Rees, "John Constable and the Art of Geography," *Geographical Review*, 1976, vol. 66, p. 59.

24. Ibid., pp. 59–61; quoted from John Constable, in C. R. Leslie (ed.) *Memoirs of John Constable*, London, Phaidon, 1951, p. 272. On Constable and science, see also

E. H. Gombrich, *Art and Illusion*, Princeton: Princeton University Press, 1961, especially part I.

25. Rees, "John Constable and the Art of Geography," op. cit., p. 59. On the role of science in Ruskin's thought, see Denis E. Cosgrove, "John Ruskin and the Geographical Imagination," *Geographical Review*, 1979, vol. 69, pp. 43–62.

26. With the exception of the second and the sixth, these are respectively, the titles of the following articles: Fels, op. cit., Rolston, "Can and Ought We to Follow Nature?" op. cit., Rolston, "Is There an Ecological Ethics?" op. cit., and Simonsen, op. cit. The second and sixth are chapter and section titles from Meeker, op. cit.

27. Kinnunen, op. cit., pp. 47–8.

28. Elliot, op. cit., p. 91.

29. Rolston, "Can and Ought We to Follow Nature?," op. cit., p. 23.

30. Rolston, "Is There an Ecological Ethic?" op. cit., p. 107. Rolston is quoting the last three words from Aldo Leopold, "The Land Ethic," *A Sand County Almanac*, New York, Oxford University Press, 1949, p. 223. In these articles Rolston is more concerned with moral than with aesthetic value.

31. Meeker, op. cit., pp. 124–5.

32. Biese, op. cit., p. 357.

33. Val Routley, "Critical Notice of John Passmore, *Man's Responsibility for Nature*," *Australasian Journal of Philosophy*, 1975, vol. 53, p. 183.

34. Elliot, op. cit., p. 91.

35. Rolston, "Is there an Ecological Ethic?," op. cit., pp. 100–1.

36. Routley, op. cit., p. 183.

37. Another possible qualification is that the justification offered here supports positive aesthetic appreciation of kinds of natural things but not of natural particulars. I doubt this because, given the role of aesthetic goodness in scientific description, categorization, and theorizing, I suspect that scientific knowledge as a whole is aesthetically imbued such that our appreciation of particulars is as enhanced as is that of kinds.

38. Positive aesthetic appreciation of unfamiliar landscapes such as volcanic mountains and tropical jungles was probably greatly enhanced by the scientific discoveries and writings of Alexander von Humboldt. It is noteworthy that his *Ansichter der Natur* [1808] went through three editions and was translated into nearly every European language by the time of his death in 1859. For a brief discussion of Humboldt's influence on the aesthetics of nature, see Edmunds Bunkse, "Humboldt and an Aesthetic Tradition in Geography," *Geographical Review*, 1981, vol. 71, pp. 127–46.

39. Concerning positive aesthetic appreciation of life, Darwin is particularly important. It is sometimes contended that Darwin's work had an adverse effect on the appreciation of nature. For example, Rolston notes: "After Darwin (through misunderstanding him, perhaps), the world of design collapsed, and nature, for all its law, seemed random, accidental, chaotic, blind, crude." "Is There an Ecological Ethic?" op. cit., p. 107). I agree that this may involve misunderstanding and think there is insight in Romanenko's remark that "everything, which before the days of Darwin had borne the stamp of 'divine origin,' the beauty of nature included, was passed down to the earth from heaven" (op. cit., p. 141). For example, prior to Darwin's demonstration of the transmutability of species these important categories of nature could be viewed as God-given. Darwin's work shows how they are the result of the human endeavors of scientific discovery, generalization, and decision. In addition, the expurgation of divine design effected by Darwin's work undercuts the grounds for certain kinds of negative aesthetic judgments about certain aspects of nature. Darwin's view that evolution has no overall direction and that all life forms must be accounted for in the same natural terms, gives no basis for viewing some as aesthetically inferior to others. As Stephen Jay Gould remarks, in light of the view that evolution "does not lead inevitably to higher things . . . The 'degeneracy' of a parasite is as perfect as the gait of a gazelle." See Stephen Jay Gould, *Ever Since Darwin*, New York, W. W. Norton, 1977, p. 13.

40. Meeker, op. cit., p. 119.

41. Rolston, "Is There an Ecological Ethic?," op. cit., p. 108.

42. It may be thought that a conclusive objection to this justification is simply that it tends to justify positive aesthetics, a position that is somewhat implausible. In short, the objection is that since there is much in the natural world that we do not find aesthetically good, any justification of the position must be incorrect. I agree that there is much in the natural world that appears to many of us not to be aesthetically good. However, this fact itself does not constitute a conclusive objection, for the justification provides the means of showing how the fact is consistent with the positive aesthetics position. First, as suggested by Rolston's remark that "we do not live in Eden, yet the trend is there," it is understandable if at the present we do not find all the natural world essentially beautiful. If our positive aesthetic appreciation of nature follows and is dependent upon the development of science, then it is to be expected that at this point in time there is much in the natural world that we do not yet find aesthetically good. Moreover, this is especially to be expected if the most relevant "science" is ecology, for it is not only a comparatively recent development but has yet to achieve the status of a mature science. For useful discussion, see Robert T. McIntosh, "The Background and Some Current Problems of Theoretical Ecology," in Esa Saarinen (ed.) *Conceptual Issues in Ecology*, Dordrecht, Reidel, 1982, pp. 1–61. Second, although the correct categories for the aesthetic appreciation of the natural world are natural categories, there are other categories in terms of which we do, as a matter of fact, occasionally perceive nature. When nature is perceived in such categories, there is, according to this justification, no reason why positive aesthetic appreciation should result. Indeed, when so perceived, much of the natural world may appear aesthetically second-rate—bland, dull, insipid, incoherent, chaotic, and the like. Whether or not certain of these other categories should also be accepted as correct categories for the natural world is another issue. Although this cannot be pursued here, I, as suggested previously, am inclined to think that they should not be so accepted—at least not for virgin nature (and not within the scientific world view).

NED HETTINGER

Objectivity in Environmental Aesthetics and Protection of the Environment

INTRODUCTION

The beauty of the environment provides significant motivation for protecting it. Whether it is preserving wilderness areas, protecting the rural countryside from sprawl, or opposing the cutting down of a neighborhood tree, environmental beauty is a prominent concern. I believe that aesthetic considerations can help justify environmental protection as well. I call such aesthetic defenses of the environment *aesthetic protectionism*. Environmental degradation is a serious problem in large part because it involves the destruction of substantial aesthetic value. Indeed, if wilderness, the rural countryside, and neighborhood trees had little aesthetic value (or negative aesthetic value), both the practice of—and justification for—environmental protection would be seriously weakened.

There are many reasons not to make aesthetics central to defending the environment. Many consider natural beauty to be a weak and trivial value compared with the utilitarian values used either to protect the environment (for example, health and recreation) or to exploit it (for example, jobs and growth). Gary Varner suggests that natural beauty is at best a tiebreaker:

> An attempt to justify a ban on logging in the Pacific Northwest's remaining old-growth forests solely in terms of these forests' special beauty would be on very shaky ground if the ban would cause economic dislocation of thousands of loggers and mill workers.... It is only in this context (i.e., other things being equal) that aesthetic considerations seem compelling.[1]

Others have argued that because natural beauty counts for little when determining how we should treat humans, we should be skeptical that it amounts to much in determining how we should treat the environment.[2] Many people think that aesthetic value is anthropocentric and instrumental (that is, a value reducible to pleasurable experiences for humans) and that the best defenses of nature should be intrinsic.

Perhaps the most important worry about aesthetic defenses of the environment—and the focus of this essay—is the common assumption that beauty is in the eye of the beholder and therefore that aesthetic responses are subjective and relative. If judgments of environmental beauty lack objective grounding, they seemingly provide a poor basis for justifying environmental protection. One legal analysis early in the environmental movement describes this concern well:

> [There is a] common judicial belief that aesthetic evaluations and standards are a matter of individual taste, which varies from person to person, and are thus too subjective to be applied in any but an arbitrary and capricious manner.... One person's judgment on aesthetic matters is as good as another's...no aesthetic judgment is more or less reasonable than any other....Any aesthetic regulation would simply impose one person's taste on another who legitimately holds a different viewpoint.[3]

One of the first philosophers to note this problem contended that

> If beauty in nature or art is merely in the eye of the beholder, then no general moral obligation arises out of aesthetic judgments....A judgment of value that is merely personal and subjective gives us no way of arguing that everyone ought to learn to appreciate something, or at least regard it as worthy of preservation.[4]

Even if we reject the view that aesthetic judgments are generally subjective and relative, we may think that judgments about *environmental* beauty are subjective and relative. A common view in the philosophy of art is that even though art is substantially objective, the aesthetic appreciation of nature is either thoroughly relative or much less constrained than the aesthetic appreciation of art.[5] Consider the following statement of this view from a highly regarded introductory aesthetic textbook:

> A great mountain (Mt. Fuji, Grand Teton) would probably strike us as noble and strong, or expressive of nobility and strength, but it is perfectly conceivable that it might strike an observer from an alien culture as comical or agonized. In the case of a natural object, such as a mountain, such relativity of perception is no real problem, because the mountain itself isn't really noble or comical. We can only say that there are different ways to regard the mountain.... It is harder to swallow such relativism when it comes to the expressive properties of artworks.... What I am suggesting is that the emotional qualities that artworks express are not dispensable facts about them, although the emotional qualities *are* dispensable facts about natural objects.... Edvard Munch's *The Scream* is truly frightening.... The fact that *The Scream* might strike a viewer from another culture as cheerful...should not make us think that *The Scream* is a cheerful painting.... There is no real fact of the matter about whether Mount Fuji is noble or whether it is comical.[6]

Although in this passage John Fisher limits his comments to the expressive features of natural objects, others have extended this claim of subjectivity and relativity to other aesthetic properties of nature and to judgments about natural beauty in general. Such relativism seems to be problematic for those hoping to use the environment's aesthetic value to support environmental protection.

In the almost fifty-year-long dispute over protecting Alaska's Arctic National Wildlife Refuge from oil development—although there clearly are other issues at stake—the aesthetic value of the refuge has figured prominently. Former U.S. Interior Secretary Gail Norton regards the refuge as a "Godforsaken mosquito-infested swamp shrouded in frozen darkness half the year," whereas former U.S. President Jimmy Carter judges it to be a place of "solitude, unmatched beauty, and grandeur." If these aesthetic judgments are merely matters of personal taste, one neither better nor worse than the other, then the aesthetic character of the refuge cannot play a legitimate role in determining its fate.

Or consider this example: A community wanting to preserve its rural character argues that great aesthetic value will be lost when its tranquil tree-lined roads, interspersed with farmhouses, small fields, and ponds—symbolic of human harmony with nature—are replaced with an aggressive, cluttered, and gaudy strip-highway sprawl of auto dealers, gas stations, and parking lots, so symbolic of our society's careless exploitation and disregard of the natural world. In response, the developers maintain that the elimination of the monotonous weed-infested dirt roads and their replacement with useful and well-built stores will offer great aesthetic value and express and reward hard work, determination, and entrepreneurial ingenuity. Environmental aesthetics needs some type of objectivity if it is to help us adjudicate between developers who like strip malls and environmentalists who do not. Without some ability to distinguish between better and worse aesthetic responses, the appeal to aesthetic considerations has little use in environmental decision making....

OBJECTIVITY AS CONSTRAINED PLURALISM: BETTER AND WORSE AESTHETIC RESPONSES TO NATURE

Carlson's views have been central to the debate over aesthetic responses to nature.[7] He brings objectivity to environmental aesthetics by arguing that environmental aesthetic appreciation (and judgment) should respond to what the aesthetic object is rather than what it is not. He argues that because science is our best guide to the nature of the natural world, an aesthetic response to nature should be guided by a knowledge of science or natural history more generally (much as an aesthetic response to art should be guided by a knowledge of art history). Because science is objective, an environmental aesthetic informed by science will be objective as well.

Many people disagree with Carlson's scientific monism and argue that acceptable nature appreciation can be guided by emotional, imaginative, or other cognitive resources besides science. Rejecting scientific monism need not mean that nature can be aesthetically appreciated in any arbitrary way one wants. To deny that there is only one correct type of response to an environmental aesthetic object—or to nature more generally—is not to accept that all aesthetic responses (or types of aesthetic response) are equally good. Carlson's science-based appreciation of nature is not the only position that allows for objectivity, nor—as we shall see—is aesthetic protectionism always best served by a scientifically informed aesthetic response.

Carlson frequently insists that the "appropriate" or "correct" or "true" aesthetic appreciation of nature must be guided by science. Therefore, aesthetic responses to nature not informed by science or natural history must be "inappropriate," "incorrect," or even "false."[8] But I believe that it is not helpful to confine our assessment of aesthetic responses to nature to choices like "correct or incorrect," "true or false," or even "appropriate or inappropriate." We need many more criteria to determine better and worse in aesthetic responses to nature, criteria that are contextually sensitive and not rigidly hierarchical. Consider that a scientifically uniformed aesthetic response may in fact be acceptable. For example, even though a child or an uneducated adult may not know that a glacier is a river of ice, there is nothing incorrect, false, or even inappropriate about their being impressed by the sight of a calving glacier. Nonetheless, informed responses often are better responses. Knowledge about the nature of glaciers can broaden our response to them. For example, we might begin to listen for and hear the groaning of the ice as it scrapes down the valley.

I believe the most plausible position on objectivity in environmental aesthetic appreciation is a "constrained pluralism" that permits many better and worse aesthetic responses to environment and that distinguishes between better and worse in a variety of ways (and not simply as correct or incorrect, true or false, based on science or not based on science, or appropriate or inappropriate).[9] Constrained pluralism falls between a naive monism that insists on uniquely correct and appropriate aesthetic responses to the environment and an "anything-goes subjectivism" that regards all aesthetic responses to the environment to be equally valid.[10] We shall see that such a view has sufficient objectivity to be useful to aesthetic protectionism.

To my knowledge, everyone working in environmental aesthetics distinguishes between better and worse responses to environment,[11] including thinkers with drastically divergent approaches to aesthetics from science-based (cognitive) theorists like Carlson to emotional-arousal theorists like Carroll and imagination-based theorists like Brady. Ronald Hepburn has discussed how we might think about better and worse aesthetic responses to nature without being constrained by naive realist-sounding phrases like "the correct or true way" to appreciate nature.[12] Hepburn focuses on the difference between a "trivial and serious" aesthetic appreciation of nature, but I think it important to appeal to additional distinctions between better and worse ways to appreciate environments.[13]

Consider the difference between deep versus shallow or superficial responses: In his critique of Carlson's scientific monism, Carroll suggests that depth in an aesthetic response might include either the length of time that a response can continue or the intensity of the response's involvement at one time.[14] The so-called scenery cult is an excellent example of a shallow appreciation of nature. A well-developed literature criticizes the inability of many people to appreciate unscenic nature as being an aesthetic vice.[15] For too many people, nature appreciation is limited to appreciating nature's dramatic landscapes. For them, nature appreciation means driving though a national park, stopping only at scenic viewpoints for snapshots and gift shops for picture postcards of the scenery. This is a lazy type of nature appreciation interested only in "easy beauty" and the "picturesque" and in visual appreciation rather than a deeper, multisensuous engagement. This critique suggests that the better aesthetic responses involve more senses than just sight.[16] Better responses are lively and active (perceptually and otherwise), rather than feeble and passive.[17] Contrast appreciating a mountain lake by gazing at it from the shoreline with appreciating the lake while swimming in it. Or compare watching through a window with experiencing a storm while being outside in the midst of it.[18]

Discriminating responses are better than undiscriminating ones. Attentive responses are better than inattentive ones or inappropriately attentive responses (for example, those people who are so focused on finding a particular flower that they miss the aesthetic qualities of the forest at large). Mature responses are better than immature ones; unbiased responses are better than biased ones. Consider the self-indulgent response that appreciates a rainbow as "placed here just for me!" Patient and careful responses are better than hasty ones; perceptive responses are better than confused ones. Thoughtful and reflective responses are better than unthinking ones, such as the stereotypical response to deer as cute and reminiscent of Bambi. Knowledgeable responses are better than ones that distort, ignore, or suppress important truths about the objects of appreciation.[19] Consider, for example, the romanticized appreciation of wolves that ignores their predatory lifestyle. Or consider the aesthetic judgment of the English poet John Donne about mountains, based on the seventeenth-century view that God originally made the world a smooth sphere but then deformed it in punishment for human sins: "Warts, and pock-holes on the face of th'earth."[20]

Some aesthetic judgments of nature are indeed true or false, correct or incorrect, appropriate or not, but many aesthetic responses to nature are better or worse than others on very different grounds. Accordingly, we should not assume that there is only one legitimate type of aesthetic appreciation of the environment (as if this were necessary for aesthetic protectionism). Nor should we feel forced into the belief that any type of aesthetic response to and judgment about the environment is acceptable. Instead, we should be open to a plurality of types of response to nature, some of which are better or worse than others. It is my contention that such a critical pluralism is sufficiently objective to make the aesthetic appreciation of nature a serious and worthwhile activity and one that enables viable aesthetic protectionism.[21]

ARGUMENTS FOR RELATIVITY IN ENVIRONMENTAL AESTHETICS

Next I consider the views of those who doubt the objectivity of environmental appreciation and argue for relativity in environmental aesthetics. Their principal argument is that nature appreciation lacks the kind of objectivity found in art appreciation and that the appreciation of art is far more constrained than the appreciation of nature. I examine whether this alleged deficiency in objectivity exists and consider whether it is a problem for aesthetic protectionism.

John Fisher defends the value of aesthetically appreciating the sounds of nature while arguing that such appreciation is far more relative than the appreciation of music.[22] Although he does not argue that we can generalize his analysis of the relativity of aesthetic judgments about nature's sounds to judgments about other natural features, I see little reason to believe that his arguments apply only to the appreciation of nature's sounds. In fact, Malcolm Budd presents similar arguments for the relativity of environmental aesthetics responses in general.[23]

Fisher distinguishes between two dimensions of objectivity. The first is that all aesthetic appreciation, including nature appreciation, should be guided by the aesthetic object ("guidance-by-object requirement") and the second is the "agreement criterion," according to which aesthetic judgments are universal in that proper aesthetic judgments are true and require agreement from other perceivers who are sensitive, rational, and appropriately placed.[24] Fisher accepts the first and rejects the second and argues that agreement does not follow from the guidance-by-object criterion because an aesthetic response can be guided by an object's characteristics at the same time it is underdetermined by them. Although he thinks this underdetermination is also true of the appreciation of art objects, aesthetic judgments of nature's sounds "will be many times more underdetermined than are typical judgments of art or musical works."[25]

Malcolm Budd agrees that an aesthetic appreciation of nature has a freedom and relativity that an appreciation of art does not have: "The aesthetic appreciation of nature is thereby endowed with a freedom denied to artistic appreciation."[26] Fisher notes that unlike artworks (including music), natural sounds are not intentional objects created to be appreciated in certain ways. This fact leads him to conclude that "the person who listens to nature is simply free of the criteria that govern appreciation of music and that function to rule out many possible ways of listening."[27] Budd makes the same claim about the appreciation of nature in general: Nature appreciation, he argues, is looser than art appreciation because nature was not designed for the purpose of aesthetic appreciation, and thus its appreciation is released from the kinds of constraints that such design places on art appreciation.[28] For example, cubist paintings are not intended to be judged in terms of their representational accuracy, and to judge them in this way is a mistake. In contrast, nature does not intend us to appreciate it in one way or another.

That artists design art objects for aesthetic appreciation may well constrain the proper appreciation of artworks in ways that nature appreciation is not constrained. The truth of this claim, however, depends on accepting particular theories of art. It is not clear that formalists would assent to it, and the claim assumes a significance for artists' intentions that anti-intentionalists may reject. Even if we grant the claim (as I do), it is arguable that intentional design not only constrains the appropriate aesthetic response but also opens avenues for new interpretations and types of appreciative responses. There may well be a greater number of appropriate appreciative responses to Marcel Duchamp's *Fountain* than there were to that toilet when it was sitting in a warehouse. Or consider the difference between appreciating a moose and appreciating a painting of a moose. The painting of a moose would have all sorts of meanings that a moose itself does not (of course, the moose in nature also has meanings that the painting would not have). The interpretation and evaluation of a moose painting involve issues of artistic intent and style, and the cultural context of the painting both constrains and complicates its appreciation. The lack of artistic intent regarding the object of nature appreciation removes some of its complexity, which may actually limit the number of appropriate responses to it.[29]

Both Fisher and Budd note the relative lack of framing in nature compared with art. Nature does not come with a frame around it (as does a painting and artworks more generally), and there are many different and legitimate ways to frame it. Unlike art, in which the artist (or the art category) frames the aesthetic object, the appreciator chooses how to frame the aesthetic experience of nature. For example, we do not look at the back of a painting or tap it to see how it sounds, even though these are permissible approaches to appreciating a natural object like a tree. Budd argues that—in contrast to art appreciation—there is no proper level of observation for nature. We can look at nature though a telescope or a microscope or with our unaided eyes. He also argues that there are no proper or optimal conditions for observation: we can observe nature when it is foggy or clear, bright or dark, from near or far. Budd also claims that we may use any sense modality or mode of perception: We can choose to look, hear, touch, taste, or smell natural objects. In general, Budd contends, we are free to frame nature as we please. Thus "there is no such thing as the appropriate aesthetic appreciation of nature" (as there is with art).[30] This is because "the range of its aesthetic properties or aesthetically relevant appearances...[are] typically indefinite and open-ended in a manner uncharacteristic of works of art."[31] Budd concludes that the attempt to find a model of nature appreciation that tells us "what is to be appreciated and how it is to be appreciated—something we have a good grasp of in the case of works of art" is "a chimerical quest."[32]

Although these claims have some validity, they clearly are problematic as well. Budd overstates the freedom involved because he overlooks constraints on how we may frame the appreciation of natural objects. Once we settle on a particular natural object as the object of our aesthetic attention, we rule out many other framing choices. For example, we should not appreciate trout swimming in a mountain stream with a telescope or a microscope; there are better and worse levels of observation in such cases. Aesthetically appreciating a cliff is not best done from an airplane six miles high or from a mobile home on a pitch black night; there are better and worse conditions of observation. Are we really free to use any of our senses to appreciate a mountain? Glenn Parsons notes that "smell, touch and taste require close proximity and mountains are generally not the sort of things we can feel or taste; at best one can feel or taste one small part of a mountain."[33]

Fisher claims that how we frame nature is partially arbitrary: "One can, of course, choose principles of framing, but I do not see how they could fail to be partially arbitrary, even if natural in one respect or another."[34] Fisher argues—again in contrast to musical appreciation—that the appreciation of natural sounds lacks institutional conventions that determine and guide appropriate appreciation. So besides there being no artist to frame the aesthetic object, there also are no social conventions to help frame the appreciation of nature (natural sounds) as there are for artworks (music).

> I see no way to raise the status of my framing to that required to make my judgments objective without claiming that we have conventions—not just typical or

understandable responses—for listening to the sounds of nature....[This] would not be a plausible claim about acts of listening to nature in our society.[35]

There are no nature (natural sound) critics in the mold of art (music) critics.[36] Thus Fisher argues that *what* we should listen to in nature, for *how long*, and in *what way* are generally choices we can make freely. He illustrates framing relativity with the following examples:

> Suppose you are sitting in a hot tub in a city in the Arizona desert listening to the sounds around you. Do you just listen to the Western Warblers and the wind in the fruit and palm trees or do you (should you) also notice the sounds of hot tub jets and popping bubbles making a pleasant hissing on the water? Do you add or ignore the sounds of ventilator fans spinning hot air from the attics and occasional jet planes overhead? At Niagara Falls do I strain to hear birds in the forest over the constant roar of the water....In the Tuscan countryside do I ignore the high pitched whining of mosquitoes? Shall I just focus on the loons from across the lake in Minnesota or shall I strain to hear others from more distant parts, and do they go together with the chattering of squirrels and the buzzing of flies?[37]

"Nature does not dictate an *intrinsically* correct way to frame its sounds in the way that a composer does," and "there is a large multiplicity of structures and relations that we might hear and all seem equally legitimate."[38]

I think Fisher and Budd have made a good case for framing pluralism in regard to aesthetic responses to environmental sounds and beauty more generally. The aesthetic appreciator clearly has great freedom (and, in many ways, greater freedom than with artworks) in framing the experience of nature's sounds and its other aesthetic objects, and this results in a multiplicity of appropriate appreciative acts and judgments. Fisher and Budd are right that there is not only one correct way to frame and aesthetically appreciate nature.

Does this plurality of appropriate aesthetic responses to the environment present a problem for aesthetic protectionism? We might not think so, as the aesthetic freedom to focus on one loon or forty—or to listen to the wind in the trees alone or along with the warblers—would seem to have little relevance to using environmental beauty for policy. Whether I look at mountain through the fog in the early morning light or during the middle of the afternoon on a perfectly clear day or whether I concentrate on the smell of the mountain's spruce trees after the rain or savor the taste of its wild huckleberries does not seem to threaten aesthetic protectionism. If all the many acceptable ways to appreciate nature were aesthetically positive and of greater value than what would replace them as a result of environmental degradation, then pluralism would not compromise aesthetic protectionism. Furthermore, acknowledging the multiplicity of acceptable ways to frame and appreciate nature is compatible with judging there to be a multiplicity of incorrect ways to do this as well (and both Fisher and Budd give us some grounds for making such judgments).

Nonetheless, certain kinds of pluralism in environmental aesthetic response can be a serious problem for aesthetic protectionism. Let us start with framing relativity: Just how arbitrary is the framing choice supposed to be? Specifically, does the freedom to frame apply to whether or not human sounds or other human effects should be part of our appreciation of a natural environment? Should human intrusions be included in our appreciation of the environment? If there are no better or worse ways to frame these aesthetic responses, then we have a problem with using typical environmentalist judgments about natural beauty to protect the environment.

Consider the following environmental policy disputes: Should airplanes be allowed to fly over the Grand Canyon? Should helicopters be allowed to transport hikers into remote areas of Alaska's Denali National Park? Is snowmobiling in Yellowstone in the winter acceptable, and is it compatible with cross-country skiing? Should a developer be allowed to put an automobile racetrack next to a cypress-swamp nature preserve? In each of these cases, environmentalists have argued that engine noises degrade the natural tranquillity and

substantially lessen the area's aesthetic value. But if the framing of sounds is arbitrary, then antienvironmentalists can insist that such intrusive human sounds be framed out of the experience. The developer can ask those listening for owls in the swamp to ignore the sounds of the nearby Friday-night races. Yellowstone skiers can be asked to frame out the stench and whine of snowmobiles. Hikers in the national parks can simply ignore the buzz of aircraft overhead. A similar argument can be made concerning other human intrusions into nature. The developer can ask those hiking in the forest to ignore the trophy homes on the ridgetops. And if there are no better or worse ways to frame these aesthetic experiences, why shouldn't they?

One response is to claim that we may be unable to frame out these human intrusions, at least not without special psychological training. But the deeper claim is that we should not frame them out, at least not in our overall assessment of the aesthetic value of these environments. Such an assessment must include these sounds, smells, and sights. An aesthetic response to and an evaluation of environments that suppress these sensual properties is aesthetically impoverished. To use some of the earlier distinctions, such a response would be superficial, inattentive, biased, and/or distorted. In these cases, it is fitting and natural to include—and even focus on—these human-caused sensual intrusions in our assessment of the overall aesthetic value of these environments. To ignore them would be like standing in Wyoming's Snake River valley and refusing to look to the west. This would not be an acceptable way to aesthetically appreciate Grand Teton National Park. Aesthetic judgments about environments that frame out human intrusions are similarly distorting. A developer who insists that putting a skyscraper in the Snake River valley will not detract from the aesthetic beauty of the valley and the neighboring Grand Teton National Park because "one can simply frame it out" is relying on a mistaken conception of the freedom of framing choices in environmental appreciation. Do Fisher's and Budd's accounts of framing freedom and relativity justify this antienvironmentalist argument? I hope not.

What accounts for the intuitively plausible judgment that such a framing choice is not legitimate? One possibility is to appeal to the ideas of natural salience and natural framing. Carroll uses these ideas to explain how "being moved by nature" (that is, an aesthetic-emotional arousal to nature) can solve the problem of aesthetic focus.

> Certain natural expanses have natural frames or what I prefer to call natural closure: caves, copses, grottoes, clearings, arbors, valleys, etc. And other natural expanses, though lacking frames, have features that are naturally salient for human organisms—i.e., they have features such as moving water, bright illumination, etc. that draw our attention instinctually toward them.[39]

The loud roar of engines or a towering skyscraper rising from a valley and blocking the view of a mountain will naturally draw our aesthetic attention, and it is awkward and forced to appreciate these environments while trying to ignore these human intrusions or to leave them out of our overall aesthetic assessments. The suggestion to remove them is similar to a symphony companion saying, "Don't worry about that foul smell or the machine-gun fire outside, just listen to the music."

These ideas of natural salience and framing also provide a way to respond to Stan Godlovitch's argument against giving the human scale a special place when aesthetically appreciating nature.[40] Godlovitch contends that typical, human aesthetic responses to nature are "sensorily parochial" and that the temporal and spatial scale-dependencies of our aesthetic responses to nature are arbitrary. He would have us aesthetically appreciate, presumably equally, all of nature, great and small, and all natural processes, long and short. Thus he argues that smashing ice blocks heaved up by a river is no less aesthetically offensive than bulldozing the Navaho sandstone castles of Monument Valley, Arizona. True, the ice melts each spring and reforms the following winter, but those monuments also will crumble and rise up again. "If we were giants, crushing a rock

monument...would be no more aesthetically offensive than flattening the odd sand castle is to us now. If our lives were measured in seconds, shattering ice blocks would count as momentously coarse as using Bryce Canyon as a landfill pit."[41]

Such a view is clearly problematic for aesthetic protectionism. If environmental aesthetics is to be useful in environmental policy, it must be able to help us identify more or less aesthetically positive environments or natural objects. It certainly cannot agree that as much aesthetic value is lost by crushing ice blocks in a river as by destroying thousand-feet-tall sandstone monuments. Note that the "equal beauty thesis" (that is, all of nature is equally beautiful)—although it is an objectivist claim—is a problem from the perspective of aesthetic protectionism. The fact that an environmental aesthetic is objective does not guarantee that it will be useful in environmental policy disputes, and it does not ensure that it will be helpful to aesthetic protectionism.

Godlovitch is right that our aesthetic experiences and judgments depend on scale (just as Budd and Fisher are right that what aesthetic properties we experience and what aesthetic judgments they support depend on how we frame our acts of nature appreciation). Hepburn illustrates this point: "The mountain that we appreciate for its majesty and stability is, on a different time-scale, as fluid as the ripples on the lake at its foot."[42] But this should not make us think that the (scale-dependent) aesthetic qualities we enjoy in the mountain cannot be appropriately appreciated. Clear-cuts are a paradigm of environmental, aesthetic disvalue, but on a longer time scale, they are merely temporary blips in an ongoing and aesthetically exciting process of forest recovery. But this should not lead us to agree with the forest-industry executive that they are not ugly because we should adopt a time scale of two hundred years.

My response to Godlovitch is that given the kind of creatures that we are and the temporal and spatial scales on which we operate, some dimensions of our framing choices are not arbitrary, and certain scales are more or less natural and appropriate. Simply because aesthetic qualities can be made to vanish and aesthetic judgments undermined by taking a different perspective does not mean that these qualities do not exist and these judgments are inappropriate given the perspective we are taking. Nor should we believe that all perspectives are equally appropriate. Some framing of environmental appreciation is awkward, forced, and myopic. Given the kind of beings we are and the legitimate purposes of aesthetic appreciation, some perspectives, scales, and framing choices—including Godlovitch's "any scale at all" and the antienvironmentalists' demand to frame out human intrusions and to appreciate nature from irrelevant or distorted scales—are not acceptable

The kind of aesthetic relativity that is most worrying to aesthetic protectionism may not be framing relativity but a relativity that affects our evaluation or judgment of aesthetic value. Perhaps it is inappropriate to suppress the whine of the snowmobile, the buzz of the helicopter, and the silhouette of the Teton valley skyscraper from our environmental aesthetic evaluation. But motor enthusiasts may claim that they find these sounds appealing, and developers may claim to enjoy the sight of a large building silhouetted against the Grand Tetons, and they both may insist that environmentalists' intuitions about the negative aesthetic character of these humanizations are just one aesthetic response, no more or less appropriate than the aesthetic responses of those who enjoy these human effects. Here is how a "wise-use" activist explained it:

> To elevate "natural quiet" to the status of a physical resource is ludicrous. Other sounds in the rest of the public land can be appreciated, and must be acknowledged as a positive part of the experience. For example, I appreciate the sound of a chain saw. To hear a chain saw in the distance as I'm hiking along a trail warms my heart.[43]

Fisher admits that he sometimes finds such relativity regarding the aesthetic value of natural sounds to be correct: "I may find the 'coo coo' sounds of

a flock of doves to be extremely harmonious and to express a soothing calm. A friend may find the same sound insistently obtrusive."[44] He also provides evidence that suggests differences between city dwellers and others concerning how favorably or unfavorably they respond to animal sounds.[45] A good case for the relativity of judgments of nature's aesthetic value can be found in J. A. Walter's "You'll Love the Rockies," an account in which this English visitor to the American West justifies his "disappointment" with the Colorado Rockies.[46]

I do not deny the possibility of *some* (perhaps even significant) relativity in aesthetic value judgments about nature. Differences in circumstances, contexts, and perspectives will motivate and perhaps justify conflicting judgments about aesthetic properties and value. Perhaps the Grand Tetons will appear puny rather than majestic to someone who grew up in the Himalayas or comical to one contemplating the meaning of the French word *teton*. The sound of an approaching snowmobile may well be soothing (rather than obnoxious) if one is lying hypothermic in the snow waiting for help or if one is the owner of a snowmobile rental business threatened by a proposed ban on snowmobiles in national parks. Clearcuts may not be eyesores to those who hunt the deer feeding off the new growth or to the loggers who cut the trees.

I suspect that the right course here is to accept some plurality in environmental aesthetic evaluations and perhaps even some conflicting evaluations. Nonetheless, we should resist an anything-goes relativity concerning such evaluative responses. Finding criteria for evaluating better and worse evaluative responses should be our goal. For example, standing before the Grand Tetons for the first time and being amused by the thought that they look like breasts—although not "incorrect," "false," or even necessarily "inappropriate"—is a worse response than, for example, being awed by their soaring height from the valley floor and imagining the geologic pressure necessary to create them.[47] Along with multiple acceptable environmental aesthetic evaluations, we should acknowledge a number of unacceptable evaluative responses. The negative aesthetic value judgment about swamps as bug-infested wastelands is a stereotyped and ignorant aesthetic response that would be rejected by someone who knows something about swamps and is aware of the ecological services of wetlands and that because the water is moving, the bugs are not bad at all. Developers whose stereotypical view of swamps leads them to believe that putting a racetrack next to a swamp nature preserve is unproblematic need not be taken seriously because their evaluation is founded on a misunderstanding of swamps. . . .

CONCLUSIONS

Environmental aesthetics is important to environmental protection. Although they present significant worries for aesthetic protectionism, environmental aesthetic relativity and subjectivity do not cripple it. I have argued that we need to develop and justify accounts of better and worse aesthetic responses to the environment that avoid both an anything-goes relativism and the idea that only one type of environmental aesthetic response is acceptable. Legitimate pluralism regarding environmental beauty does not prevent distinguishing between better and worse aesthetic responses. Environmental aesthetics contains numerous resources for objectivity that hold promise for justifying a significant role for judgments of natural beauty in environmental protection. A knowledge-based environmental aesthetic can be useful to aesthetic protectionism, but it is not the only useful environmental aesthetic, and it does not guarantee beneficial environmental results.[48]

NOTES

1. Gary Varner, *In Nature's Interests* (New York: Oxford University Press, 1998), p. 22.

2. "But if a doctor cannot make a decision regarding who gets a heart based on aesthetics, how can environmentalists ask thousands of loggers to give up their jobs and way of life on the basis of aesthetics?" See J. Robert Loftis, "Three Problems for the Aesthetic Foundations of Environmental Ethics," *Philosophy in the Contemporary World* 10 (2003):43.

3. Samuel Buford, "Beyond the Eye of the Beholder: Aesthetics and Objectivity," *Michigan Law Review* 73 (1973):1438, 1442.

4. Janna Thompson, "Aesthetics and the Value of Nature," *Environmental Ethics* 17 (1995): 293.

5. Philosophers who take this view include Malcolm Budd, *The Aesthetic Appreciation of Nature: Essays on the Aesthetics of Nature* (Oxford: Oxford University Press, 2002); John Fisher, "What the Hills Are Alive With—In Defense of the Sounds of Nature," *Journal of Aesthetics and Art Criticism* 56 (1998):167–79; and Kendall Walton, "Categories of Art," *Philosophical Review* 79 (1970):334–67. Interestingly, one philosopher who responds to this literature and defends objectivity in environmental aesthetics argues for the reverse claim: "The objectivity applicable to disputes about natural beauty may be said to be, if anything, more robust than that characteristic of art." See Glenn Parsons, "Freedom and Objectivity in the Aesthetic Appreciation of Nature," *British Journal of Aesthetics* 46 (2006):35, n. 49.

6. John Fisher, *Reflecting on Art* (Mountain View, Calif.: Mayfield, 1993), pp. 338–39 (emphasis in original). Fisher is arguing here for the importance of the artist in understanding expression in art and for the relativity of nature's expressive properties only as an aside.

7. Allen Carlson, *Aesthetics and the Environment: The Appreciation of Nature, Art and Architecture* (New York: Routledge, 2000).

8. Sometimes Carlson uses the language of "depth" versus "superficiality." This is how Glenn Parsons attempts to fill out Carlson's theory: "The aesthetic appreciation of something is deeper and more appropriate the more informed it is by knowledge of what that thing is. It follows from this that appreciation that does not involve scientific knowledge of natural things . . . is less deep and appropriate appreciation." Aesthetic responses to natural objects that are not informed by science are limited to the perception of "aesthetic properties that are peripheral to aesthetic appreciation and therefore less important in assessments of aesthetic value" and character. These properties are "somewhat superficial" when compared with the "more central" aesthetic properties available when appreciation is informed by scientific knowledge about the natural object. Appreciation so informed will allow us to "apprehend aesthetic properties that are manifest in *all*, or virtually all, of the perceptual appearances of that object." See Parsons, "Freedom and Objectivity in the Aesthetic

Appreciation of Nature," pp. 34, 35, n. 49 (emphasis in original).

9. "Objectivity" is a supercharged concept in philosophy that can mean many different things. Perhaps at its most basic it means "letting the object be one's guide, rather than the subject." It can mean that there are right and wrong answers to questions about a subject, which fits with Carlson's "true/false, correct/incorrect" language. It can also mean that some judgments are more or less rational and justifiable than others, which is the type of objectivity that Brady strives for in her account of aesthetic appreciation of nature. See Emily Brady, *Aesthetics of the Natural Environment* (Edinburgh: Edinburgh University Press, 2003), chap. 7. In this section, I sketch examples of (and criteria for) objectivity in the broad sense of their being distinctions between better and worse aesthetic responses to nature. This includes both Carlson's and Brady's types of objectivity and more.

10. Compare Brady's notion of "critical pluralism" in *Aesthetics of the Natural Environment*, pp. 79–81.

11. Perhaps the philosopher who comes closest to not making this distinction is Thomas Heyd, whom Carlson characterizes as a "postmodernist" regarding aesthetic appreciation, a position that puts no limits on aesthetic relevance. But even Heyd accepts some limits: Information is relevant to the aesthetic appreciation of nature only if it sustains aesthetic attention and does not thwart it. See Thomas Heyd, "Aesthetic Appreciation and the Many Stories About Nature," *British Journal of Aesthetics* 41 (2001):125–37.

12. Ronald Hepburn, "Trivial and Serious in Aesthetic Appreciation of Nature," in *Landscape, Natural Beauty and the Arts*, ed. Salim Kemal and Ivan Gaskell (Cambridge: Cambridge University Press, 1993). Like Carlson, Brady, and Eaton, Hepburn sees the need to distinguish better and worse in order to give aesthetics a role in environmental policy. "When we seek to defend areas of 'outstanding natural beauty' against depredations, it matters greatly what account we can give of the appreciation of that beauty.... We must be able to show that more is involved in such appreciation than the pleasant, unfocused enjoyment of a picnic place or a fleeting and distanced impression of countryside through a touring-coach window, or the obligatory visits to standard...snapshot-points" (p. 65).

13. Brady wonders why serious responses are necessarily better aesthetic responses than more playful ones. She asks why seeing a hill as like a giant's head and thus focusing on its huge, looming, and distinctive shape is a worse aesthetic response than a geological focus on the type of rock that constitutes the hill. See Brady, *Aesthetics of the Natural Environment*, pp. 167–68.

14. Noël Carroll, "On Being Moved by Nature: Between Religion and Natural History," in Kemal and Gaskell, eds., *Landscape, Natural Beauty and the Arts*, p. 259.

15. See, for example, J. Baird Callicott, "The Land Aesthetic," in *A Companion to A Sand County Almanac*, ed. J. Baird Callicott (Madison: University of Wisconsin Press, 1987), pp. 157–71; Yuriko Saito, "The Aesthetics of Unscenic Nature," *Journal of Aesthetics and Art Criticism* 56 (1998):102–11; and Carlson, *Aesthetics and the Environment*, chap. 3.

16. See Brady, *Aesthetics of the Natural Environment*, pp. 123–28.

17. Holmes Rolston argues that the best aesthetic responses to nature must involve "participatory experience" (in addition to being scientifically informed). See Holmes Rolston III, "Does Aesthetic Appreciation of Landscapes Need to Be Science-Based?" *British Journal of Aesthetics* 35 (1995): 374–85.

18. John Muir once enjoyed a windstorm by climbing to the top of a one-hundred-foot-tall Douglas fir tree: "One of the most beautiful and exhilarating storms I ever enjoyed in the Sierra occurred in December, 1874.... When the storm began to sound, I lost no time in pushing out into the woods to enjoy it. For on such occasions Nature has always something rare to show us, and the danger to life and limb is hardly greater than one would experience crouching deprecatingly beneath a roof.... Toward midday...I gained the summit of the highest ridge in the neighborhood; and then it occurred to me that it would be a fine thing to climb one of the trees to obtain a wider outlook.... I made choice of the tallest of a group of Douglas Spruces...they were about 100 feet high, and their lithe, brushy tops were rocking and swirling in wild ecstasy...never before did I enjoy so noble an exhilaration of motion...while I clung with muscles firm braced, like a bobolink on a reed. In its widest sweeps my tree-top described an arc of from twenty to thirty degrees, but I felt...safe, and free to take the wind into my pulses and enjoy the excited forest from my superb outlook." This quotation is from chap. 10 of Muir's *The Mountains of California* (1894).

19. Hepburn, "Trivial and Serious," p. 69.

20. Quoted in Rolston's "Does Aesthetic Appreciation of Landscapes Need to Be Science-Based?" p. 375.

21. One significant worry is that this pluralism, although "critical," might allow for conflicting aesthetic judgments about nature in cases that make a difference to environmental policy.

22. Fisher, "What the Hills Are Alive With." Despite arguing for a great freedom from constraints in the appreciation of natural sounds, Fisher concludes that nature's sounds "merit serious aesthetic attention both theoretically and experientially" (p. 177). He says little if anything about the implications of his views for aesthetic protectionism. Fisher's main concern in this paper is to show that judgments about natural sounds can be aesthetic even though they do not satisfy the agreement requirement (discussed later).

23. Budd, *The Aesthetic Appreciation of Nature*, chaps. 3 and 4.

24. Fisher, "What the Hills Are Alive With," pp. 171–72.

25. Ibid., p. 177. Interestingly, in "The Value of Natural Sounds," *Journal of Aesthetic Education*, 33 (1999):26–42, Fisher acknowledges widespread agreement that natural sounds are preferable to nonmusical human-caused sounds and provides an argument justifying this preference.

26. Budd, *The Aesthetic Appreciation of Nature*. p. 108.

27. Fisher, "What the Hills Are Alive With," p. 177.

28. Budd, *The Aesthetic Appreciation of Nature*, p. 108.

29. Similarly, a sand sculpture produced by an artist would have many meanings that the same pattern produced by nature would not have.

30. Budd, *The Aesthetic Appreciation of Nature*, p. 109.

31. Malcolm Budd, "Objectivity and the Aesthetic Value of Nature: Reply to Parsons," *British Journal of Aesthetics* 46 (2006):268.

32. Budd, *The Aesthetic Appreciation of Nature*, p. 147. Budd's language, and the interpretation of his views given here, might suggest that he rejects any sort of objectivity about nature appreciation. This is not the case by any means. Budd argues for better and worse in nature appreciation in a number of ways. A major part of his view is that one should appreciate nature as nature, and this rules out both narrowly formalistic appreciations of nature and appreciating nature as if it were art (see pp. 1–23). Budd also argues that sometimes mistaken beliefs about the kind of natural thing that one is appreciating can lead to a "malfounded" appreciation and can result in "aesthetic deprivation" whereby one misses "something aesthetically valuable" (p. 23). In his reply to Parson's critique in "Freedom and Objectivity in the Aesthetic Appreciation of Nature," Budd says, "Even if, as I hold, the idea of the aesthetic value of a gazelle is indeterminate, I regard its bounding movements in flight as being 'objectively'

graceful" ("Objectivity in the Aesthetic Value of Nature," p. 268). And in the preface to his book he says, "The view I recommend…[allows] that aesthetic judgments about nature can be plainly true" (p. x).

33. Parsons, "Freedom and Objectivity in the Aesthetic Appreciation of Nature," p. 31.

34. Fisher, "What the Hills Are Alive With," p. 173.

35. Ibid., p. 174.

36. I am not convinced that nature appreciation lacks significant conventions that specify better aesthetic appreciation. Many people explore natural areas with naturalists or nature guides of various sorts, and most would agree that doing so improves the aesthetic appreciation involved.

37. Fisher, "What the Hills Are Alive With," p. 173.

38. Ibid., pp. 173, 176 (emphasis in original).

39. Carroll, "On Being Moved by Nature," p. 251. Carroll argues this framing happens without using the type of scientific information that Carlson claims is needed to fix the aesthetic focus.

40. Stan Godlovitch, "Icebreakers: Environmentalism and Natural Aesthetics," *Journal of Applied Philosophy* 11 (1994):15–30.

41. Ibid., p. 18.

42. Hepburn, "Trivial and Serious," p. 77. In contrast to my arguments, Hepburn refuses to favor some perspectives over others.

43. Quoted by Todd Wilkinson in "Who Really Belongs to Their 'Silent Majority'?" *Bozeman Daily Chronicle*, October 5, 2002, p. A4.

44. Fisher, "What the Hills Are Alive With," p. 171. Fisher's relativism also is manifest in his endorsement of John Cage's claim that "what is more angry than the flash of lightning and the sound of thunder. These responses to nature are mine and will not necessarily correspond to another's" (p. 178, n. 24). Note that Fisher is not a pure relativist. As mentioned earlier, in "The Value of Natural Sounds," he accepts and attempts to justify the common idea that natural sounds are generally of greater aesthetic value than (nonmusical) human-caused sounds. Accepting the guidance-by-object requirement is another way that Fisher moves away from an anything-goes relativism. Presumably to him, ways of listening to nature's sounds that are not guided by the object are inappropriate. (It is not clear, however, what such a requirement rules out.) Another constraint that Fisher accepts is that we should not listen to nature in the same way we listen to music, for music is an intentional object and Fisher thinks that that should have a dramatic impact on how we appreciate it (p. 176). He also states that although aesthetic objects

(whether art or nature) underdetermine judgments about them, "this does not mean that any critical or interpretive judgment is properly assertable" (p. 172). He concludes his article by claiming that although "there are few constraints on appreciation of such sounds" (that is, environmental sounds), this does not "make responsible criticism and discourse about the objects of appreciation impossible" (p. 177). Fisher needs to explain further why his brand of relativism does not undermine criticism and to determine how compatible his views are with aesthetic protectionism.

45. Fisher, "What the Hills Are Alive With," p. 178, n. 24.

46. J. A. Walter, "You'll Love the Rockies," *Landscape* 17 (1983):43–47.

47. Perhaps such a judgment can be justified by Budd's requirement to appreciate nature as nature or Yuriko Saito's requirement to appreciate nature on its own terms and to let nature "speak for itself." See Yuriko Saito, "Appreciating Nature on Its Own Terms," *Environmental Ethics* 20 (1998):135–49.

48. Versions of this essay were presented at the University of Montana, the College of Charleston, and a meeting of the International Society for Environmental Ethics. I thank John Fisher and Dan Sturgis for their helpful comments and suggestions.